Three Stooges FAQ

Baltimore's Hippodrome was the September 1947 venue for one of the most unlikely pairings in show biz history: the headlining Stooges and "Velvet Fog" jazz vocalist Mel Torme. Plus, more musical acts and a "wolf's-eye view" movie, too!

Photo courtesy of Ted Okuda

Three Stooges FAQ

Everything Left to Know About the Eye-Poking, Face-Slapping, Head-Thumping Geniuses

David J. Hogan

APPLAUSE
THEATRE & CINEMA BOOKS
An Imprint of Hal Leonard Corporation

Published in 2011 by Applause Theatre & Cinema Books
An Imprint of Hal Leonard Corporation
7777 West Bluemound Road
Milwaukee, WI 53213

Trade Book Division Editorial Offices
33 Plymouth St., Montclair, NJ 07042

Images are from the author's collection unless otherwise specified.

Printed in the United States of America

Book design by Snow Creative Services

Library of Congress Cataloging-in-Publication Data

Hogan, David J., 1953–
   Three Stooges FAQ : everything left to know about the eye-poking, face-slapping, head-thumping geniuses / David J. Hogan. — 1st paperback ed.
       p. cm.
   Includes bibliographical references and index.
   Includes filmography.
   ISBN 978-1-55783-788-2
   1. Three Stooges films–History and criticism. 2. Three Stooges (Comedy team)
I. Title.
   PN1995.9.T5H64 2011
   791.4302'80922—dc23
                                                                2011030907

www.applausebooks.com

For Larry Fine
and Suzanne Ridgeway

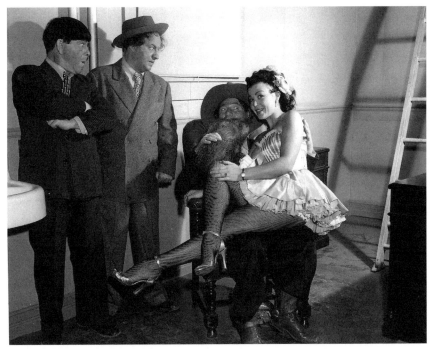

Moe Howard, Larry Fine, Shemp Howard, Suzanne Ridgeway

Contents

Acknowledgments

The author thanks

Larry Fine, for taking the time to tell me things;

Moe Howard, for being patient;

Gary Lassin, for image access, and for keeping the faith with the fabulous Stoogeum;

Teresa and Mark A. Miller, for friendship, encouragement, and images;

Ted Okuda, for friendship, encouragement, information, and images—and for filling me in on Four Eleven Forty Four;

Ron Penfound, Cleveland's Captain Penny, for being nice to kids;

Rob Rodriguez, for friendship, and for getting this whole thing rolling;

the art and editorial staffs at Applause, for encouragement and jobs well done;

www.threestooges.net, for being the only Stooges site you'll ever need;

and

Kim, Patrick, Rachel, and Ian, for being patient.

Maybe They Were Geniuses

The foundation of the legendary comedy act known as the Three Stooges—the shining, warm-to-the-touch sweet spot—is the work the team did from 1934 to 1957, as employees of Columbia's two-reel unit. In little fifteen- to eighteen-minute films shot in as many as four days and as few as one, Moe, Larry, Curly, Shemp, and Joe created the body of work that has ensured their immortality—to the dismay of moms everywhere.

Throughout their careers the boys did numberless live appearances, but most of those went unrecorded, and the roster of people who saw the boys first-hand dwindles by the day. Almost inevitably, then, the 190 short films are what make the Stooges "the Stooges."

What the Stooges Are—and Are Not

This book explores the boys' personas and comic technique in discussions of individual shorts, but we should pause here to consider their appeal. They were aggressive, physical comics from vaudeville whose humor was based on personal and bodily insult. Short, dumpy, and (after a while) middle-aged, they never traded on youthful innocence, like Stan Laurel or Harry Langdon; or on subtle, mutual fondness, like Stan Laurel and Oliver Hardy. They never projected a comically dignified elegance, like Charley Chase, nor did they traffic, like Buster Keaton, in stoic existentialism. They seldom explored surrealism, as the Marx Brothers did, and they lacked the physical grace and sheer inventiveness of Charlie Chaplin. Although very effective with dialogue, the Stooges never were glib patter comics like Bob Hope or Danny Kaye.

And unlike Thelma Todd or Mabel Normand, they certainly weren't beautiful.

As you watch the Stooges, you get the impression, from time to time, that the boys are fond of each other—usually when one of them appears to have taken a fatal tumble from a window, and the two who remain burst into tears. Most always, though, their comedy was built around interpersonal conflict. On screen, the boys were violent, petty, and antagonistic. Simple carelessness often brought unpleasant consequences. The Stooges were opportunists who regularly stole from and swindled each other. But the boys took quick offense at the slights and hostility of strangers, and banded together to gain the upper hand on those unlucky troublemakers.

Among comics of the Stooges' era, only Bob Hope rivals the boys for enormous, and unwarranted, sexual self-confidence. Many great screen comics seem almost androgynous (Langdon comes to mind), but the Stooges were ferociously heterosexual. Puffed up with delusions of their sex appeal, the boys pursued anything in skirts—and nearly always got the brush-off or a slap in the face.

Like all great comics, the Stooges didn't quite grasp how the world works, as witness those frequent collisions with women, as well as with cops, employers, banks, insurance companies, landlords, and even the stray dog on the corner.

Things often failed to work out for the boys, who never appeared to *care* that their understanding of the world was limited and unsatisfactory. They'd squash each other, and be squashed by other people and by the system itself, and they always came back for more, having learned nothing from their earlier missteps and punishments.

So why are they funny? On the one hand, we laugh because the Stooges embody many of our worst instincts, such as the desire for petty revenge. They do things that—wow!—we really wish *we* could get away with.

On the other hand, we love the boys because they knew how to end up on the side of the angels, whether by helping a family regain a stolen deed, struggling to become gentlemen, or (miraculously) getting the best of professional criminals and handing them over to the cops.

Despite the failings of personality that were built into every script, we knew that the Stooges were *good*.

How This Book Works

Organization of chapters is discretionary but not cavalier. Because the boys' first Columbia short, *Woman Haters*, is about male-female relations, Chapter 3 became "The Stooges and the Fairer Sex." Short number two, *Punch Drunks*, is about boxing—hence the theme of Chapter 4, "The Stooges and the Sporting Life."

In all, I identified thirteen overriding themes in the Stooges' two-reel work, for thirteen "theme" chapters (of fifteen), which you can examine in the table of contents.

Within each chapter, relevant shorts are discussed in chronological order. Exceptions to this are when a short was remade or reworked later; in such instances, discussion of the later short follows immediately after discussion of the original.

At appropriate places within each chapter, sidebars celebrate actors and actresses who made important contributions to the Stooges' career.

The main body of the book begins with biographical and early-career information about the Stooges, plus notes on Columbia Pictures, the studio's two-reel department, and the importance of short subjects to studios and exhibitors. These chapters are not extensive. Family members and the boys themselves wrote about the Stooges' lives, and some excellent books (noted in the bibliography) detail the workings of Columbia's two-reel unit.

Following the main text, you'll find a a filmography of the 190 shorts and a useful bibliography.

What the Shorts Mean

Throughout the book, an attempt has been made to place the boys' films in the context of their times. A film is archaeology. Observe it carefully and you learn a lot about the society and the larger world that produced it. When America was on the ropes during the Depression, the Stooges were often jobless and hungry. Shorts made immediately before and during World War II reflect the tenseness of those days.

Later shorts riff on Cold War anxiety, increased American interest in leisure and better living, and the national preoccupation with technology and Futurism.

Often, of course, the Stooges simply reacted to other movies, such as the horror films, *films noir*, and westerns that helped inspire some of the boys' more memorable two-reelers.

Because a major studio produced the Stooges' shorts, film technique is always competent, and frequently outstanding. The book calls attention to especially smart and fruitful uses of camera movement, lighting, editing, blocking, and other technical elements.

Let a Professional Do It

The greater part of *Three Stooges FAQ* was researched and written over a period of five months. I watched at least one short a day for some 150 consecutive days. That's a lot of Stooges in a relatively short time, and although I'd seen every one of the 190 many times in the past, I never stopped laughing. I always looked forward to putting down my thoughts, and moving on to the next film.

Throughout my viewings, one thing, more than any other, struck me about the Three Stooges: their professionalism. In this, they were peerless. Even as their budgets and shooting schedules were slashed, the boys maintained their respect for their audience. Quality varies among individual shorts, of course, but I never saw a lazy performance from Moe, Larry, Curly, Shemp, or Joe.

When I corresponded and spoke with Larry Fine in the early 1970s, he didn't give me tips about how to be funny, and I didn't ask. That's not the sort of thing that can be passed on verbally, or in a letter. In order to *be*, you must *do*.

Nothing is more difficult than comedy. Even experienced film comics occasionally struggle for laughs. You have your script, a director, and a supporting cast. The crew is ready. You know your cues, your lines, and your marks. The director says "Action."

Be funny.

What a boggling command. Who, really, can do that? Almost nobody. But from March 27, 1934 to December 20, 1957, the Stooges rose to the occasion. Fractious and unblushingly direct, they insisted that we laugh.

Despite the obvious evolution of automobiles, clothes, and even language over the many decades, the Stooges' shorts haven't become dated. The simplicity of the boys' comedy and the forcefulness of their personalities contribute to a timelessness that ensures an enduring popularity.

They set out to make us laugh, and we laughed. We *still* laugh, and our children and grandchildren and *their* children will laugh, too.

It's enough to give a whole world of mothers the heebie-jeebies, and that, I suspect, is how the Stooges would have wanted it.

David J. Hogan
Arlington Heights, Illinois

The Three Stooges

A Biographical and Career Timeline

T he extraordinary professionalism of the Three Stooges came from the boys' long experience as song pluggers, backstage helpers, and comic performers in vaudeville, on Broadway, and in early sound cinema. The timeline that follows notes selected high points in the lives and careers of Moe Howard, Shemp Howard, Curly Howard, Larry Fine, and Joe Besser—all of whom appeared in two-reel comedies produced by Columbia Pictures, and were billed as The Three Stooges.

Vaudeville (and its cousin, burlesque) was "variety" entertainment presented in networks of theater chains—such as Loew's and Keith-Orpheum—which, in those days before cross-country air travel, were dominant in the east and Midwest. The circuits were connected by train.

Vaudeville theaters (many of which doubled as movie theaters) ran live acts much of the day and into the night. Top acts would headline, with lesser acts filling out the bill. Because of the theaters' long hours of operation, the venues were hungry for talent. Opportunity existed for the able, but most vaudevillians remained relatively obscure. Some topped the bills, or came near to the top. A few made the transition to Broadway and to radio. And a very few stepped up to movies, gaining vast audiences. But even for featured acts, fame was relatively brief: Who today recalls "International Juggling Humorist" Billy Rayes or the "Cantonese Capers" of Larry and Trudy Leung? Vaudeville performers who remain popular and fondly recalled today—such giants as Milton Berle, Abbott and Costello, Mickey Rooney, Bob Hope, Jack Benny, Buster Keaton, and the Three Stooges—are special and rare.

Doggedness was vital to survival and success on the vaudeville circuit. Depending on one's budget, train travel could be pleasant, or cramped and uncomfortable. Just to get from here to there ate up a lot of time. Backstage, many theaters were dumps with dirty, primitive dressing rooms and awful accommodations. (A notable exception recalled by Moe is the still-gorgeous Palace Theater in Cleveland, which was as grand backstage as it was out front.)

While on the road, stars lived in hotels. Lesser lights made do with lesser hotels, or boardinghouses. It was showbiz, but it wasn't glamorous. For all, it was a job, and for some, it was a grind.

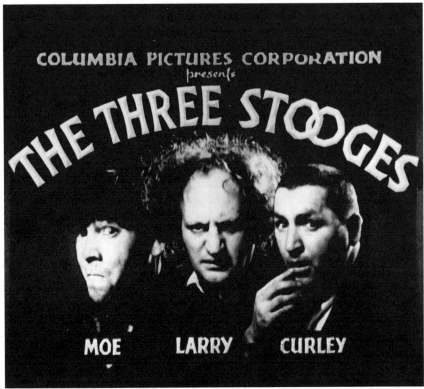

Get ready to laugh: Columbia Three Stooges title card, 1934–1936. Note the short-lived spelling of "Curley."

Most vaudevillians gulped greasy, inexpensive food, and had to contend with demanding theater managers, horny showgirls, abusive patrons, and acts that waited for moments to upstage rivals. The performers who prospered were the ones who loved their art. They didn't love many aspects of "the life," but they loved what they did on stage.

Moe, Larry, Shemp, Curly, and Joe loved it, and developed distinct personas that jibed in intriguing ways with their real selves.

Moe: an inherently serious performer with a sharp interest in the numbers side of the business, the group's de facto leader, and the one who was prudent enough to end up with a gorgeous estate above Sunset Boulevard. On stage, he seemed comically boyish with his sugar-bowl haircut, yet he was startlingly pugnacious and impatient, quick to poke and slap those he considered rivals or inferiors.

Larry: a habitué of racetracks who loved fine clothes as much as he loved the ponies. He and his wife were for many years residents of Hollywood's highly regarded Hotel Knickerbocker. In performance, Larry was faintly absurd with his frizzed-out curls and blandly smiling face, but he was one of the most brilliantly "reactive" comics of the 20th century. He never purposely stole a scene, but he was always up to something amusing, even when physically situated in the background.

Shemp: a famously funny Hollywood raconteur. Mickey Rooney told the fine historian Ted Okuda that whenever he spotted Shemp holding court in a restaurant, Rooney and his group invariably requested a table nearby, so they could listen in, and laugh. Although Shemp dealt professionally in a fast-talking worldliness, his real-life persona was kind and approachable. He was probably the most purely brilliant of all the Stooges, with a remarkable facility to think on his feet and ad lib.

Curly: the "baby" of the Howard brothers, an antic lover of life often described (rather too glibly) as a "man-child." He was connected to family, and found his greatest pleasures in women, dogs, and automobiles. A fine dancer and a comic with astoundingly inventive physical skills, he influenced generations of comics that came later, from the great Lou Costello to Jim Carrey. Curly's stage persona was apparently a reflection of his true personality, with hyper energy, boundless enthusiasm, and a lovable quality that friends, family, and his public found hugely endearing.

Joe: like Shemp, he was impressively successful for years as a solo before he became a Stooge, working as a headliner in vaudeville and on Broadway. Stout and balding, he exploited his cherub's face and body with cheerful cleverness. His carefully developed "sissy kid" persona slayed live audiences, and made him a refreshing addition to a latter-day incarnation of the Stooges.

Here, in short form, is how the Stooges learned to become the Stooges.

March 17, 1895: Samuel Horwitz (Shemp Howard) is born in Brooklyn, New York.

October 1, 1896: Ernest Lee Nash (Ted Healy) is born in Kaufman, Texas.

June 19, 1897: Moses Horwitz (Moe Howard) is born in Brooklyn, New York.

October 5, 1902: Louis Feinberg (Larry Fine) is born in Philadelphia, Pennsylvania.

October 22, 1903: Jerome Horwitz (Curly Howard) is born in Brooklyn, New York.

August 12, 1907: Joseph Besser (Joe Besser) is born in St. Louis, Missouri.

1909: Moe has casual encounters with young performer Ted Healy.

1912: Moe and Ted Healy work together in an all-girl diving act.

1914: Moe travels to Jackson, Mississippi, to perform on a riverboat, the *Sunflower*.

1916: Moe and Shemp appear at New York's Mystic Theater as Howard and Howard; their mainstay piece is "A Study in Black," a comic routine done in blackface.

Moe Howard, sophisticate.

Summer 1916: Curly's .22 rifle accidentally discharges as he holds it in his lap. The bullet shatters a bone in his ankle, and Curly will have pain and a slight limp for the rest of his life.

1916–22: Shemp and Moe work the vaudeville circuit as a double.

1917: Larry Fine plays violin and dances in his own, modest Philadelphia stage act. He also works as a song plugger, selling sheet music to vaudeville performers and others.

1918: Eleven-year-old Joe Besser works as a song plugger.

1919: Joe is a singing usher, food vendor, and occasional performer with a traveling carnival.

1919–23: Joe travels with magician Howard Thurston as an assistant, audience "plant," and stagehand.

1922: Moe parts from Shemp to team with Ted Healy.

1923: Joe assists stage magician Madame Herrmann.

1923–25: Joe assists aerialist Queenie DeNeenan.

c. 1925: Larry Fine encounters boyhood pal Eddie Laughton, who also is in show business. Years later, Laughton works with the Stooges in many two-reel comedies, and as their straight man in live appearances.

1925: Shemp and Larry join Moe and Ted Healy; the act is called Ted Healy and His Racketeers.

1926: Larry Fine marries Mabel Haney. • Joe gets into vaudeville as a "stooge" for comics Alexandria and Olsen. He begins to experiment with his "sissy" character.

1926–28: Larry Fine is part of a vaudeville trio, the Haney Sisters and Fine. The act mixes jazz and classical music with dance.

1927: Moe takes a temporary leave from show business following the birth of his daughter. He works as a home developer and a seller of distressed merchandise.

1928: Joe teams with straight man Richy Craig.

April 1928: Joe is signed by the Paramount Publix theater chain as a featured player on the vaudeville circuit.

June–November 1928: Joe headlines *Main Street to Broadway*, an ambitious musical revue.

c. 1929: Larry is a solo at Chicago's popular Rainbo Gardens club.

1929: Roughneck Irish comic Ted Healy and Shemp and Moe do a comedy act in Chicago. Healy sees Larry's act and invites him to join himself and the others. The new act is called Ted Healy and His Three Southern Gentlemen. They have success with two special bits, "A Night in Spain" and "A Night in Venice."

1930: After performing at a Hollywood party, Healy and the Stooges are approached by representatives from MGM, Columbia, and Warner Bros. • Moe, Shemp, and Larry split with Healy over a contractual matter, and briefly play the vaudeville circuit as the Three Stooges. • Joe signs with the RKO Keith Theater circuit, and headlines with straight man Sam Critcherson and, later, Lee Royce.

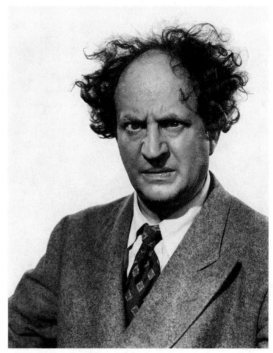

September 28, 1930: The first film of Ted Healy and His Stooges, a Fox feature called *Soup to Nuts*, is released.

1932: Shemp, Larry, and Moe join straight man Jack Walsh in a vaudeville act alternately known as Three Lost Souls and Howard, Fine & Howard. Shortly, Moe and Larry return to Ted Healy. • Curly leaves his gig as comic conductor of the Orville Knapp Orchestra to join Moe, Larry, and Healy.

Larry Fine, nonplussed, as usual.

• Shemp and Joe Besser become friends when they appear together, with Ted Healy, in a stage show called *The Passing Show of 1932*. • When Healy is offered more money elsewhere, he leaves *The Passing Show of 1932* and takes the Stooges with him. Shemp leaves the act to go solo. • Curly joins Ted Healy and Howard, Fine & Howard.

1932–46: Shemp stars and co-stars in dozens of shorts and takes prominent supporting roles in features. He works with W. C. Fields, Abbott and Costello, Olsen and Johnson, John Wayne, Maria Montez, Lionel Atwill, Patsy Kelly, the Andrews Sisters, Broderick Crawford, and many other notables.

July 6, 1933: Healy and the Stooges appear on movie screens in *Nertsery Rhymes*, an MGM short in two-strip Technicolor (shades of red and green).

August 25, 1933: Release date of *Turn Back the Clock*, a Lee Tracy–Mae Clarke feature with Healy and the Stooges in support.

August 26, 1933: Release of *Beer and Pretzels*, an MGM short starring Ted Healy and His Stooges.

September 16, 1933: Release of *Hello, Pop!*, an MGM short designed for Ted Healy and His Stooges.

Curly Howard, in uncommon repose.

October 14, 1933: MGM releases *Plane Nuts*, a comic short starring Ted Healy and His Stooges.

October 20, 1933: *Meet the Baron*, an MGM comedy feature starring Jimmy Durante and featuring Ted Healy and the Stooges (Moe, Larry, Curly), is released.

November 24, 1933: Ted Healy and His Stooges are given major exposure with the release of *Dancing Lady*, a Clark Gable–Joan Crawford musical feature.

November 25, 1933: Release of *Myrt and Marge*, a feature-length adaptation of a popular radio show, with Myrtle Vail and Donna Damerel, and with Ted Healy and His Stooges in featured roles.

Early 1934: Ted Healy, who already has done solo film work, tells the Stooges he wants to break up the act.

January 5, 1934: *Fugitive Lovers,* a light drama starring Robert Montgomery and Madge Evans, with Ted Healy and His Stooges in support, is released by MGM.

March 1934: On behalf of Larry and Curly, Moe signs a contract with Columbia following an encouraging meeting with Columbia chief Harry Cohn and production head Sam Briskin. A few hours later, Larry, acting on behalf of Moe and Curly, signs a contract with Universal. Because of the timing, the agreement with Columbia stands. The contract stipulates that Columbia owns all film rights to the Stooges, present and future—even in media not yet invented.

Shemp Howard, man about town.

Spring 1934: Ted Healy threatens to sue the boys and Columbia over the use of the name "Stooges" but does not follow through.

May 5, 1934: *Woman Haters,* the first Three Stooges short produced by Columbia, is released.

May 12, 1934: *The Big Idea,* an MGM short starring Ted Healy and His Stooges, is released.

June 1, 1934: Premiere of *Hollywood Party,* a feature-length all-star MGM revue starring Jimmy Durante, with Healy and the Stooges in bits (Healy as a reporter, the Stooges as autograph hounds).

1934–37: Joe stars in extravagant musical revues that climax with *You're in the Army.*

December 31, 1937: Ted Healy dies in Los Angeles, California, from injuries suffered in a bar beating.

March 25, 1938: Columbia releases Joe's first film, a starring-vehicle short called *Cuckoorancho.*

Spring 1938: Joe and straight man Lee Royce play vaudeville.

1939: Larry, Curly, and Moe appear on Broadway in *George White's Scandals.*

June 5, 1939: The boys begin a very successful tour of the British Isles at London's Palladium.

May 24, 1940: Universal releases *Hot Steel,* a Richard Arlen feature about steelworkers; it is Joe's first feature, and he has a prominent supporting role.

Early 1940s: Joe is a frequent guest on radio's *The Jack Benny Program.*

1941–45: The Stooges tour extensively with the USO, doing shows at U.S. Army camps and other stateside military installations.

1943–44: Joe further develops his "priss" persona with Olsen and Johnson in the duo's Broadway revue *Sons O' Fun.*

1943–45: Curly suffers a series of minor, undiagnosed strokes. Doctors warn him about his weight, hypertension, and potential heart trouble.

October 27, 1944: *Open Season for Saps,* Shemp's first solo starring short for Columbia, is released. His co-star is Christine McIntyre.

1944–47: Shemp continues to star in his own series of Columbia two-reelers.

1945: Shemp Howard fills in for ailing brother Curly during the Stooges' personal appearances.

April 17, 1945: The Stooges hit the screen with co-star with Mary Beth Hughes in *Rockin' in the Rockies,* a Columbia B-picture.

March 16, 1946: Poverty Row studio Monogram releases *Swing Parade of 1946,* an all-star musical revue, with the Stooges in support of Gale Storm and Phil Regan.

May 6, 1946: During filming of *Half-Wits Holiday,* Curly suffers a serious stroke that ends his career. The short sees release on January 9, 1947.

1946: Shemp is called back to the Three Stooges, and returns with the understanding that he will film with the act only until Curly recovers.

March 6, 1947: *Fright Night,* the first Stooges short featuring Shemp, is released. Curly will not return to the act, and Shemp will continue with the Stooges until his death in 1955.

July 17, 1947: Release date of *Hold That Lion!,* the only film that captures all three Howard brothers—Shemp, Moe, and Curly—on screen together.

Late 1940s: The Stooges have successful runs at Minsky's Burlesque in New Orleans.

February 1949: *The Three Stooges* No.1, a handsome comic book from St. John with art and story by Norman Maurer and Joe Kubert, hits America's newsstands and candy stores.

September 8, 1949: Columbia releases *Waiting in the Lurch*, the first of Joe's two-reel series. Joe will headline his own series until 1956.

1950–52: Curly is institutionalized at intervals for health reasons.

January 18, 1952: Curly Howard dies of a heart attack at Baldy View Sanitarium in San Gabriel, California.

1952–53: Joe shoots thirteen episodes of *The Abbott and Costello Show*, appearing as Stinky, a bratty, whiny kid in a Buster Brown suit (Joe is in his mid-forties).

November 22, 1955: Shemp Howard dies in Hollywood, California, of a sudden heart attack. Moe's first inclination, to become The Two Stooges, is nixed by Columbia. Moe then considers African American comic actor Mantan Moreland as the third Stooge, but he and Columbia ultimately go with veteran vaudeville and film comic Joe Besser.

Joe Besser, from solo star to Stooge.
Photo courtesy of Mark and Teresa Miller

May 3, 1956: *For Crimin' Out Loud*, the final Stooges short with new footage of Shemp, is released.

June–November 1956: In order that Moe and Larry fulfill their current contract, and exhibitors receive their allotted supply of Stooges comedies, Columbia releases four shorts in which contract player Joe Palma doubles for Shemp.

January 31, 1957: The first Stooges short with Joe Besser, *Hoofs and Goofs*, is released.

December 20, 1957: After wrapping the shoot of *Flying Saucer Daffy*, Columbia two-reel producer-director Jules White informs the Stooges that the studio has fired them. This ends the boys' relationship with Columbia as two-reel stars.

1959: Columbia releases *The Three Stooges Fun-O-Rama*, a compilation of Stooges shorts featuring Joe Besser. • Columbia packages the Stooges' shorts for local-TV sale. The package is picked up by stations around the country, and although the Stooges receive no payment, they experience an enormous burst of new popularity.

Ted Healy (second from right) and His Stooges, *Beer and Pretzels* (1933); the perturbed theater manager is Edward Brophy.   *Photo courtesy of Mark and Teresa Miller*

June 4, 1959: Release date of *Sappy Bullfighters*, the final Stooges short to reach theaters.

1959–65: The Three Stooges (Moe, Larry, "Curly-Joe" Joe DeRita) star in six feature films, five for Columbia and one for 20th Century-Fox.

1960–73: Joe Besser does comic and dramatic guest shots on episodic television.

July 1, 1960: Columbia releases *Stop! Look! And Laugh!*, a feature-length compilation of Stooges shorts from the Curly years, with wraparounds and bridges featuring Paul Winchell and the Marquis Chimps. The film so angers Moe that he fires the Stooges' longtime manager.

1962–65: Joe Besser is a regular on *The Joey Bishop Show.*

1965: The Stooges film live-action intros for *The New Three Stooges*, a TV series dominated by new Stooges animated cartoons.

1969–70: Moe, Larry, and Curly-Joe film *Kook's Tour*, a low-budget, comic travelogue. The film is never completed.

January 9, 1970: Larry suffers a debilitating stroke that ends his career. He manages to recover significantly and becomes a popular speaker on the college circuit.

1973: *Stroke of Luck*, Larry Fine's autobiography, is published.

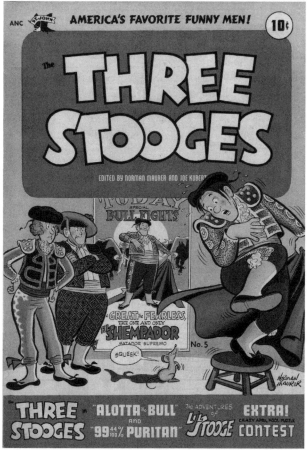

The Three Stooges No. 5, 1954, St. John Publishing. Cover art by Norman Maurer.

Photo courtesy of Mark and Teresa Miller

November 1974: Columbia releases *The Three Stooges Follies*, a feature-length compilation of shorts starring the Stooges and others, plus snippets of Columbia serials.

January 24, 1975: Following a second stroke, Larry Fine dies in Woodland Hills, California.

May 4, 1975: Moe Howard dies in Los Angeles.

1977: Posthumous publication of Moe's autobiography, *Moe Howard & The Three Stooges.*

August 30, 1983: The Three Stooges receive a star on the Hollywood Walk of Fame, at 1560 Vine Street, near Hollywood Boulevard. Joe Besser attends the ceremony, which draws the largest crowd ever to witness an unveiling on the Walk.

1984: Joe Besser's autobiography, *Not Just a Stooge*, is published.

1985: Joan Howard Maurer's *Curly*, a biography of her uncle, is published.

March 1, 1988: Joe Besser dies in North Hollywood, California.

1996–2011: Noted producer-director team the Farrelly Brothers (Peter and Robert) doggedly pursue development of an all-new Three Stooges comedy feature.

April 24, 2000: ABC-TV airs a made-for-television biopic, *The Three Stooges*, with Paul Ben-Victor as Moe, Michael Chicklis as Curly, Evan Handler as Larry, John Kassir as Shemp, Laurence Coy as Joe, Peter Callan as Curly-Joe, and Marton Csokas as Ted Healy. Executive producer is longtime Stooges fan Mel Gibson.

One-sheet poster for the 1960 compilation film that caused Moe to fire the Stooges' manager.   *Photo courtesy of Mark and Teresa Miller*

2

The Columbia Two-Reel Department

Purpose, Product, and Personnel

C olumbia Pictures began in 1919 as C.B.C. Film Sales Company, named for founders Jack Cohn, Joe Brandt, and Jack Cohn's younger brother, Harry Cohn. Brandt and Jack Cohn set up offices in New York; Harry organized and oversaw film production in Hollywood.

Harry was brusque and crude, but he also had a sense of what moviegoers wanted to see and a feel for how his company might profitably fit into the film-studio hierarchy of young Hollywood. He recognized that MGM and Paramount existed at the summit of the industry, and that a great gaggle of small companies struggled at the bottom. Cohn wanted to claim the middle ground. He was willing to work with small budgets, but his dream was to spend on quality material. Only with pictures that people wanted to see could Columbia—which owned no theaters of its own—break through the exhibition stranglehold of the major studios.

C.B.C. produced successful shorts films in the early 1920s, picked up additional partners in 1922, and changed its name to Columbia Pictures in 1924. The studio had initially established itself on so-called Poverty Row, on Sunset Boulevard between Gower and Beachwood. "Gower Gulch" is what the industry called the area, for its plethora of two-bit production companies. But by 1923, Cohn could stand at the foot of Gower and gaze north, directly at that symbol of naïve hope and aggressive business, the HOLLYWOODLAND sign. Cohn probably liked that.

Harry never saw reason to move; he simply expanded. Columbia built stages and offices in Gower Gulch and, in late 1934, purchased a forty-acre tract in Burbank that was dubbed "the Columbia Ranch." The natural exteriors of the Burbank property were utilized for westerns and other adventure films, and newly constructed false-front streets suggested a variety of time periods and places. With these physical plants, and Harry Cohn's insistence on good quality on a budget, Columbia Pictures established itself as a mini-major, on par with Universal and RKO, yet still looking up at MGM, Paramount, Fox, and Warner Bros. Cohn frankly preferred it that way. The studio was large, but not so

Harry Cohn, co-owner and absolute ruler of Columbia Pictures. *Photo courtesy of the Stoogeum*

large that it couldn't be firmly controlled day-to-day by a single man: Harry Cohn.

Columbia's earliest films were shorts, but its experience with them as support for features began in 1933, with the studio's "Musical Novelty" series. After a young but experienced short-comedy director named Jules White had a false start as head of the department in 1933, he returned a year later, to oversee production of "two-reelers"—comic films that typically ran from fifteen to eighteen minutes. White would not leave until Harry Cohn ordered the unit shut down in December 1957.

It Was a Business

Vital to an understanding of the unit's operation is that it created *product*. At a time when going to the movies could be an all-day affair, short subjects (which included comedies, cartoons, newsreels, and travelogues) were important parts of exhibitors' schedules. Many two-reel comedy acts, such as the Stooges and Andy Clyde, and Warner Bros.' Joe McDoakes *one*-reel shorts, were enormously popular, and had drawing power that existed independent of whichever feature-length film(s) might be at the top of the bill.

The first comic signed to a two-reel Columbia contract was Leon Errol, who made just five shorts at the studio before leaving for greener two-reel pastures at RKO. The Three Stooges—picked up in 1934 following their unique success as patsies for MGM comic Ted Healy, made their studio debut in a 1934 Musical Novelty short called *Woman Haters*. (Many sources refer to these as "Musical Novelties," but the films' title cards use the singular.) The team would make another 189 two-reelers for the studio. Discussions of those 190 films form the core of this book.

During the twenty-four years of the unit's operation, comics with various backgrounds in burlesque, vaudeville, and film went in and out. Included were some greats on the down side of their careers, such as Harry Langdon, Buster Keaton, and Charley Chase. Others, such as Monte Collins and Tom Kennedy, and Gus Schilling and Richard Lane, had had individual careers before being teamed by Columbia, expressly for two-reelers. Still others, like El Brendel, were novelty comics. (The novelty of Brendel, who was inexplicably popular, was that he spoke in a faux Swedish accent.)

Once-and-future Stooge Shemp Howard had a solo series at Columbia, as did future team members Joe Besser and Joe DeRita.

Producer-director Jules White ran a successful factory. Studio bean counters let him know which acts were coming in, and which were on their way out. Over the years, forty-three series were produced. Many amounted to just one or two shorts. Many others saw a half-dozen or fifteen. Columbia's two most prolific two-reel acts, the Stooges and Andy Clyde, produced short comedies by the score.

How the Stooges Fit In

Some Columbia two-reel stars, such as Walter Catlett, worked mainly in the studio's features, and did shorts only when their schedules permitted. Others, like the Stooges, worked primarily in shorts, and made features only occasionally.

The Stooges typically filmed thirty to forty weeks a year. Their first contract called for $7,500 per short, or $2,500 apiece. Although the lack of TV residuals caused Moe to publicly complain many years later that the act never was given a raise, remarks by Larry and others undercut that claim. Pay boosts did come periodically, and were reasonable.

Once shooting obligations were met, the rest of the year was the boys' to use for lucrative stage engagements and other live appearances. (Not all of the studio's two-reel contract stars enjoyed this generous arrangement.) The Stooges also were permitted to make features (when there was outside interest, which was seldom) for other studios or independents, as they did for Monogram with *Swing Parade of 1946*, and for Jack Schwarz Productions with *Gold Raiders* (1951).

The shorts' four-day shooting schedules were tight but not impossible. Until the early 1940s, reasonably complex location shoots in and around Los Angeles, and on the "Columbia Ranch" in Burbank, were common. Directors had time enough to set up and execute ambitious tracking and dolly shots. The number of supporting players in individual Stooges shorts of this period could reach twenty-five.

As the years went by, two-reel schedules were decreased to three days, and then to two. Location shooting was dropped, and "exteriors" were created on ill-disguised sound stages. Expansive standing sets became rarer, and the shorts became set-bound, often talking place largely in a single apartment or office.

For reasons of budget and release schedules, remakes and redos were endemic from the 1940s onward. The Stooges remade or reworked many of their shorts during the Shemp and Joe Besser years. Elsewhere in the unit, a short made by one comic might be redone by another. Whatever the arrangement, a remake picked up extensive stock footage from a previous short and usually set aside just a single day to shoot new scenes and inserts.

Bookings

Exhibitors who booked Columbia feature films were obligated to run the studio's two-reelers. But Columbia was happy to see its shorts booked in support of features from any other studio. A booking was a booking, and it meant rental revenue and continued exposure for the studio's two-reel stars. Release schedules were determined far in advance, for exhibitors' knowledge and convenience, and for Columbia's profit projections. Shorts were released up to a year after being shot, though from three to six months was most common. Regardless, exhibitors relied on shorts to fill out their bills, and Columbia (and other studios) obliged.

Although fans and even some historians refer to Columbia shorts and others as "episodes," they were not—at least not in the TV-oriented sense we understand today. Rather, they were discrete motion pictures, produced, marketed, and exhibited individually.

Important People We Never Saw

Vital to the factory's smooth function was its stable of contract producers, directors, and writers. (Key supporting actors and actresses are discussed in sidebars throughout the book.)

Jules White (born Weiss, in Hungary; 1900–85) headed the unit as executive producer, and directed hundreds of shorts. An imaginative filmmaker when time and budget allowed, he later became perfunctory (his managerial responsibilities remained paramount to him), and although he was the most prolific of the Stooges' directors, he fell victim to his fondness for blunt violence, and was far from the best.

Assisting White with production duties was **Hugh McCollum** (1900–68), who ran his own unit within the department, bringing taste and a keenly developed story sense to his work from 1937 to 1952, when long-simmering differences with Jules White—and White's desire for more power—led to his dismissal. McCollum finished his career as producer of *The Range Rider* TV series.

Jules White's older brother, writer-director **Jack White** (1897–1984) came to Columbia in 1935, after producing more than three hundred comedy shorts, dating to 1920, and writing and directing scores more, as far back as 1917. Invariably credited as **Preston Black** when he directed the Stooges and others, Jack White guided many of the Stooges' classics, including *Disorder in the Court, A Pain in the Pullman, Ants in the Pantry,* and *Grips, Grunts and Groans*. His grasp of physical gags was peerless, and he coaxed unusually nuanced performances from his players. As two-reel production at Columbia began to wind down in the 1950s, Jules White took over direction, and Jack was handed the unenviable task of writing new sequences to bridge stock footage used in remakes.

Charley Chase (1893–1940), though a brilliant star comic actor in silent and talkie shorts for Hal Roach, was miscast at Columbia as a series star, where his famously elegant, understated wit was made loud, and as a director, because his sophisticated sensibilities and interest in music and song were ill suited to the Stooges. Still, one short that he made with them, *Violent Is the Word for Curly*, is an undeniable gem.

Canadian native **Del Lord** (1894–1970) began in films as a director with Mack Sennett, with credits going back to 1920. After further experience at

Producer-director Jules White (center) with the Stooges and players on the set of *Fifi Blows Her Top* (1958). *Photo courtesy of the Stoogeum*

Roach, Educational, and Paramount, Lord joined Jules White at Columbia in 1935. Of all of the Stooges' directors, Lord probably possessed the greatest visual flair and comic timing. *Pop Goes the Easel, Hoi Polloi, Three Little Beers, False Alarms, A Plumbing We Will Go, All the World's a Stooge,* and *Healthy, Wealthy and Dumb* are indisputable high points of two-reel comedy. Lord came to produce many of the Columbia shorts he directed, and stumbled only when he scripted, for his narrative sense was choppy, and not nearly as unified as his vision as a director.

Other directors, notably **Harry Edwards** (1889–1952) and **Charles Lamont** (1895–1993; later very successful as one of Abbott and Costello's most frequent feature directors), directed a small handful of Stooges shorts.

Edward L. Bernds (1905–2000) is the wittiest and most astute director of Columbia two-reelers to arrive after Del Lord, and one-ups Lord with his considerable skill as a writer. He began his career in 1929 in sound, as a recordist, engineer, and mixer. By 1946, Columbia agreed that Bernds was ready to direct, and he was assigned to the Stooges' *A Bird in the Head* (1946). These initial assignments were difficult because Bernds was a novice director, and because he had to manage the physical deterioration of Curly Howard—something that he accomplished with ingenuity and grace. Bernds came into his own as a director of the Shemp films, notably *Pardon My Clutch, Fuelin' Around, Out West,* and other amusing western spoofs, and *Brideless Groom* (1947), one of the best of the boys' entire output.

Bernds scripted many shorts that he directed, arriving at a winning combination of a more subdued form of Jules White's knockabout and Del Lord's pacing and visual inventiveness.

Simultaneous with his Stooges work, Bernds began to direct small B-pictures (such as entries in the "Blondie" and "Bowery Boys" series), and was out of shorts after 1952. He was close to producer Hugh McCollum, and when McCollum was fired, Bernds left, as well. Later Bernds credits (direction and script) include a vivid juvenile-delinquent melodrama, *High School Hellcats* (1957), and a lively pair of science-fiction thrillers, *World Without End* (1956) and *Return of the Fly* (1959). Ed Bernds retired in 1965 and published an autobiography in 1999.

Bernds was one of the Stooges'—and the entire two-reel unit's—most important writers, but others were equally significant. **Clyde Bruckman** (1894–1955) earned a place in film history with an extraordinarily fruitful association with Buster Keaton during the Keaton glory years of the 1920s. A co-writer (with Buster) on Keaton's 1926 masterpiece, *The General,* Bruckman also is credited, with Keaton, as co-director of that film. He co-scripted *The Navigator* (1924) , wrote the story for Buster's *The Cameraman* (1928), and helped adapt David Belasco's play *Seven Chances* for Keaton's 1925 screen version.

Alcoholism began to get the better of Bruckman in the mid-1930s (he needed help from W. C. Fields to direct Fields's 1935 comedy, *Man on the Flying Trapeze*), and writing—an essentially solitary craft—became more congenial for him. While with the Columbia shorts department from about 1935 to 1953, Bruckman wrote dozens of the Stooges' shorts, including such classics as *Three*

Little Beers, Half Shot Shooters, You Nazty Spy!, In the Sweet Pie and Pie, Brideless Groom, and *Pardon My Clutch.*

Bruckman was a skilled gag man of vast experience, with a flair for intricate jokes as well as physical spectacle. He freely borrowed from his own earlier work, and from the work of others. (He was sued by former associate Harold Lloyd for appropriation of material from *Movie Crazy* [1932] for use in a minor 1945 Universal feature called *She Gets Her Man.*)

Bruckman wrote episodes of *The Buster Keaton Show* in 1950, and did scripts for *The Abbott and Costello Show* a couple years later, but finally reached the end of his tether in 1955, when he shot and killed himself with a handgun he had borrowed from . . . Buster Keaton.

Felix Adler (1884–1963) worked as a writer from 1925 to 1958, beginning at Mack Sennett and moving to Columbia in 1934. His first script for the Stooges was *Men in Black* (1934); after that, Adler wrote more than seventy shorts for the boys (considerably more than a third of their total), as well as many for other Columbia two-reel stars. He remained active until the unit was shuttered in 1957.

Three Little Pigskins, Uncivil Warriors, I'll Never Heil Again, Malice in the Palace, Scrambled Brains, and *Self Made Maids* are among Adler's more successful efforts. On the other hand, he's also responsible for *Don't Throw that Knife, Flagpole Jitters,* and the intriguing but much-debated *Cuckoo on a Choo Choo.*

With Ed Bernds, **Elwood Ullman** (1903–85) made the most pointed transition to features following considerable time with two-reelers. Ullman began as a writer in 1925 and joined Jules White's unit in 1936. Like other contract writers, Ullman came up with scripts and gags for many of the studio's two-reel stars. Blessed with a facility for comic dialogue as well as physical gags, Ullman wrote Stooges scripts that "read" particularly funny. His work with the boys includes *Termites of 1938, Violent Is the Word for Curly, We Want Our Mummy, Calling All Curs, A Plumbing We Will Go, Crime on Their Hands, Dutiful but Dumb, Studio Stoops,* and *Yes, We Have No Bonanza.*

Ullman walked away from shorts in the early 1950s, never mentioning during subsequent job interviews that he had worked with the Stooges or any other two-reel acts. With that part of his professional past blocked out, Ullman was able to write features for Abbott and Costello, the Bowery Boys, and Ma and Pa Kettle.

Ullman returned to the Stooges with scripts for five of the boys' feature films of the 1960s, and even wrote one for Elvis (*Tickle Me,* 1965).

Writer **Searle Kramer** (1910–85) collaborated with Elwood Ullman on two of the boys' best, *We Want Our Mummy* and *Yes, We Have No Bonanza.* As a solo, Kramer wrote the Stooges' sublime "battle of the sexes" short, *Healthy, Wealthy and Dumb.* Much later, he wrote episodes of *I Dream of Jeannie* and *The Flying Nun.*

Finally, if there was a "sixth Stooge" during the boys' Columbia tenure, it is **Joe Henrie** (1908–85), an extraordinarily clever sound effects technician who eventually headed that department at the studio. But even after becoming an executive, Henrie personally supervised the resonant sound effects that gave the Columbia shorts their distinctive sonic flavor.

Edward Bernds and the boys, with one of many exhibitors' awards.

Henrie was a friend of director and former sound man Ed Bernds, and understood the comic value of an appropriate, well-timed sound effect. The Stooges and the other two-reel stars took falls, absorbed punches, swallowed too fast, were assaulted by tools, had hairs plucked from their heads—endured all manner of physical insult that Henrie augmented with sounds created with plungers, plucked violin strings, sandpaper, a wide assortment of ratchets, and many other devices. His contribution to Columbia's two-reel unit is imaginative, and hugely important.

Throughout this book, you'll find remarks about contributions made to individual shorts by the unit's talented cinematographers, art directors, editors, and composers.

Alternate Incarnations

In 1949, Columbia offered earlier shorts for theatrical showing as *Comedy Favorites*; simultaneous 16-millimeter release was designed for the home market.

Around 1950, a home-projector manufacturing company called Excel Movie Products licensed Stooges and Andy Clyde shorts for home use with Excel's 16-millimeter projector. The shorts were abridged versions running on reels ranging from fifty to two hundred feet, frequently with new titles (one Excel-release Stooges short, for example, is called *Heavy Gunners*—perhaps an abridgment of *Half Shot Shooters*).

Another 16-millimeter outfit, Official Films, licensed a variety of Columbia's two-reelers for nontheatrical exhibition in schools, churches, and similar venues.

A 1956 theatrical compilation called *Columbia Laff Hour* combined shorts starring the Stooges, Hugh Herbert, Andy Clyde, and Vera Vague.

TV Renaissance

The Stooges' shorts were released by Columbia's TV subsidiary, Screen Gems, for local-TV showings in 1959. The boys didn't see a dime from this sale, but TV audiences didn't know that. The shorts were hugely successful in local markets, and were particularly attractive—and brand new—to youngsters who had never seen the boys before. This success led to the period of the Stooges' greatest and most lucrative popularity, and to all-new feature films (with veteran comic Joe DeRita as the third Stooge) that continued well into the 1960s.

Very shortly after the initial release of Stooges shorts to TV, a second block of shorts, Columbia's "Hilarious Hundred" (the actual number was two hundred) packaged unedited two-reelers by Andy Clyde, Vera Vague, Billy Gilbert, Hugh Herbert, Buster Keaton, El Brendel, and others for TV syndication. (Like the Stooges, these stars received no money from the sale.) The Hilarious Hundred were picked up by many local stations, but didn't fare as well as the Stooges package.

In 1959, Columbia released a theatrical compilation of the Besser shorts, *Three Stooges Fun-O-Rama*. (Content varied from theater to theater, depending upon which Besser prints were in local circulation at the time.) *Fun-O-Rama* was followed in 1960 by *Stop! Look! and Laugh!*, a feature-length compilation of snippets from the Curly years, with miserable wraparound footage and bridges featuring ventriloquist Paul Winchell and the Marquis Chimps. Once again, the Stooges received no money. Moe was so furious that he fired the Stooges' longtime manager, Harry Romm, who had taken producer credit on the film.

Later still, when young people who had first seen the Stooges on TV were in college, Columbia released yet another compilation, *The Three Stooges Follies* (1974).

The Home Theater Era

Columbia began to collect and market Stooges shorts during the VHS years in pricey packages of four or five films on each tape, typically grouped around a theme. The changeover to DVD was natural, and followed the VHS model until 2007, when Sony/Columbia began an affordable DVD release of every Stooges short, in chronological order, as a multiple-volume rollout called *The Three Stooges Collection.* By the time the collection was into the Shemp years, fans were able to own Stooges shorts that had never before been available for home use. Sony/Columbia completed the DVD set in the spring of 2010 with *Volume Eight: 1955–59,* which completed the Shemp run and returned the amusing shorts with Joe Besser to the public eye.

A 2011, Canada-only DVD release combined all eight volumes into a single boxed set.

Sony/Columbia issued a handsome collection of Buster Keaton's Columbia shorts in 2006, so his Columbia work, like the Stooges', has been carefully preserved. But the rest of the two-reel unit's output is not available for easy viewing. Except for 16-millimeter copies held and occasionally screened by collectors, and a few beat-up prints that circulate as bootleg DVRs, many hundreds of shorts with commercial as well as historical value sit in limbo.

3

The Stooges and the Fairer Sex

In which the boys learn that a pretty girl isn't always like a melody; jealous husbands are bad news; women are often brighter than they look; sometimes the best brides are war brides; sometimes the deepest love comes when you're clinically insane; if you have to brain a dame, a rifle butt is better than a length of pipe; the best secretaries are named Miss Lapdale; and under the right circumstances even a gorilla can look pretty sexy.

I n 1934, at the beginning of the Stooges' tenure at Columbia—and for one film only—executives were not completely sure of how to showcase them. As we've seen, Columbia was a "minor major" that hadn't the resources to make use of the boys' talents in the MGM manner. But Columbia had established a "Musical Novelty" shorts series in 1933, and had the services of a vivacious blonde starlet named Marjorie White. A Canadian native who stood just 4'10", White had energy and screen presence to spare. (She also had a wisecracking, New York-style attitude that belied her Canadian origins.) During 1929–31, she'd been under contract to Fox Film Corporation, appearing in nine pictures. White sang and danced, and knew her way around a page of dialogue. She'd had leads and second leads in comedies and musicals at Fox, and found similar success later in pictures for First National, Universal, Paramount, and RKO.

Even more promising from Columbia's point of view is that White held her own on screen with bombastic, well-established male comics. She was sterling in support of First National star Joe E. Brown in *Broadminded* (1931) and easily kept pace with RKO's high-energy comedy-team sensation Wheeler and Woolsey in *Diplomaniacs* (1933).

White arrived at a propitious moment. The Roaring Twenties had come and gone, and the notion of the emancipated jazz baby who smoked, worked at a job, and necked with whomever she pleased had been diminished by the Depression. But movie audiences had become accustomed to smart, sassy dames, and White fit the mold. It wasn't unreasonable, then, that the Three Stooges were designated as the fourth Musical Novelty entry, which would co-star Marjorie White. The boys would be properly introduced, and White—for whom Columbia had high hopes—would receive an amiable showcase.

All of that being said, the Stooges' inaugural Columbia effort, *Woman Haters*, is among the two or three most perplexing shorts they made at Columbia. It's also atypical, in the extreme, of their subsequent output.

The premise is simple. The boys are charter members of the Woman Haters, a vociferously misogynistic bunch who've decided that women are the bunk. But Larry falls for Mary (White) and then must hide his marriage from Moe and Curly. So far, so familiar, but get this: Larry plays a fellow named Jim. Moe is "Tommy" and Curly is "Jackie." Oh, it gets better. Jerome Gottler's lively script is entirely in rhyme, and so we're treated to contrived dialogue the likes of this soliloquy from "Jim": "Fellas, I'm tellin' ya, ya got me all wrong! I was minding my own business when that woman came along! . . . You don't think I'd fool around with a sappy dame like that! Her eyes are like a cat and her hair is like a rat!"

And so it goes, as Moe and then Curly fall prey to White's charms. The short's director, Archie Gottler, was Jerome Gottler's dad. Archie directed only a few short films, and worked mainly as a songwriter. No surprise, then, that one of his tunes, "My Life, My Love, My All," is warbled repeatedly in the course of *Woman Haters'* nineteen minutes fifteen seconds.

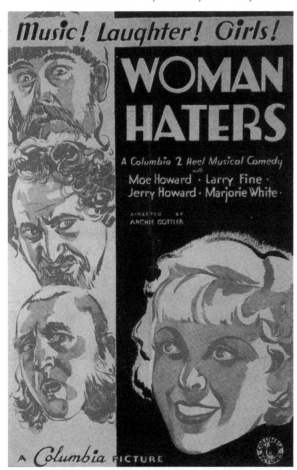

In the end, the aggressive bride doesn't take any guff from her husband's pals: "This man's my husband, we were married a coupla hours ago, and the agreement that you fellas signed is fake and it don't go, 'cause everybody's cheated, I can prove it and I know!"

Longtime Stooge fans will be happy to see blustery actor Bud Jamison as the leader of the *Woman Haters*; we'll meet Bud numerous times in the course of this book. Some sources claim that later stock-company regular Emil Sitka (who would have been about twenty at the time of *Woman Haters*) has a wordless bit as a beat-up husband, and although the actor might be Sitka, the short doesn't show up on any Sitka filmography, nor could this writer uncover any occasion when Sitka mentioned the film.

Prominent display of talented but ill-fated starlet Marjorie White in poster art for the Stooges' first Columbia two-reeler, a "Musical Novelty" called *Woman Haters* (1934).

For real novelty we have future three-time Oscar winner Walter Brennan, cast as a conductor on the train where most of the short's action plays out. Brennan nearly always looked elderly, no matter his real age; here, he appears merely middle-aged—and as thin as a reed, too.

The film offers a few hints of the boys' future greatness. When Moe sinks his teeth into Curly's bare foot, Curly lets out with a ferocious "Woop woop woop woop woop woop woop!" Curly also reprises one of his gags from the Healy days, loudly whacking his derby on his head and moving his arm like a machine gun. Moe pokes eyes and administers plenty of slaps—one of which, in fact, is a startlingly violent backhand of a sort that we'll rarely see again.

Most satisfying of all is that Larry, in the boys' very first Columbia short, lets loose with one of his best-liked signature lines: "I'm warnin' you!"

Bliss.

Sadly, all was not blissful for talented Marjorie White, who was killed in a Santa Monica car crash on August 21, 1935, just fourteen weeks after the release of *Woman Haters*. The short was the last time audiences would see her on film. Just four years earlier, Columbia lost Robert Williams, its most promising young leading man, to appendicitis.

These losses were serious blows to Columbia's spirit and to its bottom line. Fortunately, the Stooges were now on the lot, ready to pitch in.

THE BOYS' NEXT BATTLE WITH THE GENTLER SEX TAKES SHAPE IN THEIR twenty-second Columbia short, *Three Dumb Clucks* (1937). Besides giving us a rare opportunity to enjoy Curly in a dual role (as himself and as his dad), the film is usefully instructional in the ways of intergender warfare: Sometimes the skirmish isn't direct but oblique, with one party or the other utilizing proxies to carry out the dirty work. In this case, a blonde cutie named Daisy (Lucille Lund, recalled as Boris Karloff's miserable wife in the 1934 Universal thriller *The Black Cat*) enlists the aid of her unnamed boyfriend (Eddie Laughton) and henchman Chopper (Frank Mills) to knock off her wealthy bridegroom right after the marriage. The groom, you see, is Pa (Curly), a naïve, lovestruck oil magnate who's divorced Curly's Ma in order to marry the gold digger. Daisy, with her squeaky-girlie voice and habit of addressing Pa as "Popsie," is nothing if not transparent. But Pa is hopelessly in love, and even agrees to shave off his muttonchop sideburns after Daisy complains about them. Of course, clean-shaven Pa is a dead ringer for Curly.

Scripter Clyde Bruckman and director Del Lord have fun with the dead-ringer gag in a protracted sequence involving Pa, Curly, Daisy's henchmen, an elevator, and a staircase. Laughton and Crusher just can't figure out how Pa can get from here to there so quickly! The elevator door closes on Pa and a second later he's on the other side of the lobby, poking his head from the stairwell. This goes on for quite a while, with many double takes, running up and down the stairs, and trips on the elevator. To everybody's credit, the sequence is hilarious—neither too long nor too short. It's well edited (by Charles Nelson), and impeccably played by all.

Three Dumb Clucks opens, like numerous Stooges shorts, in prison, where the boys are doing hard time for an unspecified crime. Ma's letter about Pa reaches them there, so they've gotta break out. But how? "How about the tools?" Larry offers. Moe is puzzled: "What tools?" Larry pulls back one of the mattresses and patiently explains, "The tools we've been usin' for the past twenty years!" Sure enough, the space beneath the mattress is as well stocked as a good hardware store.

Later, Pa tells the boys to keep their noses out of his love life, so their best chance to save him is at Daisy's penthouse, where the wedding will take place. Daisy can't wait to say her vows and then herd Pa to the balcony, where he'll be shoved over. The boys eavesdrop as Laughton details the scheme to Chopper. Moe is impressed: "That guy thinks of everything!" Larry is almost relieved: "I'm glad they made up their minds."

Following the elevator bit, Pa is safe but the Stooges end up treed on a flagpole. Laughton topples it and sends the boys on a fourteen-floor drop (earlier stock footage makes the distance look more like *fifty* floors). A store awning breaks the boys' fall, and they tumble off the canvas and right onto Pa. Disaster averted!

Although the term "gold digger" was coined in the American West in about 1830, audiences of 1937 understood it as a staple of Depression-era entertainment; the older man–younger dame trope was always good for easy laughs, and in perilous economic times, it had the ring of truth. Columbia's young star Barbara Stanwyck played such parts for drama in the early 1930s (*Forbidden, Ladies They Talk About,* and, most famously, *Baby Face*), while Warner-First National successfully exploited the word in the lighthearted musical *Gold Diggers of 1933*, and in two follow-ups.

That Pa's scheming paramour is a gold digger named Daisy may have been no accident, for the money-hungry, faintly pathetic society girl in F. Scott Fitzgerald's 1925 novel *The Great Gatsby* has that name. But there's nothing murderous about Fitzgerald's Daisy. To find that quality, Bruckman may have recalled the Ruth Snyder murder case of 1925–27, a sordid tale that remained fresh in the cultural consciousness ten years later. Snyder was a reasonably attractive housewife living in Long Island City, New York. She schemed with her boyfriend, a corset salesman, to murder the innocent Mr. Snyder. They did so, but with such ineptitude that the public was as shocked by the nature of the crime as by the scheme itself. (Mr. Snyder was cracked on the head with a sashweight, smothered, and strangled with piano wire.) Ruth Snyder was the most infamous murderess of the day. She remains celebrated, in part, because of "The Eternal Blonde," a lively account written by Damon Runyon for Hearst's *New York Journal American,* and because Tom Howard, a *Chicago Tribune* reporter covering Snyder's execution by electric chair for sister paper the *New York Daily News,* smuggled a camera into the death chamber at Sing Sing and snapped

Snyder just as the electricity slammed her body. It's a scarifying image that was published across the nation. (Howard's brazenness inspired a 1933 Warner melodrama starring James Cagney, *Picture Snatcher*.)

One part gold digger, three parts killer, the Daisy of *Three Dumb Clucks* is amusing, but the essential nature of the characterization is rooted in dark soil indeed.

When *Three Dumb Clucks* was remade in 1953 as *Up in Daisy's Penthouse*, screenwriter Jack White adapted Clyde Bruckman's script for the original, altering nothing fundamental and retaining the key gags. He added only a few bits of business, such as Larry's innocent unraveling of Moe's suit jacket, which begins when Larry offers to get rid of a loose thread.

Shemp brings plenty of vigor to his dual role, though, not surprisingly, his interpretation of "Popsie" is more jaded and biting than Curly's. That's in keeping with Shemp's persona, but so is the fact that Shemp is no less a sucker for a good-looking gold digger.

Daisy is played by Connie Cezan, who is funny, saucy, and—partly through no real fault of her own—faintly disreputable. Cezan was pretty in an aggressively sensual way; her wide-set eyes are enormous, and her mouth looks as if it were designed according to a template associated with the erotic arts. If actress Carolyn Jones (a remarkably sexy woman herself) had had a sister who was even hotter, the sister would have been Connie Cezan.

As in *Three Dumb Clucks*, the avaricious bride-to-be has a pair of thuggish friends (Jack Kenney and perennial western heavy John Merton) who plan to shove Popsie off the balcony and into eternity.

First, though, the boys check out their dad's plush private quarters. Larry treats his hair and scalp with generous splashes of Popsie's expensive liquor while Shemp sponges at a stubborn spot on a pair of pants. *Sponge, sponge, rub rub.* The spot doesn't want to go away. (Shemp breaks the fourth wall when he grabs a bottle and cracks, "Cleaning fluid! How convenient!") As in other comedies, including the Stooges' own *Rip, Sew and Stitch*, the stain is a blob of sunlight, so Shemp's incessant rubbing takes a predictable toll on the pants.

Up in Daisy's Penthouse is among the best and most pleasing of the Stooges' remakes. Other than the boys' fall onto the canopy and stock footage of the view from the balcony to the street, the short is comprised of freshly shot material. Henry Freulich crisply photographed Charles Clague's handsome sets, and adequate numbers of extras were hired to fill out the penthouse sequence. Two stock-company players appear, Joe Palma, as a thug who guards the lower staircase; and Suzanne Ridgeway, who has a silent but eye-filling bit as a maid.

Finally, we have the title itself. *Up in Daisy's Penthouse.* Innocent, yes, if you don't believe in suggestiveness or double entendre.

What was that address again?

KEY THEMATIC THREADS POP UP AGAIN AND AGAIN IN THE STOOGES' COMEDIES. One of the funniest and best explicated is the boys' dogged, endlessly optimistic quest to elevate themselves to wealth. Sometimes they nearly make it, via illegal means or through a serendipitous meeting with a member of high society. Other times, they grab the gold ring because of something that they, against all odds, have managed to accomplish themselves. The last is what motivates *Healthy, Wealthy and Dumb* (1938), in which Curly wins a $50,000 write-the-slogan prize from the Stik-Fast Glue Company, sponsor of radio's *Coughin' Nails Cigarette Program*. The money isn't just a windfall but a life-saver, because the boys (as usual) live together in a single cramped room, and Larry cheats Moe at cards just to scare up spending money.

When Curly opens the miraculous notification letter, he immediately demonstrates his ability to handle great wealth, happily exclaiming, "Pie a la mode with beer chasers, three times a day!" And Moe is nothing but fiscal prudence personified: "Let's go places and buy things!"

Shortly, the boys are ensconced at the ritzy Hotel Costa Plente, run by an officious, self-important manager (James C. Morton) and prowled by the suspicious hotel dick (Bud Jamison). The manager is particularly proud of items that furnish the boys' swank room. "This bed goes back to Henry the Eighth," he boasts. "That's nothin'!" Curly retorts. "We had a bed that went back to Sears Roebuck the third!"

Soon, of course, the bed is destroyed, along with a frightfully expensive Ming "vahse" that Moe accidentally shatters with a board. (Shocked at smashing the "five thousand dollar gadget," he demands of Larry, "Why didn't you hand me a softer board?")

As the appalled manager stands with the boys in the midst of the destruction, a telegram arrives for Curly. It's a lengthy, itemized tally of tax deductions that has whittled the $50,000 prize to four dollars and eighty-five cents. "They'll put us in jail!" Larry swoons.

Although the manager doesn't get a look at the letter, he wisely tells the hotel dick to stand guard in the corridor.

The Stooges are in big trouble—but wait! Salvation may be just up the hall in the form of three good-looking dames (Lucille Lund, Earlene Heath, and Jean Carmen) who get wind of Curly's dough. If these gals don't come up with some cash in a hurry, they're going be thrown out of the hotel, so they slip into some glad rags and pass themselves off to the boys as three rich, lonely widows.

The "meet cute" is accomplished with help from the girls' capuchin monkey, Darwin, who is sent to invade the boys' digs. Curly spies the little beast after swilling champagne and becomes convinced he's got the DTs. Darwin retreats into a pair of pants that Larry has thrown on the floor. Larry scoffs at Curly's claim of "gorillas," only to receive a profound surprise when he picks up his clothes: "My pants bit me!"

The three couples are engaged in short order—each imagining they're hoodwinking the other—but the betrothal ends when the boys repeatedly open the door and splash their fiancées with frigid ice water from the champagne bucket, imagining that the girls are the snoopy detective.

After the first drenching, the no-good dames discover that the boys are broke. With a sublime lack of conscience and self-awareness, Lucille Lund (the girls are never named, though at least one reference book provides names) spits, "How do you like those chiselers, double-crossin' us!" At the fadeout, the girls promise to give the boys big kisses, only to crack heavy vases over their heads, knocking them silly.

In this particular war with women the Stooges are obviously, deeply complicit in their own undoing. They're out of their depth, not simply in the fancy hotel—where Curly mistakes the bathtub for a rowboat and Larry insists it's a horse trough—but in the scheming department, where they're mere apprentices compared to the cynical, vastly experienced gold diggers.

Typical of shorts directed by Del Lord, *Healthy, Wealthy and Dumb* unspools without a single wasted frame. Searle Kramer's script is simultaneously absurd and plausible, and crackles with funny dialogue. As the hotel employees, Morton and Jamison express marvelous outrage, and the three girls, particularly the only brunette—sloe-eyed, gum-chewing Earlene Heath—are hilariously crass. Although far from geniuses, these gals are practically *destined* to get the upper hand on the Stooges.

Healthy, Wealthy and Dumb was remade virtually scene for scene, with Shemp, as *A Missed Fortune* (1952). America's male-female dynamic had evolved in the intervening years, but you wouldn't guess it from Jack White's script (adapting Searle Kramer's original piece). The boys still think fifty grand is enough money to set them up for life, and the three gold diggers down the hall still want the fifty grand, and they still have a monkey, too.

Despite its faithfulness to its source material, *A Missed Fortune* has remarkably little stock footage: the insert of the Hotel Costa Plente sign; the stunt player's leap onto the top of the canopied bed and subsequent fall; Larry in the bath; a close-up of Darwin, and a later shot as he scrambles into Larry's pants.

The major changes are in casting. The boys' familiar antagonist, Vernon Dent, replaces James C. Morton as the hotel manager, and aggressive character player Stanley Blystone, as the hotel dick, is a good, menacing replacement for Bud Jamison. The scheming dames are played by French-Canadian actress Nanette Bordeaux (who worked with the Stooges a few times in the 1950s); tall, button-eyed Vivian Mason; and another Stooges stock-company player, the black-haired and frankly carnal Suzanne Ridgeway.

As for plot details, what had been a slogan competition is now the *Mystery Motor Jackpot Contest* (which broadcasts on station BURP). More significantly, the girls don't discover that the Stooges are paupers.

The boys add a few cute gags. When the hotel manager shows off the frightfully expensive Ming vase, Shemp sagely observes, "No wonder it costs so much for a ming coat!" And when Moe mashes Larry's top hat down over his eyes, Larry panics, even when the hat is removed: "Fellas, help me! I'm goin' blind, I'm goin' blind!"

"What's the matter?"

A bit of a dust-up in *A Missed Fortune* (1952), a satisfying remake of *Healthy, Wealthy and Dumb*. The actresses (from left) are Nanette Bordeaux, Suzanne Ridgeway, and Vivian Mason.   *Photo courtesy of the Stoogeum*

Larry, coyly: "I had my eyes closed!" Larry used that gag many times, and always with enthusiasm.

Director Jules White (scripter Jack was one of his brothers) notches up the violence; in a single bit, Moe gives Shemp simultaneous backhanded slaps, an eye poke, a nose masher, a stomach punch—and then gives Shemp's nose a good bite! Larry gets banged around more than in the original short, as well. All in a day's work during the endless war with women.

WHEN PREPARING TO DEAL WITH *THREE MISSING LINKS* (1938), ONE IS TEMPTED to discuss it as a "Stooges Abroad" comedy (the protagonists are at work in Africa). Although that decision could be justified, the most plangent themes of Searle Kramer's episodic screenplay are love and sex—of the forbidden variety, no less.

Larry, Curly, and Moe are janitors at Super Terrific Productions. They show up at the office of studio boss B. O. Botswaddle (James C. Morton) and proceed to tear the place apart—*and* so impress B. O. with their innate primitiveness that they win roles in his next picture, *Jilted in the Jungle*. And so it's off to Africa (amusingly simulated on a slightly ratty Columbia sound stage), where the boys run afoul of a witch doctor named Ba Luni Sulami (John Lester Johnson) who gives Curly a fistful of "love candy" in return for future ownership of Curly's skull. "Make big strong love!" the witch doctor promises. Because Curly is head over heels for Super Terrific leading lady Mirabelle Mirabelle (Jane Hamilton), and apparently less enamored of his skull than we imagined, he accepts the candy.

Curly has been selected to play the gorilla that wishes to mate with aloof white goddess Mirabelle. Larry and Moe are on hand as cavemen whose job it is to defend Mirabelle's honor. In an inevitable mix-up, a real gorilla (Ray "Crash" Corrigan, credited as "Naba") stumbles onto the set and is mistaken for Curly. Moe and Larry beat the gorilla with abandon, only to regret it.

Finally cornered in a hut by the real gorilla, Curly tries to distract the ape with love candy, nibbling some of the stuff in the process. Earlier in the short, Curly has insisted that he's "the Robert Taylor type." Because the love candy works, what was then an idle boast now becomes reality: "Dahling!" Curly exclaims, arms outstretched to the confused monkey, "I love ya!"

But the gorilla has as little interest in Curly as Mirabelle does, so the short fades out as Curly pursues the monkey into the jungle.

Although *Three Missing Links* comes early in the Stooges' Columbia output, it's something of a "greatest hits" reprise: Larry and Curly carelessly catch Moe in a crossfire of rotated mop handles; Moe rubs mud in Curly's face; Curly runs headlong into palm trees (twice); somebody throws something that shatters an expensive-looking pane of glass; Larry squashes Moe's hand with a sledgehammer; Curly drops to the floor, pivots on his shoulder and imitates "a chicken with its head cut off!"

Viewers attuned to sexual symbolism can ponder the meaning (or lack) of the boys tucked up, tight as sardines, in the same tent, as well as the lion that causes them to suggestively chortle in their sleep as it licks their bare feet. And then there's Curly's frustration with tent stakes that continually pop out of the ground after Curly has labored to insert them. All right, then.

Chief among the wiggy sex stuff is the parody of awful jungle thrillers in which a white princess is expected to mate with a gorilla. The director of *Jilted in the Jungle* carefully explains to the boys that the movie "has no leading man"— just a gorilla. So in a parody within a parody, gorilla-man Curly is jilted by the princess even as he hits on the real gorilla.

Girl/gorilla love was not without precedent in Hollywood. In 1930, the Hays Office, Hollywood's censorship body, banned an independently made exploitation picture called *Ingagi*, "the wonder film" with "a million thrills from heart of African jungle" [*sic*]. By combining silent, real-life safari footage with new scenes, director William Campbell strung together a peculiar melodrama in which the native Africans (older footage) are very dark, and the particularly good-looking "African" gals (new footage) are coffee-colored. Audiences took special note of the buxom, topless cutie who tussles with the sex-crazed gorilla of the title.

Ingagi had one important (non-jungle) predecessor, *Seven Footprints to Satan* (1929), in which a gorilla lusts after gorgeous Thelma Todd, but Campbell's pastiche was influential on its own, inspiring a litter-load of imitators: *Savage Girl* (1932), *Beast of Borneo* (1935; "The Weirdest Triangle Ever Filmed!"), *Love Life of a Gorilla* (1937), and *Forbidden Adventure in Angkor* (1937).

The best and most famous of these prewar interspecies love stories are *Murders in the Rue Morgue* (1932) and *King Kong* (1933). In the first, crazed Darwinist Bela Lugosi transfuses gorilla blood into kidnapped streetwalkers, and hopes to eventually engineer a mating. And *Kong*, of course, is pure sex, pure love story—never mind the gross disparity of size between Kong and his radiant, blonde obsession (Fay Wray).

Director Jules White failed to take full advantage of comic actor Monte Collins (who's funny nonetheless as Super Terrific's director), and allowed former model Jane Hamilton be as expressive as a post when she might have been encouraged to mug a little. The short rides mainly on the considerable energy of the Stooges, and the enthusiastic playing of black actor John Lester Johnson. Johnson was a onetime light-heavyweight boxer who took stereotyped bits in mainstream films and much better roles in black-cast movies. He's undoubtedly best-remembered as the uncivilized title character in the 1933 Our Gang comedy *The Kid from Borneo*, who cries "Yum yum, eat 'em up!" as he chases after Spanky. Next to attentions of that sort, unwanted kisses from a gorilla don't seem so awful.

THE STOOGES' UNQUENCHABLE HETEROSEXUALITY SUGGESTS THAT THEIR frequent mistreatment of innocent women (that is, women who don't unfairly provoke them) is completely unintentional. That quality allows their female-directed violence to keep its comic edge without becoming nasty, and it's also at the core of *Cookoo Cavaliers* (1940). Sick and tired of the San Diego fish business, the boys try to make a go of it in Cucaracha, Mexico, after purchasing a beauty salon that they think is a saloon. After all, as Larry sagely notes, "There's a lot of money in makin' homely dames beautiful!" Unfortunately, they rip, rub, and tear the hair from the heads of their first customers, who are beautiful to begin with.

The gals are Juanita, Conchita, Pepita, and Rosita, hostesses at a local saloon. The girls' boss (Bob O'Connor, doing a very funny turn as a Mexican) brings the girls by because "gentlemen, they prefer the blondes." Curly is beguiled by Pepita (Blanca Vischer), despite his consternation at her comically weak English. Meanwhile, Larry is kneeling in a chair meant for the girls, telling a disinterested Rosita (Stooges stock-company player Dorothy Appleby) that she has "beautiful black eyes." Moe observes all of this foolishness and doesn't know which of his partners to clobber first.

Eventually, Rosita gets a manicure when Moe cuts her nails with an enormous pair of shears, and paints what's left with a spray gun. She gets a mud pack, too, which the boys shape into what looks like an African anthill, and then can't remove without clobbering it with a mallet.

The other three girls end up bald because Larry has carelessly mixed hair remover with the peroxide solution. The short fades out as so many Stooges misadventures do, with the boys scrambling into the middle distance as an angry gunman takes potshots at their derrieres.

A beauty parlor, that esoteric domain of women, was an unavoidably absurd place for the Stooges to operate, not merely because of the boys' ignorance but because beauty salons have traditionally built their clientele on referrals. Bald, angry women don't give good referrals. Because the Stooges' shorts played before movies of all types, women accounted for a significant proportion of the boys' original audience. Patrons of beauty parlors themselves, they would have simultaneously laughed and cringed at the Stooges' ineptitude. Cosmetics maven Elizabeth Arden began an aggressive, nationwide expansion of her beauty parlors in about 1934. Any town that had had only one independent shop soon had many. And makeup itself evolved. Beauty historian Pauline Weston Thomas notes that by the 1930s red nails and deep red lipstick became popular, supplanting the suntan craze of the '20s. Salons existed not just to transform women but to teach women how to beautify themselves and stay current.

Attitudes about hair, as well, were transformed in the '30s, in large measure by platinum-blonde actress Jean Harlow. Her striking, shimmering hair color subsequently identified Depression and late-Depression personalities as diverse as Toby Wing, Thelma Todd, young Betty Grable, Ginger Rogers, Barbara Pepper, and orchestra leader Ina Ray Hutton. Little wonder that the saloon owner who runs into the Stooges asks that his dark-haired beauties be transformed into blondes.

Beauty, though, informs only the second half of *Cookoo Cavaliers*. The short's first half is preoccupied with the boys' fish, and picks up bits from a Laurel and Hardy short, *Towed in a Hole* (1932), in which Stan and Ollie hawk "fiishh, fuh-ressh fiissh!" from their truck, tooting horns as they go. The Stooges do likewise, except that they're more careless with their horns and even more inept as fishmongers. They accidentally slap a lady in the face with a mackerel, and react stupidly to another lady's innocent question, "Do you have a haddock?" That gag had been used by the Marx Brothers, and probably dates back to eons earlier. (The lady with the question, by the way, is Anita Garvin, a statuesque beauty and frequent antagonist of Laurel and Hardy, who was by now at the end of her screen career.)

Although *Cookoo Cavaliers* is essentially two mini-shorts—one about fishmongering, the other about beauty parlors—the two sections flow together briskly and well. Director Jules White allowed the boys to ad lib and even overlap their dialogue, giving the picture a pleasingly offhand quality. What befalls Juanita, Conchita, Pepita, and Rosita is dire, but it's not difficult to imagine them back at work in a day or two, as pretty as before.

THE NATIONAL CENTER FOR VITAL STATISTICS REPORTS THAT IN 1940 THE PER capita U.S. divorce rate was two per thousand. In that long ago time, married couples tended to stay married, partly because one's sense of obligation was keenly felt, and because divorce had a stigma that has since been lost. Still, those people who did divorce in the early 1940s did so for the usual variety of reasons: infidelity, incompatibility, or the all-purpose "mental cruelty." And then there was money, which propels the plot of *In the Sweet Pie and Pie* (1941), another gem written by Ewart Adamson and energetically directed by Jules White. The overriding gag, ostensibly, is that the Stooges can be counted on to make a mess when they crash high society. That particular bag of laughs is very strong here, but what really bring the boys into the bib-and-tucker set are women, marriage, and the gals' selfish desire for divorce.

When Tiska, Taska, and Baska Jones (Dorothy Appleby, Mary Ainslee, and Ethelreda Leopold, respectively) bounce into their drawing room following a game of tennis they're met by smarmy family retainer Diggins (Richard Fiske), who has bad news. The girls' fiancés, Tom, Dick, and Harry, have been detained abroad, and can't return in time to marry the girls on schedule. Ordinarily, that wouldn't be a disaster, but if the girls are to collect a meaty family inheritance, they must be married within twenty-four hours.

Diggins has an idea: The girls will marry three convicts and then become three (rich) widows as soon as the boys are hanged a day later.

The sisters are repulsed by the newspaper image of the Mushroom Murder Gang (Larry, Curly, and Moe), but gird themselves and show up at the boys' cell anyway. "Will you marry us?" Taska loudly asks.

"*Will* we?!"

A three-in-one ceremony is performed in a flash. The boys are thrilled: "We're married!" "Brother in law!" "Niagara Falls!"

It's a long moment before they realize that their brides have ducked out of the cell, leaving them to face the hangman.

In a stroke of good fortune, somebody named Mickey Finn confesses to the Mushroom Murders. Our heroes are set free and settle in with their wives.

Now, divorce is the girls' only option. But on what grounds? Diggins has an idea: Introduce the boys into society and wait for the inevitable humiliation.

In the Sweet Pie and Pie has a fascinating patina of surrealism. Before the boys meet the sisters, they puzzle over how to escape from jail. Moe laments, "If only we had a saw."

Curly lifts up his shirt to reveal an entire selection tucked into a carpenter's belt. "You mean like these?"

Moe pulls out a particularly large one. "Is this a musical saw?"

"Soitenly," Curly says happily. "It plays 'I Hear a Rhipsody!'"

"Well, here's a rhapsody in the kisser!" *Thwap!*

The discussion degenerates into a fencing match that ends when Moe runs the saw blade across Curly's skull, destroying the teeth.

After the quickie marriage, the boys are led to the hangman, in a room filled with convicts who hoot and cheer as if they're at a ball game. One con stalks the aisles, selling programs, and a radio announcer promises to give a "jerk by jerk" description of the action.

Fortunately, the ropes break. At the Jones mansion later, Tiska is shocked when the boys show up: "How did you zombies get out jail?"

In a terrific touch, the boys sleep together in one room at the Jones place, apparently willing to wait before they assert their connubial rights. Because jail has taken away their ability to sleep in comfy beds, they pound together a triple-decker affair. The top bunk is left for Curly, who has to figure a way to get all the

Performer Profile: Dorothy Appleby
1906–90

This diminutive, very pretty brunette could be a charmer but was at her best when leveling her steely gaze at the Stooges.

A former Miss Maine who became a Broadway actress, Dorothy went to Hollywood in the late 1920s and did good work at Hal Roach with Charley Chase, and in lively support of the Stooges, Andy Clyde, Buster Keaton, and other Columbia two-reel stars. Dorothy is very funny in *From Nurse to Worse* as a perplexed medical receptionist who can't quite believe that Curly is on all fours, behaving like a dog. She's most fondly recalled, though, as Pomeroy's unhappy girlfriend in *So Long, Mr. Chumps* and, especially, as the murderously avaricious socialite Tiska Jones in the convicts-and-gold-diggers comedy *In the Sweet Pie and Pie*.

With an appeal that was intelligent as well as cute, Appleby invariably elevated her material. She retired from movies in 1943.

The boys get ideas in *In the Sweet Pie and Pie* (1941). The girls, led by Dorothy Appleby (far left), have ideas, too. The other actresses are Ethelreda Leopold and Mary Ainslee.

way up there. Moe silently watches, with a kind of dread curiosity, as Curly puts together a shaky assemblage of tables and chairs that will allow him to climb to the top of the beds. He gets there, but sends all three beds crashing to the floor as soon as he lies down.

At a dance lesson the next morning, the attractive instructor (Geneva Mitchell, in footage lifted from the 1935 Stooges short *Hoi Polloi*) says, "Do everything I do" a moment before a bee flies down the back of her dress. In the wiggling that follows, Larry ad libs a hand-clappin' jive dance that's easy to miss, and very funny.

At the buffet table that evening, Larry puts a whole chicken on his plate. Moe asks, "are you gonna eat that alone?"

"No, maybe if I wait, I'll get some potatoes!"

The girls try to force trouble when they instruct the butler to "accidentally" smash a cake in Moe's face. The butler does so, but a society matron (stock-company player Symona Boniface) insists that the butler did it on purpose. In the pie-throwing melee that follows, the guests behave even worse than the Stooges. At the end, Tiska, Taska, and Baska bombard Diggins with pies. His scheme has failed, and the girls are going to be married for a long time.

It's good to see that some institutions are sacred.

A BELATED NOTE TO ACTRESS DORIS COLLEEN HOUCK: *LOVED YOU IN* BRIDELESS GROOM. *You gave Shemp a hard time in that one, but because you're full of fire and sexy as all get out, I'd marry you in a hot minute.*

Even though you'd be hell to live with.

Houck is billed in *Brideless Groom* (1947) as "Doris Colleen." She's the brunette gal with the bullet bra and wasp waist who mashes Shemp's head in a letterpress so that he'll marry her and share a $500,000 inheritance from his Uncle Caleb. Funny as well as great looking, Houck is a regrettable example of unfulfilled potential. She was born in 1921 and worked in Hollywood from 1945 to 1947. She generally took uncredited parts (*Brideless Groom* is one of the happy exceptions), appearing as models, secretaries, showgirls, and waitresses. She's a sexy firebrand and surely one of the best female antagonists the Stooges ever encountered—and she achieved that status with just two or three minutes of screen time.

The origins of *Brideless Groom*, however tenuous, are in *Seven Chances*, a 1916 Broadway comedy by Roi Cooper Megrue. The play revolves around a young fellow who must find himself a bride *tout de suite* or else lose an enormous inheritance. The show was produced by impresario David Belasco and eventually caught the attention of MGM producer Joe Schenck, who bought it for Buster Keaton in 1925.

A key plot element of *Seven Chances* is that Buster has long pined for a particular girl who has refused his proposals for years. After receiving news of his inheritance, and of the one-day deadline for marrying, Buster proposes again and the girl continues to refuse, imagining now that he's interested only in the inheritance money.

The Stooges were seldom given to sentiment, so Shemp has been pining for no one in *Brideless Groom*. In fact, marriage is anathema to him. With Moe and Larry, he ekes out a living as a singing instructor, trying to teach gawky, tone-deaf Miss Dinkelmeyer (Dee Green) how to vocalize while simultaneously avoiding her clutches.

Spurred by news of the inheritance, and with the deadline just hours away, Shemp takes out his little black book and scrambles to find a bride. Despite Moe's irrational optimism ("When Shemp turns on the charm, no dame can resist him!"), one refusal follows another.

The clock continues to tick, but possible salvation arrives in the form of a gorgeous new neighbor, Miss Hamilton (Christine McIntyre). When a gussied-up Shemp knocks on her door, he's instantly mistaken for "Cousin Basil." Miss Hamilton smothers him with noisy kisses, and Moe and Larry, parked in the corridor, are hugely encouraged. But when the real Cousin Basil phones to tell Miss Hamilton he'll be late, Shemp is subjected to a flurry of violent slaps and punches—the last of which sends him right through the door.

By this time, news of the deadline has reached the papers. Shemp has surrendered to Miss Dinkelmeyer, but the women he's phoned crash the wedding. In the dust-up that follows, the boys are kicked around like soccer balls, but in the end, Shemp meets the deadline. "Hey, Shemp, you're married!"

Shemp: "Noo, noo!" Fadeout.

Director Ed Bernds and scripter Clyde Bruckman (adapting his own 1925 treatment of Megrue's *Seven Chances*) see that *Brideless Groom* perks along with a steady surge of verbal and visual gags. Larry is especially wonderful here: stupidly asleep at the piano, wincing when Miss Dinkelmeyer sings, nervously biting and spitting out his fingernails as Shemp makes his calls.

Shemp's struggle to retrieve the wedding ring after it drops into the wires of a grand piano is painfully hilarious, and the sequence with the justice of the peace (Emil Sitka; "Hold hands, you lovebirds!") is simply classic, as Moe and Larry take up rifle butts and bear traps in order to deal with Houck and the other marauding dames, only to become victims of their own cleverness.

Stooges regular Christine McIntyre is luscious as Miss Hamilton, attired in a black peignoir, her blonde hair provocatively arranged atop her head. Although McIntyre wasn't a tall woman, she was curvy and solid, and it's easy to believe that her blows are hurting Shemp. (The final one, in fact, did. McIntyre had been hesitant to really cut loose, but with Shemp's encouragement, she did, accidentally giving him a good clip in the face.)

Gangly Dee Green is ingratiating and very funny, but her career lasted only four years. All but one of her handful of credits are in Columbia shorts with the Stooges, Harry Von Zell, Billie Burke, and others.

And Doris Houck? She died in 1965, just forty-four years old.

See ya around, beautiful. Maybe we can go a few rounds sometime.

Via the dubious magic of stock footage, Doris returned in 1956, when *Brideless Groom* was cleverly rehashed as *Husbands Beware*. About seven minutes of all-new material establishes that Moe and Larry have made the mistake of marrying Shemp's enormous sisters (Maxine Gates and Lu Leonard, billed here as "Lou Leonard"). As ill tempered as they are massive, the brides intone, "I do" and then sock their grooms on the jaws, "just to show you who's gonna be boss around here!" The gals toss all three boys into the kitchen and command them to get busy. Moe takes a straight razor and shaves the feathers from a turkey while Shemp uses an entire container of baking powder to make muffins. Moe mistakes turpentine for salad oil and slathers it all over the denuded bird. Larry knocks a bar of soap into the coffee.

The dinner goes as badly as you might imagine: The bridezillas choke and retch on the bollixed food, and finally throw the boys out of the apartment and into the opposite wall.

Shemp croaks, "Boy, if that's married life, I don't want any part of it! I'll *never* get married!"

Moe, however, isn't going to let things lie: "But you hooked *us*, you rat, and we'll get even with *you!*"

At this point we fade to the singing lessons and subsequent bedlam of *Brideless Groom*. Although the key supporting characters are seen again, only Dee Green and Christine McIntyre are credited. Shemp's spruce-up session after he spies Christine is eliminated for reasons of time, but writer Felix Adler and director Jules White felt a need for Moe to overdub a line when he sets the bear trap on the chair—"I'll lure 'em to sit down!"—as though audiences had grown indescribably dumb since watching this scene in 1947, and needed an explicit explanation of Moe's scheme.

New footage picks up again after the wedding ceremony, via a clever swish-pan that follows the boys from left to right across the screen, and reduces Dee Green's double to a briefly glimpsed background blur. Moe and Larry triumphantly inform Shemp that his Uncle Caleb isn't dead at all, and that the whole story was a ploy to force Shemp into marriage.

Ha ha, but the joke's on them because Shemp picks up a handy revolver (the gentle justice of the peace happens to have left it lying around, I guess) and pumps slugs into his erstwhile pals' fannies.

ALTHOUGH A DISAPPOINTMENT, *HOKUS POKUS* (1949) SHOWS THE STOOGES IN a kindly, selfless light: Their pleasant upstairs neighbor, Mary (Mary Ainslee), is confined to a wheelchair, and while she waits for a $25,000 settlement from her pokey insurance company, the boys faithfully wait on her. But here's the rub: Mary is a conniver and a fraud. She's not injured at all, and secretly laughs about the boys' devotion. When her smarmy boyfriend (Jimmy Lloyd) drops by, Mary sneers, "There's three saps living downstairs who've been waiting on me hand and foot. They swear I'm a hopeless cripple!"

Performer Profile: Emil Sitka
1914–98

With a goofily malleable face, young character actor Emil Sitka found many roles in shorts and features as hayseeds, bosses, rich gentlemen, janitors, butlers, storekeepers, comic lunatics, and, most memorably, as a justice of the peace who struggles mightily to marry Shemp and Dee Green ("Hold hands, you lovebirds!") in *Brideless Groom*.

Unlike many other Stooges stock-company players, Sitka began his career at the Columbia two-reel department, in 1946. He appeared in just one short with Curly, *Half-Wits Holiday*; made his greatest impact during the Shemp years (1947–56); and continued on into the Joe Besser years with his enthusiasm undimmed.

Sitka also functioned at Columbia as an all-purpose, funny character actor adept at zany and subdued and all shadings in between. He was adept at taking falls and occasionally had the opportunity to show his dramatic skills, as in the Stooges' *Fuelin' Around*, in which, as a kidnapped atomic scientist, he's an effectively low-key counterpart to Moe, Shemp, and Larry. He and actor Harold Brauer are the only players who worked with all four iterations of the Stooges, from Curly through Curly-Joe.

Sitka was briefly tapped to be the "third Stooge" following Larry's 1972 stroke and went on to roles in television and features into the 1990s.

Emil Sitka and Dee Green, in a modest lull before the storm in *Brideless Groom* (1947). Among the women assaulting Shemp is the fabulous Doris Houck (third from right).

Photo courtesy of the Stoogeum

Deferential and accommodating, the boys are being suckered, but in the end, they inadvertently expose Mary and her scam, causing her insurance rep (Vernon Dent) to take back her check and tear it to pieces.

Like some other Stooges shorts, *Hokus Pokus* isn't at all organic but simply two protracted sequences tenuously joined together. The first segment details the boys' morning as they clean themselves up and prepare Mary's breakfast (lard-fried eggs, shells and all, and "nice cold hotcakes smothered in vinegar"). This domestic business accounts for the short's best moments as the boys lather and shave each other in a kind of rotating roundelay, straight razors carelessly dragged across tongues and down foreheads and noses. Moe pats on his favorite talcum powder, "Shlemiel No. 8" (one of many Yiddishisms employed by these Jewish comics throughout their careers), and Shemp struggles to set up a card table. Naturally, the fold-down legs won't stay up, and fiendishly snap shut on Shemp's neck and fingers, as if possessed.

Upstairs, Mary taps on a steam pipe to let the boys know she's ready for breakfast. When Moe taps back, Shemp manages to position his noggin between the pipe and the hammer. Yowch! Shemp gives Moe a good glare: "Does my head look like a steam pipe?" Moe: "No, a steam pipe doesn't have ears!"

The second portion of *Hokus Pokus* finds the boys at work as poster hangers, where they meet the dignified hypnotist Svengarlic—"He'll Steal Your Breath Away!"—and his manager (longtime character player Ned Glass). Shortly, all three boys are literally mesmerized. A sequence in which Larry acts like a cat and Shemp behaves like a monkey is mechanical and unfunny; things perk up when the boys prance on a horizontal flagpole high above the street, astonishing the crowd below. When Svengarlic is knocked cold by an errant bicycle, the boys come out of their trance. After much panic (Shemp literally pulls Moe's pants down to his ankles as he tries to climb Moe's body to safety), the pole breaks and sends the Stooges crashing noisily through the window of the insurance company, startling Mary and causing her to jump up from her wheelchair, right in front of the insurance man. Oops.

Shots of the flagpole splintering at its base were lifted from *The Taming of the Snood*, a 1940 Columbia short starring Buster Keaton. (And for you kids who don't know what a snood is, ask Grandma.)

Mary Ainslee began her film career, at twenty, with a 1939 exploitation picture called *Missing Daughters* and followed with *Mad Youth* (1940). To kick off a career with independent roadshow outfits seldom augured well for future professional development, and sure enough, Ainslee never found a profitable niche. She worked in five Stooges shorts and shows up, in stock footage, in another three. She's adequate in *Hokus Pokus*, but, at just thirty, she's already too puffy, too worldly, to play an injured ingénue.

Hokus Pokus was remade as *Flagpole Jitters* (1956). Ainslee shows up in footage from the earlier comedy, with new material establishing that she really is disabled, and a good girl, too. The boys want to earn money to pay for her operation. As Moe would have put it: *schmaltzy.*

In both shorts, a tall, handsome actor named David Bond plays Svengarlic. He's very suave, but by the late 1960s, Bond's face had collapsed in on itself and he did bits on episodic television (often for Jack Webb) as winos, snitches, and other dissolute types.

Vernon Dent is typically stolid—and impatient—as the insurance man. When he visits Mary at her apartment he's just doing his job, but the Stooges don't see it that way. After much aggressive signifyin' by the boys, Vernon pokes Larry in the eyes and slaps Shemp silly. His counterattack is comical, but considered in the context of the boys' kindness to their undeserving neighbor, it somehow seems unfair.

It's enough to make you *krekhts.*

LOVE AT FIRST BITE (1950) IS ABOUT MEMORY AND ANTICIPATION. IT'S ABOUT love, too, but for the Stooges, even when the course of love is smooth, it's bumpy. The greater part of this uneven but often charming short is devoted to the boys' flashback reminiscences about their first meetings with their European sweethearts. The girls are arriving today, together on the same ship, and the boys can't wait to greet them. But when the Stooges get drunk, Shemp is given a concrete footbath by Larry and Moe. He's held fast, and only a dynamite explosion engineered by Larry is powerful enough to propel all three boys to the ship in time.

Okay, the physics of that last part are dubious, and even the most forgiving viewers will decide that most of the sight gags that don't involve the girls are rote and mechanical: A horseshoe affixed above a doorway repeatedly drops on Larry's head; Moe flings his arms wide in happiness (twice), catching Larry and Shemp in the kissers (twice); when Moe and Larry shove at Shemp while he's cemented in the round-bottomed tub, he rocks back and forth, whacking the other Stooges with his fists. (This footage was undercranked, for fast motion—problem is, the soundtrack is speeded up, too, so the boys, in a lazy gaffe that mars more than one of their shorts, momentarily sound like chipmunks.)

A by-the-numbers approach was typical of the director, Jules White, when he decided to be competent and nothing more. Then there's Felix Adler's scripting of these bits, which doesn't give White much to work with in the first place.

A protracted bubblegum bit, however, is pretty funny: Shemp can't stop chewing the stuff (he crams fresh sticks into his mouth like a starving man), and gooey residue is everywhere—most particularly on the phone receiver, where it ensnares Moe's ear.

In more ways than one, the heart of *Love at First Bite* is the trio of flashbacks.

Larry is the first to share his memories. "I was stationed in Italy, eatin' bread and hot dogs and waitin' to be mustered out." Despite what Larry says, he's in a restaurant eating spaghetti. A fan repeatedly blows gobs of the stuff into the slack mouth of a sleeping drunk, who unconsciously chews and swallows it. Larry wraps an absurdly long strand around a meatball and creates a forkful that's as big as a baseball. (Fourteen years later, in *The Disorderly Orderly,* Jerry

Lewis brilliantly carried the gag to its illogical conclusion when the twirled pasta consumes his hand and entire forearm.)

Larry's waitress is Maria (Marie Monteil, who never rose above bits in a five-year career). She's a slender, statuesque Mediterranean beauty with dark eyes and an exuberant smile. For reasons known only to her, she finds Larry's table manners ingratiating, his clumsy flirting irresistible.

Moe's sweetheart is a pigtailed Viennese charmer named Katrina (Christine McIntyre). Moe listens as she trills "The Blue Danube Waltz," and then literally falls for her as she scrubs a floor. When Moe loses his diamond ring in a vase, it ends up on Katrina's finger (after Moe accidentally smashes the vase on his head).

As for Shemp, he was a sailor in Paris, strolling down the *Rue de Schlemiel*, "lookin' for postcards" and "anxious to see the Paris sights." He meets a tall, elegant Parisian named Fifi (Yvette Reynard), and escorts her to a sidewalk café. There, Shemp cleverly ad libs a tussle with a fly in his beer, and generally turns on the charm. A gag involving a small dog that gets beneath the table is played for suggestive laughs. Before Shemp's beer is gone, Fifi is smitten.

At a time when the boys' shorts were growing increasingly set-bound, the café sequence was shot outdoors on a good-looking set in warm sunlight. The cinematographer was Rex Wimpy, who had for many years been a top special-effects cameraman at Warner Bros. His skill brings a delightful, relaxed realism to the sequence. Shemp is ingratiating, and Yvette Reynard's enormous eyes and shy smile are strikingly emphasized. Born Yvette Sarah Heap, Reynard should have had a real career; instead, she worked only a handful of times, most often in uncredited bits.

The Stooges finish their reminiscences, but before leaving for the dock to meet their sweeties they indulge in shots of Old Panther ("Bottled yesterday"). The stuff knocks them flat, and when Moe and Larry come to, they're convinced that they've murdered the still-unconscious Shemp. In the darkest line ever written for any of the Stooges, Moe drunkenly exclaims, "Let's cremate him!"

Larry, impersonating the voice of reason, responds, "We can't do that! We ain't got no cream!" In effect, Moe goes way out of character so that Larry can utter a pun.

The two of them decide to put Shemp's feet in cement and dump him in the river. That's a pretty dark idea, too.

A silly consideration, yet *Love at First Bite* is one of relatively few Hollywood films to deal with a unique phenomenon: the war bride of World War II. Between 1939 and 1946, some 16 million American men enlisted or were conscripted for military service. Demobilization began in 1945, but many thousands of G.I.s remained abroad as occupation troops, often for years. About 750,000 foreign-born brides of American servicemen entered the U.S. between 1946 and the early 1950s, accounting for the largest upsurge of immigration to these shores since the previous great wave of the 1920s. The women came from the United Kingdom, Australia, and, as *Love at First Bite* suggests, Continental Europe. (And although the short doesn't deal with Japanese and other Asian women, 50,000 to 100,000 of them married Americans—and were not allowed to enter the States until the 1952 repeal of the Oriental Exclusion Act.)

Love at First Bite was remade, with some key variations, for 1958 release as *Fifi Blows Her Top*. By this time, of course, Joe Besser was the third Stooge, and the short gives him opportunities to utter some of his prissy, very funny catch phrases, including "Ooh, not so *haaard!*," "Ooh, you're a *snitch!*," and "Not so *loud!*"

Fifi revolves around Joe's longing for a French girl he met in Paris and planned to marry before the two were separated. He's been heartbroken ever since.

The MP who finds Joe in a bistro and drags him away from Fifi is played by former faux-Shemp Joe Palma (who has much more dialogue than usual). Another late-era Stooges regular, vivacious Harriette Tarler, is Joe's waitress. Jules White staged the opening of the bistro sequence with Joe seated at the right side of the screen, his face mostly obscured by a menu. Tarler stands in profile at the table, facing Joe, her gorgeous breasts dominating the left side of the frame. For a long moment, we don't even see her face! It's a crass gag that's eye-popping instead of funny.

Stock footage from *Love at First Bite* allows Larry to once again reminisce about Maria, and Moe about Katrina. And Joe, in a flashback sequence that puts him in a sailor suit and a widow's-peaked hairpiece, recalls sprightly, blonde Fifi (Vanda Dupre). Besser displays his innate charm and sweetness (his love seems kind as well as intense), but the sequence is marred, and jarringly so, by the insertion of sunlit stock footage (the pooch beneath the table) into the sound-stage interior material with Joe and Fifi. By this late date, producer-director Jules White was making shorts on pocket change, and there was no time or money to put Besser and Dupre into a genuine exterior, and no reasonable excuse not to take advantage of the stock footage.

Joe sadly ends his story—and then, in one of those fabulous quirks of fate that usually happen only in the movies, the boys meet their new neighbor across the hall, who turns out to be . . . Fifi! She and Joe embrace joyously, but uh oh: Fifi unhappily tells Joe she's married.

The husband, stock company player Philip Van Zandt (in a surprisingly "realistic" performance), is the jealous type, and when the boys accidentally douse Fifi with the contents of a cocktail shaker, they must hide her while they dry her dress. The husband goes in and out of the apartment, and Jules White puts together some funny, well-timed gags involving the trunk that conceals Fifi, most effectively when the boys move the trunk across the room, unaware that the bottom hasn't come with it, and that Fifi—wearing Joe's pajamas—is crouching on the floor, and about to be spotted by her husband.

During an exchange that reveals the male animal at its worst, Van Zandt buttonholes Joe and confides that he's sorry he ever married Fifi. "Me too!" Joe blurts. "I mean, why don't you get a divorce?"

"I intend to! I've got my new wife all picked out! I'm a little *sick* of this one!"

With that, Fifi rises from the trunk and goes after her rat-husband with a baseball bat, missing him and accidentally conking Larry. When she limbers up for another go, Joe helpfully takes the bat from her hands—and supplies her with a bowling ball.

At the end, the melancholy that was consuming Joe has turned to joy.

Performer Profile: Harriette Tarler
1920–2001

Tall, feline Harriette Tarler pursued a Hollywood career for just three years, 1956–59, dividing her time among television, shorts, and features. She made her mark as a dependable supporting player with the Stooges and was the most frequently seen female stock-company player of the Joe Besser era.

Harriette was shapely and seemed faintly exotic (she was born in New York City); she's particularly entertaining in *Space Ship Sappy* as a sexy cannibal on the planet Sunev; and in *Outer Space Jitters* as one of the sexy space gals who drinks battery acid and is charged with electricity.

And then there are two of the boys' most peculiar shorts, *Hoofs and Goofs* and its sequel, *Horsing Around*; in each, Tarler provides the voice of the talking horse. Is she better than the material? Yes.

She wasn't this modest in the movie! Harriette Tarler takes the boys' orders in *Fifi Blows Her Top* (1958).   *Photo courtesy of the Stoogeum*

It's easy to understand why. French actress Vanda Dupre (born 1927) was a slender, big-eyed blonde with a lilting, musical voice. She also was an adept physical comedienne whose Fifi is a force to be reckoned with. Whether wielding a bat, a bowling ball, an unplugged iron, or just the back of her hand, she's a high-energy avenger, chortling triumphantly as she gives her rotten husband what for. She's a marvel, and the brilliant star character actor Jack Warden apparently thought so, too. He and Dupre married in 1958 and remained together until Warden's death in 2006.

AS WE'VE SEEN, WHERE THERE ARE THE STOOGES AND A BEAUTIFUL WOMAN, there is often a jealous husband. That chestnut motivates *Don't Throw That Knife* (1951), a very poorly paced short that's one of the boys' worst—despite funny, energetic performances from the gorgeous wife (Jean Willes) and the furious husband (frequent Stooges player Dick Curtis).

Although just fifteen minutes fifty seconds, *Don't Throw That Knife* seems interminable. The Stooges are census takers set loose in an apartment building, where they attempt to interview a Mrs. Wycoff, only to become trapped in her flat when her violently inclined husband shows up. It seems that the Wycoffs do an illusionist act in vaudeville, which provides for a couple of not-bad sight gags: a chair that gracelessly collapses the moment Moe sits on it, and Moe's subsequent impersonation of the chair (he hides beneath a slipcover) and his collapse the moment the husband sits on him.

Dick Curtis shines when he reaches across his bed to take his wife's hand, only to react, comically pop-eyed, at the bristly hairs on the mitt he's been squeezing. (The mitt belongs to Shemp, who is found out despite his valiant effort to impersonate the missus from beneath the covers.)

The short falls apart during two sequences. In the first, Moe and Larry are entranced by the Wycoffs' trick mirrors, which distort the boys' faces and bodies. The mirrors would have been effective as a very brief bit of business—a quick startle for the boys. Instead, White stretches the gag to an astonishing one hundred seconds, an absurd length of time, particularly when the soundtrack goes nearly dead silent (the only sounds are Moe and Larry's occasional small grunts of disbelief). The distortions aren't unfunny but they're not hilarious, either. You just wonder when they're going to end.

The bit is set up when Shemp accidentally shatters one of the mirrors. It's only *after* White has tortured the gag (and us) that Mrs. Wycoff exclaims, "You fools! You've ruined my trick mirror!" Besides being a completely redundant observation, how is it that Mrs. Wycoff has elected to keep silent for so long? Why the outburst *now*? Well, that's the way Felix Adler wrote it—or if he didn't, that's the way White chose to direct it.

The other laugh-killing sequence is the climax, when Mr. Wycoff flings knives at Moe and Larry, who obligingly stand stock-still so that Wycoff can do it over and over again. As with the mirrors, the knife-throws could have had comic impact if minimized, if just one or two were thrown, and as the Stooges are moving. But a lot of time is required to set up complex gags, and White had very little of that. He also had to bring the short in at the approximate required length, so he stretched and padded.

Wycoff's final revenge on the Stooges is a trick machine gun that fires eggs, whole and broken. (I don't know—you explain it to *me*.) For no other reason except to set up yet another unfunny gag, Shemp says, "Make mine scrambled," and then patiently waits as Wycoff sets up the gun. The ridiculous pause is emphasized because White cuts from Shemp's taunt to Curtis, and then back to Shemp, who's still waiting! The payoff, three rubbery fried eggs that attach themselves to Shemp's puss, is not amusing.

Some of the dialogue is funny. When the boys practice taking the census, Shemp and Larry pretend to be a couple. Shemp, as the wife, tells Moe, "We're from the South."

"What part?"

"Montreal, Canada."

Later, Moe admonishes, "Remember, we're census takers, not ordinary idiots!"

There is some Abbott and Costello-style confusion each time Mrs. Wycoff responds to the boys' query about her name. Moe has a slight cough, so Larry and Shemp think that Mrs. Wycoff is asking Moe about it each time she says, "Wycoff." The bit goes on just long enough, and gives Larry a good comeback: "Because he don't brush his teeth, lady."

It's a crude, funny line in a short that's otherwise best forgotten.

IN 1946, MARY JANE WARD WROTE A NOVEL CALLED *THE SNAKE PIT*. THE book—which Ward falsely claimed was *not* autobiographical—chronicles the agonies of a young woman after her commitment to a mental hospital. *The Snake Pit* was the best-selling American novel of 1946, and became a hugely popular and controversial 20th Century-Fox film two years later.

During this same period, American mental-health professionals dealt with thousands of cases of post-World War II battlefield "exhaustion"—also called "battle fatigue" or "shell shock." There was a regrettable feeling of shame among many of the soldiers so afflicted, and among their families. In many cases the men hadn't been hurt physically, and family members failed to understand how or why they could be ill.

National awareness of mental illness, plus the misapprehensions of patients and family members, combined to create a climate of . . .

. . . comedy.

At least that's how the two-reel unit at Columbia saw it.

Scrambled Brains (1951) allowed the Stooges to tap into this awareness. The result isn't merely one of the boys' most peculiar shorts but (in moments) one of their funniest. On the other hand, *Scrambled Brains* is as bluntly misogynistic a film as the Stooges ever made.

Shemp has been a resident of Croakers Sanitarium (run by Drs. Hart-Burns and Belcher) for an unspecified period. It's time for him to return home, but Shemp has news: He's engaged to marry his nurse, "my beautiful Nora." She steps into the room, and although Shemp sees a svelte blonde beauty, Moe and Larry see Nora as she really is: overweight, toothless, and frizzy-haired, her eyes tiny and close-set, her voice a peculiarly piping Appalachian drawl.

Larry turns to Moe and gets the ball rolling: "Hey, ya know, I think she's uglier than *you* are!" Moe begins to agree, then gives Larry a good whack.

At the wedding later, Larry heads for the bar: "I better have another drink! I can still see her face!" Moe just grimaces.

Between Nora's first appearance and the climactic wedding, unusual things happen to Shemp. When he says goodbye at the hospital, a hand reaches down from the fireplace flue to shake his. At home, he gnaws at a hangnail and noisily spits it out before tentatively playing the piano. In an eyeblink, he swings into a rollicking boogie-woogie number—not hard to do if you have three hands. Naturally, Moe and Larry can't see the extra one. A moment later a *fourth* and *fifth* hand join the fun, bringing Shemp perilously close to a complete relapse.

When Shemp slams the cover on the keyboard, and then lifts it again, four severed fingers still play. "She won't marry me!" Shemp wails. "She'll call me Stumpy, I know it!"

At bedtime, Shemp says he can't swallow the horse pills the doctor has left for him, and repeatedly spits them out. Moe collides with a wall and spits out his teeth. A burly gent (Vernon Dent) who has a run-in with the Stooges in a phone booth spits out glass after Moe smashes a light bulb in his mouth. Soon the phone booth is destroyed, and Shemp spits out a mouthful of nickels.

Predictably enough, the phone-booth man is Nora's father, and when he shows up at the wedding and spies the boys, he's out for blood. Larry and Moe glimpse the sunlit reflection of Venetian blinds on the wall and knock themselves cold when they hurl themselves at it, as if to escape through a window. (Stan Laurel had used the shadow of a window blind for surreal play in the 1938 Laurel and Hardy feature *Block-Heads.*)

Nora rescues Shemp by flinging him over her shoulder like a sack of meal. Next stop: the joys of married life.

Central to the joke of *Scrambled Brains* is that although Nora is no Venus, Shemp is no god, either. (For a time Shemp Howard was touted, absurdly and rather cruelly, as "the ugliest man in Hollywood.") Choosiness isn't likely to pay off for Shemp (or for Moe or Larry, either). Although his perception of Nora is delusional, we don't get the impression that Shemp is mean-spirited. Mentally clouded or not, he's capable of real love—one of the few times any of the boys were allowed to express depth of romantic emotion.

Nora is played, with an enormous and engaging smile, by screen veteran Babe London, who worked in shorts and features from 1919 (when she was just eighteen years old) to 1960. Okay, London really was no Clara Bow, but she was appealing in a hefty, corn-fed way. She appeared with comics Johnny Arthur,

Eddie Lyons, Lloyd Hamilton, W. C. Fields and, famously, with Laurel and Hardy (in the brilliant 1931 two-reeler *Our Wife*).

All of that is terrific, but this is better: Babe London plays a hospital attendant in *The Snake Pit*.

IMMEDIATELY AFTER WORLD WAR II, THE NUMBER OF WOMEN IN THE AMERIcan workforce declined dramatically. Veterans returned and reclaimed their jobs, sending women back into the home and into culturally approved roles as homemakers and mothers. But many women who had earned their own money during the war effort weren't easily persuaded to forget about the sense of accomplishment and independence they had enjoyed. By 1950, the number of female workers was growing again, by nearly a million jobs a year. At mid-decade, more than a third of all American women held paying jobs outside the home.

Still, very few women achieved workforce positions of real importance and compensation. The "pink ghetto" was where most of them labored, as underpaid factory workers, in restaurants and other service businesses, and as typists, clerks, and other support staff. For many women, the best course to material comfort was marriage—a fact that, in the 1960s, encouraged the notion that by marrying, a woman bartered access to her body for a nice home, good clothes, and everything else that came with the aggressively consumerist postwar American Dream.

The slick chick who's at the center of the 1952 short *Corny Casanovas* is lively and amusing, partly because she hasn't bought into either the wage-slave paradigm *or* marriage. This sexy, big-eyed blonde (Connie Cezan) wants all the goodies without any of the bother. Hence, she's become engaged to all three of the Stooges (none of whom know the truth) with no intention of marrying anybody.

The wisdom of her decision (she's never given a name) is made clear right in the short's opening sequence, as Shemp, Moe, and Larry go through the motions of housework. It's a messy, tedious job, but Moe is sanguine about the future: "We'll soon have wives to do the housework instead of us!"

Well, a wife could hardly do a worse job than the boys, who are attacked by a Murphy bed, clean furniture with a sopping mop, and make a mess with a bucket of water. Moe is the victim of the bucket, and gets an apology from Shemp in the form of some marvelously well-recited fast patter: "Gee, Moe, I'm sorry, Moe, what can a fella say, that's all there is, there ain't no mo!" That kind of gag was old when Shemp was still in knee britches, but because only Abbott and Costello and Jerry Lewis also practiced the kind of patter comedy that had its roots in burlesque and vaudeville, what was old undoubtedly seemed fresh to many. In any case, it's awfully funny.

Because the boys plan to bring their girls over later, they have to re-cover a sofa to make it presentable. Larry cuts through the bolt of fabric Moe holds, accidentally shearing through Moe's new sport coat. Shemp carelessly hammers an upholstery tack into the top of Moe's hand, but Larry redeems himself (and, it seems, saves the day) by loading tacks into a carbine automatic, which blasts the tacks into the sofa back quickly and neatly. Naturally, Larry and Shemp begin to quarrel over who gets to shoot next just as Moe bends over the sofa. The next minute is devoted to yanking the tacks, one by one, from Moe's abused arse.

It gets worse. Moe swallows some tacks and the other boys try a rescue. "The tacks won't come out!" Larry says.

Shemp offers, "They went in, maybe they're income tax!"

Following some personal cleanup (during which Moe inadvertently lathers his face with Shemp's ebony shoe polish and then makes Shemp drink the stuff), the boys show up, one by one, at the girl's apartment. As each suitor arrives, the girl hides the previous one in the back of the apartment. Each Stooge arrives with an engagement ring (the stone in Larry's is so small he presents it with a magnifying glass), and Shemp brings a bonus: a portrait of himself, which causes the girl's kitten to shrink back and growl.

When Moe and Larry accidentally meet in a back hallway, they drag each other into the living room, where they discover Shemp. The girl takes a cake in the face while the boys enact a primal scene: men fighting to claim a woman. Moe knocks Shemp flat and inflates Larry's abdomen with air that he busily pumps in with a fireplace bellows. When Moe steps on Larry's stomach, he brings forth a belch of soot that turns Larry's face as black as a golliwog's. But Larry grabs the fireplace shovel, gives Moe a couple of smart cracks on the shins, and proceeds to beat him senseless. Finally, Larry is so pooped that the sexy schemer—by now cleaned up and ready to move on—takes the shovel and uses it to clobber Larry. All three boys are down for the count.

The good-looking dish brushes her hands together and makes for the door, laughing, "So long, suckers!"

Corny Casanovas marks a solid, declarative victory for women. The girl is a schemer, but the Stooges' hubristic dream of marrying in order to gain a slave softens her villainy. In essence, the boys get just about what they deserve.

When the short was remade in 1957, scene for scene, as *Rusty Romeos*, Connie Cezon (note the altered spelling of this very funny actress's surname) was brought back. This time, she has three names—Mary, Sally, and Mabel—one for each of her suitors. The remake swells with stock footage; director Jules White shot only as much new material as was needed to get Shemp's replacement, Joe Besser, into crucial scenes. Even the climactic meeting of the boys at Connie's apartment is accomplished via a combination of five-year-old footage of Cezan with Moe, and Larry, and new stuff with the actress and Joe. Connie was a bit fleshier than in 1952, but she still looked good in the same black dress, and is certainly as conniving as before.

This time, though, at a period when the married-gal ideal was affixed to the bedrock of American expectations, our shapely schemer doesn't walk out scot-free. No, this time Joe (who in real life occasionally demurred at some of the violent bits of business that were expected of him) takes that magical carbine and riddles Connie's derriere with tacks—and then whacks her bottom with the butt of the gun, just for good measure.

Score one for the Stooges. Somehow, though, it ain't as funny as it was the first time around.

"PHILANDERER" IS THE NOUN FORM OF "PHILANDER," WHICH MEANS TO CARRY on sexually with numerous women (often women other than one's wife), with no

Performer Profile: Connie Cezan
1925–2004

Curvy stage and screen actress Connie Cezan (real name: Cezon) was blessed with enormous, pretty eyes—eyes that looked so much like Bette Davis's that Cezan's career never developed (although she did work, years after the two-reel era, as Bette's double during the shoot of *Dead Ringer*).

Almost invariably cast opposite the Stooges as a sexy schemer, Connie shines in *Corny Casanovas* as a gold-digging gal who's simultaneously engaged to Moe, Shemp, and Larry; and in that short's remake (with new footage of Connie), *Rusty Romeos*. Her beautifully insincere signature line in both, as she greets each of her fiancés in turn: "I knew you were coming so I baked a cake!"

Naturally, Connie ends up wearing it.

Following an on-again off-again stint on TV's *Perry Mason* as Perry's receptionist, Connie retired from the screen in 1964. She later owned a cat-boarding business called Connie's Kitty Kastle.

Saucer-eyed Connie Cezan plays not-so-hard-to-get in *Corny Casanovas* (1952).

Photo courtesy of the Stoogeum

intention of marrying any of them. It's from the Greek word *philandros*, which also inspired a common 18th-century name, Philander.

Observe Larry at work in the 1952 short *He Cooked His Goose*, and you'll understand why parents don't name their sons "Philander" any more. Larry plays a prosperous pet-shop owner who fills his days with sexual intrigue: horsing around with his sexy secretary, Miss Lapdale (Theila Darrin), romancing Shemp's girl, Millie (Angela Stevens), and scheming to wreck Shemp's relationship with Millie by sending Shemp (who needs a job) to model men's underwear for Moe's wife, Belle (Mary Ainslee).

In today's parlance, Larry thinks he's too smart for the room, and for a while it looks as though he's right. Shemp does indeed run afoul of Moe but manages to set things right by exposing Larry and handing him over to Moe for a good beating and a little Stooges-style gunplay.

The deliberate and complex structure of *He Cooked His Goose* is nicely accomplished, marking the short as one of the better and more unusual collaborations of writer Felix Adler and director Jules White. The added fillip of Larry as the central, motivating character puts an ostensibly gentler face on the proceedings. But *this* Larry (attired in a heavy, badly fitted wool suit ensemble topped off with a ridiculously oversized "Southern colonel's" tie, sweet-talks his victims even as he sets them up for disaster. Oh, what a two-faced rat!

The script makes amusing incidental use of the pet-store setting. When Moe drops by on a presumably friendly visit, Larry offers him coffee. Moe declines but says he'll have a little of that birdseed. He munches a handful, and then bursts into beautiful birdcalls. Later, Larry introduces Shemp to Cedric, the world's only trained clam. Cedric, nestled in Larry's palm, obediently claps out the number of days in a week, and then demonstrates "what we do when we don't like someone" by giving Shemp a good squirt in the kisser.

When Larry has to make a phone call, he dials . . . and dials and dials and dials. "Whew, what a long prefix!" he says.

Other physical gags are pretty cute. When Larry slips on a golf ball at Millie's, he executes a face-crunching fall, with hilarious body English and no stunt double. (This is one of those moments when we're reminded that Larry, a onetime boxer, was a fine athlete.)

At home, Moe struggles unsuccessfully to prevent his Christmas tree from falling onto his head. Wife Belle secretly wishes he'd fall and break his neck. (Maybe there's some wisdom behind Larry's determination never to get married!) When Moe accidentally swallows a string of lights, he opens his shirt to reveal his chest, which glows as if under a fluoroscope.

At Millie's apartment, Shemp accidentally pours water on Millie's little dog, and hurries to rectify his lapse by twisting the pooch (a cleverly cut-in flexible prop dog) like a dishrag to wring out every drop.

Later, Shemp visits Belle to obligingly show the two-piece underwear ensemble (a horror of tassels and mismatched patterns), artfully prancing like a Parisian runway model. Shemp's skinny legs and sock garters are especially attractive touches. When Moe unexpectedly arrives, Shemp hides beneath a bearskin rug and then scurries up the fireplace flue. Moe hears a noise, investigates, and is rewarded with a brick that drops resoundingly onto his forehead.

As the climax approaches, Larry clocks Moe by opening a door in his face; a little later, Shemp does the same to Larry. (There's a particularly sharp bit of timing after Moe is smacked by the door: He staggers down the corridor and turns a corner just as the elevator at the end of the corridor opens to reveal Larry. They miss seeing each other by inches.)

Starlet Mary Ainslee is intentionally unsympathetic as Belle, but actresses Angela Stevens and Theila Darrin are delights. Stevens, a tall blonde cast here as (probably) a redhead, was under contract at Columbia during much of the 1950s. Science fiction fans know her as Richard Denning's sexy, good-natured wife in the Sam Katzman-Columbia production *Creature with the Atom Brain* (1955), and she's positively revelatory in an earlier, independent picture, *Without Warning* (1952), as a sensual good-time girl who accepts a ride from a serial killer. Much of Stevens' other work was in westerns. A former model who fell into acting (it never was her ambition), Stevens was a skilled, low-key actress with an ingratiating manner. When Larry shows up at her apartment, she notes, with a subtly expressed mix of mild resignation and withering distaste, "*You* again."

Brunette Theila Darrin's bit as Miss Lapdale is brief, but Jules White wisely allowed her to make the most of it. She sways into Larry's office in a form-fitting skirt and sweater that leave little of her astounding figure to the imagination. As she takes down Larry's letter (while sitting on his lap, of course), she perpetrates what may never have been accomplished by anybody, before or after: She steals a scene from Larry Fine—and it's as simple as slowly running her tongue over her lower lip as she scribbles on her pad. Because *He Cooked His Goose* was released on July 3, theaters from coast to coast must have had to crank up the air conditioning in a hurry after Darrin's clever, attention-getting ploy.

The short was remade in 1957 (for 1959 release) as *Triple Crossed*, with Joe Besser in the Shemp role. Changes to the original are slight and don't alter the thrust of the story. When Moe investigates the fireplace, we clearly hear Shemp's exclamation, and this time Moe doesn't shoot at Larry but merely tears his hair out by the roots.

Mary Ainslee and Theila Darrin come back but in stock footage only. The credits note Ainslee as "Ainsley," while Theila Darrin is credited under what had by then become her professional name, Diana Darrin.

Angela Stevens comes back in stock footage, too, and—rather delightfully—in a couple minutes of new footage with Besser, written by Warren Wilson. (The sequence catches Stevens in the kitchen, where Joe presents her with a turkey that isn't quite dead.)

Stevens also looped new dialogue over her earlier footage, saying "I have a date with Joe" instead of "with Shemp"—though her mouth clearly says "Shemp."

Mary Ainslee didn't return at all, but her voice did, in scenes with Joe that feature an uncredited Connie Cezan, who was shot only from behind. (Because a sliver of Cezan's face is visible, viewers who are familiar with her features will

Performer Profile: Diana Darrin
b. 1933

Voluptuous, angel-faced Diana Darrin began her film career in 1952 (as Theila Darrin) and remained active until 1963, before returning for another flurry of work in 1973. She was relaxed and confident on screen and served the Stooges well in roles as secretaries, girlfriends, and even a luscious space babe.

The acting ability of starlets working in the two-reel unit was generally high, but Darrin was particularly skillful. TV and features allowed her to show a dramatic side (she has featured roles in a few girls-in-trouble melodramas), and she brought considerable comic flair to her work with the Stooges. And as we'll see elsewhere in this book, she played cleverly to the camera and always to her advantage.

Genre fans recall Diana as a nurse in a pair of 1957 releases, *The Incredible Shrinking Man* and *The Amazing Colossal Man*. Like some other starlets of the day, Darrin deserved a much more significant career but was typecast because of her physical charms.

Diana Darrin enchants the boys—and will later steal a scene from Larry—in *He Cooked His Goose* (1952). At this early stage of her career, the actress called herself Theila Darrin.

Photo courtesy of the Stoogeum

recognize her.) Connie's blonde hair is more platinum and noticeably longer than what Ainslee wore in the old footage, and Connie's figure is better, too. Nevertheless, the Ainslee-Cezan stuff is cut together pretty cleverly, and Connie picked up a paycheck—but what an unrewarding assignment!

Philandering doesn't pay, but uncredited day work at Columbia was no gold mine, either.

GENTS IN A JAM (1952) IS WRITER-DIRECTOR EDWARD BERNDS'S COMBINATION of domestic comedy and jealous-husband mayhem. The short's first half is given over to the Stooges' maladroit attempts to paint an apartment belonging to their landlady. Shemp stirs the paint and blithely slathers the stuff all over the rug; Larry brings equal vigor to his attack on a door molding and Moe's shoe, leg, and face. Shemp paints *around* a table radio rather than take the trouble to move it. (When he does, at Moe's angry suggestion, he neglects to unplug it, creating a frightful tension that shortly sends the radio hurtling through a window.)

In the kitchen later, Shemp struggles to get the upper hand on a pair of faucets that give out with water only when Shemp *isn't* there with his bucket.

The boys have offered to paint because they can't pay their rent, and now the apartment is a wreck. Their landlady, Mrs. McGruder (Kitty McHugh), is ready to throw them into the street—until Shemp receives a telegram from his wealthy Uncle Phineas, who's coming for a visit. Mrs. McGruder allows the boys to stay.

Existing parallel with the boys, the landlady, and Uncle Phineas (Emil Sitka) is a young couple, the Duggans. The husband, Rocky (the very large Mickey Simpson) is a professional strongman who tears telephone books in half. When his attractive wife (Dani Sue Nolan) visits the boys to borrow a cup of sugar, Shemp accidentally steps on her hem and strips her of her skirt.

In the action that follows, Rocky chases the boys up and down the corridors, and repeatedly knocks Uncle Phineas flat. Mrs. McGruder, the only person with a notion of how to control the situation, decks Rocky with one punch and then cuddles the addled Phineas. The two, you see, were childhood sweethearts. When they marry, Shemp will no longer be his uncle's sole heir.

Edward Bernds was a clever writer, and smartly utilizes Uncle Phineas as a sort of blind. We think the short is about Phineas' money, but the real subject is that old bugbear, man-woman relations. Moe articulates this during a rather remarkable one hundred-word monologue that he delivers to Shemp and Larry as a sort of lecture—unaware that Mrs. McGruder is standing behind him. He begins, "Scared? Of a woman? I'll tell that biddy [Mrs. McGruder] a thing or two or three! Where does she come off with that frog face? I'll tell her! Women! I tame 'em like Frank Buck tames tigers! Sometimes I'm kind to 'em [here, Moe strokes Larry on the forehead, to Larry's evident pleasure], sometimes I crack the whip and make 'em jump [Moe slaps Larry's nose]."

Moe goes on in this vein, promising that by the time he's finished charming Mrs. McGruder, she'll give the boys the apartment rent free. Naturally, Moe's bravado melts like butter in August the moment Mrs. McGruder confronts him.

His lecture becomes an unintentional joke on him, and a subversion of his cocksure sense of his masculine appeal, a little boy's illusion.

Gents in a Jam is well played by all. Kitty McHugh was a screen veteran (and sister of star character actor Frank McHugh and the less prominent Matt McHugh). Her no-nonsense performance grounds the short in a semblance of reality.

Twenty-nine-year-old Dani Sue Nolan had dark good looks and an appealingly husky voice. She's tall and lean, and you can believe that she's the wife of a strongman. Although hardly a household name, Nolan was well liked by TV producer Quinn Martin, who hired her for guest shots in many of his shows, including *The FBI, The Invaders, Barnaby Jones, The Fugitive,* and *Cannon.*

Handsome, big-boned Mickey Simpson did *Gents in a Jam* at about the midpoint of his thirty-year career. Although he worked mainly in TV westerns, genre fans recall him as a "native" tribesman in the peculiar 1952 farce *Bela Lugosi Meets a Brooklyn Gorilla.* Simpson seldom worked in comedy, but he had a flair for it: When he meets the Stooges (before everything goes south), he says, "Want me to tear a telephone book for ya?"

That's the kind of guy a gal likes to have around the house.

In 1947, a young American actor took the lead in a new play by Tennessee Williams, and proceeded to change the course of acting for a generation. The play was *A Streetcar Named Desire.* The actor, of course, was Marlon Brando. The character he played, a passionate lout named Stanley Kowalski, was impressive in concept, but as interpreted by Brando in a torn undershirt—on Broadway and, in 1951, in a hugely popular Hollywood feature—Kowalski became the template for a new breed of rebellious anti-hero.

Attracted almost against his will to a timid, sexually repressed older woman, Stanley shocks and excites her with his appetites: for sex, for dominance, for food, for understanding. As a literary figure, Stanley is triumphal and tragic. Half id and all man, he quickly became shorthand for the repellent yet alluring nature of male fury.

In 1952, who better to bring his own interpretation of the character to the screen than Larry Fine?

Nobody, that's who.

Of all the Stooges' shorts, none arouses as much debate and even disdain as *Cuckoo on a Choo Choo* (1952). Relatively short at fifteen minutes twenty-eight seconds, it nevertheless contains enough surrealism, hallucinogenic romance, alcoholism, felony theft—and purloined Tennessee Williams—to perplex and annoy even the most tolerant viewer. And yet it's not without its charms.

Larry and Shemp are ensconced inside a Pullman car they've somehow stolen from a moving train and hidden on a rail siding. The car is named "Schmow," and it's overflowing with desire. Larry is hot to marry brunette Lenore (Patricia Wright), but he can't because family tradition dictates that Lenore's blonde sister, Roberta (Victoria Horne), marry first. Larry must wait to be wed—that is, he has to wait to have sex.

Alcoholism, busted romance, hallucinations, a stolen rail car named *Schmow*—they all figure in the boys' most bizarre short, *Cuckoo on a Choo Choo* (1952). Coming along for the ride are Victoria Horne (left) and Patricia Wright.   *Photo courtesy of the Stoogeum*

The trouble is that Roberta isn't likely to marry anybody anytime soon. She's a neurotic, blubbering (and quite funny) "beanpole" (to quote Larry) who can't get her man, Shemp, to pop the question.

Shemp's troubles are twofold. First, he's an alcoholic who refuses to function in the "real" world inside the rail car named *Schmow* because he finds his DTs a more appealing alternative. This topsy-turvy nod to the dark 1945 film *The Lost Weekend* (in which the protagonist is terrified by his DTs) is an indicator of Shemp's second trouble, which to him is no trouble at all: His DTs take the form of a six-foot canary called Carrie, whom Shemp loves.

In a mild twist that further marks *Cuckoo on a Choo Choo* as a cracked oddity in the Stooges' canon, the boys don't function as a team. Rather, Moe shows up some minutes into the story, as a belligerent detective with the Penciltucky Railroad. With his badge oddly yet proudly displayed on his necktie, Moe has come for *Schmow*, and neither Larry, Shemp, nor either of the dames is going to deter him.

Larry regards Moe as yet another impediment to his pursuit of Lenore and does not greet him warmly. In a demonstration of his displeasure, Larry uses Moe's ear canal to pop the cap from a bottle of beer. Crude and boorish in his torn undershirt, and habituated to yelling with his mouth full, Larry is mainly appetite. He guzzles his beer joyously, with abandon, and even uses some of the brew to give himself an impromptu shower. He crams limburger-and-fishmeal sandwiches into his mouth so quickly he can barely chew, and speaks rudely to everybody, Lenore included.

Well, Larry is what he is, but Shemp is living on another planet. His boozing (which is accompanied by audio of whirs, bells, slide whistles, and bass drums) invariably produces visions of Carrie. She's definitely a bird yet strangely human-oid, coyly prancing in Peter Pan shoes and sending long-lashed winks in Shemp's direction. Against such formidable competition, Roberta has no chance.

Larry was understandably fond of *Cuckoo on a Choo Choo*. He seems to have had fun with this role that encouraged him to be coarse in a way that was new not only to him but to every actor in Hollywood. When Lenore slips her fingers beneath his raveled undershirt and passionately grips his back, Larry flexes his trapezius in animal pleasure, and you get the idea that Lenore might just throw family tradition out the window.

On the debit side, too many gags in *Choo Choo* are not directly related to the plot and come at us as a random mishmash. When a skunk lands on Shemp's shoulder, he calls it a "pussycat." A hideaway Pullman bed falls on Moe's head. When an electric shaver drops down the back of Shemp's shirt, he's sufficiently stimulated to plant wild kisses on Roberta and even on Lenore, who for a moment seems ready to give Larry the ozone. The shaver gag is forced and not particularly funny, but at least it brings the humor back around to the nature of the characters.

Patricia Wright was an attractive actress who toiled mainly in episodic TV in the 1950s. One of her feature credits, *Chained for Life* (1951), an exploitation vehicle for conjoined twins Daisy and Violet Hilton, is of minor interest to Z-movie buffs.

Lanky Victoria Horne was a pretty woman whose gentle, expressive features add pathos to her characterization of the miserable Roberta. Horne had a handle on neurotic types: She's very funny in *The Good Humor Man* (1950), a knockabout comedy that casts her as a new bride who's frustrated on her wedding night when the title character (Jack Carson) barges into her honeymoon suite. Horne retired after marrying star character player Jack Oakie.

Ultimately, *Cuckoo on a Choo Choo* is unable to reconcile its parts and doesn't hang together. Too much is going on and the tone is all over the place. Shemp's alcoholism isn't at all funny, and Carrie Canary (played by an unlucky but game actor named Reggie Dvorak) is just creepy.

Still, Felix Adler, Jules White, the boys, and the rest of the cast took risks here. Those risks don't completely pay off, but they are integral to a film about which nobody is going to be neutral.

THE BOYS' NEXT COLLISION WITH THE FEMALE GENDER OCCURS IN *GYPPED IN the Penthouse* (1955), a short that's not well recalled by Stooges fans—and for good reason, because it's poorly paced and has a mean streak, too. But it also has a chic, unusually handsome apartment set and a featured role for gorgeous Jean Willes, who sets the plot (such as it is) in motion.

Shemp and Larry run into each other at the ritzy Woman Haters Club 87. (It's apparently a franchise!) Inside, well-dressed gents smoke cigars, read the paper, imbibe, and complain about the dames who have made their lives miserable. Via flashback, Larry explains that he answered a lonely-hearts ad and got mixed up with a beautiful girl named Jane (Willes), who took him for a 2.5-carat engagement ring and then threw him over for another guy (Moe). In the ensuing fisticuffs, Larry took a beating.

Shemp's tale is similar, except that when he offered Jane a ring, the scheming chick (Willes again, in the same role) whipped out a handy jeweler's loupe to give the rock the once-over. The carats really hit the fan when the gal's husband (Moe again) came home unexpectedly,

In a wrap-up that's embarrassingly telegraphed, another Woman Hater (Emil Sitka) introduces Shemp and Larry to a new member—Moe of course. (We know it's Moe because he's been standing there, with his back turned, for thirty seconds.) Shemp and Larry flee, only to literally run into Jane on the sidewalk outside. She's carrying her groceries, and the boys take their revenge by humiliating her with her own milk, eggs, and flour.

Statuesque, almost regal, Jean Willes took *Gypped in the Penthouse* with more grace than the material deserves. The bit with the loupe is sharp; likewise a gag during her flashback interaction with Larry, when she lights up a cigar after he lights a cigarette.

Later, with Shemp, Willes is very funny from behind a dressing screen, where she makes chitchat while tossing her black scanties across the screen's upper edge—much to Shemp's dismayed anticipation. (Turns out she's just removing things from a dresser drawer.) And Willes sets up a cute line when she tucks Shemp's ring into her cleavage: Shemp glances at the camera and says, "There must be a way to get that ring without getting in trouble with the censor!" Oh, no, there isn't.

The climax isn't the only nasty physical gag. When Larry and Moe battle it out at Jane's apartment, Larry cracks Jane on the forehead with a piece of crockery and then shoves Moe's head square into Jane's middle, knocking her flat.

Other bits are more agreeable. Shemp (wearing one of Jane's dressing gowns after her dishwasher drenches his suit) plays Jane's piano like "that guy with the candelabra," and has a good tussle with the instrument when the ring drops inside.

When Moe shows up, Shemp dashes under the bed. In an especially good piece of physical comedy, Jane's cat follows a mouse right up Shemp's pants leg, causing Shemp to upend the bed and toss Moe across the room.

The best line goes to Emil Sitka, who addresses Moe as Moe struggles to free himself from a full fishbowl that's become stuck on his head: "Can I get you a drink of water?"

ACTRESS MAXINE GATES, WHO PLAYED ONE OF THE FRIGHTENING, ELEPHAN-tine wives in *Husbands Beware,* returned for *Muscle Up a Little Closer* (1957). This time, Gates is a sympathetic figure—in fact, she's Joe's sweet-natured fiancée, Tiny. When Tiny's ring is stolen from her locker at Seabiscuit Food Corp. ("Seabiscuit Gives You an Appetite Like a Horse"), Joe and the boys pitch in to help her find it. In the end, the culprit turns out to be another employee, Elmo (Matt Murphy). Although burly, he's no match for Tiny, who makes him cough up the ring after punting him around the company gym like a deflated football.

Joe Besser was no physical lightweight, but he seems small next to Gates, who's tall and one of those fat people who appear firm and very strong rather than doughy and helpless. As a heavyset woman working in Hollywood, Gates had to be philosophical about the sorts of roles she was offered. Whether cast as villainess or sweetie pie, she had to appear to be a good sport about it. That's certainly the case here. When the ring is discovered to have gone missing, Tiny miserably flings herself onto her bed, collapsing it and squashing Larry (who's been searching under there). At the company gym, Tiny encourages Joe to get into shape with weightlifting. She hefts a tremendously laden barbell to demonstrate proper technique. When she returns the load to the floor she says, "C'mon, Joe, pick it up!"

"Pick it up," Joe complains, "I can't even *bend*!"

When the thieving Elmo is found out, Joe is furious. "Let go of me!" Joe shouts as Tiny holds him back. "Let go of me!"

Tiny finally obeys and Joe is aghast: "Ooh, she let *go* of me!"

During her climactic drubbing of Elmo, Gates demonstrates an agile flex-ibility as she repeatedly tugs the thief to his feet and flips him over her shoulder. No double stands in for her, and Matt Murphy didn't need one either. He was a screen and TV actor only occasionally; he did most of his playacting in the ring, as a professional wrestler known as K. O. Matt Murphy. (Readers interested in observing Murphy in his element are referred to *The Best of Nick Bockwinkel,* a DVD set that includes a Murphy-Bockwinkel bout from 1965.)

As a screen actor, Murphy was a very good wrestler, delivering his lines stiffly but dishing out plenty of lively physical abuse to the boys before Tiny gets into the act. When Murphy tosses Larry across the room like a sack of meal, Larry flies into camera range in a blur, landing on his shoulder and upper arm before expertly angling himself so that he can drop his head into Moe's lap. Director Jules White framed the bit cleverly, and it's likely that somebody just out of camera range—Murphy, perhaps—helped Larry execute the flip. However the gag was accomplished, it was done without a double, and is another reminder of Larry's athleticism, which hadn't deserted him at age fifty-four.

In a protracted sequence in the company warehouse, the boys go about their work as shipping clerks, destroying fragile packages and making a terrible mess after Joe smashes a crate of raw eggs. In a pair of impressive and potentially dangerous fire gags, Joe uses an acetylene torch to send a jet of flame between

Moe's legs; Moe returns the favor by frying Joe's backside when Joe flings himself on the floor to have a temper tantrum.

Other gags are more oblique. In the short's best dialogue exchange, Larry notes that a shipment has arrived from Japan. "What's in it?" Moe asks. "Matzos," says Larry, deadpan. Moe: "Oh, just in time for Thanksgiving."

The short's preoccupation with physical fitness is a reflection of the then-burgeoning health-club industry, especially as exemplified by California body-builder and entrepreneur Vic Tanny, who favored sport coats tailored to show off his enormous shoulders. He began to hit his stride as a health-club owner after opening a unit in Santa Monica in 1939. By the end of the 1950s, the decade of his business's greatest and most visible growth, his corporation operated some eighty clubs across the country. Tanny made a special point to keep his gyms clean and modern, and to solicit female as well as male patrons. Hence the logic behind Tiny's obvious familiarity with workout equipment, and her eagerness to get Joe in on the fun.

FROM THE BEGINNING OF THE STOOGES' TWO-REEL CAREER AT COLUMBIA, AN omnipresent comic element is the boys' absurd and certainly unjustifiable confidence in their heterosexual appeal. The joke grew funnier in the 1940s, as the Stooges entered middle age, and funnier still when horse-faced Shemp and prissy Joe came on the scene.

By the late 1940s, the Stooges favor double-breasted suits—never a good choice for dumpy fellows less than five-and-a-half feet tall. But there they stand, preening, dapper and ridiculous, endlessly optimistic about their powers of seduction. Although frequently spurned, they are embraced nearly as often. In many shorts, they have girlfriends or wives, even pretty ones, and you wonder, *What got into these dames?*

The Stooges' final overtly gender-based short is *A Merry Mix-Up* (1957), a simultaneous elaboration and culmination of the boys' on-screen interactions with women. This two-reeler, number 177 of 190, marks the only time the Stooges are out-and-out objects of violent female desire. There are beautiful women in the boys' lives, and those women want them—not because Larry, Moe, and Joe are handsome or brilliant or wealthy (though they do appear to be comfortably middle-class) but because the Stooges are their men. Period.

Felix Adler's lively script borrows from a 1936 Laurel and Hardy feature, *Our Relations*, in which Stan and Ollie play two sets of identical twins who tangle with their wives and an overgrown headwaiter at a nightclub. Adler upped the ante, using as his premise three sets of identical triplets, separated since the war, who are unexpectedly reunited in the course of one momentous day.

Larry, Moe, and Joe are unmarried. With the Stooges playing *all* the brothers, we shortly meet Louie, Max, and Jack, who are amiably henpecked by their beautiful wives (Harriette Tarler, Nanette Bordeaux, and Suzanne Ridgeway). Finally, we have Luke, Morris, and Jeff, who are happily engaged to three other beauties (Jeanne Carmen, Diana Darrin, and Ruth Godfrey White).

In action centered mainly in a swanky restaurant, the three sets of brothers are slapped, rapped with baseball bats, and kicked by the women because of mistaken identity, and unjust accusations of lying and philandering. But—and this is important—the women also go after each other in a hair-pulling frenzy as they lay claim to their mates. (When Ruth Godfrey White knocks Suzanne Ridgeway's hat from her head, Ridgeway breaks character for an instant to quickly rearrange her hair!)

This is real cat-fight action, and Joe, in a verbalization of a not-uncommon male fantasy, says, "I *like* watching women fight over *me*!"

During a climax that's cleverly stage-managed by director Jules White, cinematographer Irving Lippmann, and editor Harold White, all nine Stooges appear together in the same frame. A subsequent use of doubles allows the three sets of triplets to hug and chatter, as the wives and girlfriends goggle in amazement. (The casting of all those people shot the budget to hell, so the restaurant has no customers other than the Stooges and the women.)

Then there's the waiter (Columbia contract player Frank Sully), who chases various triplets through the restaurant, demanding that they pay their bill. When he sees all nine in one room, he snaps, and beats himself into unconsciousness with the flat side of a meat cleaver.

In a nod to Paddy Chayefsky, the Stooges reprise the famed "Where you wanna go?" "I dunno, where do *you* wanna go?" dialogue from *Marty* (1955), and later make the mistake of rhapsodizing about some Cornish hens as their wives listen from the other side of the door: "Boy, are they beautiful!" "Yeah, and what beautiful legs they have!" "And young! Now there's somethin' I could really go for!"

All six actresses are alternately cuddly and mad as hell. Sexy stock-company player Suzanne Ridgeway has more lines here than in any Stooges short she ever did; her emphatic manner and angry dark eyes are highlights of this very funny film. Diana Darrin is no less scrumptious than when she was calling herself Theila Darrin, and starlet Jeanne Carmen enjoys a nice showcase as Larry's fiancée. Carmen was an accomplished trick golfer who became a pin-up model before getting into movies. Many years later, as a sexy Newport Beach matron, she claimed to have been a close friend of Marilyn Monroe and offered her own insights into the circumstances of MM's death.

All of that was highly charged, even baroque, with details far different from the cheerfully uncomplicated possessiveness that motivates *A Merry Mix-Up*, Columbia's inventive finale to the Stooges' perennial misadventures with the fairer sex.

4

The Stooges and the Sporting Life

In which the boys discover that not every bull is as sweet as Ferdinand; athletes need their daily minimum requirement of cream puffs; wild hyacinth is potent stuff; golf-course groundskeepers are awfully high-strung; a duck will outsmart you every time; the goalpost is in the other direction; "Pop Goes the Weasel" will always be there when you need it; a hatpin is okay but a left cross is better; Moe owes Shemp five bucks; and Curly is a victim of soicumstance.

Today, with professional boxing in confused disarray, particularly at the heavyweight level, it's difficult to recall that, beginning in the 1920s and continuing for some fifty years, the sport was one of America's most popular. Public interest during the prewar years wasn't just national but was a force that germinated and flourished at many levels—regional, state, municipal, and even neighborhood-by-neighborhood. Everybody had a "favorite son," and boxing became a lingua franca capable of uniting strangers. In venues encompassing small halls rented for Elks smokers to Madison Square Garden and Yankee Stadium, men boxed. Although movie stars, politicians, socialites, and other celebrities were fixtures at ringside, boxing was egalitarian, with ticket prices within the reach of the average Joe and Jane. In those years dominated by newspapers, radio, and newsreels, boxing was an Everyman diversion. Its only challenger was baseball.

Because of the Stooges' exposure in MGM shorts and features that predated the team's Columbia years, audiences were already predisposed to laugh at the notion of the boys in any kind of sporting endeavor—and none seemed more unlikely than boxing. In *Punch Drunks* (1934), the Stooges' second Columbia short (and the only one with a script credited to Howard, Fine, and Howard), Moe is a two-bit boxing promoter who can't help but notice a waiter (Curly) who goes berserk when he hears that old chestnut "Pop Goes the Weasel." Another fellow in the restaurant (Larry) has been playing the tune on his violin, inspiring Curly to mop up the floor with Moe's lunch companions. An idea is hatched: As long the strains of "Pop Goes the Weasel" are kept within Curly's hearing, he'll be unbeatable in the ring.

With Larry and violin at ringside, Curly blasts upward through the ranks, until he's matched against Killer Kilduff (Al Hill) for the championship. When Kilduff gets lucky and knocks Curly through the ropes, our brawler accidentally squashes Larry's violin (which the delusional Larry bemoans as "my Stradivarius!"). Frantic because Curly is getting the whey knocked out of him, Moe sends Larry on a mission to find something, anything, that plays the song. After much running (with humorously loud footfalls) along a business avenue (North Larchmont Boulevard), Larry finds a tabletop radio, which he breaks when the cord yanks him short. He finally comes upon a flatbed truck with an enormous speaker letting loose with, conveniently enough, "Pop Goes the Weasel." (When Larry hops into the cab and drives off, the unsuspecting guy standing in the back does a fabulous somersault onto the pavement.) Larry careens through heavy traffic and successfully crashes the truck right through the arena wall, giving Curly (by now known as "K. O. Stradivarius") the musical inspiration needed to finish off Kilduff and claim the championship.

Punch Drunks (one of a handful of pictures directed by prolific screenwriter Lou Breslow) is very nearly the first "true" Three Stooges two-reeler; the fact that the boys don't know each other as the story opens—something that would be rectified in short number three, *Men in Black*—is the only unusual element. The rhyming nonsense of *Woman Haters* is gone, a one-shot idea, and the Stooges are now, well, the Stooges. Moe is the ostensible leader, Larry is the accomplice, and Curly is the focus of the action. Granted, Moe scowls more pugnaciously than in later shorts, and Larry is simultaneously more dim and aggressive than he would be later, but Curly seems fully formed. Throughout the 1930s and '40s, his evolution was less noticeable than Moe's or Larry's. He became more lovable over time, yes, but his manic physical energy and demented way of looking at the world were in place very early on. (In *Punch Drunks* he squeaks, for the first time in his Columbia career, "I'm a victim of soicumstance!")

Support is good, especially from character actor Arthur Houseman (who made a career playing comic drunks) as the ringside timekeeper who must protect his bell from the predations of a kid who likes to throw chewing gum and spitballs. Billy Bletcher, a very short, marvelously deep-voiced actor who appeared frequently in Our Gang shorts at Roach, shows up as the ring announcer.

Punch Drunks was shot in May 1934, by which time the public had seen the tear-jerking, unintentionally parodistic 1930 Wallace Beery-Jackie Cooper melodrama *The Champ*, and digested the controversy of a 1933 heavyweight title match that was decided by a Primo Carnera uppercut that took down defending champ Jack Sharkey—and that was claimed by some to never have connected at all. Such were the hi-jinks that inspired Charlie Chaplin, Harold Lloyd, Stan Laurel, Joe E. Brown, and many other screen comics to clamber into the ring.

Curly's pretense at boxing seems hugely absurd, and yet there was at the time a real-life fighter who gives *Punch Drunks* a peculiar credibility. This was "Two-Ton" Tony Galento, a 5'8", 240-pound Jersey brawler who began a very visible pro career in 1931. In a 1939 title match with Joe Louis, Galento tagged the champ twice, rocking him with a left hook in the first round and knocking him off his feet with the same punch in the third. Galento never had a prayer of winning that bout, but his feat made him famous for the rest of his life. A fat man took the measure of a champion and staggered him. Maybe K. O. Stradivarius is a little less ridiculous than we think!

THE STOOGES' ONLY FOOTBALL COMEDY, *THREE LITTLE PIGSKINS* (1934), features a small-part actress who later beat the odds and became a superstar: Lucille Ball. She's the only Three Stooges player who accomplished this—and even at that, she swam in place during the 1930s and '40s in B-plus pictures until, nearly twenty years after *Three Little Pigskins*, she set her sights on television and became a dominant force there. (Another, lesser, future star, Lloyd Bridges, appears for an eyeblink in a montage sequence in a 1943 Stooges comedy, *They Stooge to Conga*; see "The Stooges Go to War.")

In *Pigskins*, Ball is a girlfriend of gambler Joe Stack (Walter Long), whose Tigers football team has temporarily lost three of its backs because of an auto accident. With a key game coming up, Stack has to replace his players in a hurry or forfeit $50,000 (a tremendous amount of money in 1934, when a new Ford DeLuxe coupe could be had for $555). Five hundred or $50,000, it's all surreal to the Stooges, who roam the streets as panhandlers, hoping to cadge a nickel or a dime. They find jobs carrying promotional signs while dressed as football players, and when another of the gambler's gals (Gertie Green) mistakes the boys for "the three horsemen" (*a la* Notre Dame's fabled "four horsemen" of 1924), she hurries them to meet the boss.

Naturally, the Stooges are inept at football (as are the more anarchic Marx Brothers in the 1932 comedy *Horse Feathers*) and make a hash of the contest, ensuring that Stack will lose that $50,000. The boys look tiny next to the other players on both teams, and want absolutely nothing to do with the ball. At one point, Curly stuffs the pigskin beneath his jersey, like a hunchback, and tries to *walk* it past the opposing team. My theory is that the boys are simply demoralized, not just because they're hopeless athletes but by the "numbers" on their jerseys: H^2O^2 (hydrogen peroxide!), ½, and ?

Three Little Pigskins is peppered with good gags. As the boys wearily carry their signs around Yucca Street, Moe instructs Curly to carry his "down to that red light" and then come back. Five hours later, Moe and Larry are still waiting for their pal. When Curly finally staggers back, he disgustedly explains, "That red light was a bus goin' to Boston!" A mishap with a water truck soaks the boys, and they end up at the girls' apartment in frilly nightgowns. Larry strikes a fey pose and says brightly, "Will the lady with the lucky number come and get me, please?"

The supporting cast is unusually strong. Stocky, perpetually scowling Walter Long, who plays Stack, was a veteran character man who found peculiar fame as Gus the runaway slave in Griffith's *Birth of a Nation* (1915), and became a frequent nemesis of Laurel and Hardy in the 1920s and '30s—most memorably, perhaps, as the terrifying convict called "the Tiger" in Stan and Ollie's first feature, *Pardon Us* (1931). Lucille Ball (appearing in *Pigskins* as a platinum blonde) is a blithe wisecracker, and another young actress, brunette Phyllis Crane, is cute as she quizzes Curly about his purported songwriting career. (Curly: "Did you ever hear of 'Snow, Snow, Wonderful Snow?'" Crane: "Ooh, did you write that one?" Curly: "No, but I shoveled it!")

The other platinum blonde, Gertie Green, is a special treat. Big-eyed and very pretty, she's an unusually spontaneous presence, particularly during a You-slap-me, I-slap-you gag with Moe. When she pokes his throat with her index finger, she makes his tongue stick out. He does the same to her, with the same result. Well, she finds that hilarious—and no wonder, because scripters Felix Adler and Griffin Jay knew that the bit had been a hoot when Stan Laurel and Kay Deslys did it in *We Faw Down* in 1928.

A little later, the visit degenerates into a very measured tit-for-tat squirting of seltzer—another gag with a definite Laurel and Hardy vibe. (The director, Raymond McCarey, had helmed a few L & H comedies. His older and more accomplished brother, Leo, had directed Stan and Ollie, as well as Our Gang, many times.)

Before the Stooges' shorts became set-bound after about 1941, the boys frequently shot on location. During the panhandling sequence, the camera gets a clear shot of an address—6327 Yucca Street—and the name of a business in that Hollywood neighborhood (not far from the Columbia lot on unfashionable Gower Street) that catered to movie people, Photo Players Beauty Shoppe. Pure archaeology!

The climactic football game was filmed at north-central L.A.'s then-new Gilmore Stadium, a football, baseball, and midget-car venue distinguished by a prominent "Gilmore Oil" sign. More archaeology but, alas, the stadium was torn down in 1952 to make way for the CBS Television City campus.

IN 1930, THE BRILLIANT GOLFER BOBBY JONES SAID, "COMPETITIVE GOLF IS played mainly on a five-and-a-half-inch course—the space between your ears." Uh oh. That doesn't bode well for the Stooges' luck with the game. For just that reason, *Three Little Beers* (1935) is a peerless golf comedy and arguably the best and most popular of the Stooges' two-reelers. Golfers find it hilarious, and non-golfers probably enjoy it even more, because it revels in the inherent lunacy of trying to hit a small, uncooperative ball into a tiny hole. Poster prints of the boys in golf togs are staples in barbershops coast to coast.

The boys play deliverymen for the Panther Brewing Company. Following various mishaps on the loading dock—including crowning the Panther president (Bud Jamison) with a beer barrel—the Stooges take off on their rounds, kegs piled to an absurd height on the back of the truck.

As they approach the Rancho Golf Course (a real course located on Pico Boulevard in Beverly Hills, not far from 20th Century-Fox), they feel compelled to stop. (Like all A-1 deliverymen, the Stooges are easily distracted.) The destruction that follows has become a frightful, instinctive memory in subsequent generations of groundskeepers, and the action doesn't stop there because when

Every groundskeeper's nightmare: the Stooges on the links in *Three Little Beers* (1935).

the boys flee the course, they lose their load in a hilly neighborhood, effectively stopping traffic at a busy intersection and nearly killing themselves.

Central to the humor is that although the Stooges obviously know nothing about golf, they can't wait to play. When the boys are told that the day's event is for the press only, they retreat to the men's room and return with proper I.D. held high for inspection. Moe: "Press." Larry: "Press." Curly: "Pull."

Once on the course, Curly peers into the sky, puzzled by all the talk about shooting golf. "*I* don't see any golfs!" Moe gives him a sound rap on the head. "*Look* at the golfs!" Curly says happily.

Moe takes his driver to a spilled bucket of balls and sends a large group of golfers into unconsciousness. Larry tugs at a root and destroys an entire green. When Curly can't figure how to retrieve his ball from a tree, he chops the tree down. Finally ready to drive off the first tee, Moe just nudges the ball, over and over again, until he's created dozens of horrible divots. And at a ball-washer on the seventh hole, Curly undresses and does his laundry.

All of this is beautifully staged, and it becomes funnier still because director Del Lord and editor William Lyon keep all of it going simultaneously via brisk cross-cutting. For instance, we cut away from Moe when he has just one divot under his belt, and when we cut back, he's moved from the foreground to the middle distance, the destroyed sod filling the space between like a vast moonscape. Similarly, we cut away after Curly takes his first whack at the tree, and cut back just as the tree is crashing to the ground. These are vivid examples of a film editor's crucial role in the timing and rhythm of visual comedy.

Scripter Clyde Bruckman had been an important contributor to Buster Keaton's films in the 1920s, and although he had nothing to do with a 1933 Keaton feature called *What – No Beer?*, he felt justified in lifting a gag in which Buster tries to outrun beer barrels that roll down a steep street. Bruckman felt justified because he had helped come up with the gag for a 1925 Keaton feature, *Seven Chances*, only then the beer barrels were giant boulders. Well, close enough—and isn't comedy incestuous?

As the beer barrels chase the Stooges down a modest residential street (Motor Avenue in Echo Park, northwest of downtown L.A.), we enjoy a comedy highlight of the 1930s, thanks to the boys' enthusiasm and Lord's smart decision to shoot from different points of view (top of the hill, bottom of the hill, the cab of the truck as the emergency brake releases itself, tracking shots of the madly running Stooges, tracking shots of the rolling barrels, and so on). The sequence is marred only by some poorly executed back projection when Moe hops atop a moving keg and rides it like a log roller.

The progressive clogging of the intersection (Echo Park Avenue and Delta Street) with beer barrels is a sharp set piece because we see the mess just a few times, with cutaways in between, with more barrels in the road whenever we return for another look. The payoff comes when the traffic cop (George Magrill) is violently upended by a runaway keg, his intersection complete pandemonium.

In 1998, a Wilkes-Barre, Pennsylvania, outfit that called itself the Panther Brewing Co. marketed a not-bad brew called Three Stooges Beer, with a vintage title-card image of the boys on the bottle labels and on the six-pack cases. If Bobby Jones had still been around, he would have smiled.

PROFESSIONAL WRESTLING, WITH ITS BRAZEN COMBINING OF CLASSICAL HOLDS with kidney punches and kicks to the noggin, is the traditional redheaded stepchild of sports. That was hardly less true three generations ago than now, so naturally the Stooges had to get in on the action. Like *Three Little Beers*, the boys' wrestling short, *Grips, Grunts and Groans* (1937), is particularly beloved by males of all ages.

Hoboes Moe, Larry, and Curly elude railroad dicks (with help from some very obvious stunt doubles, including a "Curly" who appears to weigh about 140 pounds) by ducking into the Hangover Athletic Club, where Curly is dragooned into becoming a sparring partner. A young boxer knocks him flat, but a popular wrestler, Bustoff (Harrison Greene), is inexplicably taken with him. Bustoff's sawed-off but very tough manager, Tony (Casey Colombo), takes note of this and hires the boys to look after Bustoff and keep him sober for the evening's match. If they pull it off, they'll get a hundred bucks, but if they fail, they'll get "a hundred slugs!"

Gravel-voiced Bustoff can't wait to go out on the town, and promises the boys that they'll "eat and drink and see plenty of pretty girls!"

They drink, all right—so much, in fact, that Bustoff gets stewed to the gills on cocktails of tequila, vodka, and cognac, rendering himself useless for the ring. Worse, the boys accidentally knock him unconscious with dumbbells, and then drop a locker on his head. Death at the hands of Tony and his crew seems inevitable. But wait! With the right outfit and some glued-on whiskers, Curly (as Moe proudly observes) "makes a sweet Bustoff."

The remainder of *Grips, Grunts and Groans* takes place in the ring, where Curly gets comically pounded around by a wrestler the script identifies as Ironhead (Tony Chavez), a well-muscled pro with plenty of slick moves, and no apparent fear of anybody named Bustoff. But it's been established earlier that Curly becomes an uncontrollable freight train when he smells wild hyacinth, and the moment Moe spots a dame with a bottle of the stuff at ringside, he lets Curly have a splash right in the snoot. Ironhead is destroyed, but because the winner is Curly instead of Bustoff, the boys must flee as Tony and his goons fire slugs at their backsides.

Clyde Bruckman's script (from a story by Searle Kramer and Herman Boxer) is clever and lively. When Curly somehow gets Ironhead on his back early in the match, Moe yells, "Pin him down!" Curly yells back, "I ain't got no pin!" Moe is flabbergasted: "He ain't got no pin!" Leave it to Larry to come up with the capper: "Get him one!"

After Curly finds a hatpin at ringside, he makes the mistake of jabbing it into Ironhead's butt and legs, which just makes the guy mad. By the time Moe gets hold of the wild hyacinth, Curly is held aloft in the dreaded propeller-spin, and on the edge of doom. But the perfume does its stuff, and Curly dispatches Ironhead with a wild flurry of illegal blows, and finally bounces his fully extended body up and down on the prostrate guy's chest, growling "Rrrff, rrrff, rrff!"

The very good-looking actress who plays the wild hyacinth lady is uncredited but noted on the studio cast list (her name is Elaine Waters); the name of another young woman, whose beer and sandwich are rudely appropriated by Curly as Ironhead twists Curly's foot the wrong way, has apparently been lost to the ages—and what a shame, because she's very funny, repeatedly standing up and objecting as Curly steals her stuff, taking a shove in the face and finally spluttering, "Well, I like *that!*"

Veteran producer-director Jack White (brother of Jules) broke into movies, as an actor, in 1910. He became a director in 1917 and a producer in 1934. He enjoyed a long and fruitful association with Columbia. His on-screen credit for *Grips, Grunts and Groans,* as on many other shorts he directed, identifies him by his pseudonym, "Preston Black."

THE STOOGES SHOT *PLAYING THE PONIES* IN MAY 1937, FOR FALL RELEASE. During filming, America was excited about a brilliant three-year-old thoroughbred named War Admiral, indisputably the greatest racehorse of the year. Sleek and elegant, War Admiral (whose sire was the formidable Man O'

War) had millions of fans. But there was a challenger in the field, a blocky, ungainly-looking four-year-old named Seabiscuit, who had won important races in New York and California in the first months of 1937. In time, Seabiscuit and War Admiral would meet, in a titanic two-horse race at Pimlico that was a sporting highlight of 1938. (Seabiscuit, the beloved underdog, won by four lengths.)

All of this happened when people called horse racing "the sport of kings," and meant it. Still credited with a noble air during those late-Depression years, thoroughbred racing developed magnificent animals that captured the public imagination. And because "high society" was more respected then than now, the public was interested in the horses' owners, too. Radio, newspaper, and newsreel coverage of the sport was enormous, and tracks thrived across the country.

It was a milieu that was at once democratic and rarefied—perfect for the Stooges. As the short begins, the boys are struggling to make a go of a two-bit restaurant called The Flounder Inn. When they overhear a couple of sharpies (Nick Copeland and Lew Davis) discussing a horse called Thunderbolt, they want in on the action—having failed to hear the beginning of the conversation, which establishes that Thunderbolt is "all run out."

After a swap—the restaurant for the horse—the boys meet swaybacked Thunderbolt and see what he's got. Not much, that's what. But during a work-out, when Thunderbolt gives himself a hot tongue after nibbling chili "pep-perinos" that Curly has liberated from the restaurant, he flies around the track to the water trough in record time.

With Larry as jockey (looking dapper despite falling onto a pitchfork the first time he attempts to mount the horse), Thunderbolt competes in a race offering a $5,000 purse. The boys have figured out that the pepperinos are what give Thunderbolt his speed, but when Larry lets the horse nibble some, Thunderbolt runs the wrong way. Finally, Moe and Curly guide Thunderbolt to a win by speeding alongside the track in a motorcycle and sidecar, a bucket of water suspended from a board in front of the horse's nose. At the conclusion, the democratic and the rarefied become one, as the Stooges and Thunderbolt bask in luxury.

Director Charles Lamont and cinematographer Allen Siegler handle the race sequence with skill that would do credit to an "A" feature, the camera car speeding to keep faultless pace with Moe's roaring motorcycle. To shoot a sequence like this one requires considerable setup and rehearsal time. That's expensive, and the fact that Columbia parted with the money suggests that the Stooges were at an early apex of their careers.

Playing the Ponies is nicely paced throughout but with no fewer than five writers contributing to the screenplay, it's very much a two-in-one proposition, neatly divided between restaurant and racetrack. The comic business at the restaurant is set-bound but comprises the short's best moments. Larry is in particularly good form, running the cash register and figuring out what a customer ate by peering at the stains on the fellow's tie (a gag lifted from a 1916 Chaplin comedy,

The Rink). Larry also has fun during an exchange with a customer ("Tiny" Lipson). Larry: "How'd you enjoy your meal?" Customer: "The soup was watery, the steak was tough, and the coffee was just like mud!" Larry offers a big smile: "Glad you liked it, don't forget to tell your friends!"

As the boys leave the restaurant for the last time, Moe's suitcase falls open to reveal a brace of silverware. Larry unsuccessfully hides a coil of wieners beneath his hat, and Curly tries to smuggle an enormous can of peanuts beneath his coat by passing off the ridiculous bulge as "a goiter." (This is especially funny because "goiter," like "grippe" and "dropsy," is one of those old medical terms you just don't hear much anymore.)

Although *Playing the Ponies* reveals no signage that would have identified the track where the expensive location shooting was done, the place is probably Pomona (today called Fairplex), a five-eighths-mile course at the Los Angeles County Fairgrounds in the city of Pomona, about thirty-five miles east of Columbia's old Hollywood studios.

A DUCKING THEY DID GO (1939) DEVOTES EVEN MORE FOOTAGE THAN *PLAYING the Ponies* to "exteriors," but this time the Stooges stayed on the Columbia lot, saving time and money by shooting a protracted duck-hunting sequence on an obvious, but handsome, sound stage, complete with a woodland pond.

Jobless, footsore, and hungry yet again, the boys steal watermelons and accidentally crack one on the head of a cop, who chases them inside an office building. The Stooges duck into the headquarters of the Canvas Back Duck Club, a hinky grift run by a pair of shifty con men (Lynton Brent and Wheaton Chambers). In a flash, the boys are on board to sell memberships at fifty dollars a pop, with 10 percent of each one going into their own kick.

The boys don't realize that there's no lodge, no club, and certainly no ducks. Full of vim, they collar a passing businessman (Vernon Dent) and give him the hard sell—which is resisted so strongly that the boys pull his suit from his body, piece by piece. No sale!

They have better luck at police headquarters, where they seduce the chief (Bud Jamison) with visions of blasting ducks at dawn, complete with helpful sound effects. The chief signs up, and so does the mayor (Casey Colombo).

When the boys report back, the con artists grab the dough but become frantic when told that the mayor and the top cop are on board. Moe blurts, "We're gonna see the governor tonight!" Lynton Brent claws his hair, his eyes popping from his skull: "The *governor*?!"

Pressed, the con men direct the boys to the nonexistent lodge. The mayor, the police chief, *everybody* bags their limit, only to discover that the lodge closed years ago, and that Curly swiped all the ducks from a nearby farmer. And the ducks are going to cost the shooters five dollars apiece. The Stooges beat a hasty retreat, leaping over a hedge and onto the backs of bucking steers that carry them into the distance. (This final footage was lifted from the boys' 1936 short *A Pain in the Pullman*, and the visual gag was reprised—with a few notes of

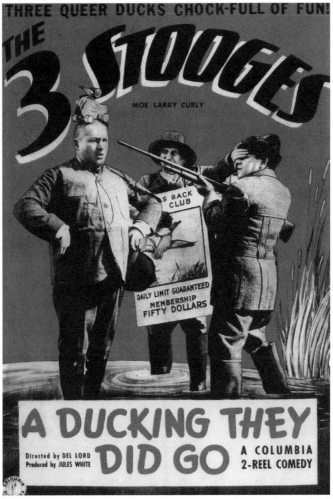

Has there been a duck born that can outwit the Stooges? What do *you* think? Marshy poster art from *A Ducking They Did Go* (1939).

Stooge-like music for emphasis—by animator John Kricsafuli in his 1992 Ren and Stimpy cartoon *Rubber Nipple Salesmen*.)

Perhaps because duck hunting isn't as obviously visual as football and boxing, *A Ducking They Did Go* is underrated today, despite being very much of a piece, with nothing that's not directly related to the plot. Wonderful dialogue comes from Curly, who by this time in the Stooges' development is as weirdly charming as he is funny. When the police chief tries to resist the boys' sales pitch, he gives Curly a hard stare and says, "Don't you know who I am?" Curly cocks his head almost into the chief's shoulder and looks him in the eye. "Your face looks familiar," he answers brightly, "but I don't know where to put it!"

Later, Curly prepares to annihilate a duck that floats serenely about four inches from the barrel of his shotgun: "Gimme a profile!" Curly instructs happily. "Smile!" Naturally, there hasn't been a duck born that can't outwit Curly, who's repeatedly spit-sprayed by quackers that drop beneath the surface before Curly can draw another bead on them.

As Curly rounds up the real ducks, Moe and Larry send inflated decoys into the air via a highly tensioned branch that they use as a catapult. (One of the decoys emits a baritone "quack" as Moe blows into it, causing him to grip the rubber thing around the neck and poke its eyes.) The inflated decoys sail through the air well enough, only to explode oddly when the police chief and others hit them with buckshot. And when Larry doesn't pay attention for a moment, he releases the branch a little too soon and catches Moe square in the face.

Del Lord's staging of this and other visual humor is faultless, with the footage given a fine rhythm by editor Charles Nelson.

The woodsy, ornate pond set is a small marvel of (uncredited) art direction, with trees, shrubs, cattails, and even a sense of morning mist. All of it was beautifully lit and shot by thirty-one-year-old Lucien Ballard; decades later he was the cinematographer on *True Grit*, *The Wild Bunch*, and many other major pictures.

Finally, *A Ducking They Did Go* has a perfectly magical moment when the boys sing "You'll Never Know What Tears Are" in sliding five-part harmony with Bud Jamison and Casey Colombo. It's a lovely rendition of a song that Larry, Shemp, and Moe performed with Ted Healy in their first film, *Soup to Nuts*, in 1930.

"LOCO AMERICANOS COMEDIANS, THE THREE STOOGES! WE HOPE YOU LIKE them, too many." That's the public-address intro the boys get at a massive bull-ring in Mexico, where their comic bullfighter and bull act will precede a genuine bullfight. *What's the Matador?* (1942) is a solid comedy, but its most intriguing aspect is that, for one of the very few times in their Columbia two-reel career, the Stooges are referred to as "the Three Stooges." (Earlier in the film, they identify *themselves* that way when they send a wire.) The gimmick makes the characters that we know as the Stooges more real—as though they exist in the everyday world outside the movie theater—but it simultaneously pushes them away from us, emphasizing that they're actors playing the Three Stooges, who are known in the fictional world, too, as the Three Stooges.

Hmm. Maybe it's just me.

Anyway, to speculate about what, if anything at all, audiences made of this unintentional existentialism is unnecessary because *What's the Matador?* has a lot of other things to grab one's attention. Bullfighting is a natural subject for physical comedy; in 1922, for instance, Stan Laurel parodied Rudolph Valentino's bullfight romance, *Blood and Sand*, as *Mud and Sand*. Although the sport has fallen dramatically out of favor, interest in it was high when the Stooges shot their comedy late in 1941 or very early in '42 (it was released in April 1942). A 1941 version of *Blood and Sand*, with Tyrone Power, was hugely popular and had been prompted, in part, by continuing public curiosity about a great matador named Juan Belmonte. The autobiography of this hero of Spain had been published in America in 1937 and was widely read. Belmonte had retired two years before, after an unmatched career highlighted by his invention of *aguantar*, by which the matador stands motionless as the bull charges, moving nothing but his *muleta* (cape) and upper body. Belmonte's peculiarly intense form of courage was universally emulated, but the initial human risks had been his and his alone. Against this, how can the Stooges measure up?

Trouble starts right away. The boys are happy to be set up with the job at the bullring but are dismayed when a beautiful Mexican woman, Dolores (Suzanne Kaaren), inadvertently walks off with the suitcase containing Curly's matador costume and the bull suit Moe and Larry wear in the act. Easy enough to find Dolores—the problem is that the boys narrowly escape with their necks after ending up inside her hacienda at the moment her jealous husband (Harry Burns) shows up.

At the arena, Jose pays off a pair of attendants (the very Anglo Eddie Laughton and Cy Schindell) so that a real bull is let loose into the ring during the Stooges' act. Because Curly thinks he's still out there with his pals, he insults the bull and taunts it to charge. (And this is a *big* animal.) When Curly looks over and sees the frantic Moe and Larry behind the safety fence, half-in and half-out of their ratty bull costume, he reacts with one of his best-ever expressions of utter dismay.

Curly goes for a bucking ride on the bull's back, and finally gets angry. With some help from a stunt double, he meets el toro forehead-to-forehead, knocking the beast cold.

The Mexican setting allows for the requisite language gags, notably an exchange with a sleepy local hombre who hears "siesta" whenever Moe says "fiesta"—and repeatedly excuses himself from Moe to take a nap. No great thinker himself, Moe nevertheless mutters, "I bet he eats soup with a knife!"

Gags inside the woman's hacienda are cute. When Dolores cries "Darling!" and looks past Curly at her husband, Curly thinks she's looking at *him* and inserts himself into her waiting arms. Jose doesn't take it well. "How *dare* you hug my wife before my eyes!" "Well, turn around," Curly suggests, "and I'll hug her behind your back!"

A later gag in which Jose reaches to the next bed to take Curly's hand, thinking it belongs to his wife, is okay but was better executed by the boys a decade later, in one of their lesser shorts, *Don't Throw That Knife* (see "The Stooges and the Fairer Sex").

Small-part actor (and silent-era writer-director) Harry Burns is appropriately wrathful as the angered husband, and Suzanne Kaaren is appealing and competent as Dolores. Kaaren was a high-jump champion who became a charter-member Rockette before getting into pictures. Today, she's recalled mainly for the three shorts she did with the Stooges (*Disorder in the Court* and *Yes, We Have*

No Bonanza are the others), and for her co-starring role in *The Devil Bat* (1941) a perverse, very entertaining Bela Lugosi vehicle.

Although the vast crowds seen in *What's the Matador?* appear courtesy of ancient stock footage, the bullring shenanigans with the Stooges were shot outdoors on a convincing set and look good. When the short was remade, virtually scene for scene, in 1957 (for 1959 release) as *Sappy Bullfighters,* matador Joe goes through his paces on a badly lit sound stage that looks even worse because a lot of the outdoor footage from the earlier film is clumsily cut in. Curly's whoops are heard for a moment as Joe rides the bull, and when director Jules White cuts to close-ups of Joe astride a fake bull, the prop barely moves, which means not only that the new footage has no hope of matching the far livelier stock stuff but that Joe's enthusiastic performance is undercut.

Like Curly, Joe is hilarious when he mistakes the wife's overture to her husband as one intended for him, and he puts his own, irritable, spin on the climactic encounter with the bull, commanding, "Don't just *stand* there, you *craazy*!" Joe Besser was virtually unequalled as a comic priss (though Joe Penner and Franklin Pangborn are contenders), and it's fun to see him with his dander up.

Strictly on its own terms, *Sappy Bullfighters* is fun. Perennial serial heavy George Lewis (a quite underrated actor) is terrific as the ill-tempered husband, and the stunningly good-looking Greta Thyssen (a former Miss Denmark who had worked with the Stooges in the recent past) is glorious as the wife. Jules White hadn't really *directed* anybody in years, so Thyssen was on her own. And that's okay because she could act and had an innate sense of comic timing. (Still, all of that kind of goes out the window when Thyssen enters a scene clad in a white, cowl-neck dress that must have been applied with a spray gun, and later,

Uh oh: A real bull has snorted into the ring. Curly stands his ground, but Moe and Larry will shortly vanish. *What's the Matador?* (1942).

Photo courtesy of Mark and Teresa Miller

as she undresses while the boys—unknown to her—are in the room with her and her sleeping husband.)

Although not the last Stooges two-reeler to be filmed, *Sappy Bullfighters* was the last to be released: It came to theaters on June 4, 1959, closing out not merely the Stooges' two-reel career but short-form comedy itself. The Stooges had outlasted everybody.

ALTHOUGH THE STOOGES NEARLY ALWAYS AVOID SENTIMENTALITY (A QUALITY distinct from the related but more sophisticated emotion, sentiment), they toy with it a few times during their two-reel career. Comic actors who fare best with it are those with personas predicated on kindness and youthful innocence, such as Harry Langdon and Chaplin.

Generally, sentimentality sits uneasily in the bag of tricks of comic actors, who are better off when they explore it gingerly, if at all. The Stooges—hardly paragons of innocence or kindness—should have avoided it completely.

The saccharine, confused script for *Even as I.O.U.* (1942) essentially *forces* the boys' empathy for a young mother (Ruth Skinner) and her little girl who have been "dispossessed" from their home. Now the two of them live outdoors, with their furniture and other belongings neatly, piteously, arrayed in a vacant lot. Although the boys have had a very bad morning trying to sell day-old racetrack tip sheets (Curly is run over by one car, and the back of his skull is cracked by another), they immediately rally to the cause of mother and daughter, and heroically try to turn the woebegone tableau into something resembling a home.

At the racetrack later, a crook who can throw his voice notices when the boys win big on a race and gulls them into buying a "talking" thoroughbred named Seabasket. Later, after the horse appears to have fallen ill, a track vet delivers a foal that sets eyes on the Stooges and says "Da da! Da da da!" The boys delightedly embrace the animal as we fade out.

If you're wondering what happened to the dispossessed mother and child, join the club. Their predicament dominates the short's first two-thirds and then is forgotten, apparently existing in the first place only so that Curly can "borrow" the kid's piggybank for a stake with which to make the winning bet.

A small, blandly pretty actress named Ruth Skinner plays the mother. She has no screen presence, and her line readings are so low key that they sound embarrassed. The little girl (whose real name has been lost) has almost no interaction with the Stooges (a real lapse by writer Felix Adler and director Del Lord), so neither of these supporting players can boost the short's flagging energy.

Patient viewers are rewarded with a few good moments. Stock-company players Vernon Dent and Bud Jamison make brief appearances as an irate motorist and a cop, respectively, and another regular, Stanley Blystone, does a lot with his small but pivotal role as the scheming ventriloquist.

Even as I.O.U. gives Larry virtually nothing to do but throws a few bones to Curly, who wanders among the mother's belongings and spies a tuba, which he delightedly identifies as "a bazooney!" When ordered to "scale that fish," he does so—like a harmonica—and when he encounters a statue of Nipper, the RCA dog, he gamely tries to strike up a conversation. Curly also mines some humor while milking a goat, but the payoff (the milk makes the little girl go "Baaa!) is as riotous as a potato pancake.

All three boys go through the motions of reprising the "Push, push, pull" gag from *Three Little Beers*, where it was better staged and infinitely funnier.

The big set piece is the group's attempt to eat dinner after Curly has innocently cooked a stuffed (as in taxidermied) fish, and everybody has a lot of trouble cutting, chewing, and swallowing. Del Lord was a skilled comedy director, but this sequence may be the most tedious and unrewarding one he ever shot.

And then there's the dispossession theme, which feels anachronistic in a short that was released nine months after Pearl Harbor, by which time unemployment had diminished and women easily found defense jobs and other positions. (The point stands even if the short was filmed shortly *before* Pearl, when the numbers of defense jobs were already increasing dramatically.) Despite these realities, Adler's script relentlessly pushes the Depression angle: Curly wonders why the mother can't get "an FBI loan," and the vacant lot happens to be located across the street from an enormous sign advertising new houses. Was this obvious irony intentional? At the very least, the juxtaposition of the sign with the unhappy mother and child is unavoidably reminiscent of photojournalist Margaret Bourke-White's famed 1937 picture of forlorn black Kentuckians (awaiting food aid after a flood) queued up beneath a billboard dominated by a smiling white family and the words, "WORLD'S HIGHEST STANDARD OF LIVING. There's no way like the American Way."

The short becomes more sensibly topical at the track, when Curly rationalizes his possession of the piggybank as "a kind of Lend-Lease"—but the joke is tepid, so who cares? *Even as I.O.U.* can be dismissed with a single syllable: Ouch.

AS DESCRIBED IN THIS BOOK'S BIOGRAPHICAL SECTION, THE STROKE THAT ended Curly Howard's career occurred on May 6, 1946, on the set during the third day of a scheduled three-day shoot of *Half-Wits Holiday* (released 1947). With obligations to exhibitors, Columbia quickly signed Shemp Howard as Curly's replacement. Skilled, seasoned, and with long experience as a solo, Shemp returned easily to the "third Stooge" role he hadn't played since 1933. His first post-Curly two-reeler, *Fright Night* (1947), had been written with his younger brother in mind, and if scripter Clyde Bruckman had to alter the script at all, those alterations were probably minor.

Fright Night returns the Stooges to the world of boxing. ("Fight night" was a mantra across America on Fridays and Saturdays, and was especially anticipated by patrons of big-city bars that had invested in television sets.)

This time, the boys have been (recklessly) put in charge of a dopey fighter named Chopper (beefy, rubber-faced Dick Wessell). Chopper has even less ability to stay on task than the Stooges, and is lazier, too—remarkable when you think about it! The boys struggle to keep him in condition and appoint Shemp as his sparring partner. Chopper doesn't feel like sparring until Larry's girl, Kitty (Claire Carleton), shows up. In a nanosecond, Kitty completely forgets about Larry and becomes Chopper's girl. Energized and eager to show off, Chopper pulverizes Shemp, who can't mount even a pretense of a defense because Moe has carelessly tied his right glove to the top rope.

Bad-tempered emissaries from the Stooges' boss, Big Mike, arrive to announce that Chopper *will lose* the big fight—Big Mike's orders! The boys are unable to get rid of Kitty, so their only hope of getting Chopper *out* of condition is to use Kitty against him. In short order, the boys are feeding Chopper cream puffs ("S'my favorite fruit!" he says happily) while the big lug begs Kitty to read him more poems "about love." Larry is ecstatic: "By fight time he'll be as soft as putty!"

But on the night of the bout Chopper learns that his opponent, Gorilla Watson, has stolen Kitty. (Fickle, isn't she?) Now he's rarin' to go all over again. Gorilla shows up a minute later, so eager to pulverize Chopper that he lands a jab against a brick wall, breaking his hand.

The fight has to be called off, and the Stooges are delighted because they think they're off the hook. But with no fight, Big Mike (Harold Brauer) stands to lose a hundred grand. He blames the Stooges, and the subsequent chase, in a dingy warehouse packed with crates, is a highlight of the Shemp years.

Unlike producer-director Jules White (who was comfortably and happily locked in as head of Columbia's prolific two-reel unit), *Fright Night* director Ed Bernds wanted to graduate to features—and ultimately did. He excelled at shorts that had good stories with logical plot progressions, and he was skilled at knockabout and other sorts of physical action. In the warehouse, Big Mike and a small army of his henchmen pursue the Stooges through a maze of stacked crates. Columbia's two-reel shooting schedules during the mid-1940s were three days—the equivalent of a two-week shoot for an eighty-minute feature. That's fast but not impossible for an experienced "B" unit (Monogram, PRC, and lesser Poverty Row producers cranked out fifty-five- and sixty-minute features in a week). Still, Bernds's three days were far from generous, so it's to his great credit that he devoted precious time to the setup of an overhead POV shot on the warehouse set, giving us panoramic views of the action below and emphasizing the place's maze-like quality. Editor Paul Borofsky understood what Bernds was up to; he cut between close-ups, medium shots, and the overhead view with a beautiful, easy rhythm. What could have been just another foot chase becomes something exciting and almost epic.

The boys and their antagonists dash around crates and between them; climb on top of them and slither beneath them. In a particularly funny moment, Larry carefully peers around a crate, unaware that the fellow in front of him—on whose shoulder Larry's hand is resting—is Big Mike!

When bricks slide onto the head of a thug named Moose (Cy Schindell) and knock him cold, Moe hides behind canvas and manipulates Moose's head and shoulders as Big Mike stops to chat.

Cleverly tossed mothballs and the blunt end of an axe put an end to the hoodlums, who get off a single gunshot as police arrive. The bullet pierces a can of red paint, which drips onto Shemp, convincing him that he's been hit. When Shemp collapses, Moe wants to get a doctor, whereupon Larry utters the most hilariously unlikely line ever heard in a Stooges short: "Wait a minute! I studied medicine for three years!" (Take a moment to think about that statement.)

Larry puts his head to Shemp's chest. "Ooh! He's gone!"

Moe is heartbroken: "The poor kid! And I owe him five bucks!"

"Wait a minute" Shemp says, suddenly back from the dead. "I heard that! Gimme the five!"

In 1955, Shemp and the other Stooges did a remake of *Fright Night* called *Fling in the Ring*, comprised mainly of footage from the earlier film. Dick Wessell (now credited as "Richard") and Claire Carleton return but in stock footage only. Credited scripter Jack White wrote a few minutes of new footage (Clyde Bruckman's name does not appear), and Jules White is credited as director; no credit at all is given to Ed Bernds.

This time around, pop-eyed Frank Sully, who alternately screeches his lines or delivers them flatly, plays Big Mike. Perhaps he's dispirited because he's not as big a player as the original Big Mike, who stood to lose a hundred grand. *This* Big Mike is on the hook for just ten. On the other hand, the extra ninety grand probably went toward his very cool apartment, chicly furnished in mid-century Space Age style, courtesy of art director Edward Ilou.

Before the climactic chase in the warehouse, the Stooges wedge (the new) Big Mike's head in a door, which allows them to tweak his nose, pull out his eyebrows, and paint his face. Big Mike's imprisonment also removes him from the chase sequence, which carries on with stock footage of the earlier Big Mike, actor Harold Brauer, now demoted to one of his own henchmen. Very Kafka, very Philip K. Dick.

The red-paint business at the end is eliminated. Shemp merely knocks himself out with the axe after dispatching the bad guys, and then loses his pants as Moe and Larry drag him away.

Fling in the Ring is as much an exercise in brutal, faintly imaginative cost cutting as it is a comedy. White and the Stooges shot the new footage during just one day, filling another slot on the release schedule and spending very little. Eight years had passed since *Fright Night*, so if anybody in the audiences thought that they'd seen essentially the same short before, they may not have been positive about it. If filmmakers can get away with that, it's a pretty good trick.

5

The Stooges on the Job

In which the boys brew some hooch; have trouble with tassels; educate America's youth; sell Bloop Soup; join Annie and Fannie in a Turkish bath; swipe an ice cream truck; discover that small Chinese antiques are awfully fragile; coax water to run uphill; varnish a cowboy's lid; cook weenies on the 97th floor; dress beautiful women in furniture; find love amidst the hounds; go places and eat things; meet the crazy man in Room 81; and stand up for democracy.

In 1934, MGM released a sanitized version of *Men in White*, Sydney Kingsley's Pulitzer Prize–winning 1933 play about the professional and personal lives of young doctors. In a sort of "answer" comedy that broadly burlesques rather than satirizes, the Stooges' third Columbia comedy, *Men in Black* (1934), casts the boys as belligerent hospital interns who loudly claim to labor "for duty and humanity!" In reality, they're holy terrors who squander precious time with nurses and careen through the hospital's crowded corridors on horses, go-karts, and on a bicycle built for three. They administer anesthesia with a mallet and play tic-tac-toe on a patient's abdomen. And when Moe has a visible nervous breakdown, his eyes bulge, he laughs maniacally, and he whacks the head of an unconscious patient like a vibraphone.

Men in Black plays at an undisciplined anarchy that writer Felix Adler and director Raymond McCarey borrowed from the Marx Brothers. Oh, hell, they *swiped* it from the Marx Brothers, without realizing or caring that the Brothers' chaos was tightly disciplined and sprang from what Marx Brothers historian Joe Adamson calls their "point of view." The Stooges simply wanted to entertain— which is one reason why they thrived on screen for far longer than the Marxes. A point of view can be expressed to an artist's satisfaction, and to the familiarity of audiences, in relatively few films, but well-executed pure entertainment that avoids complexities is less likely to wear out its welcome. Although the Stooges never achieved the artistic heights of the Marx Brothers—whose greatest films, *Monkey Business* (1931), *Horse Feathers* (1932), and *Duck Soup* (1933), predate *Men in Black*— they didn't fade after the 1930s, either, and maintained their active star status well into the 1960s. Longevity is often correspondent with simplicity.

With a supporting cast of twenty-five and good production values, *Men in Black* (1934) has a certain ambition; Columbia was obviously enthusiastic about its new contract players. Although the short avoids or just can't manage satire, it succeeds as a grab bag of pugnacious entertainment and was honored with an Academy Award nomination for Best Short Subject of 1934. (The award went to *La Cucaracha*, a Technicolor rumba musical; the other nominee was *What, No Men!* with "Swedish" dialect comic El Brendel.)

More important than the Academy nomination, though, is that *Men in Black* is the first of many shorts in which the Stooges bumble about in the world of work, driving bosses and other authority figures to distraction, annoying and even abusing clients, and generally doing a half-assed job. As doctors, they can't visit the director of medicine (Hal Roach veteran Dell Henderson) without destroying the glass in his office door, and their touch with patients is completely ham-handed, particularly if the person is at all challenging. "The crazy patient in room 81" is played by another Roach alumnus, Billy Gilbert, with gravel-voiced, schizoid certitude: "You know," he intones, hunched and shifty-eyed, "once I was crazy! [He grabs his nightgown.] You see that buttonhole? *Rats* used to come out of that!" He finally scares the Stooges right out of the room.

A Western Union messenger (Bob Callahan) who has a telegram for the Stooges leaves not only without a tip but without a half-dollar he's pulled from his own pocket. (The boys take the guy with the old double-or-nothing ploy, in which Curly—whom Moe describes as "tongue-tied"— calls heads or tails with a strangled "Hunghh!" That response is Moe's cue to show the coin to Curly and ask, "Is *that* it?" Well, of course it is.)

Because Felix Adler and the boys were trying things on for size at this early juncture, dialogue in *Men in Black* is hit-or-miss. A typical exchange—"How did you find that patient in 66?" "Under the bed!"— provides a timid laugh. On the other hand, the Stooges perform a wonderful nonsense-word bit when Moe demands a succession of mysterious surgical instruments: "*Tsimmis!* [a Yiddishism] Anacon! Sennaturner! Anaconapooner! Feemanol! Anasonic!"

Appropriate words ensure effective communication, which is something the Stooges seem doomed never to achieve. In *Men in Black*, the symbol of the boys' antipathy to work is in fact a communication device: the hospital's enormous wall-mounted intercom, an elaborate, flashing horror that looks like something out of *Metropolis* by way of *Undersea Kingdom*. So often does it bark, "Calling Dr. Howard, Dr. Fine, Dr. Howard!" that the boys are at last inspired to attack it with mallets and claw-like fingers until finally its heart—a small, trembling cylinder—squirms on the floor before them. The Stooges pull guns and blast the thing to pieces.

Humanity has been served.

During a Fireside Chat in 1935, President Roosevelt noted that, for the first time since the Depression began, "the relief rolls have declined." True enough, but unemployment stood at 21.7 percent in 1934 and 20.1 percent for '35. Those are terrifying numbers.

Although the Stooges weren't satirists, they were frequently topical. Witness, for example, the opening moments of *Pop Goes the Easel* (1935), in which the boys tramp the sidewalk with homemade signs, begging for work. Moe seeks a position as a social secretary (Depression or not, the Stooges are nothing if not optimistic). Larry wishes to be a bridge instructor, and Curly just advertises that he's starving.

Interest in the boys' plight is almost nil, and when it's not, it's just unhelpfully smart-ass: A well-dressed fellow (William Irving) with an ice-cream-slurping kid in tow listens patiently as Curly explains that he hasn't had any food in days. "Well, don't worry," the fellow counsels, "it still tastes just the same."

Larry is unable to answer a question about bridge when a passing motorist poses one, and Moe, disgusted with himself because he can't spell "chrysanthemum" on command, tosses his "social secretary" sign to another bum (who is promptly greeted and hired by a woman in a limousine). Every job seeker has a story about "the one I almost landed," and this is Moe's.

The Stooges *want* to be "on the job" but fate, the general state of the economy, and their own very apparent limitations conspire against them. Then Moe comes up with an idea that, in a sane society, would be a good one: The boys grab brooms from inside a notions store and begin to sweep the sidewalk outside. Whoever owns the place will note their industriousness and is sure to give them jobs! But the Stooges and employment—even when the boys *have* employment—never add up to any kind of sanity, so the storeowner imagines the boys are *stealing* his stupid brooms. The boys run off in a panic, a plainclothes cop (Louis Mason) in pursuit until they lose him inside an art studio.

Although *Pop Goes the Easel* subsequently chronicles the Stooges' fish-out-of-water misadventures in the world of art, the short's overarching preoccupation remains jobs. A lack of them has led the boys to the studio, which isn't a museum or a gallery but a place of business owned by a Professor Fuller (Bobby Burns). He employs a young, pretty assistant (Phyllis Crane, oddly but appealingly attired in a tutu), and together they teach drawing, painting, and sculpting.

Felix Adler's script is sprightly. When Curly spies two people drawing, he exclaims, "Oh, a pair of drawers!" The short includes an early instance of Moe's deadly invitation to "Pick out two," and the boys have some more fun with nonsense words, including "Eanar" (which is what Larry feels is needed to fix somebody else's painting; when there's no job, Larry *creates* one).

When Curly commits a faux pas, he philosophically says, "Easel come, easel go!" But Moe is not amused: "Easel outta here!"

Inevitably, the boys horse around with a blob of clay. After a while, Curly is stopped in his tracks. "Look!" he says in amazement, "We made somethin'!"

Soon, of course, wet clay is flying everywhere: into the boys' faces, onto Professor Fuller's door (he keeps saying, "Come in!"), and even onto the comely bosom of a beautiful model (Geneva Mitchell). In a sequence that's nicely choreographed by director Del Lord and sharply played by Ellinor Vanderveer (famed as the concerned mother in Our Gang's *Washee Ironee*), an elegant society matron serenely examines a wall of paintings—bending, standing, moving laterally as clay thuds above her, next to her and, at last, right onto her fashionably garbed derriere.

The short's highlight comes when the plainclothes cop begins to stalk around the studio. Thinking quickly (for once), the Stooges greet him in drag, looking winsome in wigs and frilly tutus. In falsetto, Curly introduces Moe as "my mother," to which Moe pipingly responds, "Spread out!"

Meanwhile, Larry (who calls himself "Crumette") coyly seduces the cop by nuzzling his cheek and tickling under his chin. Drag humor has been well-mined, particularly by British comics, but with the possible exceptions of two who came much later, Divine (Harris Glenn Milstead) and Brit comic Dick Emery, nobody did it better or funnier than the Stooges—a minor point of interest because there is no real tradition of Jewish drag comedy, although a contemporaneous Jewish-American comic, Milton Berle, got laughs by playing women.

PARDON MY SCOTCH (1935) IS PREDICATED ON THE (REAL-LIFE) FACT THAT Prohibition is being repealed state by state. A druggist (Al Thompson) is furious with his liquor wholesaler, J. T. Walton (James C. Morton), because legal booze isn't going to be available in time to help the drugstore's suffering bottom line. *Everybody* is thirsty for the good stuff but J. T. just can't accommodate.

While the druggist argues into the phone, three carpenters he's hired go to work on the installation of a door-and-frame unit in a new wall on the store's second floor. Larry, Curly, and Moe *look* like carpenters, and they tell the guy not to worry. It's a simple job. What could go wrong?

Problems start right away when the boys can't agree on the difference between left and right (the problem is that they're facing each other as they argue). When Curly takes a portable framing saw to a two-by-four, he fails to notice that he's cutting through the table beneath. Larry is oblivious and busy elsewhere, but Moe is standing on the table, which folds in on itself like a drop-leaf when Curly finishes, sending Moe crashing to the floor. (The painful accident cracked ribs on Moe's left side.)

More wayward sawing sends Moe *through* the floor and flat on his back into the drugstore below. In the sequence that follows, one of J. T.'s desperate salesmen (Nat Carr) becomes convinced that the Stooges are Scottish distillers after the boys mix together whatever they find on the shelves behind them and optimistically offer it to him as a pick-me-up. In a delightful burst of improbability, the concoction tastes like quality Scotch, and in short order the boys are delivered—in kilts, no less—to a posh dinner party at J. T.'s house.

Given the demand for liquor, a move from carpentry to the liquor business is professional progress, but when the boys attempt to replicate their formula, they blow up their mammoth keg and inundate the house with foam.

Scripter Andrew Bennison and director Del Lord have fun with a variety of sight gags. As the boys prepare their first batch of hooch at the drugstore, they strain it through a wicker chair—and dissolve the wicker. When they shake the stuff in a rubber boot, it rumbles ominously, and when poured it spits and sparks.

At the dinner party, the salesman introduces the boys as McSniff, McSnuff, and McSnort. The other guests pretend not to notice that Curly's kilt is up to his crotch, and that Larry's brushes the floor. (Only Moe's looks more or less proper.) An awful singer named Senor Cantino (Billy Gilbert) is the featured entertainment, and the Stooges signal their displeasure by flipping grapes and a banana into his mouth, and finally by sending a whole pineapple sailing at his head.

The boys' variation on the Highland fling (they call it the "Lowland Shim") is ridiculous, and when they move to the elaborate dinner table, Curly spears two breadsticks and manipulates them on the table like little shoes (previously done by Fatty Arbuckle and Chaplin) until Moe puts breadsticks on his own forks and uses them to poke Curly in the eyes. Curly somehow finds a hero sandwich, but he can't eat it because the bread separates and bites his nose. Finally, Moe causes Curly to topple backwards in his chair, pulling the tablecloth and food onto the floor and all the guests along with him. (The gag is especially funny because it unfolds in an odd sort of slow motion, with a brief pause when Curly reaches a tipping point that suggests that maybe the disaster won't happen after all.)

Dialogue sparkles, too. Larry orders a phalanx of pipers to start tooting by saying, "Play on, Macduff!" (possibly the most erudite Stooges joke ever), and the boys impersonate Scots (improperly referred to throughout the short as "Scotchmen') by hooting, "Hoot mon, hoot mon, hallelujah!"

People who watch *Pardon My Scotch* attentively are rewarded by a quietly brilliant throwaway gag that says a lot about salesmanship in the world of work. Behind the soda fountain is a small sign that reads, "Ice Cream. 3 Flavors." Well, who could resist *that*?

Now we know part of the reason why the druggist struggles without booze sales, and why he hasn't the means to hire carpenters more proficient than the Stooges. He's just got no head for business.

AMONG THE MYRIAD, FASCINATING JOYS PROVIDED BY THE STOOGES IS THE remarkable plasticity of their characters. Although always "Larry, Curly, and Moe" (or Shemp or Joe), their circumstances change wildly from short to short. Few external things are definite in the Stooges' universe. Stars slip, galaxies collide. What will tomorrow bring?

The status and nature of the boys' employment are particularly malleable. The Stooges change occupations like other people change socks. Some might say that's emblematic of the restlessness of the American spirit, or of the conspiracy against the working class. Then again, maybe the boys are just too dumb to hold a job for more than a week or two.

In *False Alarms* (1936), the Stooges are Los Angeles firemen. (America had no firefighters in 1936, just firemen.) When you have spare time, dig up a copy of the civil service examination for fireman. Look it over. It's difficult material! Candidates have to be smart to join the department, and they have to know a lot of stuff. So just how is it, then, that Moe, Larry, and Curly are part of L.A.'s

Station 61? (Director Del Lord shot on location at that station, situated in the 5000 block of W. 3rd Street in L.A.'s crowded Fairfax district.) Maybe one of the boys is married to the captain's daughter. Maybe they're *all* married to her. At any rate, they're at Station 61, where they drive the captain (Stanley Blystone) buggy. "Just why did you three half-wits join the fire department?" he demands. Of course, the more pertinent question is *how?*

The Stooges sleep through fire alarms. They accidentally lock themselves in the station bathroom. They'd rather horse around with dames than work. When they do try to get down to business, everything goes wrong, as when Curly carelessly unrolls lengths of hose and the hoses are run over and severed by streetcars. (The clanging, rushing cars were part of the now-defunct Los Angeles Railway, aka the Yellow Car Line. The route outside the fire station is the 3 Line.)

The boys' ultimate sin is to make off with the captain's brand-new '36 Ford coupe. They weave it in and out of traffic and over-rev the engine. They punish the suspension by roaring across broken vacant lots, and take corners on two wheels. Their abuse of the car is particularly, painfully, funny because the deliveryman has advised the captain to treat his new ride carefully, and to "take it easy the first five hundred miles."

By the time the captain has reason to exclaim "That's my car!," you know things aren't going to end prettily.

False Alarms is wonderful for many reasons. John Grey's linear, incident-packed script is one of the best the boys ever worked with. Physical gags and verbal humor are unusually well balanced. When Larry starts to slide down the pole at the station, Moe grabs a fistful of curls and pulls him back up (a terrific physical gag that betrays no wires or other lifting device). And after a key is accidentally dropped down a sink, Moe bodily upends Larry and bangs his head into the tiny drain hole, demanding that he get the key back.

Elsewhere, Curly meets three girls, including a chubby giant named Minnie (the charming and enthusiastic June Gittelson). Minnie's alarmingly physical playfulness intimidates Curly; trapped in a corner, he can only cower and defensively squeak, "Okay, Hercules!" Later, he phones Moe at the station: "You better come right over, you're missin' one of the *biggest* things of your life!"

Moe and Larry's arrival thrills Minnie: "Let's go places and eat things!" The entire group shoehorns itself into the captain's car, forcing an awful-sounding groan from the tortured suspension.

The subsequent joyride was shot with enormous confidence by director Del Lord and cinematographer Benjamin Kline, on location (probably along 3rd, Larchmont, and LaBrea). A camera car follows the speeding coupe as it weaves across streetcar tracks, tailgates other cars, and finally performs a startling ninety-degree turn at an intersection to avoid a collision. (Charles Hochberg's rat-a-tat editing is especially effective during this sequence.)

Inside the car, one of the girls covers the eyes of Curly (who's driving) and stupidly says, "Guess who this is!" Eager to play along, Curly takes his hands from the wheel, much to Moe's dismay.

The boys struggle to master the intricacies of the fire pole in *False Alarms* (1936).

After the coupe smashes into a light pole, Moe is the only one standing; his companions are nowhere in sight. Comes a muffled cry: "Oh oh, woo woo!" "What was that?" a bystander asks. "That's the other five people that were with me," Moe explains, "but I can't find 'em!" He looks left, he looks right, he even looks straight up. When he raps on the mangled trunk lid, the unseen Curly brightly chirps, "Come in!"

In a discarded sequence from an early *False Alarms* script, the boys' carelessness allows the wrecked car to catch fire.

For lovers of old L.A., *False Alarms* is a special treat, with many minutes of exteriors that reveal Fairfax-area streets and businesses of 1936: Safeway Market, Silvertown Tires, Ozark Drugs, Wilshire Club Market, Max Factor Salon (with Art Deco entryway portholes), Carl X. Folsom Modern Motor Service.

It's all long ago and far away, but here it is, the working city, preserved.

THE FIRST HALF OF *SLIPPERY SILKS* (1936) FOLLOWS THE STOOGES DURING A typical day on the job as furniture makers in Manhattan: Larry accidentally pours wood glue on the floor and traps Curly's feet on a pair of clumsy boards. Moe shoves Curly into an open barrel of finishing nails and then picks up a claw hammer for a little impromptu surgery on Curly's backside. An enormous plank falls on Moe's head, and later the same enormous plank falls on the boss's head.

A customer (Vernon Dent) who has witnessed some of the commotion asks the boss (Robert Williams), "Are you certain this work will be in competent hands?" Curly pipes up, "Soitenly, we're *all* incompetent!" (Just to hammer home the point, Curly optimistically adds, "We're not as dumb as we look around here!")

The customer has arrived with a special job: He wants an exact duplicate of an ancient Chinese cabinet. The delicate original is small enough to be easily held in both hands. Oh, and it's valued at $50,000.

The boys get to work. First, a close call, when the cabinet is launched like a shot put from the end of an unstable board, causing Moe to execute a lunging, panicked circus catch that Jim Thorpe couldn't have pulled off. Then disaster: While Moe and Curly argue, Larry stares at the cabinet in impotent horror as the delicate piece moves on a conveyor belt into the thin, vicious blade of a band saw, which slices the curio neatly in half. Gahh!

Aghast, Larry moans, "We'll have to work all our lives for this!"

Outside, cops put the grab on the Stooges—not because of the debacle with the Chinese whatsit but to tell the boys that they've inherited their late uncle's chi-chi business, Madame de France, a popular Fifth Avenue fashion house. (Location shooting for *Slippery Silks* took place in Hollywood—on Gower Street near the Columbia lot and at the intersection of Wilcox and Cahuenga.)

Slippery Silks then slides easily into its second portion as the boys bring their cabinetmaking abilities to the world of high fashion.

Not surprisingly, haute couture was staggered by the Depression. But the industry caught a break in the mid-thirties when the Duke and Duchess of Windsor—a couple whose storybook romance fascinated the world—popularized waisted jackets and dresses in smart, traditional wools and tweeds that could be duplicated at reasonable cost for mass production. (Hart Schaffner & Marx, for example, prospered by sending such pieces to countless haberdashers and department stores.)

When the Stooges mount a fashion show, many of the first ensembles (all of which are the work of the previous owner) are tweedy and sophisticated. The show also includes a subtly provocative white swimsuit that recalls the hugely popular Jantzen line, and a floor-length, Harlowesque negligee ensemble very much in step with designs by influential Hollywood costumer Adrian.

The boys' own creations are worn by brave models who struggle to look elegant in ziggurat-like catastrophes obviously modeled after vanities and dressers—unbecomingly narrow at the shoulder, comically wide at the floor—complete with pull-out drawers with powder puffs. (One especially ornate outfit has a handy drop-drawer in the rear.)

Unsurprisingly, the society dames clamor for the new look. One of them, the unexpectedly adventurous Mrs. Morgan Morgan (Symona Boniface), is thrilled to be given an immediate fitting, but everything goes south when her husband shows up. Naturally, he's the guy who used to own the Chinese cabinet.

The short climaxes with a creampuff fight that's hilariously staged by director Jack White (credited as Preston Black) and played by the Stooges with great and messy enthusiasm. A gag that begins with a spring-loaded ladies' glove display has a particularly satisfying payoff.

White offers the requisite violence (Moe traps Larry's nose between the blades of a scissors and Curly laughs, "He looks like a V-8!"), but *Slippery Silks* ultimately succeeds because of scripter Ewart Adamson's clever central concept. Tables, cabinets, eveningwear, whatever, it's all equal to our trio of imaginative craftsmen.

A SNAKE-OIL SALESMAN WHO CALLS HIMSELF DR. BRIGHT (FRANK MILLS) HAS traveled from city to city, looking in vain for salesmen to hawk Brighto ("Brighto Brightens Old Bodies!"). Now he's set up shop in Los Angeles, and *still* nobody responds to his ads. How can this be? His secretary (Betty McMahon) explains, "Well, since prosperity's back everybody's working!" That's the optimistic premise of *Dizzy Doctors* (1937), in which the Stooges don't have jobs because they don't *want* them. And why should they? As Moe says to Curly and Larry moments after expressing a desire for breakfast (it's eleven in the morning and the boys are just waking up), "Our wives *can't* get breakfast and work at the same time!" Well, naturally not. And as Curly reflects, "We looked for a job one day last year!"

That's not nearly enough of an effort to satisfy the boys' wives (June Gittelson, Ione Leslie, and the six-foot Eva Murray), who shoo the boys from the one-room apartment. Get jobs or else.

At Dr. Bright's, the Stooges are immediately sold on Brighto's commercial possibilities.

MOE
Brighto! Brighto! It makes old bodies new!

LARRY
We'll sell a million bottles!

CURLY
Woo woo woo woo woo woo woo!

Once out on the street (effective location shooting by Del Lord, probably around Sunset and Fairfax), the boys buttonhole potential customers and stage impromptu product demonstrations that even the shifty Dr. Bright wouldn't recommend: They shine shoes (the stuff dissolves leather); they clean a spot from the uniform of policeman Bud Jamison (the Brighto leaves a smoking hole in the fabric); and, most famously, they polish the elegant touring car belonging to Harry Arms (Vernon Dent), the superintendent of nearby Los Arms Hospital. The boys kneel at the curb with their bottles of Brighto and go to work on the car's finish. (Their wives would be proud—maybe.) Curly applies the stuff in up-and-down strokes, Larry makes nice big circles, and Moe follows the contour of a fender. Harry Arms returns just as the boys realize that the Brighto is taking the paint right off. Frequent Stooges antagonist Vernon Dent got really upset with the boys many times but seldom with more fury than here: "If I ever catch you guys again I'll tear you limb from limb!"

The boys escape into the hospital, where they deliver obnoxious patter via the intercom system, ride gurneys through the corridors as if they were driving midget race cars, massage the contents of two bottles of Brighto into the scalp of a patient (A. R. Haysel) who's been hospitalized for dandruff, and relieve him of his hair. When they run into the superintendent again, a quick gurney ride (complete with unfurled sail) takes them to their apartment building. They leap through the window and land in bed, which is right where they were when the story began.

Writer Al Ray came up with good bits of business. When the boys literally run in circles to hawk Brighto, Curly pauses to hitchhike, getting down on his knees when a fellow in an American Bantam—the smallest American car of the day—rolls by. At the hospital, the boys try to give a hapless fellow in a wheelchair a traffic ticket, and they use a slug of Brighto to awaken a sleeping patient (Frank Mills again, doing double duty), who angrily tells them that he'd wanted to "break Rip Van Winkle's record! Put me back to sleep!" With heavy mallets, the boys oblige. And in a gag that the Marx Brothers would have liked, Curly says that someone on the phone "wants to know what to do for inflammation!" "Why call us?" Moe says irritably. "Tell him to dial Inflammation!"

Dizzy Doctors was shot during four days in December 1936, when the U.S. economy was on the mend. But Treasury secretary Henry Morgenthau soon talked President Roosevelt into authorizing a sharp pullback of federal stimulus spending (the Fed feared inflation), and the economy collapsed all over again during August–September 1937. *Dizzy Doctors* had been released five months earlier, so the assertion of Dr. Bright's secretary—"everybody's working!"—hadn't seemed too foolish to audiences, but by late summer the remark had become painfully ironic. Real economic growth wasn't seen again until U.S. industry ramped up military production in 1938–39, in anticipation of war.

Fortunately for Morgenthau, he and FDR were on the same page about matters other than economics; notably, they had a shared distaste for American neutrality in the inevitable tussle with the Axis. If not for that philosophical bond, *Morgenthau* could have been the one running in circles, yelling, "Brighto! Brighto!"

TASSELS IN THE AIR (1938) TAKES ITS TITLE FROM ANOTHER OF CURLY'S PEC-cadilloes, à la his violent reactions to "Pop Goes the Weasel" (*Punch Drunks*) and wild hyacinth (*Grips, Grunts and Groans*). This time he can't abide tassels. We're not told why, but we *do* learn that the only way to calm him is to tickle his chin. But unlike the "Weasel" tune and wild hyacinth, tassels don't figure into either the plot or the climax of *Tassels in the Air*. Curly's tasselphobia is simply a condition, like flat feet or Tourette's.

In the meanwhile, the boys go about their work as painters and handymen in a high-rise. Unfortunate things happen when they mix up door stencils: Their boss (Vernon Dent) falls down an elevator shaft and their temporary office is identified as belonging to the famed Parisian interior designer Omay. Because of Curly's struggles to learn pig Latin, an unwitting potential client, Maggie Smirch (Bess Flowers), mistakes Moe for Omay. In short order, the boys are wrecking things at the Smirch's elaborate house and disrupting Mrs. Smirch's bridge game. When the real Omay (Jean De Briac) shows up, it's the *boys* who feel insulted. They stomp from the house in a self-righteous huff to prepare a paint-can booby trap that backfires on them.

Class, as well as jobs, is a central preoccupation of Al Giebler and Elwood Ullman's script. When Mrs. Smirch tells husband Thaddeus (Bud Jamison) that she wants to engage Omay to redecorate the house, Thaddeus is compelled to remind her that "before we came into all this money I was just a letter carrier." He's an easygoing guy who recoils at his wife's ambition to mingle with the upper crust; he just wants to sit in his easy chair and read the paper. When the Stooges show up to begin their work, Thaddeus eagerly asks if he can help, so Moe dismissively sends him off to prepare a batch of "spotted paint." Thaddeus, although integral to the short's theme, has as much relevance to the plot as the tassel thing, and spends the rest of the film happily puttering in a corner, pouring paint through a colander to make spots, and thinking he's succeeded when some of the stuff gets on his Dalmatian.

Tassels in the Air was the first of five Stooges shorts directed by one of screen comedy's greatest and most unsung actors, Charley Chase, who borrowed elements from his own 1933 Hal Roach short *Luncheon at Twelve* (in which he stumbles into a job as an interior decorator without having a clue as to what a decorator does). The low-key intelligence he brought to shorts in which he starred and frequently directed for Roach in the 1920s and early '30s informs his later work as a director. Chase had a fine working relationship with Columbia producer Hugh McCollum but was disliked by department head Jules White, who was put off by Chase's easygoing nature on the set.

Because of Chase, the major set piece of *Tassels in the Air* is paced and played in ways noticeably different from those choreographed by the Stooges' other directors. The boys' heedless application of paint to an antique table that once belonged to Louis XVI ("Oh, second hand, eh?" Larry sneers) *reads* like many other of the boys' big comic scenes—Moe accidentally paints Larry's butt, Larry carelessly paints with Curly's sandwich, Curly takes a bite out of Larry's brush, and so on—but Chase stages the sequence with an easy, measured grace that transforms the boys' usual pistol-quick action-reaction style into a slower progression of small disasters.

When Moe swallows a mouthful of paint because of a misplaced coffee cup, he spits the stuff out and unintentionally catches Larry flush in the face. In a typical short, Larry would react in an instant with an angry "Hey!" before a rapid cutaway to Moe. But in Chase's hands the moment is prolonged and made funnier, as Larry pauses to gaze unhappily at the camera, very much in the manner of Chase's Roach-studio comrade, Oliver Hardy.

Curly has a particularly good moment when he eagerly salts and tries to eat a cuckoo-clock counterweight that looks like an ear of corn ("I thought it was a Golden Bantam!"), and Chase pulls off a fine, almost subliminal gag when the Smirches' butler (John Ince) quickly strides by, allowing the briefest of glimpses at his back, where one of the boys has stenciled "NOT RESPONSIBLE FOR HATS AND COATS."

Because the boys have slathered paint on the metal chairs in the card room, Mrs. Smirch's dress is torn from her backside when she stands up. When the other women stand, their chairs remain affixed to their bottoms, twitching behind them like bustles. Moe, ever-observant, mutters, "Somethin's goin' on here, boys." Yes: the collision of working-class anarchy and strained, nouveau riche gentility.

IMMEDIATELY FOLLOWING *TASSELS IN THE AIR*, CHARLEY CHASE WAS BACK TO direct *Flat Foot Stooges* (1938), working this time from his own story and script. Despite the up-to-the-minute nature of the short's title (a pun on the title of a 1938 Slam Stewart-Slim Gaillard jazz hit, "Flat Foot Floogie" [from "floozie"]), Chase deliberately looked backward this time, casting a pair of former Mack Sennett Keystone Kops in supporting roles, relying heavily on a maiden-in-distress subplot, and evoking a semi-rural, small-town atmosphere where the fire department still operates a horse-drawn steam engine.

The department consists of the elderly chief (Chester Conklin), a couple other old duffs—and Larry, Moe, and Curly, who represent youthful energy and imagination. Curly, in fact, has invented a semi-automatic drop-down harness that he insists will get the dapple-gray horses, Annie and Fannie, ready for action in an eyeblink.

It's a cute innovation (that doesn't work, as things turn out), but it's still wedded to an old technology that irritates the hell out of Reardon (Richard Curtis), an outsider who wants to sell the department a brand-new pumper truck. To ensure a sale, he drops a can of gunpowder into the engine's boiler—which ultimately leads to his entrapment, along with the chief's pretty daughter (Lola Jensen), in a conflagration that blazes in the fire station's second floor. (The fire starts when a duck that's been eating the gunpowder lays an explosive egg.)

Charley Chase never worked for film-comedy pioneer Mack Sennett, but he was obviously taken with the Sennett style of big-scale, outdoor slapstick. This fondness is very apparent during the short's protracted and elaborate climax, which begins with Annie and Fannie racing off without the wagon (and with the *Stooges* in harness). In short order, townsfolk run to the station to help the boys, and subsequently pull the wagon in the wrong direction, *away* from the fire.

When a wheel falls off, the boys replace it with a length of fencing, and the mad dash continues—still traveling the wrong way. Finally realizing their error, the boys and their helpers execute a screeching U-turn and head back to the blaze. With the Stooges lost amidst a sea of extras, the sequence (shot by a fast-tracking camera car) effectively replicates Sennett's style of "crowd" comedy. A pleasing, intimate break comes during a medium close-up on Curly, who gaily plucks wildflowers as he runs and happily offers them to Moe.

The planted gunpowder finally destroys the pumper, but the group salvages a net and catches the chief's daughter when she leaps from a window. (Sneaky Reardon appears in a window first, and although the rescuers set up beneath him, they immediately shift to the girl when she calls for help. Reardon can't stop his jump, which knocks him cold and leaves an enormous crater in the dirt.)

Mack Sennett liked to mix his large-scale set pieces with sentiment, and Chase indulges in a bit of that early in the short, when the Stooges take Annie and Fannie to a Turkish bath to spruce them up so they'll win first prize in a beauty contest at a picnic. Sweet, almost maternal here, the Stooges don't quite seem like themselves.

Horse-drawn engines, picnics, damsels in distress, old comics with walrus mustaches—*Flat Foot Stooges* is a real time machine. It's also one of the least typical of the boys' shorts, and isn't particularly satisfying, either. Larry, Moe, and Curly are very urban creatures, and although they functioned effectively in Old West and other historical settings, small-town Americana doesn't suit them at all. The Stooges of 1938 were aggressively modern, so Chase's attempt to cast them in an earlier comic mold is novel instead of consistently funny.

A few gags, though, are very much in the Stooges' style. One of the horses neighs at Curly as he industriously buffs her hoof, causing him to blush like a callow manicurist and say, "You know we're not supposed to flirt with the customers!" And after the fire has started in the rooms directly above the boys, Moe asks Curly if he smells anything. "No," Curly says, "especially smoke!"

A sequence involving an unwanted firehouse mouse has some promise but falls apart when the off-screen handler of a bulldog sent by the boys to eliminate the rodent treats the pooch too roughly. You just feel bad when the dog is abruptly spun onto the floor after being ejected through the doors of a cupboard. Curly's initial idea, though, to catch the mousie in an enormous bear trap, is visual and very funny. Excess, with a patina of cruelty—*that's* more like the Stooges we know.

ONCE UPON A TIME, MOTORISTS WHO DROVE INTO SERVICE STATIONS GOT service—and lots of it. Gas, water, oil, air, a clean windshield—the works. "Super service!" That's what the Stooges happily shout to customers in the opening sequence of *Violent Is the Word for Curly* (1938), an energetic, superior short written by Al Giebler and Elwood Ullman, and directed by Charley Chase. (The title is a pun on the title of a 1936 Paramount feature, *Valiant Is the Word for Carrie*, which concerns the romance of a young man and woman, and the benign influence in their lives of a former prostitute.)

The Stooges' boss (Bud Jamison) steps across the street for lunch, and the boys are left in charge. Uh oh. When three Teutonic professors roll in for gas, the boys' eagerness to serve becomes a frantic, choreographed dance, rhythmically punctuated with cries of "Super Service!," "Riight!," and Curly's lusty "Swing it!" But their enthusiasm is a little careless: The professors are sprayed with water, and then smothered in dust when Curly has a titanic struggle with a snaking air hose. Because one of the profs gets particularly filthy, Moe shouts, "Take it easy, field marshal!" and buffs the indignant fellow's bald pate with car wax. Finally, Moe accidentally blows up the professors' automobile (Curly has been filling the radiator with gasoline, and Moe takes a lighted match to see what's what). The Stooges panic and swipe a nearby ice cream truck, unaware that the professors' suitcases have been tossed inside. Later, attired in gowns and mortarboards, they're welcomed at Mildew College as the highbrow new instructors: professors Feinstein, Frankfurter, and Von Stupor.

Less stodgy, more fun—that's the Stooges' plan for higher education in *Violent Is the Word for Curly* (1938).

Mildew is an all-girl college where Coach Benson (Pat Gleason) has been knocking his head against the wall trying to get funding from a wealthy alumnus, Mrs. Sufferin Catsby (Gladys Gale), for an athletics program. Nearly thirty-five years before Title IX guaranteed female high school and college students equal access to (among other things) athletic facilities, Benson is revealed as a man with a vision. But despite the fact that Mrs. Catsby's pretty daughter (Marjorie Dean) wants to play basketball on a proper court, Mom is fixated on high culture—hence her engagement of the stuffy brainiacs from Europe.

The boys successfully pass as the educators, despite a few faux pas, most noticeably Curly's flirtation with a girl in the front row: "Say, I'll meet you in the gymnasium over by the dumbbells! You'll know me, I got a hat!"

The film's highlight is "Swingin' the Alphabet," a delightful nonsense song led by the Stooges, with the students adding some reet-to-the-beat harmonies. According to film and music historian Richard Finegan, the tune is a variation of "The Spelling Bee," an 1875 song by successful American music publisher and songwriter Septimus Miller. Charley Chase, who had a pleasing singing voice and frequently incorporated songs into his Hal Roach shorts, may have sung the tune to his children. For the Stooges, he adapted it into a brisk fox trot, transferring the deliberate rhythms of the service-station sequence to a less destructive and more logical purpose.

"Bee A bay, boy A bee, bee eye bickey bay, bee I bo . . ." the song begins, progressing through various consonants of the alphabet. Larry and Curly could sing, and although the vocals of all three boys were looped in post-production, only Moe's were handled by a professional singer.

"Swingin' the Alphabet" is bouncy good fun, but for sheer grotesqueness that's weirdly predictive of such later horrors as *Cannibal Holocaust*, it's impossible to find anything in the Stooges' films to match the sequence in which Curly, who's been removed frozen stiff from the back of the stolen ice cream truck, is thawed by Moe and Larry on a giant rotisserie over an open fire. The quite functional device is constructed of tree trunks and heavy branches. Curly is literally tied to the spit. Larry turns the enormous crank but visibly struggles because of Curly's heft. And when Curly is left facing the fire for a little too long, he's singed. For real. What a way to make a living!

THE UNCOMPLICATED NATURE OF DOGS IS ONE REASON THE STOOGES SEEM well suited to play veterinarians in *Calling All Curs* (1939). The simplicity of the pooch mind and habits lends itself easily to knockabout comedy. Further, it's no stretch to suppose that Curly Howard—inveterately fond of dogs and women—enjoyed the shoot of *Calling All Curs*. The short features dogs of all breeds, sizes, and ages. The set overflows with them, and is full of pretty women playing nurses, too. Curly must not have known where to look first.

During an operation that might give pause to the Mayo brothers, Larry, Moe, and Curly—plus a bevy of beautiful nurses and an array of very elaborate instruments—carefully extract a thorn from the paw of Garçon, a champion, full-size black poodle owned by a regular client, Mrs. Bedford (Isabelle LaMal). When a pair of no-goods (Lynton Brent and Cy Schindell) pass themselves off as reporters and then kidnap Garçon, Curly is unworried. "Here's his collar and leash. All we gotta do is refill it!"

Moe and Larry know it's not going to be that easy. Following an embarrassing misadventure with another dog clumsily disguised by the boys to resemble Garçon, the real pooch is located and rescued, and the dognappers are collared.

Writers Elwood Ullman and Searle Kramer (working from a story by Thea Goodan) provide the boys and director Jules White with plenty of good material. In a great moment that plays without dialogue, Curly strides into a central corridor and eagerly follows a pretty nurse (who's unaware of his presence). Another nurse exits another door, and Curly reverses course to follow *her*. Then yet another nurse enters the corridor, causing Curly to execute another one-eighty. You get the impression that this could go on all day.

While scrubbing for the operation, Larry pulls out a pair of gaudily striped socks and begins to launder them. Curly stoops to insert his hand into the glove a nurse holds for him, only to miss completely and fall onto the floor. At dinner with the patients, Curly has trouble with another sandwich that wants to bite his nose—only this time the sandwich is made with oversized dog biscuits. Then Moe looks at the plate of dog food Curly has served him and asks, "Since when do I look like a dog?" "I dunno," Curly answers, "I ain't seen you lately!"

In a fancifully bizarre bit, Curly cracks wise to Moe's voice at a wall-mounted intercom, only to be smacked in the face by a fist that pops right through the speaker. The fist belongs to Moe, whose head soon fills the speaker frame. When Moe admits he's stuck, Curly feels free to begin pulling out Moe's eyebrows, hair by hair.

As the boys wait with the phony Garçon in Mrs. Bedford's drawing room, they help themselves to her liquor cart. When their deception is revealed (the maid's vacuum cleaner sucks the tremendous piles of mattress stuffing right off the phony Garçon's body), Mrs. Bedford faints and Curly makes his escape by tethering the mutt to the cart and riding it right out of frame. Eventually, phony Garçon helps the boys track down the real dog.

Although no supporting players are credited on screen, Columbia cast sheets note five starlets who appear as nurses. They're all easy on the eyes, but one, a nineteen-year-old charmer named Dorothy Moore, is especially appealing. Dark blonde or possibly a redhead, she has vividly flirtatious interactions with Curly, during which real voltage seems to crackle up there on the screen. Curly shot longing gazes at a lot of actresses during his career but never with the eagerness he shows to this sweetly pretty kid with the slim shape and shy smile. And Moore, unless she was a one-in-a-million acting prodigy, appears to reciprocate those feelings. After asking for equipment at the start of the operation sequence, Curly catches Moore's eye. She returns his gaze from beneath her lashes, looks away, and then looks at him again. When he moves a bit, her eyes follow him.

Pretty Dorothy Moore (middle nurse) and Curly struck sparks in *Calling All Curs* (1939). It's all too much for the flop-tongued patient.

Later, Curly flutters his fingers beneath her chin, which triggers another intriguingly believable round of flickering gazes and shared smiles.

I discuss this not simply to express a viewer's pleasure at obvious mutual attraction between two people but to refute some of the Stooges' more unsympathetic critics, who claim that the boys were one-dimensional actors incapable of subtle expression. A good actor draws from life and from the heart, and that's precisely what I think was happening during the last week of 1938 on the set of *Calling All Curs*.

IF THE PIPES IN YOUR HOME SPRING A LEAK WHEN YOU'RE THROWING A RITZY party, and you need a plumber, you *really* need a plumber. That's probably why Mrs. Hadley (Bess Flowers) doesn't look too closely when the Stooges roll up in a truck marked "Casey the Plumber." How could she know that the boys are just unemployed layabouts who've stolen the truck to elude the cops? That's the motivating premise of *A Plumbing We Will Go* (1940), one of the Stooges' greatest shorts, and the one that Curly cited as his personal favorite.

The protracted sequence in which Curly frantically labors to stop up a gush of water while standing in a bathtub is practically folklore, a kind of shared memory of American experience. Curly has accidentally yanked a shower faucet handle right off the wall, so, armed with an array of water pipes of various lengths and configurations, he optimistically applies himself to stopping the leak. He happily screws a pipe directly into the gushing wall faucet, an act that eliminates the flood from the wall by unhelpfully transferring it to the outlet of the new pipe. Well, simple to fix *that*, with *another* length of pipe screwed onto the first one. Success! But, oh no, now the water spurts from *that* pipe! This goes on in Sisyphean fashion, as Curly unthinkingly, and with increasing panic, adds more lengths of pipe, including some that have *two* open ends instead of just one, which send water spraying simultaneously in opposite directions. By the time Curly thinks he's finally conquered the problem, he realizes that he's trapped himself in a labyrinthine weave of pipe that surrounds him completely and stretches higher than his head. There's no place to squeeze through, no hope of escape, and Curly's infantile frustration is at once funny and pitiable. Caught by his own misplaced ingenuity, he's doomed to starve, or maybe just hyperventilate himself to death. He's enthusiastically labored to build the better mousetrap, only to discover that *he's* the mouse. Unobserved, unappreciated, with no boss present to praise him for good intentions, help him, or even acknowledge his existence by laughing at him, Curly is the forgotten laborer.

If there's ever been a better visual metaphor for the frustrations of work, I'd like to see it.

The sequence picks up added humor, and a certain cynical pathos, because director Del Lord and editor Arthur Seid freely cut between Curly's predicament and the other boys' activities. Each time we return to Curly his situation is worse than before, so we're delighted by the evidence of his growing failure, and satisfied by its inevitability.

Curly has created his private hell in a second-floor bathroom. Two floors below, Moe and Larry stare at a small leak that drips from a pipe running just below the basement ceiling. They soon make the leak worse, of course, and in the bargain manage to puncture an enormous steam pipe that runs from the furnace.

The basement is now filling with water, but Larry has an idea: "Hey, I once saw a guy shut the water off in the front yard!" Moe is pissed off about the whole situation and snarls back, "When I want your advice, I'll ask for it!" Pause. "Hey, go shut the water off in the front yard!"

After snagging the handle of a spade in Moe's suspenders, tugging on it, and nearly breaking Moe's spine when he releases his grip, Larry scurries up the steps and outside, where he begins to dig a hole that will eventually be the size of a bomb crater. Larry, though no less wrongheaded in his fix-it notions than Curly, has more moxie, and rudely tells the butler (Wilson Benge) to "Beat it!" when the fellow protests the ruination of the lawn.

Eventually, Curly manages to fall through the bathroom floor all the way into the basement and right on top of Moe. By subsequently connecting the water to an electrical pipe Curly has pulled from the basement power box, the boys manage to upset all the appliances in the house. The kitchen's overhead bulb fills with water, and the stove sends forth a lusty spray, to the comical dismay of the cook (Dudley Dickerson). In the parlor, Mrs. Hadley and her guests are inundated when she demonstrates her "new television receiver." "Okay, Niagara Falls," the unseen announcer shouts, "take it away!" The ensuing gush of water from the screen is so powerful it knocks people right off their feet.

The watery-appliances set piece is, along with Curly's entrapment, the other great gag from *A Plumbing We Will Go* that everybody seems to know. Dudley Dickerson, a wonderful actor skilled at verbal and physical comedy, takes hilarious, repeated pratfalls on the wet kitchen floor (he eventually attires himself in a rain slicker but keeps falling down anyway). Finally—and famously—Dickerson mutters, "Dis house has sho' gone crazy!"

A Plumbing We Will Go opens with the boys on trial for chicken theft and their acquittal by a judge (John Tyrrell) who quickly loses patience with them. A subsequent run-in with a cop (Bud Jamison) ends badly for the officer, and when the boys come across a Professor Bilbo (veteran comic Monte Collins), an illusionist whose "magic" pistol shot is supposed to transfer his pretty assistant from one cabinet to another, Curly somehow ends up inside the cabinet with the girl, who looks a little perplexed by Curly's shameless flirting. A second magic shot transfers all three boys into the *other* cabinet.

The circularity of Elwood Ullman's lively script is revealed in two segments that comprise the conclusion: when Mr. Hadley returns home and we—and the boys—recognize him as the judge; and when the hapless Mrs. Hadley—having engaged our old friend Professor Bilbo as the afternoon's entertainment—is shocked when the magic shot releases a surge of Stooges from the skinny cabinet, followed by a seething mass of running policemen and capped with a roaring phalanx of motorcycle cops.

A Plumbing We Will Go makes excellent use of a standing mansion set and numerous sunny exteriors on city streets and the suburbs. Even a sound-stage setup (for the lawn in which Larry busily digs) is unusually well lit—another proficient job by Benjamin Kline. By any standard, this is an accomplished, good-looking film.

The short was remade in 1949 as *Vagabond Loafers* (a cute but pointless title pun that has nothing at all to do with this tale of plumbing). Although director Ed Bernds reshot much of the original in order to seamlessly incorporate Shemp, the nature of the plumbing-related mayhem is virtually unchanged. Sharp-eyed viewers, though, will note with some relief that the nasty, asbestos-covered steam pipe of the original film has been replaced by a modern one of stamped tin.

Elwood Ullman's revised script adds a great new bit in the basement: As Moe struggles with the leaking overhead pipe, water from it collects in a bucket below. When the bucket fills, the essentially idle Larry puts his newspaper aside,

Performer Profile: Bud Jamison
1894–1944

Burly, baby-faced Bud Jamison excelled at playing cops, bosses, high-society types, and butlers. Even when cast as a servant, he exuded a don't-mess-with-it authority that he frequently expressed with a menacing glare and sometimes a short punch to the jaw. Although Bud's speaking voice was pleasant, even charming, that voice could be turned to a growl of menace in a heartbeat.

His featured role in *Woman Haters*, the Stooges' first Columbia short, came after a lengthy movie apprenticeship that stretched back to 1915. Jamison worked with many of the great comics of his era: Harry Langdon, Snub Pollard, Charlie Chaplin, and Edgar Kennedy—work that took him to Essanay, Hal Roach, Mack Sennett, RKO, First National, and, by 1934, Columbia.

In addition to his frequent Columbia outings with the Stooges, Bud worked there with Clark and McCullough, Tom Kennedy and Monte Collins, Buster Keaton, Andy Clyde, El Brendel, Charley Chase, Harry Langdon, Vera Vague, and others.

Bud is particularly well remembered for his roles in *Crash Goes the Hash*, as the thieving butler, Flint; and *A Ducking They Did Go*, as the police chief who displays a charming tenor in a song scene with the Stooges.

Jamison was a Christian Scientist who refused treatment for an infection that quickly worsened and took his life at age fifty.

Perennial flatfoot Bud Jamison finally gets his hands on the boys in *A Plumbing We Will Go* (1940).
Photo courtesy of the Stoogeum

carefully dumps the contents of the bucket on the floor, resets it in place, and then goes back to his newspaper.

A significant new twist is a subplot concerning a pair of brazen art thieves (Kenneth MacDonald and Christine McIntyre), who cut a "Van Brocklin" from its frame during a party hosted by the Norfleets (Symona Boniface and Emil Sitka). The thieves hide the painting in one of the Stooges' spare pipes and get the drop on the boys and the others in the Norfleets' basement. "Count to a hundred," MacDonald warns, and the Norfleets' butler, Wilkes (Herbert Evans), quaveringly recites, "One, two, three . . . ." Mrs. Norfleet can't believe what she's hearing and exclaims, "Oh, *Wilkes!*"

The standoff ends when MacDonald is startled by Larry, who's been accidentally doused with flour, ghost-like, by cook Dudley Dickerson (who reprises his role of nine years earlier).

Shemp distinguishes himself from the more manic Curly with ad libs: When he rousts Mr. Norfleet from the shower in order to work, he impatiently listens as Norfleet demands, "Who *are* you?" Full of swagger, Shemp comes back with, "Who am I, I'm the plumber, get outta here! Who am I, that's a hot one!"

A Plumbing We Will Go (plus much of *Vagabond Loafers*) was retooled yet again, after Shemp's death, for release in 1956 as a miserable pastiche called *Scheming Schemers*. Scripter Jack White provided brother Jules (Ed Bernds had moved on to features by this time) with another subplot, explicated in brief new footage: the eagerness of Mr. Norfleet (Emil Sitka again) that the boys retrieve his wife's diamond ring from the drain of a bathroom sink. Shemp is noticeably absent as Moe and Larry search for the ring (footage from *Vagabond Loafers* doesn't appear until more than four minutes into the story), and that absence is foolishly made all the more apparent when Larry and Moe separately ask, "Where's Shemp?" Yikes.

Joe Palma does the third of his four turns as what some fans call "fake Shemp," bumbling with pipes and tools, being careful not to allow the camera a glimpse of his face. A single line of vintage Shemp dialogue is looped over Palma's sequence, and Larry loops over his own dialogue from *A Plumbing We Will Go*, replacing "We can't plug a pipe while it's leakin'!" with "We can't find a ring while it's leakin'!" Audiences probably never noticed.

Kenneth MacDonald (looking considerably older than he did in 1949) returns as the art thief. Christine McIntyre appears in stock footage only and is doubled from the back (none too well) in one or two quick setups featuring MacDonald.

The climax of *Scheming Schemers* takes place at a dinner buffet rather than in the Norfleet basement. A few pies are hurled about (courtesy of footage lifted from *Half-Wits Holiday*, 1947), and the thief is captured.

The tag line that dominates the one-sheet poster for *Scheming Schemers* says, "A floodtide of fabulous fun." If you buy *that*, I know some good plumbers you might like . . .

HOW HIGH IS UP? (1940), WHICH FOLLOWS THE STOOGES AS THEY ENDURE A disastrous day as high-iron workers, is among the more linear and naturally flowing of the boys' shorts. Although divided into two distinct segments (the boys on the ground and the boys on a skyscraper's unfinished ninety-seventh floor), the story moves from the first segment to the second logically and without undue contrivance. The boys work out of (and live in) a truck that's the HQ of Minute Menders, Inc., a shoestring operation that, on this particular day, tries to drum up repair jobs by puncturing ironworkers' lunch boxes when the workers aren't around. But, oops, the workers *are* around, and to escape, the boys run to a nearby construction site, where Curly identifies the three of them as "the best riveters that ever riveted,"

Naturally, Curly is petrified of heights. When Moe tells him to stop looking down at the street, Curly says, "I can't help it, I *belong* down there!" That answer encourages Moe to get physical, nearly toppling Curly right off the narrow girder. Because Curly won't shut up about being terrified, Moe helpfully blindfolds him. Later, Curly accidentally kicks over a pail of grease while laboring as the bucker-up man who holds firm the rivets that Moe guns in from the other side. Every vibration from Moe's rivet gun repeatedly sends Curly sliding backwards, bringing him closer and closer to the end of the girder, and oblivion.

Meanwhile, one story below, Larry uses his coal forge not to heat rivets but to cook weenies. When the foreman (Edmund Cobb) shows up, Larry meekly gets back to the rivets, and when he tosses one upward, Curly assumes it's another weenie and catches it with a bun before gamely munching on it.

Eventually, the construction company owner (Vernon Dent) leans back against a girder the boys have worked on, only to recoil in horror as the girder, and many others around it, gives way and collapses with an awful crash. Dent looks up and sees a crazy-quilt of girders that have been riveted together every which way. Then the boys carelessly drop a hot rivet down the back of the guy's shirt. The parachute that Curly has insisted on bringing with him comes in handy as the Stooges leap into space, drop right into their truck, and speed away.

The short's opening sequence is clever and purely visual: The boys are crammed together in bed, asleep, whistling and snoring. An enormous bumblebee drops in and out of Curly's mouth (disaster is narrowly averted), and when a city worker opens a hydrant, we see that the boys' "bed" is just a mattress they've laid beneath their truck. They sleep on as the hydrant gushes water, oblivious as the mattress is rapidly carried by the current that courses next to the curb. Director Del Lord and cinematographer Allen Siegler smoothly track with the mattress as it floats along. The horizontal nature of the sequence later provides a pointed, and almost certainly unintentional, contrast with the severe vertical nature of the scenes atop the skyscraper. Then again, because the boys and the mattress are as close to the ground as possible—which sets up another sort of visual contrast—maybe all of this wasn't unintentional at all.

New York skyscraper construction succumbed to economic drought in the early 1930s (the Empire State Building, for instance, had been topped off in

1931)—so just what was it that inspired writer Elwood Ullman to create a high-iron adventure for the Stooges in 1940? The answer is the highly publicized November 1939 completion of Rockefeller Center, which was commemorated when John D. Rockefeller drove the final rivet—a silver one.

How High Is Up? finds much of its humor in the precisely ordered ritual of rivet construction. Ironically, high-iron rivet work was virtually extinct by 1940, having been superseded in the 1920s by electrical arc welding, which is less expensive and gives better results. But where's the physical humor in arc welding, beyond, perhaps, an unexpected brush fire in someone's hair?

Ullman and Lord get the rivet scenes mostly right. Typically, a riveting gang (crew) was comprised of four men: a hoister, a rivet heater, a riveter, and a bucker-up man. The bucker-up man, who stationed himself on the side of the girder opposite the riveter, used a tool called a dolly bar, which he positioned in the open end of the rivet hole before leaning his entire weight against it. Curly's antics, though a burlesque of actual rivet technique (instead of a dolly bar he uses a helmet on his head), rightly suggest that the bucker-up had an extraordinarily demanding job requiring not just physical strength and coordination but continual attentiveness, because the hot rivets—like the laughs in this short—keep on coming.

IN LATE-DEPRESSION 1940, NATIONAL JOBLESSNESS STOOD AT 14.6 PERCENT, or 8.1 million total unemployed. People who landed temporary jobs as census takers considered themselves fortunate. They were getting paychecks—and they had to work hard for them, asking precise questions about age, employment, income, marital status, and much more.

Harry Edwards and Elwood Ullman's episodic, nicely chugging script for *No Census, No Feeling* (1940) establishes that the boys will earn four cents for every person they interview, so they're eager to rush to and from as many interviews as possible. Moe stands on a man's front stoop and asks that perfectly reasonable question, "Are you married or happy?" The man suddenly ducks, and Moe is smacked in the face by a piece of flying crockery. Okay, that answers *that* question.

Inside the kitchen of a swank house, Curly makes time with a pretty maid (Marjorie Kane) and then puts on a chef's hat and begins to putter at the sink. That's Moe's cue to come inside and start an interview, unaware that he's talking to his pal. Curly reveals, "There was a litter of three—and I was the one they kept!" Well, that kind of idiocy sounds very familiar to Moe, and an instant later he's assaulting Curly's nose with a lemon squeezer and running a cheese grater up and down the side of his face.

In the living room, Moe spies a man dozing on the couch, his face covered by newspapers. Moe asks about the circumstances of the fellow's birth and Larry responds, "I was one of a litter of three."

Moe scowls. "Now don't tell me you're the one they kept!"

Larry: "Nah, I'm the one they threw away!"

Moe beats on the newspaper, only to discover that the resting man *isn't* Larry, who's been goldbricking, out of Moe's sight, on another couch.

"One of a litter of three, eh?" Moe says as he squeezes Larry's head in the heavy door of a wardrobe. "A three-litter man, eh?"

Larry's outraged shrieks bring the lady of the house (Symona Boniface), who immediately falls under the boys' scrutiny.

> MOE
> How old are you?

> LARRY
> What address is this?

> SYMONA
> One hundred and two.

> MOE
> You don't look a day over eighty!

> SYMONA
> Young man, I'm twenty-nine!

> MOE
> Oh, yeah?

> SYMONA
> Well, how do I look?

> MOE
> Oh, you look like a million!

> LARRY
> Ah, she can't be that old!

Despite the boys' rude examination of her teeth to determine her age, they're invited to the game room to fill out a couple of foursomes for that most complex of card games, bridge.

As you might expect, neither Moe nor Larry are well suited to the pastime, and things only get worse when Curly, back in the kitchen again, unwittingly spikes the punch with lip-puckering alum. In a few minutes the bridge fiends all look like perplexed suckerfish, their mouths contracted into absurd "kiss me" shapes. In the best of the sequence's many gags, an index finger that Larry has stuck in his mouth to free his lips gets stuck, giving him a brief moment of raw (and beautifully played) panic. Puckered party guest Vernon Dent gamely soldiers on, saying things like "I redobbo!" and "Wotuzay?" (Having utilized very few close-ups to this point, Del Lord employs them very well during this sequence, so that the puckered faces have a heightened comic impact.)

Once outside, it's back to business when the boys rush to a football stadium (the field at USC) where—at four cents a head—they can really clean up. The Stooges find uniforms and bluff their way past a guard. Larry: "Quarterback!" Moe: "Halfback!" Curly (with a football stuffed between his shoulder blades): "Hunchback!"

On the field, the census taking dissolves into a melee of shoves and flying ice cream. The angry players finally chase the Stooges off the field and into the neighborhood beyond.

In the opening sequence of *No Census, No Feeling*, a merchant (silent-comedy star Max Davidson) unrolls his awning and is surprised when the sleeping Stooges tumble out and collide with the sidewalk. Some bedroom! No wonder four cents a head is so enticing.

AN ACHE IN EVERY STAKE (1941) PUTS THE BOYS TO WORK FOR THE ZERO ICE & Coal Company, as icemen who deliver to home iceboxes. The Stooges ought to know that the successful iceman organizes his load and plans his route carefully, in order to complete his deliveries so that (and this is important) the ice doesn't melt first. But, the Stooges being the Stooges, they're not particularly good icemen.

The visual and existential centerpiece of the short's first half is a dizzying set of concrete steps leading from the street to the home of a lady who's been calling for her ice. Curly hefts a big block with his tongs and races up the steps, arriving at the top with only a cocktail-size ice cube to present to the unhappy customer. Then Moe has a brainstorm: He, Larry, and Curly will run a relay with *two* blocks of ice, so that one full-size block will remain by the time the load reaches the top. Of course, when Curly, the third man in the relay, finally staggers to the summit, he's holding *two* ice cubes.

Okay, that didn't work, so Moe's big brain comes up with a better idea: Take the icebox from the house down the stairs to the wagon, load the ice into the icebox, and then carry the icebox up the steps to the house!

Inevitably, ice and ice box get away from the boys and repeatedly ambush an amiable fellow (Vernon Dent) who can't get his birthday cakes home without being made to fall into them.

The ice and ice box are finally delivered—and then the cook quits. The mistress of the house, Mrs. Lawrence (Bess Flowers), is distraught, but the boys magnanimously volunteer to prepare dinner. Curly stuffs a turkey with unshelled oysters, and in the dining room, Larry uses his enormous tongs to drop single ice cubes into people's drinks. Curly dances with a guest (Symona Boniface), only to have trouble when a sofa string attaches itself to the seat of his pants, causing him to bounce around like a jack-in-the-box. Later, and with marvelous gaucherie, Curly fishes with his hands in the punch bowl. When he's startled by Moe, he upends the bowl and sends a torrent of punch cascading down Mrs. Lawrence's back.

The short's verbal highlight comes when Curly, having been ordered by Moe to "shave some ice," proceeds to do just that, conscientiously covering the ice block's lower part with a bib, applying lather, and going at it with a straight razor. As he plays barber, Curly makes with offhand small talk that's priceless: "You're new in the neighborhood, aren't you? Once over lightly, yes. Tell me, is it as warm in the country as it is in the summer? Are you married or happy? . . . Say, did you have a pink tie on? No? Well, here's your lip."

A birthday cake the boys put together causes the sides of the oven to ominously expand and contract (à la the ominous cake in the 1932 Our Gang short *Birthday Blues*). When Larry accidentally deflates the cake with a fork, Moe decides to plump it up with natural gas. "Thirty-eight pounds, OK!" Curly announces. Moe considers the number of guests: "Pump in four more slices!" When Mr. Lawrence—who is of course the hapless guy victimized earlier by the Stooges—blows out the candles, the gassy confection explodes. What a party!

Lloyd French, who worked at Hal Roach (frequently with Laurel and Hardy) as an assistant director, director, and writer before he scripted *An Ache in Every Stake*, moved to Warner Bros. not long after *Ache*, so the short is his only credit with the Stooges. That's a shame because he grasped the boys' comic style and added a bit of Hal Roach's unique, but equally working-class, point of view.

In 2001, film historian Jim Pauley discovered that the steps seen in *An Ache in Every Stake* are located in the Silver Lake district of Los Angeles, between 2257 and 2258 Fair Oak View Terrace. As late as 2004, the steps were virtually unchanged. The towering steps that figure prominently in a fabulous Laurel and Hardy short, *The Music Box* (a 1932 Hal Roach production), are also located in Silver Lake, between 923 and 935 Vendome Street.

ONE OF THE MORE TOPICAL STOOGES SHORTS, *DIZZY PILOTS* (1943), IS ALSO one of the most unrewarding. The boys are the Wrong brothers, aeronautical engineers who hope to sell their new biplane, the *Buzzard*, to the army—never mind that by 1943 *nobody* was developing new biplanes. (That's just one reason why the boys are the *Wrong* brothers.)

The greater portion of the short involves the boys' struggles to get the *Buzzard* up and running in their workshop. Comic byplay with the plane's propeller is forced and unfunny: When Moe tries to coax the prop into motion, he conveniently stands to the side of the blade, just so that it can strike him in the stomach, whirl him around a few times, and then send him flying across the shop.

The main comic diversion of the workshop sequence is set in motion by an enormous tub of rubber compound that the boys have prepared as a sealant. The goo is thick and black and looks very hot. When Moe falls into it, he's almost instantly immobilized. He yells to Larry and Curly to pump hydrogen beneath the rubber so that the stuff will inflate and allow it to be cut away from his body. (The inflated Moe is wonderfully grotesque and looks like an ebony Tweedledum, with a panicked face above an enormous, spherical body.) But before he can be cut free, the hydrogen sends him rising to the ceiling, where he becomes stuck. Curly thinks he can effect a rescue with a lasso but only manages to get the rope around Larry's neck and nearly strangle him. Larry and Curly finally get hold of Moe, only to lose their grip. When Moe begins to float away, he says—via looped and completely superfluous dialogue—"Oh, I'm floating!"

Once rescued (Moe plummets into a well after Curly blows the rubber to smithereens with a shotgun), Moe and the boys do a demonstration flight for two representatives (Al Thompson and Harry Semels) sent by Sky Aircraft. Although the boys are aeronautical engineers, they don't know how to fly, which leads to much confusion in the cockpit. It's all pretty rote. When Moe says, "Throw out the clutch," Curly obeys, and not in a good way. Further, some of the comic effect of the flying sequence is undercut because stock footage of the looping biplane includes more than one aircraft, and is obviously from an air show.

There are a couple of good bits while the boys fly. Larry takes a blast of loose tobacco in the kisser when he tries to roll a cigarette for Moe, so he just hands Moe a cigar. And when the plane goes into a spin, Moe and Curly are thrust very close together, which prompts Larry to inquire, "Hey, are you two guys goin' steady?"

When the *Buzzard* does a loop and turns over, more unnecessarily looped dialogue informs us, "We're turning over!" With that, the boys fall from the cockpit into the well.

The final quarter of *Dizzy Pilots* puts the boys in uniform and in basic training, in footage lifted from the early portion of their 1940 short *Boobs in Arms*, with Richard Fiske as an exasperated drill sergeant. (See "The Stooges Go to War.")

Although *Dizzy Pilots* is weak, it does have a couple of points of interest. Publicity photos snapped on the set show the boys in a sort of conga line with actors Thompson and Semels, plus Columbia starlets Judy Malcolm and Sethma Williams. The images suggest that the sequence (possibly a musical interlude) was filmed but, for reasons unknown, was killed before the final cut. Elimination of the sequence would have caused *Dizzy Pilots* to run short, which may be why the *Boobs in Arms* footage is tacked onto the end.

Early in the short, the boys are informed via telegram that they'll be drafted if their plane can't cut the mustard. The telegram is a static insert with voice-over dialogue by Moe. The insert provides a rationale for the *Boobs in Arms* sequence, and may have been a last-minute fix after the footage with the actresses was cut.

The most unusual aspect of *Dizzy Pilots* is that the Stooges do not play Americans. Writer Clyde Bruckman and director Jules White take pains to establish that the boys are citizens of a country called Moronica. Further, Sky Aircraft is not based in the USA but in the Republic of Cannabeer, P.U. At a time when America fielded superior, recently developed combat aircraft the likes of the Lockheed P-38 Lightning and the Grumman F6F Hellcat, Columbia felt a need (or was *instructed* to feel a need) to avoid any suggestion that the Stooges and the *Buzzard* represented any part of America's airborne war effort.

FOOD AND SLAPSTICK COMEDY HAVE A LONG AND STORIED RELATIONSHIP. THE formalized confines of a diner or restaurant, where people who go to eat food are comically upset when they end up wearing it, has provided venues for violent comedy since movie comedy began. The Stooges play the proprietors of eating establishments in numerous shorts, and although *Busy Buddies* (1944) isn't one of the best of those, it's nevertheless agreeably, innocuously funny.

Promoting themselves as hipsters (or "hepsters," if one wishes to be accurate about the jargon of 1944), the Stooges call their place the Jive Café, where people in a hurry can grab "a speed feed" and "a short snort." But despite the attempts to relate to the Lindy hop crowd, it's pretty much business as Stooge-usual. Curly struggles to make hotcakes for a customer (Vernon Dent), squirting himself with batter before inattentively sending the plate out with a pot holder on top of the stack. When Dent attempts to eat the cakes he bends his knife and fork and nearly chokes. (Dent, a beloved regular in Columbia shorts starring the Stooges and others, is unusually thin here. He was diabetic, so his temporarily drawn appearance may have been the result of dieting.)

Back in the kitchen, live-in hens lay eggs (including hard-boiled) to order. Two fried eggs that get away from Curly plant themselves on Moe's face, and when the yolks pop out, Moe looks like a burglar, or an albino raccoon.

One gag—pouring hot water through a raw chicken in order to make a bowl of chicken soup—shows up in many of the boys' comedies. It's funny on its own terms (the boys are cheap and aren't above cheating their patrons), but many of today's viewers have forgotten (if they ever knew at all) that meat was severely rationed during World War II. No, the boys don't mind gypping their customers, but they almost have no choice!

Some of the best laughs are provided by the incidental signage on the café's walls: "Cups of coffee—10 cents." "Saucer coffee—5 cents." Then there's the one that challenges, "Can U take it? Try our hash."

Larry keeps himself busy hand-painting a large new sign with the heading "Jive Diner 4 Bits." The rest of the sign is glimpsed only a couple of times and very briefly, but thanks to the miracle of the PAUSE button, we can see that the boys specialize in "Bloop Soup, Reet Meat, Jake Cake, and Hava Java."

Conflict enters the picture in the guise of an irate pie salesman (Fred Kelsey), who becomes even more surly when he drinks a cup of Larry's paint, thinking it's coffee. The guy demands ninety-seven dollars in back payment. If he doesn't get it, he'll take over the restaurant—a stretch of fiscal reality but sufficient to give the Stooges special motivation to protect their business. The salesman also demands the return of pies already delivered, and he gets his wish because Curly has inadvertently tied his apron to the pie shelves behind him. When he moves forward, the gooey pies fly from the shelves, right into the salesman's face.

Following a brief interlude as poster hangers (the boys calculate that they won't earn ninety-seven dollars until 1992), Moe enters the very urban Curly in a cow-milking contest offering a hundred-dollar prize.

Much is made of practice attempts to milk a bull, each of which abruptly ends when the animal butts Curly back over the fence and onto his head. (Because we hear but never see Curly's interaction with the justifiably upset bull, the situation is all the funnier.) Moe and Larry's attempts to catch their pal in a blanket as he sails overhead are fruitless.

At the contest, Moe and Larry disguise themselves as a cow, inserting the neck of an enormous jug of milk into a rubber glove that protrudes from the bottom of the costume. Curly tugs happily, the fake cow bobbing up and down as if its spine were made of rubber. But the defending champion (burly Eddie Gribben) catches on, and the boys scramble off in disgrace.

If there's a lesson in all this, it's that the Stooges should stick with what they think they know best—in this instance, serving watery soup and running up big bills they have no hope of paying.

IT IS THE DREAM OF MERCHANTS AND RETAILERS TO "CUT OUT THE MIDDLE man" by providing themselves, promptly and at minimal expense, with the product they sell. That's the premise of *Booby Dupes* (1945), which casts the boys as fishmongers (as in the earlier *Cookoo Cavaliers*). Once again taking the basic premise and a gag or two from Laurel and Hardy's 1932 short *Towed in a Hole*, the Stooges make their way through the streets in a truck, blowing a horn to alert potential customers. "Hey, Harry James!" Moe says when Larry blows a note right into his ear. Larry responds with coquettish modesty: "Oh, I'm not *that* good!" Moe agrees: "You said it!" and gives Larry a quick thumping.

When the boys discover that a gaggle of kittens has eaten their fish, they decide to buy a boat and catch their own. Ah, simplicity itself! Unfortunately, the boat is a wreck foisted on them by a con man (John Tyrrell), and once the boys get the tub in the water, their stupidity and carelessness make everything worse. Finally, taking on water and sinking, they tie a white rag to a pole to alert a plane that drones overhead. But the rag has a stain that resembles Japan's Rising Sun, so the plane's pilot starts dropping bombs.

Writer-director Del Lord (working with the Stooges for the final time) crams *Booby Dupes* with gags, but the ultimate humor lies in the Stooges' inability to come together and cooperate in pursuit of a common goal. That flaw of character and will is fundamental to the boys' humor—as it is, of course, to Laurel and Hardy's, as well. Because much of *Booby Dupes* is shot in a small, hideously false-looking studio tank with black water shimmering in the glare of multiple arc lamps, the boys' foolishness seems magnified.

The short's protracted first portion, however, puts the boys on dry land as they troll the streets and then steal navy uniforms that they (inexplicably) feel they'll need if they're to be proper sailors and fishermen. Moe and Larry swipe their threads right off the rack, but Curly's belong to an ill-tempered captain (Vernon Dent) who has dropped off his uniform for cleaning. Attired as an officer, Curly saunters onto the sidewalk and quickly scores with a couple of babes, one of whom (Rebel Randall) happens to be the captain's none-too-loyal girlfriend. At a beach (another perfectly awful sound stage), Curly has to bury himself in the sand when the real captain—by now wearing Curly's too-small clothes and looking like Buster Brown—comes looking for his girl. The chick dryly observes, "My, what a uniform *does* cover up!" The captain isn't amused and vows to rip apart the joker who stole his duds.

A threat like that suggests that the aggressor will pursue the Stooges all the way to the story's conclusion, but in a contrived and awkward twist, the captain is simply removed from the plot after his struggle with Curly sends him head-first into an ice-cream wagon. Because the camera setup establishes that Dent must approach and fall into the wagon from right to left, the negative had to be flopped for printing: "ICE CREAM" is visibly backwards on the side of the cart. The cart's proprietor, in a wordless bit that's so brief it's almost nonexistent, is former silent-comedy star Snub Pollard.

At the boat, Curly's foot goes through the deck and onto Moe's head. Moe finds an enormous monkey wrench and uses it to twist Curly's nose. Moe's hindquarters are chewed by the propeller, and as Moe stands on deck, Larry and Curly drive nails into the bottom of his shoes as they struggle to patch the hull.

When a suitable spot to fish is finally reached, Curly throws out the anchor—and just the anchor, because no line is attached. Moe is cracked on the head with a board as Curly tries to subdue a leaping, spitting fish that's been tormenting him.

The boat takes on water and Moe yells, "Bail out!" Larry responds with an especially funny line: "I haven't got my parachute!" Curly decides to drain the boat by drilling holes in the hull (he calls his hand drill "a water letter outer!").

The kerfluffle with the pilot—"They're Japs, all right, let 'em have it!"—gives the short its wartime creds. After the first bomb falls, Moe flails at the sky and shouts out a rare instance of self-referential dialogue: "Hey, it's the Stooges!" Curly attaches his phonograph's turntable to the propeller, and the boat (a painfully obvious miniature that can't be longer than six inches) zips to safety.

Actress Rebel Randall, a onetime Powers models who became popular later as hostess of *Jukebox U.S.A.* and *America Calling* for the Armed Forces Radio Services, is effortlessly sexy as the captain's girlfriend. Perfectly gorgeous and of Amazonian proportions, she exists partly to provide pointed visual contrast to Vernon Dent (large and stout) and Curly (short and stout). Although Randall took small parts and uncredited bits in pictures for sixteen years, she was famous mainly for being famous, making news with her marriages, divorces, a remarriage, and an annulment.

All of that sounds like a lot of work. Me—I'd rather fish.

If I could get a little cooperation.

FOR A BRIEF PERIOD AFTER CURLY LEFT THE STOOGES, THE BOYS' FILMS OCCAsionally looked bad: small, cheap, and set-bound. Like every other studio, Columbia was hurt by postwar inflation, salary demands of top-flight stars, and an understandable (and short-lived) trepidation about audience reaction to Shemp. To Columbia's credit, studio promotion of the act didn't flag and helped ensure that the Stooges remained the centerpiece of the studio's two-reel unit. But Columbia's obvious interest in the act came with a built-in on-screen paradox, as the Stooges were forced into increasingly small physical spaces.

Between 1947 and 1949, before television became a real threat, Columbia and Jules White reasoned that the boys had the potential to remain solid earners whether or not their shorts looked good. There simply was no need to spend money on elaborate, time-consuming exteriors, as in the '30s and early '40s. There wasn't even a need for intricate sound-stage setups. So for a year or two, many Stooges shorts had that malnourished air suggestive of Hollywood's Poverty Row.

In comic content, *Sing a Song of Six Pants* (1947) is a typical Stooges outing: The boys antagonize each other before banding together to fix the wagons of crooks who threaten them, and who threaten the larger society, too.

Six Pants, in which the boys play proprietors of a tailoring and dry cleaning shop, looks simply awful. As imagined by art director Charles Clague and cinematographer Henry Freulich (who could not have reacted gaily to the budget restrictions), the Stooges' Pip Boys shop (from the real-life Pep Boys chain of auto-parts stores) is a small and grimy space that fronts on a flatly lit urban street constructed on a remote corner of a sound stage. Director White didn't bother with camera movement, going instead with static setups that simply record the action, and that encourage the Stooges and other characters to stand in one place or simply walk in and out of frame. Granted, time is needed to rehearse complex blocking, and to properly pull the focus on the damn camera, but a no-style short like this one abuses not just the Stooges but audiences, too. Many moviegoers made special points to attend programs because the Stooges were part of the evening's entertainment. Those people deserved better.

Having established that none of this was the Stooges' fault, we'll acknowledge that *Sing a Song of Six Pants* has some clever Felix Adler dialogue that the boys deliver with snappy enthusiasm. When a police detective (Vernon Dent) dashes into the tailor shop to ask whether they've seen fugitive safecracker Terry Hargan, Shemp appraisingly lifts one of the cop's lapels and says, "Where did you ever get this mess?" Dent: "I bought it here!" Shemp must backtrack in a hurry. "Oh what a beautiful messterpiece!" But the boys won't be happy until the cop buys a brand-new outfit. "This coat's two hundred percent wool!" Shemp declares.

"Two hundred percent?"

"Yeah, these sheep led a double life!"

Shemp also has a funny exchange with Moe, who bemoans the dunning letter that's come to them from Skin & Flint Finance Company (I. Fleecum, President). "We're gonna be paupers!" Moe wails. "Paupers!" Shemp snorts, "Are you kiddin'? We're not even married!"

And then there's Hargan's girlfriend (Virginia Hunter), who engages Shemp in a discussion of "henna color" dye, "a sort of brown reddish" she explains. The impatient Shemp doesn't get it at all: "Yellow turnip, blue cucumbers . . . !"

The best bit of dialogue involves diminutive character actor Phil Arnold, who stops by to pick up a jacket. Shemp eyes Arnolds's standard-issue fedora and says,

Performer Profile: Harold Brauer
1909–90

Variously credited (or not) as Tiny Brauer, Bill Brauer, and Harold Brauer, this stocky character player with the lived-in face and streetwise vocalese was active in films and television for twenty years but worked only sporadically, with most of his activity coming during 1946–49. Many of his appearances are in serials and B-westerns, but he was cast in Columbia two-reelers as early as 1946.

Brauer was not a prolific supporting player to the Stooges but has the distinction of working with all four iterations of the group: in shorts with Curly, Shemp, and Joe, and in the later feature films with Joe De Rita.

He's an agreeably dim Big Mike in *Fright Night*, impotently chasing the Stooges round and round crates in a warehouse; as Terry "Slippery Fingers" Hargan in *Sing a Song of Six Pants*; and overconfident thug Butch McGee, who is put into a baby carriage by the Stooges in *Three Loan Wolves* and pushed into traffic for his trouble.

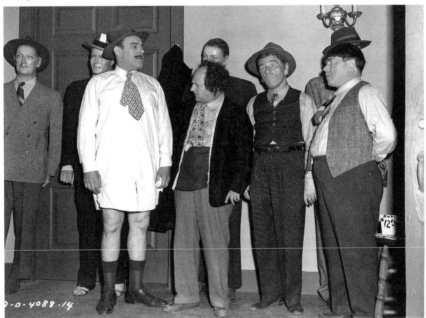

Larry wonders whether something is amiss with the mannequin (Harold Brauer) in *Sing a Song of Six Pants* (1947). *Photo courtesy of the Stoogeum*

"Who made that hat?" Without a beat Arnold comes back with, "My mother," which Shemp tops when he casually responds, "I thought so."

A razor blade that ends up in the bristles of a whisk broom causes the boys to inadvertently slice the back of Arnold's coat into neat vertical strips. Arnold returns later to say that his wife loves the coat and wants the boys to make a pair of pants to match. (At this, the Stooges are astonished and fall backwards onto the floor, a hopelessly out-of-date "big foot" cartoon gag.)

The thief Hargan (Harold Brauer) has earlier disguised himself as a mannequin to escape the cop, and now he's back with a couple of his boys to retrieve a slip of paper that has the combination to a safe. Hargan hangs Shemp on a revolving coat rack and pummels him but ends up on the short end because Shemp's swinging feet repeatedly catch him on the chin. Another of the thugs (Cy Schindell) has his pants pressed by Larry—while Cy is still wearing them. (The five or six iron-shaped burns that crisscross the hood's butt exemplify Jules White's predilection for a frankly sadistic sort of slapstick.) Larry finally sticks Schindell's head in a big trouser press to fry his skull, and then knocks him cold with a heavy board.

The boys won't get the reward for capturing Hargan (the cop says *he* does), but Shemp finds a bundle of "green stuff" in Hargan's jacket. After the cop leaves, Shemp begins to count: "three hundred, four hundred, five hundred. Hey, how'd that lousy fifty get in there?" He crumples the bill and throws it to the floor—and a split second later, all three boys hurl themselves on top of it.

Sing a Song of Six Pants was remade in 1953 as *Rip, Sew and Stitch*. Just nine seconds shorter than the earlier film, it is in fact virtually the *same* film, scene by scene, frame by frame. Writer Jack White (no credit is given to Felix Adler) squeezed in a few moments of new dialogue after brother Jules made room by engineering early fadeouts for a couple of existing scenes.

This time around, the boys don't fall back embarrassingly at the conclusion of the shredded-coat business but merely agree to have the shredded pants ready the following day. Shemp cracks, "That guy's mother must've raised him on shredded wheat!"

Fresh mayhem is added, too. Moe pokes Shemp in the stomach and then yanks him away by hooking his finger in Shemp's mouth. Later, as Moe holds a hammer, he looks at Shemp and inquires, "Do your knuckles hurt? . . . They will!"

A clumsily disguised double fills in for Harold Brauer during a single quick shot, but Cy Schindell returns as the henchman—an intriguing trick because Schindell had passed away three years before this quasi-pastiche was made. Terry Hargan's girlfriend is eliminated altogether.

Rip, Sew and Stitch was shot during a single day that couldn't have extended much past lunchtime.

IF DENTISTS REALLY DO SUFFER A HIGHER SUICIDE RATE THAN THE AVERAGE (study results vary), even the most severely depressed will feel loads better about themselves after observing the Stooges deal with patients in *The Tooth*

Will Out (1951). Written and directed by Ed Bernds (who prepared the short simultaneously with the one immediately preceding it on the release schedule, *Merry Mavericks*), *The Tooth Will Out* is focused and funny for most of its running time. It has two failings, however: a poorly paced sequence in its second half (forgivable), and a weak, ho-hum ending (a bit of a bungle).

Bernds and cinematographer Fayte Brown shot the opening sequence on Columbia's sunny "Old New York" backlot in Burbank, to suggest the year 1910 or thereabouts. After being chased down the street by an angry cook (Emil Sitka), the boys hide in a cut-rate school of dentistry. The professor (Vernon Dent) and his alarmingly buck-toothed gal Friday (Margie Liszt) offer a one-week course of study ("Five dollars apiece or three for twenty-five") that isn't exactly designed to produce top-notch tooth-yankers. The denture that the boys must make in order to graduate somehow turns out to be a fanged, ill-tempered horror that (via cleverly executed mechanical effects on a tabletop) can snap and spin around. When it senses that all three boys are about to pounce, it distracts them by beginning to sing: "Bum bum bum bum—" and the boys immediately jump in with three-part harmony: "I made a lucky strike when I found you—"

"Bum bum bum bum—"

"The girl of my dreeems—"

At this, the teeth (voiced by Vernon Dent) complain, "Hey, hey, one a' you guys is flat!" The boys point fingers and begin to apologize before recoiling, terrified, when they realize what's happening. A moment later, the denture has locked itself onto Shemp's finger, to the accompaniment of a sound effect that suggests a grizzly bear masticating somebody's ulna.

By passing off a perfect sample denture as their own, the boys graduate and head west. They use a drill to torture their first patient (Slim Gaut) during an interminable three-and-a-half-minute sequence that might have been funny for twenty seconds. As filmed, it's just exhausting.

Things perk up when the local bad boy (Dick Curtis) strides inside, bulling up to the boys and displaying his gun. "You know what happened to the last dentist that worked on me? That's him there—notch number nine!"

Larry puts an enormous wad of ether-soaked cotton into a toilet plunger and sticks the whole thing over the gunslinger's face. Moe says, "Now count to ninety!"

"One . . . *zzzz.*" (Larry lifts the plunger and stares at it in mild astonishment.)

When Shemp carelessly grabs a book called *The Amateur Carpenter*, he "sandpapers the chest." Larry warns him to be careful of the guy's tattoo. Shemp: "He had a tattoo?" Then it's time to "varnish the lid," which means that Curtis's hat is practically glued to his head. Moe finally catches on that something is awry when Shemp haltingly reads aloud, "Take a finishing nail and put putty" and so forth. (Yes, Shemp pronounces "putty" as "puty.")

The Stooges finally do what they're supposed to, but when Curtis wakes up, he shouts that the boys "got the wrong tooth!" As the Stooges dash through the door and out of frame, Curtis falls to the floor and awkwardly fires after them. And that's it. The end. There's a word for this sort of comic denouement: *perfunctory*. Plus, you won't laugh.

Bernds muffed the final gag but was smart when he decided to shoot much of *The Tooth Will Out* in medium close-up, framing the boys from the waist up—neither so close that peripheral content is lost, nor so far away that subtleties of the boys' reactions, and other visual details, are neglected. The approach creates a friendly, easy intimacy that pulls the viewer emotionally closer to the Stooges, and more deeply into the story.

Cinematographer Fayte Brown (who specialized in B westerns until moving into shorts as his career wound down in the early 1950s) brings a sunny freshness to the backlot exteriors, and an unusually broad palette of warm gray tones to the interiors.

If only the short had an ending!

ALTHOUGH THE STOOGES' NEXT "AT WORK" ADVENTURE, *LISTEN, JUDGE* (1952), follows a plot very similar to that of the previously discussed *An Ache in Every Stake*, it differs sufficiently so that it should be looked at now, in chronological context, rather than as a remake.

In a reworking of the opening of *A Plumbing We Will Go*, the boys are on the hook for stealing chickens. But Judge Henderson (Vernon Dent) thinks the officers have no case and acquits the relieved defendants. But the jig is up when a chicken worms its way from beneath Shemp's coat and into the judge's face. A short while later and many blocks away, the Stooges resume their work as itinerant, door-to-door fix-it men. A frazzled woman (Kitty McHugh) hires them to repair her doorbell, and by the time Stooges are done, the doorbell is still broken and an interior wall looks as if it's been mauled by mutant woodpeckers. On top of that, the lady's dinner party has been completely ruined—not least by a gas-filled birthday cake that explodes in the face of an influential guest.

Elwood Ullman's script is a salad of venerable gags that seems fresh in the Stooges' hands. In an early bit of business smoothly choreographed by director Ed Bernds, Kitty McHugh does a beautiful "scream take" before deftly catching a falling vase that Larry has inadvertently knocked from the top of a tall curio cabinet. Rather than be contrite about this narrowly averted disaster, Moe barks, "You'll have to beat it, lady, we got a lot of work to do!"

Indeed. Larry and Moe struggle on opposite sides of a wall to get hold of the wiring that controls the doorbell. By the time the tug of war is over, Moe has been pulled through two walls and into the next room. Shemp and Larry are aghast: "A gopher!" (Their reaction suggests why the Stooges are fix-it men and not zoologists.) They rap Moe on the head, bringing forth a yelp of pain. Larry marvels, "Hey, that gopher sounds like Moe!"

The boys move the curio to hide the mosaic of holes they've punched in the wall, and sweep plaster and other debris beneath a rug. But the cook (Emil

Sitka) has quit because of profound abuse visited on him by Moe, so the boys take over in the kitchen.

In a thorough, and no less funny, reshoot of the kitchen sequence from *An Ache in Every Stake*, Shemp separates two eggs ("I guess that's far enough") and inserts an unopened can of tomatoes into the turkey. Fortunately, Moe happens by and tears off the label. Does Shemp expect people to eat paper?

Shemp shows off his skill with ad libs as he vigorously dusts the turkey with flour and continues to violate it with foreign objects. Satisfied at last, he pulls up the turkey's zipper and pops the whole thing into a 650-degree oven.

Larry serves canapés to the guests, advising (with all the elegance of a racetrack tout), "I just got a flash from the kitchen. You better fill up on these!"

The once-plump turkey comes out of the blazing oven looking like a Hiroshima canary, so there's nothing left to eat but the birthday cake—which Larry and Shemp have pumped full of kitchen gas. A faintly pompous guest named George Morton (John Hamilton, at liberty between seasons one and two of *The Adventures of Superman*) blows out the candles and ends up smeared in frosting, vowing to *never* support the judge for reelection. The Stooges escape by crashing head-first through a window. (As you enjoy Columbia films from this period, listen for the studio's extraordinarily distinctive stock sound effects: the sharp, short crack of a handgun; the heavy, expelled-air *oof!* of a falling body; and the thick, subtly musical crash of shattering glass.)

Production values are high, with handsome interiors and well-lit sound-stage "exteriors." (The cinematographer was Ellis Carter, whose best credit is *The Incredible Shrinking Man*, 1957.) The four-day shooting schedule was standard for this period, and the budget allowed for a sufficient number of good-looking, well-dressed extras in the dinner-party sequence. The boys are lively and enthusiastic, and Hamilton, Dent, and McHugh add considerable artistic weight.

Listen, Judge is a smart, ingenious triumph of recycled ideas.

DURING THE 1952 REPUBLICAN NATIONAL CONVENTION, HELD AT CHICAGO'S International Amphitheatre on June 7–11, 1952, two delegate ballots were needed for retired General of the Army Dwight D. Eisenhower to soundly defeat Senator Robert Taft from Ohio. Ike, who didn't even announce a party affiliation until shortly before campaign season, was a fresh face in politics, and thus a finger in the eye of the old guard personified by Taft. Although first-ballot voting was close, Eisenhower buried Taft in the second tally, leaving some bitter division within the party.

At the same venue ten days later, Illinois's Democratic governor Adlai Stevenson needed three ballots to eliminate his most powerful party rival, Tennessee senator Estes Kefauver.

Party hacks—or delegates, if you prefer—held enormous power in those days, and back-room dealing, particularly when it took place between contentious ballots, was active, and not at all like the democracy that America's kids learned about in school. (The liberal and erudite Stevenson was handed

Alabama senator John Sparkman—a vocal segregationist—as his running mate. Imagine *that* back-room confab!)

Felix Adler's script for the Stooges' only overtly political short, *Three Dark Horses* (1952), was filmed during the final week of August, late enough to allow revisions that reflected what had occurred in Chicago the previous month. And indeed, the short's central conflict turns on the Stooges' betrayal of the political operators who have made them delegates and paid them for their votes.

Three Dark Horses was released in October 1952, an unusually brisk turn-around for the Columbia two-reel unit. But then, this short was highly topical, so release before Election Day (November 4) was essential.

A pair of shady political operatives (stock player Kenneth MacDonald and perennial movie and TV thug Ben Welden) are desperate for "three delegates who are too dumb to think and will do what we tell them," ensuring that their candidate, Hammond Egger, secures the nomination. (The face on the Egger campaign posters belongs to Bud Jamison, the beloved Columbia two-reel stock-company player who died in 1944.) After observing the Stooges assault each other while working in the office as janitors, the politicos know they've found their dupes. With Egger in office, MacDonald and Welden—and many others, it can be presumed—will cash in on a crooked "oil-grab" scheme.

During the convention, the boys stuff themselves with room service . . . and switch votes on the sixty-fifth ballot after discovering that Egger is a crook. Exultant back at the hotel, they whoop and throw confetti. Moe wonders how long it takes to cut all that paper into such tiny pieces with a scissors. Larry knowingly informs him that that's not how confetti is made. The paper is cut with razor blades.

When MacDonald and Welden show up to beat the Stooges with baseball bats, the boys maneuver them into the bathtub, jump in on top of them, and begin to take a bath with their clothes on.

Democracy is saved, and the American republic staggers onward.

Some special care seems to have been taken during filming. The two key sets, a political office and the boys' hotel room, are detailed and well furnished. And director Jules White seldom moved his camera as freely as here, sweeping gracefully around furniture for dolly-ins on the faces of the boys and their manipulators.

A rich variety of gags ensures that *Three Dark Horses* perks along. Shemp bites Moe's finger so Moe clamps his munchers on Shemp's nose. Welden's toupee is sucked off his head by the boys' vacuum cleaner, and is a dusty horror when it's finally retrieved. Larry slaps it back where it belongs and is ready to secure it in place with hammer and nail. Moe asks Larry if he's crazy. "You wanna punch a hole in this man's toupee?" When Moe finds a pot of glue, Shemp looks at Welden's bald head and says, "Okay, Moe, slap a shine on that honeydew!" Filthy dirty and dripping with glue, Welden is too outdone even to defend himself.

In a brightly clever sequence, the Stooges amuse MacDonald with a bit of convention-style playacting, complete with patriotic musical fanfares, a calling of the roll, some debate with a querulous delegate (from "Rico Puerto"), and Moe's call to clear the aisles: "Order, order!"

"I'll have a steak and French fries!" Larry says cheerfully.

At the hotel, as a parrot waddles inside the boys' dinner turkey, Larry initiates an off-screen discussion with Moe: "I'm goin' fishin'."

"Ya got worms?"

"Yeah, but I'm goin' anyway!" (This sort of lowbrow, burley-q wit is what compelled Hollywood to invent Audrey Hepburn.)

Once the parrot is cozy inside the turkey, Larry does a fabulous take each time a cracker is mysteriously snatched from his fingers. Meanwhile, at the far right edge of the frame, Moe arranges the lank hair at the sides of Shemp's face into a flapper's bob that recalls Louise Brooks. Why is Moe doing this, and why is Shemp letting him? Because it's funny.

The biggest laugh in *Three Dark Horses*, however, is a bitter one, when delegate Moe tells the boys to ignore the political speeches: "Don't be a chump, you chump! You can't believe all that stuff! It's a *campaign* promise!"

The republic still staggers on, just a little more slowly, now.

IN *PARDON MY BACKFIRE*, THE STOOGES OWN THEIR OWN GARAGE AND, NO, they don't know what they're doing. But the early postwar period was a good time to get into auto repair, so who are the Stooges to buck a trend? Independent garages grew rapidly after the war, in sheer numbers and in overall share of car-repair work. While in the service, thousands of men had learned how to repair various sorts of engines. Upon return to civilian life, some went to work as mechanics for existing businesses, and those with the entrepreneurial spirit opened garages of their own. By 1953, when *Pardon My Backfire* was released, new-car dealers handled less than 50 percent of car repairs. The lion's share of jobs went to neighborhood guys. Guys like Larry, Shemp, and Moe.

The central dilemma of the short is this: The boys have been engaged to Hettie, Nettie, and Bettie for ten years, and Papa (Fred Kelsey, in his final appearance with the Stooges) lays down the law: Marry my daughters within the week or get lost! At the garage, the boys pick up a radio bulletin (voiced by director Jules White) about three escaped cons, whose capture will bring a reward of fifteen hundred dollars. Boy, if only the Stooges could get their hands on those guys! Well, they do, and in the battle royale that follows, the boys' garage becomes a veritable chamber of horrors that proves to be the crooks' undoing. Reward money assured, the boys can marry their sweeties!

Pardon My Backfire was the Stooges' second and last short filmed and released in 3-D, a gimmick that hits Hollywood like the flu every thirty years or so. (*Spooks* was the boys' first.) Indie producer Arch Oboler kicked off the craze in 1952 with *Bwana Devil* ("A lion in your lap! A lover in your arms!"). Warner Bros. jumped in with a hugely successful 3-D thriller, *House of Wax* (1953), and Universal offered the excellent *It Came from Outer Space* (1953). The ball was rolling.

Emphatic, hard-sell poster art for *Pardon My Backfire* (1953), the last of two Stooges shorts shot and released in 3-D.

The action of *Pardon My Backfire* is split between lively domestic scenes and mayhem at the garage. The gags are typically Stoogian except that many are directed right at the subjective camera—at *us*. In such moments, we *become* Shemp or Larry or one of the criminals. Finger pokes, punches, squirts of oil, an acetylene flame, knives, and other things are directed outward, into the audience.

Budget dictated that the solid-object 3-D gags be wire based, which kills the effect, and for two reasons: First, the wire rigs force the actors to grip and throw each object as if it were a paper airplane (this looks especially silly when the object is a knife); and second, the rigs cause the objects to slowly float toward the camera, without real menace.

You're apt to get the most laughs from Felix Adler's "flat" gags, as when "Oh, Susannah" blares from the radio at the supper table, and the Stooges and their fiancées (Diana Darrin, Angela Stevens, and Ruth Godfrey White) do a complex roundelay of food-passing in rhythm to the music.

At the garage, the boys get to work on the cons' damaged car. The gang's leader (Benny Rubin) instructs his sexy girlfriend (Barbara Bartay), "Go flirt with those men to make them hurry!" Yeah, that'll work!

Later, as the chick unknowingly walks around with a greasy work glove stuck to the back of her dress, Moe takes an enormous file to Larry's forehead, scraping the tool back and forth with enough vigor to raise sawdust. (The sound effects here are especially wince inducing). Shemp carelessly sets the seat of Moe's pants on fire ("Say, I smell garbage burning!"), and Moe runs a whirring portable grinder against the ass end of one of the thugs (Frank Sully). And in an especially nasty gag, a stiff wire that snakes its way up from an engine enters Larry's nostril and exits from his ear. He must grip the wire and then slowly, excruciatingly, pull it back through his head and out his nose.

Phil Arnold, playing a tiny fiend who loves knives, is particularly funny, and sexy Barbara Bartay (who worked exclusively in two-reelers until her final credit, the 1956 Rock Hudson vehicle *Never Say Goodbye*) sizzles as the moll.

The standard opening and closing titles were replaced for *Pardon My Backfire* with live action of the Stooges' heads against a black background, floating toward the camera before the boys wave canes in our faces. The unique "The End" card displays the words in handsome script overlaid on a "dimensional" still photo of the garage.

Columbia's two-reel unit filmed a third 3-D short, *Down the Hatch* (1953), a vehicle for contract player Harry Mimmo. Although paired for exhibition with a 3-D feature, *Drums of Tahiti*, *Down the Hatch* was released "flat," in late November 1953, because the 3-D craze had died.

And so we say goodbye to auto repair and to the Stooges in 3-D.

ALTHOUGH TWO- AND EVEN ONE-DAY SHOOTS BECAME A FACT OF LIFE AT Columbia's two-reel unit in the 1950s, the Stooges' 188th short, *Oil's Well That Ends Well* (1958), looks anything but shoddy. To the contrary, it's unusually good-looking; Irving Lippman's photography is especially handsome. The short is also among the boys' funniest later efforts. Directed by Jules White in just two days in August 1957 from a spirited script by Felix Adler, the short balances physical gags with a logical, linear plot. Most pleasingly, *Oil's Well That Ends Well* provides Joe Besser with a splendid showcase that makes one long all the more for the later Larry, Moe, and Joe feature films that never were.

The boys, once again playing brothers, learn via letter that their ailing "Pa" needs an operation that he's unable to pay for. He reminds the boys of his longtime belief that priceless uranium is in nearby Red Dog Canyon. Outfitted with food and equipment, the boys dig and poke at the rocks, insult and smack each other, and nearly kill themselves with dynamite. Finally, the Geiger counter suggests that they've struck a rich vein. The next morning the boys find an oil well, too. They're rich! (And Pa can have his operation.)

As in some other Stooges shorts, *Oil's Well That Ends Well* supposes that one of the boys possesses a supernatural power, a kind of benign white magic. Here, the talent belongs to Joe, whose habit of wishing for things inevitably leads to the wishes coming true. (We said the plot was linear, we didn't say it was realistic.) After Pa's letter arrives, Joe wishes he had a hundred dollars so he could grubstake the expedition to Red Dog Canyon. A subsequent shoving match with Larry knocks over an end table that has a hundred-dollar bill neatly taped to the underside.

A minute later, Joe wishes he had a cigar, and when he opens a package "from your pal, Felix" (Adler, of course), he finds a top-notch corona inside. But Larry steals it, prompting Joe to wish that the stogie would blow up in Larry's face. It does just that, giving Larry a blackened puss and Joe reason

The boys take a coffee break while hoping to cash in on the uranium boom in *Oils Well That Ends Well* (1958). *Photo courtesy of the Stoogeum*

enough to be a little scared of his ability (and an opportunity to reflect on the fact that Felix isn't much of a pal after all).

While placing dynamite in the uranium field, Moe loses patience with Joe and repeatedly insists that he go sit down. Joe walks to the camera, frowns right at the lens, and silently mouths, "I hate him!" and then gives that angry little fist waggle of his. It's a great bit.

Once, twice, Joe is about to unknowingly sit on Moe's detonator plunger, only to shuffle back to make another suggestion. Will the dynamite blow? Admittedly, this ain't as nail-biting as, say, *The Wages of Fear*, but the sequence does build a nice level of comic tension that's relieved when Joe finally plunks his butt on the plunger. *Kaboom!*

The boys discover oil the next morning when an outdoor water pump covers Moe's face in a sudden spurt of crude. Larry excitedly calls it "earl," and Joe insists it's "an oil geezer!"

Joe perches on the open pipe and is suddenly sent aloft by the gusher (Joe appears in close-ups, oil swirling around his head and shoulders, and an unrecognizable Curly appears in very brief snippets of long shots from *Oily to Bed, Oily to Rise*). The geyser stops when Joe wishes it would, then starts again when he changes his mind. He happily exclaims, "Well, oil's well that ends well!"

Like many Stooges shorts, *Oil's Well That Ends Well* is topical, taking as its springboard the "uranium boom" of the day. After World War II the Atomic Energy Commission unwisely offered bounties to members of the public who located uranium. Four big strikes near Moab, Utah, in 1954 energized thousands of people, and by 1955–56 the boom was on, with more than eight hundred mines operating in Utah and elsewhere. (The cover of the July 1955 issue of *Popular Electronics*, a special "Uranium Prospecting Issue," is dominated by a crisp illustration of a serious young man who prods a rock with his Geiger counter.) Not surprisingly, the federal government neglected to remind people that uranium is toxic—fatally so with prolonged exposure. Ironic, then, that some of the Stooges' real-life counterparts later became sick and even died because of the riches they pulled from the earth.

Now what kind of a way is that to make a living?

6

The Stooges Out West

In which our two-gun cowpokes are assaulted by their Ma; take a lesson from Shakespeare; reveal a new use for cheese; catch a fish that looks like Moe; rebound nicely after their heads are squashed; do battle with their own six-guns; hang out in Dead Man's Gulch; ride a bicycle built for three; assault each other with celery; buy a hundred thousand tons of gold for a hundred bucks; see a ghost; and learn to hate ukuleles.

In 1935, Hollywood released 147 westerns. Some, like *Annie Oakley* with Barbara Stanwyck, are well-mounted "A" pictures. A few are interesting mainly for historical reasons, such as *Hop-A-Long Cassidy*, with William Boyd (Hoppy's first screen appearance), and *Tumbling Tumbleweeds*, with Gene Autry. The majority are gallant "B" westerns, which flourished in the 1930s and '40s.

Today, when new westerns are rare, it may be difficult to appreciate the climate that encouraged the remarkable gush of "oaters" that helped define Hollywood two and three generations ago, and contributed mightily to the industry's financial well-being. But consider: The year 1885 is to 1935 what 1960 is to 2010. A western released in 1935 wasn't confabulating about some hazy, long-forgotten past. To the contrary, an Oklahoma woman in her mid-fifties would have vivid memories of those days. The Old West was very much alive in '35.

Given westerns' rugged settings (with natural locations and standing sets plentiful in and around Hollywood), colorful accoutrements, and possibilities for action (as well as a relative cheapness to produce), the genre was a natural fit for screen comics: Keaton (*Go West*), Laurel and Hardy (*Way Out West*), Harold Lloyd (*The Eastern Westerner*), Harry Langdon (*The Fighting Parson*), Charley Chase (*The Tabasco Kid*), Roscoe "Fatty" Arbuckle (*The Roundup*), and Chaplin (*The Gold Rush*, a *north*western).

The Stooges' first Columbia western, *Horses' Collars*, was one of that group released in 1935. It's lavish and pleasingly long (more than eighteen minutes), with rugged-looking sets, superior costuming, and a cast of about twenty that includes supporting players, bit actors, and extras.

As in many comic westerns (such as the aforementioned *The Eastern Westerner*), the Stooges are fish out of water, having traveled from the east on orders from their employer, noted P.I. Hyden Zeke (Fred Kelsey), to prevent a local heel from swindling a young woman out of her land. Despite being outsiders, the boys don't seem overly intimidated. They pull off some fancy shooting and freely crack wise to the weasel, Double Deal Decker (frequent western player

Fred Kohler), and his henchman, Lobo (Leo Willis). The beleaguered young lady is Nell Higginbotham (helium-voiced Dorothy Kent).

The boys avoid big trouble at the climax because Curly slips into a windmilling frenzy whenever he sees a mouse—*any* mouse. It's a deus ex machina that returns, with variations (wild hyacinth, tassels, etc.), in later shorts. Only cheese can stop Curly's spasms—hence the now-famous lines, "Moe, Larry, cheese! Moe, Larry, cheese!" Whether Roquefort or Camembert or another variety (Curly always voices a preference), great chunks quickly stuffed into his mouth calm him.

Scripter Felix Adler and director Clyde Bruckman (a brilliant gag writer whose directorial career was winding down because of alcoholism) go for broke and keep piling on the comedy. When Decker challenges Curly to draw, Curly struggles to free his revolver, which dangles from the front of his pants like an uncooperative penis. Larry tosses a match that ignites Lobo's furry white chaps and turns them black, a small disaster that Larry celebrates by commenting, "Boy, you look ten years younger!" Moe creates a shower of quarters when he shoots a five-dollar gold piece out of the air, and all three boys go at each other in a celery attack that's almost startling in its ferocity. (Yes, *celery*.) And when the Stooges go to crack Decker's safe, Curly stares at the dial, sandpapers his fingertips, and turns on a radio (remember, this is the Old West).

In an exceptionally well-staged bit, Curly accidentally relieves a fellow of his toupee and tosses it aside. It lands, momentarily unnoticed, on the hand of a drunk (Bobby Callahan), who does a sidesplitting take when he sees the hairy horror resting there.

On the dance floor, the boys separate Decker from his expandable wallet when Moe pulls it taut on its chain and Larry and his dance partner (June Gittelson) tango through with a pair of shears. When Decker catches on, Moe plays the wallet like a concertina, joining Larry and Curly in soulful three-part harmony: "You'll never know what love is/'Til you cry like you maaade me cryyy!"

Decker grabs the boys to string 'em up. Moe says, "Hey, take it easy, that's silk!" Larry piteously protests, "Wait a minute, I gotta go home!"

As Moe and Larry twist in their nooses in the background, Curly spies a mouse and mops up the place with Decker and Lobo. Moments later, stuffed with Limburger, he's calm again, but when he exhales, Larry, Moe, and Nell collapse. Curly takes a sniff and does the same.

As we'll see, the boys return again and again to westerns during their two-reel career. Sagebrush and horses suited them: Their western shorts are almost invariably slick and sharply amusing. *Horses' Collars* is a fine way to kick off the fun.

LIKE *HORSES' COLLARS*, *WHOOPS, I'M AN INDIAN!* (1936) IS A WELL-MOUNTED film, with a cast of about twenty and the additional appeal of lively outdoor sequences. This time, the boys are clad in buckskin, making mischief in the rugged Pacific Northwest with a two-bit gambling gaff in a saloon. One heavy bettor is

Pierre (Bud Jamison), a burly French-Canadian trapper who tears off Larry's moccasin and discovers the magnet that controls the boys' makeshift roulette game.

The Stooges take to the woods. As Moe and Larry sit in the high branches of an enormous fir tree, Moe wants to know what happened to the money from the roulette scam. Curly answers, "I threw it away so I could run faster!" Moe reacts with a slap that causes Curly to execute a beautiful three-sixty on the branch, his body held in place only by the backs of his knees. A moment later, the two of them tumble to the ground and onto Larry, whose bow gets hung up crosswise on Curly's neck. Curly begs for help. Moe says, "Hold still, Daniel Boone"—and then gives the bowstring a good yank and lets it go against Curly's throat (sound effect provided by a pluck of a meaty string on a standup bass).

The short's central sequence concerns the boys' lakeside efforts to snag some fish for dinner. While Moe angrily tells the small fish he catches to go back and get their big brothers, Curly finds a club and some chewing tobacco. He explains, "When they come up to spit I'll hit 'em on the head!"

Moe finally lands a thirty-pounder that Curly accidentally releases back into the lake. Fortunately, a cabin (that belongs to Pierre!) is well stocked with grub, but the Stooges must hide and disguise themselves as Indians (Curly is the squaw) when Pierre and the sheriff come around. The boys greet the white men. Larry: "How." Moe: "How." Curly: "*And* how!"

A convenient bicycle built for three allows the boys to escape back to the saloon (which is apparently the only place the Stooges know how to get to). Close behind is Pierre, who gets a good look at Curly and becomes smitten. With his thick neck and heavy forearms, Curly is hilarious, playing his new role like a Parisian coquette, simultaneously egging Pierre on and pushing him away. Pierre finally hefts his prize onto one shoulder and carries him upstairs. "For you, I have the grand surprise!" Pierre says happily. Curly answers, "So have I, if you only knew it!"

Upstairs, Curly continues to flirt— twisting Pierre's ears and swooning at a new flannel nightie—unaware that his wig has become caught on a wall peg. Pierre lunges at him in a fury, and they both fall onto the bed, which collapses and disgorges Moe and Larry. All three boys beat feet along the wooden sidewalk and into the first door: the county jail.

An important aspect of the Stooges' on-screen personas, which is keenly apparent in the rugged setting and tough physical gags that propel *Whoops, I'm an Indian!,* is that although the boys are short (like many screen comics), they aren't small. There's nothing puny or wasted about them. Moe and Curly are obviously solid, and Larry's former life as a boxer gave him a nicely sculpted (if slightly bowlegged) physique. In this physical regard, the Stooges were very different from, say, the wispy Harry Langdon or the painfully thin Robert Woolsey (of Wheeler and Woolsey). Robust men, the Stooges literally throw themselves into the business of slapstick.

Benjamin Kline's sunlit, high-contrast photography evokes cool air and the scent of pine, and the gag men (Searle Kramer and Herman Boxer, story; Clyde

Bruckman, script) don't let up for a moment. Curly looks spiffy in his skunkskin cap (which shows up in later shorts), and Bud Jamison seems to have had a good time as the perpetually bad-tempered Pierre.

Whoops, I'm an Indian! reveals not just the Stooges' sturdy physicality but their lightly cynical, very urban sensibility that subtly underscores the anachronistic nature of their presence in the North Woods. In the first saloon sequence, the boys uncork the spiel that lures the suckers:

> MOE
> We pay 10 to 1!
>
> CURLY
> 20 to 1!
>
> MOE
> 30!
>
> CURLY (with fiendish exuberance)
> 40!
>
> MOE (under his breath)
> What's a' matter with you?
>
> CURLY
> What's the difference, they can't win anyway!

Whether on Fifth Avenue or in the middle of nowhere, these guys have what it takes to be survivors.

WHEN THE STOOGES BREAK UP A BAND OF CATTLE RUSTLERS IN *GOOFS AND SADDLES* (1937), they not only continue their streak of superior shorts with a western theme but draw on and perpetuate some of America's most cherished myths about the west. The short also evokes Gene Autry and Shakespeare. Oh, and soap operas, too. That's a lot to accomplish in a seventeen-minute film that was shot in just four days, but with help from Del Lord and writer Felix Adler, the Stooges pull it off.

The Indian Wars are winding down, but General Muster (Ted Lorch) has his hands full with cattle rustlers. It's time to call in his three best scouts: Buffalo Billious (Curly), Wild Bill Hiccup (Moe), and Just Plain Bill (Larry, named for a popular radio soap opera of the day). Precisely how the boys earned their reputations as the best, and why the general believes it, is never addressed. Even the Stooges themselves seem a little uncertain. "And don't forget, boys . . ." the general intones.

"Yes?"

"The entire west depends upon you!"

"Noo!"

Well, at least the Stooges *look* the part, dressed in rugged outfits that combine military uniforms and buckskin. Out in the woods they think they hear something. They put their ears to the ground, and an instant later, their heads are squashed by the wheels of a stagecoach (a gruesomely funny effect achieved with dummies and a quick edit). Larry dusts himself off and sagely observes, "Look, wagon tracks!"

"And fresh ones, too!" Curly adds.

After locating the rustlers' base of operations, the boys pull a Macduff to the thieves' Macbeth by disguising themselves as ambulatory vegetation. When one of the gang (Hank Mann) investigates, the bushes sidestep him when his back is turned, hit him on the back of the noggin with a club, and grab the head of his axe, turning his own leverage against him and causing him to do a terrific, brain-rattling somersault.

Disguised later as professional gamblers, the boys arrive in the nearest town, where the rustlers' boss, Longhorn Pete (Stanley Blystone), outsmarts them in a poker game. After being trapped inside a small cabin that Pete and his gang shoot to pieces, the Stooges discover that the meat grinder Curly has been using to make himself lunch is capable of firing bullets (even full belts of them), like a teeny, greasy Gatling gun.

Goofs and Saddles—its title is a play on *Boots and Saddles,* a 1937 vehicle for Gene Autry—utilizes only two, very brief snippets of stock footage: a long-shot exterior of the rustlers and one of the cavalrymen who save the day at the climax. Otherwise, the short is logistically ambitious, with another good-sized cast, more excellent exterior shooting by Benjamin Kline, and a well-staged chase in which Moe and Larry, guiding a wagon's team, actually ride the galloping horses. Del Lord's decision to squeeze a few more bucks from the budget for a speedy camera car (rather than position Moe and Larry on fake horses in front of a process screen) pays off handsomely. The saloon interiors and costumes are good-looking, as well, so *Goofs and Saddles* has the competent production values of any B-western of the period.

Former Keystone Kop Hank Mann shot his knockabout scenes just a month shy of his fiftieth birthday. Athletic, expressive, and a master of comic timing, he's a special treat, and in a parallel universe he could have contributed mightily to many of the boys' shorts. But Mann spent nearly his entire long career in features, so *Goofs and Saddles* and the earlier *Men in Black* (see "The Stooges on the Job") comprise his only work with the boys.

As to western myth, it's no accident that the Stooges play scouts—men who, then as now, were among the most admired figures in Old West lore. The boys are clearly based on William "Buffalo Bill" Cody, a particularly accomplished buffalo hunter, Indian fighter, and scout who was awarded the Medal of Honor in 1872 for heroism while a civilian attached to the 5th Cavalry in Nebraska.

Not just the real deal, Cody also was a showman and shrewd self-promoter who happily allowed novelist E. Z. C. Judson (writing as Ned Buntline) to elaborate on his legend. In 1873, Cody was invited to tour back east in Judson's play *Scouts of the Plain,* and ten years after that, Cody mounted his own ornate touring show, "Buffalo Bill's Wild West." By 1900, Cody was reckoned one of the most famous people in the world. The Stooges traded on his legend, and their clever, gentle burlesque does nothing to diminish it.

A QUALITY OF THE STOOGES THAT IS SELDOM, IF EVER, DISCUSSED IS THEIR innocence—about particular situations, and about their place in the world. Although selfish, spiteful, and inclined to violence, the boys are essentially guilt-less. They abuse each other terribly but never *intentionally* direct their negative energies toward people who don't deserve to be assaulted. The fact that the Stooges' mayhem very frequently sucks in people who are completely blameless (think of the bystanders at the boys' marathon pie fights) gives a lot of weight to the word "intentionally," and suggests three things: first, that the boys are childishly impulsive; second, that they are constitutionally unable to anticipate the consequences of their actions; and third, that they have a fundamental misunderstanding of the world and how it works. It's for all of these reasons that the boys are continually at odds with society, and why they frequently make dumbheaded decisions based on incredibly naïve—but innocent—assumptions.

So it is that when the Stooges dig up bundles of bank notes and bonds, and sacks of coins, in *Yes, We Have No Bonanza* (1939), they assume the money is part of nature's bounty. Their internal wiring prevents them from considering for an instant that other people might have come by it illegally and buried it. Some of the bonds are gold bonds, and Curly says delightedly, "Gee, ain't nature wonderful!"

See?

Of course, somebody *did* bury the money, saloon owner Maxey (Dick Curtis) and his bank-robbing associate, Pete (Lynton Brent). Maxey is a big, surly sort who employs the Stooges' very pretty fiancées (Jean Carmen, Lola Jensen, and Suzanne Kaaren) as entertainers, bullying them because their father owes him a lot of money.

The Stooges work at the saloon, too, as bartenders and waiters. They take a lot of abuse from Maxey, partly because they're incompetent and partly because Maxey just feels like it. He's wired *not* to be innocent.

The money provides the Stooges and their girls with a way out, but the outraged Maxey and Pete understandably want it back. A wild chase in which the crooks' car pulls the boys' wooden horse through the streets climaxes when Moe tosses a beehive into Maxey's lap, causing the car to plow right through the wall of the city jail (an excellent mechanical effect), where the sheriff (Vernon Dent) is waiting.

The boys succumb to gold fever when Pete stupidly pays for a drink with a stolen twenty-dollar gold piece and explains it away by saying, "Oh, it's some-thing I just dug up." Naturally, the boys take him literally, and soon they're outfit-ted as prospectors, complete with mule, provisions, and tools. This is a lengthy, beautifully played sequence devised by co-scripters Elwood Ullman and Searle Kramer, and very well directed by Del Lord (on the nicely redressed "woods" set from *A Ducking They Did Go*). Curly cuts a side of beef and discovers that the bones can be played like a xylophone. Larry ruins his axe on a rock (one of the most unpleasant sound effects you could imagine) and disgustedly tosses the

Performer Profile: Lynton Brent
1897–1981

Like John Tyrrell, former architect Lynton Brent brought a pleasing face and "man on the street" charm to more than 250 film roles undertaken between 1929 and his retirement in 1950. He did many more features than shorts, taking supporting roles—some credited, others not—as reporters, henchmen, cops, clerks, and sneaks.

Brent worked frequently at Monogram and RKO and settled in at Columbia around 1935, where he appeared in two-reelers starring Harry Langdon, Buster Keaton, the Glove Slingers, and the Stooges. He makes a brief but important appearance as Mr. Amscray in *I'll Never Heil Again*, and gets good face time in *So Long, Mr. Chumps* as the prison guard whose puss is painted by Curly.

In *Cookoo Cavaliers*, Brent plays the amiable Pedro Ruiz, who sells the boys a beauty salon in Mexico; and he shines in *A Ducking They Did Go* as the con man who is horrified when the Stooges inform him they've sold a phony duck-club membership to the governor.

Hard guy Lynton Brent puts the boys on their guard in *Yes, We Have No Bonanza* (1939).

Photo courtesy of the Stoogeum

rock aside, accidentally striking Curly in the head. Curly thinks Moe did it, so he uncorks from twenty feet and wings the rock right into Moe's temple.

A backswing of Curly's pick drives the blade into Moe's coccyx (a real wince-inducer), and Moe retaliates by bringing his pick down squarely on the top of Curly's skull, bending the blade as if it were melted licorice.

A little misunderstanding with dynamite causes the boys to believe they've blown up their patient mule, Yorick (more of the bard!), but the explosion exposes the hidden loot.

The title of *Yes, We Have No Bonanza* comes from Curly's ad-libbed riff on a popular song, "Yes, We Have No Bananas." The short has big-scale action, but some of the best laughs are subtle throwaways. Maxey cheats at solitaire, and Larry greets a regular by silently inviting him to cut a deck of cards. Larry looks at his own card, grimaces with surprise, and yells to Moe to "draw one!" You get the feeling Larry does this—and loses—all the time.

But to return to the fundamental nature of the Stooges: At the prospecting site, Curly informs Moe that he's loaded the eggs "on top of the burro so they'll be nice and fresh in the sun!" Oh dear, it's not only the rules of society that the Stooges don't understand but the very laws of nature, too.

JULES WHITE AND CLYDE BRUCKMAN'S *ROCKIN' THROUGH THE ROCKIES* (1940) places the boys in the unlikely role of protectors of white maidenhood. They're showbiz "hoofers" who have assumed the guise of Indian scouts in order to lead a wagonload of female performers—"Hells Belles, Direct from Three Hot Weeks in Kansas"—across the Sunflower State westward to San Francisco, a distance of more than two thousand miles. Well, five months have gone by, winter has arrived, and the Escrow Indians are prowling around the camp, intimidating the Stooges and eyeballing the women. "Me makum whoopee!" one brave leeringly suggests. Chief Growling Bear (Dick Curtis) tells his man to take it easy and then looks back over his shoulder at the gals. "Not bad," he admits.

Pretty funny stuff, but we must remember that so-called "miscegenation" laws were still on the books in the American South (and would be until 1967). The purported threat encouraged hatred and loathing not just in Dixie but in such supposedly cosmopolitan cities as Chicago and Boston. The bigots' greatest fear, of course, was that black men would take up with and "violate" white women, but "red men" fooling with Anglo-Saxon females also strikes a negative, if potentially more humorous, chord. The theme propels many westerns, some good and others not so good, including John Ford's 1956 masterpiece, *The Searchers*. Although audiences of 1940 (and later) got a chuckle from the horny Escrow Indians, a shudder runs beneath the laughter like a tripwire.

The very pretty Belles (Linda Winters, Lorna Gray, and stock-company standout Dorothy Appleby) are chaperoned by a towering, hatchet-faced harridan called Nell (Kathy Sheldon), who would probably kill the boys if she didn't think they might be useful. None of them are ever around until somebody rings the dinner bell, and they're completely hopeless as scouts. Curly (back in his skunkskin cap) loudly complains, "I'm sick and tired of lookin' for Indians! Let 'em look for us for a change!"

The first of a pair of successful set pieces begins with a heavy snowfall that forces the boys and the Belles inside the flimsy canvas prop used in the troupe's productions of *Uncle Tom's Cabin.* The boys' snoring shakes the canvas like cheesecloth, and Moe is finally awakened by Curly, who barks in his sleep. Ordered to go outside to bring back the bear hide so he can sleep in it by himself, Curly fashions snowshoes from guitars. Clad only in his nightshirt, hands clasped behind his back like the most relaxed of skaters, Curly happily slides across the snow, warbling "La la lee la. . ." It's a completely endearing glimpse of an eccentric man-child who lives in his own world. Curly has at least one such interlude in nearly all of the ninety-seven shorts he made at Columbia with Moe and Larry. The moments are always brightly amusing, and never fail to confirm that Curly Howard was one of the screen's best and most inventive comics.

The set piece concludes back inside the flimsy cabin, where there's some confusion about the bearskin—it seems that Curly left the door open and allowed a real bear to come inside.

The other set piece is the boys' attempt to go ice fishing. (The sequence may also have been shot on the woodsy set created for *A Ducking We Will Go,* re-dressed yet again.) The air seems very cold, and the snow-dusted "ice" that covers the water appears real. After much travail, Moe snags a big one. Hey, Larry and Curly have a big one on their line, too! The two of them tug mightily and pull Moe right into his hole and beneath the ice. Larry and Curly keep pulling and hit the fish on the head with an iron bar. Curly exclaims, "Hey, that fish looks like Moe!"

Larry: "It *is* Moe!"

Stand by for retribution.

When the Indians finally broach the cabin, they dash head-first into a massive snowbank that Curly created earlier by thoughtlessly poking at the canvas ceiling with a broomstick.

With the Indians held fast, the Belles—virtue intact—hop aboard the wagon, and the boys literally set sail. Next stop: San Francisco!

AS THESE WORDS ARE WRITTEN, GOLD IS SELLING FOR A JILLION DOLLARS AN ounce—or possibly even a million.

Well, not really, but it's selling for a lot. (It'll also sell for a lot *less* after a while, but that's another story.) The Stooges, like many other people, can't resist the lure of that glittery metal and fall hard when a street hustler (Eddie Laughton) offers them the deed to the fabled Lost Mine: "A hundred thousand tons of pure gold, worth thirty-five dollars an ounce! Think of it!"

As best they can, the boys *do* think of it, and fork over their last hundred dollars. Soon, they're out west with Curly's new invention, a gold finder that's an unholy combination of Geiger counter, surface-to-surface missile, and crossbow.

(The boys are delighted when a letter from a manufacturer informs Curly that the gadget is "incomprehensible and utterly impractical." He's a success!)

Just by chance, the gadget finally leads the boys to the Lost Mine, where they discover countless gold coins—only to run into a pair of greedy prospectors.

That's the quick version of *Cactus Makes Perfect* (1942), in which we have the opportunity to meet the boys' mother. (Larry, Curly, and Moe once again play brothers.) Ma is very tall and square-shouldered, with breasts like droopy melons and a foghorn voice. Like Curly, she's accident-prone and easily frustrated. And she's played by Monte "Monty" Collins, the veteran screen comic who co-wrote this short with Elwood Ullman. If Collins's talents were insufficiently exploited in *Three Missing Links* (see "The Stooges and the Fairer Sex"), they're on full display here. Ma is an eye-opening creation: part loving mother, part disciplinarian, part rogue grizzly. Impatient to rouse the boys from slumber, she tugs a rope that's connected to the upstairs bed, which rotates on a central pivot, like a rotisserie. Although Ma pulls and pulls, and the bed goes round and round, the snoring boys don't fall out. Only centrifugal force sends them flying across the room, and even then they sleep on, piled atop one another like puppies.

During their morning ablutions, Moe generously takes a straight razor to Curly's kisser. He gets hung up on a tricky spot on Curly's throat, swiftly rotates the blade around Curly's eye sockets, and thoughtfully shoves it into Curly's nostrils, to get at those bothersome nose hairs.

Curly, meanwhile, can't wait to start the new day: "I'm gonna change my socks, what an experience!"

Out west, the boys locate nothing but tin cans, and tangle with a grabby saguaro cactus that leaves a mosaic of spines in Curly's butt and gives Larry an amorous hug.

When Curly is down to his last arrow, he ties it to his arm and is launched right along with it, flying through space like a drunken flying squirrel before finally landing with a thud against the mine's boarded entrance, his head caught just inside. Here, director Del Lord lets his inner Jules White come out as he devotes more than a minute of screen time to Moe's unintentional torture of Curly with a crowbar that's intended to free Curly's head. Larry wants to blast, but Moe insists they can just shove Curly through into the other side. Larry shrugs, "Well, it'll take longer but go ahead."

As Curly disappears down the shaft, he emits a gorgeous, two-note "Wohohohoho, woahhhhh!" shriek, with the second note augmented by a rich echo.

Deep in the mine, the handles of Larry and Curly's shovels abuse Moe's head, but all is forgiven when Curly discovers a lever that disgorges the coins. Moe says, "Boy, won't Ma be happy!"

Larry agrees. "Yeah, we'll take her right outta the kitchen!"

Curly: "And move the stove in the dining room!"

The boys stash their cash in the enormous safe of an abandoned hotel (Moe and Larry enter first, ring at the desk, and are greeted by Curly), but they've been followed by a couple of desert rats (Vernon Dent and Ernie Adams), who instigate some mischief with dynamite that puts the Stooges right through a wall.

Although the pair's names aren't heard on the soundtrack, the script calls them Red and Stumpy, intriguingly close to the Ren and Stimpy cartoon heroes of the 1990s. In 1993, a Ren and Stimpy parody comic book called itself *Red and Stumpy*.

Cactus Makes Perfect gives us another opportunity to admire Curly's skunkskin cap and to ponder the boys' incredible naiveté. And not enough can be said in praise of Monte Collins as Ma, who helps us understand the cruel tricks of genetics.

THE PLOT OF *PHONY EXPRESS* (1943) IS NO MORE OR LESS CONTRIVED THAN that of any other Stooges short, but the elements don't jell. Although competent, it's also rote and mechanical, and a rare disaster for Del Lord. One explanation may be that everybody, Lord included, pushes too hard. You can almost read their minds: *Look at us! We're doing funny! Funny!*

The Stooges are vagrants—and apparently very accomplished ones, because their criminal lassitude is commemorated on a Wanted poster devoted just to them. Over in Peaceful Gulch, Red Morgan (Bud Jamison) and his gang are terrorizing the citizenry, and the town's leading lights are afraid that an enormous payroll will be stolen. The only thing to do (and this is the short's funniest notion) is to run the photograph of the three vagrants in the local paper, and claim that they're famed lawmen on their way to clean up the town.

Of course, the Stooges have no idea of the scheme. Nevertheless, Red Morgan and his gang are cowed when the boys fumble into town. Eventually, though, Morgan realizes that "Wild Bill Hiccup" and his boys are phonies, so he brazenly takes the payroll that the city fathers have been so worried about. In a climactic showdown in an isolated cabin, the Stooges recover the loot and put the arm on the crooks.

Broadly sketched, *Phony Express* seems to have promise. Mistaken identity is a sure-fire laugh getter, and Lord has the services of the estimable Bud Jamison. Things begin to go awry when the boys are mistaken for patent-medicine shills and are ordered by the local sheriff (a gaunt Snub Pollard) to produce something to relieve his lumbago. Larry and Curly huddle in the back of the wagon, mixing "this and that" into a beaker and coaxing the fizzing, sparking result into a bottle. After the sheriff takes a swig, his handlebar mustache goes into a vigorous twirl. Lord holds on this static, ho-hum gag a little too long, finally breaking off for a ho-hum shot of the lawman knocked back onto his butt. Weak tea, indeed.

The boys pile into the wagon, which is reduced to a speeding, skeletal frame after the sheriff tosses the bottle in their direction and causes a sweet explosion. The gag is unexpected, and you're likely to laugh in genuine surprise. All regard to writers Elwood Ullman and Monte Collins (again credited as "Monty"), who almost compensate for the flat bit of business with the mustache. A physical gag built around a loose floorboard that swings upward to catch Moe on the underside of his chin when Curly innocently steps on the other end is another inventive, well-played moment.

The rest of *Phony Express* is very up-and-down. At the local saloon, the swinging doors catch Moe in the face. Righto. Later, Larry and Curly do the venerable about-face right-face gag and repeatedly conk Moe's head and pinch his neck with their rifle barrels. In the woods, Moe is hit again and again with swinging tree branches. And a protracted sequence involving bear traps that catch some of Red's gang is poorly paced and flatly executed. The gag isn't constructed to offer a surprise, but it doesn't engender real anticipation, either. You can guess precisely what's going to happen at the payoff, and it does: Four guys clutch at their ankles and howl because Del Lord said, "Okay, howl."

The short's worst sin is a dreadful violation of internal logic, when the city fathers—who know the boys are frauds—deputize them to guard the bank. The plot point is so skewed that the viewer actively *thinks* about it and is taken right out of the story.

But the boys are game, regardless, and after the bank is knocked over, Larry and Moe tether Curly to a rope and take him into the woods like a bloodhound. There's much scrambling on hands and knees, and loudly insistent baying and barking—most of the latter looped into the soundtrack during post-production and sounding like it. Although Curly is enthusiastic, the bit goes on much too long, and you start to feel bad that Curly the character and Curly the man are being abused so. Mercifully, the gag has a cute payoff, as Curly follows a skunk into its den (the camera stays outside so we can only hear the mayhem). After a pregnant pause, Curly emerges with—yes!—another skunkskin cap.

Phony Express was filmed in the first half of 1943 (for November release), and we see the early stage of Curly's physical decline, which culminated in the career-ending stroke he suffered almost exactly three years later. His performance here is generally bright, but his face has become lined and noticeably thicker, and some of the light has gone out of his eyes. A climactic moment, when he's trapped inside a hot stove with bullets exploding all around, should have been a laff riot, but Lord's close-ups on Curly's face (in profile) show a man in anxious puzzlement rather than all-out comic terror. Curly seems a little lost.

On the other hand, he's beautiful when he spies a box of mothballs and happily gobbles them: "Ah, peppermintees!" He also plays well opposite tall actress Shirley Patterson, who is alluring as a saloon girl in league with the gang (and who is amusingly irritated when Curly carelessly dumps his beer down her back while they dance).

The final shot of *Phony Express* is a dispassionate examination of the stove as bullets explode inside and the whole thing twirls across the cabin floor like a sparking Roman candle. The image is funny in the abstract, but what about Curly? Is he hurt? How is he going to get out of there? Is he going to be killed? We can only guess.

Phony Express got the remake treatment in 1951, as *Merry Mavericks*. Because the source material is flawed, it's reasonable to expect that the remake will be as bad, or worse. Ah, surprise! Because of the inventiveness of writer-director Ed Bernds, and enthusiastic playing by the entire cast, *Merry Mavericks* is far superior to its inspiration. The plot setup is identical, and snippets of stock footage are used (the town under siege—which already was stock footage back in 1943—and the dubious brainstorm of the city fathers vis-à-vis the Stooges' jobs). But everything else is reshot, reworked, and given a fresh perspective. Because Bernds loved to mix genres, *Merry Mavericks* isn't just a western but a spook comedy, too, in which the Morgan gang fiendishly terrorizes the Stooges with a variety of ghastly masks and other gruesome disguises. Sequences in which the boys race from room to room, hurl themselves onto beds and through doorways, and cower as *something* touches them on the shoulder are fast-paced and smartly visual. With nothing weak or extraneous to get in the way (the business with the medicine wagon is jettisoned; likewise the "bloodhound" and bear trap business), *Merry Mavericks* accomplishes its plot points while giving the audience a real ride.

The gleeful mixing of genres suggests another of Bernds's strengths as a writer: his fond understanding of movie conventions and his eagerness to satirize them. Among his notable additions to the remake is a stalwart lawman (Paul Campbell)—tall, good-looking, and very much in the mold of the impossibly competent heroes of B-westerns—except that as conceived by Bernds, the fellow, Cassidy (a riff on "Elmer," another Bernds creation played in another western short by Jock Mahoney), is a foolish incompetent with a knack for showing up *after* the Stooges have done all the heavy lifting. He mainly stands around, looks handsome, and makes pronouncements that nobody cares about.

He's certainly nowhere nearby when the gang is scaring the hell out of the Stooges, particularly when one of the group (prolific B-western heavy John Merton, who plays a member of Red's gang in *Phony Express*) stalks around as a headless Indian chief. This gives Larry fits and some fine, panicked dialogue: "I saw his head! Where it wasn't!"

Perennial blonde starlet Marion Martin, captured here at age forty-three and revealing a delicious, slightly *zaftig* sexiness, is very engaged as the dance hall floozie in league with Red (who is played with a smooth sneer by handsome B-western and serial actor Don Harvey).

Director of photography Allen Siegler gives the short's relatively simple flats beautiful, faintly sinister shadows and textures, but *Merry Mavericks*, like so many comic films, really hits pay dirt when it riffs on sex. With Red's gang subdued, Shemp asks, "Moe, what'll we do with the girl?"

"Ahh, throw her to the dogs!"

At that, Shemp and Larry exchange a quick glance and then launch into loud vocalizations of canine lust: "Woof, woof, woof! Awooo!"

Marion Martin looks on, slightly bemused but unworried because at least she's fallen into the hands of guys who appreciate her.

THREE TROUBLEDOERS (1946), A REWORKING OF A 1945 HARRY LANGDON AND El Brendel short called *Pistol Packin' Nitwits*, is the last western in which Curly appears. It was shot in May 1945, a few months after Curly was diagnosed with hypertension linked in part to his weight. Not long after the diagnosis, Curly suffered one or more mild strokes that, although not completely debilitating, slowed his reactions and made memorization of dialogue increasingly difficult for him. Dieting altered the contours of his face, and his flagging energy caused changes to the pitch and cadence of his voice.

Columbia made clear to Moe, the group's de facto leader, that a radical slow-down of the boys' output was unacceptable. The release schedule had already declined in 1945, and the studio insisted that it not slip further.

Curly soldiered on. The heroic thing about *Three Troubledoers* is that Curly looked at Jack White's script, saw that he was the focal character, and turned in a lively, enthusiastic performance. And because the short is particularly pointed in its spoofery of the conventions of B-westerns, director Ed Bernds was in his element, and Curly responded to him particularly well.

The situation seems grim. Local bullyboy Badlands Blackie (Dick Curtis, who plays essentially the same part in *Pistol Packin' Nitwits*) insists that innocent Nell (Christine McIntyre) marry him—and to ensure that she does, Blackie has kid-napped her father. If Nell wants to see her "pappy" alive again, she'll say, "I do."

Dick Curtis jumps into Blackie as joyously as a retriever jumps into water. He uses his size to leer and intimidate but adds unmistakable overtones of radio ventriloquist Edgar Bergen's dim-witted associate, Mortimer Snerd. Blackie is aggressively insistent about the coerced marriage, and dead serious about his threats against Nell's dad. On the other hand, he displays childlike delight when Nell acquiesces on any small point at all, prematurely referring to her as "Mrs. Blackie" and fishing for compliments by asking, "Ain't she purty?" And when he laughs, the sound that comes from his diaphragm is pure Snerd: "Yuh huh!"

Although based in Skullbone Pass, Blackie has made himself a malignant presence in Dead Man's Gulch. When the Stooges wander into town, Blackie immediately victimizes them. But when he tosses Curly's gun belt into a black-smith's blazing forge, the exploding bullets cause Blackie to retreat, firing blindly before he topples backwards into a horse trough. That's enough for the city fathers, who appoint Curly sheriff and Moe and Larry his deputies.

Curly's attempts to hone his shooting skills don't go well at all (he aims at one target and inevitably hits another), so Moe insists that the boys develop a long-range weapon, a sort of 19th-century bazooka. After a few run-ins with Blackie and multiple failures of the new weapon, the boys break up the wed-ding by *throwing* the bazooka onto the ground, exploding the shed that holds Nell's dad.

In B-westerns, bad things often happen at sunset. In comic acknowledgment of this, the late-afternoon sun above Dead Man's Gulch periodically plummets in the sky, only to just as quickly return to its starting point. The gag is optically clever and agreeably absurd.

Performer Profile: Dick Curtis
1902–52

When 6'3" Dick Curtis levels his serpent's stare at the Stooges, you know the boys are in big trouble. Narrow-eyed, with high cheekbones and full lips, Curtis almost inevitably arrives on the screen with a built-in swagger perfected during a thirty-year career that includes appearances in *Tell It to the Marines*, *King Kong*, *The Cross of Lorraine*, and *My Six Convicts*. Kids who flocked to B-western matinees came to know Curtis as the frequent, and violent, nemesis of cowboy star Charles Starrett; their throat-clutching fights are practically legendary.

With the Stooges, Curtis appeared as the idiotic Nazi, General Bommel, in *Higher Than a Kite*; a trigger-happy cowboy with a bad molar in *The Tooth Will Out*; a professional knife thrower who resents the Stooges' innocent attentions to his wife in *Don't Throw That Knife*; and brain-dead gunslinger Badlands Blackie in *Three Troubledoers*.

Emphatic and very focused on the screen, Curtis is among the Stooges' greatest antagonists.

Curly is unmasked and Badlands Blackie (Dick Curtis, with revolver) isn't pleased in *Three Troubledoers* (1946). Other players, from left: Christine McIntyre, Blackie Whiteford, Ethan Laidlaw.
Photo courtesy of the Stoogeum

The short is boosted further by some cute, if unremarkable, set pieces: Curly hides in a haystack and barks his head off when one of Blackie's men says he thinks he heard a dog; Curly pummels a dummy dressed to look like Blackie, only to be shocked when the real Blackie steals in and takes the dummy's place. After two of Blackie's boys lock an iron collar around Curly's neck, Moe and Larry fruitlessly pound on it (and on Curly) with a mallet and chisel, before finally trying a crowbar, in a brief reprise of a central gag from *Cactus Makes Perfect*. Later, Curly delays the wedding with a giddy impersonation of the justice of the peace.

As the climax draws near, Bernds and editor Henry Batista have fun with aggressive cross-cutting between the bridal party (and a most miserable Nell) and Moe and Larry, who furiously pedal a bicycle built for two (with many falls and other mishaps along the way, all played to a frantic version of Rossini's *William Tell* overture).

The ironic payoff for Curly, after all his sweat and risk, is to be insulted by Nell's father (Sam Lufkin) when Nell announces her intention to marry Curly. "What, *him?*" Pappy exclaims. "I'd rather be dead!"

By this time, Curly's patience and essentially sweet nature have run their course for the day. "Anything to oblige!" he says as he hands Pappy a lighted stick of dynamite. In a panic, Nell grabs the TNT and thoughtlessly tosses it toward the Stooges, who are blown to kingdom come.

No good deed goes unpunished.

IN *OUT WEST* (1947), THE STOOGES ARE TENDERFOOT EASTERNERS WHO HAVE come to the frontier for Shemp's health—specifically, for an inflamed vein in his leg that is quickly mistaken by local bad boy Doc Barker (Jack Norman) for an enormous vein of gold. In a grim turn, we learn that Barker has killed the father of local beauty Nell (Christine McIntyre) and taken over her saloon. Once again, we have the extortionate marriage proposal: If Nell doesn't trip to the altar, Barker will knock off her imprisoned lover, the Arizona Kid (Jacques O'Mahoney). (Barker is probably named for Arthur "Doc" Barker of the notorious Depression-era Barker gang that was supposedly headed by Arthur's mother, Kate "Ma" Barker.)

The Stooges put on a good show of being tough guys, and Shemp even takes Barker for five hundred bucks in a poker game that's been rigged against him, by surreptitiously intercepting the aces that one of Barker's cronies passes beneath the table. In time, the boys slip Barker a mickey, lift his keys, and free the Kid, who returns with the cavalry.

By 1947, screenwriter Clyde Bruckman had been in the business for nearly thirty years. Always ready reuse any of his own gags, he also showed unflagging inventiveness. *Out West* could have been very tired stuff, but Bruckman and director Ed Bernds mine laughs from some familiar territory. Barker swills the mickey and immediately screams for water; Larry finds a fire hose on the wall (a cute anachronism) and uncoils it at a dead run, only to run out of hose and—with help from a stunt double—execute a fabulous over-the-top flip flat onto his back.

While the Stooges hammer away at the lock on the Arizona Kid's basement cell, Nell sings "The Last Rose of Summer," a quite sad Irish ballad, to cover the racket (as always, Christine McIntyre's pure soprano is a joy). Downstairs, the boys' exertions with mallets, crowbars, and other tools aren't getting anywhere at all. When Shemp gets in Moe's way, Moe says, "Hold your ear," and then busily tries to separate the ear from Shemp's head with a hacksaw.

The Kid is finally freed (carefully smoothing his hair before departing) and hurries to the nearest fort, where he tells the colonel (Stanley Blystone) that it may already be too late. The colonel gravely pronounces, "Son, never in the history of motion pictures has the United States Cavalry been too late!"

As in *Three Troubledoers*, aggressive cross-cutting (between Nell, the Stooges, and the approaching cavalry) gently mocks genre conventions even as it heightens tension. The climax is a less elaborate reprise of the warehouse sequence from *Fright Night* (see "The Stooges and the Sporting Life"), in which the boys are pursued around boxes and crates before subduing Barker and his goons with a well-tossed stick of dynamite.

A couple of visual jokes—the cavalry running backwards when the danger is over, and a freeze-frame of a tossed coin while Shemp readies his gun to shoot it—don't work, but Bruckman and Bernds score big when Shemp innocently discusses his vein with Barker, as the two of them examine a drawing done back east by Shemp's doctor. "You know something," Barker says thoughtfully, "I could do things with a vein like that. . . . If it's near the surface we'd use twenty men with pick and shovel." Shemp reacts with silent horror. "If it's any deeper, we'll use dynamite." As you might expect, Shemp's reaction to this apparent casual sadism is priceless.

The comedy's final shot, the embrace of the reunited young lovers, reinforces that *Out West* is as much about the genre as it is about the Stooges.

The enjoyable froth of *Out West* was recycled for a 1954 remake, *Pals and Gals* (one of the least evocative Stooges titles ever). Christine McIntyre, no less beautiful than seven years earlier, returns as Nell for some new scenes involving her sisters, Zelle (Norma Randall) and Belle (Ruth Godfrey), who are the captives this time around. John Norman returns as Doc Barker in stock footage only and is credited as Norman Willes. In an unsettling twist devised by scripter Jack White so that Barker can be removed from the new storyline, the villain drinks the Stooges' mickey—and dies! "Heart failure," somebody hastens to explain. Viewers are further unsettled a few minutes later when Barker is carelessly allowed to reappear in stock footage of Nell's song.

Stanley Blystone, looking a little tired just two years before his death, returns as well—this time as one of Barker's boys.

It's all a bit dizzying. Some sources note that *Pals and Gals* was shot in a single day. If true, Jules White and his cast and crew worked like carpenter ants.

The wagon-chase sequence from *Goofs and Saddles* is lifted wholesale, with director Jules White adding new footage of Shemp and the boys in the back of the wagon. This leads to one odd moment: When Shemp uses his cupped hands as "binoculars" to eyeball the approaching bad guys, his mouth moves—probably with ad libs—but the soundtrack has no dialogue. Do we have a lip reader in the house?

At the conclusion, Nell is reunited with her sisters, everybody embraces, and the audience goes home happy, knowing that the Stooges won't spend the night alone.

IN JACK SCHAEFER'S FINE 1949 NOVEL *SHANE*, THE TITLE CHARACTER PATIENTLY explains to a young boy why a competent gunfighter has no need to carry two six-guns.

Well, Elmer, the Arizona Kid (Jock O'Mahoney), never picked up on that wisdom because he carries a pair of guns, and quite flashily, too, in the first of writer-director Ed Bernds's western parodies with the Stooges, *Punchy Cowpunchers* (1950). Trouble is, Elmer usually forgets to load them fine shootin' irons and neglects to tie the holsters to his thighs (the rawhide strips just dangle impotently). When he does have bullets, he struggles to hit what he aims at. But sweet Nell (Christine McIntyre) loves him—even though he's not keen on marriage and leaves nearly all of the cleanup of Coyote Creek to Larry, Shemp, and Moe.

The town is in the thrall of "the Killer Dillons" (as a dramatic title card informs us when three of them turn from the bar to glare at the Stooges). They're a rough, uncouth bunch led by—who else?—Dillon (Kenneth MacDonald), a clever smoothie who knows that the boys are Army spies from Fort Scott. He wants them killed so that he and his cohorts can rob the local bank without interference. A bit of disguise allows the boys to stay out of the gang's clutches for a while, but Moe and Larry are eventually captured and hogtied. Shemp, meanwhile, locks himself inside the bank safe, with explosive consequences for the Dillons.

Punchy Cowpunchers has a nice, linear progression, opening with the boys going about their duties as cavalrymen at the fort and running afoul of their burly sergeant (Dick Wessel). They accidentally conk him with horseshoes and generally try his patience: When Shemp is ordered to shoe a horse he sidles up to the beast and coyly inquires, "What size, madam?" The sarge is handed an opportunity for revenge when the colonel (Vernon Dent) asks that he find three men who can travel to Coyote Pass and root out the Dillon gang. The colonel portentously notes, "They will probably never come back!"

In short order, the boys are out of uniform and swaggering around Dillon territory in cowpoke duds. Like Harpo Marx in *Monkey Business*, the boys make a comic effort to "get tough." At the bar, Moe watches a Dillon pop the cap off his beer by levering the neck against the bar rail; Moe blithely opens *his* bottle on Shemp's teeth. Shemp recovers and orders a milkshake "with sour milk," and then makes a valiant effort to display his shooting prowess after one of the Dillons has fanned his six-shooter to obliterate a line of bottles on the bar. But Shemp can't even free his gun from its holster, managing only to let his pants and chaps drop to the floor. But Shemp isn't the giving-up kind: "I'll have it in a minute . . . ," he says in embarrassment. The boys finally crack the Dillons on the head with bottles. Elmer shows up a moment later, looking heroic with both guns drawn but of absolutely no help at all. With a practiced flourish, he smoothly twirls his six-shooters this way and that, forward and backward, before allowing them to drop into their holsters. (Kudos to Jock Mahoney!) The Stooges observe this with all the grave interest of the little boy in *Shane* and twirl their own guns with the finesse of circus clowns. Shemp gets thoroughly hung up, and his gun finally hangs from his finger like an angry vole. "Look at this, look at this," he ad libs in an aggravated mutter, "get it off, will ya?"

At the climax, Bernds and editor Henry DeMond put together some virtuoso cross-cutting between the Stooges' battle with the Dillons (some of which takes place in yet another warehouse inspired by *Fright Night*); the rest of the gang's scramble to crack the safe; Elmer's gallop through the night ("He fell off again!" one title card explains); and Nell's heroic efforts to protect her virtue when one Dillon after another invades her sitting room. Bernds successfully maintains the frantic pace for nearly three minutes, ensuring that the climax is as exciting as it is funny.

Although Bernds never was averse to the Stooges' brand of knockabout violence, in *Punchy Cowpunchers* the boys turn relatively little abuse on each other. Instead of continually attacking with no reason other than a quick laugh, the boys work from within the plot, to service it and allow their actions to be motivated by it. The Stooges aren't simply *farceurs* in *Punchy Cowpunchers* but legitimate components of plot that help construct the narrative even as they parody it. This is Bernds's most subtle acknowledgment of B-western conventions and the smartest example of his success as a satirist.

The always-game Christine McIntyre sees as much physical action as anybody, decking the Dillons with roundhouse blows. McIntyre could throw a punch as convincingly as any stuntman, and she lays out the villains like fallen timber. But because Nell is a lady above all, a delicate creature in the finest tradition of mid-Victorian refinement and decorum, she gets the vapors after each punch and retreats to her bed to fall into an appropriate faint. (After her third encounter, Nell toddles not to her bed but to a small couch, where she faints and hits her head, with a splendidly hollow conk, on a decorative knob. She takes a quick moment to rub her bruised noggin, and then faints again.)

Punchy Cowpunchers warrants careful observation because bits of business happen at all widths and depths of the frame, often simultaneously. The funniest single moment, though, is a static camera setup and a dead throwaway—look away for an instant and you'll miss it. It's a silent bit at the bar, where mixologist Shemp prepares a drink for a surly-looking cowboy (Blackie Whiteford). The cowboy glowers at the martini glass Shemp has set before him, disdainfully

Christine McIntyre has eyes only for the bumbling but handsome Elmer, the Arizona Kid (Jock O'Mahoney) in *Punchy Cowpunchers* (1950). This was the first of writer-director Ed Bernds's splendid western parodies.   *Photo courtesy of the Stoogeum*

plucks out the swizzle and olive, and tosses them to the floor. Where does Shemp think he is, Delmonico's? (The sequence begins in long shot, as Shemp faces Whiteford and ad libs the story of the Three Bears! When we cut in closer, Shemp is suddenly silent.)

Vincent Farrar's setups are crisply lit and shot; every frame is handsome without being showy. Henry DeMond's cutting is superior.

Jock Mahoney executes some marvelous stunts, including a forward flip when a glass crashes against the back of his head, and he's hugely eager to spoof his good looks. Elmer is one of the best roles Mahoney had before he became a TV and B-movie star. He's one of many reasons why *Punchy Cowpunchers* rides tall among the Stooges' two-reelers.

SO-CALLED ADULT WESTERNS, WHICH PLUMB THE PSYCHOLOGY OF THEIR central characters, began to be recognized as separate from other westerns in about 1950. Three releases from that year have special significance. *Broken Arrow* suggests that American Indians had humanity and legitimate disagreements with white settlers. *The Gunfighter* explores the fatalistic mindset of a professional gunman, and *Winchester '73*, the first of Anthony Mann's famously grim westerns of the 1950s, plumbs the dark territory of obsession and familial hatred.

And then, in 1952, audiences were mesmerized by the real-time drama of Fred Zinnemann's *High Noon*, in which an aging sheriff who has been deserted by his deputy and his townspeople must stand alone against four vengeful killers who will arrive on the noon train. Compelling and psychologically bleak, *High Noon* transforms the sunlit streets of a small western town into an ironic metaphor for isolation, cowardice, and loss.

A cultural phenomenon as well as a superior movie, *High Noon* inspired admiration, argument (hard-line conservatives condemned it for being un-American), and, inevitably, parody. The film was sent up by *MAD* magazine as "Hah! Noon!," and those other great bellwethers of American thought, the Three Stooges, had a go with their final two-reel western, *Shot in the Frontier* (1954). This is a reasonably ambitious comedy, written by Felix Adler and directed by Jules White, that looks good and plays well despite a meager three-day shooting schedule (at the Columbia Ranch in Burbank) in late October 1953. A comically brisk pace, some clever gags, sunlit exteriors, and animated performances distinguish it.

As in many of the Stooges' comedies, the boys have inexplicably hooked up with three babes, Ella, Bella, and Stella (Vivian Mason, Ruth Godfrey, and Diana Darrin, respectively). Just as the couples exchange wedding vows, word arrives that the Noonan brothers are on their way to town to rub out the Stooges. The boys want to skedaddle but are shamed by their new brides into staying. That being settled, the local troubadour (grizzled B-western sidekick Emmett Lynn) helpfully pipes up with, "Say, I'll go over and order you some coffins."

Told, like *High Noon*, with a minimum of dialogue, *Shot in the Frontier* is a succession of satisfying visual gags. At the wedding, the troubadour nails Moe with a half-full bag of rice, and then lets him have it with a pair of shoes. When the lean, black-clad Noonans begin to prowl the streets, Shemp nervously pours himself a drink—into his hand. Later, he hooks his suspenders onto his boot heels to create a catapult, sending a rock square into a Noonan forehead. (Inevitably, Shemp gets turned around and propels a rock into *Moe's* forehead.) Larry carelessly loads a rifle with balloons, which create some pretty pops when Larry fires but don't do anything to deter the killers.

In the set-piece battle, which begins with the Stooges and the Noonans firing at each other from opposite sides of the street, those excellent Columbia gunshot and ricochet sound effects are put to fine use—and with some real drama, as when the Noonans shoot great chunks from the tombstones the boys use as shields (ominously, the Stooges are in front of an undertaker's establishment).

When the battle moves into the open street, Shemp shows off some of his fancy footwork before being decked with one punch. Larry launches his head into a Noonan midsection, only to be flattened because the killer has hidden a stove plate beneath his shirt. Moe deftly avoids a pair of roundhouses (an expertly staged stunt) and then grabs the Noonan and falls with him to the ground—rolling from the shadowed foreground of the frame alll the way into the sunlit background (it's a nice deep-focus shot engineered by cinematographer Ray Cory), and then rolling back again. And then more rolling into the far-off sunlight, and then back yet again! This goes on for a while, and is hilarious in its absurdity.

Goodness (if not intelligence) ultimately triumphs, and the boys are reunited with their brides. But there's still that pesky troubadour—a send-up of singer Frankie Laine, whose (off-screen) vocalizing of "Do Not Forsake Me Oh My Darling" dominates *High Noon* and became a big hit. The old bugger who serenades the Stooges is truly awful, and Moe finally grabs the guy's guitar and smashes it over his head. Undeterred, the old coot whips out a ukulele and carries on singing.

Well, sonic torture is a small price to pay after you've made the west safe for civilization.

7

The Stooges Rewrite History

In which the boys fracture Donizetti; peddle lemons to the suckers; stick their little tootsies in the water; bring the Pilgrims the gift of jive; play the mating game; invoke Jim Crow; get skewered in a box; check out the Giva Dam; meet a cheerful executioner; make with the Yiddish; come back from Paris with postcards; and listen to the director.

R ecent years have brought numerous "alternate-reality" studies of World War II, the Civil War, notable political and technological developments, and other pivot points of the past. The best of these "what if" books and essays are thoughtful and engaging, with qualified historians working from foreknowledge and other insights that were unavailable to original participants. But what if you didn't want to extrapolate seriously about historical events? What if you made movies and you just wanted to goof on history?

Then you'd be Columbia's two-reel department, and you'd put the Stooges in the wayback machine.

Most screen comics do costume films. The equation is usually irresistible: zany modern sensibility collides with the past to produce laughs. In the Stooges' era, major comedy stars enjoyed great success with costume comedies, for instance, Laurel and Hardy in *Way Out West*, Red Skelton in *Du Barry Was a Lady*, Danny Kaye in *The Court Jester*, Bob Hope in *The Princess and the Pirate*, Abbott and Costello in *The Naughty Nineties*—the list continues for nearly as long as history itself.

Intriguingly, no such tradition existed at Columbia's two-reel department. Buster Keaton did a Civil War farce, *Mooching Through Georgia* (1939), and the unit produced a quartet of unrelated western shorts: *Back to the Soil* (George Sidney and Charlie Murray, 1934); *Garden of Eatin'* (Slim Summerville, 1943); *Pistol Packin' Nitwits* (Harry Langdon and El Brendel, 1945); and *Rootin' Tootin' Tenderfeet* (Max Baer and Maxie Rosenbloom, 1952). The rest of the unit's output, spread over a quarter century and among forty-five series (other than the Stooges), is contemporary, revolving around fractured marriages, miserable vacations, mistaken identity, haunted houses, escaped criminals, and similarly familiar comic fodder. If the Stooges—as urban and modern in their sensibilities as any other comics on the lot—flourished in costume pictures, many of the others could have, too. But the fact is that nobody else had the Stooges' box-office appeal or staying power. Although the boys' historical comedies were shot on standing sets that had been put up for features, and utilized period costumes and props pulled from the respective studio departments, the films nevertheless required more time and care than a short with, say, two sequences in an apartment and one in an office. It was the Stooges' popularity that made the extra investment in costume comedies worthwhile. The boys reciprocated by demonstrating their comfort with historical settings of all sorts.

The Stooges' first jump into historical comedy is *Restless Knights* (1935), their sixth Columbia two-reeler, and their first with director Charles Lamont, who went on to great success as the director of features with Abbott and Costello and Ma and Pa Kettle. Lamont shapes *Restless Knights* so that it's brisk and aggressively violent, and gets considerable mileage from grand standing sets built for *A Royal Romance* (1930).

Contrary to a misapprehension perpetuated by many Web sources, *Restless Knights* does not have a medieval setting; rather, it's set centuries later, in what looks like the first quarter of the 17th century, in the European monarchy of Anesthesia. "Entry of the Giants," the Baroque-style fanfare by studio composer Louis Silver that plays majestically over the short's opening and closing title cards, is another obvious indicator of the time period.

The boys are petty noblemen appointed by the queen (Geneva Mitchell) to be her personal guard. That rankles the ambitious prime minister, Boris (George Baxter), who has designs on the throne. When he and his co-conspirators abduct the queen, the Stooges risk their lives to find and rescue her.

Boris and his cohorts have the costumes, swords, and skill of seasoned musketeers, so Larry (the Duke of Mixture), Moe (the Fief of Drum), and Curly (the Baron of Brainmatter) have their hands full.

The short is essentially a succession of polished set pieces. The first begins as the boys slide into the throne room like base runners, to meet the queen. "From where came you?" the elegant lady inquires.

"Paris," says Larry.

Curly: "Show her the postcards!"

Moe adds that they were "looking over the Paris sights."

For reasons unknown, the queen is impressed with these dim fellows and brings them into her inner circle. Hideously bent rapiers held aloft, the Stooges declaim:

LARRY
All for one!

MOE
One for all!

CURLY (as he gives the queen a flirtatious wave)
I'll take care of myself!

Four gorgeous courtesans enter to stand by their queen. "I'll take the blonde!" Larry says.

"I'll take the brunette!" Moe exclaims.

That leaves Curly: "I'll take the black and tan!"

If we're quoting a lot of dialogue here, it's because writer Felix Adler is very generous with it. *Restless Knights* was Adler's fourth outing with the Stooges, and the veteran screenwriter, whose Hollywood career began in 1924, was very important in the Stooges' development, particularly as individuated characters. With this short, Larry begins to cede obvious leadership to Moe, and Curly develops further as the truly anarchic member of the team.

The second set piece in *Restless Knights* involves a pair of burly wrestlers (Bud O'Neill and James Howard), whose grappling inspires the Stooges to demonstrate their moves, too. In the free-for-all that follows, Moe handles Curly like an unloved handball, and Larry is head-butted by Moe and later tossed across the enormous hall and right onto the queen's throne (with an assist from a poorly disguised stunt double).

But where is the queen?

Set piece number three is the boys' valiant but doomed duel with Boris and his men, and subsequent preparation for their execution by crossbow. Lined up against a wall with Curly and Moe, Larry hopefully says, "Maybe they'll miss us!"

Curly cheerfully notes, "That'll be an arrow escape!"

Whew! The boys are pooped, but the queen is safe in *Restless Knights* (1935).

Photo courtesy of the Stoogeum

The silhouette of a babe who undresses in a nearby tower window distracts the bowmen, and the boys make their getaway—which propels us into the final and most complex set piece, the rescue of the queen from the castle's wine cellar and surrounding catacombs. The sequence unfolds on gorgeous, low-ceilinged sets with dramatic arches and evocative shadows—"A"-picture cinematography, with marvelous chiaroscuro lighting, by Benjamin Kline.

The scheme calls for Curly to taunt the turncoat guards, one by one, into running through an archway, where Moe and Larry wait with clubs. Inevitably, the last guard trips and falls, so Moe and Larry carelessly club each other.

Dark-eyed Geneva Mitchell, a former Ziegfeld Girl, is at once majestic and approachable as the queen, and looks good even when her dignity is upended. Gruff character player Stanley Blystone, who appears in many Stooges shorts, steals a scene or two as one of Boris's musketeers. But George Baxter, as Boris, is given surprisingly little to do, and frankly doesn't make much of an impression. Character player Jack Duffy has a featured bit as an aged, comically toothless guard (Duffy was only fifty-three at the time!), and forty-one-year-old Walter Brennan—another young fella who invariably looked like he'd been born in the Mesozoic era—dominates the deathbed scene that opens the story when he informs his sons of their royal bloodline. Brennan's performance is appropriately sober—until he raises his hand and cracks the boys with the first three-across face slap of their Columbia careers. Now *that's* historic.

IN A SOP TO THE STOOGES' FANS AND COLUMBIA'S EXHIBITORS DOWN SOUTH, the handsomely produced *Uncivil Warriors* (1935) opens and closes with studio composer R. H. Bassett's appealing arrangement of "Dixie"—but that's about the only break the Confederacy gets because "Dixie" segues for a few bars into that abolitionist favorite "The Battle Hymn of the Republic." The studio tried to throw southern audiences a bone before writer Felix Adler and director Del Lord suggest that dopes and fools staffed the Confederate army.

Then again, the Union side isn't depicted as a hothouse of genius, particularly since the army's most accomplished spies are the Stooges. At an outdoor bivouac, the general explains to the boys that they're being sent on a dangerous infiltration mission disguised as Confederates: Lieutenant Duck (Larry), Captain Dodge (Moe), and Major Hyde (Curly)—and yes, the moment each boy hears his new name he does what the name suggests.

It's a long donkey slog into rebel territory, and Moe wonders aloud if they've reached the right place. Curly looks around and expansively says, "Well, being as there's no other place around the place I reckon this must be the place, I reckon!" This line—probably a chestnut from burlesque and vaudeville—is so good that Curly uses it again in a fine 1939 short, *We Want Our Mummy*.

Once in the presence of the unsuspecting and amiable Colonel Butts (Bud Jamison), the boys easily coax important information about the numbers of rebel troops and field pieces. Moe slyly jots it all down on a small piece of paper, only to have it literally go up in smoke when Curly uses the paper to roll a cigarette. Moe (darkly): "Do you know what that paper was?"

Curly: "Hot?"

During filming, Curly was unaware that the tobacco immediately spills from the end of his hand-rolled smoke; when he lights it, the paper burns in a flash, startling Curly and nearly frying his nose. His reaction was retained for the final cut.

In a bit of a disappointment, *Uncivil Warriors* slows to a crawl after the boys are introduced to the colonel's daughters (Phyllis Crane and Celeste Edwards) and the sisters' friend (Jenifer Gray). The ladies' project for the day is to bake a cake, which gets bollixed up when Crane unknowingly tosses a torn potholder into Curly's cake pan. The boys subsequently struggle to chew and swallow the cake (for a too-obvious reason, the girls aren't eating, and are content with coffee). The gag might have been a hoot if kept to a few cuts that consumed just a few moments, but instead it turns into a complex set piece with multiple camera setups, too many boy-it's-hard-to-chew-this close-ups, and gratuitous remarks (mostly made off-camera) from the girls along the lines of, "You certainly like that cake!" and "Do you like that cake?"

Okay, we get it: The cake is awful, the girls have no idea, and the boys don't want them to discover the truth. The bit finally climaxes when the boys cough up a blizzard of feathers. The Stooges revisited the potholder-cake bit in a 1950 short, *Three Hams on Rye*. The gag is no funnier the second time around.

Impatient male viewers are mollified—a lot—by the trio of appealing young actresses who share the sequence with the Stooges. Pretty Phyllis Crane and Celeste Edwards are charming and natural. Black-haired Jenifer Gray is particularly striking, and summons a suitably confused reaction when Curly lifts a piece of his cake to her coffee cup and asks if he can dunk.

In due course, a reasonably clever rebel intelligence officer, Colonel Philbert (Ted Lorch), shows up and eyes the Stooges closely. Colonel Butts brags of Philbert, "He can smell a spy a mile away!" Curly whispers to Moe, "I'm glad he can't smell 'em any closer!"

Philbert makes the Stooges jump through hoops (and puts Curly into a hoop skirt) by claiming to have met several of the boys' relatives and spouses. The payoff to all this is the presentation by Curly (by now in that hoop skirt) of "her" son—a swaddled black baby. It's an uneasy kind of laugh but a laugh, nonetheless.

The boys flee to the woods and take cover inside a hollow log that turns out to be a camouflaged rebel cannon. Following a quick flight back to their own lines, the Stooges land dead center on the general's table, dazed but full of useful intelligence.

Look at the previous sentence again. It may be the only time ever that "useful intelligence" and "the Stooges" will appear in close proximity.

A STONE MONUMENT IN PLYMOUTH, MASSACHUSETTS, COMMEMORATES THE British religious separatists who died there during the winter of 1620–21 as they struggled to establish a settlement following a difficult voyage across the Atlantic. After a brief stop in late November 1620 at what is now Provincetown, the Pilgrims' ship, the *Mayflower*, landed at Plymouth four weeks later. The men and women on board, numbering just over one hundred, were greeted by six inches of snow and a landscape that was completely wild: no shelter, no systems for delivery of food and water—nothing except native Patuxet Indians.

Although that first winter was, by Cape Cod standards, a mild one—it was mainly rainy and blustery—nearly half of those who had completed the sea journey died. A lack of adequate shelter was an obvious problem, and food was scarce. Scurvy took some, and depredations by Indians, who developed an understandable resentment of the Pilgrims' forays into their hunting grounds, further depleted the settlers' numbers. (Indian aggression grew so serious that Pilgrim graves were tamped flat, to prevent the Indians from seeing how dramatically the settlement had shrunk.)

Many more settlers died between 1621 and 1623, but by 1630, the situation at Plymouth had improved considerably.

Naturally, the Stooges are perfect for this dramatic historical setting. *Back to the Woods* (1937) supposes that a British magistrate (John Ince) is so fed up with the boys' mischief that he orders them exiled to Plymouth. (His first idea is fifty-five years apiece at Margate Prison, but his bailiff [Bud Jamison] points out that shipping the three to the New World will cost a lot less than feeding them for decades at Margate.)

Dumped at the colony, the boys soon ogle three gorgeous sisters, Faith (Harlene Wood), Hope (Ethelreda Leopold), and Charity (Beatrice Curtis, adorable in anachronistic Harold Lloyd-style eyeglasses).

The girls' father (Vernon Dent) is unimpressed with the Stooges, but a bigger problem is that Chief Rain in the Puss (Ted Lorch) wants "five thousand shekels." If he doesn't get it, he'll close off the hunting grounds.

The demure girls wail in unison, "We shall perish of hunger! O woe is us, O woe is us!"

The Stooges volunteer to venture onto Indian land to hunt. They tangle with the Indians, but ingenuity and a lot of dumb luck allow the boys to escape to a life of (one assumes) faith, hope, and charity.

Back to the Woods has plenty of lively violence: Curly bangs the stock of his musket on the ground and brings down an enormous turkey, which drops from the sky and onto Larry's head like a sack of cement. A little later, the boys make a catapult of a tightly sprung branch and pelt the Indians with rocks, mud, a fish, and a hornets' nest.

Hand-to-hand fighting is resolved when the Stooges shovel hot coals down the backsides of the Indians' breeches.

Although all of that is funny, the short is at its best during a sequence dreamed up by writer Andrew Bennison (working from a story by Searle Kramer) and thoughtfully directed by Preston Black (Jack White): Moe has brought Faith, Hope, and Charity a music box, and as it plays the three couples dance a graceful, slowly paced minuet that's enlivened by Moe and Larry's careless habit of swinging their boot heels into Curly's rear. White's staging of this lengthy, frankly enchanting sequence mixes long and medium shots with judiciously utilized close-ups, for an interlude that's courtly not simply in subject matter but in execution.

In time, the Stooges take a break by dancing with each other, and when the music box picks up the pace, the boys strut like jive hipsters, whose syncopated steppin' is timidly mimicked by the intrigued girls.

Faux Old English dialogue is dropped in throughout the story. Pinned by the gaze of the magistrate in England, Larry tries to explain: "Ya seeith, it was like thisith!" When Moe takes a carelessly swung branch in the face he says, "Why don't ye look where ye swisheth?" Even Chief Rain in the Puss instructs his braves, "Giveth them the works."

If there's an ill portent amidst the charm and humor, it's that *Back to the Woods* is the first Stooges short to utilize stock footage from one of the boys' earlier films, in this case, a canoe's speedboat-quick escape across a lake, which comes from *Whoops, I'm an Indian* (see "The Stooges Out West").

IN ANCIENT ERYSIPELAS, EMPEROR OCTOPUS GRABUS ORDERS ALL REDHEADED women aged eighteen to twenty-two to present themselves at the palace, for inspection as potential brides. One such lovely, Diane (Marjorie Deanne), hides in the shop of potters Mohicus, Laricus, and Curleycue. The boys fight for her freedom but all four are finally dragged before the nearsighted emperor (Vernon Dent). Diane (whom the emperor calls "Diana") is able to make herself scarce (in fact, she disappears from the whole film), giving Curleycue the opportunity to slip into drag and divert Grabus. When the emperor declares that he and Curly (with whom he wishes to be left alone) are married, all three boys beat feet and leap through the nearest window.

Matri-Phony (1942) plays on historical accounts of the excesses of Caligula, Commodus, Nero, and other Roman emperors, which have sparked the public imagination for centuries, particularly since the late-18th-century publication of Edward Gibbon's *The History of the Decline and Fall of the Roman Empire*. Gibbon proposed that a sort of moral rot helped speed the empire's fall—and moral rot certainly seems to be the chief characteristic of Grabus. Portly, oversexed, and fumbling with comically anachronistic eyeglasses, Grabus claims to want marriage—though of course what he mainly wants is to get laid, even when the object of his desire is a disguised Curly.

Grabus is funny because his horniness makes him optimistically eager when the Stooges are horrified. Here are four people representing two camps, working in direct opposition to each other—and the emperor has no clue. The comic sexual tension is heightened because, after a while, Curly starts to buy into his own deception, coyly giggling and allowing himself to be seduced when Grabus flirts with him.

Writers Monte Collins (who also plays the emperor's aide) and Elwood Ullman produced a script that, though slick, probably didn't require a great deal of creative effort. A gag like a meal that fights back (a crab that steals Curly's olive and then squirts him with a pickle), though funny, was nevertheless venerable by 1942. In a later sequence that goes on and on in search of yoks that are never going to be there, guards repeatedly poke the boys in the keisters with spears. (The sound effects man must have worn out the violin pluck that signals a sharp poke.)

A "human puppet" gag involving an unconscious guard (Cy Schindell) is pretty well executed but can't recover from a stupidly forced setup: Grabus has ordered Schindell and the rest of the guards to arrest the Stooges immediately—so why does Schindell promptly sit down on a bench in front of a curtain? So that the Stooges can conk him on the head and move his head and arms in order to convince another guard that he's conscious, that's why. This is not organic humor.

Schindell and the Stooges would do the gag more skillfully five years later, in *Fright Night.*

Matri-Phony achieves better results with small, offhand gags, as when Larry lights a cigar with a Zippo. The short's dialogue is better still. When Curly is outfitted in drag, Moe unwisely tells him, "Go on, get sexy," and Curly's sighting of the crab on a buffet table causes him to exclaim, "A tarantula!" Later, he cheekily calls Grabus "Ocky."

Even familiar comic dialogue plays well here:

GRABUS
Even without my glasses I can see you're *ravishing*!

CURLY
I bet you say that to all the boys!

Pretty Marjorie Deanne, a perennial bit player during her brief career, is lively but exists only to propel the Stooges into action. She's a device, a human prop, which is a common fate of good-looking women in slapstick comedy.

Matri-Phony is distinguished by Dent's peerless enthusiasm as Grabus, and by some peculiar technical screwups. When a bit player moves out of frame in close-up, his entire head goes out of focus. A few moments later, editor Paul Borofsky uses outtake footage for a cutaway, suddenly reversing Moe and Larry's positions in the frame and showing Larry with a wine goblet that he wasn't holding an instant earlier. Cinematographer George Meehan's lighting is crisp but too emphatic: When somebody waggles a sword blade at the bottom of the frame, the sword's enormous shadow waggles on a wall at the *top* of the frame, like the shadow of an errant boom mic.

And then there's the voice of director Harry Edwards, shouting an instruction during the final shot: "Hey, Larry, grab hold and hold on!"

Larry immediately obeys, showing professionalism in a short that could have used a little bit more of it.

THE STOOGES' SECOND CIVIL WAR COMEDY, *UNCIVIL WAR BIRDS* (1946), OPENS with a rousing rendition of "Dixie" over the main titles. The short is a lovely one that faded from TV broadcast in the late 1960s and didn't reappear until more than a decade later, with studio-authorized re-releases of Stooges comedies to home video.

Television had wanted no part of the short because of a brief sequence in which Larry, Moe, and Curly mingle with Union soldiers while in blackface—with Curly in the stout "Mammy" role. If the Stooges can now be regarded in any way as controversial, this sequence in *Uncivil War Birds* is the reason.

The "blacked-up" humor of American minstrelsy (practiced by white and black performers alike) has a long and dubious history that dates to the 18th century. Minstrel shows became particularly pervasive across the South in the early 19th century as the region's cotton economy grew increasingly dependent on the labor of slaves.

The original Jim Crow was a blackface character portrayed in the 1830s by Thomas Dartmouth Rice, a white entertainer who called himself Daddy Rice. In Rice's most celebrated song-and-dance routine, Jim is a servile, foolish bumbler. In time, of course, "Jim Crow" became the shorthand term for racial segregation and the laws that enforced it. Beyond the essentially unfriendly visual nature of blackface, then, the tradition has a linguistic link to the most miserable and embarrassing interlude in all of American jurisprudence. As late as the early 1950s, such films as *Torch Song* (Joan Crawford), *I'll See You in My Dreams* (Doris Day), *Father Is a Bachelor* (William Holden), and *Somebody Loves Me* (Betty Hutton) included blackface numbers, without irony.

The Stooges' blackface turn, though by definition racial, isn't overtly racist. The boys don't become complete caricatures. They're just the Stooges with blackened pusses.

Is the sequence funny? Curly in Mammy guise is a startlingly funny image. So, objectively speaking, the sequence is funny. Of course, there's nothing objective about comedy in the first place, particularly not when race is involved. What tickles me may not tickle the person sitting next to me.

On other levels, *Uncivil War Birds* is a mixed bag. Opening and closing exteriors are sunlit delights, with the boys in muttonchop sideburns and handsome period costumes on a gorgeous antebellum-style estate, romancing their belles on the day that war is declared.

Because their (unspecified) state has divided loyalties, Moe and Larry enlist in the Union army, and Curly shows up in Confederate gear. During the remainder of the short, the area is combed by troops from both sides, prompting the boys to switch uniforms and claim each other as prisoners as it suits their chances for survival. The premise, as well as a very brief snippet of stock footage, is borrowed from Buster Keaton's 1939 Columbia short, *Mooching Through Georgia* (which takes place in Kentucky—go figure).

Philip Tannura's photography of the opening and closing sequences is perfectly gorgeous, "A"-picture quality, but he can't do much with the gray

Performer Profile: Vernon Dent
1895–1963

Authoritative Vernon Dent was beleaguered and bedeviled by the Stooges in more than fifty shorts. Sometimes a mere victim of circumstance; other times an irascible father, businessman, or other authority figure, Dent was physically imposing, yet he occasionally expressed a bit of pathos, as in *Malice in the Palace*, where he veers wonderfully from menace to blubbering misery as Hassan Ben Sober, a would-be big operator who is really just a doorman at the Oasis Hotel.

Vernon began his film career with Mack Sennett 1919, working mainly as a "heavy" opposite such comics as Hank Mann, Harry Gribbon, Harry Langdon, Billy Bevan, and Andy Clyde. He came to Columbia in 1935 and remained there until his retirement, doing most of his work for the two-reel unit but lending his authority to bits in B-features, as well.

He's priceless in *Dizzy Doctors* as a man who witnesses the Stooges use "Brighto" to inadvertently remove the finish from his car; as the absurdly goose-steeping Nazi fifth columnist in *They Stooge to Conga*; and as Emperor Octopus Grabus in *Matri-Phony*.

Chronic diabetes took Dent's sight in the 1950s. He passed away in 1963 at sixty-eight.

Roman romance about to run aground: Vernon Dent as grabby Octopus Grabus, who falls for Curly in *Matri-Phony* (1942).   *Photo courtesy of the Stoogeum*

sound-stage barn and smokehouse that figure in the action of the short's very long middle section. In these scenes, *Uncivil War Birds* looks low budget and even a little careworn.

Three gorgeous, enthusiastic starlets (Faye Williams, Eleanor Counts, and Marilyn Johnson) play the boys' fiancées (Mary Belle, Ringa Belle, and Lulu Belle, respectively). Also featured in the cast of more than twenty are such familiar players as Ted Lorch, Cy Schindell, and Joe Palma, as soldiers, and a lanky young actor and future producer named Maury Dexter, who's good as an excited dandy who announces that war has come at last.

Although Moe utters a surprisingly sexual line ("Y'all done ejaculated a mouthful!"), the short's two funniest moments are purely visual: All three boys, in Confederate uniforms, casually stroll through the front door of a mansion and blithely grab apples from a side table. The camera dollies back with them to reveal that the place is crammed with Union troops, much to the boys' shock. Later, when Curly is about to be executed by a Union firing squad, he's put in place against a wall, and an instant later he's quietly, magically, standing with the riflemen.

Although not feeling well by this time, Curly seems very much his "old self" in this short, which is reason enough to celebrate *Uncivil War Birds*.

SQUAREHEADS OF THE ROUND TABLE (1948), WHICH OPENS WITH A HANDSOME title card done up in Old English letters, is the first Stooges short to feature Philip Van Zandt, a highly skilled dramatic actor with a flair for dark comedy. Handsome in an imperious, almost feral way, Van Zandt (who is billed here as "Phil") is ideally cast as the Black Prince, a nobleman who schemes with Sir Satchel (Harold Brauer) to murder King Arthur (Vernon Dent), take power, and coerce beautiful Princess Elaine (Christine McIntyre) into marriage.

Although writer-director Ed Bernds invokes the legendary King Arthur, who (if he actually existed) ruled Britain in the early 6th century, the handsome sets and costumes of *Squareheads* suggest the late 12th century, the period of Richard the Lionheart. In fact, the sets were constructed for a 1946 Columbia adventure starring Cornel Wilde, *The Bandit of Sherwood Forest*; as numerous retellings of the legend make clear, Robin Hood was a great supporter of Richard.

As for Elaine, life is complicated by her romance with a lowly commoner, Cedric the blacksmith (the appealing and unassuming Jacques O'Mahoney). When Cedric finds troubadours Moe, Shemp, and Larry in his shop, all four agree to become allies, and see that Cedric wins Elaine.

Of course, the Black Prince is a formidable obstacle, and Elaine's father is another. After some close scrapes, Cedric and the boys expose the Black Prince's conspiracy.

Squareheads is one of the best shorts of the Shemp era, and is in the top rank of the Stooges' entire two-reel output. It has many delights, chief among them Christine McIntyre. Always beautiful, always funny, and invariably a good sport, she didn't have nearly enough opportunities to show off her trained, bel canto-style operatic soprano. Here, though, she exchanges musical bars with the Stooges during a serenade attended by the lovestruck Cedric. Working with Donizetti's sextet from the tragic opera *Lucia di Lammermoor*, the Stooges express Cedric's love in music (while inadvertently abusing each other with their instruments): "Oh, Elaine, Elaine, come out . . . the big boy is here/We see the coast is clear. . . ."

Elaine responds in kind, proclaiming her love in song and finishing by adding that she'll "raise the shade, the lovely shade/When the coast is clear." McIntyre's trill of a voice, plus the elegant, décolletage gown she wears, add up to joy.

Set pieces and dialogue are strong. In the opening sequence, the Stooges use Cedric's shop to remove Shemp from the chest piece of a suit of armor. "I was always poppin' rivets," Shemp explains, "so I had my tailor spot-weld me!" (Like Elwood Ullman and others who wrote for the Stooges, Bernds loved anachronisms. When one of the king's guards pauses in his nighttime rounds, he inserts his key into a night watchman's clock.)

A pair of burly guards sent to find Cedric invades the shop. Cedric doesn't seem to be around, and the boys explain that they're just troubadours. To demonstrate, they launch into (without being asked, of course) a little three-part harmony: "Soo, we stuck our little tootsies in the waater/And *ducked* under the waves, we did, ha *haa*!"

Is this brilliant? Probably, yes.

The boys finally meet Cedric and cast their lot with him. Following the serenade—which Bernds shot at eye level as well as from a dramatic higher vantage that shows off the good-looking courtyard set—the Black Prince spirits Elaine from the bedroom, leaving the king to take her place inside. The boys toss gravel against the window to catch Elaine's attention and finally attach a note to a rock, which catches the king flush in the forehead.

After climbing a trellis, Shemp enters the room and speaks to the figure hidden beneath the bedcovers, assuming the person to be Elaine. "[Your father's] got a puss like a snappin' turtle!" Shemp chortles, greatly amused by his own wit.

Captured (after the king has taken a thumping fall when he tries to pursue Shemp back down the trellis), Cedric and the boys are looking at a night in the dungeon, followed by morning appointments with the headsman. That fellow sits at a grinding wheel, putting a fine edge on the blade of his axe. Satisfied, he cheerfully says, "See you tomorrow, bright and early!"

The Stooges don't find execution an appealing prospect:

MOE
I'm gonna get myself a cheap lawyer!

SHEMP (mournfully)
And I just bought two new hats!

> *LARRY*
> I *can't* die! I haven't seen *The Jolson Story!*

A medium-size loaf of bread sent by Elaine contains chisels, mallets, a hacksaw, and an enormous sledgehammer. The boys don't make any progress on the bars at all but escape when their cell door mysteriously drifts open. ("I feel a draft!" Larry says.)

The boys leave the tools for Cedric and head upstairs, where they conceal themselves in armor and make ready to perform a rattly soft-shoe to Stephen Foster's "Old Folks at Home." But before they begin the number, Shemp and Larry wonder what they're going to do for music. "Turn on the radio," Moe says. "Are you kiddin'?" Larry responds. "This is ancient times!"

Moe: "This is an ancient radio!"

Fruit thrown by the Stooges into the heralds' trumpets prevents the sounding of the fanfare that the Black Prince has designated as the signal to murder the king. When the heralds finally summon sufficient lungpower to dislodge the fruit, the stuff splatters the Black Prince and Satchel.

Cedric and Elaine are reunited, but the king is appalled that his daughter wishes to marry "a lowly smith." Shemp sets Arthur's mind at ease: "Take it easy, king! Millions 'a women marry Smiths every year!"

Phil Van Zandt (by now billed as "Philip"), Vernon Dent, Jock Mahoney (by now the star of TV's *The Range Rider*), and Christine McIntyre return in a few minutes of new scenes, shot in two days, for the 1954 remake of *Squareheads, Knutzy Knights*. Felix Adler's script adds little that's really significant, other than that the Stooges are specifically summoned to cheer up Elaine, who pines for Cedric, who's gone missing.

The Black Prince is behind the disappearance, of course, aided once again by Sir Satchel, played by actor Harold Brauer in old footage and by Joe Palma—who looks nothing like Brauer—in new scenes. (Although nearly all of *Knutzy Knights* is six-year-old footage by Ed Bernds, only Jules White is credited as director.)

White's take on the fruit-in-the-horns gag is longer and less funny, and he reshot the "marry a Smith" joke—also to lesser effect.

Adler's mini-script offers one pretty funny line, uttered by Larry when the boys' shenanigans fail to cheer up Elaine: "I can't understand it! This routine killed 'em in Cucamonga!"

On its face, *Knutzy Knights* is nearly as funny as *Squareheads of the Round Table,* but a new title slapped onto footage that audiences have seen before isn't enough to give producer-director White a pass. (Only the exigencies of the business side of filmmaking, and the need to meet a release schedule, can do that.)

If there's any fresh interest here at all, it's in the one-sheet poster: Christine McIntyre, seated in a leg-art pose, dominates the lower right, while the boys' heads sprawl across the top. Moe and Shemp are recognizable, but Larry looks like Larry (vaguely) with a lot of Curly DNA. It's very odd.

Because Vernon Dent's chronic diabetes was beginning to seriously bother him by the early 1950s, *Knutzy Knights* is the last Stooges short in which this marvelous comic actor appears in new footage. The loss of his talents was a significant blow to the quality and élan not just of the Stooges' shorts but also to the entire output of the studio's two-reel unit.

FIDDLERS THREE (1948) IS A MILD EXPERIMENT IN GENRE-MIXING AND STYLE, as well as the second consecutive Stooges short to take advantage of the fulsome sets built for *The Bandit of Sherwood Forest*. Once again cast as troubadours, the boys spend their days entertaining King Cole (Vernon Dent), who is indeed a merry old soul. Amiable and white-bearded, he laughs heartily at the Stooges' antics and songs. In vignettes shot by cinematographer Allen Siegler against heavy gray, intentionally stark backgrounds, the boys' songs are visualized: Shemp, in storybook facial makeup, plays Jack Be Nimble and nearly fries his rear on a candlestick; in another, Larry is a mannish Little Miss Muffet (when the spider shows up, a wire rig pulls Larry upward and out of the frame, and a woman's scream is overdubbed on the soundtrack). In the final vignette, Moe (the Pieman) and Shemp (Simple Simon) tangle over pastry, with Moe uncharacteristically admitting defeat with an anguished "Waughh!"

The vignettes are novel, and while scripter Felix Adler and director Jules White get points for style, the little tableaux aren't nearly as funny as the king's uproarious laughter suggests. At best, they're good for a smile.

Almost as if in anticipation of this, the vignettes are preceded by a smiling command from the king, to the Stooges and his court: "Everybody laugh!"—and they do, for a tedious fifty-three seconds. Although an accomplished professional filmmaker, Jules White had a curious habit of defying conventional comic wisdom by milking gags way beyond their shelf lives. Whether to fill time or because he honestly thought that a whole lot of something is always better than a little, this sort of force-fed stretching shows up frequently in Stooges shorts and in other two-reelers directed by White. (See, for example, the discussion of *Don't Throw That Knife* in "The Stooges and the Fairer Sex.")

As to the plot of *Fiddlers Three*, the Stooges search the palace for Princess Alicia (Virginia Hunter) after she's been spirited away by evil court magician Murgatroyd (Philip Van Zandt; the script spells the character's name as "Mergatroyd," a less common but acceptable variation). During a disastrous attempt to shoe Sue the mule ("Shoeing Sue we must do! Shoe shoe shoo shoo shoo woo woo!"), the boys are kicked through a wall that abuts the dungeon hiding place of Murgatroyd's cohorts, who keep an idle eye on the trussed-up princess.

The climax of the short involves Murgatroyd's frustrated attempts to perform a sword-in-the-box trick for the king, unaware that the Stooges have climbed through the box's false bottom from a rope ladder hanging in the dungeon below. When the boys can no longer stand being poked, they burst from the box and accuse Murgatroyd of kidnapping Alicia. The princess is saved!

Aside from the ill-conceived laugh-or-else business, the gags in *Fiddlers Three*, though familiar, are agreeably funny. When Alicia first goes missing, the king barks, "Notify the FBI . . . Flanagan, Brannigan and Iskovitch!" While the boys labor to get shoes on the mule, Shemp is pushed onto a bed of hot coals and takes great pleasure when he plunks his behind into a tub of water, sending up great clouds of steam. A moment later, Shemp bends over the mule and thoughtlessly extends his own foot backwards, which is promptly nailed with a shoe by the inattentive Moe.

When Shemp plays with a bellows that emits a baritone, "Bee Ohh, Bee Ohh!" the short is giving us a sonic reference to the advertising and marketing phenomenon of body odor (BO), a term that was dreamed up by Odor-Ro-No deodorant in 1919 and adopted later by many products, including Lifebuoy soap and Listerine.

Murgatroyd's assistant is a leggy, very tall chorus-girl type (Sherry O'Neil), and in a smart running gag, the kidnappers, the Stooges, and even King Cole are distracted whenever she walks by. Adopting Groucho-like crouches, with hands folded at their backs, the men follow wherever the girl leads, the soundtrack humming with a muted chorus of wolf whistles.

Beautiful Sherry O'Neil was a startling physical specimen: lithe and blessed with a very slender, vaguely unconventional face. She has no dialogue in *Fiddlers Three*, but by the 1960s she was a busy TV actress. She's very funny, for example, as a rumpled and bespectacled "plain Jane" war correspondent whose looks appall a gaggle of sailors in "Beauty and the Beast," a 1963 episode of *McHale's Navy*. The men change their tune after O'Neil falls into the water, loses her specs, and emerges from her quarters wearing only a blanket.

The Stooges' ordeal inside Murgatroyd's magic box goes just where you expect it to, but you laugh anyway. An enormous, snaggle-toothed saw rakes Larry's head, then his butt, and finally his crotch as he struggles to avoid the sharp teeth. The saw is long and flexible, and so there's much whipsaw action inside the box as Larry and Moe use the blade to exchange slaps in the face. Outside, Murgatroyd hefts a mallet to hammer a sword into an unseen obstruction (Moe's head), and then pulls out a blade that's collapsed into a comic squiggle, like half-dried pasta. Still pressing on, Murgatroyd executes a flourish and removes the saw—with one of the boys' boxer shorts hanging from the end. The usually imperturbable Murgatroyd is mortified: "Ohh, sire!"

Fiddlers Three was shot in four days. Jules White spent a single day in the spring of 1953 shooting new footage for a remake, *Musty Musketeers* (1954). Composer Hugo Friedhofer came up with some oddly programmatic music for the opening sequence, while Jack White wrote a few minutes of new scenes that, among other things, introduce the boys' beautiful fiancées, Tillieth (Diana Darrin), Millieth (Norma Randall), and Lillyeth (Ruth Godfrey White).

Vernon Dent (in his penultimate Stooges short) returns as King Cole, and a mute actress named Wanda Perry hides her face behind a fan as she doubles for the absent Virginia Hunter. Columbia player Frank Sully does his rubber-faced shtick as the king's attendant, and the Stooges engage in a ferocious swordfight with Murgatroyd (Van Zandt, back for more) and his accomplices. In that sequence's best moment, a madly dueling Larry is forced backwards almost onto the floor, where his left hand inserts itself into a heavy vase—which turns out to be a terrific weapon!

With Murgatroyd vanquished, the Stooges' gals arrive to greet their heroes. A stationary camera and very poor blocking kill the final sequence, in which each group of three runs to the other from opposite sides of the frame. When all six meet in the middle, they bonk their heads and collapse in a lovestruck heap.

Meanwhile, audiences aren't exactly collapsing with laughter.

THE STOOGES' FIRST CAVEMAN COMEDY, *I'M A MONKEY'S UNCLE* (1948), BEGINS with a title card that invokes Darwin and monkeys, and that expresses a hope that the monkeys won't be insulted by what they're about to see. Well, let's put it this way: The monkeys will have no reason to feel inferior after observing the Stone Age Stooges at work and play.

Anticipating the 1960 arrival of *The Flintstones*, the short offers an inventive catalogue of anachronisms: Shemp ignites a fire with his "trusty rock lighter"; Moe combs his hair with the stiff spine of a fish skeleton and then pats on his favorite scent, "eu de Colonna" (for comic Jerry Colonna); cavegirls speak and act like silly high schoolers, and the milkman shows up, with his own cow. After Moe and Larry bathe (Larry just *flicks* a drop or two on his face and then shivers wildly, as if he's been completely immersed), the boys take their palm-frond towels from a towel rack and rub themselves dry.

The short's physical action is a sort of "greatest hits" compilation that's familiar but energetically presented. When Shemp chops wood, a good-sized log flies upward, out of frame, and returns a long moment later as kindling that cracks him on the head. Larry does his "I can't see! I can't see!" routine, and Moe undertakes long and heroic battle with a saucy duck in a sequence that reworks Curly's epic clash from *A Ducking They Did Go* (see "The Stooges and the Sporting Life"). At the climax, the boys dispatch a trio of enemy cavemen by firing mud, rocks, eggs, and even a skunk from their tree-branch catapult. (Naturally, Moe is accidentally victimized by one of these missiles, after Larry is stung by a bee and releases the branch too soon.)

The Stooges are at war because of women. Moe is frankly obsessed with a cave cutie named Aggie, invoking her name as he fitfully sleeps during the short's opening sequence. Moe mumbles happily and pats the sleeping Shemp, and then turns to Larry, pulling out big tufts of hair as if they were flower petals. Larry awakens after the painful second tug and stares at the sleeping Moe—who's still making with the pillow talk—and then looks around in confusion, as if he's going to find an explanation for Moe's lovestruck assault. (Look carefully at Larry during this throwaway moment; his body language and facial expression are priceless.)

When Aggie (Virginia Hunter, somewhat more lively here than in *Fiddlers Three*) shows up with her girlfriends, the boys grab enormous clubs and—in the best fantasy-caveman fashion—conk the girls on their heads (to wonderfully resonant sound effects) once, twice. The gals just keep giggling. Aggie says, "Let's just ignore them, girls!"

Introductions are finally made, and the boys greet Aggie and her friends, Maggie (blonde beauty Nancy Saunders) and Baggie (the tall and pleasantly plain Dee Green, who has her finest moment in the boys' 1947 triumph *Brideless Groom*; see "The Stooges and the Fairer Sex").

The instant Shemp gets a look at Baggie he takes off as if pursued by a sabre-toothed tiger, but Baggie is determined. She races after Shemp and brings him down in a crushing tackle, staking her claim to him. Whether he likes it or not, Shemp has acquired a mate.

When the ladies' outraged former boyfriends arrive on the scene, Cy Schindell shouts a particularly funny line: "You stole our girls, you horse thieves!" (Joe Palma and Bill Wallace play the other intruders.)

The aforementioned skunk turns the tide of battle. The victorious Stooges hoot like monkeys and embrace their women.

Okay, monkeys *will* be insulted.

The then-standard four-day shooting schedule was observed for *I'm a Monkey's Uncle*, so gags are developed carefully, and the boys have time for funny asides, as when Larry unwisely says to Moe, "Hang up my towel to dry—and *don't* wrinkle it!" You can guess what happens next.

Because Jules White and writer Zion Myers (White's co-director on MGM's very peculiar "Dogville" comedy shorts of the early 1930s) do workmanlike jobs, it's a shame that *I'm a Monkey's Uncle* is undercut by a dreadful sound stage tricked up as a Stone Age landscape. A pond reflects every one of the multitude of lights needed by cinematographer George Kelley (whose name is misspelled by some sources as "Kelly") to illuminate the stage. Trees and foliage are impressively good-looking, but when your eye wanders to the middle distance, the only thing you see out there is a featureless, light-gray void.

White insisted on the sound stage for budgetary reasons, of course, but it's really not his fault. He knew better than many other executives that a buck was always precious at Columbia.

In a rare occurrence, the redo of *I'm a Monkey's Uncle, Stone Age Romeos* (1955), is funnier than the original. White and writer Felix Adler accomplish this with about seven minutes of new material that bookends footage from the earlier film and establishes the Stooges as present-day explorers who strike a lucrative deal with the Museum of Natural History and its curator, B. Bopper (Emil Sitka, wearing eyeglasses for the legally blind). The boys—handsome in suits and nicely trimmed beards—assure Mr. Bopper that they'll return from their expedition with proof of what Bopper strongly suspects—that Stone Age men still exist in remote corners of the world.

Six minutes of new setup lead right into footage from *Monkey's Uncle*, with a few sequences shortened or cut altogether. This time, there's no milkman and no bathing sequence. The boys' morning spruce-up is truncated, and some funny byplay between Shemp and Baggie is gone. The climactic battle remains, however, and as the girls run to embrace the Stooges (which is the last shot of the earlier short), the scene momentarily fades to white, and we realize that we've been looking at a movie screen in B. Bopper's office. As the boys promised, they've returned with the footage Bopper wanted so badly.

When Bopper steps from the office to cut the boys a check, the Stooges loudly congratulate themselves for putting one over on him. They're confident (and rightly so) that Bopper is too dumb to realize that *they* are the men in the caveman footage, and that he'll never see through their phony beards.

But Bopper overhears, and like any reasonable museum curator, he pulls a revolver and perforates the Stooges' asses before accidentally shooting himself in the foot.

Anytime the boys imagine they're too smart for the room, and then get found out, is good fun, and an important part of the Stooges' appeal. We empathize

Don't forget to tip your hairdresser. Moe's Stone Age beauty regimen in *I'm a Monkey's Uncle* (1948).   *Photo courtesy of the Stoogeum*

and identify with them only in degrees. If they're hungry, we remember what hunger feels like. When their bosses or wives kick them around, we share their frustration. But because we're invariably invited to feel superior to the boys, we don't mind when they get caught in their own hare-brained deceptions, and are punished. We laugh because we'd never do anything as dumb.

Of course we wouldn't.

Stone Age Romeos would be a small gem if not for another instance of Jules White's maddening habit of milking gags longer than a stupid farmer milks a dry cow. When the boys produce a map in Bopper's office, White holds on a close-up of the paper—with a dead-silent soundtrack—for an absurd fifty-two seconds. Apparently, the audience must be allowed time to read the names of such places as the Hot Sea and the Tot Sea, Giva-Dam, Mish Mosh, and Udopia. The names are cute, but White's treatment is dreadful. Better to have offered a brief insert of the map and then let the boys explicate the silly names in dialogue. At the very least, Shemp could have taken a funny slap after saying something inappropriate about Giva-Dam.

Those fifty-two seconds can never be returned to us, nor can they be completely redeemed, but they do give us an opportunity to chuckle at some Yiddish humor. Shmow Lake isn't far from the Schnozzle Mts. (sic), and there's a mysterious place up north called Ferblongent. The last is an incorrect spelling of the Yiddish *farblondget*, or *farblondzhet*, which means confused or bewildered—but it sounds funnier in Yiddish, doesn't it?

Stone Age Romeos was released in 1955. At that time in American pop culture, very little mass media that appealed to children exposed Jewish and gentile kids to the pleasures of Yiddish. Harvey Kurtzman's *MAD* magazine was a significant exception. The Stooges' two-reelers were another. In this, the films have a certain cultural uniqueness. You might even call them *bateitik*.

WHEN THE SMILING EGYPTIANS (MOE, SHEMP, AND LARRY) MAKE THE MISTAKE of selling a lemon of a used chariot to a captain in King Rootentooten's guard, they're dragged to the palace for punishment. Rootentooten (Vernon Dent) is unimpressed by what he sees: "Who are these sand fleas?" he demands. A few minutes later, the boys are saved from death because Shemp maladroitly (and mostly accidentally) extracts a tooth that's been bothering the hell out of the king. Installed by the grateful monarch as royal chamberlains, the Stooges enjoy ancient Egypt's version of the life of Riley—at least until the perpetually angry captain (Ralph Dunn) decides to get rid of them.

That's the setup to *Mummy's Dummies* (1948), which spins historical humor from popular interest in Egyptology. The tomb of the young, doomed 18th Dynasty monarch King Tutankhamun had been opened in 1922. People around the world were fascinated by the tomb's exotic beauty and riches—as well as by rumors of a curse. Various comic short films and animated cartoons of the 1920s and '30s used ancient Egypt and mummies as springboards, but the best straight-faced treatment was Universal's *The Mummy*, a 1932 vehicle for Boris

Karloff. Universal followed up in the 1940s with a successful "Mummy" series starring Lon Chaney, Jr. The most recent of those thrillers, *The Mummy's Curse*, had been released in 1944, just four years before *Mummy's Dummies*. (The Stooges themselves had already had fun with mummies, in 1939's *We Want Our Mummy*; see "The Stooges Abroad.")

A mummy figures only marginally in *Mummy's Dummies*, but its appearance is striking—not least because the mummy is Shemp. As the captain and his men chase the boys through the bowels of the palace, Moe and Larry clamber into a wicker basket (which they subsequently negotiate through the corridors with the aid of a very 20th–century periscope). Shemp is left to his own devices and finally hides in a standing sarcophagus. When the captain pulls it open, he's startled to see a mummy, its partially unwrapped face (which fills the screen) in stygian shadow, the pupils of the eyes disquietingly illuminated by intense pin-pricks of light. Artful treatment by cinematographer Allen Siegler and Shemp's strong features combine to create an ominous image that wouldn't be out of place in any of the period's dead-serious horror thrillers.

Far removed from ancient Egypt, yet the foundation of an amusing sidelight of *Mummy's Dummies*, are used cars. Because of wartime production needs, no new cars were manufactured in America between 1942 and 1945. The absence of new models gave a tremendous boost to dealers in used cars—after all, a shopper could easily be induced to trade his tired '34 model for a used '40 or a '41. Buyer eagerness encouraged a lot of price gouging and other unscrupulous dealings. Late-model autos that looked good cosmetically were often wrecks under the skin, and many buyers drove home with overpriced cars that were frankly dangerous. Gouging continued after the war and was aggravated by col-lusion between new- and used-car dealers. (MGM's very popular "Crime Does Not Pay" two-reel series warned consumers of this chronic problem in a bluntly shocking 1941 entry, *Coffins on Wheels*.)

When Larry busily coats a chariot in new paint that Moe will pass off as "original," the situation set up by scripter Elwood Ullman and director Ed Bernds doesn't just give Larry an opportunity to slather his paint brush across Moe's butt and face—it's also a cheerfully cynical comment on the state of the used-car buying experience.

The Stooges quickly close and lock the gate after the captain wheels his purchase from the lot—and promptly gets wet paint on his hand and then steps right through the chariot's rotted floorboards. We're in ancient Egypt, but the scene played out every day on Crenshaw Boulevard's "auto row" in L.A., and on similar thoroughfares across the country.

Sets seen in *Mummy's Dummies* are handsome but not eye-filling, so the supporting cast counts for a lot. Vernon Dent is perfect as the mercurial Rootentooten, and Philip Van Zandt brings oily calculation to his role as the royal tax collector, who conspires with the captain to cheat the king out of revenue. Actress Dee Green, with blacked-out teeth, plays Rootentooten's dumpy daughter, who scares the pants off the boys when the king announces she's available for marriage. Familiar Columbia starlet Suzanne Ridgeway looks smashing in a silent bit as a slave girl.

Finally, in a scene that says much more than what we actually hear, attractive bit player Jean Spangler (as a slave) has an amusing exchange with Shemp:

SHEMP
Some perfume, sister, what brand do you use?

SLAVE GIRL
Sphinx.

SHEMP
I know, but what brand do you use?

Beneath the bandages, Shemp is all man: forward, obtuse, and angling to make a little history at night.

8

The Stooges Puncture High Society

In which the boys run afoul of a gopher bomb; abuse a flower named Bess; recycle plenty of pies; break the old man's heart; get into some bad spumoni; fantasize about skunk; eat a powder puff; make like woodpeckers; cool off a half-dressed dame; watch poppy seeds walkin'; and put the "M" in moron.

So here come professors Richmond and Nichols down the street, walking along Larchmont Boulevard, with the afternoon sun burning into their black waistcoats and opera hats, the HOLLYWOODLAND sign on the San Gabriels behind them, and they're not thinking about the movies. No, they're thinking deep thoughts, and they're talking about the inherent nature of man.

For reasons that are going to remain unclear, Richmond (Harry Holman) has convinced himself that if he takes a man "from the lowest strata of society" and turns him into a gentleman with exposure to a new and improved environment, then *something* besides just Richmond's theory will be proved correct. Nichols (Robert Graves) says hogwash—*heredity* is the determining factor in appropriate behavior and socialization and all the other swell things that encourage learned older men to walk around L.A.'s Windsor Square neighborhood in waistcoats at noon.

Meanwhile, at the curb, the Stooges are garbage men struggling to master their trade. Empty cans have a way of getting loose from Curly and soaring over the truck to pelt Moe and Larry on their heads. Richmond and Nichols walk into this noisy mayhem, and a bet is forced: If Richmond can turn *these* three into gentlemen, Nichols will hand over $10,000. If Richmond fails, Nichols walks away with ten Gs of Richmond's money (which, during the Depression, could have kept a family of five going for, oh, eight years).

For their part, the Stooges are horrified at the prospect of becoming gentlemen. "It'll break the old man's heart," Moe laments.

Director Del Lord and writer Felix Adler keep *Hoi Polloi* (1935) humming along like a well-greased locomotive. You watch the short with the intention of taking notes and you have to hit PAUSE over and over because the jokes and the gags fly at you with the speed and force of a thousand mailbags hurled from a thousand locomotives. *Hoi Polloi* is so fabulous it's exhausting.

Installed at Professor Richmond's mansion, the boys try to learn table manners, read aloud, and pick up some respectable dance moves. But when they're introduced to society at a posh party, Richmond learns—like the earlier Henry

Higgins and the later Humbert Humbert—that human beings are not clay that can be formed into a work of art intended to suit an arrogant, presumptuous artist. Either willingly or (most maddeningly, as with the Stooges) unwillingly, your subject will defy you, and you will have failed.

Performer Profile: Phyllis Crane
1912–82

Petite, dark-eyed Phyllis Crane is a delightful presence in numerous Stooges shorts of the 1930s, bringing a combination of innocence and mischief to her roles. A native of Calgary, Canada, she undertook her movie career in 1928 and worked steadily in shorts and features until her retirement in 1937. In features, Crane's talent was wasted in uncredited bits; the noticeable roles came in shorts. She's amusing in *A Pain in the Pullman* as the dreaming girl who gets a kiss from Curly; quite adorable in a tutu in *Pop Goes the Easel*; and is wonderfully bright-eyed and spontaneous in the society comedy *Hoi Polloi*. Fans probably recall her best from the last, in a hilarious scene in which she corners Moe on a sofa and gets New-Agey before there was a New Age: "You must believe in the hypothesis of occult power!" she breathes.

Phyllis's two-reel career took her to Educational, Pathé, Lane Comedy Corporation, and Columbia. She worked with many comics other than the Stooges, including Andy Clyde, Buster Keaton, Monte Collins, and Tom Kennedy.

During cocktails, sparkly Phyllis Crane (right) brings out the best in Moe in the Stooges' peerless "society" comedy *Hoi Polloi* (1935).   *Photo courtesy of the Stoogeum*

But the boys try to please. During an imaginary meal, Curly lifts his pinkies when he slurps coffee from his saucer, and Larry eats beans with a knife. Moe becomes the professor's proxy, vigorously slapping his pals to keep them in line. Finally, Curly refuses to speak with his mouth full, pleasing Richmond until Curly slips a finger into his teeth and says, "Say, ya ain't got a toothpick on ya, have ya, bud?"

When the pretty dance instructor (Geneva Mitchell) tells the boys to do everything she does, and then is sent into frantic gyrations by a bee sting, Moe does backflips, Curly's hand becomes a cobra that nearly bites him, and Larry gets the feeling and slips into a hand-clappin' jive shuffle.

On the dance floor at the party, a sofa spring attaches itself to the seat of Curly's tuxedo pants and turns him into a jack-in-the-box because his gargantuan partner (Blanche Payson) keeps knocking him on his ass. Larry loses a shoe (he wears no socks, by the way) and mounts a search on his hands and knees, getting under the dancers' feet and making them fall. Curly accidentally unravels Moe's jacket, eats a lipstick, and then tries to steal the silverware.

When the boys are introduced to the skeptical professor Nichols, Larry sidles forward and says, "Brother, can you spare a nickel?"

Bad breeding is apparently catching because the social set ultimately takes its cues from the Stooges—poking, slapping, punching, and whinnying—turning against each other like a roomful of perverse two-year-olds. Richmond's theory of environment just got run over by that locomotive we mentioned earlier.

Harry Holman—kindly looking and inhumanly patient—is one of the best actors the Stooges ever worked with. His soft but eccentrically modulated voice is a particular treat. Starlet Phyllis Crane, as Richmond's wide-eyed daughter, is so sweet and so subtly funny—so *with* all the gags—that you want to eat her up like a good sorbet. Dorothy Moore, Curly's special friend in *Calling All Curs* (see "The Stooges on the Job"), is decorative as a dancing guest, and Stooges regular Bud Jamison plays the butler. He has no lines but glowers at the Stooges with unconcealed hatred, and is there at the end to help Nichols and Richmond crown the boys with bottles.

Temporarily down for the count, the Stooges will return from whence they came, happily unimproved by their flirtation with high society, which is comprised of nothing, after all, but hoi polloi.

The Stooges have another go-round with the environment vs. heredity question in a clever redo called *Half-Wits Holiday* (1947). It was directed in May 1946 by Jules White, from a script by Zion Myers, so it's more bluntly, viscerally violent than Lord's *Hoi Polloi*. Professor Sedlitz (Ted Lorch) catches the backswing of Moe's sledgehammer full in the belly, and when lunch is served, the boys run right over the butler, Sappington (Emil Sitka, in his first appearance with the boys), leaving the imprints of their shoes on his face.

This time, the proponent of environment is Vernon Dent's Professor Quackenbush (an oddly explicit nod to Groucho Marx), and he has a daughter, Lulu (former Powers model Barbara Slater), who strikes Moe and Larry's fancy.

During a funny seduction scene at lunch, Moe promises to smother Lulu in furs: "Only the best for you. Mink, skunk, porcupine!" Moe thinks he's playing handsy with Lulu beneath the table, but the other hand belongs to Larry, who's similarly smitten.

Curly reprises the raised-pinky gag from *Hoi Polloi* and swipes the silverware, too. And when the frustrated Quackenbush pulls out his hair, Curly eagerly picks up the tufts and slaps them onto his shorn skull.

The boys' society debut is nicely mounted, though not as elaborately as in *Hoi Polloi*—budgets during the late '40s were noticeably slimmer than before, so the lighting is a little harsh, almost perfunctory, and the short lacks the visual richness that the plot demands. Still, the cast includes plenty of willing bit players and extras, and White keeps things perking as the party devolves into an all-out pie fight. (In a cute throwaway aside at the beginning of the sequence, guest Symona Boniface—particularly wonderful in this short—mentions to Lulu, "I'm allergic to pastry.")

The boys are just happy not to be workingmen anymore. "You know," Moe explains to a guest, "this is our first entrée into society. We find it very delightful!"

Unhappy guests reflect on the wreckage of the climactic pie fight in *Half-Wits Holiday* (1947), the last Stooges short to star Curly Howard. Gooey victims include Emil Sitka (between Larry and Moe) and the redoubtable Symona Boniface (second from right). Note the shadow of the mic boom above Symona (not visible in the film itself). *Photo courtesy of the Stoogeum*

Larry is compelled to add, "So different than our first party at the reform school!"

The gag that's dear to every Stooges fan involves a pie that Moe has taken away from Larry and tossed onto the ceiling as Symona approaches. She's intrigued by the boys and wants to chat; cutaways to the pie as it gradually loses its grip on the ceiling establish why Moe is visibly agitated. "Young man, what's wrong? You act as though the sword of Damocles is hanging over your head!"

Moe gets the heck out of there, and when Symona looks up, the gooey pie finally gives in to gravity and drops onto her face. When she flicks a gob of it aside, the gob catches another guest, and the pie fight is on.

Curly appears tired and sluggish in *Half-Wits Holiday*. His history of small strokes finally caught up with him. Pencil notations on Jules White's script reassign portions of Curly's dialogue to Larry or delete it altogether. On the scheduled final day of shooting, Curly had one more sequence to do, the pie fight. When he didn't respond to the assistant director's call, Moe found him slumped in a chair. Moe's daughter, Joan Howard Maurer, relates that Curly's "head drooped onto his chest, [he was] unable to speak, tears rolling down his cheeks." This stroke was a bad one and ended Curly's brilliant career. The great comic had fought heroically and lost, but at least *Half-Wits Holiday* is funny, solid, and ambitious.

After Joe Besser joined the team, *Half-Wits Holiday* was remade, scene for scene and with plentiful stock footage, as *Pies and Guys* (1958). Jules White directed once again, and his brother Jack wrote the script—that is, as much that was needed to redo Zion Myers's original, which isn't much at all.

Beautiful Greta Thyssen takes the Lulu role, and solid character players Milton Frome and Gene Roth come aboard as the professors. Barbara Slater appears in stock footage (reduced to a nameless guest), and Emil Sitka returns for a few new scenes as Sappington. Regular player Harriette Tarler has a good bit as Countess Shpritzvasser, who eventually has pie trouble.

And then there's the reprise of the "moron gag," which was in bad taste in *Half-Wits Holiday* in 1947 and in crummy taste in 1957, when *Pies and Guys* was shot. Shortly after meeting the boys, the professors remark that the three seem to be morons. "*And* we're organized!" Moe proclaims proudly. He pulls out an "AAM" button, the "Amalgamated Association of Morons." And then the boys strike medically spastic poses and chorus, "We are morons tried and true/Now we'll do our yell for you!—Gnghh, aghh, rowrr, nyaaa, oowowwer!"

Morons, get it? (All right, it's hard not to smile at this, but really!)

Where *Half-Wits Holiday* was noticeably less opulent than *Hoi Polloi*, *Pies and Guys* is a careworn version of *Half-Wits*. Shooting schedules for "new" shorts were by this time two days, so nobody was authorizing fancy shmancy sets and decorations. Nearly the entire pie fight is stock footage in which the women's 1947 fashions look absurdly out of date, particularly in contrast to the chic outfits worn by Thyssen and Tarler. Those two actresses, and Joe (who's game but obviously not comfortable with flung pastry), participate in the fight via close-up inserts; the same goes for Frome and Roth.

Editor Harold White cuts it all together well enough, so he should get a raise. Greta Thyssen, though, needs a talking-to because she closes her eyes long before the pie with her name on it hits home. But with a two-day schedule, Jules White should be doing retakes?

ANTS IN THE PANTRY (1936) MIGHT EASILY BE PLACED IN THE "ON THE JOB" category of Stooges shorts but for the fact that the silly vicissitudes of high society—and the boys' dismantling of them—are emphasized with gleeful fervor. The boys are inept exterminators whose boss has sent them out to drum up business, but their primary comic function here is to screw up a stuffy luncheon put on by society dowager Mrs. Burlap (onetime silent-screen idol Clara Kimball Young).

You may ask: Just how do exterminators drum up business? By planting vermin throughout a house and then ringing the doorbell to ask if the house has been infested by vermin, that's how. Larry sprinkles ants on a gorgeous white cake, and Moe drops a mouse into Mrs. Burlap's pump when she goes upstairs to change her shoes. Curly sprinkles ants onto Mrs. Burlap's sheets, and Larry prowls around like that man from St. Ives, a sack full of mouse-eating cats flung across his shoulder. (Humorously, the head of one patient kitty pokes from the burlap.)

Mrs. Burlap doesn't want her guests (the short has a generous cast of thirty) to know that exterminators are about, so she dresses the boys in foxhunt outfits. Thus attired, the Stooges blend in perfectly.

Right.

Shortly, (real) mice are literally flying all over the place, via wonderful wire work, landing on guests' shoe tops and on their shoulders. Armed with hammers and spray guns of Flit, the Stooges pursue their quarry. When a rodent slips down the back of a guest's dress, Curly invites her to dance and then swings and shakes her so violently that the hapless mouse tumbles onto the floor. Larry scrambles along on his hands and knees, eager to mash the mousie, but brings his hammer down on guests' toes, instead.

When Moe notices later that Larry still has the cat-sack, he orders him to get rid of it. Larry obeys by stashing the pussies inside an upright piano, moments before Professor Repulso (Bud Jamison) sits down to play "The Blue Danube Waltz." "Da da da da da, mrow mrow mrow mrowr!"—and so on, until Moe literally upends Larry and shoves him inside the piano to extract the cats. When the piano falls forward, cats fly everywhere and Larry is trapped inside. Moe tugs on his pal and only succeeds in removing his pants.

The pandemonium horrifies the guests, but one of them, Mrs. Burlap's kindly friend Clara (appealingly played by Isabelle LeMal), thinks quickly and congratulates the hostess on finding such wonderful entertainment!

Partly because "Preston Black" was the pseudonym Jack White used when he directed, White's enormous contribution to the Stooges' career is often

Ants in the Pantry (1936) casts the boys as exterminators who bring their own vermin to every job. Here, Moe discreetly issues last-minute instructions; Curly has doubts about a pussy.

overlooked. The situation has been compounded because Jack's brother, Jules, played a more visible role in the boys' development, and Jack was directing during the same period as another fine talent, Del Lord. But Preston Black/Jack White was a big gun. When his name appears in the credits, settle back because you're going to have fun.

Like *Hoi Polloi* and other superior Stooges two-reelers, *Ants in the Pantry* unreels at a breathless velocity. Individual sequences are beautifully paced, and editor William Lyon cuts them together with marvelous energy and rhythm.

Al Giebler's script is a treasure, not simply situationally but in dialogue. The Stooges aren't commonly thought of as dialogue-driven comics, but because Giebler hits on twelve cylinders this time out, the boys are the verbal equals of any nearly anybody in the business. Early on, Larry enters the house holding a nasty-looking spring-loaded trap. Moe says, "What's that for?"

"Ya never can tell," Larry answers, "we might meet up with a bear!"

Moe: "Yeah. Meet my bare hand!" Slap!

Mrs. Burlap gets her first look at the Stooges and says to the butler (Vesey O'Davoren), "My word, Gawkins, what *are* these?"

In the kitchen, Moe flirts with the pretty maid (Helen Martinez), who responds by saying (with a charming Spanish accent), "I like you, too, you beeg brave mouse catcher!"

Curly gets upset when Larry feeds him rat poison in a test of its potency:

CURLY
What does he think I am, a rat?

MOE
Yeah! What about it?

CURLY (suddenly meek and conciliatory)
Well, you don't have to tell everybody . . .

Later, Larry and Curly make idle chitchat in an effort to blend in with the upper crust:

LARRY
Say, whatever happened in 1776?

CURLY
What street?

The conclusion of *Ants in Pantry*, in which the boys join the real guests on a foxhunt, is a bit of a non sequitur but a funny one. Although Moe shows up on a horse, Curly has been given a burro and Larry straddles a bicycle. Because Curly has a cold he can't smell the skunk that he thinks is the fox. He stuffs Mr. Skunk into a burlap sack—there's a lot of "sack" and "burlap" in this short—and then opens it for Moe and Larry, who promptly faint dead away.

Fifteen years later, producer-director Jules White, working with writer Felix Adler, went back to the well and created a good-looking remake called *Pest Man Wins* (1951). Because of available stock footage from the earlier film and two others, *Pest Man* was shot in just three days rather than the usual four. The setup is virtually the same as in *Ants*, except this time it's the boys themselves, and not a boss, who come up with the idea of letting vermin loose in a house.

Gags play out similarly, with Margie Liszt as Mrs. Castor, the earnest hostess; cute Nanette Bordeaux as the maid; and Vernon Dent as the pianist, now named Mr. Philander.

After Mrs. Castor hires the boys, she warns, "Gentleman, [the guests] must not know what you're doing!"

Larry proudly responds, "You're a cinch, lady, we don't know what we're doin' ourselves!"

In the original short, Curly's hand gets caught in a heavy valise as Moe hurries to close it. That sequence is a good one, but Shemp plays it here with even more energy, and Adler's script invents a couple of new ways for the valise to bash Moe in the face.

When Mrs. Castor announces a buffet, the final minutes of *Pest Man Wins* become a pastiche of new footage and pie-fight stock sequences lifted from *Half-Wits Holiday* and *In the Sweet Pie and Pie*. The former short supplies the pie on the ceiling and Symona Boniface's famed "sword of Damocles" remark; the latter brings Eddie's Laughton's pie-interrupted account of his battle with a lion. New players Shemp, Nanette Bordeaux, and others are cut in via inserts.

In an uncharacteristic lapse while shooting new footage, Jules White neglected to get adequate coverage of one of his bit players, veteran comic Heinie Conklin, so a close-up insert of Conklin as he takes a pie had to be created in an optical printer, a process that invariably brings ugly, noticeable grain

Performer Profile: Nanette Bordeaux
1911–56

Helene Olivine Veilleux was born in Quebec, where she came by her charming French accent naturally. Nanette dipped a toe into movies in 1938 and became more steadily active after 1948. Following uncredited bits as maids and French girls, Nanette started at Columbia's two-reel unit in 1949. She brought her big eyes and Gallic charm to comedies with Schilling and Lane, Wally Brown, Bert Wheeler, Wally Vernon and Eddie Quillan, and others.

Of her fifteen Columbia shorts, Nanette appeared with the Stooges in eight. Highlights: a sexy gold digger in *A Missed Fortune*, Fifi the maid in *Pest Man Wins*, and a saucy French showgirl in *Loose Loot*.

Her final acting job was with the Stooges in *A Merry Mix-Up*. Nanette died of pneumonia in April 1956, just weeks after that short's release.

Another gig as exterminators in *Pest Man Wins* (1951), but first: a pause to make a little time with pretty maid Nanette Bordeaux. How can she resist such charm?   *Photo courtesy of the Stoogeum*

to the film stock. When editor Edwin Bryant cuts back to a medium shot (which is how White shot Conklin in the first place), the sudden clarity is startling.

Stooges fan Fredric March, on the Columbia lot to shoot *Death of a Salesman*, asked permission to visit the *Pest Man* set. Jules White naturally obliged, and took great pleasure observing March's struggles to stifle his laughter.

Overall, *Pest Man Wins* is better than good, and is a pleasing poke at pretension.

BACK IN THAT INNOCENT AGE OF 1938 (WHEN THE NAZIS WERE ALREADY BEGINning to take over Europe, and American farmers victimized by banks and the Dust Bowl were soberly burying their parents and children), a male "escort" was a perfectly acceptable accoutrement to a wealthy lady's trousseau. The escort's presence, at functions public and private, never carried so much as a *hint* of impropriety—he was on hand simply for appearance, and to see that the lady had a visible partner at the dinner table and on the dance floor. If the lady needed some minor item, such as a handkerchief or a light for her cigarette, her escort would provide it. An escort made a lady complete.

It's just this kind of thinking that gets Mrs. Van Twitchell (Bess Flowers) into a bunch of trouble in *Termites of 1938*. (The title is a play on the very popular *Gold Diggers of 1933/35/37* musicals produced by Warner Bros. Over at Hal Roach, his Rascals did a fine musical send-up called *Our Gang Follies of 1938*.)

Mrs. Van Twitchell's grumpy husband has made a point to leave for a hunting trip on the eve of a big soiree thrown by another society lady, Mrs. Sturgeon (Dorothy Granger, a charter member of the Screen Actors Guild). Mrs. Van Twitchell wouldn't think of attending the party alone, so she instructs her maid to dial Acme Escorts. Well, the maid misreads the phone listing and confuses "Escorts" with "Exterminators."

It happens.

Mrs. Van Twitchell is suddenly on the line with Moe. He's not hearing so well just then because his latest invention to annihilate mice—a tangle of strings attached to the trigger of a miniature cannon—has gone off and blown his head through a wall. (The gag is a good payoff to a sequence that director Del Lord stretches for too long.)

When Mrs. Van Twitchell asks for one of the Acme's best men, Moe says, "We're *all* pest men!" The fundamental misunderstanding continues: Mrs. Van Twitchell says "dance" and Moe hears "ants." She asks about "fees" and Moe hears "fleas."

Moe is given a swank address on Laurel Canyon Drive (actually, it's the sunny Columbia Ranch in Burbank), and is told that the affair is semi-formal. He hears that part all right, so when he arrives with Larry and Curly, all three are decked out in tails.

Unlike *Ants in the Pantry*, *Termites* is more concerned with the Stooges' mischief than with the creatures the boys are hunting. Guided by Curly's stethoscope, Larry periodically inserts the heavy bit of a gigantic electric drill into parts of walls where it doesn't belong, nearly boring holes into people's heads and squirting their faces with Flit when they turn around to see what's going on.

At the de rigueur dinner-table sequence (amusingly written by Elwood Ullman and Al Giebler, and warmly photographed by André Barlatier), Moe eyes an Amazonian blonde and cracks, "Siddown, Shortie, stuff's here and it's mellow!" Mrs. Sturgeon and her guests reluctantly take their cues from Sir Wafflebottom (Bud Jamison), who imitates everything the Stooges do because he thinks they're typical American "college chaps." Napkins end up hanging from collars and bodices, and everybody blows on their silver before buffing it on their sleeves. Moe covers his knife in mashed potatoes that he uses to trap his peas, and later uses corn holders to spear his tiny squab, so that he can gnaw at it like a pork rib. Hostess and guests do likewise.

When Mr. Van Twitchell unexpectedly returns home and discovers that his wife has become a victim of the giant drill (you have to see it to understand it), he dispatches the boys with one of their own gopher bombs, blowing their jalopy to flinders and reducing them to tatters.

A few miscellaneous points: In a break with tradition, the boy's theme, "Listen to the Mockingbird," plays over their first scene and is heard again at the end—innovations, possibly, of musically oriented co-producer Charley Chase. New music by Columbia staff composers Howard Jackson and Raphael Penso softly underscores the dinner sequence.

Latter-day sources identify actor Robert Fiske as Mr. Van Twitchell, but the actor we see is older than Fiske and not nearly as tall. Whoever he is, his name has apparently been lost in the vapors of film history.

At least one source credits an actress named Willa Pearl Curtis with the role of Mandy, Mrs. Van Twitchell's maid, but the part is played by Etta McDaniel, Hattie McDaniel's sister (and a dead ringer for that Oscar-winning actress, too).

When Curly voices his conviction that he can use his piccolo to lure mice, he holds a copy of Robert Browning's *The Pied Piper of Hamelin*. The book is the handsome 1936 Grosset & Dunlap edition, with cover and interior art by famed *New Yorker* and children's book illustrator Roger Duvoisin.

Termites of 1938 was remade at Columbia in 1946 as *Society Mugs*, with Shemp Howard and Tom Kennedy. Christine McIntyre has the Bess Flowers role, and Rebel Randall takes over for Dorothy Granger. And Bess, with nearly another twenty years of her remarkable career ahead of her, appears in the remake, too—as a party guest.

THREE SAPPY PEOPLE (1939) EXISTS AT THE CENTER OF OPPOSING CULTURAL and comedic forces. It's a screwball comedy (gorgeous, nutty heiress does wacky but ostensibly endearing things)—as well as a more forceful criticism of the idle rich than most feature-length screwball comedies cared to be. When the central supporting character receives her comeuppance, we laugh but also feel vindicated: This character's humiliation is well deserved, and we take an uncharitable satisfaction in it.

The screwball comedy genre, although celebrated for a sleek sophistication, isn't far removed from some of the coarser conventions of comic two-reelers.

Performer Profile: Bess Flowers
1898–1984

It is likely that no Hollywood actress put together more screen appearances than elegant Bess Flowers. Married to an assistant director and, later, to a Columbia studio manager, she owned a beautiful and extensive wardrobe that endeared her to casting directors in need of "dress extras" for sequences in night clubs, society parties, theater audiences, and other sophisticated venues. So prolific was Bess—she had about eight hundred screen appearances—that she came to be known as "Queen of the Dress Extras."

Patrician-featured and blessed with a pleasing voice, she was 5'8"—too tall to reasonably expect a career as a leading lady. Her considerable beauty was refined rather than flashy, and she was a marvelous foil for the Stooges in four shorts: *Termites of 1938*, *Tassels in the Air*, *Mutts to You*, and *A Plumbing We Will Go*, in which she's variously drenched in water, shoved upward through a staircase and smacked in the face with a wet rag, and sees her dinner party descend into chaos.

She worked continually in shorts and features from 1923 to 1965, her hair changing from brunette to an elegant silver. Bess was invariably lovely and always a pleasure to encounter.

Termites of 1938: Genteel society matron Bess Flowers is at a loss when Curly's appalling table manners are taken up by Lord Wafflebottom (Bud Jamison).   *Photo courtesy of the Stoogeum*

In *Bringing Up Baby*, the essential menace of Cary Grant making a fist, and then relenting a bit before deciding to push his palm into Katharine Hepburn's face so that she topples backwards through a doorway, is fundamentally little different from Moe maliciously throwing a pie at a snooty dowager.

The "madcap heiress" figure of *Three Sappy People* (the title is a riff on a popular song, "Two Sleepy People") is Sherry Rumsford (Lorna Gray), a clinically manic whirlwind who's ready, when we meet her, to disappear from her own birthday party to take a ride on a submarine. She has time to pursue such nonsense because, in late-Depression 1939, she doesn't work and doesn't need to. If you develop a modest dislike for her on sight, scripter Clyde Bruckman would have said you're on the right track.

Sherry's husband (the fine character actor Don Beddoe) is sufficiently concerned about his wife's state of mind to engage three famed psychiatrists, Drs. Ziller, Zeller, and Zoller. The docs are out of their office, but the Stooges, struggling to fix the doctors' switchboard, pick up the call and hurry right over after hearing that "money is no object." Money would be good because, as Curly says with noticeable embarrassment, "It's Gertie, she's gonna have . . ." [a baby]. And that's all we hear of Gertie, who's named for the wife of Curly's brother Shemp.

As Columbia's two-reel budgets inched south throughout the 1940s and '50s, the output of director Jules White grew increasingly perfunctory. However, when budgets were still generous, he showed (or felt *inclined* to show) a fondness for graceful dolly shots and other evidence of filmmaking skill. *Three Sappy People* looks like a nicely budgeted feature film. In fact, of all the boys' Columbia shorts, it may be the best looking. Generously populated with extras who fill unusually handsome mansion interiors and beautifully landscaped exteriors, and lushly photographed by George Meehan, the comedy is completely convincing in its depiction of the public's idea of the trappings of scatterbrained wealth. So skillfully is all this put together, in fact, that the opening sequence, in which Sherry gaily drives her new Plymouth roadster into a drawing room packed with guests, is as "real" as it is startlingly comic: The stunt driver comes in quickly and expertly brakes inches from a wall.

As the thin story develops, the boys do gags that they'd done before or would do again: Curly shaves at the luncheon table, and then struggles to eat a powder puff that's fallen onto his biscuits; Moe and Larry spike the punch until it steams and bubbles like witches' brew; the boys fail to get a reflex reaction from Sherry's leg when they tap her knee with a tiny mallet, but Moe must eat Curly's leg when a tap sends it catapulting into his face.

Curly makes his much-loved lunch request—"Some burnt toast and a rotten egg," because "I got a tapeworm and that's good enough for him!" (Tapeworm humor is one comic neighborhood that screwball comedies did *not* explore.) When Moe threatens to tear out Curly's Adam's apple, Curly cheerfully replies, "I'll make a note of it!" Moe snatches Curly's pencil, so Curly pulls out a bigger one. The cycle is repeated until Curly scribbles with a pencil that's as big as a butcher's salami.

Even the Stooges are a little out of their comfort zone when they encounter a manic society girl (Lorna Gray) in *Three Sappy People* (1939). The socialite's husband (Don Beddoe, left) is mortified.   *Photo courtesy of the Stoogeum*

A gooey, climactic food fight, which is preceded by the boys' maladroit attempts to eat corn-wrapped tamales (a kind of food they've obviously never encountered before), is lively. We're particularly pleased when the fed-up Mr. Rumsford brings an enormous, very heavy birthday cake down on his wife's head, shocking her into blessed silence.

For all its virtues, *Three Sappy People* has a fundamental problem: Actress Lorna Gray isn't up to the requirements of her role. She's beautiful and has some sparkle, but until the climax her excited laughter sounds embarrassingly forced and false. If White filmed the script sequentially, Gray got better as the four-day shoot went along; if White shot out of sequence, the actress exhausted her gifts in the first day or two, and had nothing left for the comedy's early scenes.

To an industry that paid scant attention to shorts in the first place, the performance isn't one that could have lifted Gray to the next professional level.

FULLER BULL IS UPSET. HE'S ANGRY. AND HE'S MAD AS HELL, TOO! THE STAFF that he derisively calls his "newshawks" cannot get close to prominent socialite Mrs. Van Bustle and the new man in her life, the oily Prince Shaam of Ubeedarn.

The pair's high-society romance is one of the biggest stories of the year, and Bull's paper, the *Daily News,* has come up dry. But its rival, the *Star Press,* has an early scoop that makes the *News* look foolish. Fuller Bull's only hope of topping the *Star* is to be first with a photograph of the lovebirds—a ferocious challenge because the prince has hired free-swinging bullyboys to protect the privacy he enjoys with Mrs. Van Bustle.

Crash Goes the Hash (1944) asks whether anybody in town is capable of getting in, snapping a picture, and getting out. Is there, huh, is there?

Why, soitenly.

Of course, the Stooges' qualifications as reporters exist only in Fuller Bull's imagination: After accidentally lowering a window onto the mangled foot of one of his assaulted reporters, Bull (Vernon Dent) looks down at a truck from the Star Cleaning & Pressing Co. The truck's right-side rear door is open, leaving only the left one visible, so what Bull sees is: "Star Press."

Oh boy! Not only does Bull have a shot at upstaging the *Star,* but he may be able to do it with three of its own men. Naturally enough, Moe, Larry, and Curly are swayed by the promise of a hundred bucks, and are right on board with Bull's scheme.

Felix Adler's premise is fun because it reminds us that, in pre-television America, journalism was a war. Big-city newspapers had to deliver the goods— once, twice, and even three times a day—or perish. A city as big as New York had a dozen dailies, and even burgs the size of Cleveland had two or three. Cutthroat competition led to some great scoops as well as to a lot of sensationalism and cheese. Readers ate it up.

At the Van Bustle mansion, the boys make a mess of a dinner after convincing the butler, Flint (Bud Jamison), that they're the chef and waiters Mrs. Van Bustle has called for.

Central to the humor in the kitchen is the homophonic relation of "canapés" (which the boys need to prepare) to "can a' peas." Moe has the clearest notion of a canapé: "You mean the toast with the lace curtains!" Larry, however, is completely as sea and diligently searches the cupboards for a can of peas. Lacking toast, he discovers dog biscuits that, when slathered with the peas, look just as appetizing as you'd expect.

In the drawing room, Curly busies himself with lemonade, accidentally pouring some down the naked back of a female guest and then wetting her décolletage after she angrily turns to confront him. Shortly, Curly is tossing ice cubes into the glasses with his bare hands and swigging the lemonade nearly as fast as he can prepare it. Mrs. Van Bustle (Symona Boniface) is horrified, particularly when Curly says, "Have a lemonade? Ten cents apiece or three for a quarter!"

In the setup to Larry's best bit, the prince (Dick Curtis) and Mrs. Van Bustle cuddle on a loveseat. Larry spies them and goes for the photo by levering himself onto a baby grand—only to be pinned by the noisily collapsing lid. "I faw down!" he meekly explains.

Meanwhile, back in the kitchen, an escaped parrot creeps inside the cooked turkey, a gag that also shows up in *G.I. Wanna Home* and *Three Dark Horses.*

Director Jules White milks the payoff—the turkey's upright waddle along the dinner table—way beyond its humor quotient; the shtick plays better later, when the parrot-turkey briefly toddles behind the boys as they creep along a dim hallway.

Things come to a head when the boys snap a photo of the prince and Flint, who are busily robbing Mrs. Van Bustle's safe. Following a major tussle (in which Bud Jamison clenches his fists and grimaces with the delightful élan of a silent-screen heavy), the boys come out on top. Mrs. Van Bustle is so grateful that she picks up Curly like a doll (with help from a wire rig) and proclaims that she'll marry *him*.

Symona Boniface and Dick Curtis—as dependable as the seasons—are great fun, as is that other stalwart, Bud Jamison. When he indignantly tells the boys that they remind him "of the Three Stooges," he isn't just noodling with the fourth wall; he's unintentionally acknowledging a splendid, shared professional history. Regrettably, *Crash Goes the Hash* is Bud's last work with the Stooges. Illness forced an early retirement, and he passed away in 1945.

MICRO-PHONIES (1945) IS ABOUT MUSIC, ARTIFICE, AND IMPERSONATION.

Music: Alice Van Doren (Christine McIntyre) is determined to sing on the radio. Her father doesn't like the idea, even though Alice brings skill and feeling to renditions of Strauss's "The Voices of Spring" and the "Sextet" soprano part from Donizetti's *Lucia di Lammermoor*. She's obviously spent years in study and practice; if "work ethic" isn't her middle name, it should be.

Artifice: Alice is a longtime friend of the woman who has the authority to hire her, so rather than audition in person and create a sense of obligation, Alice transfers her voice to a record. She intends for this simulation to fulfill the requirements of an audition. The record becomes an indication of the honesty of Alice's character, and also propels the Stooges into Alice's life and aspirations.

Impersonation: Curly (a bungling plumber) attends a society party dressed as a Spanish coloratura named Senorita Cucaracha—complete with high comb and mantilla—because he's been mistaken for, well, a dame who sings. For the entertainment of an audience of swells, he mouths the lyrics to the two pieces noted above as Larry and Moe (also bungling plumbers) impersonate classically trained singers, Senors Mucho and Gusto, one a bass and the other a tenor. In addition, Moe impersonates a person who can play the flute.

When the record is destroyed (Moe angrily shatters it on Curly's head because Curly tells him to be careful with it), Alice stands behind a curtain to sing "live." Although their impersonations are exposed by an ill-tempered violinist (Gino Corrado) who has run afoul of the boys earlier, Alice's friend Mrs. Bixby (Symona Boniface) hires Alice on the spot. Even Alice's staid father (Sam Flint) is won over.

Sound effects technician and sound editor Ed Bernds was given his first opportunity to direct in the spring of 1945 when he was assigned to the Stooges' *A Bird in the Head*. *The Three Troubledoers* was next; *Micro-Phonies* is the third of the many Stooges shorts Bernds would direct over the next seven years.

A Bird in the Head (see "The Stooges and the Fantastic") was shot in April 1945 and caught the chronically ailing Curly during one of his down periods. He's physically and comedically stronger in *Three Troubledoers*, and stronger still in *Micro-Phonies*, which was filmed in June 1945. Bernds was understandably concerned about the future of his budding career as a director, and when he appealed to producer Hugh McCollum to release *Micro-Phonies* before the other two, McCollum agreed. This artistic alliance was broken up when two-reel department head Jules White fired Hugh McCollum in the spring of 1952; Bernds elected to leave as well. The final McCollum-Bernds Stooges short is *Gents in a Jam*.

Bernds wrote as well as directed *Micro-Phonies*—never mind that the one-sheet poster erroneously credits Harry Edwards. So strong is the script, and so game is Curly, that the short remains hugely popular. Although not one of their very best, it's nevertheless a lot of fun and has a special, manic energy. Curly's first lip-synch to McIntyre's angelic voice, at the radio station, is absurdly hilarious: He clamps his lips tight during pauses in the lyric and then opens his gob like an abruptly raised window when McIntyre's voice returns. When he fastens his gaze on the microphone located in front of and slightly below him, he looks like a mad scientist admiring an illicitly obtained human brain. Of course, we know he's not supposed to be singing, and yet we can see that he's a slave to the music. His inner soprano wants out.

Christine McIntyre, Hugh McCollum's lover and arguably the most dependable of the Stooges' many regular collaborators, may never have been more beautiful, and brings sparkle and dignity to what amounts to a quietly dramatic role. Symona Boniface also performs "straight." The aforementioned Gino Corrado (whose name is misspelled on the title-card credits and on the one-sheet poster as "Carrado") is wildly aggressive as Spumoni—he foolishly smashes his violin over Moe's head when the boys interrupt his practice and he comes at Larry with a saber, which Larry deftly parries with a mic stand. At the party, the Stooges sabotage his singing by flipping cherries into his throat, and Spumoni returns the favor by sending a well-aimed banana flying across the room and into Curly's mouth as Curly pretends to vocalize.

Veteran player Fred Kelsey is a perfect picture of exasperated authority as the boys' boss, and Frank Mayo has a funny bit as a guest who flirts with Senorita Cucaracha, and who later gets smeared with cherries because he has the bad luck to be holding a bowl of them while in the vicinity of Spumoni. And we have another opportunity to enjoy lovely Bess Flowers, who has a silent bit as a party guest.

The short's title notwithstanding, the Stooges are phonies only in their transparent impersonations. The truth is that there's nothing phony about them at all. When the highbrow guests pelt them with records in the final scene, it's not because the boys are fakes. It's because they're annoyingly real.

Performer Profile: Christine McIntyre
1911–84

Of all the Stooges' many supporting players, none is more beloved than beautiful and vivacious Christine McIntyre. Familiar to many movie fans as the heroine of B-westerns (many from Monogram), she found her best roles, and her greatest moments, at Columbia's two-reel unit, which she joined in 1943. She supported Andy Clyde, El Brendel, Hugh Herbert, and many more of the studio's contract comedy stars, but none so vividly as the Stooges.

Blonde, sparkling-eyed, and shapely, Christine had a musical speaking voice—an outgrowth, no doubt, of her Chicago training as an operatic soprano. She sang beautifully, with expressiveness and color, in the brilliant tones of the classic bel canto sopranos.

Highlights of McIntyre's time with the Stooges are too numerous to cover here; see comments in discussions of individual shorts in the main body of this book. A few, however, must be mentioned: the aspiring, and brilliantly talented, vocalist in *Micro-Phonies*; the scheming, murderous dame in *Crime on Their Hands* (a rare turn as a villainess, and a deliciously funny one); the sweetly singing Princess Elaine in *Squareheads of the Round Table*; and the negligee'd Miss Hopkins in *Brideless Groom*, who mistakes Shemp for a masher and literally punches him through a door.

Christine retired from movies in the early 1950s and married radio producer J. Donald Wilson.

Of the Stooges' leading ladies, none were more frequently seen, more lovely, or more talented than Christine McIntyre. *Micro-Phonies* (1945) showcases her shimmering soprano voice—which Curly (passing himself off as "Senorita Cucaracha") has been channeling at a party.

Photo courtesy of the Stoogeum

9

The Stooges and Showbiz

In which the boys take a big gal to the big city; experience hairy romance; lay eggs; get berth marks; choke on Dixie; forget to write; have trouble at Niagara Falls; meet a freak from Abba Dabba; go "blue"; tussle with Freud; contemplate eternity; and end up on the cutting-room floor.

When the Stooges shot *Movie Maniacs* in 1935, talkies had been around for just eight years. The technology had become very sophisticated in the interim, but Hollywood still was home to a horde of stage-trained directors, writers, actors, and elocution coaches whose experience with dialogue had given them a certain value in sound's early days. The importation of stage folk happened because of some reasonably logical thinking by studio executives, but the fallout from the influx was a lot of stilted dialogue marked by formalized sentence structure, absurdly precise enunciation, and pseudo-British accents. And because of the need to express emotion to people seated in row T of legit theaters, stage actors in Hollywood were happy, when encouraged, to do a lot of declaiming: pose, gesture grandly, overact in the close-ups.

Romantic scenes could be particularly dire. "Oh, dahling!" "Yes, my sweet!" "I cahn't *express* how I've *longed* for this moment!"

Big-budget "A" pictures were frequently guilty of this sort of thing (particularly if the setting was one of great wealth), imagining that such falseness imparted class and an elegant worldliness. Audiences went along with it, but moviegoers also liked more "real" personalities, like Harlow, Gable, Cagney, and Stanwyck.

Comedy, the least respected and most difficult of all film genres, gave numberless comics opportunities to have fun with the conventions of movie drama and melodrama. A very amusing, pre-sound example is Stan Laurel's 1922 solo short *Mud and Sand*, which sends up the snorting eroticism of Rudolph Valentino's very popular *Blood and Sand*. (Stan calls himself Rhubarb Vaselino.) Nineteen years later, writer-director Preston Sturges excoriated his Hollywood contemporaries with *Sullivan's Travels*, the picaresque adventures of a maverick director who's fed up with Hollywood's fakery and sets out to discover the "real" America—only to learn that he's nearly as ignorant as everybody else in the picture business.

Movie Maniacs (released 1936) falls neatly between those two points and is no less merciless than Laurel or Sturges in its observations. Mistaken for studio executives sent to Carnation Pictures ("From Contented Actors") by the New York office to shake things up, the boys unintentionally intimidate general manager Fuller Rath (Bud Jamison) and meddle so grossly in a romantic scene directed by German martinet Cecil Z. Swinehardt (Harry Semels) that the director stalks off the set. (Just for starters, Curly lights his match on the bare sole of Swinehardt's leading lady [Mildred Harris] as she languorously reclines on a divan.)

Swinehardt takes offense when Larry and Curly stand behind the actors (Kenneth Harlan plays the leading man) and insert their arms in front of the pair, to demonstrate the kind of "life" that self-appointed director Moe wants to see. The sight of the slender Harris gesticulating with Curly's beefy forearms isn't quickly forgotten, and Curly does a sublime bit of business (possibly an ad lib) when he adjusts Harris's bodice and girdle.

Harlan, meanwhile, recites his plaintive dialogue—"I have no money!"—whereupon Larry inserts his hand into Harlan's pocket and comes out with a big bill.

A bit later, Curly takes over the female role himself, looking hideous in a birds' nest of a blonde wig, bee-stung lips, and sexy peignoir. As he awaits his paramour, Larry (who enters the room, shuts the door behind him, and *then* knocks), Curly idly uses an enormous pliers to noisily pluck his eyebrows.

Moe dragoons three starlets (one of whom is played by a tall and very beautiful girl named Althea Henley) to demonstrate the proper way to give and receive a kiss, in a cute, innocuous sequence that, years later, was occasionally axed by local TV stations.

Director Del Lord's staging of the forepart of the short, as the boys travel cross-country in a boxcar filled with furniture, is smart, acknowledging the cramped quarters without restricting the Stooges' movement. The sequence is superior, with a couple of especially good moments. In one, Larry gets grease on Moe's white slacks after he's been ordered to iron them. His solution? Slather them with so much white paint that they stand up by themselves.

The other funny bit is a dialogue exchange:

CURLY

How are we gonna get in pictures? We know nothin' about movies!

MOE

There's a coupla thousand people in pictures *now* know nothin' about it. Three more won't make any difference.

This would seem to support a remark by the gifted and supremely cynical screenwriter Ben Hecht: "A movie is never any better than the stupidest man connected with it." And writer Felix Adler's crack about "Contented Actors" is a pretty obvious dig at the bovine acquiescence of many stars and other actors to studio demands.

The supporting cast of *Movie Maniacs* is strong, with Bud Jamison veering nicely from fear to outrage, Heinie Conklin and Blackie Whiteford as energetic studio guards, and diminutive Hilda Title as a hilariously smart-ass script girl.

At least one production still exists of the boys standing amidst the burned-out wreckage of a sound stage. This is a remnant of an early version of the script (discovered in 2001 by historian Brent Seguine) that casts the boys as screenwriters named Howard, Fine, and Howard who manage to burn the joint down.

Movies about movies are intentionally self-referential, but *Movie Maniacs* has a special piquancy because the actors who play Swinehardt's cornball stars, Kenneth Harlan and Mildred Harris, had been names during the silent era. Harlan enjoyed a fleeting acquaintance with glory in the mid-1920s but fell out of favor even before the advent of sound.

Mildred Harris came to short-lived stardom around 1920. She was defined more by celebrity than by true fame, because she married Charlie Chaplin in 1918. After divorcing him in 1921, she quickly began an affair with Edward, Prince of Wales (later King Edward VIII and, later still, the Duke of Windsor). By 1925, Harris was cast as second female leads, and her prestige slipped even further after that. *Movie Maniacs* is Harris's last on-screen credit. She took a few more jobs, all uncredited, and died of pneumonia in 1944 at age forty-two.

Now *that's* a Hollywood story.

IN 1932, TWO YEARS BEFORE THE STOOGES BEGAN THEIR ASSOCIATION WITH Columbia, director Jules White did his only work for producer Hal Roach, the knockabout comedy king whose contract players included Laurel and Hardy, Our Gang, and Charley Chase.

One of the top teams at Roach was Thelma Todd and ZaSu Pitts, a female "odd couple"—Todd blonde and jaw-droppingly good-looking; Pitts dark and with a cultivated mousiness. White directed them in a two-reeler called *Show Business* (1932), in which the girls (much like Stan and Ollie in a 1929 Roach short called *Berth Marks*) board a train and create chaos. The girls shortly run afoul of an unpleasant Broadway star (Anita Garvin, a tall, dark, and imposing beauty who was a member of the Roach stock company and a frequent antagonist of Laurel and Hardy).

Thelma and ZaSu have sneaked their capuchin monkey aboard, and in the course of the night aboard the train, the monkey gets loose and the girls make terrible rackets as they try to situate themselves in their upper berth. All of this raises the ire of Garvin (who plays herself!) and causes no end of headaches for the troupe's beleaguered manager (Monte Collins).

Although a Santa Monica preview of *Show Business* went acceptably well, White and Roach disagreed about some of Jules White's cutting decisions—and that was the end of White's career at Roach.

Surviving credits for *Show Business* note White as producer-director. No writer is credited, but a reasonable guess is that it was White himself or his brother, Jack.

In any case, Jules (producer) and Jack (writer-director, as "Preston Black") revived the whole idea for the Stooges as *A Pain in the Pullman* (1936). Instead of regal Anita Garvin, the boys' nemesis is an aging star named Paul Paine (James C. Morton), a preening, grandiloquent fop who won't stop reminding everybody that he's the idol of millions. That plays all right until the Stooges' monkey, Joe, mischievously lifts Paine's toupee in the presence of assorted showgirls.

Bud Jamison takes the Monte Collins role as the troupe's manager and awakes in his berth with a start, cracking his head on the low ceiling whenever his name ("Johnson!!") is shouted, which is frequently. The same thing happens whenever the Stooges make a commotion, another frequent occurrence. By the end of the film, Johnson has more concussions than an unprotected quarterback. The frequent shouting for "Johnson!!" may have made an impact on German émigré Billy Wilder, whose 1959 comedy, *Some Like It Hot*, has a long sequence aboard a train, where the cry for "Bienstock!!" (the manager of the all-girl band that's aboard) becomes a running gag

A Pain in the Pullman is slick and unfailingly funny. Jack White mixes his shots well and accomplishes a beautiful tracking shot as the boys run to the train station, the trunk that they hold between them banging into pedestrians and knocking a ladder from beneath a workman.

As they do in just a small handful of their shorts, the boys play "the Three Stooges." Here, they're hoofers who are desperate for a job, and when their booking agent calls from Goldstein, Goldberg, Goldblatt, and O'Brien with good news, the boys are thrilled. (O'Brien, played by Yiddish dialect comic Jesse DeVorska, makes the call.)

After "lights out" aboard the train, Curly passes the berth of a pretty girl (Phyllis Crane) who talks in her sleep, cooing, "At last you're here. Kiss me, darling. . . . Come to my arms."

This is sufficient to stop Curly dead in his tracks.

"Why didn't you write?" the slumbering girl wants to know.

Curly: "I didn't know your *address!*"

After one more entreaty for a kiss, Curly leans into the berth, and an instant later Johnson is awake again, rubbing his noggin.

Bobby Burns reprises his bit from *Show Business* as a drunk who stares in inebriated horror at the monkey's tail and takes shaky aim with scissors each time the appendage comes through the curtains and uncoils in front of his nose.

The Stooges' maladroit exertions to clamber into their upper berth is familiar comic stuff that plays brilliantly. Moe and Curly repeatedly toss Larry up and in, where he cracks his head and inevitably falls out. Another attempt boosts Larry into the berth across the corridor, which is occupied by a giant of a woman (name not known) who patiently, if violently, hurls the boys where they belong. Once settled (more or less), Moe indignantly complains about the possibility of "berth marks." And for those of you who like to keep count, *A Pain in the Pullman* is the first Columbia short in which Moe snarls, "Wake up and go to sleep!"

When the train stops after Johnson and the monkey get tangled in the emergency brake, the boys are tossed from the caboose and over a hedge, where they ride bucking bulls into the distance. The same footage, beginning with the

Performer Profile: James C. Morton
1884–1942

Balding and imperious, James C. Morton began the most prolific part of his career in 1930, putting together about two hundred appearances, mostly uncredited, until his early death at fifty-eight.

Comedy fans recall Morton best for his many roles in Our Gang shorts, notably as the tormented radio station manager in *Mike Fright*. Morton also worked many times with Laurel and Hardy.

With the Stooges, he's wonderful in *Healthy, Wealthy and Dumb* as the hotel manager who is appalled when the boys destroy one of his rooms; a vain movie star in the train comedy *A Pain in the Pullman*; the irascible father of the boys' fiancées in *The Sitter Downers*; and, most memorably, the hapless court clerk in *Disorder in the Court*, who witnesses Moe shoot his toupee full of holes after it's been stripped from his head by Larry's errant violin bow.

Recipe for disaster in *A Pain in the Pullman* (1936): the Stooges, a train, a monkey in a sailor suit, a big-headed actor (James C. Morton, in dark suit), and a short-fused chaperone (Bud Jamison).

Photo courtesy of Ted Okuda

cutaway from the train, is utilized for the non sequitur conclusion to *A Ducking They Did Go* (see "The Stooges and the Sporting Life").

A Pain in the Pullman played so well that Columbia remade it as *Training for Trouble*, a 1947 vehicle for contract comics Gus Schilling and Richard Lane.

ACTORS LAUGH VERY HARD IN *LOCO BOY MAKES GOOD* (1942). THROUGHOUT much of this rather desperate short, supporting players and extras laugh and laugh. Picture the laughter as a wave, enormous and roaring toward the beach— and when it gets there, the wave is just a dribble, a sad thing, because it was laughter created from very little worth laughing about.

Loco Boy Makes Good doesn't fall apart, but that's only because it never properly comes together in the first place. Some fundamental mistakes account for its undoing. Chief among those is that the film flirts with sentimentality, utilizing the dire situation of an old woman as its pivot point. Mrs. Brown (the name of the kindly-seeming actress has been lost) is months behind on the note the bank holds on her run-down hotel. The Stooges are touched by the lady's plight, and contribute an apparent fortune, and a lot of sweat equity, to transform her place's ground floor into a très élégante supper club. Mrs. Brown is so pitifully grateful she nearly blubbers.

Illogic is another problem. Felix Adler and Clyde Bruckman's script establishes that the hotel has had no business because it's become run-down and shabby. The transformation wrought by the Stooges is impressive (and considerably more protracted in the original script), but the hotel's past would seem to militate against the likelihood of an opening-night parade of well-dressed swells led by influential gossip columnist Waldo Twitchell (John Tyrrell).

A sign on the sidewalk ballyhoos the featured act, Nill, Null & Void, "3 Hams Who Lay Their Own Eggs." It all happens inside, at the Kokonuts Grove (a weak play on Boston's famed Cocoanut Grove club, where 492 people were killed in a fire that occurred on November 28, 1942, about eleven months after the January 8 release of *Loco Boy Makes Good*.

Twitchell (who is modeled, of course, on famed columnist and broadcaster Walter Winchell) watches with great, and unjustifiable, glee as the boys play piano, attempt some (intentionally) weak jokes, and threaten to sing "She Was Bred in Old Kentucky But She's Just a Crumb Up Here."

Backstage, Curly carelessly puts on a coat belonging to Balbo the Magician (Vernon Dent, who's wasted in a single, brief scene). As Curly dances with Twitchell's attractive friend, Miss Stompandale (Dorothy Appleby), the coat regurgitates a parrot and then a rabbit. The parrot lands on a society matron (Ellinor VanDerveer) and terrifies her, which sends the crowd into amused hysterics. The rabbit is deposited beneath a serving tray as waiter Larry strides by, and when the drunken diner (Eddie Laughton) lifts the lid, he's so horrified he falls off his chair.

By now, the place is a shrieking bedlam of laughter. (One person who wasn't laughing was comic Harold Lloyd, who sued Columbia, claiming the magic coat idea had been appropriated from the script he and Vincent Lawrence wrote for a 1932 Lloyd comedy, *Movie Crazy*. Lloyd was awarded $40,000.)

When the fabulous coat disgorges an egg, Curly dances over to the drunk and plops the cackle fruit in the fellow's hand, so that when the guy goes to swat a fly on his forehead, he covers himself in eggy goo.

With that, Twitchell and the other patrons laugh so hard and so helplessly that you begin to wonder if the Stooges will have to bring out the chest paddles.

You're also waiting for something funnier than "kind of cute" to happen.

There are bright spots. Curly happily eats a bar of soap, his mouth ringed by the rich foam of a hydrophobic. He collects the goo with a swirl of his index finger and slurps it into his mouth. Aahh, tasty!

During the remodeling sequence, Moe sizes a heavy board by neatly cracking it over Curly's skull and then uses the back of Curly's head to drive a nail. Rolls of linoleum that refuse to lie flat prompt some cute gags.

At the supper club, Dorothy Appleby displays her edgy, don't-mess-with-me charm, and is amused when Curly does his backward shuffle on the dance floor and then dances sideways and even on his knees.

After Balbo's coat disgorges a herd of white mice, some of the rodents crawl up Moe's pants, causing him to drop his drawers so that he can frantically pick the critters from his long johns. (This is funny, but, as throughout, the crowd's laughter is just over the top.)

Finally, Curly discovers that an endless rope of scarves he pulls from his sleeve culminates with a skunk. That's good for a grin, but please: Hold the hysterics.

IN AN INCIDENTAL WAY, *THREE LITTLE TWIRPS* (1943), IN WHICH THE BOYS JOIN the circus, is a commemoration of a uniquely colorful type of entertainment that was already fading from the American scene in that wartime year. The modern circus, a familiar and much-loved institution with roots in 18th-century Britain, had become a major provider of entertainment across the United States a century later. In an expanding America where huge numbers of people lived far away from urban areas, the circus's lively exoticism was eagerly anticipated. By about 1910, more than *thirty* shows toured the country by train, respecting each other's territory as they crisscrossed the continent. The Horwitz brothers and Larry Feinberg were boys during that period, and they undoubtedly knew and enjoyed the circus, particularly large ones like Ringling Brothers and its rival, Barnum & Bailey, which had the name recognition and attractions needed to set up in big cities.

In *Three Little Twirps*, when Curly sticks his face through a circus poster featuring a gorilla, he becomes a grinning caricature of a frankly bizarre sort of entertainment that, although on the wane, still had a hold on America. Curly's exuberant face atop the ape body establishes a link between him and the broad spectrum and history of American show business—of which he and the other Stooges were important parts.

Curly-Gorilla is a cute gag on strictly visual terms, but it's also a layered one that movie audiences of 1943 would have immediately understood: Just five years before, in 1938, the by-then combined Ringling Brothers and Barnum & Bailey circus introduced the captive Congolese gorilla called Gargantua the Great, whose immense popularity ("The World's Most Terrifying Living Creature!") literally saved RBB&B during the late Depression. The fact that Curly-Gorilla has a goofy body is only half the joke; the rest of it is that he isn't at all terrifying.

Mr. Herman (Stanley Blystone), the short-fused circus manager who doesn't care for the boys' inept way of hanging his posters, reasons that he can still get his money's worth, and punish the boys at the same time, by "welcoming" them into the circus family. When the boys enter the grounds, Curly recalls, "Say, I haven't been at the circus since I got out of the fourth grade!"

Moe: "Yeah, that was last year!"

A sequence in which the boys scalp circus tickets right on the midway works nicely because of good timing and Curly's impossible-to-resist offer of dollar tickets for a quarter—while Moe and Larry try to unload theirs for fifty cents. But too much time is devoted to an unfunny, vaguely unpleasant bit with Chester Conklin as a nearsighted duffer whose job it is to slaughter unlucky circus horses for lion food. Larry and Curly are fooling around inside a long-necked, droopy-butt horse costume, so guess what?

Curly's sexually ambivalent encounter with the skinny bearded lady (Hank Bell, with uncredited female overdubbing) is hilarious, particularly when the hirsute gal flirtatiously says, "You remind me of my seventh husband!" Curly shoots back, "You remind me of a girlfriend in Detroit, but you look more like her stepfather!" This is comic dialogue with rhythm and bite: Why is "Detroit" funnier than "Minneapolis"? Why is "stepfather" funnier than "father" or "dad" or even "old man"? It just is, so kudos to writers Monte Collins and Elwood Ullman, and to Curly, who delivers the line so well.

Finally, imagining they're bona fide circus performers, the boys excitedly bound onto the sawdust attired in ridiculous tights and feathered headdresses. They look like Koo Koo, the plumy table dancer in Tod Browning's *Freaks*—and that allusion isn't far-fetched because the Stooges' jobs are to be human targets for the spear-tossing horror known as the Untamed Sultan of Abba Dabba (Caucasian actor Duke York, in blackface and black*body*).

Curly soon reaches his fright quotient, and climbs the trapeze pole with the Sultan right behind. When Curly unwisely steps onto the narrow high wire, the Sultan shakes it, sending Curly into a propeller spin that climaxes with Moe and Larry exhorting Curly to let go because they've got a net. Naturally, the net is paper and Curly plummets right through it, leaving an enormous sinkhole to mark his passage.

Harry Edwards, directing the Stooges for the second and final time, does a workmanlike job. *Three Little Twirps* isn't quite good enough to inspire you to go to the circus tomorrow, but it may bring back some pleasant memories of circuses past.

AS DESCRIBED EARLIER IN THIS BOOK, THE STOOGES WERE CREATURES OF THE stage for years before they considered working in film. They performed as a live act (or *acts*, given the changes in personnel) throughout the entirety of their careers, initially in vaudeville and on Broadway and then, during breaks in their shooting schedules after 1934, on stage, in nightclubs, and even stadiums.

The Stooges worked live after '34 not just for the lucrative payouts but because, like most performers who begin on the stage, they thrived on that "high wire" form of performance: no retakes, no edits that might fix a fluff after the fact, no opportunity to do it again tomorrow when you're feeling fresher—just rows of expectant faces, and you with nothing but your material, your talent, and the adrenaline rush that simultaneously gratifies and terrifies you.

Gents Without Cents (1944) invokes some of that. It's a peculiar short because the Stooges step out of their familiar character- and story-driven mode to become people who live to perform, and who do so in a context devoid of story. *Gents Without Cents* is all about "the act."

The boys didn't execute this shift for art's sake but because of studio economics. In 1943, they worked with director Ray Enright (later to become known for his westerns) on a piece of Columbia wartime fluff called *Good Luck, Mr. Yates*, in which a soft-spoken teacher (Jess Barker) at a boys' school desperately wants to go to war. When he believes he will, he tells people so and then must explain himself to girlfriend Claire Trevor and everybody else when things don't work out as he'd hoped.

Like many patriotism-lite movies of the period, *Good Luck, Mr. Yates* is dotted with morale-boosting variety acts supposedly staged for the benefit of soldiers and war workers. The Stooges—who shot their sequence at a sound-stage ship-yard in front of extras cast as shipbuilders—did not make the final cut. The footage was probably eliminated for reasons of running time, though the entirety of *Good Luck, Mr. Yates* consumes a mere seventy minutes.

Regardless, the footage is a record of the boys' version of that fatalistic old chestnut of inevitable, unavoidable violence, "Slowly I Turned," also known as "Niagara Falls." In the bit, variously credited to (or claimed by) Joey Faye, Harry Steppe, and others, Curly has a chance meeting with a down-and-out stranger, played by Moe, who laments losing his wife to somebody named Larry. Moe says he tracked Larry across the country and finally caught up with him at Niagara Falls.

You probably know the rest: The words "Niagara Falls" send Moe into a spasm of violence directed against the hapless Curly. This happens two or three times (Curly forgets to stop saying "Niagara Falls") until, finally, Moe and Larry meet again. Curly naturally anticipates more mayhem, so he's puzzled when the enemies greet each other like old pals. But when Curly says the magic words, *both* guys turn on him: "Slowwly I turned, step by step, inch by inch, and then I grabbed him," and so on.

The footage was in the can, bought and paid for, so Felix Adler and Jules White made it the centerpiece of *Gents Without Cents*. The short's framing device casts the boys as struggling performers who hook up with a trio of cute, acrobatic hoofers who live upstairs (Lindsay Bourqua, Laverne Thompson, and Betty Phares—billed on the short's title card as "Lindsay • Laverne • Betty").

Prominent among the new material are the boys' sterling harmony vocal on "We Just Dropped By to Say Hello" and L L & B's athleticism, which the girls display in an acrobatic dance number. Of the three women, dark-haired Betty Phares shows particular sparkle.

In the framing segment's wrap-up (shot outdoors and thus at odds with the artificial look of the rest of the short), the Stooges and the gals are newly married and on their way to—say it with me—Niagara Falls. Curly gets caught outside the car, which lurches after him in rhythm to the group's call of "step by step, inch by inch." So concludes a fluffy appetizer of a short that has some historical interest and not a great deal more.

RHYTHM AND WEEP (1946) IS SUPERFICIALLY SIMILAR TO GENTS WITHOUT Cents, as it incorporates a stagy Army induction sketch that had been written in 1944 for another project but never filmed. That earlier project was *Gents Without Cents*.

Dizzying, isn't it? Wait, there's more: The sketch, in which Curly refuses to undress for Sgt. Moe, turns up in an earlier Columbia short, *General Nuisance* (1941), with Buster Keaton as the recruit and Monte Collins as the frustrated examiner.

To say that *Rhythm and Weep* has a plot is probably too generous, but the short does have a *premise* that's somewhat more energetic than the tiny engine that motivates *Gents*. Once again, the Stooges are performers, and this time they're not just struggling but completely hopeless—as in: without hope. There's nothing to do but climb the city's tallest skyscraper and jump off. (The rooftop and cityscape cyclorama were at Monogram, a few blocks east of Columbia, on Sunset.) Before they can do that little thing, they have to wait in line behind three beautiful but discouraged dancers who are already poised on the ledge, ready to leap into eternity. The Stooges quickly get cozy with the three girls, Hilda, Wilda, and Tilda (Gloria Patrice, Nita Bieber, and Ruth Godfrey, respectively. Cast lists in some secondary sources transpose Patrice and Bieber's roles).

The group investigates piano music coming from elsewhere on the roof. The pianist is a millionaire (Jack Norton) who defies his family by dabbling in theater. He has a new show, plenty of money to bankroll it, but no cast. On the spot, the Stooges and the girls audition and win the jobs.

All three actresses were highly trained dancers, and their rooftop numbers—one ballet and the other jumpin' modern—are perfectly lovely.

Jack Norton, one of two men in Hollywood who worked mainly in "drunk" roles (the other was Arthur Houseman), is ingratiating in a straight characterization. Well, *almost* straight: The payoff gag involves a place called Dr. Dippy's Retreat.

Curly's worsening illness is very apparent throughout the short, and a lot of dialogue and other business that would have gone to him is handled by Larry.

The venerable "three watches to tell time" gag is performed by Larry, and in the army sketch, pills that the two-year-old script describe as being popped into Curly's mouth by Curly are put there instead by Moe.

Curly shows his stuff earlier during an exchange with Moe that's probably the closest the Stooges ever came to what people used to call "dirty" humor. It happens as the two of them look waayy down at the street from their perch on the ledge:

CURLY
Look look look look! Those two men down there! They're
my uncles!

MOE
Your uncles?

CURLY
Yeah!

MOE
They look like ants!

CURLY
They got aunts in their—

Before Curly can say "pants," a slap from Moe cuts him short—and precludes a letter from the studio censor.

Viewers watching the final scene of *Rhythm and Weep* are apt to wonder why Patrice, Bieber, and Godfrey wear men's suits. Felix Adler's full script includes a sequence in which the gals impersonate the Stooges (returning a favor, as the boys don tutus to briefly impersonate the girls). Jules White shot the sequence but the footage was cut, providing yet another sideways link to *Gents Without Cents*. Fortunately, adorable production stills can be enjoyed at Ms. Bieber's very appealing Web site, www.nitabieber.com.

The *Rhythm and Weep* one-sheet poster identifies ballerina Moe as Larry, and vice versa. You'd think that after an association of twelve years, Columbia's promotional department would get it right.

BACKSTAGE INTRIGUE INSTIGATES THE ACTION OF *THREE HAMS ON RYE* (1950), written by Clyde Bruckman and directed by Jules White. Larry, Moe, and Shemp are incompetent stagehands who also have small roles in a new Broadway revue produced by B. K. Doaks (Emil Sitka), an irritable Type-A personality who has suffered ten consecutive flops. Those failures tickle the hell out of a snarky theater critic named Nick Barker, who loves to pan Doaks's shows.

Doaks tells the Stooges to forget about their paint chores (as much paint gets on the boy's faces as on the theatrical flats) and instead see that Barker doesn't sneak into the theater from backstage.

Performer Profile: Ruth Godfrey White
1922–85

This dark blonde daughter-in-law to two-reel producer-director Jules White dabbled in film, appearing with the Stooges between 1946 and 1957 and working once with Andy Clyde.

Pretty in a wholesome, unassuming way, Ruth was a trained dancer who came to Columbia after an association with choreographer Jack Cole. White (who sometimes worked under the name Ruth Godfrey) is charming in her first film role, as an aspiring performer in the Stooges' *Rhythm and Weep*. In later shorts such as *Pardon My Backfire*, *Musty Musketeers*, *Pals and Gals*, and *A Merry Mix-Up*, she's a pleasing girlfriend or fiancée.

Although not in the first rank of the boys' stock company players, White was invariably an appealing, thoroughly professional presence.

Larry plays by ear in *Rhythm and Weep* (1946), to the amusement of (from left) Ruth Godfrey White, Moe, Jack Norton, Nita Bieber, Gloria Patrice, and Curly.   *Photo courtesy of the Stoogeum*

Plot point: Barker often operates in disguise, and because the Stooges don't want him to pan any of *their* future performances, *they'll* be in disguise, too. In a surreal touch, Larry disguises himself in a floor-length black coat and a stovepipe hat that rests on his shoulders. He looks like Uncle Fester by way of Abe Lincoln; Shemp spies him and is convinced that Barker's disguised himself as" a black banana."

Naturally, the boys start cracking each other over the heads, and accidentally assault their boss, too. Meanwhile, Barker gets into the theater.

The comic centerpiece of *Three Hams on Rye* is an Old South sketch that climaxes Doaks's show. The star (Christine McIntyre, who looks stunning as a Southern belle) has supposedly baked a cake that she offers to five suitors (the Stooges plus bit players Danny Lewis [father of Jerry] and Brian O'Hara). Because Moe and Shemp have carelessly baked a pot holder into the cake, the treat is almost impossible to cut, let alone eat, and soon the stage is a whiteout of regurgitated feathers—a reprise of a gag the boys performed in one of their 1935 releases, *Uncivil Warriors* (see "The Stooges in History"). Jules White keeps the gag going for more than three minutes, pulling it off because of the Stooges' enthusiastic playing (Shemp and Larry's facial contortions are particularly funny) and competent cutting by Edwin Bryant.

As the curtain falls, Doaks is in despair at the audience's laughter, but Nick Baker (Ned Glass) rushes backstage to congratulate the producer on a brilliant piece of satire. (An easily pleased critic is Mr. Baker!)

Good bits that are incidental to the plot include a mock-seduction of Shemp by a saucy showgirl (Nanette Bordeaux), whose insincere attentions encourage Shemp to coo, "Come wiz me to ze Casbahdor!" Larry and Moe have a lively duel with dripping paint brushes, and all three boys harmonize nicely on their own composition, "Jane" (which is heard, as "Nora," in *Scrambled Brains*; see "The Stooges and the Fairer Sex").

A sure-fire laugh (and another moment of surrealism) is set up when Shemp pauses at a backstage door marked "Dangerous. Keep Away!" "Dangaroos," Shemp reads haltingly. "Kipawa." He opens the door and is greeted by a burly arm with a fist sporting a boxing glove. Pow! Right in the kisser.

Who *was* that? Is the gag theatrical or just theater? What is the boxing glove's motivation? Who let the Stooges near Broadway in the first place?

What is art?

THE STOOGES' FINAL SHOWBIZ SHORT, *SWEET AND HOT* (1958), HAS SINGING and dancing and some slapstick, plus invocations of Freud, quack psychiatry, "Daddy issues," and child abuse.

What a peculiar recipe.

Of all the boys' two-reelers, *Sweet and Hot* inspires the most vitriolic comment. Some outraged viewers threaten suicide or murder, or both. One of the milder fan-site reactions reads, "After viewing this, I'm the one who needs therapy. . . ."

Plus-size cutie Muriel Landers is Tiny, a naturally gifted vocalist and dancer whose stage fright has caused her to sequester herself on the family farm. Her old flame Larry (apparently playing himself) is a hit in big-city show business and comes by to say he knows a psychiatrist who can cure Tiny's stage fright. After that, she can join his act.

The shrink is Moe, who looks like he's having fun as Dr. Hugo Gansamacher (*gansa macher* is Yiddish for a "big shot" or other influential person, but the expression can be used sarcastically to suggest a person of bloated self-regard who actually accomplishes very little). The doc is an energetic caricature who arrives complete with mangled syntax and a burlesqued German accent. (He makes self-important pronouncements like "Plees, mein time ist linament!")

With sodium pentathol administered via an enormous needle (which Gansamacher wields with too much relish, recalling some real-life bad-boy German doctors), Tiny regresses to her childhood on the farm. Her father (Moe) loves to hear her sing and perform. Her guileless rendition of "I'm a Little Teapot" is cute; likewise her turn at a sawhorse "piano," where she sings the Stooges' longtime theme, "Three Blind Mice."

But Tiny freezes after Uncle Louie (Larry) and Uncle Joe innocently come by to watch. Daddy becomes enraged (and I use that word advisedly), uncoils a bullwhip (!), and chases his 300-pound little girl around the haystacks, threatening to *force* her to perform.

Meanwhile, Sigmund Freud, wherever he was by this time, was nodding gravely.

Gansamacher, for all his apparent idiocy, nevertheless gets to the bottom of Tiny's fears, giving her the confidence she needs to become a star.

Like *Gents Without Cents* and *Rhythm and Weep, Sweet and Hot* is a pastiche. It was released on September 4, 1958, by which time audiences had already seen Muriel Landers in a solo short, *Tricky Chicks* (released October 24, 1957). In that

Larry, Joe, and Muriel Landers combine nightclub style with a bit of vaudeville in the charming and underrated *Sweet and Hot* (1958).   *Photo courtesy of the Stoogeum*

one, Muriel and slender gal pal Bek Nelson are nightclub entertainers who are mistaken for Red spies. In a key sequence, Muriel wears a showy dress and belts out "The Heat Is On."

Jules White designed *Tricky Chicks* as the kickoff to a new two-reel series to star Landers, but when word came that the unit would shut down at the end of 1957, the idea died. However, Columbia still had Landers's services, so for two days in August 1957, White brought Muriel and the boys together, picking up the solid (and very smartly arranged) performance of "The Heat Is On," and using the same set (with Muriel in the same dress) to introduce Larry and Joe into the number. Larry plays his violin, and Joe does a charming soft-shoe.

For all of its oddness, *Sweet and Hot* has a lot to like. To see Moe out of character is novel and amusing, particularly since his new persona doesn't prevent him from doing knockabout with Joe and Larry.

The short has a strong feel of the gentler aspects of vaudeville that Besser obviously found congenial, because he's lively and bright-eyed throughout.

Muriel Landers was by this time an experienced singer-actress who had been Ray Bolger's song and dance partner. She had a beautiful face, a pleasant speaking voice, and a charmingly graceful dance style. When you watch her act, you think *professional.*

As a vocalist, she wasn't Peggy Lee, but she wasn't chopped liver, either—and anyway, Peggy Lee couldn't do comedy.

Landers is especially funny when Larry extols the virtues of the big city to Tiny: Whatever Larry says causes Tiny to shake her head in disinterest—the shows, the clothes, the excitement, the food. At the last, Landers's eyes dart upward, emphatic but understated, and with exquisite timing.

In a particular kindness, White saw that Landers receives a special title card, "Also starring Muriel Landers."

Sweet and Hot is a departure for the Stooges, but it's well made and entertaining. By no stretch is it the "worst" Stooges short—and anyway, "worst" is a terrible, and undefinable, word.

There is a "least" short made by the boys, but *Sweet and Hot* isn't it.

10

The Stooges Go to War

In which America's best go off to see the sea; become citizens of Televania; annoy the Sarge; send the Afrika Korps to the North Pole; make the Cold War hot; bid a friend au reservoir; get sick of watermelon; laugh themselves to death; and fry in hell.

More than 4.7 million American troops were under arms during the United States' 1917–18 involvement in World War I. At war's end, nearly all U.S. officers and men became eligible for discharge. A standing army still had to be maintained, of course, and this was seen to, in part, by a 1919 Congressional act authorizing one- and three-year army enlistments.

In 1920, Congress passed the National Defense Act, which authorized the U.S. armed forces to prepare for war.

But preparation was strictly theoretical. Who was there for America to fight? From that high of 4.7 million troops in 1917–18, the American Regular Army shrank to 200,000 by 1920, and to 150,000 in 1921—partly because the government wanted it that way and partly because many men who would otherwise have considered becoming career soldiers knew that pay was low and promotions scarce. Army service was a dead end.

Between 1921 and 1936, only 137,000 American men were under arms, despite Japan's illegal 1931 occupation of Manchuria and the growing bellicosity of Hitler's Germany. The world was becoming more dangerous, but Washington seemed not to notice.

How can we underestimate, then, the significance of Larry, Moe, and Curly's presence in the peacetime army? Pass the ammunition and praise the Stooges!

The boys' first "service" comedy, *Half Shot Shooters*, was released in 1936. The opening sequence catches the Stooges in 1918, where they sleep through a frightful German artillery barrage. When Moe and Curly start a commotion, Larry says, "Pipe down, you guys, you're spoilin' the whole war for me!"

The irascible Sgt. McGillicuddy (Stanley Blystone) doesn't take easily to that sort of attitude. He gives black eyes to Larry and Curly and twists Moe's arm like a piece of licorice. And then: Armistice! The boys are discharged, but before they leave, they tell McGillicuddy "*au reservoir*" by cheerfully assaulting him.

Flash forward to 1935. Depression. No jobs. And for the threadbare Stooges, no food. After they annoy a prosperous restaurant patron (Vernon Dent, in his first appearance with the Stooges) by staring at him from the sidewalk outside, he tells them that right over there, on the third floor, "they're looking for men. Just tell 'em you want to sign up!"

Inside, Curly is the only one who notices the army recruiting poster, and when he tries to say something, Moe tells him to shut up.

McGillicuddy strides in a moment later. He's still a sergeant (slow promotions indeed!), and he remembers the boys right away—after all, it's hard to forget the jokers who pulled out your underarm hairs and smacked your behind with a nail-studded board.

Curly tries to make nice: "Your mother and my mother are both mothers!"

After absorbing some rough treatment from McGillicuddy that momentarily kills their hearing, the Stooges have an interview with a general (Harry Semels).

> GENERAL
> Where were you born?
>
> CURLY
> Upstairs, in the front room!
>
> GENERAL
> Were you born in this country?
>
> LARRY
> No, Milwaukee!

Ignorant of such things as death, Curly happily awaits the big noise in *Half Shot Shooters* (1936).

Finally, the boys are assigned to practice with a gunnery crew but are away on an errand when the other soldiers are dismissed. (The admiral's flagship is in the target area, so practice is canceled.) Moe wonders where everybody went. Larry offers, "Maybe it's between halves!"

The boys merrily rotate the sleek, enormous gun on its base and elevate the barrel from zero to ninety degrees to zero and all points between. When they start firing, they manage to accidentally explode a smokestack, a barracks building, a very long bridge, and the admiral's flagship (which they think is a dummy ship being sailed by remote control).

When the horrified McGillicuddy returns, he forces a smile and gently shepherds the boys in front of the cannon. "Now line up there in a straight line," he says brightly. "Hold it, and look pleasant!"

McGillicuddy fires the gun, and only the boys' smoking boots show that they ever existed at all.

Half Shot Shooters is in the pantheon of the Stooges' Columbia two-reelers. Preston Black (Jack White) moves briskly from one sharp Clyde Bruckman gag to the next, maintaining the narrative at a satisfying canter.

But White knows when to slow down, too. At the cannon (a gorgeous prop on a handsome sound stage), much is made of the boys' attempts to load the thing. They arrive with a dolly-load of shells and powder, harmonizing on "You'll Never Know What Tears Are"—as if they're about to trim the roses instead of throw a shell two miles.

There's more vocal harmony when they think they've properly set the range: "Gun range okay! Gun range okay! Gun range okkaayyy!"

After a quick huddle and some football audibles, Curly shuts his finger in the breech, and Larry barely gets his head out of the cannon's mouth before the gun goes off.

Stock footage of the ravaged targets is integrated into the main action almost perfectly. When the barracks go up, Moe says (with no little worry), "I don't know where that landed but I hope it didn't hit the pool room!"

Truly, here are soldiers who have America's best interests at heart.

Half Shot Shooters is one of the funniest service comedies of the period— maybe *ever*—and augured well for the boys' subsequent war-related shorts.

BY THE LATE 1930S, WASHINGTON'S ANTICIPATION OF GERMAN ESPIONAGE AND the U-boat threat (the Battle of the Atlantic would begin in 1939) carried real weight. A lot had happened in Europe since the 1935 release of *Half Shot Shooters* and the March 1938 shoot of the boys' second war-related short, *Three Little Sew and Sews* (1939). German legislation of 1935 intimidated and harassed Germany's Jews. The following year, Hitler's adventurism took his troops illegally into the Rhineland, a demilitarized buffer zone separating Germany from France; and, as an ally of Fascist revolutionary Francisco Franco, to Spain, where Hitler's generals observed the efficacy of new German tactics and equipment in real combat.

Mussolini's Italy, another Fascist nation with dreams of conquest, attacked helpless Ethiopia in 1935, and became an ally of Germany two years later. The thunder of coming war was unmistakable; the question in the public mind was whether America would become actively involved. To many in Washington, the issue was *when.*

Throughout *Three Little Sew and Sews*, it seems clear that the boys are sailors who rescue America's submarine program from German spies. Yet because no Hollywood film had previously lampooned Hitler or his criminal government, and because there was no war when *Sew and Sews* was filmed in late March 1938, the conniving foreign power is unnamed. Further, the Stooges aren't Americans but citizens of the Republic of Televania.

Why this obfuscation?

Officially, at least, America (echoing with a lot of bluster from loudmouthed isolationist politicians) was merely displeased with Nazi Germany. Further, Hollywood still benefited from films that were profitably exported to that nation. Although Jewish studio heads, including Columbia's Harry Cohn, were upset by developments in Europe, there was no sense—at least for the moment—in antagonizing the Germans.

It was from this combination of politics and business that the Stooges, for this short only, are Televanians.

In all respects but name, however, they're as American as a '38 Plymouth.

Inveigled by Curly into joining the navy, the boys labor as tailors instead of as true seamen. But when the uniform of an admiral shows up in the shop one day, Curly slips it on after finding a party invitation in the pocket. Moe and Larry, also impersonating officers, tag along.

The host, Count Gehrol (Harry Semels), recognizes immediately that the admiral is an imposter, and so to ferret out information—and maybe gain access to submarine secrets—Gehrol sics the beautiful Olga (Phyllis Barry) on Curly.

Things go well for our hero, and then not so well, and after a while all three boys are captives aboard a submarine stolen by Olga and Gehrol. When the sub seems fated to become the spies' permanent property, Televanian artillery and bombers save the day—sort of.

Three Little Sew and Sews is a joy to watch because of Curly's comic exuberance and physical vitality. He's irrepressible and charming and radiates health the way the sun radiates solar rays. He's a benevolent force of nature.

Working from a hilarious script by Ewart Adamson, director Del Lord finds plenty for Curly to do. During an early interlude in which Moe and Larry cool their heels in the brig, Curly catches their attention from a window opposite their cell. There, he does a delicious pantomime of his plans for the evening, playing himself *and* the girl he intends to make time with. He demonstrates his approach (some pointing to his admiral's stripes) and how he'll ask the girl to dance (a little bow followed by a twirl of two fingers aimed at the floor). She's shy (an embarrassed tugging on imaginary hair and obvious pleasure at being asked by so fine a gentleman). Finally, Curly goes into a fanciful dance, making silent, imaginary conversation and enjoying himself hugely.

Even the wonderful Lou Costello, who was greatly influenced by Curly, could not have done this pantomime more inventively. The sequence is brilliant, and you know you're looking at a genius.

At the party, the highly persuasive Olga seduces "the admiral" on a sofa. As always, Curly is fiercely heterosexual yet as shy as a bluebird. He writhes and groans so ecstatically that if the seduction goes on much longer he's going to have to excuse himself to change his pants.

After Curly unknowingly sits on his lit cigar, he invites Olga to take a seat on his lap. We glimpse some ominous wisps of smoke as Olga asks, "Do you smell rubbish burning?" Curly is puzzled: "Smells like somebody's fryin' onions!"

Curly suddenly dumps Olga onto the floor—a move that causes a thick sofa spring to attach itself to his singed ass. Curly wants to be free of the thing, but each time he struggles forward on the polished floor, the spring violently pulls him back onto the sofa, and finally flat onto his face, upsetting an end table that loudly conks his head. (The sudden sideways flip of this piece of furniture was pure serendipity, and Curly's head takes a real, if slight, knock.) A party guest (Vernon Dent) can't stop laughing—indeed, Dent's laughter is almost certainly genuine; there's real merriment in his eyes.

Aboard the stolen sub, Gehrol (with pistol), a scarily menacing Olga (with knife), and the boys perform a roundabout pursuit at the base of the periscope. Curly's windup with a length of pipe conks Olga, and his follow-through takes out the Count.

The sub's subsequent drift to the ocean floor, courtesy of gorgeous footage from a 1937 Richard Dix vehicle called *Devil's Playground,* sends Curly into a panic of gasps, eye rolling, and frantic gesturing. Moe says, "Hey, what's the matter with you?"

Curly: "I'm practicin' for when we run out of air!"

After the sub finally surfaces, a Televanian shore battery hurls mammoth shells just inches from Curly's nose. Inside again, he miraculously catches a bomb dropped from a plane right through the sub's open hatch. The admiral soon comes aboard and wants to know how the boys subdued the spies. Curly demonstrates by giving the "dud" bomb a good whack. Kaboom!

In the short's final moments, the boys are angels, wings and all, who serenely fly through the heavens. Behind them, bewinged but nevertheless shaking his fist and mad as hell, is the admiral.

"Hey, step on it," Curly shouts in alarm, "look who's comin'!"

Politics are fleeting, but the quarrels of officers and enlisted men are eternal.

CHARLIE CHAPLIN'S *THE GREAT DICTATOR* (1940) IS A SAVAGELY FUNNY POLITI-cal satire in which a mild barber (Chaplin) is transformed into Adenoid Hynkel, the blustering dictator of a nation very much like Nazi Germany. Although long at 128 minutes, *The Great Dictator* is a milestone of film comedy and an indicator of the savagery that can be perpetrated against deserving targets by clever comic minds.

The Great Dictator was released on October 15, 1940, and is commonly considered Hollywood's first satiric exploration of Hitler. However, the Three Stooges' *You Nazty Spy* (1940) began to play theater dates nine months earlier, on January 19.

In this startling, viciously funny two-reeler, a cadre of industrialists in the European nation of Moronica deposes the king and installs an incompetent paperhanger, Moe Hailstone, as the country's puppet leader. Yet as things develop, Hailstone thrives in the role and becomes an irrational and dangerous dictator. Fellow paperhangers Larry and Curly are initiated into power as well, filling out the bumbling triumvirate that rules Moronica.

In a bit less than eighteen minutes, *You Nazty Spy* establishes that Hailstone imprisons the powerful and the weak on the flimsiest of pretexts, that he's a burner of books, and that he personifies a lot of what had been happening in Europe since *Three Little Sew and Sews*.

German troops achieved *Anschluss* (union) with Nazi-friendly Austria in 1938. Later that year, Hitler humiliated British prime minister Neville Chamberlain by forcing Chamberlain to accept a promise that Hitler's planned takeover of the ethnic-German Sudetenland, a part of Czechoslovakia protected by treaty, was his final territorial ambition. Chamberlain returned to Britain, where he proclaimed "peace in our time."

But Hitler wasn't done. He erased Czechoslovakia from the map with a 1939 takeover of Bohemia and Moravia. In August of that year, Germany signed a non-aggression pact with Russia, neutralizing the only threat to Germany from the east.

On September 1, 1939, German *blitzkrieg* (lightning war) forces drove east into Poland. Britain and France declared war—at last—on September 3, the same day that Russia, exercising a secret protocol to its agreement with Germany, punched westward to take its share of Poland.

And in the Atlantic, Nazi U-boats initiated attacks against British convoys and warships, and mined British waters.

The United States, though officially neutral, accelerated its rearmament.

As far as producer-director Jules White and writers Felix Adler and Clyde Bruckman were concerned, Germany had by now become the unwholesome center of human affairs, and Hitler was a simultaneously fearsome and absurd figure who begged to be stripped bare via lampoon.

The industrialists of Moronica "create" Moe Hailstone for their own ends, but in Germany, it was Hitler—a man determined to wage war—who snookered the greedy captains of industry, encouraging them to make a deal with the devil in anticipation of the spoils of German rearmament.

A Moronican manufacturer, Mr. Ixnay (Richard Fiske), complains to Moe that "there's no money in peace!" Moe ponders this, acquiring a temporary toothbrush mustache when his finger strays across ink. "We must extend our neighbors a helping hand!" he finally declares. "We will extend them *two* helping hands, and help ourselves to our neighbors!" This reasoning parallels Hitler's bald claim that the rationale for the march into the Sudetenland was to protect the ethnic Germans who lived there. The later takeover of Austria was explained, in part, as another "helping hand" gesture.

When a diminutive bellboy (midget actor Little Billy) hauls an everyday citizen into Moe's lavish office, we're handed a visual joke about the few who terrorize the many—this is a midget, after all, and the citizen is very tall. Further, the hapless citizen's arrest is predicated on utter nonsense: The bellboy found him walking with a chicken. Dictator Moe is intrigued. How did the citizen acquire the chicken? From an egg. And where did the egg come from? A chicken.

Curly (by now the image of the obese and vain Hermann Göring) cries, "A vicious cycle. Remind me to kill a cycle!" (kilocycle)

Moe scowls at the midget's captive and shouts, "Put him in a concentrated [sic] camp!" There were plenty of concentration camps in Germany by 1939. In 1933 alone, fifty of them, including Dachau, were established.

This demented talk of helping hands and camps and chickens is amusing in the cracked way that was intended, but the laughs are queasy. The Stooges and Jules White, all Jews, knew that what they were lampooning was pernicious and frightening.

More idiot's logic follows, as Moe has a notion to throw the prisoner to the lions.

Unfortunately, there aren't any.

> MOE
> Why have we no lions?
>
> CURLY
> Because there's no bones in ice cream!

At that, Moe has a babyish temper fit, a take on Hitler's well-known (and much-feared) insensible rages.

Later, Curly explains that "[Moe's] a little grouchy. He got up on the wrong side of the gutter this morning!"—a smarting reference to Hitler's common origins in Austria, and his poverty-stricken young adulthood in Vienna.

Moe's secretary (Lorna Gray) is actually Mata Herring (*matjeshering*, Yiddish for marinated herring), a spy and the daughter of Moronica's deposed king. In disguise as Mata, she conjures a magic eight ball and instructs Moe to "sit right down behind it." There's no reason to believe that Adler and Bruckman were not aware of the Nazi hierarchy's nonsensical fondness for the occult, particularly numerology, cosmology, neo-paganism, and a crackpot notion that Germany was established by superhuman émigrés from Atlantis. Given all of that, the mesmeric effect on Moe of Mata Herring's eight ball is almost believable.

In a related scene that can't be described as anything but horrifying, a peek through a magic telescope allows Moe a godless vision of himself and his two pals in hell, hogtied on a spit that's lazily turned over a roaring flame by grinning demons who are roasting them alive. The boys' shrieks, and Harry Davis's chiaroscuro lighting, momentarily remove *You Nazty Spy* from the realm of comedy and make an unashamed appeal to our love of revenge.

Back in the "real world," Curly rhapsodizes about blintzes and sour cream (a Jewish treat), anticipating what he calls a "blintzkrieg." He demonstrates a startling fondness for booze, too—much like Göring, whose appetites for food, drink, women, and opium were unrestrained and enormous. In the beautifully computer-colored version of *You Nazty Spy* released to home video in 2004, Curly preens in a rose-colored tunic (sagging with medals, front and back) and baby-blue breeches. He's an absurd vision, and yet the real Göring wore a variety of oddly hued, custom-made uniforms, including one in powder blue. He also rouged his cheeks, much to the amusement of the Nazi inner circle and the German people.

When Moe speaks in mock-German (and very skillfully, too), he slips in *Shalom aleichem* (Yiddish for "Peace unto you"), and, according to the very useful www.threestooges.net, he even says something in Yiddish about his belly button.

Everyday German is sent up when Moe burlesques the language's guttural aspect and even the word *Ja*, which sends Larry into a spasm of "*Ja! Ja! Ja*, man! Hallelujah!"

The language also gets a mild raking when we meet Moe's lissome, tutu-clad secretary (dancer Florine Dickson), who does ballet leaps and pirouettes as she relays her message. Her name is Miss Pfeffernusse—*pfeffernusse* being a much-loved German Christmas spice cookie.

When the citizens of Moronica finally rise up in open revolt, the boys beat feet to a remote exterior corner of the ministry—where they are eaten by lions.

Lorna Gray, as Mata Herring, is gorgeous to look at and gives a smoothly understated performance that's a nice change from her frantic posturing earlier in 1939, in *Three Sappy People* (see "The Stooges Puncture High Society").

In *You Nazty Spy*, the Stooges are no longer Moe, Larry, and Curly. They don't play "the Three Stooges," as in some of their showbiz shorts, and they don't play "everyday" people, either (such as Moe's railroad detective in *Cuckoo on a Choo Choo*). Here, they're fresh characters altogether, and although you struggle to find empathetic threads in the boy's bloodthirsty craziness, you laugh nevertheless. Even though Moe and the others take to corrupt power with alarming ease, you appreciate the performances *and* the dead-serious motivation that underlies them.

ON JULY 1, 1940, CONGRESS PASSED BURKE-WADSWORTH, BETTER KNOWN AS the Selective Training and Service Act. President Roosevelt signed the legislation into law on September 16, establishing the first peacetime draft in U.S. history. Compulsory call-ups began at the end of October.

The law required all American men between twenty-one and thirty-five to register for a national military draft lottery. On the day the bill was signed, Europe had been at war for a year and two weeks, so it's understandable that many young American men experienced an uneasy feeling. The United States was not actively fighting, but it had aligned itself with England, which, alone among the major western European nations, other than those that had declared neutrality, hadn't fallen to German forces. (France had been invaded in May 1940 and capitulated in an embarrassing six weeks.)

The American Lend-Lease program provided Britain with enormous amounts of materiel and other aid, but none of that accounted for British grit. The aerial Battle of Britain that riveted the world during the summer of 1940 was won by England because Germany's fabled *Luftwaffe* had been unable to break Britain's air defense. Still, tension ran high, and common thought was that Hitler's planned invasion of England—across the English Channel from Occupied France—would merely be postponed rather than abandoned.

The United States, having lined up on the side of the angels, monitored all of this with intense interest. Although the shouts of American isolationist politicians grew more strident, armed conflict with Germany seemed inevitable.

The Stooges' fourth service comedy, *Boobs in Arms* (the title a spin on the popular musical *Babes in Arms*), was released on December 27, 1940. Shooting dates have been lost, but a guess would place filming between June and September 1940—plenty of time for writer Felix Adler and director Jules White to be aware of the worsening European situation and the coming influx of green recruits into the U.S. military.

And, boy, the Stooges are as green as they come.

They end up in the army by way of a misunderstanding that causes them to be unfairly abused, which prompts them to react aggressively—a familiar Stooges trope. Their victim is a young man named Hugh Dare (Richard Fiske), who takes a fall when the Stooges literally (and innocently) run into him on the sidewalk. Dare is a big, robust fellow with a big, robust temper. He's not interested in apologies—and to demonstrate, he gives Curly a couple of good socks on the jaw. But like so many antagonistic types who stand taller than the Stooges, Dare lives to regret his pugnacious attitude and absorbs a sweet beating before the boys dump him backwards into a sidewalk freight elevator.

The Stooges run into Mr. Dare again at the Dare apartment—a calamitous development that's pure chance, as the boys have been peddling greeting cards throughout the building. They are surprised (but willing) when the unhappy Mrs. Dare asks them to pretend to romance her, so that her husband becomes jealous. The mister comes home, sees the Stooges, and wants to kill them all over again—a situation very like one faced by greeting-card salesmen Laurel and Hardy, who meet a married woman in *The Fixer Uppers* (1935).

The boys carelessly hide in a line for a recruiting station, and not long after, posted to a nearby base and wearing natty new uniforms, grab a seat in the sunshine.

LARRY
What a life!

CURLY
Nothin' to do but live off the fat of the land!

MOE
And eat and sleep!

Their reverie is interrupted by their new drill sergeant—and you know who it is, don't you?

For much of the rest of *Boobs in Arms*, Sgt. Dare tries his hardest to injure and embarrass the boys, only to be outsmarted at every turn. He gets some traction when he thrusts his bayonet into practice bags after the boys have clambered inside and then tries to flood the bags with a hose, only to collapse in frustration when the bags serenely sprout umbrellas. (Dare's oft-repeated lament is "Everything happens to *me*!")

In time, Dare and the Stooges are in a shooting war somewhere in Europe, which was expertly simulated on the Columbia Ranch with mud, shell holes, and shattered trees. As in *Half Shot Shooters*, the boys sleep like babies through a frightful artillery barrage. (The implication, of course, isn't that the boys are courageous—just that they're too dumb to be scared.)

Orders to fire a shell loaded with experimental laughing gas go slightly awry after Curly gets his head stuck in the cannon's barrel and then rotates the weapon straight up. The exploded shell reduces the boys to uncontrollable laughter that continues even after enemy soldiers—who wear distinctly Germanic *Pickelhaubes* (spiked helmets)—surround them. "I think we're captured!" Moe laughs. Larry stops howling long enough to exclaim, "They'll probably shoot us!"

The Stooges—*still* laughing—finally get the better of their captors, only to be barraged by friendly fire. Moe laughs, "Our own army is bombarding us!" Larry laughingly comes back with, "We'll be killed!" (That laughing gas is amazing stuff!)

Artillery shells whistle through the enemy HQ, and an especially enormous one zips between the boys' legs and carries them—yes, still laughing—through a window and up into the clouds.

Although the boys achieve mixed results as soldiers, you get the impression that they're really better off in the service, because they just can't hack it in the outside world. As they struggle to sell their greeting cards, they run around like ants and annoy everybody they buttonhole. One unsympathetic gent (Lynton Brent) blows smoke in their faces, and a pretty girl (Guatemalan actress Blanca Vischer) turns out to be a tiger cat when she decks all three boys with a single punch.

The Stooges are oddly undeterred, and even after they push Dare into the void beneath the sidewalk, Curly happily recites for him what the boys call

Performer Profile: Richard Fiske
1915–44

Has there ever been a drill sergeant more frustrated than the ramrod young soldier of *Boobs in Arms*? Driven next door to insanity by the Stooges' ineptitude, the sarge finally snaps and decides to bayonet them to death (fails) and then drown them (fails again). Fiske's frustration is a beautifully constructed monument to hopelessness that's all the funnier because the Stooges don't aggravate him with any malicious intent. He's as much a victim of himself as of the boys.

From 1938 until he left Hollywood for the army in 1942, Fiske appeared in nearly ninety features and shorts, all but a few produced by Columbia. Tall and good-looking, with a strong, masculine voice, he was equally effective in light and adventurous roles. Columbia recognized his potential early, moving him from bits to featured roles in westerns and serials. He was that relatively rare breed—a handsome young character player with leading-man potential.

While part of the 9th Infantry Regiment, Lt. Fiske died in combat in Le Croix, France, on August 10, 1944. He was posthumously awarded the Bronze Star and the Purple Heart and was interred at the Brittany American Cemetery and Memorial in Normandy.

Boobs in Arms (1940): The boys have a little trouble with the manual of arms, to the mild annoyance of their drill sergeant (Richard Fiske). Soon, the sarge will be in complete, hysterical meltdown.
Photo courtesy of the Stoogeum

Number Twenty-two: "Greetings little shut-in/Don't you weep or sigh/If you're not out by Christmas/You'll be out the Fourth of July!"

Or as soon as your hitch is up.

Other comics followed the Stooges into the service with features released a year later, in 1941: *Buck Privates* (Abbott and Costello), *Great Guns* (Laurel and Hardy), *Caught in the Draft* (Bob Hope), and *You're in the Army Now* (Phil Silvers and Jimmy Durante).

I'LL NEVER HEIL AGAIN (1941), THE FIRST OF ONLY TWO SEQUELS THE STOOGES ever made at Columbia, is a follow-on to *You Nazty Spy* (the two films are separated in the release schedule by eleven shorts and eighteen months). Moe is once again Moe Hailstone, dictator of Moronica; Curly and Larry reprise Göring and Goebbels, respectively. The script, as before, is the work of Adler and Bruckman, and Jules White returns as director.

I'll Never Heil Again vibrates with energy—with more, perhaps, than *Nazty Spy*—but its satirical content isn't up to that of the earlier film, and the script offers little opportunity for further development of the principal characters. Curly is still overstuffed and vain, Larry is still ineffectual, and Moe is familiarly aggressive, incoherent, and childishly temperamental.

Sic semper tyrannis! The startling—and queerly satisfying—final shot of the Stooges' second anti-Hitler comedy, *I'll Never Heil Again* (1941).

However, two bits of dialogue bring *I'll Never Heil Again* a little closer to the level of *You Nazty Spy*. First, a minor witticism, when Moe commands Curly to sit by shouting, "Plotz!"—Yiddish for a collapse caused by excitement or surprise.

The other piece of dialogue has weight and the authority of brutal truth. It comes when Hailstone grows particularly impatient and shrieks, "I am not *interested* in the *people*!"

The effect is a bit stunning.

I'll Never Heil Again was released on July 11, 1941. The precise shooting dates are unknown, but we have a clue: Moe's allies include not just Stalin (Don Barclay), Chiselinni (Cy Schindell), and a Japanese emissary (Duncan Renaldo, ten years away from world fame as the Cisco Kid) but a fourth person, too, a hookah-smoking Middle Easterner identified as the Bay of Rum (Jack "Tiny" Lipson). Some Web sources carelessly hazard that this character represents Turkey or Romania, but a better guess is Iraq, where Rashid Ali al-Gaylani had been in and out of office as prime minister during the early part of 1941, finally seizing power by coup on April 1. Rashid Ali was fiercely anti-British, and made diplomatic overtures to Hitler's government. Alarmed by this, and by the possibility of interference in Britain's administration of Palestine, British troops entered Iraq on May 2. That gave Rashid Ali exactly a month to agitate and make news—which suggests an April 1941 shoot of *I'll Never Heil Again*.

The plot that drives *Heil* is one of intrigue. The industrialists who installed Moe in power now want him gone and approach the deposed king's daughter, Princess Gilda (Mary Ainslee), for help. She agrees to pass herself off as a clairvoyant in order to gain access to Moe's inner sanctum, where she'll leave a bomb disguised as a billiard ball.

The princess enters a conference room where the puns and non sequiturs fly thick and fast. Moe announces that his armies have taken Paregoric and Pinochle. Then he wants to know whether he has control of the dikes of Holland. Curly answers, "Soitenly! And the van Dykes of Amsterdam and the Updikes of Rotterdam and the Hunchback of Notre Dam(e)!"

When the phone rings, a female voice wants to know, "Have you got anything on tonight?"

Curly: "Not a thing!"

Caller: "You'll catch cold! Goodbye."

Moe gravely inspects a map of Europe, which director Jules White holds on, with a dead-silent soundtrack, for a ridiculous forty-seven seconds. The map is marked with Great Mitten, the Cant Sea, Slap Happia, Jerkola, and other strategic points, but Hailstone is more interested in engaging his allies in a tug-of-war over a globe. An enormous, oddly feather-light globe figures in the most brilliant, and horrifying, sequence of Chaplin's *The Great Dictator*, but the Stooges' treatment is hyper-literal: Hailstone's globe is rock hard and shatters to pieces when cracked over his skull.

Moe eventually subdues Chiselinni with a judo flip and maneuvers the Bay of Rum right out the window. But the conspirators' explosive billiard ball goes off when Moe and Curly angrily throw it back and forth. It's all eerily prescient of the failed July 1944 bomb plot against Hitler.

In the morbidly funny final scene, the boys are dead, their heads neatly stuffed and mounted on a wall at the king's palace.

Readers with a grasp of World War II chronology will already have noted the irony of the July 11, 1941, release date of *Heil!* Just three weeks earlier, on June 22, Hitler had turned on Stalin, sending three million German soldiers across the Russian frontier on a drive toward Leningrad and Moscow. For the next few months, Operation Barbarossa promised to be Hitler's greatest triumph, but it would prove to be his worst mistake, and his undoing.

Metaphorically, his head would become a trophy just as surely as Hailstone's.

THE JANUARY 1, 1943, RELEASE OF *THEY STOOGE TO CONGA* COINCIDED ALMOST exactly with the one-year anniversary of America's entry into World War II, which followed the December 7, 1941, Japanese attacks on Pearl Harbor, Hawaii, and Clark Field, the Philippines. The United States, Great Britain, and other Commonwealth nations declared war on Japan the following day, and on December 11, Germany and Italy (stupidly) declared war on the United States.

During the next four months, Japanese forces ran riot across Asia, taking Siam, Malaya, and Hong Kong; Manila, the Solomon Islands, and Singapore; Rangoon, Bataan, and Corregidor.

In May 1942, a month after a mainly symbolic but psychologically devastating U.S. air attack on Tokyo, the U.S. navy halted its Japanese counterpart in the critical Battle of the Coral Sea. In June, carrier-based U.S. planes soundly defeated a powerful Japanese fleet in the Battle of Midway. This was the turning point of the war in the Pacific. Henceforth, the Japanese would fight a defensive, rather than an offensive, war.

As for Germany, Hitler's forces in Russia had raced as far east as Sevastapol during the summer and early autumn of 1941 but suspended the assault on Moscow at the end of the year because of brutal winter weather. The *Wehrmacht* endured the winter and mounted a second offensive in the spring of '42. Although this thrust made considerable progress, it was less successful than that first assault a year earlier. The winter had given Stalin time to regroup.

Ominously, the May 18, 1942, edition of the *New York Times* reported that German forces had murdered more than 400,000 Jewish civilians across Eastern Europe. If Larry, Moe, and Curly—and the rest of the Jews in Hollywood—were aware of this (which is certainly likely), it would have inevitably increased their anti-German fervor and colored the nature of their creative work.

With all of the above in place before mid-1942, *They Stooge to Conga* was designed to revolve around German and Japanese operatives working out of a New York City mansion, where the Stooges have come to fix a doorbell. Inside, the boys discover a portrait of Hitler and a short-wave radio, which they use to bollix instructions to a German U-boat skulking near New York harbor. (Germany's Operation Drumbeat, which kicked off late in 1941, positioned

"Nose to the grindstone" gone literal in *They Stooge to Conga* (1943), which is almost certainly the most fiendishly violent of the Stooges' Columbia shorts.

U-boats up and down America's eastern shore, from Cape Hatteras to St. Lawrence. Ordinary Americans were unaware of the scheme.)

Moe steps into a picture frame to impersonate Hitler, and the boys quickly dispose of the German spy (Vernon Dent, whose Iron Cross is as wide as a Memorial Day pancake) and the German's monosyllabic Japanese accomplice (Lynton Brent, sporting heavy glasses and buck teeth, and who says almost nothing except "So?" and "So!")

The boys' deft handling of the Axis agents is amusing but a little perfunctory because writers Elwood Ullman and Monte Collins and director Del Lord seem to have been much more concerned with slapstick—*violent* slapstick. Some of it—as when Larry tugs on wires and rips an entire wall to hell, or when he and Curly yank Moe right through the wall—is familiar enough. But other gags are downright sadistic.

Moe ratchets Curly's nose with an enormous manual pipe threader and then shoves Curly's face into a whirring grinder.

When Curly struggles to reach wires atop a phone pole, his wicked climbing spike jabs at least six inches through the top of Moe's head, into Moe's ear, and into Moe's eye. You exclaim out loud ("Eww!" "Gahh!" and "Oh, !†x!!#¢" are typical reactions), but you don't exactly laugh.

Moe finally encourages his pal to scoot the rest of the way with a jet of acety-lene flame aimed at Curly's bottom. Once there, Curly puts a "hot" wire on his tongue and is shortly electrocuted and blown through a window.

Whew!

The script is clever about Axis perfidy: Dent strokes a globe and then looks at his Japanese ally. "So den ve divide der vorldt in haff!" he pronounces. "Of course, Chermany gets der bigger haff!"

Vernon Dent is appropriately pompous and dim-witted (he goose-steps from room to room), and Dudley Dickerson is energetic and funny as an innocent cook who backs into a hot waffle maker after the phone explodes in his ear. In a montage sequence, young Lloyd Bridges appears in stock footage (possibly from *The Lone Wolf Takes a Chance*) as a fellow whose phone doesn't work.

And because of all the excitement, we never do learn whether the boys fix the doorbell.

OTHER THAN THE SMALL NOVELTY OF THE STOOGES IN BEARDS, *BACK FROM the Front* (1943) is pretty much business as usual—and that's mostly good. Because of a sensible strategic decision by producer-director Jules White, the manic satire of the boys' "Hitler" shorts is absent. The Hitler comedies had been well received, but, as the lesser novelty and slight falloff in quality of *I'll Never Heil Again* suggests, the premise wasn't indefinitely sustainable. Moe Hailstone would have lost his edge and worn out his welcome.

At the beginning of *Back from the Front*, the boys are identified as Pinky (Moe), Blinky (Larry), and Stinky (Curly); thankfully, we never hear those names again. The monikers exist only so that writers Jack White and Ewart Adamson can set up a euphonious rhyme with the names of the boys' sweethearts, Tizzy, Lizzy, and Dizzy (Sally Cairns, Ruth Skinner, and Adele Mara, respectively). With much ado about being "off to see the sea," the Stooges inform the girls that they've decided to do their bit for Uncle Sam in the U.S. Merchant Marine.

A civilian arm of the U.S. Navy in peacetime, Merchant Mariners are military personnel during war, so although the boys' happy announcement may now seem "cute" and suggestive of only modest danger, audiences of 1943 knew that this was perilous service. One in twenty-six Merchant seamen died during the war (the highest casualty rate of any service). Death came from wounds, drown-ing, fire, freezing, and starvation.

More than 215,000 seamen—a dramatic increase from the prewar total of 55,000—successfully moved countless tons of much-needed equipment, supplies, and personnel to hot spots around the globe. (According to American Merchant Marine at War [www.usmm.org], seven to fifteen tons of supplies were needed to support one U.S. soldier for one year.)

Much of the materiel, such as fuel and ammunition, was highly dangerous. The bravery, and utility, of the Merchant Marine during World War II can scarcely be overstated, particularly during 1942 (the likely shooting date of *Back from the Front*), when cargo ships lost to German submarines and other vessels outstripped U.S. shipbuilding capacity by a factor of about 2.3 to 1. (That ratio would be reversed during 1943.)

Audience understanding of the great importance of the Merchant Marine immediately marks the boys as brave and selfless. Further, when their merchant ship is torpedoed, the boys' only foolishness is between themselves. After climbing aboard a German raider, they give remorseless focus to the elimination of the raider as a fighting ship. The raider is the SS *Shickelgruber*, a possibly intentional misspelling of "Schicklgruber," the surname of Adolf Hitler's father, Alois, until Alois was thirty-nine. Although Adolf never had the name (he was born when Alois was nearly fifty-two), Americans and other Allies took delight in its garble of syllables.

The boys lure German sailors into cargo nets, drench them in baked beans, conk their foreheads with a block and tackle, and just rap them over the skulls, to be carried away by Curly and Moe as the sailors fall unconscious over the boys' shoulders. A great laugh comes when Larry tries this tactic on a very tall, very fat sailor (Jack "Tiny" Lipson) who obediently falls unconscious and drapes himself over Larry, whose legs immediately buckle. Until Moe and Curly rescue him, Larry is helplessly squashed.

The climactic confrontation in the captain's quarters, during which the Stooges briefly reprise their impersonations of Hitler, Göring, and Goebbels, is good, unsubtle fun. Hitler-Moe barks, "Blow out your brains!" The flustered captain (Stanley Blystone) can only respond, "But mein Führer, we are Nazis, we haff no brains!"

In the end, the boys simply grease the deck outside the captain's door and wait for Blystone and the others to slide over the edge and into the sea. And to be sure the job is complete, Moe picks up a section of railing and throws it onto the Germans below. We don't see them, but their cries suggest that Moe—a patriot, after all—has ensured that they will go to watery graves.

Of the supporting cast, Blystone and Vernon Dent (as a sneak who had been aboard the boys' merchant ship and arranged for its sinking) are emphatically pompous and menacing. And Adele Mara, a pretty brunette who enjoyed a minor but prolific career in second leads and the occasional B-picture lead role, is expressive and good-humored as Dizzy.

Frank Capra famously pondered *Why We Fight*. Well, for freedom, of course, and for Dizzy and all the rest of the loved ones who wait at home.

But in a coda that was scripted and never filmed, the boys return and discover that their girls have cheated on them!

HIGHER THAN A KITE (1943) CASTS THE BOYS AS AMERICAN EXPATS IN BRITAIN who hope to aid the RAF in the war effort, but instead of flying, they're exiled to the motor pool, where their biggest challenge is to repair the colonel's car. They make a mess of it, raising the ire of their supervisor (Duke York, in his only Stooges role as a normal fellow instead of a monster or half-human goon). In the second part of this conspicuously two-piece short, the boys literally ride a bomb into a German army headquarters and subsequently make life miserable for some top Nazis.

Higher Than a Kite is easy to like. It's funny and fast-paced, and although its two distinct stories are strung together with the thinnest thread of glue, it doesn't fail in its mission to make us laugh.

That the boys serve with the RAF rather than with the Army Air Corps is peculiar, but there is a plausible explanation. When the Stooges' previous wartime short, *Back from the Front*, was in preparation, the Columbia front office killed the first-draft script, claiming that the navy would take offense. Nobody enjoys an edict like that, so it's probable that scripters Elwood Ullman and Monte Collins and director Del Lord sidestepped potential objections to *Kite* right from the jump, allowing the Stooges to be an embarrassment to the RAF instead of to the U.S. Army.

So it is that, at "A Flying Field Somewhere in Somewhere," the boys abuse each other with a vacuum cleaner, a chain vice, exhaust soot, a superheated forge, and a hammer.

Some of the action is surreal: As Curly prepares to work on the colonel's engine, the barely opened hood swallows his crowbar with a liquid gulp. A little later, when a jacked-up tire rotates against Moe's chest and propels him and his creeper backwards into a large section of pipe, trapping his head, that same crowbar is maladroitly used by Larry and Curly in an obviously painful attempt to free him.

When the mess the Stooges have made of the car is discovered, the boys race across the airfield and into a "sewer pipe" that turns out to be a blockbuster bomb. Taken aloft (via stock footage of a B-25) and dropped over a German target (by a stock-footage B-17), boys and bomb land unexploded in the office of Field Marshal Böring.

Curly tries to eat a hand grenade (he thinks it's an avocado) and then tosses it through a window, where it explodes and reduces the German soldiers outside to their swastika-festooned long underwear.

The boys play Chinese checkers with the pins in Böring's plotting map, making a mess that appalls Field Marshal Bommel (Vernon Dent), who arrives on a tiny wooden scooter because he's "only got a 'A' card" (the lowest-priority American gasoline-ration classification).

"Der 28th Division iss in der Red Sea!" Bommel cries as he scans the map. "Und der Afrika Korps iss in der North Pole!" Böring (Dick Curtis) is speechless.

Fortunately, Bommel has arrived with new plans "from der Führer. He got them from a new astrologer!"

Bommel soon discovers Larry, who has disguised himself in drag so that he looks like an unnerving combination of Veronica Lake, Carmen Miranda, and, well, Larry Fine. "I am Moronica!" Larry coos in seductive falsetto.

Bommel is smitten. "Ach, a lady! Well, bizness could wait! Come here, my liddle edelweiss! Sit on my lap!"

Larry looks dubious. "*What* lap?" (At this, Dent does a beautiful slow burn, with a glance at the camera, in the manner of Oliver Hardy.)

Moe (by now in a purloined German uniform) senses it's time to grab the plans and leave. "Pardon me, general, I think I know the froleen. [To Larry:] Did you ever play football for the Giants?"

Larry grabs the plans from Bommel but not before having more fun at the field marshal's expense: "I love every chin on your face!"

Found out at last, the boys beat a retreat, with a portrait of Hitler stuck to the seat of Curly's pants. Böring dearly wants to bayonet this cheeky American but can't because each time Curly turns around, Böring sees the Führer, and goes into the reflexive "Heil, Hitler!"

But on the street outside, a U.S. Marine bulldog outside sees Hitler, too, and attaches himself to Curly's butt as the boys make their escape.

Yes, the bulldog, like the Stooges, is a long way from home. We'll hope that stock footage of *something* waits to fly boys and pooch back to safety.

WHEN A SHERIFF SOLEMNLY INFORMS A MOTORIST THAT FUGITIVE JAPS ARE ON the loose *and* that an ostrich has gone AWOL from a nearby circus, you can guess that the bird, anyway, is going to account for some of the laughs in *The Yoke's on Me* (1944).

The goofy-looking thing ends up in a barn occupied by the Stooges, who have purchased a busted farm because they can't pass the army physical. Other than a goose that likes to bite Curly's nose, the place has none of the livestock that's been promised—not even a horse. So Moe straps Curly and Larry into plow harness and makes about four inches of progress on a barren patch of field. Handily enough, the barn has a cache of blasting powder that Moe plans to use to prepare the field.

The ostrich gobbles some of the powder and then lays huge, ostrich-style eggs that are as stable as a jigger of nitro.

And who can resist throwing eggs during the climax of a Stooges short?

Another laugh comes from a snippet of poorly enunciated, unscripted dialogue, so you have to be ready to listen closely. When the wily old duff (Emmett Lynn) who's unloaded his farm on the Stooges has trouble starting his car, he mutters, "Git up! Go on! Bastard."

Oops.

Well, Mr. Lynn kicked Hollywood's Production Code right in the shins with that one and got away with it.

"Bastard" might have gotten a laugh in the big cities but wouldn't have gone over well at all in America's wide-open spaces, where godliness was a loudly proclaimed virtue. Wide-open spaces in, say, Colorado and Arizona, Arkansas and California, Utah and Wyoming, where respect and decorum mattered—and where the United States government illegally imprisoned Americans of Japanese ancestry.

Spurred by race-baiting senators and other politicians, and mindful of growing public paranoia about spies and saboteurs, President Roosevelt signed

Executive Order 9066 on February 19, 1942, authorizing the interning of some 120,000 Japanese—men, women, the aged, and children—living in America. About 60 percent of those arrested and imprisoned were U.S. citizens. (Some resident-alien Germans and Italians also were arrested.)

Local opportunists seized Japanese businesses, homes, automobiles, and other assets. Many white businessmen welcomed the forced disappearance of their hardworking competitors.

Internees were shipped to ten Inland War Relocation Camps in the states noted above (plus others), arriving with only what they were able to carry. The prisoners lived in plain wooden barracks with common-area latrines, surrounded by barbed wire and armed guards. Depending on location and time of year, the internees suffered extremes of heat or cold.

The Yoke's on Me, besides mining laughs from ostriches and bastards, looks for humor in the Stooges' run-in with Japanese "escapees" from a nearby camp. The uncredited Asian bit players (probably Chinese Americans) are costumed in sinister-looking, penal-style coveralls and want to kill the Stooges—never mind that internees wore civilian clothes and were teachers, truck farmers, and owners of hardware stores, and not soldiers.

A protracted bit involving grinning jack-o-lanterns carved by the Stooges, and subsequently—and illogically—worn by the Japanese as disguises, is elaborated

Interned Japanese civilians inexplicably become pumpkinheaded killers in *The Yoke's on Me* (1943), the least funny and intrinsically most unpleasant of the Stooges' war-years shorts.   *Photo courtesy of the Stoogeum*

on by writer Clyde Bruckman and director Jules White when the *Stooges* put on pumpkinheads, too, "so they'll think we're on their side!"

Finally, the boys pick up those TNT ostrich eggs and face the Asian fiends. "If we gotta die," Moe says, "at least we'll scramble some Japs with these eggs!" And they do, killing the Japanese. (Sprawled unmoving on the barn floor and hanging limply from beams and rafters, they certainly appear dead.) The Stooge's success as a three-man death squad removes the sting of their earlier rejection by the army.

All of this dubious patriotism is leavened by some bright moments. Arriving on the farm, Larry says, "I don't see a single cow!" Curly adds, "I don't even see a married one!"

Wordplay that begins with "goose" leads to gooses, gander, Goostapo, and propagander. Curly accidentally conks his own head with a hatchet when he tries to get the abusive goose but gently fills a narrow hole with water to free a trapped gosling.

After Curly pulls feathers from the ostrich (to a symphony of violin plucks), he slides into a graceful, very funny Sally Rand fan dance, using plumes to coyly cover his derriere.

Because of a minor but efficient cinematographer named Glen Gano, who worked mostly in two-reelers, *The Yoke's on Me* has the crisp, pleasingly sunlit look of a feature film. Gano's sound-stage work with the weirdly lurking Japanese is effective, too, with shifting shadows and a heavy sense of menace.

Asian menace.

DURING THE WAR, TYPICAL ANTI-AMERICAN CARTOON PROPAGANDA FROM Japan depicted Yanks as cucumber-nosed giants with enormous hands and feet, wavy blond hair, and peculiarly ovoid eyes. If these ogres weren't treading on the Japanese flag, they were slaughtering innocent Japanese children and forcing themselves on petite, horrified Japanese women. The cartoons encouraged Japanese to cringe and to remember this: Americans are monsters.

Such is propaganda.

In the opening scene of *No Dough, Boys* (1944), an American G.I. stands in triumph above three Japanese soldiers, his rifle high in his arms, the Japanese small and ineffectual at his feet. One of them weakly holds a shred of white cloth intended to indicate surrender.

We see a moment later that the tableau has been set up inside a photographer's studio, and that the Japanese are models wearing makeup. In fact, they're the Three Stooges.

Three Japs have escaped from a bold but failed submarine attack against the American mainland. So trouble begins when the boys break for lunch next door. The restaurant proprietor (Brian O'Hara) naturally assumes that the three uniformed Japanese at his table are the fugitives (what would *you* think?) and immediately tries to kill them.

Wow, some lunch break.

The boys escape after shoving the guy onto a hot stove. In a dingy alley behind the restaurant, Curly idly leans against an unmarked door and falls through into a gorgeously appointed mansion that apparently fronts on the next block. An overstuffed Nazi fifth columnist named Hans (Vernon Dent) happily greets the boys (who identify themselves as Naki, Saki, and Waki) and introduces them to three good-looking women who are accomplished Nazi operatives, Delia Pumpernickel, Amelia Schwartzbrot, and Celia Zwieback (Kelly Flint, Judy Malcolm, and Christine McIntyre, respectively).

Moe absorbs these yeasty names and remarks, "They're very well bread!"

The boys' demonstration of Japanese acrobatics doesn't go well, and things get hairy when the real Japanese show up. After a lot of mayhem, the Ratzis and Japs are subdued, and democracy (or at least the block) is saved.

No Dough, Boys is dominated by the long acrobatics sequence. The set piece is very funny and recalls some of the nonverbal knockabout that the Stooges and many other vaudeville clowns thrived on in the 1920s and '30s. Central to the gag is that the boys are graceless and clumsy but that they work hard to mount what they think is a good pretense of competence, constantly yelping "Hip! Hup! Ho!" as they bounce around on the balls of their feet and endlessly toss a handkerchief back and forth among themselves in an intriguing but idiotic round-robin.

Larry executes an exuberant and hilariously clumsy cartwheel (he lands, more or less, flat on his back), and Curly drops to the floor and rotates on his side and then imitates a barking seal. When Moe lies on his back and bravely attempts to flip Curly over his body, the trick finishes with Curly seated on Moe's face.

Hans insists on a ju-jitsu demonstration, which ends badly for Fräuleins Pumpernickel and Schwartzbrot, who are twirled like dolls by Moe and Larry. The boys don't really know what they're doing, but Fräulein Zwieback is an old hand at ju jitsu—as Curly discovers when he's flung so hard through the living room wall that his head pokes outside, where it's assaulted by a woodpecker. (Christine McIntyre diligently practiced the arm and leg moves that allow her to rotate and spin the much heavier Curly, but it's a shame that Felix Adler's script gives this wonderful actress almost nothing else to do.)

The climactic face-off with Hans and the real Japanese involves a pie, a lot of squirted seltzer water, and plenty of punching. In a gag that would be better executed in the boys' 1949 short *Who Done It?*, the Stooges and even one of the Japanese take turns switching the lights off at critical moments of the battle, plunging the room into utter blackness in which the mayhem is heard but not seen.

The short generally dismisses any pretense of satire, though Adler and White show their teeth when Moe (speaking with a mangled Japanese accent) promises Hans that the acrobatics have "falling, spilling of brains and blood. Velly beautiful!"

That's a good jaundiced joke. Another good one is considerably more gentle, and is taken right out of the Stan Laurel playbook, as Curly duplicates Stan's "white magic" when he packs his fist with tobacco, lights it, and happily puffs on his thumb.

A guy who does his duty deserves a good smoke.

COLUMBIA RELEASED THE ESPIONAGE COMEDY *FUELIN' AROUND* ON JULY 7, 1949, barely more than four months after a captured German V-2 rocket—named by its American operators *WAC-Corporal 1*—was fired to an altitude of 248 miles, becoming the first device to broach outer space. Barely more than two months later, on May 3, 1949, the United States successfully test-fired a rocket of its own design, the *Viking*, and on May 14, President Truman authorized the establishment of a rocket test range at Cape Canaveral, Florida.

Audiences couldn't help but notice the timeliness of *Fuelin' Around*, in which spies who have parked themselves in bushes across the street from a handsome suburban house make a critical boo-boo: Peering through binoculars, Captain Rork (Philip Van Zandt) gets a good look at Larry and mistakes him for Professor Sneed, inventor of a "super rocket fuel." Rork excitedly blurts, "There's no mistaking that magnificent head of hair!" The allusion to physicist Albert Einstein is underscored when the real Professor Sneed (Emil Sitka), long white hair artfully askew, sticks his head in to see how the Stooges are doing with laying his new carpet.

After an arduous day of slicing each other's toes and eyeballing the professor's daughter, Hazel (Christine McIntyre), the boys are kidnapped when they leave the house. Via skillfully utilized stock footage of an airplane and a European locomotive, Larry and his "assistants" are quickly spirited to the State of Anemia, an Eastern Bloc hellhole with a capital that looks like an 18th-century stone fortress by way of comic operetta: Larry even mistakes a gaudily uniformed general (Vernon Dent) for a doorman.

As the boys stall for time inside a well-equipped lab, Shemp (who's been staggered after pulling a heavy flask onto his head) sticks the end of a funnel into Moe's sleeve instead of into a beaker. Director Ed Bernds sets up the gag as a two-shot before cutting to a close-up on Moe's face in the instant before his eyes dart upward. Whatever it is that's dribbling down his arm, it doesn't feel good, and Moe jumps up in a panic, whacking the already addled Shemp.

Completely by accident, the boys synthesize something that wants to burn a hole through the table. Moe exclaims, "If you put this stuff into an airplane, something's *bound* to happen!"

The boys are thanked for their contribution to Anemian science. "Oh, think nothing of it," Larry says amiably as he heads for the door. "Drop us a line and let us know how you come out."

But when the general produces the real Professor Sneed and his daughter and locks them in a basement cell, the boys are left in the lab above to await the firing squad. In a pretty smart stroke, Larry uncorks the "fuel" and burns a hole in the floor—which he promptly falls through.

The group escapes in a jeep that Shemp fuels with Larry's concoction. Blowback from the exhaust reduces the general and a coterie of Anemian soldiers to their long johns, which are covered in medals—a good dig at the Soviet propensity for ostentatious military adornment.

The special nature of *Fuelin' Around* is that it's a showcase for Larry, who is the pivot point of the plot. This time, "the Stooge in the middle" is the engine that drives the action. It's easy to forget that the Stooges were accomplished actors, but we're reminded of that in this short, particularly when Larry briefly tries to pass himself off to Sneed as the head carpet layer, and later as he struggles to impersonate the professor. There's a pleasingly offhand quality to Larry's line readings. He doesn't recite but *reacts* to changing situations.

The sense of reality is heightened by Elwood Ullman's smart script and by Bernds's crisp direction. With a solid contribution from editor Henry Batista, Bernds effectively mixes close-ups, two-shots, and three-shots, while utilizing the frame from back-to-front as well as from side-to-side.

The European-style Anemia exteriors were filmed on an ornate standing set. It's an impressive setup, with a curved cobblestone street lined with shops and apartments that culminates at the foreboding stone headquarters/prison.

The Stooges stock company is terrific here, with Dent and Van Zandt asked to do broad burlesque turns, while Sitka and McIntyre—rather unexpectedly—take perfectly straight roles. Their solemnly understated performances wouldn't be out of place in a feature-length thriller.

Christine McIntyre has a nice opportunity to turn on her irresistible charm in a jailhouse sequence played with a handsome young newcomer billed as Jacques O'Mahoney—well known later as Jock Mahoney. He's cast as a lovestruck guard (wearing another of those comic-opera uniforms) who's concerned about Hazel and her father. So that the professor can lift the guy's keys, Hazel shamelessly beguiles him, complimenting him on his dimples and his curly hair and telling him he ought to be in pictures. The fellow puffs up like a pampered peacock, and by the time he saunters off (only to conk himself twice on a hanging lamp), he's completely smitten—and the professor has the keys to the cell.

Fuelin' Around was remade, with new footage and a slightly altered storyline, for 1956 release as *Hot Stuff*. Most of the key footage is retained but plays out in a fresh context under the direction of Jules White. In Felix Adler's reworked script, the boys are no longer carpet layers but agents of Urania, a nation locked in fierce political combat with Anemia. Larry and the others simply *pose* as laborers in order to guard Sneed and his daughter.

Shemp died before *Hot Stuff* was filmed, so he appears only in stock footage from *Fuelin' Around*. Scenes with Sitka, McIntyre, and O'Mahoney are also pickup footage from the earlier comedy. However, Philip Van Zandt reprises his role as Captain Rork for a new expository scene with actor Gene Roth, who is cast as Rork's blowhard, alcoholic superior.

New footage with the Stooges is highlighted by a protracted office sequence at Urania's Department of the Inferior, where the boys get their orders. Big-eyed

An unfriendly nation that wants a new rocket-fuel formula barks up the wrong tree when it assumes Larry can provide it, in *Fuelin' Around* (1949).

Connie Cezan and stolid Evelyn Lovequist are Uranian intelligence officers; naturally, the boys are gaga for them, and let fly with typically gross and clumsy flirting.

Cezan had already made her mark with the Stooges in a succession of blonde-floozy roles. As befits her position of Uranian authority, her hair is darker in *Hot Stuff*, and she's all business. When she explains that the boys will impersonate carpet layers, Larry retorts, "Wait a minute! I can't lay carpet!"

Cezan coldly asks why. "I'm not that rugged!" Larry laughs uproariously at his joke (it *is* pretty funny), giving Moe an opportunity to pour an entire bottle of India ink down his gullet.

As is typical of the Shempless Shemp comedies, Larry and Moe carry more of the narrative than usual. The reason for Shemp's absence from the briefing sequence is established in a hallway setup, when Shemp (Joe Palma, shot mainly from behind while wearing a bearded disguise) is distracted by dark-haired knockout Suzanne Ridgeway, whose hip-swinging sashay along the corridor encourages Palma to follow after her.

Dunked in the Deep (1949) is the Stooges' final war-oriented short with all-new footage. The film also brings the Stooges into a new kind of conflict: the Cold War.

U.S.-Soviet relations went south after 1945, when Moscow's expansionist ambition became very clear. Politicians in both countries leapt into a war of words intended to create vivid distinctions between the respective ideologies.

Dunked in the Deep is neither disliked nor loved. People recall it mainly for a funny line of dialogue and for visual gags related to a spy's method of smuggling secret microfilm out of the country: He hides it in hollowed-out watermelons. The short was filmed at the end of 1948 or very early in 1949 for November 3 release.

Scripter Felix Adler was very obviously influenced by particular events of 1948. In March, the supposed suicide of a progressive Czech politician, Jan Masaryk, promised even tighter Soviet control of Czechoslovakia and the rest of Europe's Eastern Bloc. And then came June and the Soviets' purposely provocative blockade of eastern Berlin (the portion of the city it had received as war spoils in 1945). President Truman responded by mounting a tremendous American effort that air-dropped supplies into the city. The blockade was broken and the Soviets abandoned it the following spring, but the lines of U.S.-Soviet antagonism had become clear.

Inevitably, American fear of Communist infiltration and subversion began to grow. Later in the summer of 1948, a rumpled *Time* magazine senior editor and admitted self-rehabilitated ex-Communist named Whittaker Chambers accused a former mid-level State Department employee of Communist ties and espionage. The accused was Alger Hiss, a patrician easterner who had left State in 1947 to head up the Carnegie Endowment for International Peace. Chambers said that he and Hiss had been Party members in the 1930s, when Hiss was already in government employ.

The House Un-American Activities Committee (HUAC) took up the case. Particulars of Hiss's defense fell apart when Chambers revealed that he possessed more than sixty typed and handwritten pages of internal, low-level State Department correspondence from the spring of 1938—pages that had been purloined and copied by Hiss and later given to Chambers for safekeeping. If HUAC wanted proof, Chambers said, microfilmed copies would be found

Performer Profile: Gene Roth
1903–76

Late in his life, this very tall and husky character actor was reduced to tears as he was feted at a convention of film fans. A busy actor who was nevertheless largely anonymous throughout his forty-five-year screen career (1922–67), Roth was astounded and touched that he *had* been noticed, and enjoyed, by many.

Sometimes using the names Gene/Eugene Stutenroth, he got billing in serials and a few other small films but worked mainly without credit until getting heavily involved in television after the mid-1950s.

Roth made his first appearance with the Stooges in *Dunked in the Deep* (1946) as Bortch, the stowaway/spy whose microfilm has been appropriated by the Stooges. Famous line: "Giff me dat fillum!"

He's amiably monstrous as the Grand Zilch of Sunev in *Outer Space Jitters* and has fiendish fun with Joe Besser in *Quiz Whizz*, when he sits Joe on his lap and makes him eat a cigar.

Skilled at comedy, Roth also could be dead-serious dangerous, as he demonstrated in numerous supporting roles on TV's *The Untouchables*.

By 1949, America was engaged in a new kind of war: a Cold one. Here, Communist spy Bortch (Gene Roth) puts the boot to the boys aboard a lurching freighter in *Dunked in the Deep*.
Photo courtesy of the Stoogeum

inside a hollowed-out pumpkin on Chambers's farm in Westminster, Maryland. Chambers wasn't lying.

The Stooges' adversary in *Dunked in the Deep* is a tall, husky European spy named Bortch (Gene Roth). He probably doesn't own a farm, but he got the idea for the watermelons from somewhere. He's lively and deceptively affable: an eager drinker prone to vaguely sinister fits of laughter that culminate with glimpses of an awfully big knife. If director Jules White wanted a personification of duplicitous Soviet perfidy, he got it from Roth, an experienced actor who was most active in westerns during his long career.

Larry, Shemp, and Moe are alert and engaged throughout, and although the political humor begins and ends with Bortch, the film benefits from a nicely dingy cargo-hold set and some good laughs. After the spy has tricked the boys onto the ship that will take him to his own country, he jovially announces, "I got a secret for you. I am a stowaway and *you* are stowaways, hahahahaha!" The boys crack up, too, until Moe says, "Hey, what're we laughin' for?"

Shemp carelessly sets his hammock on fire and has a problem with a damp porthole. All three boys get seasick after eating Bortch's salami. Shemp, his face as pale as a bag of flour, makes a retching noise and leans against a water bucket, sending a small stream onto Moe—who, naturally enough, thinks he's been vomited on. The gag is tasteless, but you'll laugh.

Bortch sleeps with his watermelons—one cradled in each arm and the third beneath his head. The boys swipe two of them, but Larry winds up trapped beneath Bortch's head after using his own noggin to gently shove the pillow-melon free.

Moe and Shemp discover the microfilm. Bortch awakens and gets a stranglehold on Larry, and then launches into what becomes an amusing refrain: "Giff me dat fillum!"

When Moe and Larry try to clobber Bortch with a swinging block-and-tackle rig, they only conk themselves. Shemp has some fun when he leads the spy on a merry, well-choreographed zigzag chase among stacks of crates, and he's more agile than you'd expect after his feet become trapped in the watermelons.

Finally, Moe just *walks* the block and tackle over to Bortch and lets him have it.

Shemp opens that damned porthole one last time, and instead of taking a blast of seawater he's splattered with mud. "Land, land!" he cries exultantly.

A redo, *Commotion on the Ocean* (1956), is the fourth and last "fake Shemp" two-reeler cobbled together after the beloved comic's death. The film picks up much of the footage from *Dunked in the Deep*, though it ignores Shemp and Bortch's chase amidst the cargo, and also drops an amusing bit in which the boys make the mistake of violently cracking Brazil nuts against a crate of blasting caps.

Bortch's motivation is the same as before. Gene Roth returned with Moe and Larry to shoot a few minutes of mainly insert footage that helps explains the new premise: The boys are would-be reporters chasing after a big scoop. All of *that* is established with still more stock footage, from the opening sequence of *Crime on Their Hands* (1948; see "The Stooges and the Law").

Felix Adler's reworked script unwisely reminds us that Shemp is dead when Moe says, "I wonder what became of that Shemp?" Well, Shemp does appear briefly in new footage (all of which was shot in one day) but in the person of fill-in actor Joe Palma, who staggers behind Moe and Larry while dressed as Shemp, his forearm awkwardly covering his face.

A completely new sequence with sexy stock-company player Harriette Tarler pays off weakly when Moe and Larry—plus Roth, who essentially fills in for Shemp—cough up sawdust when they try to eat a purloined stuffed fish.

Because the Cold War had become hotter between 1949 and 1956, *Commotion on the Ocean* was even more politically timely than it had been when the story was called *Dunked in the Deep*. The USSR shocked America and the world by exploding its first atomic bomb in the summer of '49. The Korean War of 1950–53 had come and gone, but tensions on the Korean Peninsula ran high, and China, a key player in that war, was recognized as a deadly enemy.

The world situation was grave, but if not for the Stooges' patriotism, it would have been worse—and a lot less funny.

The Stooges
and the Law

In which the boys meet a big kitty; flee from an Angel; waste five good slugs on a divot; cheat Uncle Sam; make a deposit at a pet cemetery; invest in smog bags; get tight with a talking gorilla; study the sweet science of decapitation; work magic with a trectahomlachtameter; become beer barons; bark for dollars; play hide-the-poison; make little ones out of big ones; and have an adventure that never was.

Disorder in the Court (1936) is one of four Stooges two-reelers that Columbia inadvertently allowed to fall out of copyright in the 1960s. (*Malice in the Palace, Sing a Song of Six Pants,* and *Brideless Groom* are the others.) Because *Disorder in the Court* is the oldest of the four, the public-domain TV prints that float around on "budget" home video (often as a part of documentaries or spurious "Stooges Rarities" collections) are particularly scratched and dark, with muddy audio. Columbia's official video release is the only way to see this lively two-reeler by writer Felix Adler and director Preston Black (Jack White).

It's a saucy, sexy comedy about nightclub dancer Gale Tempest (Suzanne Kaaren, probably best remembered for the feature *The Devil Bat*), who stands accused of shooting a mug named Kirk Robin (from the British folk poem "Who Killed Cock Robin"). The Stooges, fellow club employees, are defense witnesses.

The Stooges function mainly as disruptive elements designed to kick court-room decorum in the pants. When the DA (Harry Semels) stands, the boys use chalk to play tic-tac-toe on his chair. When he sits down and then bolts to his feet again, the boys continue their game (with great vigor) on the tail of his jacket.

In a beautiful sequence, a short-fused court clerk (James C. Morton) mounts a persistent but doomed attempt to swear Curly in as a witness: "Doyousweartotellthetruththewholetruthandnothingbutthetruth?" It all comes out in a hilarious rush (Morton is wonderful), and Curly can't understand a single syllable. The clerk tries again and then once more.

The problem is compounded because Curly has to raise his right hand and place his left on the bible. Simple enough, except that Curly has stepped to the stand holding an umbrella and wearing his derby. Clerk: "Raise your right hand! Place your left hand on the bible!"

Judge: "Take off your hat!"

If Curly were an octopus he might be able to pull this off, but during this long, amusingly choreographed interlude it appears that he'll *never* get to his testimony.

When the judge allows Gale to reenact the shimmying dance she performed on the night of the murder, the Stooges play a cute honky tonk number, "Push 'Em Up." Shapely Suzanne Kaaren wears a black, low-cut costume that looks like a particularly revealing one-piece swimsuit. On top of that, the pretty actress is obviously braless, which rivets the attention of the male jurors.

The boys' accompaniment becomes a little too vigorous. Curly, on bass fiddle, loses his grip on his bow and launches it sideways into the mouth of the exasperated clerk. A minute later, after Moe accidentally swallows a tiny harmonica, Curly and Larry rhythmically press his abdomen and pump his arm, producing a not-bad rendition of "Have You Ever Seen a Lassie?"

The tormented clerk is victimized again when Larry's errant violin bow plucks the toupee from the fellow's head. Larry sees the toup hanging from the end of his bow and shrieks, "A tarantula!" (Curly simply says, "A field mouse!") After Larry shakes the ragged thing to the floor, Moe grabs the bailiff's revolver and blows off a few rounds.

"Tarantula?" he says disgustedly. "I shot five holes in a divot!"

The judge says simply, "Gentlemen, you must control your killing instincts!"

A parrot that is apparently part of the defense repeatedly croaks, "Read the letter!"—a letter that's attached to the bird's leg. In the end, all is explained: An egg named Buck Wing (from buck-and-wing, a style of tap dance) is the killer. Gale is free!

Disorder in the Court is equal parts visual and verbal. Defense attorney Bud Jamison opens with transparent compliments to the "intelligent" jury. Cut to the jury box, where we see a collection of nappers, slack-jaws, and mouth-breathers. (Two of the good-sport jurors are Jenny and Solomon Horwitz, parents of Moe, Shemp, and Curly.)

A little later, Jamison stumbles into the arms of an alarmingly homely female juror (Mack Sennett veteran Alice Belcher). "Broadview 9-9772," she whispers with horrifying seductiveness, "after five o' clock!"

The defense claims that because the action of the murder gun is so stiff, Gale couldn't possibly have pulled the trigger, which would "take the strength of a mule!" Jamison hands the gun to Curly and asks him to demonstrate.

"I'm no mule!" Curly says indignantly.

Moe: "No, your ears are too short!"

Disorder in the Court is the first Columbia short to spell "Curly" correctly on the main title card (instead of the previous "Curley"). It also introduces a redesigned Lady Columbia, seen for the first time on her famous pedestal.

OILY TO BED, OILY TO RISE (1939) IS GROUNDED IN CRIMINAL FRAUD AND THE Stooges' eagerness to repay a kindness. The short captures the boys at their best—as performers and as likable characters. *Oily to Bed* isn't just hilarious but quietly, honestly sweet.

When the short was filmed in March 1939, two-bit sharks prowled the nation's small towns and rural areas, looking for easy land deals that could be negotiated with impoverished or disenchanted farmers. Three such guys are Clipper (Dick Curtis), Briggs (Eddie Laughton), and an unnamed driver (James Craig, who later found B-movie stardom). For the moment, the con men are canvassing near a small town called Fairport. Their most recent mark is the Widow Jenkins (Eva McKenzie), a sweet-natured lady who has sold her farm for fifty dollars an acre after the crooks lied and told her a dust storm was coming. As soon as the chiselers can get to Fairport and record the deed, the farm will be lost.

Fate—and the hope of a free meal—brings the Stooges to the widow's door. She happily feeds them, and the boys offer to do chores as payment. They subsequently discover three things: The place is rich with oil, the widow has sold the land for a song, and she has three beautiful daughters. Inspired, the boys track down the crooks and take back the deed.

When Jules White directed *Oily to Bed*, the stars were in alignment: He had the then-standard four-day shooting schedule; a cinematographer (Henry Freulich) who got good results in sunny exteriors; the Stooges, who were at or near their peaks as performers; a solid supporting cast; and an eventful and richly verbal script by Andrew Bennison and Mauri Grashin.

The boys' early encounter with a young farmer (Richard Fiske) ends with the careless destruction of the farmer's saws and a remarkable, blubbery temper fit thrown by Curly, who's driven crazy by the trap door of a wagon that won't stay closed. He flings himself on the ground and cries, "Moe, Larry, I'm so *aggravated, Moe, Larry!*"

A running gag is Curly's habit of making impossible wishes that annoy Moe but nevertheless come true: a meal, a car (a complete misunderstanding), and cigars (which Curly and Moe discover in the car's back-seat storage compartment). As all three boys light up, Larry forgets that he's driving and allows the car to drift toward a cliff edge. "Hey, don't look know," Curly says pleasantly, "but I think we're about to be killed!"

At the Jenkins place, the boys pause on the porch after their meal.

LARRY
Boy, isn't this a beautiful spot?

CURLY
You said it! It brings out the wood nymph in me! You know, I
wish we could meet three beautiful girls so we could settle
down out here!

Cue the return of the Jenkins girls, April, May, and June ("Three of the *prettiest* months of the year!" Curly grins), who have been busy in town winning a beauty contest. Let's pause here to note that every available source confuses the credits for the actresses who play the sisters. The error is easily rectified by careful observation of the order in which the Widow Jenkins introduces her girls.

For the record, the proper credits are Dorothy Moore (April), Adrian Booth (May), and the barely glimpsed Linda Winters aka Dorothy Comingore of *Citizen Kane* fame (June). Miss Moore is the adorable actress who apparently attracted Curly's real-life attention during the shoot of *Calling All Curs* (see "The Stooges on the Job") and who is romanced by him in this short.

After volunteering to take a look at the Widow Jenkins's water pump (the farm's water tastes like coal oil), the boys release a geyser of black gold, which they stop by positioning Curly atop the naked pump spindle, like a cork. When the geyser blows again, Curly (or rather, his stunt double) is taken aloft with it in a fabulously good mechanical effect.

Remember that free car? It belongs to Clipper and the other con men, who spot it and jump inside to confront the Stooges (after Curly wishes he could meet the bums who swindled the widow). Because of the mess made by the oil, the Stooges are dressed in the widow's clothes—bonnets and all—but Clipper is so pissed he's ready to clobber somebody, "dame or no dame!" The boys recover the deed and then flip the crooks backwards onto the road.

Back at the Jenkins place, a justice of the peace (Victor Travers) shows up.

Curly wishes for quintuplets and suggests a Canadian honeymoon (a cute nod to the famed Dionne quintuplets of Ontario, Canada).

Farm deeds, good deeds—it all adds up to happiness.

FROM NURSE TO WORSE (1940) IS KICKED OFF BY THE STOOGES' FRIEND JERRY (Lynton Brent), who sells insurance. But because he's not really their friend at all, he pitches this idea: For twenty-five dollars down and fifty a month, he'll write a policy on Curly. The only thing Moe and Larry have to do after that is to march Curly to the insurance office and tell the examiner that he's insane. On the spot, the company will write a check for five hundred simoleons.

Momentarily overcome by the prospect of easy money, the boys forget—if they ever knew at all—that this is called insurance fraud, and it's against the law. In two shakes of an Airedale's tail, Moe and Larry attempt the scam. Curly is with them—tethered to a leash and larking about on all fours, barking and growling. Yikes, he thinks he's a dog! He's so enthusiastic that you wonder about his mental state—more than usual, that is. Moe just wants the check. "C'mon, Hydrophobia," he says impatiently, and gives the leash a good tug.

The examining doctor (Vernon Dent) is indeed convinced that Curly is nuts and announces—before anybody has a chance to bring up the five hundred bucks—that Curly must be operated on at once.

"Don't worry, it won't hurt," the doc says reassuringly. "I'm just going to take the top of your head off right there"— a bisection that's alarmingly low on Curly's forehead. Unable to get a second opinion, the boys beat it, becoming fugitives in an adventure that will involve doctors, nurses, the dog pound, a persistent cop, babies, Bellevue, and a crematory. Oh, and a little frontier justice.

Insurance companies hate like hell to pay out on false claims. The great humor of *From Nurse to Worse* is that even after Curly-dog breaks character and escapes, the doctor is convinced that no fakery is going on. You get the idea that the boys can have their money, no problem with that at all, as long as they let the doc take a double-scoop from Curly's brain.

Performer Profile: Cy Schindell
1907–48

Flat-faced, pugnacious Cy Schindell excelled in many Stooges shorts as excitable thugs, henchmen, and cops. He amassed scores of appearances between 1934 and 1942, was absent from the screen while in the Army in 1943, and picked up where he left off in 1944.

Schindell worked in serials and A- and B-pictures (he's a leopard man in *Tarzan and the Leopard Woman*) but devoted the better part of his energies to Columbia shorts starring the Stooges, Charley Chase, Billie Burke, Schilling and Lane, Sterling Holloway, and others.

Fans recall him fondly as the hapless thug, Moose, who gets conked on the head by bricks in *Fright Night*, only to be manipulated by the Stooges like a slack-jawed marionette. And he's all over the screen in *Mutts to You* as a persistent cop who chases the Stooges every which way through a hospital, halts with the boys at the maternity-ward window to admire the babies, and then comes to his senses and resumes the chase.

Schindell was taken by cancer when he was just forty-one.

When the boys' insurance scam goes awry in *From Nurse to Worse* (1940), officer Cy Schindell is vigorous in pursuit.
Photo courtesy of the Stoogeum

Self-preservation, and the boys' loyalty to each other, turns them into fugitives. In the back of a dogcatchers' truck, Curly communicates with the rest of the dogs before the whole gang—dogs and Stooges—forms a conga line of mutual back-scratching (fleas, you see).

Finally nabbed by a cop (Cy Schindell) right outside Bellevue, Curly is dragged inside and prepped for brain surgery. As Moe and Larry lead the flatfoot on a fast chase through the corridors, Curly manages events so that the doctor, and not he, is on the verge of having his brain pan opened.

Footage lifted from *Dizzy Doctors* (see "The Stooges on the Job") kicks off the final sequence, in which the boys literally run into Jerry and fix his wagon.

From Nurse to Worse has nice turns by numerous Stooges regulars. Vernon Dent is at once genial and slightly demented as Dr. D. Lerious. The alphabet soup on his office door—M.D. CCC. FHA. WPA. A.W.O.L.—is one of many affirmations in the boys' shorts of their support (or Jules White's or Columbia's or somebody's) of President Roosevelt's New Deal.

Johnny Kascier appears as an innocent orderly who just wants to deliver a meal, only to be repeatedly flattened in collisions with the boys and burly Schindell. (Kascier's falls are fabulously good.)

Another orderly (Dudley Dickerson) hurls himself through a window when the Stooges, stacked three-high beneath a sheet on a gurney that's to be sent to the crematory, stir and talk.

Pretty Dorothy Appleby brings her expressive face and eyes to her role as the receptionist who's the first to be nonplussed by the barking Curly. And Cy Schindell has his best role ever with the Stooges, enforcing the law with physical vigor and dim-witted determination. He slips, he falls; he takes fingers in the eyes and stops a swinging door with his face. As written by Clyde Bruckman (story by Charles L. Kimball), the role has nothing in particular to recommend it. The part is all about its potential—which Schindell, to our delight, uncovers.

The whole mess would never have happened at all if the boys had been unable to scrape up the money for the policy. Moe knows his pals are holding out, and for starters he forces Curly to undo about seven vests and unlock the padlocked purse that hangs against his chest. With that accomplished, Moe aims a sinister glare at Larry. "You're next. Shoot the money to me, honey."

What have we learned?

You can't insure against human nature.

DIOGENES, ONE OF THE ORIGINAL CYNICS, SEARCHED ACROSS ANCIENT GREECE for an honest man because he wanted to satisfy himself that no such creature existed. The Stooges, although roundly buffeted by life, are not cynics, so they cry right along with the weeping young woman (Dorothy Appleby) who tells them that her sweetheart, Percy Pomeroy, is in the local jail for theft. "[B]ut he didn't do it!" she insists. "He's honest! Honest, he's honest!" Are the boys willing to set him free? (A surviving production still suggests a deleted sequence in which the Stooges and Appleby are joined by a crying cop, played by Bud Jamison.)

To engineer the freedom of a stranger is the central challenge of Clyde Bruckman and Felix Adler's *So Long, Mr. Chumps* (1941, from *Goodbye, Mr. Chips*), and it ties in nicely with another one dreamed up for the boys by a fellow named B. O. Davis (John Tyrrell). While working as street cleaners, the boys find oil bonds belonging to Mr. Davis and return them. For reasons that are rather obscure, Davis promises the boys five large if they bring an honest man to him. (Apparently the *Stooges'* honesty is inadequate to win the prize.)

The boys try the old wallet-on-a-string gag and turn up nothing but dishonest men. The only honest man, as Moe notes with no little disgust, is a dog that brings the wallet back to them and then leads them to the unhappy Miss Appleby. At last, a chance to find a bona fide honest man! Naturally, the best way to rescue the fellow is to do it from inside the jail, so the boys set off to get themselves arrested.

They kick a cop in the pants and provoke laughter from a passerby. The cop arrests the passerby.

Curly corners a citizen against a wall, pulls a gun to stick him up, and then orders Moe and Larry to "get a cop!" When they return, the tables have somehow been turned, and it's Curly who stands against the wall at gunpoint. The cop is pleased: "It's Gyp! Gyp DePeople!"

Inside a precinct station, the boys confess awful crimes to the desk sergeant (Vernon Dent), who genially laughs them off. As the old saying goes, the boys "couldn't get arrested in this town." But when they tackle a station cop so that he's not brained by a falling light fixture, they're busted for assault and promised a year in jail.

Moe makes a vain appeal to reason: "We gotta be home for dinner!"

In a heartbeat, the Stooges are in striped prison uniforms that director Jules White turns into clever visual counterpoint to the innocuous street cleaners' uniforms the boys wore earlier. After various misadventures inside prison walls, the boys locate Pomeroy (Eddie Laughton). Before everybody paints their uniforms black, to pass as guards, we see that the number on Pomeroy's is 41144. That's a riff on Four Eleven Forty Four, or 4-11-44, "lucky numbers" beloved by black American "policy" (numbers-racket) bettors of the late 19th and 20th centuries. In folklore, the numbers may also have sexual connotations pertaining to penis size. Years later, Jules White and Felix Adler pulled the little joke again by noting, incidentally, that the address of the sexy gold digger of *Gypped in the Penthouse* (1955) is 41144.

So Long, Mr. Chumps is comprised of two major set pieces: the boys' exertions as street cleaners and their time at the jail. Street cleaning is prole work of a low sort, but the boys pursue it with diligence—well, except for Curly, who empties his dustpan beneath a lifted divot of sod. Larry accidentally pokes Moe in the arse with his paper spike, and Curly has trouble getting rid of a piece of flypaper until he deposits it on Moe's face.

In an especially exuberant display, Curly frolics on grass that's been saturated by in-ground sprinklers, flinging himself onto his stomach from a dead run and sliding like an otter.

In the joint, Curly steals the lunchmeat from a guard's sandwich and replaces it with a stripe of paint. Another guard (Lynton Brent) is outraged when Curly gets paint on his face. Neither contrite nor vindictive, Curly simply says, "Oh, pardon me, there's a white spot!"—and slaps his brush against the guard's puss until the guy is as black as coal.

Performer Profile: Eddie Laughton
1903–52

British-born Edgar Laughton had been a boyhood friend of young Larry Fine. He started his Hollywood career in 1935 and put together more than two hundred screen appearances in fifteen years. Laughton stayed busy in features as a general-purpose actor, usually in small supporting roles. His dapper good looks and pencil mustache brought him many roles as desk clerks and partygoers, as well as parts as thieves, kidnappers, loggers, and ordinary Joes.

He also was a frequent straight man for the Stooges during the boys' live appearances.

In shorts with the Stooges, Laughton is well recalled as the jailed innocent man, Pomeroy, in *So Long, Mr. Chumps*; and as the socialite partygoer of *In the Sweet Pie and Pie*, whose retelling of his safari encounter with a lion is continually interrupted by pies that collide with his face. "*Never*," he says finally, "have I been in such a lion fight!"

Eddie Laughton, in his best role with the Stooges, as the wrongly imprisoned Pomeroy in *So Long, Mr. Chumps* (1941). Although not visible here, the number on Pomeroy's uniform is the fabled Four Eleven Forty Four.   *Photo courtesy of the Stoogeum*

Later, the boys need keys to free Pomeroy. Curly addresses a guard (Bruce Bennett) who's preoccupied with a phone conversation with the warden.

CURLY
Can I borrow your keys?

GUARD *(to warden)*
Yes, of course, go right ahead!

CURLY
Thanks!

GUARD
You're welcome, no trouble at all, don't even mention it!

CURLY
He's a swell guy!

Pomeroy will go free, and in a surprise run-in with B. O. Davis, the boys learn that their generous patron has been arrested for fraud. For the moment, the boys' world almost seems a just one. But at the end of the film the Stooges are back in the prison yard, methodically breaking rocks on Curly's head, serving the rest of their time for a crime they didn't commit.

Moe, after listening to Pomeroy's unhappy sweetheart earlier in the film, is sufficiently astute to sum up a perennial situation that exists beyond the boundaries of this or any other movie. "Maybe she's right," Moe says. "Maybe all the honest men *are* in jail."

WITH *THREE SMART SAPS* (1942), WRITER CLYDE BRUCKMAN AND DIRECTOR Jules White recall a lot of the injustice-against-the-individual theme of *So Long, Mr. Chumps.* The victim this time isn't just an "ordinary" citizen but a prison warden, victimized by the corrupt local political machine and made an inmate of his own prison. Meanwhile, the pols have turned much of the place into a chi-chi casino.

Improbably enough, the Stooges are engaged to the warden's daughters, Stella, Nella, and Bella. (Maybe Dad came to like the boys after running into them in an official capacity, who knows?) As in the earlier comedy, the Stooges decide that they can do their most effective rescue work from the inside, so they contrive to get themselves arrested—and that's difficult. They hurl rocks at a storefront, unaware that the display glass in unbreakable. (The rocks just bounce off and crack Moe's skull.) When they try to get into the casino through the back door, they're rapped by somebody's fist.

And then, in a propitious lapse of security, the door just *falls* open. The boys collapse inside and locate the unhappy warden (John Tyrrell). He's locked up but hands across a camera. Snap enough pictures of what's going on, he says, and he can get out and the girls can marry.

During a lengthy and wonderful sequence that's part crime exposé, part send-up of the idle rich, the boys accomplish their mission.

Three Smart Saps takes its title from *Three Smart Girls*, a popular 1936 Universal vehicle for singing star Deanna Durbin. The *Saps* title suggests a certain fluffiness of attitude, and while the short has its fluffy moments, its emphasis on wrongful political imprisonment of an honest official is an obvious reaction to what had been going on in Europe for the better part of ten years, and with particular fervor since Germany's 1940 invasion of France and nearby nations and its subsequent establishment of Vichy and other puppet governments. The warden's predicament is a more pointed explication of the topsy-turvy justice that informs *So Long, Mr. Chumps*.

The boys snap pictures throughout the casino and especially on a dance floor, where friends of the corrupt political machine shake their tootsies. Curly ends up in a borrowed suit that's too large and loosely basted, so Larry positions himself behind a curtain with needle and thread, ready to do repairs on the fly as Curly dances past. But in an ill omen, Larry's hiding place has a liquor cart, which Larry reacts to with a happy "Ah, spirits!"

In the short's funniest and best-directed sequence, Curly has trouble with a trouser leg and must dance his gorgeous partner (former Powers model Barbara Slater) over to the curtain. Rakishly seating himself backwards on a chair so that he can extend his leg to Larry, Curly makes small talk until the amiably lubricated Larry accidentally jabs his leg with a needle. Curly yelps from the other side of the curtain and his lower leg shoots up, catching Larry in the face. When Larry collapses, his weight comes down on the leg and pulls Curly inexorably downward on the chair. Larry's continued fumbling finally sends Curly to the floor, his chair flipping from beneath his arms and conking him on the head.

There are a number of wonderful things about this sequence: Curly's brave pretense of normalcy, Larry's brilliant physical comedy, and the work of Jules White and his editor, Jerome Thoms (who later edited *The Naked Kiss* and other films by Sam Fuller), who deftly cut back and forth between both sides of that curtain, letting the gag build and climax, and giving it literal weight—you can almost feel the press of Larry's body on Curly's trapped limb.

Despite this disaster, the boys snap all the pictures needed to bring down the whole criminal enterprise.

In a cute coda, the Stooges prepare to depart for their honeymoon. Some violent gags with thrown shoes are funny (and not at all unexpected), but in an oddly amusing throwaway that has no immediately apparent payoff, Curly's pants are held up with a chain and padlock (in an earlier scene, he can't find his belt). In the final shot of *Three Smart Saps*, the newly married Curly waltzes toward the camera, his padlocked pants clearly visible.

Isn't there a law against preventing a man from enjoying his wedding night?

WITH *DIZZY DETECTIVES* (1943), JULES WHITE AND FELIX ADLER MIX 'N' MATCH a couple of can't-miss propositions: the Stooges as inept police patrolmen and a brazen burglary ring headed by someone—or something—known as the

Ape Man. With regard to the latter, the short is very much in the venerable "spook" mold, especially because most of it plays out at night, inside an eerie antiques store, where one of the many useful items for sale is a guillotine.

A community leader named Mr. Dill (John Tyrrell) gives Police Commissioner I. Doolittle (Bud Jamison) a good dressing-down about the department's inability to squelch the Ape Man gang. The Stooges happen to witness his scolding and are thus handy, so the commissioner sends them out to solve the case.

Something fishy is going on at the Bruckman Building (yes, *that* Bruckman), and as Moe, Larry, and Curly fumble to locate a pass key, the door behind them is quietly opened by an enormous gorilla (onetime serial and western star Ray "Crash" Corrigan).

At this, any pretense of realism goes right out the window, and you can't keep from smiling like the village idiot. In the spooky interior—cleverly designed by Carl Anderson and lit in luscious shadow by Benjamin Kline—the gorilla fades into the woodwork as the boys nervously explore. A gag that involves Curly, a dark room, a cat's tail, and a rocking chair is satisfying because Curly plays it well ("I'm not afraid," he mutters to himself. "Only babies are afraid.") and because White postpones the payoff long enough to put you on edge. As an element of narrative, the gag's noisy climax is a propulsive device that throws you into the next scene.

Because the boys have let themselves be convinced that the Ape Man is just a criminal in a costume, when they finally run across the gorilla, they eagerly pull their guns and kick it in the ass. They feel pretty good until the monkey bends the guns' barrels like warm taffy.

Uh oh.

The rest of the gang arrives (led, of course, by Mr. Dill), and the boys are at a disadvantage until the gorilla drinks a bottle of nitroglycerine.

Like many Stooges' shorts, *Dizzy Detectives* lets us enjoy the boys' familiar ineptitude even as the plot places them on a moral plane higher than the ones occupied by other characters. Dill is a fraud and a reprobate, puffing himself up with faked outrage as he connives to discredit the commissioner and take his job. And the commissioner might at least be expected to have doubts about Dill, but because he doesn't, he's just another lazy bureaucrat sequestered in an office. Whatever the Stooges' myriad failings, fakery and pretentiousness aren't among them.

Of course, a lack of pretension is no guarantee of competence. Moe is excited to be a cop mainly because of the prospect of free apples. When he asks Curly why he doesn't have his gun, Curly says he gave it to the landlady's baby to play with.

Later, just as Curly slides his neck beneath the (rubber) blade of the guillotine and thoughtlessly pulls the release, the ape angrily knocks off the head of a mannequin and sends it skittering across the floor to Moe and Larry, who faint dead away.

The nitroglycerine explosion that puts an end to Dill's mischief rather grue-somely severs the head of the ape, which somehow retains the power to snarl when Curly picks it up. If the boys wanted to give up law enforcement after this strange adventure, would you blame them?

In yet another instance of Columbia's ingenious and endless recycling of comedy, *Dizzy Detectives* was remade at Columbia twice as solo vehicles for contract comic Joe Besser: *Fraidy Cat* (1951), in which Joe is an investigator with the Wide Awake Detective Agency; and the heavily stock-footage *Hook a Crook* (1955). In both, the ape is played by veteran "gorilla-suit man" Steve Calvert. Dan Blocker appears in new footage shot for the remake.

A GEM OF A JAM, THE BOYS' TENTH AND FINAL RELEASE OF 1943, REPRISES MUCH of the spooky business of *Dizzy Detectives*. This time, though, the creeper isn't a gorilla but Curly.

Writer-director Del Lord's script starts strongly, with the boys in hospital whites, scrubbing for an operation.

> CURLY
> I think it's a bad case of spectusonthefloorus.
>
> MOE
> Then we should use plenty of sulfathiazode.
>
> LARRY *(thoughtfully)*
> I wouldn't say yes, I wouldn't say no.
>
> CURLY
> Would you say "maybe"?
>
> LARRY
> I *might*!
>
> MOE
> So be it!

With that, the boys get to work—cleaning a doctor's office. They're in a hurry, so Larry deposits the *smutz* from his dustpan beneath a chair cushion. Moe slyly pulls back a secret zipper in the rug and empties his pan there.

In a tremendously good, and unexpected, visual gag, Curly denudes his feather duster when he carelessly dusts an unshielded table fan. *Rrrr!* goes the soundtrack, and Curly is left holding the stump of a handle. His expression is priceless: What happened?

After Curly's head becomes stuck in a fishbowl, Moe and Larry hustle him to a fluoroscope. In a very clever visual effect, a goldfish happily swims in and around Curly's ribs.

Curly is worried. "Have I got somethin'?"

Moe: "Nothin' I can't catch!"

Sirens suddenly sound outside on the street below, and three thugs invade the office. One of the intruders, Joe (John Tyrrell), has been shot, and his pals order the "doctors" to fix him up. After much stalling, Curly accidentally steps on

Performer Profile: Dudley Dickerson
1906–68

Black actors had a tough time in studio films of the 1940s (only black-cast independent pictures offered "real" roles), but Dudley Dickerson was able to act silly while preserving his considerable dignity.

Dickerson played innumerable chauffeurs, porters, waiters, red caps, and cooks from 1934 until his last film in 1959. But broadly written roles became scarce after 1950, and Dudley spent the last decade of his life working in sanitation.

He has a fine moment in *Hold That Lion!* as a Pullman porter who innocently uses the tuft of a lion's tail as a shoeshine dauber, and as a night watchman who reacts badly to a pasty-white Curly in *A Gem of a Jam*.

Far and away his most famous role with the Stooges is in *A Plumbing We Will Go* as the mystified but resourceful cook, who is sprayed by every appliance in the kitchen and must finally resort to boots and slicker just to move in and out of the room. Dickerson's funniest and most famous line comes from that short, too: "Dis house has sho' gone crazy!"

Dudley Dickerson struggles to keep his cool after Curly has a bit of a mishap in *A Gem of a Jam* (1943).   *Photo courtesy of the Stoogeum*

the gurney's release pedal and tilts Joe backwards—and right through the open window. The patient drops noisily into a trashcan behind a cop (Fred Kelsey).

The guy's pals return, by which time Moe and Larry have secreted Curly beneath a sheet to pass him off as Joe. Moe demands that Larry hand him a sulfademis, which is apparently Latin for "hand drill."

When the gurney tilts back a second time, nearly spilling Curly onto the street, Moe is steamed: "What's the idea tryin' to get away before us?"

From here, *A Gem of a Jam* strides into its second part and becomes a traditional spook comedy. Another office holds merchandise belonging to a theatrical-novelty company, which provides many opportunities for scares. Cinematographer John Stumar's lighting is shadowed and atmospheric, and Del Lord's pacing is as good as his feel for gags. A night watchman (Dudley Dickerson, in one of his most fruitful collaborations with the Stooges) is terrified when he backs into a mannequin; in many TV prints, Dickerson's shout of "I'm losin' my mind!" is excised from the soundtrack. The line was restored by Columbia for home-video release.

A little later, Dickerson does some more wonderfully reactive comedy when he and Curly engage in a tug-of-war from opposite sides of a rubbery doorknob.

After a fall, Curly is covered in so much gooey white paint that he looks like Lon Chaney, Jr. as the Mummy. As the paint stiffens, Curly *shuffles* like the Mummy, too, scaring Moe and Larry in a maze of crates and sneaking behind the watchman, who thinks Curly is a mannequin. "You sho is ugly!" Dickerson pronounces.

The centerpiece of all this comes after Curly sits down near Dickerson, who raises his arm from the floor and takes one of Curly's hands. In a moment, the two hands—one deathly white, the other a contrasting brown—busily twiddle their thumbs. After a while, the two thumbs silently battle each other. When Curly falls off his perch, Dickerson looks at him face to face, his hair expanding with a *boinngg!* to force the inside of his cap upward into a comical bulge.

The thugs stumble into the arms of the cops, and the night watchman dashes straight through *two* closed doors. Moe and Larry follow, with Curly chasing after as best he can.

The bifurcated nature of *A Gem of a Jam* feels natural rather than jarring, and Lord's script gives equal weight to verbal and visual jokes. An enormous jack-in-the-box that shocks Larry when he opens a lid is simultaneously weird and amusing. Later, Larry flattens Moe with a heavy club, thinking he's nailed one of the crooks. He races back around the crate the way he came and tries to tell Moe all about it.

"I just knocked a guy cold *right there!*"

Moe lets Larry have it with the same club. "Now *you're* right there!"

And so are we, laughing.

OVERT "SPOOK" ELEMENTS DOMINATE WRITER-DIRECTOR DEL LORD'S *THREE Pests in a Mess* (1945), one of the last Stooges shorts to capture Curly in his robust glory. The short also merits a nod because it casts perennial good girl

Christine McIntyre as a con artist who tries to seduce Curly because she and her associates erroneously believe Curly has won a $100,000 sweepstakes. McIntyre (whose character goes unnamed) feigns tears in front of the boys, sobbing, "I'm just a poor little orphan. Nobody loves me and I have no food." Alone with the conniving dame, Curly reveals that he needs to collect a hundred thousand *flies* in order to convince a patent attorney to take a second look at his absurdly complicated flycatcher (which has a tiny staircase that leads to a platform from which exasperated flies will leap to commit suicide).

With that peculiar logic exhibited by many criminals, suddenly the *girl* is the injured party: "Not dollars!" she yelps angrily. "Why, you double-crosser!" The girl's cohorts (Brian O'Hara and Robert Williams) chase the boys into an office, where Curly accidentally sends a rifle slug into a mannequin, which topples onto the floor with an unappetizing *thonk*. The panicked Stooges stuff the "corpse" into a sack and beat it out the window.

The boys struggle with the mannequin to a pet cemetery, where they intend to bury it. But the caretaker (silent-era star Snub Pollard) phones the place's owner, Mr. Black (Vernon Dent), at a masquerade party. Black and two associates arrive at the shadowy cemetery dressed as a fiend wearing a top hat and a black cloak (Mr. Black, get it?), a devil, and a skeleton.

Fans who enjoy *Three Pests in a Mess* are forgiving of the comedy's bifold nature, which suggests the Scotch-taping of one short (the grifters' interest in Curly's bank account) to another (the spooky stuff). Del Lord didn't usually write the shorts he directed. This one glides along on good gags and sharp pacing, but the failure of the two halves to jibe confirms that Lord was stronger with staging than with story structure. That's not uncommon among filmmakers, and it doesn't diminish the short's amusing peculiarities.

The Ever Rest Pet Cemetery is a fabulous sound-stage set (by Charles Clague) that's rife with hooting owls, chirping crickets, and creepy shadows designed by cinematographer Benjamin Kline. Although a blank scrim that's visible behind artfully placed trees and shrubs makes the set appear more theatrical than "real," the total effect is also *weirder* than reality, and somehow better.

In a stir of conscience, Curly looks at the "dead man" and soberly says, "Do you think *he* was somebody's pet?" Before the boys have time to ponder that one, odd things start to happen. The frightened caretaker hides in a sack that Curly mistakes for *the* sack—only to be given a good fright when the sack kicks him in the rear. The skeleton (actor unknown) plops his hands onto Larry's shoulders, sending Larry (in a clever combination of stunt work, mechanical effect, and undercranked camera) into a burrowing dive beneath a shed. In a cute touch, the bemused skeleton peers into the hole and then scratches his head, with a sound like bone on hollow bone.

Meanwhile, the devil (Heinie Conklin) pinions Moe's neck between the tines of his pitchfork and then uses it to stab Moe in the rear.

When the cemetery phone rings, Curly answers it and then, like the Philip Morris bellboy, goes off in search of Mr. Black:

CURLY
Caall for Philllip Blaackk!

MR. BLACK
I'm Mr. Black.

CURLY
Phone, sir.

Curly waits for a half-beat, as if expecting further instructions or a tip, and then yanks Black's hat down around his eyes when he realizes the insanity of what he's been doing.

Crooks, plaster corpses, and goblins aside, the funniest and best-played gag of *Three Pests in a Mess* is a race-based guilty pleasure that's set up when Christine McIntyre angrily hurls a bottle of ink that noisily conks Moe and blacks his face. He staggers backwards from the office and bumps into Larry, who complains, "What's the idea, porter?" When he sees that the "porter" is Moe, he launches into mocking laughter before dropping to one knee and opening his arms, Jolson-style. "Mammy!" he says heartily. Moe drops to one knee, too, and answers "Pappy!"—before giving Larry a couple of good slaps. "Get away from here! Whaddaya mean, 'porter'?"

The joke isn't a tasteful one, but it's better than murder.

A bad night at the pet cemetery in *Three Pests in a Mess* (1945). Note the headstone held by Curly, marked with his real name, Jerry. That's Vernon Dent in black and Heinie Conklin as the Devil. No record of the skeleton exists. Creepy, eh?

Pardon My Terror: The Stooges Short That Never Was

On April 9, 1946, Ed Bernds completed a final draft of a Stooges script, called *Pardon My Terror*, to be shot later that spring for 1947 release. Four weeks after Bernds finished his script, Curly Howard suffered a serious stroke that ended his career; *Pardon My Terror* would never be a Stooges comedy. Years later, Bernds explained to historians Ted Okuda and Ed Watz that, except for Curly, everything was in place for the filming of *Pardon My Terror*: sets, costumes, props, and most of the supporting cast. Bernds explained that the situation had turned into a "pay or play" dilemma by which, according to Screen Actors Guild rules, players had to be paid whether or not they performed. With actors' salaries in the mix, as well as the specter of dressed sets sitting unused (more wasted money), plus the two-reel unit's sacrosanct production and release schedules, Bernds had no choice but to hurriedly rewrite *Pardon My Terror* for Gus Schilling and Richard Lane, a recently signed Columbia-contract comedy team with an opening in their schedule. We'll get to the Schilling and Lane version shortly. First, let's look at the script as it was written for the Stooges.

Heiress Alice Morton (Christine McIntyre) is terrified. Her grandfather, Jonas, has gone missing in his own mansion, and she fears that he's been murdered. Because she's first in line to inherit Jonas's estate, she fears that she'll be killed next. Desperate, she reaches out to the Wide Awake Detective Agency and involves Larry, Curly, and Moe in a double scheme of deception. Another would-be heiress, a beautiful black widow named Wanda (Lynne Lyons), conspires with her lover, Grooch (Kenneth MacDonald), to steal the estate. Wanda believes her charms are sufficient to handle the detectives, and on the off chance she can't, Grooch has rigged an innocuous-appearing settee to put out ten thousand volts. It's a trap with the Stooges' names on it.

Following unnerving run-ins with the peculiar butler, Jarvis (Philip Van Zandt), and a hard-punching goon called Luke (Dick Wessel), plus unexpected encounters with Jonas's corpse (which seems to turn up everywhere) *and* a close call for Curly when the seductive Wanda poisons his drink, Jones (Vernon Dent) turns up one more time—alive! He reveals to Alice and the boys that, with a loyal assist from Jarvis, he faked his death in order to force Grooch and Wanda to show their hand.

In a climactic melee, the schemers are subdued and Jonas hands the Stooges $10,000 in cash. That puts an exciting cap on the evening—which turns shocking when the boys unknowingly sit on what Bernds's script notation describes as the "hot-seat settee."

From the outset, we see that the boys aren't cut out to be detectives. They sleep at their desks, and their carelessness with guns nearly kills their landlord (Emil Sitka) and the janitor (Dudley Dickerson). Once at the mansion, the boys are victimized by mysterious boxing gloves that shoot from behind

Gus Schilling (left) and Richard Lane had never worked together as a team until the Columbia two-reel unit made them one—with good results. Their antics in *Pardon My Terror* (1946), from a lively script originally fashioned for the Stooges, are energetic and very funny.

bookshelves, and scare each other silly when they patrol the corridors. Larry finally admits that he and Curly are mice, not men. Moe pulls an enormous piece of Swiss cheese from his pocket and says, "All right. Let's have a bite to eat and get to work!"

Moe tells Curly to yell "It's warm in here!" if he has any trouble. Curly is so flummoxed by Wanda's seduction that he falls off the couch and spills his drink, and then stares in horror as the poisoned pills smoke on the carpet.

"It's warm in here! It's warm in here!"

Bernds intended that most of the considerable physical action of *Pardon My Terror* be given to Moe and Larry. Their dialogue is vital to the exposition; Curly's lines are brief, and he's more reactive than active. With hindsight, it's apparent that Bernds was compensating for Curly's declining memory and physical condition.

Gus Schilling and Dick Lane signed with Columbia in 1945, after Schilling's long experience in burlesque and movies and Lane's time in the circus, vaudeville, and films. Their signature Columbia theme, heard during the opening and closing titles of their shorts, is "Merrily We Roll Along"—which nicely sums up *Pardon My Terror*. Schilling is a prissy, scaredy-cat type, and Lane is the pompous, aggressive straight man. The two are energetic and very funny, particularly Lane's gruff cowardice and Schilling's catch phrase, "Ooh, you *hurt* me!" Schilling is game and very physical, particularly during the boxing glove bit, during which he absorbs a lot of punches while suppressing the instinct to flinch in anticipation.

Christine McIntyre, stunning in a mink stole, is appealingly soft-spoken, and Lynne Lyons, a slinky brunette, makes a sensational statement in a low-cut, midriff-baring gown. She's an amusing femme fatale, and you wish that Curly could have worked with her.

The script's mouse-and-cheese gag was eliminated for Schilling and Lane, and the comics have a dialogue exchange that isn't in the original script:

> SCHILLING
> I gotta get back to the office, I forgot something there!
>
> LANE
> You forgot something?
>
> SCHILLING
> Yeah, I forgot to stay there!

Otherwise, the script was filmed as written, with dialogue and gags designed for three simply divided among two. Researcher Brent Seguine discovered the final draft in the Jules White file at the Academy of Motion Picture Arts and Sciences Library in 2003.

Pardon My Terror would have been an above-average Stooges comedy. As things worked out, it's a footnote to Stooges history—and compelling evidence that Schilling and Lane deserve to be rediscovered.

WITH *IDIOTS DELUXE* (1945), ELWOOD ULLMAN AND JULES WHITE GET RIGHT down to it: Moe is on trial for attempted murder—by axe.

It's reasonable to assume that Moe isn't going to do hard time, but his predicament is undeniably surprising, particularly since the people he's allegedly tried to kill are Larry and Curly.

That, plus an effectively utilized flashback structure, gives *Idiots Deluxe* some distinction. (The title comes from a popular play and film, *Idiot's Delight*.)

Moe's nerves are shot. We don't learn why. They just are. He explains this to a judge (Vernon Dent)—or at least he tries during interludes when the bandaged Larry and Curly aren't angrily heckling him from the gallery. What he needs most, he says, is peace and quiet.

Cue the flashback, in which Moe is a complete basket case, huddled in a chair beneath a blanket, angrily telling the quietly padding housecat to "quit stomping around!"

Meanwhile, Larry and Curly are in the parlor, rehearsing their act, the Original Two-Man Quartet. The boys make a lot of noise as they play multiple instruments (Larry has the bass drum's mallet strapped to his heinie). Worse, the gratingly idiotic tune they play sounds like something you'd hear at one of the less-reputable carnivals in Alabama.

Moe is frantic with agitation, and loses his temper when Larry loses the slide to his trombone, which flies into the next room and grips Moe around the neck.

Either fearful for their own safety or out of concern for Moe, Larry and Curly suggest a getaway to the country, where there's quiet and "fresh air." Larry takes a deep breath and immediately launches into uncontrolled hacking—a sort of local in-joke aimed at Angelenos, for whom smog (still called "haze" in those days) was already a serious problem.

At an isolated cabin deep in the woods, the boys make lunch, most of which is eaten by a brazen bear that repeatedly sticks his snout through an open window at the kitchen table.

Curly sits on a bear trap, Moe is brained by a rock that Larry stupidly hikes like a football, Curly accidentally conks Larry with a shovel, and Moe is shot in the ass when his pals mistake him for the bear.

In a final insult, the bear steals the boys' car.

Back in the courtroom, the judge dismisses the charges. Grateful, Moe asks if he can take Exhibit A—his axe—which he uses to chase Larry and Curly from the court.

The humor is *Idiots Deluxe* isn't at all expansive. The courtroom scenes are efficient and relatively brief, so most of the action takes place in and close to the boys' cabin. With nothing extraneous—no girls, no game warden, no hidden loot—the short focuses on the boys' interaction with the bear and with each other. Because of that, and because the boys have no one to play off of other than each other, *Idiots Deluxe* is very organic. Events that unfold with a progressive logic are motivated by Moe's medical condition, and by the character flaws of all three Stooges. This is far from the boys' best short, but it's pleasing in its purity.

Ullman's script has some especially funny dialogue. When Moe imagines that the bear is eating Curly, he says to Larry, "Do you want that bear to eat him alive? Get out there and help him!"

Larry: "That bear don't *need* no help!"

After Moe's rifle accidentally discharges and brings down a turkey, Curly stands with his arms extended, looking into the sky. He explains, "[I'm] waitin' for the dressing and the cranberry sauce!"

In a stroke of demented genius, Ullman and White put together a courtroom discussion between Moe and the judge that's the film's comic highlight.

MOE
But I'm a sick man. A *very* sick man. I've had two very serious operations. [stands and lifts his shirt to show judge] And this one here, for crushed grape seeds, right here . . .

JUDGE
Oh, I have one exactly like that!

MOE
You have?

JUDGE
Let me show it to you! [lifts shirt] See here?

MOE
Oh, that's a bum job! That's like hem-stitching with a picot
edge! [laughs]

JUDGE
Eh— [frowns] Sit down, we'll continue with the testimony!

The sequence is particularly funny because Moe and Vernon Dent do half-turns away from the camera as they discuss their invasive surgeries, forcing us to imagine what the post-surgical wreckage looks like.

Idiots Deluxe is a remake of a 1935 Tom Kennedy and Monte Collins short, *Oh, My Nerves* (directed by Del Lord), in which Monte tries to relax on a fishing trip that's ruined by the rest of the family, especially his obnoxious brother-in-law (Kennedy).

Also, *Idiots* is the first Stooges short to feature the mask of theatrical Comedy (from Thaleia, one of the nine *mousai* [muses] of ancient Greece) on the opening and closing cards, an image that would continue until the team's final two-reeler.

The 1957 remake of *Idiots Deluxe, Guns a Poppin!* (a goof on *Hellzapoppin*), is the fifth Stooges short to co-star Joe Besser, and the first of those to pick up stock footage from one of the team's earlier comedies. Directed by Jules White, with new scenes (shot in one day) scripted by brother Jack, *Guns* makes liberal use of footage from the earlier short. White and his editor, Saul Goodkind, cut between old and new with reasonable grace, but twelve years had passed since *Idiots*. Although Larry appears virtually unchanged, Moe is noticeably older.

The courtroom setup and Moe's medical condition are unchanged. Vernon Dent and the bear return via stock footage. Some of the business with the bear is cut, but we again witness the animal greedily eat Moe's eggs and potatoes and use its remarkable tongue inside a jar to get at the last bit of Moe's beloved honey.

Many gags from the earlier film are reshot with Joe, who cooks eggs by breaking them with a hammer and joins Moe and Larry to slather his breakfast with endless condiments.

Paradoxically, Joe is at his best during scenes that depart from *Idiots Deluxe* and that undercut the purity of the premise. The local sheriff (Frank Sully) is hot on the trail of outlaw Mad Bill Hookup (Joe Palma, in a rare credited role). There's much shooting into and out of the cabin, and Moe is repeatedly squashed beneath the door when the sheriff and Hookup kick it down. When Hookup uses Joe as a human shield in order to fire from the cabin's window, he rests his gun hand on the top of Joe's head; recoil from each shot causes his hand to thump Joe's skull. "Ooh, that *hurrts!*" Joe exclaims before knocking Pickup's hat from his head.

When Larry loudly howls like a wolf (a thoroughly contrived gag), Joe comes back with, "Not so loud! . . . Don't *yell* at me!"

Jack White's best gag—to which Moe probably contributed dialogue—is inside the besieged cabin, when Moe pulls a rifle and gets the drop on Hookup.

HOOKUP
That's a nice gun you have there!

MOE
Yeah, I got it for my bar mitzvah!

HOOKUP
Can I see it?
[Moe hands it over and Hookup uses it to give Moe a ferocious crack on the forehead]

JOE (indignantly, to Hookup)
Whaddaya tryin' to do, break his gun?!

Hookup is finally subdued, but the boys are so excited by the fat reward that they allow the outlaw to escape. Moe stalks toward the camera: "Oh, my nerves! My nerves!"

BEER BARREL POLECATS (1946) COMBINES INGENUITY WITH A BARELY CONcealed panic, as Curly fell ill before filming and was unable (at least for a while) to handle the rigors of a four-day shooting schedule. Columbia's front office would not (and could not) dramatically scale back the Stooges' release schedule, so producer-director Jules White had to punt. Some scenes already scripted by Hal Roach alumnus Gilbert W. Pratt were scrapped and replaced with stock footage from two Stooges shorts released in 1941. However, many of Curly's scripted scenes remain.

Throughout the approximately eight minutes of new footage in *Beer Barrel Polecats*, Curly is professional and amusing. If you'd never seen him before, you'd think he was an okay comic. But of course, Curly Howard was brilliant, so to see his genius diminished by illness is at once sad and peculiar.

The short's premise—that the boys cannot find beer anywhere and so decide to brew their own—is obscure today but would have been well understood by beer drinkers of the 1940s. Wartime rationing of sugar, and shortages of barley and other grains, cut into domestic beer production (the problem was far more severe in Europe; Britain was particularly thirsty). Also, large beer manufacturers began to purchase smaller rivals in the '40s, not necessarily for beer brands but to gain access to distribution systems. With this consolidation, many favorite beers disappeared. The shortage was reasonably severe and had a negative impact not just on restaurants and taverns but on businesses of other sorts. The

July 31, 1943, issue of *The Billboard* reported that jukebox plays in Houston were down 25 percent during May and June. The magazine said, "Shortage of beer was given as the main reason."

When the boys decide to make their own beer, they become bootleggers, an occupation that, beer shortage or not, is illegal. They brew up a batch of Panther Pilsner, adding nine cakes of yeast (three apiece, without the other boys' knowledge) rather than the required three. "We *all* put the yeast in," they chorus woefully after their brew foams out of control.

The boys fill 185 bottles that pop their caps and explode because they've been set too close to the stove. (This is a protracted and quite wonderful mechanical effect that's made better with clever sound effects and well-timed cuts to the boys being drenched by the spray.)

A moment later, the boys are in jail. Curly has made the mistake of trying to sell a bottle to a cop (which is what Stan Laurel does in the first Laurel and Hardy feature, *Pardon Us*, 1931—scripter Gilbert W. Pratt used to work at Roach, remember?). Amazingly, Pratt's *Beer Barrel Polecats* script includes a lengthy, never-filmed prison-classroom sequence that frankly plagiarizes a virtually identical sequence from *Pardon Us.*

Not long after the small keg that Curly has smuggled inside beneath his coat explodes under the hot lights in the mug-shot room, the boys are in striped pajamas and wondering how to break out.

In the rec room, a tough con (Joe Palma) tries to goad Curly into punching him—a mild gag based on a deleted scene from *Pardon Us*—and Moe trips and falls onto his ice cream cone.

Except for a brief coda, the remainder of *Beer Barrel Polecats* is stock footage from *In the Sweet Pie and Pie* (hi-jinks inside the boy's prison cell) and *So Long, Mr. Chumps* (rockpile and painting gags, and the boys' search for "Pomeroy"). Eagle-eyed viewers will notice an inconsistency in the numbers on the boys' uniforms, and everybody will wonder who the hell Pomeroy is and why the Stooges want to break him out.

This sloppiness isn't intentional. It was born of desperation.

The short's final minute establishes that forty years have passed. Vernon Dent is still the warden, and the bearded Stooges are finally free. (A vaguely similar old-age sequence that was to wrap up *Pardon Us* was filmed and discarded.) Curly says the first thing he's going to do is find "a tall, big beautiful bottle of beer!" In palsied slow motion, the aged Moe pokes Curly's eyes, and Larry summons enough strength to give him a rap in the stomach. Moe and Larry shove Curly back into the arms of the warden and go off to find "a coupla beautiful blondes."

And that's *Beer Barrel Polecats*, held together with spit and paste, and ready to bring déjà vu to a theater near you.

THE WORD "QUACK," TO DESCRIBE AN UNETHICAL DOCTOR OR A PERSON WHO pretends to be a doctor, dates to 16th-century Britain, when "to quack" meant to peddle. A quacksalver was a peddler of useless, fraudulent medicines and other nostrums. Quackery flourished concurrent with the rise of mass media in the late 19th and early 20th centuries, particularly in the United States. Broadsheets, newspapers, magazines, and radio advertised tonics, pills, salves, herbs, enemas, and other items and techniques with purported abilities to cure everything from dropsy to cancer. Although Teddy Roosevelt signed the Food and Drugs Act in 1906, and the Food and Drug Administration was officially established in 1930, credulous, sometimes desperate people remained susceptible to promises of good health.

A former coal miner and insurance salesman named Harry Hoxsey became emblematic of faux medicine for profit. He opened his first herb-based cancer clinic in Taylorville, Illinois, in 1924, and twelve years later opened one in Dallas that became one of the world's largest privately owned cancer-treatment centers. According to the FDA, which finally banned all Hoxsey activity in the United States in 1960, Mr. Hoxsey was a quack.

As *Monkey Businessmen* (1946) begins, the Stooges are nearing the end of a bad day on the job (the boys are ungifted electricians). Worn out, they take Curly's nest egg and go somewhere for a rest. They end up in a spa *cum* clinic operated by an unctuous, well-spoken fellow who calls himself Dr. Mallard (Kenneth MacDonald, in the first of many appearances with the Stooges). The business model Mallard follows with all his patients is to "run them ragged and take them for every nickel they've got!"

Larry, Moe, and Curly not only cough up their dough but suffer the indignities of early wakeups, punishing exercise, inadequate food, and the physical bullying of Mallard's burly nurses (Cy Schindell and Rocky Woods). After a lot of running around and a near-death experience in a steam room, the boys escape.

Monkey Businessmen has acquired a mournful reputation among fans because of Curly's evident illness. The short regularly turns up on "worst" lists; it's not reviled, it's eulogized. And that's peculiar because *Monkey Businessmen* is a sharply paced, well-written adventure that, frankly, shows Curly to good advantage. He's physically confident and expressive, and although his speech is slower than during his prime, he seems engaged.

The short marks former sound man Ed Bernds's first experience as a director. In his 1999 autobiography, he says that Curly functioned at a child's level during the shoot, and that Moe coached his younger brother through his sides, line by line. More than one source claims that, on screen, Moe's elbow visibly pokes Curly, as if to say, "It's your line!"

There's no reason to doubt that Moe coached Curly, but claims of obvious cueing are nonsense. It just isn't there. Curly knows his lines. Further, in many scenes he's downright nimble, taking the staged slaps and conks with aplomb.

Bernds wrote the script, which is peppered with solid gags. In the opening sequence, electrician Moe tugs on a cord and pulls a lamp off a desk in the next room. The irate client (Fred Kelsey) makes a futile grab for his phone and ends up tipped backwards in his chair. When Kelsey gets the boys' boss on the phone, the boss is so angry that the cord sizzles and burns.

At the clinic, Curly mounts futile attempts to make time with the stunning Nurse Shapely (regular player Jean Willes, making her Stooges debut). After she finally tosses him through a closed door, he yells from the floor, "I can take a hint!"

Performer Profile: Jean Willes
1923–89

A tall, shapely stunner with high cheekbones, feline eyes, and an enticing aura of worldliness, Jean Willes worked in pictures and on TV from 1942 to 1976. She looked smashing as a redhead or brunette and occasionally burned up the screen as a blonde, too. Off and on throughout her career, she was billed as Jean Donahue, which was her real name.

While with Columbia's two-reel unit in the late 1940s and '50s, Willes stayed busy with the Stooges, Joe De Rita, Andy Clyde, Bert Wheeler, and others. She's especially fun in the Stooges' *Don't Throw That Knife*, inviting the boys into her apartment by saying, "Walk this way," and then giving every male in the audience something to think about.

Willes grabbed showy bits in "A" pictures and good featured roles in B-plus productions like *5 Against the House* and *The Crowded Sky*. Although Jean Willes never became a name, she was apparently beloved by casting directors and was that relative rarity: a working actress who always worked.

"Rest farm" employee Nurse Shapely (Jean Willes) arouses the boys' baser instincts in *Monkey Businessmen* (1946), one of the best of Curly's later shorts.   *Photo courtesy of the Stoogeum*

Larry and Curly are excited by Mallard's promise of private nurses and coyly cuddle up to Schindell and Woods without looking at them. They only glance at each other, sharing goofy, conspiratorial grins.

Silent-era great Snub Pollard jumps into a nice role as a gout patient who is miraculously cured when Curly falls onto his foot.

The short's best sequence involves another oversized nurse, George (the comically expressive Wade Crosby). Moe and Larry are masquerading as surgeons, and their patient (a trembling Curly) is hidden beneath a sheet on the table. Moe tries to bluff his way out of the jam and maybe get rid of George in the process.

> MOE
> By the way, I'll need a trectahomlachtameter!

> GEORGE
> Got one right here!

> MOE
> That's a big one! . . . Say, I'll also need a hamadanaseenafarin!

> GEORGE
> Got one comin' right up!

> MOE (to Larry)
> That guy's got everything!

Bernds's directorial debut is impressive. He obviously found his own script congenial because plot and gags unfold at a pleasingly steady clip. Scenes are imaginatively blocked, and effective use is made of people and objects in the middle ground for some lively compositions. Pullback shots that allow funny situations to be revealed at the director's discretion are utilized smartly.

The only odd moment comes at the climax after the steam room door explodes off its hinges, freeing Moe and Larry from a sweaty fate. The master shot of all three boys (Curly has been watching from a distance and then begins to move forward) is intercut with a hazy, very tight, and badly framed close-up on Curly's head and shoulders as he continues to move to his beleaguered pals. The insert isn't necessary, and its poor visual quality suggests not just steam but that the close-up was created in an optical printer, as if Bernds felt he had failed to get necessary coverage.

But he hadn't missed anything. His coverage is fine.

Monkey Businessmen ends with a thousand-dollar reward from the grateful gout patient. Moe and Larry dream of dames, food, and Monte Carlo.

Curly just wants to take a rest.

AMBROSE ROSE, "DECEASED MILLIONAIRE JUNK DEALER," HAS LEFT HIS CONsiderable estate to his nephews, Moe, Larry, and Shemp. The boys' lawyer (Emil Sitka) at Cess, Poole & Drayne hasn't been able to bring the boys and their money together because the estate's executor, a crooked investment banker named Ichabod Slipp (Kenneth MacDonald) has proved to be a slippery eel indeed. The boys have a terrible tussle with him at his office, and Slipp ends up on the loose, the subpoenas that they brought with them torn to shreds.

The Stooges know that Slipp is leaving town.

They also know which train he'll be on.

Hold That Lion! (1947) is one of many excellent Stooges shorts that feature Shemp. *Fright Night*, his first Columbia two-reeler with Moe and Larry (he'd been on the studio's roster as a solo), had been the team's ninety-eighth Columbia release; *Hold That Lion!* was number one hundred. That number seems propitious in retrospect because *Hold That Lion!* is the only time all three Horwitz brothers—Moses, Samuel, and Jerome—appeared on screen together.

This bit of comedy history takes place when Moe, Larry, and Shemp search the train's Pullman cars for Slipp. They realize that the crook may be in disguise, so a well-dressed fellow who leans back in his seat, his face covered by a bowler hat, catches their attention. The boys lift the bowler and see that the passenger is sleeping with a clothespin on his nose. When they remove the clothespin, the man bursts forth with noises that audiences find very familiar: *Woo woo woo woo woop! Rrruff, rruff!* The sleeping man is Curly, who, according to director Jules White, paid an impromptu visit to the set, inspiring White to cast him in the cameo (the bit is not in Felix Adler's *Hold That Lion!* script).

Other sources report that White closed the set so that only the Stooges and Curly were present, but at least five extras who play other passengers are in the scene, too, and a couple of them, in character, visibly react to Curly's outburst.

As one might expect, the interlude is poignant as well as funny. Curly's final starring short, *Half-Wits Holiday*, had been released on January 9, 1947. First-run engagements of *Hold That Lion!* began on July 17. Fans had certainly not forgotten about Curly, but they'd no longer been seeing him with the accustomed regularity. This was a homecoming.

Always a nice-looking man, Curly was now handsome, with a pleasingly slimmed face and grown-out wavy hair. The boys replace the clothespin and the bowler and move on, giving Curly to the ages.

Hold That Lion! has a ferocity that bubbles from inside Kenneth MacDonald's Slipp, a schemer who is brazen in his self-righteous violence. He bursts into his own office three times, claiming to be looking for Slipp ("Aha, Mr. Slipp, at last I catch you in your office!"), and then beats the hell out of Larry, then Moe, and finally Shemp (who offers a hilariously inept demonstration of shadow-boxing and feints until he finally bores Slipp, who just clocks him).

Moe and Larry revive to discover Shemp slumped against a wall with a fishbowl wedged over his head. They struggle to free him.

SHEMP (hollowly)
Dubadubadubagowdegowbow!

MOE
What'd he say?

LARRY

Dubadubadubagowdegowbow!

Moe and Larry become preoccupied with objects on Slipp's desk, and for the next *twenty-five seconds*, Shemp silently, desperately struggles behind them with the suffocating fishbowl. He twists it this way, he twists it that way. He lowers his head and tries to pull it off like a turtleneck; he raises his head and tries to take it off like a hat—and again, in silence. No bit of business from the boys' two-reel career at Columbia is more skillfully played or designed.

The train sequence is highlighted by the boys' unexpected run-ins with a lion, which occur in a crate (the boys duck into it to hide—separated from the animal by a pane of glass, at Shemp's request—and immediately wonder who smells so awful). They also meet the big kitty in the Pullman corridor and finally in their berth.

In an unused compartment, a porter (the wonderful Dudley Dickerson) quietly polishes travelers' shoes. When the lion (a handsome and marvelously well-trained beast, by the way) hops quietly onto the next seat, Dickerson obliviously uses the tuft of the cat's tail as a shoe-polish dauber—that is, until the lion growls. Dickerson's understandably panicked, shrieking reaction as he struggles in vain to escape through the window is racialist (as distinct from "racist"), but

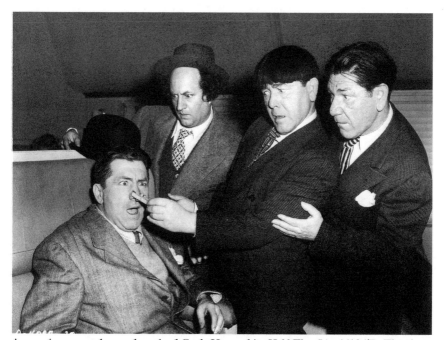

A surprise cameo by newly retired Curly Howard in *Hold That Lion!* (1947). The short came very early in Shemp's Columbia run as one of the Stooges and makes clear that he was a splendid replacement for his youngest brother.   *Photo courtesy of the Stoogeum*

there's nothing demeaning here. The porter is no less terrified than the Stooges or anybody else who sees the lion.

Veteran comic Heinie Conklin has a funny bit as a conductor who suspects that the Stooges have no tickets. (He's right.) Moe cheerfully directs him to a drawing room, opening the door to reveal the shadow of a young woman who brushes her hair. Moe closes the door behind the conductor, and in a moment the soundtrack rings with girlish screams. "Eeee! Go away!"

The conductor (unseen behind the door) can only yelp, "Ow! Take it *easy,* lady!"

The boys absorb a lot of physical abuse from the hard-punching Slipp during a chase among maze-like crates in the freight car but prevail when Moe tosses aside a hammer (he's been using it as fan to revive Larry) and catches Slipp right in the forehead.

In a wonderful coda, Moe begins to divide up the bundles of moolah.

MOE

Here's one for you, one for you, and there's one for me.

SLIPP *(weakly)*

Oohhh . . .

MOE

(as he gives Slipp another rap with the hammer)

And one for you!

For reasons humorously unexplained, Shemp suddenly gets huffy about the bundle of bonds: "I want it now this minute—*tk! tk!*—that's what I want, *rright now!*"

Moe: "Well, you got it!"—an eye poke, that is, and a quick shove into a crate of eggs.

Shemp looks at himself and mutters, "How d'ya like that, I feel like a piece a' French toast!"

Shemp catches Moe and Larry in their pusses with raw eggs, but they laugh it off and assure Shemp they're not angry.

But they are.

When *Hold That Lion!* was reworked, with considerable stock footage, as *Booty and the Beast* in 1953, the Stooges were becoming victims of their own success. They regularly topped exhibitors' polls as Hollywood's most popular two-reel stars and brought many industry awards home to Columbia. Producer-director Jules White, always under the gun about budget, decided for the first time to use stock footage from an earlier Shemp short to pad out a new one. Audiences apparently didn't mind, and the practice became more frequent (and more blatant) over the next four years.

Approximately the first half of *Booty and the Beast* is new material, with Kenneth MacDonald returning, this time as an unnamed crook who tells the

Stooges a tall story about losing the key to his mansion, inveigling them to break in and blow an upstairs safe. (His satchel, which is full of burglar tools and explosives, isn't his at all, he explains. And his own satchel had a paper with the safe's combination!)

Dialogue among the boys establishes that their old man blew many a safe in his day, and so after some trouble getting into the house (Larry falls face-first into a muddy flower bed) and painful mishaps with a gigantic drill, the boys expertly rig the in-wall lockbox with TNT connected by a halo of wires to a bottle of nitro. Frankly, it's a thing of beauty. If the old man didn't teach the boys the trade, they sure observed him carefully.

The safe goes up with a tremendous boom. The crook grabs the loot, grins at the unconscious Stooges, and takes off.

But as in *Hold That Lion!*, the boys remember that the guy mentioned taking a train. They hop aboard—which is where footage from *Lion* begins. Simple redubs that replace "Slipp" with "him" maintain the crook's namelessness.

Booty and the Beast is a superior redo. Jack White's script for the first half is sharp and snappy, and brother Jules directed with considerable energy. If there's an anomaly here, it involves the cinematography. Fayte Browne's lighting for the new sequences is crisp and clean, while George Kelley's, for the earlier *Lion*, is more textured and atmospheric. Although a noticeable stylistic discrepancy, it's a forgivable one.

Hold That Lion! was redone yet again as *Loose Loot* (1953), which was the first Stooges short released after *Booty and the Beast*. Jules White was a clever and talented guy, and he also had more than a little gall.

In a happy turn, *Loose Loot* is another gem, with most of the *Lion* footage of the confrontations in Slipp's office returning, and Jack White again scripting new sequences. Kenneth MacDonald is once again Mr. Slipp, but now he's a greedy theatrical impresario—who nevertheless has managed to become administrator of the Ambrose Rose estate. And he has a hulking accomplice, Joe (doughy-faced Tom Kennedy, who had starred in his own series of Columbia two-reelers).

Kennedy is a fine foil. When Larry slips one of the big man's punches, Kennedy's hand collides painfully with a steam pipe and swells to enormous size (a silly prop hand that's nevertheless very funny). Kennedy sticks his damaged paw into a sink, raising steam as his fist returns to normal size. Larry, like a prey animal that allows itself to be hypnotized by the predator, stares at the restored hand with intense interest—until Kennedy uses it to punch Larry in the eye.

Kenneth MacDonald's new footage climaxes when the boys lever a chairback around his neck after he's made the mistake of sticking his head through a hole in the door. For the next couple of minutes, Shemp slips into a carnival pitchman mode, passing overripe fruit to Moe and Larry and furiously ad lib-bing: "That's it, pitch 'em in there! . . . Ah, the little fat man with the porcupine haircut, go ahead!" and so on.

Performer Profile: Suzanne Ridgeway
1918–96

When dark-haired Suzanne Ridgeway rounds a corner in the backstage area of a theater in the Stooges' *Loose Loot* and the boys stare after her, she's wearing an abbreviated tutu and heels—and looks as good going away as any woman who ever lived. Haughty, imperious, and frankly carnal, Suzy is sex personified.

Very nearly all of her more than 140 screen appearances are uncredited and without dialogue. She worked mainly in features, where cast lists note her in roles the likes of "saloon girl," "nightclub table extra," "girl in cantina," "party guest," "café extra," and "girl at dance joint."

The boys eyeball the ever-alluring Suzanne Ridgeway in an amusingly misleading publicity still from *Loose Loot* (1953). In the film, Napoleon (Johnny Kascier) inhabits the picture frame.
Photo courtesy of the Stoogeum

Early in her career she was fresh-faced and girlish, and became startlingly attractive as she entered her thirties. In a working environment that was pitiless to actresses who were no longer ingénues, Suzanne kept plugging, becoming sexier and more assertive as she approached forty. Genre fans recall her as the ill-fated "native girl" Korey in *From Hell It Came*; she also appears in some bona fide Hollywood classics: *Gone With the Wind*, *Citizen Kane*, *The Best Years of Our Lives*, and *Around the World in Eighty Days*.

From 1948 to 1957, Suzanne appeared in eight shorts with the Stooges. When she has dialogue, she uncorks with a sharp, aggressive voice that brings fresh dimension to her obvious physical charms. She gives the Stooges some hell in the boys' identical-triplets comedy *A Merry Mix-Up*, and has a fine time beating Moe to a pulp in *Rumpus in the Harem*.

And although she has no lines in *A Missed Fortune* (1952), she looks sensational in a variety of chic ensembles—each of which the boys drench with ice water.

Suzanne called it quits in 1959, the year she turned forty-one, after a featured role in *The Purple Gang*, a violent crime thriller starring young Robert Blake. In it, Suzanne is billed as Suzy Marquette, the only time she used that name professionally.

When Shemp gets conked by a vase after stepping too close to Slipp, he shrugs it off with a merry, "A bulls-eye in reverse! Well, apple sauce!"—as he palms a gooey apple against Slipp's forehead.

The backstage theater setting allows a variety of gags involving pretty showgirls. When one of the beauties (the invariably delicious Suzanne Ridgeway) walks past the boys, Shemp eyeballs those fabulous gams and forgets about his mission to locate Slipp. Later in the short, Ridgeway, Nanette Bordeaux, and a blonde showgirl (the actress's full name is unknown) get the boys' goat by playing pickle in the middle with the satchel of dough. The sequence is cheerful and charming, partly for its exuberant energy and partly because Bordeaux calls the other girls by their real names: "Catch, Suzy! . . . Mary, over here!"

The visual highlight of *Loose Loot* is an exceptionally funny, crisscrossing chase in a backstage corridor that takes Slipp, Joe, and the Stooges in and out of various doors. Jules White's camera is intentionally stationary, so the sequence is all about choreography, timing, and Edwin Bryant's unobtrusive edits. Two of the Stooges and Slipp run one way. All three boys, and Slipp and Joe, dash another way. All three boys and Joe go this way. Shemp, all alone and chased by no one, walks verrry slowly from one door to the end of the corridor, where he disappears. Then Moe, hurrying from background to middle ground, chases Suzanne. An instant later, Moe *and* Larry chase Suzanne straight across the hall. "Oooh! Eee!" says Suzanne.

By the time all of this is concluded, you're going to have a stomachache—and not because you ate too much pizza.

Justice and laffs win the day in *Hold That Lion!*, *Booty and the Beast*, and *Loose Loot*—the Stooges' crime-comedy trifecta.

THE LONG AND FRUITFUL COLLABORATION OF DEL LORD AND THE STOOGES concluded in 1947, when the former Keystone Kops player directed the boys in *Shivering Sherlocks* (1948). The short's first half is alternately inventive and familiar; the second is deeply atmospheric in the manner of Bob Hope's 1940 feature, *The Ghost Breakers*, with horror elements that are played for scares rather than for laughs. Although a protracted buildup steals time from the scary material, *Shivering Sherlocks* is nevertheless a fondly recalled gem of the Shemp years (and Lord's only professional interlude with Shemp). At the very least, it's an unusually good-looking example of fast, low-budget filmmaking.

Internal logic and story construction, though, are other issues, because *Shivering Sherlocks* ain't got any of either. Questioned as robbery suspects for no other reason than that they're hiding in a garbage can, the boys later help out at a diner owned by Gladys (Christine McIntyre). Larry has a run-in with a surly customer, and the boys are able to identify the leader of the gang from a photo displayed by a police detective (Vernon Dent) who has already struggled to give them lie detector tests.

A little later, the boys accompany Gladys to check out her deserted family homestead because—out of the blue—a prospective buyer has sent a purchase letter.

Did we say "deserted"? Ensconced inside the shadowy place are the real robbers (Kenneth MacDonald and Frank Lackteen), who saw the Stooges' picture in the paper and have been wondering how to find and get rid of them.

The boys are spied upon, chased, shot at, and nearly turned into cold cuts by the machete belonging to a brute called Angel (Duke York).

Finally, Shemp gets a brainstorm and drops empty barrels onto the crooks as they run beneath him, sending the thugs crashing through a window just as the police arrive.

Consternations:

- Why have the Stooges folded themselves into a garbage can?

- How do the boys identify the leader of the gang from a photograph? They've never seen him before.

- Who wants to buy Gladys's creepy house?

- Why does that person want to buy it?

- Why does that person want to buy it now?

- Who can swallow the coincidence of the thugs hiding in Gladys's long-deserted house?

- What malevolent god sends Gladys and the Stooges to the house while the murderous crooks are inside?

- Has any bunch of crooks ever been handed an easier opportunity to bump off witnesses?

- Why are police right outside, waiting to scoop up the crooks like minnows?

Lord may have shot expository footage that was later cut, but no supportive evidence of that has been uncovered. And anyway, the interlude at the diner (another "greatest hits" package, with fried eggs on the face, a feisty clam in the clam chowder, and other familiar gags) could easily have been shortened to accommodate scenes designed to make sense of the plot.

At the night-shrouded old house, Gladys's key doesn't work. Shemp spies a rifle barrel poking from an outside wall and mistakes it for a pipe that he might use to break inside, and then can't figure out what happened when he goes to grab it after it's been retracted inside again.

Meanwhile, Larry strolls from inside the house with a crowbar that he thinks might be handy for forcing the door. (To grasp the wonderfulness of Larry, read that sentence again.)

Now the narrative and visual tones change radically. We see the hunchbacked Angel (Duke York) as a moving, misshapen shadow on a wall and then (following a graceful pullback shot) in the flesh, dimly but fixedly absorbed in hacking chunks from a piece of railroad tie. Kenneth MacDonald stands over him and

says (in that marvelous Karloff voice of his), "Angel—strangers in the house."
No exclamation point, just a fact, like *mice in the cellar.* Angel looks up. "Urhrr?"
MacDonald gives a small nod.

"Urhhr!" Angel responds, and lumbers off with his machete.

MacDonald watches like a satisfied parent before putting his hand on Frank
Lackteen's shoulder. "He'll do a nice *quiet* job."

Performer Profile: Duke York
1908–52

Giant-sized Duke York played some of the Stooges' most unforgettable antagonists but
was often obscured beneath "scare" makeup: the wild hair, hunchback, and buck teeth
of murderous Angel in *Shivering Sherlocks*; the deathly pale, raccoon-eyed "goon" in *Who
Done It*; in blackface as a Rhumboogie "native" in *Some More of Samoa*; and in facial fur as
Lupe the wolf man in *Idle Roomers*.

York was a pleasant-looking fellow, and you can get a look at his natural features as
the impatient military chauffeur in *Higher Than a Kite*.

During a film career that began in 1933, Duke appeared in more than one hundred
tough-guy and oddball roles. Serial fans know him as King Kala in *Flash Gordon*.

A broken romance prompted York to commit suicide in 1952 at forty-two.

In another moment, Shemp will see Angel (Duke York), a blade, and some alarming orthodontia in
Shivering Sherlocks (1948).   *Photo courtesy of the Stoogeum*

Because of the sinister nature of the setup and Allen Siegler's rich, shadowed photography, Angel's pursuit of the boys is almost unnerving, and it's a relief to laugh when Shemp opens a door to admit the killer, thinking he's admitting Moe and Larry; and when Larry—so terrified he's been struck mute—spreads his hands to show Moe that *he's* not gripping his shoulder.

And then there's Gladys: gagged and tied to a chair in an empty room, sensing that someone is behind her but unable to turn around. Angel creeps nearer and the soundtrack is utterly silent for an unbearable twelve seconds. At the last instant, just as Gladys sees him, Angel is distracted by the boys' voices and shuffles away.

All of this is meaty stuff, and people who first saw *Shivering Sherlocks* while children never forgot it.

Still, there are those consternations noted above. Jules White remembered them, and when he brought the short back for 1955 release as *Of Cash and Hash*, his brother Jack wrote new expository scenes that plug a lot of holes.

Christine McIntyre (in her final new footage with the Stooges), Kenneth MacDonald, Frank Lackteen, and Stanley Blystone (as the nasty diner customer) reprise their roles from seven years before—a surprising amount of effort for just five or six minutes of new footage. Vernon Dent and Duke York (who died in 1952) return via stock footage. Old footage and new are cut together pretty well, though White's direction is noticeably more perfunctory than Lord's except for a beautifully composed shot in which the nose of a truck (extreme right foreground of the frame) suddenly pulls in front of a car (middle ground). Very brief new sequences inside the house aren't as visually textured as the originals.

As for plot, the Stooges are able to identify MacDonald because they've been caught in the middle of a gun battle (which opens the short) between the gang and guards from the armored car. And they can identify Lackteen, too—not simply because he's involved in the shootout but because he makes the mistake of showing up later at the diner.

The simplest of devices brings Gladys and the boys to the house, and for a logical reason: When Lackteen dashes from the diner, Gladys and the boys hop into Gladys's car and follow him.

Scotch-taping old and new footage invites narrative mistakes, such as Lackteen's despair at ever finding the boys (1948) when he's just located them at the diner (1955). And you may notice that the actor is clean-shaven in the diner but wears a gangster's pencil mustache inside the house.

The original soundtrack can't accommodate every alteration to the plot, so a few lines of dialogue are clumsily redubbed.

Although *Of Cash and Hash* makes okay sense as narrative, it lacks the disquieting image of Angel's shadow, and shortens Gladys's ordeal in the chair to just a few moments. In cleaning up the exposition, Jules White sacrificed some flair.

CRIME ON THEIR HANDS (1948) IS ACES BECAUSE IT FEATURES A GORILLA. Nothing more is needed for true comedy. You can keep your chimps and your capuchins and your baboons—give me a gorilla every time. These great apes are mild, even timid, by nature, and we can all agree that movies have misrepresented them as killers, but that's only because they're bigger and stronger than we are. We're afraid.

On the other hand, as Shemp discovers in this short, a gorilla is a good guy to have on your side.

The Stooges are janitors at the *Daily Gazette*, but what they really want to be is reporters. When editor J. J. Cameron (Charles C. Wilson) steps out for a bite, the boys take a phone call from a squealer (Lester Allen) who has information about the stolen Punjab Diamond. In a flash, the boys transform themselves into investigative reporters.

Writer Elwood Ullman and director Ed Bernds naturally grasped industry trends. Hard-boiled crime pictures had come into vogue after the war, often in the form of moody, existential noir melodramas, such as Fritz Lang's *Scarlet Street* (1945). Essentially lighthearted "series" adventures featuring Boston Blackie, Charlie Cahn, The Falcon, and others were also popular, largely because audiences enjoyed knowing what to expect from those characters. And the wisecracking big-city reporter—probably best exemplified by actress Glenda Farrell in the popular Torchy Blane films of the 1930s—was a movie-industry chestnut by 1948.

Crime on Their Hands fulfills expectations because Elwood Ullman's script doesn't deviate from the Stooges' usual personas, and because it lets us observe the boys in an unfamiliar situation: at odds with serious, coldblooded killers. The script makes sure we grasp the danger by including a violent scene in which the squealer is shot through the glass of a phone booth as he spills his story to the boys. The assassination is sufficient to give the short an unquestionably ominous and sinister air.

The squealer's tip leads the boys to the waterfront and a smoky dive called Squid McGuffey's Café. Dapper (Kenneth MacDonald) and Bea (Christine McIntyre) hang out in the back room. Because she mistakenly believes the boys are cops, Bea quickly hides the diamond in a dish of candy mints. Well, Shemp enjoys mints, so as soon as he swallows the diamond, and the boys are exposed as would-be reporters, Dapper and his right-hand man, Muscles (Cy Schindell, who died of cancer not long after the short was completed), lock Moe and Larry in a closet and prepare to perform a little impromptu switchblade surgery on Shemp.

I can hear you out there: *What about the gorilla, huh? What about the gorilla?*

The gorilla's name is Harold, and he's in the charge of a cheerful Cockney named Hawkins. (The name of the very funny actor who plays Hawkins has been lost.) Harold is a big mother who eats so much of the tavern's food that Squid (George Lloyd) is sorry he ever allowed Hawkins to stash the monk in the back room. Now he just wants Harold gone.

Despite their innate cowardice, the Stooges try their best to fit into Squid's café. Larry and Moe pull down the forward brims of their hats; Shemp does the same with his straw boater. Less than imposing at about 5'4" apiece, the boys nevertheless swagger across the floor, flipping coins, à la George Raft in another nod to crime-movie convention.

The usually demure Christine McIntyre is a revelation as Bea: a sexy vision in clinging black, her blonde hair piled atop her head, her mouth heavy with crimson lipstick. (Yes, the short is in black and white, but what other color would her lipstick be?) Bea is a man eater who doesn't care who gets hurt or killed, or why.

Kenneth MacDonald's Dapper is one of the actor's greatest inventions: smooth (dapper, if you will), calculating, and willing to gut Shemp like a flounder in order to retrieve the rock. Even hard-as-nails Muscles flinches and says, "Ain't ya even gonna give him anesthetic?"

Dapper looks mildly annoyed. "So you're going to get technical, eh?"

Moe and Larry have been locked inside a closet that backs onto the rear of Harold's cage. They find tools (a heavy bag of them falls on Larry's head) and get to work on the wall with a hand drill and a blade-like compass saw. Harold is understandably perturbed when the saw's wicked point jabs him in the rear, so he bounces Larry right back into the closet. This is bad because Moe has as little patience as Harold, so the terrified Larry becomes a ping pong ball who's bounced back and forth, taking head shots from Harold and even worse ones from Moe, until he's so addled that he can longer summon the words to warn Moe about the monkey.

> LARRY
> Moe, there's a . . .
>
> MOE (hits Larry on the head with a hammer)
> Quiet!
>
> LARRY
> There's a bi—there's a big thing . . .
>
> MOE
> Listen! Listen, you!
>
> LARRY (addled)
> Yeah . . .
>
> MOE
> Ya afraid to go by yourself?
>
> LARRY
> Yeah . . . There's a big . . .
>
> MOE
> All right, I'll take you by the hand!
>
> LARRY
> Yeah, yeah!

Performer Profile: Kenneth MacDonald
1901–72

With a voice like Boris Karloff's, the lean face and figure of an unwillingly aging matinee idol, and the smiling charm of a crooked Bible salesman, pencil-mustached Kenneth MacDonald excelled at cheats, con men, robbers, kidnappers, and all manner of smarmy schemers.

A proficient actor with credits dating to 1931, MacDonald made strong impressions in B-westerns and found lasting fame opposite the Stooges. He has the distinction of being Ichabod Slipp, a central character in *Hold That Lion!*, the only film to feature all three of the Howard brothers—Moe, Shemp, and Curly. MacDonald also is a memorable crumb in *Three Dark Horses* (as a crooked politico); *Crime on Their Hands* (as a diamond thief who prepares to filet Shemp like a halibut in order to get at an accidentally swallowed stone); and *Studio Stoops* as Hollywood kidnapper Dandy Dawson.

MacDonald voluntarily slowed his career after 1955 but worked steadily on television and in movies until 1970, most notably as a semi-regular—as, of all things, a distinguished judge—in the long-running *Perry Mason* TV series.

Shemp waits as Dapper (Kenneth MacDonald) scrapes the ol' whetstone prior to some impromptu surgery in *Crime on Their Hands* (1948). Ray Corrigan is inside the gorilla suit.

Photo courtesy of the Stoogeum

MOE
Little boy! Come on!

LARRY
But, Moe, ya gotta listen to me!

MOE (to Harold)
How do you like this, too scared—Yaahhh!

LARRY

Gaahhh!

The sequence is directed with perfect emphasis by Bernds and sharply edited by Henry DeMond. The entire bit accounts for thirty-five seconds of brilliantly funny comic business that few comics could have equaled. Moe and Larry display their gifts for impeccable comic timing, and Larry shows his stuff as a skilled, wonderfully physical actor.

Harold leaps through the hole in the wall, deftly dispatches Muscles and Dapper, and then investigates the trussed-up Shemp. Because most of the short is comprised of medium two- and three-shots, Bernds's decision here to come in very close on Shemp's face as the gorilla breathes all over him is mildly startling as well as dramatically sound. Ray Corrigan (as Harold) plays it beautifully, simultaneously curious and ferocious. Shemp is wonderful, too, his eyes betraying real terror and his words a panicked babble when Harold uses Dapper's knife to slice through the gag.

In a great touch that's calculatedly funny because it's patently fake, Dapper and Muscles, partially out of sight behind the makeshift operating table, come to, only to be tossed into the air like salad by the annoyed Harold, their arms and legs as floppy as dummies' limbs, their squawks of shock and awe cleverly dubbed into the soundtrack.

Harold's well-placed poke to Shemp's stomach pops the diamond free just as the cops arrive with J. J. Cameron to clean up the mess.

CAMERON
Did you knock these crooks out all by yourself?

SHEMP
That I did, boss, that I did!

HAROLD (rising to embrace Shemp from behind)
I helped!

SHEMP
My buddy!

Crime on Their Hands was remade, on the cheap, as *Hot Ice* (1955). Opening footage at Scotland Yard (in which the boys identify themselves as correspondence-school detectives) is lifted from a 1948 short, *Hot Scots*. The greater portion of *Crime on Their Hands* is reused, though new sequences and bridging inserts written by Jack White and directed by brother Jules attempt to paint over the old wallpaper. Squid McGuffey's Café becomes a British hotel, and when the boys search one of the rooms, they reprise the conk-your-head-on-the-bureau-drawer gag. They investigate further by pulling back bedclothes and uncovering a bleary drunk (Harry Wilson, a onetime stand-in for Wallace Beery), whose lived-in face scares them right out of the room.

Sexy Barbara Bartay (who is terrific with the boys in *Pardon My Backfire*, see "The Stooges on the Job") looks smashin' in a form-fitting sweater but lets loose with the most godawful impersonation of a Cockney accent anybody has ever heard. (The actress's origins are in Eastern Europe, so the fault is more White's than Bartay's.)

Christine McIntyre and Kenneth MacDonald return for a few expository inserts, and in a poorly handled moment, actor Joe Palma walks into frame behind MacDonald to "double" the late Cy Schindell as Muscles.

Harold the Gorilla returns in stock footage only, with a new insert explaining that Dapper and the gang have kidnapped him from a circus for ransom. (If it were that easy to kidnap a gorilla, everybody would be doing it!)

Some details of décor between old footage and new don't match, and the lighting of the new scenes is noticeably flatter than in the original.

Although clever in a vaguely cynical way, and a bit of a boon for chest men thanks to Miss Bartay, *Hot Ice* is tepid stuff.

THERE ARE MANY WONDERFULLY STRIKING IMAGES IN *WHO DONE IT?* (1949), and here are two of the best: the topple of Emil Sitka's dead-white corpse from behind a secret panel, nearly into our laps; and Christine McIntyre, the Stooges' perennial leading lady, as she seduces the camera in a black, off-the-shoulder gown. She's the "bad girl" in this short, and although you're concerned when she attempts to poison Shemp's champagne, you can't tear your eyes from Christine. Whatever your gender, you find her just as compelling as she is amusing.

Who Done It? is the Stooges' reworking of the 1947 Schilling and Lane short *Pardon My Terror*. As discussed earlier in this chapter, Ed Bernds had written that one for the Stooges, only to be forced to rework it when Curly entered the final phase of his illness.

Bernds wrote (as well as directed) *Who Done It?*, retaining many of the *Pardon My Terror* plot points and gags and adding some inventive twists. The boys are again detectives, and our first glimpse of them is hilarious: Their office phone, in tight close-up at the right of the frame, rings loudly, and when Bernds pans up, we see the Stooges glumly sitting in a line against the far wall, trussed up like Christmas turkeys. Right away we have doubts about the name of their business: Alert Detective Agency.

In *Pardon My Terror* the imperiled millionaire fakes his own disappearance, but in *Who Done It?* old man Goodrich (Sitka) is an undisputed victim who is violently choked and pulled through a secret panel by a wild-haired, raccoon-eyed giant (Duke York) whom the boys later call the Goon.

The Stooges show up at the Goodrich place with a large glass-plate camera that sports an absurdly long focus bellows. When Shemp gets a load of McIntyre though the viewfinder, the bellows develops a mind of its own, extending itself to within inches of her body and shuddering with ill-concealed desire, roving up and down her fabulous figure, and twisting itself like an overheated Turkish Taffy to get the best possible look. Shemp is as determinedly horny as Christine is premeditatedly sexy, and you begin to wonder what might happen next if the two of them were completely alone.

The rest of the criminal gang (played with arrogant surliness by Ralph Dunn and Charles Knight) is more prosaic than McIntyre and the Goon but no less murderous. They're not brought to heel until old man Goodrich (who's miraculously alive) flicks off the lights during a tense showdown, giving the Stooges a chance to gain the upper hand.

The poison sequence is a comical back-and-forth of unconcealed intentions, as McIntyre drops poison pills into Shemp's bubbly, and each of them subsequently switches the other's glass—or pretends to—when the other looks away. Shemp confidently slugs back the poison (after toasting McIntyre with, "A coupla pip pips, a barbecue, and a what have you!"), certain that he's given her the bug juice. But after a moment he hiccups into a spasm of peep-peep-peeps, *tk tks tks*, gurgles, and tongue-tied choking. McIntyre looks smugly satisfied in insert close-ups, but in two-shots with Shemp she can barely suppress her laughter.

Goodrich turns up alive but worse for wear, shakily telling the Stooges, "They tortured me to get my money! I'm a lover of fine music! They tied me up and made me listen to singing commercials! I thought I'd go mad!"

The climactic battle that unfolds in pitch blackness is dramatically punctuated by muzzle flashes, lit matches, angry and frightened faces, glimpses of fists, and shattering vases.

Most of the atmospheric photography of Ira Morgan, and the handsome art direction of Charles Clague, returns in the stock footage that dominates the remake, *For Crimin' Out Loud* (1956), the last Stooges two-reeler with new footage of Shemp, who had been dead for more than three months when the short was released on May 3, 1956.

Felix Adler and Jules White came up with about four-and-a-half minutes of new footage to open the short; the remainder is from *Who Done It?*, with some minor edits for time.

The entire supporting cast except for Emil Sitka (who shot a quick insert in which he identifies himself as a threatened councilman) exists only in stock footage. Duke York, in fact, had been deceased for more than four years by the time *For Crimin' Out Loud* was cobbled together.

In a small variation from the original, the boys run the Miracle Detective Agency ("If we solve your crime, it's a miracle."). Moe carelessly tosses a boiling test tube down the back of Larry's pants, Shemp files a suspect's toupee under "D" (for dandruff), and all three boys take time to compliment a sexy "newsboy" (Barbara Bartay), who answers with a gravel-voiced (and overdubbed), "Gosh, fellas, thanks a lot!"

Later, Moe wants everybody to be in synch with the clock. He tells Larry, "Look at your watch!"

Larry: "Okay, but you'll hafta wait'll I go the pawn shop!"

HUGS AND MUGS (1950) IS VERY CLEAR ABOUT TWO POINTS: CRAZY THINGS happen when guys let the little head tell the big head what to do; and the Columbia two-reel department was experiencing an interlude of enforced austerity, as this is one of the most poverty-stricken of all the boys' shorts. The unit occasionally rented inexpensive stage space away from the Columbia lot, and that's the case here. *Hugs and Mugs* was shot in three days at Darmour Studios, a long, two-story building that filled somewhat less than half of the 5800 block of Santa Monica Boulevard. Built around the time of World War I, Darmour had been home to Mickey Rooney's Mickey McGuire shorts in the late silent era. Harold Lloyd also filmed there. The building sat vacant for many years before it was razed for new construction in the 1990s.

Supposed exteriors on the sidewalk outside the Stooges' upholstery business are flat gray and virtually featureless; the set looks like something designed by a minimalist theatrical troupe. Furniture and other props fill out the shop interior adequately well, but Vincent Farrar—a competent director of photography—was given no time by producer-director Jules White to accomplish much of anything with the lighting, except more of that perfunctory, flat gray.

The Stooges get mixed up with three beautiful dames (Christine McIntyre, Kathy O'Malley, and, in her first short with the Stooges, Nanette Bordeaux) who are freshly released from prison for fur theft. They stole pearls, too, and have tracked them to the boys, who made a blind purchase of the girls' parcel at an express company auction. (The Stooges think the pearls are phony).

Each of the sexy thieves attaches herself to one of the boys and flirts outrageously. During the seductions, Larry admits to O'Malley (who spent 1948–50 at the two-reel unit and then worked in TV until 1998) that he polishes his head with floor wax. Shemp makes the mistake of letting Bordeaux know he's ticklish.

Just as the boys are convinced to hand over the pearls, the shop is invaded by three goons (Joe Palma, Pat Moran, and Blackie Whiteford) who say the pearls belong to them.

The Stooges—by now madly in love with girls they'd never seen until five minutes earlier—tussle violently with the thugs and finally subdue them by using hot irons to administer third-degree burns to the interlopers' backsides. That frantic, noisy abuse (Shemp even burns himself because he can't tell his own ass from anybody else's) is strictly, dispiritingly mechanical. The comic imagination of Clyde Bruckman's script and White's direction is as chintzy as Darmour itself.

The three actresses are amusing when they unexpectedly indulge in punching, ink-squirting, foot-stomping, eye-poking, and more Stooge-like behavior. But then, out of left field, comes the revelation, described by McIntyre, that all they want to do is return the pearls "to their rightful owner."

Say what?

For fifteen minutes these broads have carried on like Bonnie Parker, and in an eyeblink they're Deanna Durbin. Credulity is stretched further when the gals proclaim real love for the boys. The sentiment just doesn't scan, and neither does this short.

As LAID OUT IN *STUDIO STOOPS* (1950), B.O. PICTURES HAS A NEW HOT PROPerty, a starlet named Dolly DeVore (Christine McIntyre). The studio chief has her in tow when he barges into his publicity department to demand a big buildup of Dolly in advance of her next picture, *Kiss the Moonbeams Off My Elbow* (a play on the 1948 Joan Fontaine thriller *Kiss the Blood Off My Hands*).

Well, that shouldn't be too tough, except that the guys in the office are the Stooges, and they're custodians, not studio flacks. But because they've just changed into their street clothes, they look the part (if you don't look too closely).

Moe practically vibrates with confidence and big ideas, and in a moment Shemp and Larry are on board, brainstorming right along with him. (No "imposter syndrome" troubles these boys!) The newspapers will be told that Miss DeVore has disappeared, "when all the time she'll be holed up at the Clinton Arms Hotel!"

"She'll be on the front page of every newspaper in the country!"

"It'll be colossal!"

That's sufficient information for kidnapper Dandy Dawson (Kenneth MacDonald) and his toadie, Tiny (Charles Jordan), who lurk in the corridor outside and listen through the door. (Their presence begs the question, *What happened to the guards at the studio gate? They're supposed to prevent lowlifes like these two from entering the lot.* Wait. Maybe Dawson has been on the lot all along. Maybe he's a crooked focus puller or a minor executive in the two-reel unit.)

Studio Stoops is another completely successful comedy by Elwood Ullman and director Ed Bernds. The boys are witty and enthusiastic, and Bernds and cinematographer Vincent Farrar tell the story with effectively utilized dolly-ins, dolly-outs, and brisk pans. Bernds had no more time to shoot this short than anybody else would have had, so what we're watching is talent, craft, and ingenuity.

Ullman's script has some priceless situations and dialogue. In the boys' newly refurbished office, Shemp types out a press release as Moe breathlessly dictates the copy. "Flash! June 22nd," Moe begins, and goes on for sentence after sentence, during which Shemp types almost nothing. Moe pauses to catch his breath before continuing with "and . . ."—which sends Shemp into a protracted frenzy of noisy, violent typing.

> MOE (suspiciously)
> Read that back.

> SHEMP (squinting at his work)
> Ogula gobblea yackabena foockatimin aharadja paranikmonheeha, June 22nd!

> MOE
> Get away!!

When things get hairy at the hotel, Larry has a thought.

> LARRY
> Hey, you'd better bolt that door in case our adversaries come back!

> MOE
> Good idea! [beat] "Adversaries"?

> LARRY
> Yeah!

> MOE
> Since when did you get so smart?

> LARRY
> Oh, I been smart all the time, only *you* didn't know it! Say! When I come back I'll give you the password!

> MOE
> Brilliant! What'll it be?

> LARRY
> "Open the door!"

The highlight of *Studio Stoops* is Shemp's misadventure inside a zippered garment bag. He staggers from a closet right through a window and onto the ledge outside—and promptly falls off. His friends scream in horror and then reflect. "Poor Shemp," Moe says sadly.

Larry: "And he had his good suit on, too!"

Shemp has rescued himself by reaching through a window to grab a phone attached to a scissors-style extender. He calls the hotel room and Moe sends down a rope. Shemp alights on a balcony occupied by a beauty enjoying a sunbath. "Hiya, toots, mind if I drop in?"

At this, the kidnappers show up. Dawson's ankle becomes tangled in Shemp's lifeline and the captain arrives, but only because Larry has thrown pastry into his face to get his attention.

If there's a "sweet" element to this action-packed short, it's the transformation of Dolly DeVore from ice queen to sweetie-pie. And the change isn't because of gratitude only; when she thinks Shemp has been killed, she's truly bereft.

Ullman and Bernds borrowed the hanging-on-the-telephone gag from a Buster Keaton short directed for Columbia by Del Lord in 1941, *So You Won't Squawk*. The business with the wardrobe bag comes from *Feet First* (1930), in which Harold Lloyd is held fast inside a laundry sack that dangles above a scaffold.

Stand by while B.O. Pictures' new publicity geniuses put their heads together to persuade us that benign theft of comedy is a colossal idea.

SLAPHAPPY SLEUTHS (1950) WAS RELEASED ON NOVEMBER 9, 1950, A MONTH after *Studio Stoops*. If the latter short suggests that the Shemp era was purring right along, *Slaphappy Sleuths* is a step backwards. It's an amiable but minor effort with good patter and performances, one inventive visual gag, and a lot of familiar-seeming slapstick. Jules White directed it with an emphasis that, even for him, is blunt and heavy-handed, and that confirms the superior skills of the unit's other mainstay, Ed Bernds.

Once again, the boys are investigators—or as Fuller Grime (Gene Roth), the general manager of the Onion Oil Company, puts it—"three brainy but stupid-looking private detectives [who can] pose as gas station attendants." A robbery gang has been making off with the receipts from dozens of Onion stations, and Grime wants it to stop.

He stares at the Stooges and adds, "Well, you fellas are certainly stupid-looking enough, but about being brainy detectives, that's open to conjecture!"

"Oh, thank you!" chorus Moe and Larry.

Shemp: "I'll button mine!"

That's a great line by Felix Adler, who put the script together with a lot of silly enthusiasm.

> FULLER GRIME (to Moe)
> You were in the service, weren't you?
>
> MOE
> That's right.
>
> GRIME
> Did you ever get a commission?
>
> MOE
> Nah, just straight salary!

A minute later, Shemp has something caught in his tooth. His pocketknife is too big to use to dig it out, so without a moment's hesitation he carves an enormous spear of wood from the edge of Fuller Grime's coffee table and whittles it into a toothpick.

Subsequent scenes at an Onion gas station bring the boys into contact with the gang, whose leader (Stanley Blystone) effortlessly raids the till.

But the crooks' car leaks oil, and in the short's best gag, the boys trace the dark smear from the service station to the inside corridor of an apartment house, where the oil leads right to an apartment door.

Once the boys are inside, White wisely does nothing to emphasize the fact that the gang's roadster is inexplicably parked in the living room. It's just there. That's clever, so a tip of the Onion Oil cap to White and Adler.

The remainder of the apartment sequence is blunt slapstick. Stanley Blystone, who was about fifty-six when the short was filmed, is as physical and blustery as he was fourteen years earlier in *False Alarms* (see "The Stooges on the Job"). His vigor helps compensate for some tepid gags, notably the bit in which the boys torture his head after inserting it into an enormous woodworking vice.

Shortly after, Shemp becomes tangled in one arm of Blystone's coat, which sets up the venerable gag in which two thugs trade punches while Shemp, who revolves back and forth inside the coat, is untouched.

Pretty Nanette Bordeaux plays Blystone's avaricious girlfriend, and has almost nothing to do other than be repeatedly cold-cocked by her careless pals. Cutaways to the delicate actress's cockeyed face in unconsciousness are supposed to be hugely funny but only seem cruel.

The script apparently gave Bordeaux a good scene at the gas station—she promises Blystone that she'll keep the Stooges busy so that he can snatch the cash—but if her attempt at seduction was ever filmed at all, it's in that mythic landfill of lost footage. In the short's final cut, Blystone leaps back into the car and drives away with Nanette before we can enjoy watching her turn on the charm.

Early in the service station sequence (which is marred by a stagily distract-ing, obviously painted backdrop depicting houses and trees), Emil Sitka puts together one of his funniest performances as a young rube (alternately argu-mentative and goofy) who stops to gas up his dilapidated flivver. The Stooges reprise their "super-service" routine from *Violent Is the Word for Curly*, carelessly abusing Sitka as they labor to pamper him with a manicure, a little hair styling, a shave (Moe demands to use Sitka's tongue as a strop for a straight razor), and a shoeshine (during which Shemp gets shoeblack all over Sitka's white socks and then mutters, "Thought ya had boots on there!").

The boys manage to make popcorn in Sitka's radiator, and Moe's face is blackened when the tailpipe farts black soot into his face. Larry suggests that Moe sing "Mammy."

Lovers of defunct products will enjoy the advert plastered on the back of Moe's uniform: "Feel tired? Take Stun. Stun is nuts spelled backward." (*sic*)

Performer Profile: Stanley Blystone
1894–1956

This imposing, gargle-voiced character actor achieved immortality as the unlucky, justifiably apoplectic fire chief in charge of the Stooges in *False Alarms*. Exasperated by the boys' laziness and ineptitude—and more than a little upset when they wreck his brand-new car—Blystone shouts, threatens, and comes perilously close to murder.

Craggy and husky, Blystone amassed more than five hundred appearances in a career that began in 1924. He worked steadily for the rest of his life as a tailor-made authority figure in roles as cops, detectives, military men, gunmen, guards, and ranchers. Blystone worked with Laurel and Hardy in *Swiss Miss* and *A Chump at Oxford* and with Abbott and Costello in their breakthrough comedy *Buck Privates*.

His first appearance with the Stooges came in 1935 in *Restless Knights*. Besides *False Alarms*, he's memorable in *Half Shot Shooters* as the justifiably vengeful Sergeant McGillicuddy. In *Out West*, Blystone is a cavalry colonel who is begged not to arrive too late to prevent trouble. With dignified authority, Blystone replies, "Son, never in the history of motion pictures has the U.S. Cavalry ever been late!"

Does *this* hurt? Robber and car thief Stanley Blystone is sorry he ever ran into the Stooges in *Slaphappy Sleuths* (1950). *Photo courtesy of the Stoogeum*

That's a cute riff on Serutan ("Read it backwards"), a now-defunct laxative that was beloved by old folks.

If Moe gave Emil Sitka a Stun treatment, the footage is in the same landfill with Bordeaux's flirting.

IN HIS 1999 AUTOBIOGRAPHY, ED BERNDS ADMITTED THAT HE NEVER CARED for the sort of cringe-worthy violence that characterizes many of the Stooges' two-reelers. Bernds found Moe's signature eye poke especially unnerving and avoided it after he came to the team in 1945—just two years after the release of the boys' most violent short, Del Lord's *They Stooge to Conga* (see "The Stooges Go to War").

Bernds frequently wrote the two-reelers that he directed, and when that wasn't possible, he had a congenial, sophisticated collaborator in Elwood Ullman. But Ullman, who co-wrote *They Stooge to Conga* (with Monte Collins), let his inner fiend run riot when he scripted *A Snitch in Time* (1950), in which the boys play with a lot of sharp instruments. We'll note here that the short has no eye pokes, but that's a little like taking a moment to report that nobody got shot with a squirt gun during the Battle of the Bulge. It hardly matters.

A Snitch in Time is all about mayhem. Although perhaps not as violent overall as *They Stooge to Conga*, it comes close, and with one gag, in fact, it far outstrips the earlier film's pain quotient. *Snitch* isn't the best of the Bernds films, but it entertains with plenty of crude laughs, effective visual storytelling (as always, Bernds mixes his shots beautifully), crisp photography by Vincent Farrar, and the sharp timing of editor Henry DeMond. The supporting cast is superior.

As in many of their other adventures, the boys work with their hands, this time as furniture makers who own a business, Ye Olde Furniture Shoppe, Antiques Made While U Waite (*sic*). In a novel turn, the boys' product is beautiful. No, really: We see for ourselves that the furniture they make is lovely.

It's the *making* of the furniture that gives them trouble.

Remember, the boys work with wood, which means they routinely get their mitts on hammers, chisels, wood planes, and (cue four-note *Dragnet* theme) a table saw with a whirring blade that's the diameter of a tire from a Buick Roadmaster.

A deadline for a customer named Miss Scudder (Jean Willes) looms, so the Stooges shift into high gear to finish on time. Naturally, bad things happen when the boys work quickly. Moe watches with mild irritation as Larry struggles to insert a dresser drawer, forgetting for a moment that he's guiding a piece of wood toward the table saw blade. So that we grasp the danger, Bernds goes to a close-up of the delicate webbing between Moe's index and middle fingers as the wood is pushed to within millimeters of the blade.

When Larry accidentally planes a stripe from Moe's hair, Moe grabs the tool and planes Larry's forehead (so high, so smooth, so inviting), and then gets his fingers into Larry's curls and pulls out a gigantic tuft—just because he can. "Here, go stuff a mattress!" Moe snarls.

Shemp traps his hand in the tray of a new high chair (the gag is vaguely reminiscent of Oliver Hardy's *two-handed* trouble with a window frame in the great 1930 Laurel and Hardy short *Busy Bodies*). Shemp also has trouble with a camel's hair brush. "Must be the hump," he mutters as he flicks a glob of black paint over his shoulder and into Moe's eye, sealing it shut. Shemp and Larry try to pry the eye open with a hammer and screwdriver, a wire cutter, and pliers. Remember, this is Moe's *eye*.

The eye is finally forced open, but then Moe's palms become stuck on a varnished board. Shemp briefly uses a hacksaw to try to saw Moe's hands off at the wrist before Moe releases himself with a tremendous backward heave—which sends his hind end right into the whirring blade of the table saw. A little later, *Moe's face collides with the blade*, an outrageous gag that easily outstrips Curly's nose to the (literal) grindstone in *They Stooge to Conga*. Kids of the day—before bicycle helmets, seat belts, and moratoriums on peanut butter—loved this kind of torment. It's still funny today, but you keep waiting for the spray of blood. An anonymous 2001 post to www.threestooges.net commented, "Only *Dawn of the Dead* gives you more pain for your entertainment dollar."

Three jewel thieves have taken over Miss Scudder's boardinghouse, setting up a showdown after the boys arrive to deliver the new furniture. But first, the furniture needs to be stained, which leads to Moe drinking a cup of Larry's varnish, Shemp eating a brush that he thinks is a sandwich, and the usual all-over body-painting of Moe by his careless pals.

The three thugs (John Merton, John L. Cason, and Henry Kulky) are fearsome but bring the violence down to a reasonable level with mere punches, gouges, and gunfire.

This is Kulky's only short with the Stooges, and he appeared in it not long after abandoning his wrestling name, Bomber Kulkovich. His attempt to punch his way free of a freshly varnished chair that's attached itself to his backside is hilarious, and it's easy to see the energy and personality that kept him working continually until his death in 1965.

Tall, feline Jean Willes—who receives a nice solo credit beneath the short's title—turns what might have been a nothing role into something special, forcing the crooks to tie her up to get her out of their hair and later narrowing her eyes in simmering anger as she prepares to press a hot iron into John Merton's butt.

And then, deciding that retreat is a good idea, she gracefully dashes down the hall, executing a wonderful little hop before disappearing around the corner.

The radio bulletin that announces the gang's robbery is read by Fred F. Sears, a character actor who specialized in westerns before becoming a director. Throughout the 1950s, while with Sam Katzman's Clover unit on the Columbia lot, Sears directed many low-budget gems, including *Teenage Crime Wave*, a subdued and very affecting horror thriller called *The Werewolf*, and the fascinatingly nihilistic true story of Caryl Chessman, *Cell 2455, Death Row*. Sears also did one of the greatest and best loved of all "bad" movies, *The Giant Claw*.

DETECTIVE STORY, SIDNEY KINGSLEY'S VERY SUCCESSFUL 1949 BROADWAY PLAY, is a tightly focused drama set in a small New York City police precinct that's dominated by an unreasonably judgmental detective lieutenant. During the course of his shift, the detective's patience and (small) empathy are tried by a dim-witted shoplifter; a young embezzler; a pair of petty robbers; assorted cranks; and a perennial, much-hated adversary, an inept abortionist (at a time when the procedure was illegal). Ashamed of his origins and unbending in his black-and-white morality, the detective tries and fails to come to grips with a revelation from his wife's past and is unexpectedly killed inside the station when one of the robbers takes another cop's gun.

Except for a few process shots, William Wyler's excellent 1951 film version (with Kirk Douglas) restricts itself to the station house and a couple of ancillary rooms. Its set-bound nature is a virtue because viewers are forced to rub noses with an unending gallery of losers, misfits, and eccentrics. And in its banality of shuffling feet, endlessly ringing phones, and flimsy alibis, it finds great drama.

The Stooges' *Tricky Dicks* (1953) is a clear send-up of *Detective Story*. Felix Adler's script casts the boys as plainclothes cops and brings forth an array of oddballs fit for a zookeeper: an Italian organ grinder (dialect comic Benny Rubin) named Antonio Zucchini Salami Gorgonzola de Pizza, who speaks with an Oxford accent; an erudite little assassin named Chopper (Phil Arnold), who is unable to confess to a murder because his vocabulary is too elevated for the boys to understand; B. A. Copper (Ferris Taylor), the exasperated and dim chief of detectives; a sexy shoplifter (Connie Cezan); and an annoyingly meek little fellow (Murray Alper) in spectacles who turns out to be a self-described "thrill killer" who puts seven slugs into Detective Shemp at point-blank range.

Except for the boys having been ordered to find the killer of one Slug McGurk in twenty-four hours, *Tricky Dicks* is essentially plotless. Action is restricted to a single set that, because of careful work by art director Paul Donnelly, perfectly captures the cluttered but drab look of a small precinct house: plain desks and file cabinets, uncomfortable wooden chairs, a wall map, a fire extinguisher, a hanging row of clipboards, drab light fixtures, framed photos of cops. A barred door at the rear is the entrance to an unseen holding pen.

When the boys root through the files, it's in footage lifted from *Hold That Lion!*, making *Tricky Dicks* the third consecutive Stooges short to lift footage from that 1947 release.

Jules White and cinematographer William Whitley alternate two-shots and medium close-ups beneath flat, even lighting that suggest the plain look of *The Undercover Man* (1949) and other then-novel police "procedurals."

White's attention to detail is good, as well, particularly the fact that neither Moe nor Larry wears a sidearm in his belt holster—standard procedure when dealing with suspects in a small space.

The phones that never stop ringing in Sidney Kingsley's world go off like fire alarms at the Stooges' precinct, giving Moe a start every time and aggravating his already bad mood. He has his hands full with a lot of nonsense, but everything goes south when the thrill killer opens up with a revolver, spoofing that movie convention of the handgun that never seems to run out of bullets: The killer shoots and shoots . . . and shoots some more, expending more than *eighty-five* rounds without reloading. The gut shots he sends into Shemp have no apparent effect other than to make Shemp squirt like a sprinkler when he takes a drink.

Besides spoofing *Detective Story*, *Tricky Dicks* does homage to the quick, corn-ball verbal humor of burlesque and vaudeville.

> LARRY *(mildly)*
> Y'know, my sister was engaged to a guy with a wooden leg.
>
> MOE
> Yeah? What happened?"
>
> LARRY
> She broke it off.

And:

> MOE *(into phone)*
> Oh, hello, dear! Oh, sure, you've got nothing
> to worry about!
> G'bye, sweetheart! [beat] That was the mayor.

Later, on the phone again:

> MOE
> Oh, wait a minute, Clancy. Go ahead. You say there's
> a dead horse on Ticonderoga Street? How do you
> spell Ticonderoga? Oh, you don't know, either.
> Well, drag him over to First Street!

Shemp makes a call:

> SHEMP
> Oh, yeah, Joe, look, release that guy who stole those eleven
> bottles of whiskey.
> I *know* he's guilty, but the D.A. says we can't make a case out
> of eleven bottles!

Comedians with stage experience inevitably played well off of women, and here it's curvy Suzanne Ridgeway as a uniformed jailer who responds to Larry's impulsive kiss with a good slap.

Other gags are pure Stooges. When Moe tells Larry to take down a confession in shorthand, Larry pulls his pencil and pad up almost to his nose. And when ordered to beat a suspect with a hose, Larry flashes a malevolent grin and lashes the prisoner with a woman's stocking.

It's all part of the gritty business of law and order at (where else?) the 13th Precinct.

INCOME TAX SAPPY (1954) IS OSTENSIBLY ABOUT THE BOYS' FIDDLING WITH their tax returns in order to shortchange the Internal Revenue Service. (The department's name was formally changed from Bureau of Internal Revenue in 1953, the year this short was filmed. Assuming the general public was paying attention to that formality, the revised name would have given the short some minor topicality.)

The boys' gangly sister (Margie Liszt) gives them the crooked idea, and although it initially strikes them as a bad one, they warm to it in about nine seconds.

LARRY
Say, after all, makin' out the income tax is nothin'!

MOE
Whaddaya mean, nothin'?

LARRY
When I get through, the income tax collector'll get *nothin'*!

SHEMP
...They never can catch smart guys like us!

LARRY
We'll hornswoggle 'em!

Some tactics are decided upon. Because Moe doesn't plan to make good on money he owes, he'll write it off as a bad debt. Larry will deduct three grand for charitable donations because "charity begins at home." Shemp will write off eleven dependents: his ex-wife and ten bartenders. And so it goes, the giddy scheming of these criminal dunderheads. It's funny stuff, and well played by the Stooges in an almost "straight" acting style and conversational, even subdued, dialogue.

Although more humor might have been mined from the boys' interpretations of the federal tax code, scripter Felix Adler and director Jules White lose interest in the idea and wrap up that part of the short by establishing that the Stooges have become filthy rich by showing others how to cheat on taxes. The remainder of *Income Tax Sappy* is an agreeable but very familiar "greatest hits" comedy. For instance: Moe's palm ends up glued to Larry's head, and when Moe pulls free, an enormous tuft of Larry's hair comes with it. So fiendish is the glue that the hair on Moe's palm migrates to the end of his nose and then onto one of his eyelids.

Because Larry doesn't pay attention as he cuts a baguette for sandwiches, he ends up with a dangly horror that looks like an overstretched concertina. Moe's sandwich bites his nose, and when he threatens it, the hot dog inside leaps out of the bread and goes yelping across the floor.

During a dinner party later, Larry clumsily cuts off the beard of a guest (Benny Rubin). Moe is appalled and tries to articulate to Larry what he's done: "Arrylay, ixnay on the eardbay!" When the unknowing victim goes to stroke his murdered whiskers, Moe gets behind him and quickly substitutes a whisk broom.

Various people are assaulted by flying salad, mashed potatoes and gravy, spaghetti, and pie, while Larry does violent battle with a lobster claw that brazenly emerges from the chicken gumbo to steal his crackers.

By 1953, the boys could do this sort of thing in their sleep, and it's to their credit that they do more than just go through the motions. They're wonderful. It's the gags that are tired.

A highlight is provided by Benny Rubin, who wants to add salt and other things to his food. "A- number zix?" he ad libs in a fractured German accent. "Ja, seven sideways? Anyt'ing! You got condimintis?"

In the end, Rubin removes what's left of that damned beard and announces that he's a tax agent; burly agents Vernon Dent and Joe Palma burst in to assist in the arrest, which concludes with small fires blazing on the seats of the boys' pants.

We could say more about that, but you probably need to see it for yourself.

JACK WEBB'S *DRAGNET* WAS DETERMINEDLY STRAIGHT-FACED AND REALISTIC— so much so that, in its insistence on a lack of style, it became highly stylized. That quality was irresistible to wiseguy parodists. Writer Harvey Kurtzman and artist Bill Elder came up with "Dragged Net" for *MAD* number 3 (January–February 1953), and radio-TV satirist Stan Freberg (with Daws Butler, June Foray, and others) scored a million-selling spoken-word single for Capitol in August 1953 with "St. George and the Dragonet."

The Stooges have a go at Webb's creation in *Blunder Boys* (1955), playing rookie police detectives who have trouble with a cross-dressing hotel robber called The Eel (Benny Rubin). Moe and Larry mimic the deadpan persona of Jack Webb's Joe Friday, but contrary to the nature of those performances, which cast them in "roles" ("All we want is the facts ma'am," Moe says when the boys enroll in a criminology course), Shemp is very much Shemp, tapped by scripter Felix Adler and director Jules White to exist in counterpoint to his partners. In the opening sequence, for instance, Moe stares into the camera and holds up his badge. "I'm Farrady," he says flatly.

Larry shows a badge and says, "I'm Terraday."

Shemp displays a shamrock and giggles, "I'm St. Patrick's Day!" (Before he's through, Shemp will invoke numerous other holidays, including Groundhog Day.) All three boys are clowns in this short, but only Shemp has the extra dimension of characterization that allows him to be the clown who mocks the other two.

Benny Rubin plays his part in drag, and although he's more than a match for the Stooges, we don't have the pleasure of a good look at him. By dealing with The Eel mainly in long and medium shots—often with Rubin's back turned or his face otherwise obscured—White reduces him to a cipher who scurries about in a lumpish, vaguely sinister gray dress. Rubin's performance is lively, but you won't miss much of it if you listen without watching.

In a not-bad moment, The Eel forces Shemp to straddle a mechanical horse in a hotel workout room and turns the control to Gallup. (Yes, it's spelled that way on the machine's dial.) Shemp is bucked so violently that he's tossed straight up, his head punching through the ceiling, the rest of him left dangling in empty air. It's a surreal image, and one of the strangest in all of the boys' shorts. (When Shemp's pudgy stunt double extricates his head and falls, his "Shemp wig" comes loose and falls separately.)

Larry gets trapped outside the hotel on a high ledge (a faux night stage-and-cyclorama setup that's particularly well shot by Ray Cory), and all three boys must disguise themselves as dames in order to get *out* of a women's Turkish bath. (Now the Stooges and The Eel have something in common—a circumstance that Jack Webb never would have allowed to befall Joe Friday.) Although they're perfectly horrid (and wonderful) in towels, lipstick, and piping falsettos, the boys might have made their escape except for Shemp's loudly declared intention to "linger with the rest of the girls!"

Pure, demented fascination arises from a unique twist on the standard eye poke. Moe warns Shemp and Larry to "prepare for 81C!" The boys are horrified: "No, not that! Not 81C!" But they obey, running straight into Moe's outthrust fingers so that they give *themselves* eye pokes. The punishment administered, Moe solemnly wipes eye goo from his digits.

Pretty Angela Stevens is appealing in a subdued role as the boys' criminology instructor, and Barbara Bartay (reverting to her natural, Eastern European accent) is quite funny as a beautician who applies a mud pack to "Moella" and remarks, "I luff your bangs!"

The boys' struggle to free themselves from two pairs of handcuffs (our linked heroes look like a ridiculous, life-size charm bracelet) is a well-staged exercise in barely repressed panic. Larry is a good foil later in a gag that spoofs Jack Webb's familiar "Mark VII Limited" hallmark, but a flashback World War II combat sequence meant to suggest the boys' familiarity with danger is completely extraneous and seems to have been shoehorned in from another galaxy.

Blunder Boys is the last Stooges short released during Shemp's lifetime. The great comic passed away on November 22, 1955, barely more than three weeks after the film's November 3 release.

THE STOOGES' FINAL FORAY INTO CRIMINALITY, *QUIZ WHIZZ* (1958), CASTS them as gullible victims. Joe has won $15,000 on a TV quiz show and tells Moe and Larry that he's invested the whole amount with a stranger named John Smith.

And just what is it that has sucked away Joe's windfall?

"Consolidated Fujiyama California Smog Bags!" Joe says happily. "Filled with smog!"

The remainder of *Quiz Whizz* concerns the boys' search for the swindler John Smith, with an unlikely but darkly funny interlude in which the money-starved Stooges pretend to be the new adopted sons of a rich man, Montgomery M. Montgomery (Gene Roth).

"Oh, boy," Joe exclaims, "we'll be Montgomery's wards!"

The impersonation goes less well than the Stooges would have liked (they're nearly murdered), but they do gets their hands on John Smith (Milton Frome) and take back Joe's check.

When *Quiz Whizz* was shot on May 2–3, 1957, America had already fallen in love with Charles Van Doren, a young instructor of English at Columbia University who had been a fabulously successful contestant on a television quiz show called *Twenty One*. He unseated a longtime champion at the end of 1956, and finally "retired" the following March. His face was on the cover of *Time* magazine, and women he never met wanted to marry him.

There were other popular TV quiz shows, too, notably *The $64,000 Challenge* and *Dotto*. Because of all that, *Quiz Whizz* arrived with a certain timeliness, but Searle Kramer's script uses the quiz show phenomenon only as a device by which Joe comes into the money. The short has no quiz-show sequence.

If the boys' contract had been extended into 1958, *Quiz Whizz* would have been a very different kind of comedy, because the "quiz show scandal" gripped the nation that August when allegations of cynically orchestrated cheating began to be heard. The three programs mentioned above were implicated, and a New York grand jury convened in October to investigate.

That alone would have given the Stooges plenty of material, but the story became even more gripping in the autumn of 1959 when Van Doren admitted to a Congressional panel that he had been given answers in advance. America's intellectual sweetheart was a fraud.

Joe doesn't pretend to be an intellect, but he is the likable focus of *Quiz Whizz*. Jules White tones down the violence so that the humor is situational and character based. Of course, Joe has an opportunity to cry, "Not so *loouudd!*," and then shows another side altogether when he waves a lit cigar at Moe and threatens, "I oughtta give you a *hot face*, that's what *I* oughtta do!"

Hot face?

Montgomery M. Montgomery is in league with the swindlers, and his job is to kill the boys. Joe, Larry, and Moe show up at his mansion wearing Buster Brown outfits that recall the kiddie clothing of *All the World's a Stooge* (1941; see "The Stooges and the Youth of America"). For Besser, it was like a trip back to *The Abbott and Costello Show* during 1952–53, when he wore a similar outfit to play the neighborhood brat, Stinky. Showbiz history aside, it's just a hoot to see men in their fifties and sixties dressed this way.

The boys are greeted at the door by Lisa (Greta Thyssen), Montgomery's beautiful but murderous accomplice. She lies, "What nice boys!"

Larry: "You're not so bad yourself!"

Moe and Larry are nearly killed by Lisa during a game of blind man's bluff, and in an elaborate pantomime Joe is forced to eat a cigar that turns him a hideous, sickly white.

Smith and his pal (Harold Brauer, billed here as "Bill Brauer") show up, and the mayhem expands to encompass knives and rat poison. Lisa ends up wearing a cake, and Montgomery is knocked cold by a serving tray. Smith and his crony writhe on the floor with their own knives stuck in their rears.

Moe finds the check and shares it by carefully tearing it into three pieces— with a little extra torn away for the tax man. Only after a long beat does he realize what he's done.

Regardless, the crooks have been put down, and the Stooges have possibly not broken any laws. All is restored to what passes for normal.

Justitia nemini neganda est.

12

The Stooges and the Youth of America

In which the boys live large at the City Dump; pound on the walla; scare themselves in a dark basement; suffer a squirt named Jackie; scream for Mommy; juggle infants like rugby balls; and get Bupp'd.

Because the Stooges were not sentimental comics—no Chaplin or Langdon pathos for them—they seldom worked with children. Instinct and their years on the vaudeville circuit told them that in showbiz, kids, like dogs, are nothing but trouble. You can't use them as foils because people will think you're cruel. If you play the kids' game and make nice, you're simpering or false.

Cash and Carry (1937) is the Stooges' first Columbia two-reeler to revolve around a child. The boys got lucky because the young actor who worked with them was Sonny Bupp, an appealing nine-year-old who'd come from New York City to Los Angeles with his family in 1934. There were four Bupp kids (Ann, Jane, Tommy, and Sonny), and they all had talent and they all got into the movies.

Few child actors could top Sonny Bupp's best credit, the young Charles Foster Kane in *Citizen Kane*. But when he worked with the Stooges, that plum role was four years away. In *Cash and Carry* he's straight out of Dickens—a crippled boy who lives with his older sister in a shack at the city dump. Oh, and he needs an operation. The sister has saved sixty-two dollars, and everything will be jake as soon as she does the impossible by accumulating five hundred.

The shack happens to "belong" to Moe, Larry, and Curly, who live there as squatters when they're not prospecting in the San Gabriel Mountains above Los Angeles. Gold was first found in the range in the 1840s, and after a second burst of activity around 1910, the San Gabriels saw a third round of prospecting in the 1930s. Director Del Lord shot the exteriors of *Cash and Carry* on location in the L.A. basin, where the San Gabriels dominate the far background of many scenes.

The Stooges' first instinct is to throw the kid out on his keister (Larry says, "C'mon, beat it!"), but when they see him lean on a crutch as he begins to hobble from the table, their hearts melt and they feel ashamed. "Wait a minute, son!" Moe says. "We made a mistake! This ain't our house! We didn't have any curtains! Go on siddown, do your homework."

The studied awkwardness of those lines speaks well to the talents of scripters Clyde Bruckman and Elwood Ullman (the latter doing his first work with the Stooges), and to the gifts of Moe Howard, who was, lest we forget, an actor.

The sister (Harlene Wood) is a soulful, junior-Sylvia Sidney type whose polite humility makes you want to give her a painful pinch. But the Stooges are softies and promise they'll get all the money the boy needs.

A couple of swindlers (Lew Davis and Nick Copeland) tell the boys about a treasure buried by "Captain Kidd's kid" inside an empty house.

> CON MAN
> Just a minute! It'll cost you two hundred for the privilege of digging it up!
>
> CURLY
> Two hundred?
>
> CON MAN
> Two hundred or nothin'!
>
> CURLY
> Oh, we'll take it for nothin'!

In the end, the Stooges hand over the kid's sixty-two bucks—and throw in their jalopy, too. (The same premise was reworked by director Jules White and Jack White [adapted screenplay] in 1945 for two-reel star Andy Clyde, as *A Miner Affair*. Clyde reworked his own remake, with stock footage, in *Two April Fools* [1954], which eliminates the boy to concentrate on bank robbers.)

The map, of course, is useless, but once inside the house, the boys are intrigued because on one section of the map Walla Walla has been circled. "We'll each take a walla!" Curly declares.

During the beaver-like labor that follows, Moe is cracked with a shovel and a pick, Curly falls into a cellar, and a beam collapses on Moe's neck when he makes the mistake of sticking his head inside a broken "walla."

The dirt cellar hides another walla, which the boys rig to blow with dynamite before realizing they have no way to get out of the hole before the explosion.

Without knowing it, they've blown the hell out of a U.S Treasury vault that's lined with bars of gold and stacks of cash. Larry is goggle-eyed. "Now Jimmy can get his operation!"

Curly: "There's enough here for *all* of us to have an operation!"

Guards storm in with tommy guns, but in the end President Roosevelt (played by an obscure actor named Al Richardson, seen only from the back) pardons the boys and promises to arrange for Jimmy's operation.

This being 1937, the boys salute, and chorus, "Gee, Mr. President, you're a swell guy!"

Cash and Carry is beautiful to look at, city dump and all. Lord and cinematographer Lucien Ballard shot in gorgeous sunshine (even the shack is pierced with light), and the empty-house interior is handsome and intriguing.

Curly is captured at the peak of his comic and physical exuberance; he's wonderfully childlike as Moe prepares to set the dynamite: "Oh boy, I like

The Stooges have an audience with FDR (Al Richardson) and relate Harlene Wood and Sonny Bupp's tale of woe in the mildly syrupy *Cash and Carry* (1937).

Photo courtesy of the Stoogeum

firecrackers!" he says excitedly, his hands moving like pinwheels. "Rrrr! Phffftt! Aahhh!"

Sonny Bupp is nice to have around, partly because he's not around that much.

Sentimentality issue solved.

IN *MUTTS TO YOU* (1938), A SIGN ON THE STOOGES' APARTMENT HOUSE declares "NO BABIES OR DOGS ALLOWED." The boys wash dogs for a living but never bring their work home, so they're good on that count, but when they end up in charge of a baby they assume has been abandoned, their lives become complicated.

The brilliant comic actor Charley Chase directed *Mutts to You*, from a screenplay by Al Giebler and Elwood Ullman. Chase was an ambitious filmmaker with an affinity for complex camera setups and elaborate physical gags. As a performer, he conveyed a silly yet understated sophistication and looked for that quality in other actors. Chase directed the Stooges five times, with mixed results. His Stooges comedies haven't the rude knockabout of Jules White's efforts, nor do they trade as effectively as Del Lord's on the boys' established on-screen personalities. On the other hand, the Chase-Stooges shorts are smart, glossy, and frequently charming. *Mutts to You* is one you might screen for a friend of delicate constitution, if that friend has never seen the Stooges before.

The boys are almost innocuously childlike, conducting their dog-wash business on a makeshift conveyor belt, with jerry-rigged controls of Goldbergesque gadgets and crudely printed homemade signs. It's very like any number of business schemes put together by Our Gang—and probably no coincidence because that act, like Charley Chase, did fine work for Hal Roach.

At a water wheel, Curly pedals a stationary bike to keep the H_2O flowing. When a wooden lever is pulled, an udder of mechanical arms drops down to wash and scrub. Moe and Larry work the crude master control panel, their eyes shining like little boys', and it's easy to imagine Spanky and Alfalfa.

Among the Stooges' clients is an affluent couple named Manning (Bess Flowers and Lane Chandler), who have an elaborate misunderstanding that leads to their baby being left momentarily on the Mannings' front doorstep just as the Stooges happen by. (The good-looking, dormered Colonial is still at 111 South Norton, two doors south of West 1st Street, in L.A.'s Windsor Square neighborhood.) The boys "rescue" the kid, and after close calls with the landlord (Vernon Dent) and a cop (Bud Jamison), baby and parents are reunited. The Stooges are cleared, and the baby takes a ride on the dog-wash conveyor belt.

A few gentle gags stand out. As Curly attends to the nails of the Mannings' Dalmatian, he asks, "Did anyone ever tell you you have pretty paws?" Larry plucks a single flea from the dog's coat and deposits it on an anvil, where it's smushed by a household iron after Larry pulls a rope. A very teeny voice cries, "Ah, they got meee!"

The run-in with O'Halloran the cop is a highlight. Curly has disguised himself as the baby's mother, "Mrs. O'Toole," and although he looks like a Bulgarian washerwoman, the cop is enchanted. "That's a fine broth of a boy you have there!" O'Halloran says. "Is he on the bottle yet?"

"I should say not!" Curly answers indignantly. "He don't smoke, drink, nor chew!"

Curly's supposedly pipe-stem legs (seen in an insert; they actually belong to Charley Chase) have been filled out beneath Curly's nylons with sponges, which swell grotesquely when soaked by a sprinkler. The cop finally figures out he's dealing with imposters and takes out after them.

A little later, Moe and Larry disguise themselves as Chinese laundrymen, with Curly and the baby stashed between them in a closed hamper. Bud Jamison does a great take that combines surprise and repulsion when he stares at Larry (who brazenly stares right back).

COP
And what part of China are *you* from?

LARRY
Ibinachinaboychikslavodkabanianiotmenachik, and I don't
mean *ipsha*!

The Dalmatian and the baby are patient with the silliness on the conveyor belt; in fact, the baby seems to enjoy it. As Mrs. Manning, Bess Flowers (the only supporting player to receive title-card billing) is pretty, if a little bitchy. The Mister is played by 6'4" Lane Chandler, a handsome star of the silent era who worked mainly in westerns and on television as a supporting player until 1966.

The baby grew up.

"OH, BOYS, I'M GOING TO ASK YOU TO DO SOMETHING THAT MIGHT SAVE THE life of a little girl. Will you do it?"

Those are pivotal lines of dialogue, written by Clyde Bruckman and Felix Adler and delivered by a dead-serious Vernon Dent, in *Nutty But Nice* (1940). He's not speaking to a team of doctors or to the misfit G.I.s of Easy Company. He's speaking to Larry, Curly, and Moe.

The dialogue gives Stooges fans the shivers. Some weep. Others slip into seizures so severe that bystanders must place pencils or Nerf balls between their jaws, so that in their convulsive shock they don't injure themselves.

Women who always thought they had an active dislike for the Stooges think the whole setup is sweet.

Welcome to the Land of Saccharine, State of Corn Syrup, County of Treacle. If you forgot to pack insulin, it can be provided for you.

A banker named Williams has been abducted while holding hundreds of thousands of dollars in bonds. His little girl is so stricken by his loss that *she's literally on her deathbed*. (Me, I was always glad when the old man went away for a while, but that's another story.) The Stooges work as singing waiters at a restaurant frequented by Dr. Walters (Dent) and his friend Dr. Lyman (John Tyrrell). During the daily businessman's lunch, the boys march from the kitchen cracking jokes and singing "Yankee Doodle Soup," which they ladle from Curly's trick snare drum.

The two doctors think all of this is a scream, but when Vernon Dent gets serious, he Gets Serious. While it's novel and pleasing to see the great man in close-up, delivering portentous lines with great portent, you just know it can't lead to anything good.

The Stooges agree to go to the hospital to snap the kid out of it. They show up as burly little girls, in pretty pinafores and enormous hair ribbons. They tell nonsense nursery rhymes and crack each other over the head with their lollipops. Moe holds an inflated bladder that's as big as an eggplant and that he wields like a cudgel.

The docs and the nurse (Evelyn Young) think all of this is hilarious (mostly, it is), but the little girl (whose real name has been mercifully lost to history) just lies there, blankets up to her chin, her face down to there. She whispers:

"i want my daddy . . ."

No capital letters, that's how pathetically weak her voice and spirit have become.

For the moment, the Stooges have failed, but they leave the hospital with some clues about the kid's old man. He's 5'10", has a bald spot, and sports a tattoo on his shoulder. And he yodels. No, really.

The boys take to the streets and assault various innocent fellows who look like they might fill the bill, plucking hats from heads, tearing off sleeves, measuring with a measuring stick.

Curly stops at the curb to measure a cart horse. Moe demands to know what the heck Curly thinks he's doing.

Curly: "Don't you believe in reincarnation?"

Finally, a yodeling singer on a record played by one of the kidnappers leads the boys to Mr. Williams (a trussed-up Ned Glass) and sets up an inventive and hilarious climax in a dark basement, where the lights keep going out. Jules White's direction of all the preamble has been better than competent, but he really shines during the lights-on/lights-off business: Curly is convinced he's drowning, but he's only standing in a tub of water; he finds a staircase in the blackness, but when he lights a match, he's standing on the highest rung of a tall ladder. The lights go out and he falls. Then the lights come up again, on one of Curly's greatest moments:

> CURLY (apparently impaled by a spear)
> I'm stabbed! I'm dead! I'm murdered, I'm killed! I'm annihilated! What'll the world do without me? What'll *I* do without myself? I'm slaughtered, I'm annihilated, I'm destroyed! I'm barbecued, I'm done for! [Pause]
> [to Moe] Can you think of anything else?
>
> MOE
> No, you've covered it all!
>
> CURLY
> I'm not even wounded?
>
> MOE
> That's what *you* think!

Reliable Cy Schindell and Lynton Brent glower as the kidnappers. Moe and Larry fall down a dumbwaiter, and Johnny Kascier takes some beautiful tumbles as a guy who just wants to deliver a few buckets of beer.

At the conclusion, daddy and daughter are reunited, and the boys do sterling three-part harmony on "Home on the Range" (Curly sings especially well) before assaulting each other with whipped cream.

Which is very sugary stuff. If you still need insulin, please let us know.

IN AN UNUSUAL TURN, *ALL THE WORLD'S A STOOGE* (1941), ALTHOUGH NATU-rally dominated by the Stooges, finds its structure—and much of its comedy—in a trio of strong supporting players. The short utilizes the Stooges as if they're raucous guest stars in somebody else's comedy. The approach is refreshing, and because it's beautifully written by John Grey (*False Alarms*) and very well directed by Del Lord, it's one of the best Curly shorts of the 1940s.

The film is deceptively satiric, with a stinging, almost bitter subtext. During World War II, children in Europe were displaced from their homes by the thousands, and some social-relief agencies arranged for temporary placement of refugee boys and girls with American families. As you might imagine, in some affluent American households the refugees became perverse status symbols—living children displayed as pets for which the bubbleheaded hosts could be congratulated.

That is precisely the attitude and expectation of Lotta Bullion (Lelah Tyler), a well-fed matron who has been badgering husband Ajax (Emory Parnell, billed here as "Emery") to bring home a sweet little refugee.

Ajax (who functions in the slow-burn mode of Edgar Kennedy, and is nearly as funny) sees right through his wife's superficial rationale and wants nothing to do with the idea. But when he finds the Stooges in his car after they've had a run-in with a cop, Ajax decides to pass the boys off as "little refugees" and teach Lotta a lesson.

The third member of the comic trio mentioned earlier is the Bullions' long-suffering butler, Barters (Olaf Hytten). Though a polite and efficient servant, Barters's opinion of Mrs. Bullion's notions are no higher than Ajax's.

> MRS. BULLION *(excitedly)*
> A little waif from the war-torn battlefields of, of . . .
> *somewhere!*
> Isn't it splendid?

> BARTERS *(dryly)*
> I can't imagine anything more intriguing, Madam.

When Ajax returns home with *three* little refugees, Mrs. Bullion is ecstatic. In troop the waifs: Moe and Curly in Buster Brown outfits and Larry resplendent in petticoat and pinafore, with a huge satin hair ribbon. The "kids" are introduced as Frankie, Johnny, and Mabel (the last was the name of Larry's real-life wife). At the name "Mabel," Larry delicately props his index finger beneath his chin and does a graceful curtsy. He's quite a sight.

Mrs. Bullion is charmed and introduces the children at a society party. Curly settles on the lap of perennial society dame Symona Boniface after having smeared Limburger cheese on his chest, thinking it's salve for his cold. Symona wants to get rid of this stinky kid, and does when she jabs Curly with a straight pin that sends him flying onto a nearby loveseat. "I still don't smell so good," Curly explains (he means he's congested).

The young man (Stanley Brown) on the love seat retorts, "*I'll* say you don't!"

Performer Profile: John Tyrrell
(1900–49)

General-purpose actor John Tyrrell came from the same medium as the Stooges, vaudeville, as half of a very successful comedy and dance act called Tyrrell and Mack. A featured role in *George White's Scandals* was encouraging, but Tyrell left the variety stage in the mid-1930s to gain experience as an actor. Regional stock in New England and other theater work led him to Hollywood, where his regular features, emphatic voice, and ability to suggest sophisticated authority won him a contract with Columbia in 1935.

Tyrrell was kept busy with bits in the studio's "A" pictures and featured supporting parts in Bs and two-reelers. He worked frequently with El Brendel, Charley Chase, and Andy Clyde, as well as with the Stooges. He plays a golfer in *Three Little Beers*, a building manager in *All the World's a Stooge*, the conniving B. O. Davis in *So Long, Mr. Chumps*, and showbiz promoter Manny Weeks in *Gents Without Cents*.

Tyrrell is at his best in *Dizzy Detectives* as community leader Mr. Dill, who raises holy hell about a citywide crime wave—only to be revealed as its mastermind.

Fed-up building manager John Tyrrell (right) and dentist I. Yankum (Richard Fiske) collar the boys in *All the World's a Stooge* (1941). *Photo courtesy of the Stoogeum*

The boys have already turned lunch into a small disaster, and Ajax's patience with his refugees finally runs out after they get into his cigars. In a great moment, Larry and Moe rush into the sitting room shouting "Momm*ee*! Momm*ee*!" as Ajax follows close behind, hefting a battleaxe.

Mrs. Bullion is appalled: "Ajax!!"

All three boys leap through a window and hide behind an enormous tree, which is split vertically (in a superb mechanical effect) when Ajax tosses the axe. The little refugees dash off across the lawn, Larry pumping his muscular legs like a bowlegged track star.

Central, of course, to the comedy of *All the World's a Stooge* is the viewer's willing suspension of disbelief regarding the Stooges. Only Ajax sees that they're grownups; everybody else is convinced that these hard-bitten, middle-aged men are little kids. What marvelous absurdity!

The boys shoot craps with Barters in an upstairs bedroom, and because Barters has had to give up an article of clothing after every losing pass, he hurriedly stands in a blanket, and the boys go "Woo woo woo!" around him, Indian-style, when Mrs. Bullion sticks her head in.

During the party, Curly is invited to recite.

CURLY
Little fly upon the wall/Ain't ya got no clothes at all?/
Ain't ya got no shimmy-shirt?/Ain't ya got no petti-skirt?/
Boo, fly, ain't ya cold?

All the World's a Stooge (1941): Mama's little refugees have demolished lunch and now ponder a wish.

Parnell, Tyler, and Hytten are unusually strong comic actors. (Parnell frequently appeared in Warner Bros.' "Joe McDoakes" one-reelers, as Joe's boss.) It's unlikely that *All the World's a Stooge* was a tryout, but these three could surely have carried a domestic-comedy two-reel series of their own.

In the short's well-mounted opening sequence, the boys are window washers who end up inside a dentist's office, where Ajax mistakes Moe for the doc and insists that his aching tooth be pulled. Larry puts Ajax under with a hammer to the noggin, and Curly yanks out the patient's upper plate. "Ya stripped his gears!" Larry exclaims.

Oops. Well, boys (and girls) will be boys.

A SHADOWY NIGHT. A YOUNG WOMAN IN A PLAIN COAT BENDS OVER THE FRONT stoop of a house and leaves a basket.

"Goodbye, Jimmy!" she whispers before stealing away. "My baby!"

The Stooges discover the kid and a simple note that's signed "A Broken-Hearted Mother."

The boys are delighted.

Why are they delighted? This is a central question, and failing, of *Sock-a-Bye Baby* (1942).

Much of the Stooges' appeal lies in the boys' pragmatic approach to the world. (We said pragmatic, not "sensible.") They're good about looking after their own interests. They become resentful when other people put them in touchy situations that might bring, say, criminal charges. They *really* don't want to go to jail.

So all three boys should be hyperventilating and running around in a panic on their front stoop, bemoaning the inevitable arrival of the cops and shooting dark glances at Curly, as if the baby somehow belongs to *him*.

That would have been in keeping with the Stooges' style. But according to scripter Clyde Bruckman and director Jules White, the boys never think to call the police or even to take the kid on a drop 'n' run to the nearest precinct house. Instead, their fear of jail has apparently vanished, like dandelion fluff in a stiff wind. Brimming with fatherly gusto, they happily assume shared paternity, a job they should know they're unqualified by skill and temperament to carry out.

The next morning is devoted to preparation of the baby's breakfast. Moe looks at Curly. "What did you eat when you were a baby?"

"Weeds."

That's a good, unexpected answer, and if *Sock-a-Bye Baby* had more of that mordant sensibility, we'd all be better off. But the boys remain uncharacteristically earnest about being responsible.

They agree that babies like "soft stuff," so Larry goes to the market and returns with herring, celery, radishes, beer, and bicarbonate.

When breakfast is served, Larry exclaims, "Wait'll you see the meal we have for you! Fit for a king! Even better—fit for an airplane worker!" We know it's wartime, but Larry's unlikely remark turns him into a responsible citizen and, worse, into an "establishment" comic. Where's the anarchy? (Earlier, Curly is uncharacteristically nasty when he says, "*Ptoo* [spit] on the Japanese!")

Jimmy (played by a cute little girl named Joyce Gardner) is unhappy with the boys' offerings of enchiladas, radishes, onions, and pigs' feet. In one of the short's best bits, he squeezes an olive and sends the pimento flush into Moe's eye.

An artichoke (Curly derisively calls it "a feathered apple") frustrates the baby and makes him cry. He flings the leaves onto Moe's face, and follows up with a plate of spaghetti.

White stages the food gags well, and the boys certainly play them expertly, but because there are no surprises here (of *course* the kid will fling the food around), the bits unreel mechanically—one two three—and kind of lie there, looking wan.

The seriousness of the whole situation doesn't dawn on the Stooges until they see a newspaper headline about a kidnapped baby. *Now* panic sets in. They load Jimmy into the back of their woodie wagon and head to a remarkably undeveloped region of the L.A. basin that has a paved two-lane road linked to dirt cutoffs, a house or two under construction, and a lot of sandy soil and scrub. *Sock-a-Bye Baby* finally becomes significant but for archaeological rather than comic reasons.

Bud Jamison is enthusiastic as one of two dogged motorcycle cops on the boys' trail (most of the riding scenes are in long shot, but Bud does a wee bit of the driving himself). The basics of the chase—twisty roads, motorcycles, a speeding car, open land, plenty of dust—recall classic Mack Sennett stuff, but the action is so physically spread out that the sequence can't develop any urgency or comic rhythm.

After the boys hide their car beneath a two-window tent, Curly leans across Moe's back to tend to the baby and mashes Moe's face into the car's horn ring—just when the boys are trying to hide. It's the first belly laugh, and the film is nearly over.

The second motorcycle cop (Clarence Straight) is the baby's father. Neither he nor Bud has a beef with the Stooges. The baby is safe (the mother [Julie Gibson] abandoned the kid after a mild domestic argument), and Dad is happy—but if he has any sense he'll deliver the missus to the nearest psych hospital.

The Stooges, meanwhile, escape by running beneath haystacks, creating a funny, frankly weird image in an otherwise shockingly tame and conventional short.

THREE LOAN WOLVES (1946) IS A DISCOURAGEMENT TO FANS OF CURLY BECAUSE it captures the great man in one of his late-career "down" periods. He's uncharacteristically slim here (his suit hangs from his frame), and the stress of illness is etched in the lines in his face. Always professional, he mounts an effort to be engaged, but his features are slack. We see his body, but Curly seems to be somewhere else, unable to fully communicate with us.

Things might be more tolerable if a little blond squirt named Jackie Jackson were somewhere else, too—like Kansas City—but, alas, he's the central figure of Felix Adler's script. Jackson was a child actor who was about ten when he did *Three Loan Wolves*; he retired in 1955, after a stint as Henry Kettle in Universal's Ma and Pa Kettle comedies. If you can't recall him in those amusing films, you may have hysterical amnesia. This is a very annoying kid.

Adler's premise is that the boy—whose name is Egbert, of all things—has been cared for since infancy by the Stooges. His real father is apparently completely unknown, and a throwaway line of dialogue notes only that he's the son of someone's sister. As frequently happens with adopted children, Egbert gets older and becomes curious about his origins. Fair enough, but young Mr. Jackson doesn't act—he strikes a pose and shouts. The pose is usually dominated by a pugnacious crossing of the arms, and the dialogue goes like this: "There's! somethin'! funny! about! this! and! I! want! the! lowdown!! Now! come! clean!, where! did! I! come! from!?"

Of course, only the Lord is responsible for Jackie Jackson's lack of talent, so earthly blame for the kid's awful performance must be laid at the door of Jules White. Although White was skilled at his craft, his primary role at Columbia was as an executive who ran the two-reel unit and pushed product into theaters. No one ever called him an actor's director. He never hung out with Lee Strasberg to toss around theories about motivation. Curly was ill, so Adler's script had had to be rejiggered to give the lion's share of the physical and verbal gags to Larry. White had to find ways to include Curly in the action without harming Curly or the film. White already had his hands full, so little Jackie's ability to hit his marks and speak was good enough. Cut, print.

The Stooges tell Egbert what they know, establishing the flashback structure that consumes most of the short's running time. They run a pawnshop, where the boys' grinning faces adorn the hanging Medici balls. Larry makes loans on worthless things like a bass fiddle made of cardboard but has a fresh problem when the local street thug, Butch McGee (Harold Brauer in his first Stooges short), demands protection money.

McGee's girlfriend, Molly (Beverly Warren, an appealing Virginia Mayo type), leaves her sister's baby behind when she's unable to finagle a loan on a glass diamond.

"The bag left me holdin' the babe!" Larry explains later.

The Stooges' puzzlement about baby care is similar to the confusion they display in *Sock-a-Bye Baby*, but becomes oddly distasteful when Curly gives the infant a loaded revolver as a pacifier (the kid sucks on the barrel) and when Moe lifts the corners of his eyes to make a funny face and recites, "Japee! Japee!"

McGee is accidentally knocked senseless by bowling balls, so the boys hurry to toss him into a baby carriage and shove him into the street. When he returns with two buddies (Wally Rose and a very lively Joe Palma), Larry keeps McGee at bay with a bottle of seltzer water, and then squeezes his head in a letterpress. Curly tosses Wally Rose into a roll-top desk, and Larry dumps hot coals down the back of Palma's pants.

Curly is brought into the physical action via a stunt double who performs falls and flips.

"And that's the way it was, son," Moe explains as the flashback concludes. "Y'see, the police came and took them away, *but nobody ever called for you.*" [emphasis added]

With that, *Three Loan Wolves* ceases to be a Stooges comedy and becomes an adaptation of a lesser work by tearjerker novelist Fannie Hurst.

Ungrateful Egbert has had it up to *here*. "Oh! So! you! just! moved! in! on! me!, eh!? I'm! going! to! find! my! mother!!"

The child stalks out of frame, leaving the Stooges alone, unloved, and unappreciated.

Well, maybe we'll see a train wreck on the way home and be cheered up.

THE CENTRAL—AND OFT-REPEATED—GAG OF *BABY SITTERS JITTERS* (1951) IS that Shemp stands on his head to quiet a crying baby. Shemp was fifty-four or fifty-five when the short was filmed, so the very fact that he can stand on his noggin at all gives the stunt some minor, built-in appeal. But a visual joke that's mildly amusing the first time quickly grows stale with overuse.

True to their lot as chronic underachievers, the Stooges are professional babysitters. They've just taken up the trade, and their first job brings them to a spiffy neighborhood. "Boy, this is some joint!" Moe says admiringly. "I wish I had a house like this!" Babysitters were lucky to get a dollar an hour in 1951, so Moe's wish is apt to remain just that. As is usually the case, the Stooges must admire life's great boulevards from the side streets.

The boys are greeted by a beautiful young mother (Lynn Davis) whose carelessness with a revolver allows her toddler (David Windsor) to get hold of it and stick the barrel in his mouth. (This seems to have been a new obsession of Felix Adler.) The mother assures the boys the gun isn't loaded—but it is, of course, as everybody discovers when Shemp jerks the trigger and carves a groove-like divot in Moe's scalp.

The mom explains that the gun is kept handy in case "a certain somebody" tries to snatch Junior. Late in the short the boys meet the estranged (but mild) young husband (Myron Healey). Shemp shadow-boxes in the guy's face like a wet-brained pug but breaks off to stand on his head—again—when the baby fusses.

The husband decides he's ready to make up with his wife. She's so happy she can't stop crying, so the baby stands on—well, you know.

Despite the pushy sentimentality and forced humor, *Baby Sitters Jitters* opens with a potent laugh as the apprentice sitters feed and burp their gurgling charges and then execute a seated, simultaneous, three-way crosswise baby toss

Lynn Davis has no qualms about entrusting the Stooges with her kid in *Baby Sitters Jitters* (1951).   *Photo courtesy of the Stoogeum*

across the living room. Shemp barely catches his baby, and when he stands up a moment later he trips on the rug and *squashes the infant beneath him.*

Even though the babies turn out to be practice dolls, the gag lets you think otherwise for a long moment, perpetrating a kind of goofy nihilism that American culture wouldn't tolerate for another twenty-five years, from the likes of *National Lampoon* and *Saturday Night Live.* By going out on a comic limb, Felix Adler redeems himself for the unfunny gun gag, and Jules White gets a gold star for clever staging. And the Stooges—dig it—are cutting-edge.

Generally speaking, when the short doesn't go for schmaltz, it's funny. For example, the mother is surprised that she gets three sitters instead of one. "We work as a unit!" Larry explains.

Shemp pipes up with, "Yeah, we're Unitarians!"

After the mother leaves for her night out, Shemp steals the silver, and Larry snaps a nipple onto a bottle of Coke that keeps Junior quiet until the kid raises the bottle and sends it crashing into the back of Larry's skull. (Because the baby and Larry are in separate camera setups during the gag, Edwin Bryant's sharply timed cutting is critical.)

Shemp has his best moments in the kitchen, where he struggles with basic literacy while preparing soup. He dumps what he calls "consummatreated soup" (concentrated soap) into a pot and adds "saggy" (sage), "gloves" (cloves), "caninny" (cayenne), and "powdered bacon" (baking powder). Adler's script sets up the basic misapprehensions, but Shemp ad libs with abandon, marveling that the gloves are little ones, and muttering about the lack of pits in the saggy.

The subsequent explosion of soap bubbles from the boys' mouths is mechanical and overlong; Jules White never quite grasped that, even with the Stooges, a little might be better than a lot.

When Mom returns home, the boys are asleep. Shemp groggily awakens in the crib. Where's Junior?

"He was sleepin' here with me!" Shemp says. He looks around. "Maybe he's between the spring and the mattress."

Myron Healey, who became a dependable television actor, has far too little to do here. Lynn Davis commits a sin by allowing her voice to trail off so that she "swallows" the final words of some of her lines—an amateur's failing that Jules White, on the inevitable deadline, ignored.

Little David Windsor, the last child performer to have a central role in a Stooges short, is expressive (he's helped by some dubbed, post-production laughter and dialogue) and—okay, we admit it—he's cute, too.

13

The Stooges at Home

In which our little homebodies give nightmares to Frank Lloyd Wright; play Tarzan; beat on the boob tube; sit down for their rights; stare dumbly at a puzzle with 30,000 pieces; enjoy a three-way honeymoon; burn the plans; make Pop blow his top; and play with each other's nipples.

*T*he *Sitter Downers* (1937) is a visually inventive short that's also one of the Stooges' most socially conscious. If that sounds pretentious or inaccurate, bear in mind that "socially conscious" isn't the same as "activist." The boys never displayed activist agendas in their work, but like other screen stars (as well as the team's writers and other collaborators), their work was informed by the concerns and events of the day. In *The Sitter Downers*, the chief concerns are workers' rights (incidental) and affordable, comfortable housing (primary). It's only the passing of the years that has dulled some of the film's urgency.

Filming of this two-reeler began on Friday, May 28, 1937, by coincidence just two days after United Auto Workers organizers Walter Reuther, Richard Frankensteen, and others, including women, were badly beaten by Ford Motor Company goons sent by the company's enforcer, Harry Bennett, who took his orders directly from Henry Ford. The UAW had been demanding concessions from Ford, including a hike in the daily wage from six dollars to eight. Scotty Kilpatrick, a photographer with the *Detroit News*, snapped the bloody confrontation, which was later dubbed the Battle of the Overpass. Kilpatrick's images greatly increased public support for the UAW and for the U.S. labor movement in general.

The sit-down strike, by which workers literally sat at their posts and did nothing (i.e., produced no goods or revenue), was a particularly effective labor maneuver. Ford had been hit with one earlier in the year.

The Stooges borrow the sit-down tactic (and embody the short's title) because Mr. Belle (James C. Morton), the father of their sweethearts, refuses to allow his daughters to marry. He's not against marriage—he just hates the Stooges. Cora Belle (June Gittelson), Flora Belle (Marcia Healy, a sister of the Stooges' former partner Ted Healy), and Dora Belle (Betty Mack, a frequent co-star to Charley Chase at Roach) don't see a ray of hope until the boys' sit-down strike in the Belle living room attracts national attention. Included among the great gobs of fan mail are an offer for a free lot and another for a free, "ready-cut" house. With that, Mr. Belle allows his girls to marry—but declares, "The honeymoon starts when the house is finished!"

This moves Ewart Adamson's narrative into its reflection of the contemporaneous housing issue. Although a new home could be built for $5,000 in

Domestic bliss, delivered on-site by the truckload, in *The Sitter Downers* (1937). Spunky June Gittelson is front and center; Marcia Healy (left) and Betty Mack bring up the rear.   *Photo courtesy of the Stoogeum*

Depression-year 1937, that sum was about four times the average annual wage and was out of reach for many. One alternative was the pre-fabricated (or ready-cut) house, a notion that was made feasible in the 1830s when the Manning Portable Cottage was built by the hundreds in England and shipped to colonists in Australia. In America after 1900, the Aladdin Company, Keck Crystal, Stran-Steel, and Sears, Roebuck & Company got into the manufacture of pre-fabs. Materials costs were dramatically cut, and true do-it-yourselfers could avoid expenditures for the labor of carpenters, plasterers, and other skilled craftsmen.

When their home is delivered on-site, the Stooges discover that they must build the thing themselves. Oh, it gets better because the average pre-fab of the day had about 30,000 pieces! (Shemp Howard and Roscoe Ates face a similar challenge in a 1935 Vitaphone short, *Why Pay Rent?*) The boys make a half-assed attempt to nail piece A to piece B, but we know things won't turn out well when Moe grouses that Curly stupidly burned the plans.

Sure enough, in its framing stage the house looks like a wooden web constructed by a demented spider. And when the boys are done, the place is a mad Expressionist tangle of canted windows, hideously mismatched wallpaper, and a bathtub that clings flat to the bathroom wall. When Cora Belle tugs at a timber that looks like it doesn't belong, the whole nightmare collapses.

A pivotal gag involves Curly's predicament after a keg of nails conks him on the head and sends him to dreamland—as he stands in wet cement. Moe finally has a use for the supplier's dynamite. The explosion propels Curly straight up into a tall tree. Flora Belle skewers him with a hard look and lets fly with a Noo Yawk command: "Come down outta there, Tahzen!" When she pokes him beneath the jaw with a long board, he falls on top of her.

Adamson's script is eventful; one gag, in fact, is almost gratuitously cruel. (You'll know it when you see it.) The sit-down portion of the short, though relatively brief, leads logically to the boys' acquisition and construction of their home. Del Lord directs with his usual visual ambition, notably during his sunny Toluca Lake exteriors, which are highlighted by a complex tracking shot of the boys tooling along Clybourn Avenue in motorized kiddie cars.

They're on their way to see their girls, and although the boys aren't equipped for domestic home life, they're determined to give it a try.

BY 1946, THE DEPRESSION WAS LONG GONE, BUT HOUSING AVAILABILITY HAD become a problem again, this time because of inflation and the needs of millions of discharged young veterans who had returned home to marry and start families. Apartment vacancy rates were nil, and new-home construction had no immediate hope of meeting demand. The 1946 short *G.I. Wanna Home*, then, isn't based just on a mild pun but on a mantra spoken by millions.

Freshly discharged from the service and eager to get back to civilian life, the Stooges exist in society's mainstream, rather than as misfit outsiders. As in *The Sitter Downers*, they have sweethearts, but when they arrive at 418 Meshuggener Avenue (a cute Yiddish joke), they discover that the girls—Jessie, Tessie, and Bessie—and all their belongings have been booted to the curb. "We've been dispossessed!" the girls cry. "It's a new American custom!" (The tactic was employed by some postwar landlords to lure desperate new tenants at jacked-up rents).

The boys promise to find a home but strike out at place after place. One landlady (Symona Boniface, in an atypical role as a modestly middle-class woman) even snaps and hisses at them like a cat.

The short's cleverest moment comes with the next scene, which is a picture of quiet domesticity: Nicely dressed in suits and ties, Moe and Larry relax and read on the couch. Director Jules White slowly pulls back the camera to reveal that although the boys are in a good-looking living room, it's not a room at all but part of a neatly furnished empty lot.

This "exterior" that dominates *G.I. Wanna Home* is a nicely dressed sound stage, and although birdie sound effects and some not-bad lighting suggest the outdoors, the whole tableau looks like a theater set. And White generally directs it that way, too, in a succession of locked-down two- and three-shots that are hardly more detailed or cinematic than what a theatergoer might see from row E.

The boys' fiancées, who had figured so dramatically in the short's opening minutes, have been forgotten altogether; we won't see them again for quite a while.

In the meantime, Larry covers up for Curly's poor physical state by assuming a lot of expository dialogue and physical gags, such as climbing a tree to reach a bird's nest. Very little dialogue of any sort is given to Curly, who mainly looks tired and a little lost.

The greater part of *G.I. Wanna Home* plays out on this stage. Larry accidentally dumps eggs onto Moe's face, and a noisy parrot hops inside the boys' dinner goose. Moe sets a hot pan on Larry's back, and Curly is spooked by the barrel of a shotgun as Moe and Larry argue over the weapon. All of these gags are reprised from earlier, better shorts.

The boys' experiment in open-air living abruptly ends when a man rolls through on a tractor and destroys everything. This mayhem is perplexing, and certainly isn't funny.

The ladies return in the final few minutes as the boys show off a home they claim to have built themselves, an absurdly small, two-room affair with a minuscule bedroom bracketed by two sets of triple-decker bunk beds. Very romantic! The girls disappear into the bathroom and are not heard from again. (The actresses are Judy Malcolm, Ethelreda Leopold, and Doris Houck. The nature of their underuse by Adler and White is practically criminal, particularly because Houck showed what she could do a year later in the fabulous *Brideless Groom*; see "The Stooges and the Fairer Sex.")

The short climaxes with a poorly staged redo of the venerable collapsing bunk bed gag, which had been brilliantly executed by Jules White and the boys for *In the Sweet Pie and Pie* (1941).

By doing virtually nothing with the female characters, *G.I. Wanna Home* kicks its premise right in the rear. Without the women as living reminders of the urgency of the Stooges' predicament, the short can't build any comic tension. Ultimately, what we have is a domestic comedy in which half the cast goes missing. What a wasted opportunity.

PARDON MY CLUTCH (1948) IS A "HOME" COMEDY THROUGH AND THROUGH because, as in most homes, nothing much happens besides the small things that comprise daily life. The short is sharply funny and well versed in everyday frustration.

Shemp doesn't feel well, so a friend, Claude (Matt McHugh, brother of Warner Bros. contract player Frank McHugh), suggests that a camping trip might be what Shemp needs to bring him back into the pink. The boys, as well as their wives, are enthusiastic.

LARRY

We can camp near a lake and catch all the fish we can eat!
[to Moe] You know fish is great brain food!

Conniving, fast-talking buddy Claude (Matt McHugh, right) encourages the boys to take a trip in *Pardon My Clutch* (1948).   *Photo courtesy of the Stoogeum*

MOE
You know *you* should fish for a whale!

What's beautiful about *Pardon My Clutch* is that although there's much preparation for the trip (the organizing of camping gear, and so on), the trip never happens—at least not in this short. It's *all* preparation.

A visual and comic highlight is the boys' practice attempt to set up the tent in the living room. Moe and Larry take turns smashing each other in the puss with the roof support, and the wives are dragooned into helping out. Finally, the tent is tied off at various points in the room, but everything goes haywire when a door is opened: a floor lamp topples, a vase falls from a table, a sculpture leaps from a shelf, and the tent collapses. It's a lot of kinetic action that's well staged by director Ed Bernds and precisely edited by Henry DeMond. The cuts come at you—bam bam bam—and it's all beautiful.

Friend Claude provides the comic tension because he's really not much of a friend at all. He's an amiable heel (McHugh is wonderful) who knows the boys have no car. If they're to take their trip, they'll be obliged to fork over nine hundred bucks to buy his set of wheels, a ridiculous open touring car that was already old when bathtub gin was new.

The Stooges have never seen such a car.

CLAUDE
It's a Columbus!

SHEMP
Never mind who you bought it from, what make is it?

Before anybody can even think about camping, though, the ailing Shemp has to be roused from bed. This gives Claude another opportunity to throw his weight around, opening up his "doctor book" (he's clearly no doctor) to determine Shemp's trouble.

CLAUDE
He's got a rash! It tells you right here, a rash may be caused by excessive use of the gray matter of the brain!

MOE
Aw, it must be somethin' else!

SHEMP (confidently)
Sure, it can't be that!

Claude comes up with a bottle of pills, which scripter Clyde Bruckman uses in some time-tested and very funny gags: Moe and Larry rudely awaken Shemp from deep slumber to give him a sleeping pill, and a little later they're flummoxed by this instruction: *Take one pill every 15 minutes, then skip an hour.* In a heartbeat, the exhausted Shemp is handed a jump rope and forced to skip—while Moe and Larry compound the insult by catnapping on Shemp's bed. Wobbly in rumpled pajamas, his lank hair hanging in his face, Shemp is a perfect vision of miserable exhaustion. When he tries to put the jump rope aside, Moe and Larry suddenly awaken and yell, "Skip!!"

Claude reasons that Shemp's trouble might be a bad tooth. That brainstorm leads to a succession of well-played gags involving a tooth, a window shade, a doorknob, and much protest from poor beleaguered Shemp. Like the pills, the bum tooth is a hoary comic device that seems fresh because of the boys' high level of enthusiasm and Ed Bernds's crisp direction. His camera sense mates perfectly with his feel for comedy: Setups and cuts are invariably just as they should be.

Brightly overcast exteriors revolve around the boys' struggle to change a flat tire at the curb outside the house. Larry and Shemp foolishly jack the tire up by its hub, so that there's no way to pull it completely free once it's off the ground. "I wonder how they got the tire *on?*" Shemp ponders.

The jack collapses on Moe's shoe, inciting panic not just in Moe but in the other boys, too. Shemp pauses in the struggle to look at Moe and ask, "How is it, pretty heavy?"

The tire rolls away into a service station, where the surly attendant (George Lloyd) has to be subdued because he thinks the ancient tire is part of his stock.

Back at the car, Larry is nearly strangled by a rope thrown over the groaning load. When everybody is finally ready, the car collapses onto its frame and sends the load—and Larry—crashing to the pavement.

A wild-eyed stranger (Emil Sitka, at his nuttiest) offers the boys two grand for the car; he says he wants it for a movie. Claude forces the boys to take back their $900 so that *he* can take the $2,000—but the buyer turns out to be a lunatic who's escaped from a nearby booby hatch. A white-coated attendant (Stanley Blystone) promises the patient a nice lunch back at the home.

Claude is outdone. He stomps on his hat, and then laughs maniacally before calling after the attendant: "I want some lunch, too!"

Moe divides the nine hundred dollars three ways. Shemp kisses his dough. "Love it! Love it!" he sing-songs, and then begins to skip away.

MOE
Hey hey hey hey! Where *you* goin'?

SHEMP
I'm hungry too!

That line captures a lot of things about Shemp: his inability to be embarrassed and his highly developed sense of looking out for his own interests. Shemp did more fine Stooges shorts than can be easily counted. *Pardon My Clutch* is one of his best.

A 1955 remake, *Wham-Bam-Slam*, contains about six minutes of fresh footage; the remainder is taken from the earlier film. Actress Alyn Lockwood, who's very attractive in a lady-next-door way, returns as Petunia, one of the wives. (Seven years had gone by, and Lockwood, just three days past her forty-first birthday when the new footage was filmed on January 18, 1955, hadn't aged a day.)

New business brings the boys to the breakfast table, where Larry smothers his hotcakes in ketchup ("My favorite fruit!" he exclaims), and Shemp eats a powder puff after Petunia rather carelessly sets it on his plate. Later, a live lobster that has dropped from the fridge into Shemp's footbath assaults his toe.

Matt McHugh appears in stock footage only, identified via new dialogue as Larry's friend, Claude A. Quacker. Emil Sitka's scenes are gone.

Felix Adler and Jules White integrate the new footage almost seamlessly, so on its own terms, *Wham-Bam-Slam* is satisfying.

SELF MADE MAIDS (1950) IS A WELL-CRAFTED NOVELTY SHORT THAT CONCERNS itself with romantic courtship. So why aren't we discussing it as part of "The Stooges and the Fairer Sex"? To be sure, the Stooges *are* the fairer sex in this Felix Adler–Jules White effort and are hilarious in their roles as the dames they're romancing. But because Larry, Moe, and Shemp are unacceptable to their girls' father, and because they bodily invade the man's home, the domestic aspect seems more piquant than the strictly romantic one.

Dad (played by Moe) objects to his daughters' choices because the boys are artists. (He apparently had hoped for accountants or industrialists.) It's a familiar conflict: the pragmatic father who becomes too invested in his daughters' relationships, even as he justifiably wishes them the best possible futures.

A minor point of irony is that although the Stooges are artists, they're far from scruffy bohemians, and they're not exactly starving, either. They dress well and work together in a spacious, good-looking studio. Although we get a look at a painting done by Shemp (awful), we never see the portraits the boys are doing of their sweeties. We can only assume that the boys are competent portraitists or, at the very least, shrewd self-promoters. After all, they have clients.

But Dad still insists on finding out "just what kind of bozos" the boys are.

If the word "bozos" suggests to you that Dad has already made up his mind, you're right. No matter who might show up at the house—Pollock, de Kooning, Wyeth, Chester Gould—they're not going to measure up. Rich, famous—doesn't matter. The old man just doesn't dig the artistic temperament. In that, he embodies the conflicted American reactions to art (occasionally pleasing, if not too challenging) and artists (flighty and untrustworthy).

So who are these paragons of pulchritude that Dad defends with shouts and violence? They are Moetta, Larraine, and Shempetta, stocky matrons with big noses, carefully coiffed 'dos, fabulous manicures, and plenty of makeup. The simultaneously hilarious and creepy aspect of their impersonations is that— God help me—they're not completely unattractive. Yes, yes! they're homely, but middle-aged women of this sort once were everyday fixtures in high-level restaurants and tea rooms, capable of defying the bad hand dealt to them by nature because they were confident in their affluence.

Mascara and eyeliner are remarkable tools: Shempetta's eyes look positively gorgeous beneath a discreet half-veil. Moetta has a gifted hairdresser, and Larraine—in a pale, draped dress that's unnervingly form-fitting (and that causes her to fiddle unselfconsciously with her girdle)—carries herself with the easy self-assurance of Betty Grable.

The boys' falsettos are funny because although they're patently phony, they're not piping. It's *possible* that real women actually sound like this.

The central action of the short occurs at the girls' nicely appointed home, where Dad is understandably miffed by this invasion of jokers he considers undesirables. He chases the boys in circles, round and round, and is victimized by obstacles hidden by the Stooges behind drapes, by a cake, and by a sofa that collapses beneath him because it's not a sofa at all, but the boys kneeling in a row beneath a slipcover.

Dad, however, comes up with a gun, which he uses to shoot point-blank into the Stooges' asses. Fortunately, because the boys reside in an alternate reality where bullets smart but don't do real damage, they're just scared by the assault.

The boys finally immobilize dad in a drape and tickle his foot until he consents to the marriages.

The tarted-up Stooges, confident in their femininity as the *Self Made Maids* (1950). The boys play multiple roles in this gender-bending comedy.

Photo courtesy of the Stoogeum

His acquiescence leads us into the final scene, in which three proud papas gaze into the three-across crib that holds Moe, Jr.; Larry, Jr.; and Shemp, Jr. Flat on their backs and topped by ruffled Baby Snooks caps, they greedily suck from separate, snakelike nipples attached to a wall-mounted container of formula. Predictably, Moe, Jr. steals his brothers' nipples, squirting formula in baby Shemp's face and causing little Larry to screech in indignation.

Self Made Maids is briskly directed by White, who seems to have been inspired by the opportunities for multiple three-shots, many of which are handsomely composed as diagonals that lead the eye from the front of the frame to the rear. The homey touches of Charles Clague's art direction are also highlights.

Love, home, children. It's the American Dream, Stooges-style.

STUDIO EXECUTIVES OF THE LATE 1940S AND VERY EARLY 1950S REGARDED television as an inferior medium that made stars of radio personalities, coarse vaudeville and movie comics, and second-rate singers and nightclub comedians. TV was beneath contempt, but because it was "free," it also was a threat.

The Stooges' *Goof on the Roof* (1953) has some interesting confluences with television. First, and most obviously, it's a comedy that utilizes television—specifically, the installation of a television in a home—as central to its conflict and humor.

Second, the short came to theaters at nearly the same time as *The Robe* (1953), a biblical epic that was the first movie shot in 20th Century-Fox's proprietary widescreen process, CinemaScope. *The Robe* was released on September 16, 1953, and enjoyed a long run. It's likely that some theaters were still running the picture on December 3, the release date of *Goof on the Roof*. Because Columbia's shorts could play with features from Columbia or any other studio, it's possible that *Goof*—a low-budget short that finds humor in television—played at some theaters with *The Robe*, the technologically advanced, 135-minute "event" picture that was specifically designed to give audiences the star power and visual immersion that TV was unable to match.

Third, and perhaps most significantly, *Goof on the Roof* suggests that television was a literal and figurative fixture in American homes. The Stooges struggle to install one so that their friend Bill and his new bride will have a set when the couple returns from their honeymoon.

TV was an appliance that mattered.

Except for the unwise repetition of a forced physical gag that involves a Dutch door and buckets of water, *Goof on the Roof* is a brisk and inventive physical comedy with confident direction by Jules White and a sharp script by Clyde Bruckman (this was the veteran writer's final movie job).

The Stooges brought their "A" game when the short was filmed in mid-November 1952. Moe displays a finely honed frustration: While struggling to put the TV's guts back inside the chassis and cabinet (Shemp has taken everything out in order to retrieve his Cracker Jack ring), Moe is assaulted by a spiky wiring harness. He glares at the thing and says, "Just for that, you don't go in there!"—before he petulantly tosses the piece aside.

Larry is all about dogged determination after stepping on a control knob and bending the extender that connects the knob to the set's tuner. He attempts to hammer the tube straight by holding it against a wall but only manages to create a shocking hole—and drop the knob inside the wall in the bargain. But he's determined to retrieve this vital piece, so after a while the wall has been hammered so vigorously that it appears to have been ravaged by a crackbrained picturehanger.

Larry can't spot the knob, so he foolishly peers into one of the holes with a lighted match. Moe scolds him for inviting a fire and then carelessly tosses Larry's match through the hole.

The subsequent smoldering fire invites some good physical gags with a tiny fire extinguisher and a knotted garden hose that's attached to the kitchen faucet. The bit climaxes when Moe furiously sticks the gushing hose down the front of Shemp's pants.

Shemp, like Larry, is in never-say-die mode and makes his way with the antenna to the roof of the house, where he batters the chimney into pieces (which conk Larry after he sticks his head from a window to see what the heck is going on), and later pounds a hole into the roof with such vigor that he plummets through the ceiling below. "I faw down!" he says apologetically. (This portion of *Goof on the Roof* is reminiscent of Laurel and Hardy's *Hog Wild* [1930], in which the pair make a mess of installing a radio antenna on the roof of Ollie's house.)

Some of the Stooges' incidental gags are priceless. As the boys' day begins, they're attired in toddler-type footie sleepers, adorably decorated with bunny silhouettes. At the Dutch door later, Moe literally wrings out his jelly sandwich after Shemp has destroyed it and then smushes it into Shemp's face. Shemp stands stock-still for a beat, and then asks the existential "*Why?!*"

Big-girl Maxine Gates good-naturedly carries the much smaller Bill (Frank Mitchell) across the threshold, only to be appalled by the damaged interior. She flounces out, and Bill isn't mollified when the boys suggest that all four of them can live together.

Bill produces a revolver, and in moments the Stooges are scooting from the place on their damaged derrieres.

Television helped force two-reelers into extinction, but the medium also would be the Stooges' eventual salvation. Here, though it's just another domestic device that makes their lives miserable, and very funny.

Larry has been less than careful with a friend's wall in *Goof on the Roof* (1953), the Stooges' hilariously relentless take on the horrors of TV installation.

14

The Stooges Abroad

In which the merry travelers hold out for straight salary; outlast a firing squad; sing "Zee Lollipop Song"; make pillow talk with the rest of the girls; show a lion who's boss; run up a fat beer tab; contemplate pork chops; sniff a cork; and kick the Production Code in the shins.

 ee *Wee Wee Monsieur* (1938) opens with a static image of the Eiffel Tower overlaid with the helpful words

PARIS
Somewhere in France

Right away, we know we're abroad and that the Stooges will grace a foreign shore with their unique brand of Americanism.

Sure enough, like clueless, aging members of the Lost Generation, the boys are in the City of Light, busily working as artistes in a garret apartment. As they merrily chorus a nonsense ditty called "Zee Lollipop Song," Moe slashes away at a piece of sculpture, catching Curly in the back of the head with his chisel. Larry laboriously composes at a piano, and Curly has just painted his "masterpiece." All he has to do is sell it—which would be helpful because the boys are eight months in arrears on their rent and have resorted to a hook and line to steal from a sidewalk fishmonger.

A street run-in with a gendarme that strips the officer of his pants encourages the boys to take cover in the local Foreign Legion recruiting office. They think it's the French version of the American Legion: "Fellow Legionnaires!" they cry happily. Before you can gobble a *gougère*, the boys have agreed to a hitch with the roughest, toughest fighting force in the world. (When Curly signs the recruiting paper, by the way, we discover that his last name is "Van Dyke.")

As imagined by writer Searle Kramer and director Del Lord, the balance of *Wee Wee Monsieur* concerns the boys' misadventures at a lonely desert outpost, where they antagonize their impatient sergeant (Bud Jamison) and rescue their abducted captain (William J. Irving) from the inner sanctum of an Arab warlord named Tsimmis. (A *tsimmis* is a Jewish fruit stew, but the word's more colloquial Yiddish meaning is "big deal," as in, "Don't make a *tsimmis* out of it!")

Sequences at the Legion outpost play out in familiar "service comedy" fashion, as the Stooges march like drunken lemurs and carelessly crack the sergeant on the back of the head with their rifle barrels. Lord's staging of these bits of business is a little perfunctory, but the boys, particularly Curly, are energetic and very physical.

The ambience of the lonely desert is one of creepy desolation, due in large part to Andre Barlatier's evocatively shadowed "nighttime" photography of the minimalist but effective desert set (the name of the art director has been lost) and standing fortress sets.

The Stooges gain entry to Tsimmis's Muslim redoubt disguised as that beloved Christian sprite Santa Claus, times three. Laurel and Hardy serve in the Legion in a four-reel short called *Beau Hunks* (1931). Ollie has joined in hopes of forgetting "Jeanie-Weenie," a girl who threw him over. In *Wee Wee Monsieur,* the Stooges have no dames in their lives until *after* they're in the Legion and meet the babes who fill out Tsimmis's harem. Curly makes a little pillow talk with one of them, who drops her veil to reveal a face like a longshoreman's. (The name of the cross-dressing actor is unknown.)

A little later, a good-looking concubine (Ethelreda Leopold) catches Curly's eye:

CURLY
Where you been all my life, toots?

HAREM GIRL
Down at Toity-toid and Toid Avenah! I just got ovah!

CURLY
Oh, a landsman! Remember the old pool room?

HAREM GIRL
Yeah . . .

CURLY
Well, that's a church now!

HAREM GIRL
No kiddin'!

A "landsman," by the way, is a fellow Jew who hails from the same Eastern European region or village as you or, as here, from your borough, Brooklyn.

But Brooklyn seems far away here. Tsimmis (Vernon Dent) is a pompous tadpole who offers the captain his pick of the harem—which by this time includes the Stooges in drag, short and stocky and very unsexy but willing to perform a pretense of exotic dancing. Arm in arm and high-kicking like the Rockettes, the boys bound across the floor and clip Tsimmis right in the chops.

After the captain and the boys have a run-in with a lion (a sequence that's marred by mismatched lighting during cuts), they roll away in an ornate wagon pulled by the suddenly obedient King of Beasts.

Other than the short's Yiddish wit, ethnic humor is provided by black actor John Lester Johnson as a palace eunuch who responds to Tsimmis's command, "Find them and feed them to the lions!" with a lusty, "Yowza, boss!" We cringe at this base American humor because we should, but there's an undeniable low wit in the line's two-front defiance of culture and geography.

The boys' adventures with things Arab carry on in Del Lord's *We Want Our Mummy* (1939), the most exotic and handsome of their foreign-locale shorts. It's fondly recalled for a splendid supporting cast, rapid-fire gags and dialogue, and a nice seasoning of scares.

As we've noted in the discussion of the boys' *Mummy's Dummies* (1948; see "The Stooges Rewrite History"), laypeople's interest in Egyptology was high in the 1930s because of the 1922 British discovery of the tomb of Tutankhamen. The Stooges were just one of several comics and comedy teams that subsequently encountered mummies. This time they're private investigators hired by a pair of Egyptologists, Dr. Powell (Bud Jamison) and Professor Wilson (James C. Morton), to locate a missing colleague, Professor Tuttle.

> POWELL (to Wilson)
> Nobody in his right mind would undertake that expedition!
>
> WILSON
> It's almost certain death!
>
> POWELL
> Let's hire them before they find out about the Curse of King Rutentutin!
>
> WILSON
> Done! And if the curse does strike them, it will be a blessing to humanity!

After a $20,000 cab ride to the Egyptian desert, Curly makes smart cracks about Tunis and tuna salad sandwiches before spying a watery mirage. In inventive pantomime, he dips a toesy into the chilly water, shivers, splashes a few drops on his chest, and finally holds his nose and dunks. After some gleeful porpoising in the "water," Curly emerges from the sand and invites Moe and Larry to join him.

The boys dive through a trap door that deposits them inside the bowels of Rutentutin's tomb. The slapstick of Searle Kramer and Elwood Ullman's script now acquires a funhouse atmosphere, which becomes more pointed as the boys creep through chambers rife with sliding panels, revolving walls, canopic jars, and glyphs—all of it eerily illuminated from wall sconces holding guttering torches. (Andre Barlatier's photography is textured and interestingly shadowed, and makes the beautiful sets appear especially foreboding and larger than they are. As with *Wee Wee Monsieur*, the name of the talented art director has been lost.)

After some scary encounters with a mummy (Ted Lorch) and raspy, disembodied threats the likes of "Infidels! Prepare to die!" Curly falls onto a mummy and reduces it to dust. He must lie down and impersonate Rutentutin in order to snooker a tomb robber, Jackson (Dick Curtis). Jackson prepares to filet Curly like a Nile perch to get at jewels he imagines are hidden inside, so Curly undoes a convenient zipper.

> JACKSON
> He's burst open! [Reaches inside and pulls out a newspaper]
> "Yanks Win World Series."
> Can you beat that?
> CURLY (forgetting himself) Yeah, and I won five bucks!
>
> JACKSON
> No kiddin'! I had the Cubs and—Whaat?

Jackson and his henchmen shortly end up at the bottom of a pit, the boys locate Professor Tuttle (actor unknown), and leave with Rutentutin, whose sarcophagus is about two feet long because, as Tuttle explains, the king was a midget.

(The mummy destroyed by Curly is Rutentutin's wife, Queen Hotsytotsy.)

We Want Our Mummy has the modestly affluent look of a B-plus feature film in the same league as, say, a Charlie Chan thriller. Powell and Wilson's offices at the Museum of Ancient History are plush and detailed, with more excellent cinematography by Barlatier. The place seems to carry the dusty weight of ancient history.

The short's sound-stage "exteriors" are especially picturesque, with pleasingly arrayed sand and fake palm trees backed by tall, painted cycloramas of the larger desert. The stage doesn't look real but conveys a suitably "otherwhere" appearance and feel.

As the phony mummy, Ted Lorch is burly of body and cadaverous of face— with grasping, birdlike talons, no less— and thus plenty intimidating. And the Stooges, attired in khakis and pith helmets, convey an illusion of intrepid adventurousness. A modular, three-figure 1999 model

Their Egyptology professor never told them about this. A scary bit of business with Ted Lorch from *We Want Our Mummy* (1939).

Photo courtesy of the Stoogeum

kit by a company called Polar Lights immortalized the boys and those outfits and is a fine memento of the Stooges as they appear in one of their best shorts.

THINGS ARE HOT AND SLOW IN VALESKA, A SUN-BAKED LATIN NATION WHERE traffic cops fall asleep at intersections and nothing happens except earthquakes. The Stooges are clothing salesmen assigned to this unpromising territory, and if they're going to pay their debts and stay out of jail, they have to move merchandise. But why would anybody want a double-breasted raccoon coat?

Their sales manager sends a terse wire from the States: NO PASSSAGE MONEY UNTIL YOU GET RID OF PRESENT WARDROBE. When a local official (Gino Corrado) gets his hands on the telegram, he misreads it as "get rid of President Ward Robey," Valeska's despotic ruler. Faster than you can say *culpable como el infierno,* the boys are condemned to die at sunrise.

That's the setup to *Saved by the Belle* (1939), an amiable comedy that purrs along at about twenty-five miles per hour. The short is easy to like but impossible to love.

It's nicely mounted, and money was found for a large cast of extras to move about sleepy-looking exteriors. In addition to directing, Charley Chase (working with the Stooges for the final time) wrote the script from a story by Searle Kramer and Elwood Ullman. Only later do you realize that the judiciously placed gags have equal weight, and that a big explosion of story-related laughs never comes. Typical of Chase's restrained style, the Stooges are less violent than usual, and nearly all of the humor arises from dialogue.

When the boys are handed their unpaid hotel bill, the tab notes beer, beer, beer, beer . . . endless charges for brew. Moe wants to know, "Who had that last beer!"

Curly points to the bill: "Not me! I had *that* one, with all the foam!"

In jail later, awaiting execution, Curly busily winds an alarm clock. "We're gonna be shot at sunrise and I wanna make sure we don't oversleep!"

The Stooges have an ally in Rita (Carmen LaRoux), a rebel fighter who wants to depose President Robey. Rita's help, plus a propitiously timed earthquake, allows the boys to find safety at the rebel encampment in the hills.

The hotel owner (Leroy Mason) is also the rebel leader. He forgives the Stooges for ducking out on their bill and (at Rita's urging) reluctantly offers them commissions. Curly pulls a face. "Not me!" he says. "Straight salary or nothin'!"

At the climax, the boys commandeer a truck and elude Robey's forces by tossing hand grenades that Curly thinks are unripe pineapples. Exteriors of the madly speeding truck are well integrated with handsome back-projection shots of the boys as they fumble in the cab.

Saved by the Belle—which is sympathetic to a rebel political philosophy—makes nothing of the fact that the United States, by 1939, had already developed its habit of intrusively propping up dubious Latin American governments for hard-nosed economic reasons (Washington disingenuously called its approach the Good Neighbor policy).

The short's funniest bit is a complete throwaway: Moe is upset because Curly has affectionately grasped Rita's shoulder, so Moe carefully salts the top of Curly's hand—and *then* bites it. This is the explosion of laughter the short needs, but it's over in a moment.

WARTIME EUROPE.
According to *Dutiful but Dumb* (1941), the oppressive dictatorship of Vulgaria has perfected an invisible-ray machine.

VULGARIAN SOLDIER
We can point it at any gun and the gun goes off, *poof!*

VULGARIAN COLONEL
Well, proceed with the poofing! [Thinks for a moment] With that poofer, we could shoot the enemy before he shoots us!

The nation that controls the poofer can control the world. That's news, and that's why *Whack* magazine has sent its three worst photographers into harm's way to get exclusive photos of the machine. Momentarily alone with the device, Larry, Moe, and Curly must scurry to make themselves scarce when the soldiers return. Moe disguises himself as a floor lamp, Larry disappears altogether, and Curly crouches inside the back of a console radio.

When the Vulgarian colonel (Fred Kelsey) demands a news report, his aide (Eddie Laughton) switches on the radio—which Curly takes as his cue to whip out an industrial-strength harmonica and blow it for all he's worth, producing a frantic marching tune. A cymbal strapped to his head provides rhythm, and tiny mallets that he rakes over the radio's tubes create a xylophone effect. And for counterpoint melody, Curly plucks and strums the radio's wires like the strings of a harp. And he does all this very fast, with that special kind of vigor that's born of panic.

The colonel can't stand the racket, and orders his aide to switch stations.

The music is on *all* the stations!

Inside the radio, Curly keeps up a musical pace so frantic that it continues even when he momentarily drops the harmonica from his lips. (Think about that gag for a moment. It exists on numerous literal and philosophical levels.)

Curly finally ad libs a phony news report about the "three spies" and helpfully adds, "They ain't in here!"

The radio bit is perfectly set up by Lord in tight close-up that allows us to witness Curly's energy and inventiveness, but that also leaves the comic with almost complete responsibility for the sequence's success.

He succeeds.

Curly has two other protracted bits that put people on the floor. At a lunch counter, he's violently spun around on his stool each time he swigs from an unlabeled bottle. The stuff is potent and Curly can't stop sampling it—and each time he rotates like a top. And then, in a fresh interpretation of a gag that Del Lord did first with comic Billy Bevan (playing a mild-mannered cop) in a 1926 short called *Wandering Willies*, Curly orders clam chowder. Before you can say "bivalve," the clam is tormenting him: It steals his crackers, bites his fingers, takes all the "fishing" line he has improvised with a spool of thread, and finally gives Curly a good, lusty squirt in the kisser.

Curly is more than disenchanted. He's furious to the point of violence and empties his revolver at the offending bowl (missing every time, by the way, but spraying the back of the counter with lead and giving the counterman [Chester Conklin] cause to impotently cry, "Stop that!" [*Bang! Pow!*] "Cut that out!")

The final set piece is the best and catches all three boys in a moment of real peril. A Vulgarian sergeant (Bud Jamison) prepares the picture snatchers for death by firing squad.

> LARRY *(frantically)*
> We're supposed to have a last request!
>
> CURLY
> Yeah, this is Request Night!

Curly asks for a final smoke. The sergeant agrees but warns that once the smoke is gone—the lights will go out.

Curly reaches inside his coat and pulls out a cigar as big as a Genoa salami.

In the end, the invisible ray is forgotten, along with the entire opening sequence about the boys' attempt to snap a picture of elusive society newlyweds. *Whack* magazine doesn't matter anymore, either. *Dutiful but Dumb* is honeycombed with narrative culs-de-sac, and that's fine because the destination never mattered in the first place. Only the journey is important.

Former Olympian Bruce Bennett has a bit as a Vulgarian guard, and diminutive George Ovey (a comedy star during World War I) is hilarious in a brief bit as a hapless tourist who learns that the penalty for using a camera in Vulgaria is death. (When he's told, his shoulders give the tiniest twitch and his upper lip lifts. That's all. The word that comes to mind to describe this bit of comic acting is "sublime.")

Mr. Ovey notwithstanding, the short is almost completely dominated by Curly. Ullman and Lord played to their stars' strengths, and during the four days in 1940 when *Dutiful but Dumb* was filmed, Curly Howard was the strongest guy in Hollywood.

BY THE TIME *SOME MORE OF SAMOA* WAS RELEASED IN DECEMBER 1941, A YOUNG American anthropologist named Margaret Mead had been a celebrity for more than a dozen years. Her 1928 book *Coming of Age in Samoa* had impressed professionals with its detailed, immersive look into Samoan culture, and with Mead's close consideration of a central question about human development and behavior: Are the mindsets and actions of individuals and groups determined primarily by genetic programming (heredity) or by cultural cues (environment)? What many lay readers interpreted as the brute immorality of Samoan culture (the book explores Samoans' casual attitudes about sex) nearly obscured Mead's finer points but also brought her notoriety that spread far beyond the discipline of anthropology.

Moviegoers who spied the title *Some More of Samoa* expected not only exotica and laughs but something *extra* to justify the use of "Samoa," a place name that had become a code word for other, more interesting things.

Well, the short *is* about sex—at least as it relates to the reproduction of the puckerlips persimmon tree and the journey of the Stooges (who play tree surgeons) to the remote island of Rhum Boogie to locate a mate for a failing stateside tree.

Rhum Boogie is a fecund place that, unlike Samoa, is populated by a weird polyglot of human types: Western Europeans, Fijians, and Africans. (Genetic accuracy never was Hollywood's strong suit, particularly in matters of comedy.) Under the patronage of a millionaire whose puckerlips is ill, the boys arrive in a tiny skiff just as the craft is foundering.

"Four thousand miles, and I rowed every step of the way!" Moe exclaims.

> *MOE*
> Where's Curly?
>
> *LARRY*
> I dunno. Last night he told me he had a date with a mermaid.
> Maybe he eloped!

Curly may have had that date, but he's gone one better by taking over the whole island. The king (played by white actor Tiny Ward) has been no match for Curly's loaded dice and has had to forfeit his throne. As per Rhum Boogie tradition, the new king must marry into the family of the former monarch. Curly salivates at the sight of the king's daughters (one blonde, the other brunette) but wilts when he discovers that his bride is to be the king's sister, an overeager babe (Louise Carver) who was young when Margaret Mead's grandmother was in Sunday school.

Curly protests, and so after nearly becoming the natives' lunch ("Roast Stooge!" the cook happily yells), the boys liberate a puckerlips and jump into their boat—which slowly sinks beneath them.

Scripters Harry Edwards and Elwood Ullman fill *Some More of Samoa* with cute visual and verbal gags. When Curly puts his stethoscope to the ailing puckerlips, he gravely says, "I don't like its bark!" He injects it with his own concoction, Vitamin PDQ, which turns the little sapling into a big sap in an eyeblink. Curly is accidentally poked in the arse by his own hypo and immediately grows to about eight feet tall—courtesy of a clever but regrettably noisy hydraulic jack that allows him to fill out his overlong pants.

On Rhum Boogie, Curly has a surprising encounter with a multi-armed idol that guards the puckerlips, and Larry picks up Curly's footprints—literally.

When Moe and Larry run into a dusky native (Caucasian actor Duke York), they're inspired to spontaneously invoke *Amos 'n Andy*.

> MOE
> Hiya, Snowflake!
>
> NATIVE
> Me no snowflake! Me kingfisher!
>
> LARRY
> Oh, he's the Kingfish!
>
> MOE
> I know Amos!
>
> LARRY
> I know Andy! [high-pitched voice] Hiya, Amos!
>
> MOE [low-pitched voice]
> Hi, Andy!
>
> LARRY
> How's Lightnin'?
>
> MOE
> Ah dunno but ah think it's gonna strike any minute!
>
> LARRY
> Yeah . . .
>
> BOTH
> Hallelujah!

This little burlesque ends when the native prods the boys with a spear and delivers them to King Curly. "Don't they have large monkeys in this part of the country!" the new ruler observes.

As the boys—all three of them—are being prepared for supper, the cook (Dudley Dickerson) bastes Curly with a flour sifter and then lays his cleaver on various parts of Curly's body. "Sho't ribs! Po'k chops! Soup bone!"

Here, then, are the questions: Were Del Lord, the writers, the Stooges, and the other players products of their heredity or of their environments? What led them to the morally dubious landscape of racial humor? How did they know that cannibalism can be nearly as funny as it is horrifying? Why is Curly put off by the idea of sex with a much older woman? Why did the boys traffic in physical pain for laughs?

Why are *you* laughing?

CURLY'S FINAL TWO-REEL ADVENTURE ABROAD IS *THREE LITTLE PIRATES* (1946), a typically smart and concise short by Ed Bernds, scripted by Clyde Bruckman. The film is fondly recalled for the "Maharaja Routine," a two-person, back-and-forth stew of nonsense syllables, doubletalk, and faux Russian performed in costume.

Although one popular Internet source declares that *Three Little Pirates* is set in 1672 (a number that the claimant pulled from his or her derriere), the setting is clearly modern but on a pirate island where time has mysteriously stood still. Although the governor (Vernon Dent, in a fulsome performance) and others affect 17th-century garb and speech, the plot encompasses a pinball machine and a power drill, and the handsome sets by Charles Clague include artifacts the likes of table lamps and electrical outlets. And yet the governor has never seen a fountain pen. Curious!

The Stooges are shipwrecked garbage scow operators out of New York City. Stranded on the governor's little hellhole, they're sentenced to die because— well, just because. A sympathetic beauty, Rita (Christine McIntyre), helps them shed their sailors' duds for robes and turbans that suggest the mysterious East. Thus disguised (and claiming citizenship of the far-off islands of Coney and Long), they ply the governor with exotic gifts, like the fountain pen that the governor assumes is black ivory, and a heart-shaped raspberry lollipop. "I have seen many pigeon-blood rubies," the guv says breathlessly, "but never have I been given the raspberry!"

The governor's concubine (onetime burlesque performer Dorothy DeHaven) spills the beans about the boys, who are subsequently set up for a rough night at a joint called Black Louie's. Following a wild knife-throwing contest, more double talk, and a swell bar fight, the Stooges gain the upper hand.

Ed Bernds recalled that Moe dictated the Maharaja dialogue to writer Clyde Bruckman "crazy syllable by crazy syllable." The boys first performed the bit on film for a 1941 Columbia musical called *Time Out for Rhythm*, but the routine suggests a considerably older lineage. With its visually static nature and reliance on flip dialogue, it screams vaudeville. Although double-talk bits were staples of vaudeville and burlesque houses, the specifics of the Maharaja routine apparently belong to the Stooges alone. (For the record, and from Bruckman's April 1946 script, Moe's repartee begins, "Razbanyas yatee benee futch ah tinny herongha . . . ." At interludes, when he's looking for an answer from Curly, he'll say, "asky tasky.")

Although Curly was deeply sunk in illness by the time *Three Little Pirates* was filmed (he was stricken with a career-ending stroke just two weeks later), he's verbally and physically agile. Fewer physical demands are made of him than in the past, but when Bruckman's script calls for him to fall upside-down from a chair, Curly does it, and beautifully. He's similarly nimble with the doubletalk.

Moe and Larry put together some fine physical humor, as well, particularly when they try to drill themselves free of a cramped closet. The power drill is huge, and because it vibrates like hell, it causes the back of Moe's upper arm to steadily choke Larry, who's trapped against the wall behind him.

Actor Robert Stevens (who sometimes called himself Robert Kellard) is sturdy and menacing as Black Louie. He tells his unwilling target, Larry, not to worry about his knife throws or the maharaja's: "If either of us hits you, we lose!"

Small consolation!

Louie and his minions are surprised when Curly's errant knives

- Catch a dangerous pirate in the hip,
- Crash into a picture frame and cause the girl in the portrait to screech and drop a vase on the head of the pirate seated beneath her (a gag that works because we see the girl inside the frame for only a split moment before she reacts), and
- Cut through a chandelier column like butter and send the fixture crashing onto a pair of pirates at a table.

Larry, who has already discovered the perils of tilting Black Louie's pinball machine—an enormous mallet comes down from the rafters to conk the offender—maneuvers a pirate into making the same mistake.

Vivacious Dorothy DeHaven charms the boys in the wonkily absurd *Three Little Pirates* (1946).   *Photo courtesy of the Stoogeum*

The stuntmen and bit players (among them, favorites Joe Palma and Cy Schindell) are comically enthusiastic. When they fall, they don't just drop—their eyes roll back and they collapse in *stages*, like drunken caterpillars.

Bernds gave editor Paul Borofsky plenty of coverage, so the climactic fight cuts together very well and maintains a steady, breathless rhythm. (In Bruckman's original script, the boys and Rita escape in Black Louie's sloop, accidentally sink it, and aren't rescued until Rita shows some leg to passing speedboats.)

Brisk, lively, and unexpectedly surreal, *The Little Pirates* also reveals the extent of Curly's determination and courage. The short is as touching as it is funny.

BECAUSE *THE HOT SCOTS* (1948) IS AN AMERICAN TWO-REELER MADE STRICTLY for laughs, its conception of Scotland is out of a child's storybook: English spoken with heavy brogues, a drafty castle, men in kilts, women that men call "lassie," and much talk of ghosts and windswept moors.

Oh, and well-aged Scotch, too, which the Earl of Glenheather (Herbert Evans) offers to the Stooges. "Would ye care for a wee snifter?" the earl asks—and a sniff is *all* they get, as the earl just passes the cork beneath the boys' noses, and his own, before returning it to the bottle. (That's a wee joke about Scottish miserliness, don't ye know.)

Larry, Shemp, and Moe are newly minted correspondence-school detectives. A sympathetic inspector (Clive Morgan) at Scotland Yard has hired them to locate "some missing papers," which means they have jobs picking trash on the Yard's grounds. A memo that has blown from the inspector's window alerts them to peculiar thefts at Glenheather.

The castle has the usual sorts of suspects: the dotty earl; a sinister butler, Angus (Charles Knight); a retainer, MacPherson (Ted Lorch); and a gorgeous blonde lass named Lorna Doone (Christine McIntyre). Soon, the boys are pursued by figures in ghastly masks, conk each other over the head, appear and disappear on a sliding bed, and battle a living portrait.

It's a full evening.

Angus and MacPherson are literally unmasked. The shocker is that lovely Lorna has been in league with them.

The buildup to the castle sequences establishes that the boys are inept maintenance men whose prospects as detectives may not be bright. Larry's hedge shears cut open an enormous sack of carefully gathered paper, and Moe displays his impatience by locking his pruning shears onto Shemp's nose and pulling him through a hedge. Larry hides his gathered scrap paper beneath a lid of loose turf, and Moe figures out a way to do almost nothing at all.

When Shemp annoys him, Moe has a question:

MOE
Which would you rather have, a shoe full of dollar bills or
two socks of five?

SHEMP
I'll take the two socks!

MOE
You got 'em!
[insert sound effect here]

A little later, Shemp says, "If there's any more paper in this yard, I'll eat it!" Moe impassively watches a scrap drift from the inspector's window: "Here comes your lunch."

At the castle, the boys pass themselves off as MacMoe, MacLarry, and MacShemp. The earl introduces Lorna, so that scripter Elwood Ullman can haul out an old chestnut and hand it to Shemp: "Hi, Lorna, how ya doon?" (The joke comes full circle later, to a nice payoff.)

Shemp forgets to be a Scot when the earl offers the snifter. "Yowza, yowza!" Shemp exclaims, "that's what the man says, yowza!" The line is so "left field" that it's dazzling.

Moe quickly explains that Shemp is "from southern Scotland, south of the MacMason MacDixon line!"

"MacYowza!" confirms Shemp.

The wordplay continues:

EARL
I'm off to a gatherin' of the clan!

SHEMP
Oh, a clanbake, eh?

As is his fashion, director Ed Bernds tells the story as much with the camera as with dialogue. Because Bernds stages and shoots very smartly—two-shots, three-shots, and close-ups— the protracted tussle with the masked thieves never flags.

The sliding bed, which noiselessly glides beneath a wall separating two rooms, gets a real workout involving multiple characters. (The bed gag makes a very early appearance in *Cursed by His Beauty* [1914], a one-reel Keystone comedy with Charlie Murray and Charley Chase.)

Bernds's coverage is perfect, and Henry DeMond's cutting helps us keep everything straight as the action moves from room to room, hallway to room, and even from closet to room. However, when the film is undercranked, the soundtrack speeds up, giving the boys' voices a Munchkin quality. The anomaly could easily have been addressed with overdubs.

In the final sequence, the earl promises to reward the boys with *drinks* of Scotch, but when he opens the liquor cabinet, he finds a skeleton that noisily plays the bagpipes (the pipes being the one cliché heretofore left unexplored). The Stooges and the earl go *yikes!* and run away, and although Bernds and cinematographer Allen Siegler follow their progress with a rather elegant tracking shot with a slight dolly-in, the joke is childish and unfunny. In a scripted but unused variation, Shemp momentarily snags his clothes on the cabinet and must catch up with the others on the road, running alongside their car and then passing it as it's doing ninety. That's not a bad gag, but time or budget, or both, militated against it.

The supporting players, particularly Herbert Evans and Charles Knight, are enthusiastic and well-cast, and it's a treat to see Christine McIntyre with her blonde hair to her shoulders and showing some leg in a modified kilt. The handsome castle interiors, possibly put up for *The Bandit of Sherwood Forest* (1946), give the short a first-class look. Costumes and set decoration are also superior.

Some reference sources transpose the roles played by Ted Lorch and Charles Knight, and many are unaware that the title is comprised of three words: *The Hot Scots*. (The "The" may have been an afterthought: The wording hasn't the quick rhythm of a typical Stooges title, and it appears on the title card with "the" rendered in smallish, lowercase letters.)

When the short was remade for November 1954 release as *Scotched in Scotland*, director Jules White and scripter Jack White created just five or six minutes of new footage; the rest is bald pickup. Philip Van Zandt appears in a new opening sequence as the dean of a chintzy detective school attended by the boys, and Charles Knight and Christine McIntyre return for a few snippets of footage that make very clear the criminally collusive nature of their relationship. Ted Lorch, who passed away in 1947, returns in stock footage and is unsatisfactorily replaced by George Pembroke in a couple of new bits.

Jack White's script tosses in some oddball flying gags by resurrecting the parrot-in-the-human-skull gag from *If a Body Meets a Body* (1945); the joke shows up later in *The Ghost Talks* (1949) and its remake, *Creeps* (1956).

The *Scotched in Scotland* parrot has a habit of asking, "How ya fixed for blades?" à la Gillette's TV-cartoon mascot, Sharpie the Parrot, who spent most of the 1950s singing "How are you fixed for blades? You better look!"

The remake's final gag—which some people may have found amusing at the time—comes from the skeleton bagpiper via a couple of overdubbed lines (voiced by Jules White): "How ya fixed for liquor? Ya better look!"

MacWitty, that.

"ARABIA" TAKES IT ON THE CHIN AGAIN IN *MALICE IN THE PLACE* (1949), A broad burlesque born of America's curiosity about Arab culture and simultaneous ignorance of it. In short form, the boys are restaurant owners "somewhere in the Orient" who take back the enormous Ruttin' Tuttin (as spelled in the script) diamond stolen by the Emir of Shmow (from the Yiddish *shmo*, for "idiot"). During the course of this exceptionally well-done short, the boys fight like cats and dogs, play Santa Claus, and impersonate evil spirits. Although dominated by a single set piece that occupies only two sets, the film is smartly paced and is certainly one of the best with Shemp.

It's a routine day at the boys' Café Casbahbah until Hassan Ben Sober ("Hasn't Been Sober" for you teetotalers in the audience) and Ghinna Rumma show up. Ben Sober (Vernon Dent) is a portly fellow with beard and turban; Rumma (George Lewis) wears a heavy mustache, fez, and cummerbund. In league with Haffa Dalla (Frank Lackteen), they scheme to get their hands on the diamond. But in the meantime, they sit down for some lunch.

The Stooges hurry out to the table with their usual brand of hyperactive super service and manage to spill another order onto their new customers. Moe finds a cupcake—with a lighted candle—behind Ben Sober's ear, and Shemp cuts the spaghetti on Rumma's face as a hairdresser might do, leaving Rumma with fetching pasta bangs. Broken crockery is everywhere. As the boys clean up, Larry discovers an unbroken dish, which he promptly smashes to pieces. Well, why not?

The six-minute gag that dominates the short revolves around a fundamental misunderstanding: Ben Sober and Rumma order hot dogs and rabbit, and then watch and listen in silent horror as Larry runs back and forth from the kitchen, wielding a cleaver and chasing after a cat and a cairn terrier. He hauls each animal back to kitchen, glaring and shaking the cleaver.

During a succession of hideous—but innocent—sounds, Ben Sober, Rumma, and Moe and Shemp become convinced that Larry is chopping the animals into mincemeat for lunch. Larry delivers the food with a bright "Hot dog! When it comes to cookin', I'm the cat's meow!" Shemp weeps when the hot dog whines contentedly when he strokes it (the real dog and cat have ambled beneath the table), and Moe is stricken when the meat on his plate meows at the touch of his fork. In a particularly weird moment, the hot dog shoots out a tiny tongue that noisily licks Shemp's face. (There's enough material right there to keep the freshmen in Introduction to Freud talking for a week.) Larry looks on, puzzled, as everybody else bawls.

The misunderstanding about the food is finally resolved, but now Ben Sober is heartbroken after learning that the emir has got to the diamond first.

BEN SOBER (blubbering)
With that diamond I could have quit my job as the doorman
at the Oasis Hotel!

MOE
Hey! Spinach chin! Do you mean to tell me you're only a
doorman?

BEN SOBER
Yes!

SHEMP
Well, there's the door, man! [Gives Ben Sober a good kick]

Rumma whips out a nasty dagger.

RUMMA (sobbing, to Moe)
Will you give me five for this?

MOE
No, but I'll give you two!

RUMMA
I'll take it!
[Moe pokes him in the eyes and spins him away by
unraveling his cummerbund]

With help from a snippet of stock footage from *Wee Wee Monsieur,* the boys penetrate the emir's fortress disguised as Santa Clauses. The emir (Johnny Kascier) is appropriately cowed when confronted by a towering Santa, seated on each other's shoulders with Shemp at the top. Complemented by multiple pairs of waving arms, Shemp identifies himself as the "evil spirit" that guards the diamond. When he demands its return, the emir hands it over and then obeys Shemp's command to "stand on your head in that lily pond, until further notice!"

A face-off with a burly Nubian guard (Everett Brown) is resolved in the Stooges' favor with rotten fruit and a heavy vase. As the boys prepare to leave, they squeeze the water from the now-swollen emir.

Malice in the Palace is a superior short that's of special interest because of a lobby card and other promotional material that picture a gaunt gent with a chef's hat and handlebar mustache, who confronts Larry, Moe, and Shemp with a cleaver. The actor is Curly Howard, and his absence from the short's final cut has been a point of curiosity and intrigue for years. Film historian Ted Okuda described to me a glaring lapse in logic: Larry takes the villains' lunch order and then heads to the kitchen to prepare it. Why does he perform both jobs? In other Stooges shorts involving restaurants, Moe and Larry are the waiters and Curly the cook (as in *Playing the Ponies* and *Busy Buddies*), or Shemp handles the kitchen chores (as in *Shivering Sherlocks*).

During a visit to the Jules White Collection at the Margaret Herrick Library, Academy of Motion Picture Arts and Sciences, Okuda discovered White's copy of the *Malice in the Palace* script. As originally written by Felix Adler, Larry goes to the kitchen with the order and hands it to the chef, who says something to the effect of "Make it yourself! I'm goin' to lunch!" With the chef gone, Larry must prepare the food.

The chef role amounts to nothing at all, but it would have provided the retired Curly with a nice cameo. It's unknown whether Curly filmed the scene, but because of the promotional image—the sort that an on-set photographer doesn't shoot until a scene has been blocked and lit—the odds are good that he did.

Larry Fine's ghostwritten 1973 autobiography, *Stroke of Luck*, includes the still as a full-page image, with this caption: "Curly Howard, at the time of his illness, returns to film this scene with Larry, Moe and Shemp in 'Malice in the Palace.'"

Malice in the Palace was reworked as *Rumpus in the Harem* (1956), the first of four "fake Shemp" shorts featuring Joe Palma as Shemp that were made to fulfill the boys' contract and meet Columbia's release schedule.

Jack White completed the *Rumpus* script on December 12, 1955, and the cast gathered for new footage (shot in a single day) with director Jules White two or three days later. That places the shoot at barely more than three weeks after Shemp's death on November 22. It is impossible to imagine how Moe struggled to address another actor as "Shemp" and recite clumsy dialogue designed to explain Shemp's occasional absences from the action.

The greater part of *Rumpus* is stock footage from the earlier film, augmented with an amusing new sequence establishing that the boys' girlfriends, Jeeba, Reba, and Heeba (Ruth Godfrey White, Helen Jay, and Diana Darrin) cannot come up with individual payments of one thousand chillblainas for the "virgin tax" within a three-day deadline. This provides the Stooges with motivation to pursue the diamond.

Stock footage of the emir's palace is nicely augmented with another new sequence that begins when Moe and Larry stumble into a harem. The concubines inside (Harriette Tarler and Suzanne Ridgeway) go after the boys with a vengeance, particularly the tall, sturdy Ridgeway.

SUZANNE *(as she pummels Moe)*
How dare you invade the privacy of us fragile women! And you caught me with my veil down! [She twists Moe's ears like radio knobs, and then grips his neck in an arm lock to repeatedly lever her elbow into his face] You worm, you! I'll teach you to leave us little lambs alone!
[She bangs Moe's head on a tabletop]

Ridgeway comports herself like an athlete, aggressively shoving her hip into Moe's side as she prepares the headlock, remaining aware of the camera so that her face is displayed to good advantage. What a professional!

Larry, meanwhile, is vigorously karate-chopped about the head and shoulders by Tarler.

Joe Palma is filmed from behind throughout the short, perpetually crouching to disguise his height and obediently moving backward when White dollies in on Moe and Larry. And in a mystifying faux pas, Palma's voice remains on the soundtrack ("Ohh, yipe!") as "Shemp" dives through a window at the conclusion.

Strange things happen in the mysterious East.

Finally, remember the "virgin tax" mentioned by one of the girlfriends? Jules and Jack White, Columbia, and the Stooges knew they were treading dangerous ground with that little joke. During 1951–53, powerful producer-director Otto Preminger battled the Breen office (Hollywood's self-imposed censoring body) over inclusion of the word "virgin" in the script for *The Moon Is Blue* (1953), a light romance starring William Holden and Maggie McNamara. The Motion Picture Production Code prohibited the word. Preminger used it anyway, and

Performer Profile: Joe Palma
1905–94

Husky, potato-nosed Joe Palma was the two-reel unit's go-to guy whenever a script called for a thug, guard, western gunfighter, cop, bowman, or other potentially dangerous figure. An intimidating gaze and a firm set to his mouth made Palma ideal for such roles, and he also had a passing resemblance to Shemp Howard—which led to Palma's most-often-discussed job, that of "fake Shemp" in four shorts made to fulfill contractual and schedule obligations after Shemp's death late in 1955. Those shorts, all 1956 releases, are *Scheming Schemers*, *Rumpus in the Harem*, *Hot Stuff*, and *Commotion on the Ocean*. The films make liberal use of stock footage featuring Shemp, interspersed with new inserts involving Palma, who was shot from behind or in disguise. Next to the unknown actresses who double Jean Harlow in Harlow's final picture, *Saratoga*, the Palma/Shemp ruse may be the most intriguing instance of "career after death."

In *Shot in the Frontier*, the boys' spoof of *High Noon*, Palma is black-clad Jack Noonan, a gunslinger hardly less intimidating than the ones faced by Gary Cooper.

Palma later became Jack Lemmon's assistant, working through *The Odd Couple* before retiring.

In order to fulfill studio and exhibitor contracts, Joe Palma (far left) was drafted to double for the recently deceased Shemp in four shorts; *Rumpus in the Harem* (1956) was the first. Palma's face was never as clearly visible on screen as in this still. The seductive dancing girls are Suzanne Ridgeway (left) and Harriette Tarler.   *Photo courtesy of the Stoogeum*

the Code refused to back down. United Artists finally elected to release *The Moon Is Blue* without the Production Code seal of approval. Despite that, despite a "condemned" rating from the Catholic Legion of Decency, and despite some theaters' refusal to book the picture, Preminger's piece of fluff was a commercial success.

The Moon Is Blue was finally granted the Code seal of approval in 1961, eight years after its release. Bear in mind, then, that this 1955–56 short with the Stooges was purposely provocative.

ED BERNDS BEGAN TO DIRECT FEATURE FILMS IN 1948. DURING 1950–51, HE was tied up with B-comedies based on the *Blondie* and *Gasoline Alley* comic strips. His temporary absence encouraged longtime Stooges producer Hugh McCollum to assume the director's chair for the boys' *Hula-La-La* (1951), a short that Bernds did find time to write. Although McCollum also directed two shorts starring Hugh Herbert at this time, he helmed the Stooges only once, and that's unfortunate because he had a light, smart touch.

Set on a tropic isle, the boys' adventure freely mixes ethnic types and cultural cues into a mishmash that recalls the dubious sociology of *Some More of Samoa*. Their film-mogul boss, Mr. Baines (Emil Sitka), has purchased a South Sea isle and wants to shoot a musical there. But the natives know nothing about dancing. Because the Stooges are studio choreographers, Baines (who is humorously attended by fawning yes-men) dispatches them to the isle to teach the natives the two-step.

The boys arrive, worried by rumors of headhunting and other bad behavior. That's part of the mishmash: When *Hula-La-La* was filmed in 1951, the likelihood of headhunting in Polynesia, where the boys' adventure apparently takes place, was nil. (The practice may still have gone on, however, in Micronesia, Melanesia, Indonesia, Southeast Asia, and the Amazon.)

The island has a weak king (Heinie Conklin) and a powerful witch doctor, Varanu (Kenneth MacDonald), who speaks with the precise diction of a banker. When he tells the boys that their heads will fill out his collection of shrunken noggins, Larry is particularly upset at the thought of "hangin' all day like a smoked goose liver!" Soon, a beauty named Luana (Jean Willes) offers her help.

Hula-La-La was inspired by a flood of jungle movies that crested in the early 1950s. Columbia's "Jungle Jim" and Monogram's "Bomba the Jungle Boy" series were ongoing, and Lex Barker was playing Tarzan at RKO. Indie producer Jack Broder came up with *Bride of the Gorilla* (1951), and Arch Oboler's *Bwana Devil*, the first commercially successful 3-D feature, would appear in 1952.

In the public imagination, Africa, South America, Indonesia, and the Pacific Islands were a jumble of geography that amounted to the same thing. Moviegoers had innocent fun with jungle adventures, and suppliers of stock footage prospered.

Another historical note that's relevant to *Hula-La-La* involves the so-called cargo cults. During World War II, American soldiers were delivered to various islands—including the Solomons, the New Hebrides, and New Guinea—to create landing strips and bases, bringing with them material goods that included food, candy, lumber, medicine, and clothing. The scope and circumstances of this unaccustomed bounty, which anthropological historian Mike Jay has termed "dispensation," encouraged quasi-religious devotion on some islands after the war. Would the great god come again? Shrines and even idols were not unknown. (A postwar *New Yorker* cartoon by Charles Addams depicts a Pacific islander genuflecting before a wood idol that has been fashioned to resemble a scowling master sergeant.) On parts of some islands, locals became so preoccupied with the "white god" that useful work fell off sharply.

The Stooges discover a crate of hand grenades (left by those "white gods"), but the crate is guarded by a cross-legged, four-armed female idol. Exotic-looking actress Lei Aloha sits impassive and perfectly still, her arms bent and held out at her sides, with the arms of a second person protruding from beneath hers. The effect is good and even a little unnerving.

SHEMP
Say, that [might] come in handy in case of mosquitoes! You could slap with one hand, scratch with another, and play gin rummy with the other two! Or, you could scratch with one and slap with two!

MOE
I think I'll slap with two!

Hugh McCollum knew he had a good thing with the idol, and made the most of it with a variety of well-staged, violent gags. The idol dispenses slaps, of course, and also lays a little trap by snapping her fingers and then pointing to her own pedestal before banging Moe's head into it—with two right hands! (She congratulates herself by using two hands to shake and two others to make the boxer's overhead gesture of triumph.)

Later, after the box of grenades has migrated from the pedestal to the idol's lap, Larry is roughly grabbed by the hair from behind. Only an eye poke from Moe—with four hands flying up to cover the injured orbs—ends the confrontation.

Shemp has an amusing misadventure with a baby crocodile and its mama. Later, when Shemp is about to be beheaded by Varanu, Moe taunts the witch doctor into striking the crate of grenades with his blade. *Boom!* (Never mind that real grenades wouldn't behave that way.)

The boys finally begin their lesson in dance, wiggling and hopping spastically while the natives gracefully hula. This final tableau—a handsome panorama that expands with a graceful dolly-out—is accompanied by Ross DiMaggio and Nico Gregor's sweetly lush melody "Lu-Lu," which plays through the end of the action and over the short's "The End" card. It's all as pleasant as a travelogue.

15

The Stooges and the Fantastic

In which the boys turn on the boogie-woogie box; play footsie with an atomic zombie; get splattered with supersonic pies; do a whipped-cream swindle; bed down with a corpse; poke the audience in the eye; have dates with electronic dames; imagine their blood running in rivers; rip off a mule; meet cannibal space chicks; and nearly end up in sections.

One of the great childhood pleasures from America's past is the laugh-in-the-dark carnival ride that took you, via a small, wheeled car, through a sinister, twisting maze of glowing faces, misshapen figures that sprang from nooks in the walls, and hackle-raising shrieks and groans. None of these rides made any logical sense (which was an essential part of the experience), and the best of them cast a peculiar, dream-like spell over the brave or foolish souls who endured them. In such places—chintzy-looking in full light but so effective in stygian blackness—the rules of the everyday were brazenly suspended.

Of all the Stooges' shorts, *Spook Louder* (1943) comes closest to duplicating the laugh-in-the-dark experience. Crammed with incident yet virtually plotless, it has a special weirdness that belies its relative obscurity in the boys' two-reel output. As a wartime short, it trots out—with virtually no conviction at all—a raison d'être of spies that invade the home of a wiggy inventor, Graves (Ted Lorch), because he's invented a "death ray machine." Hired as caretakers while Graves is away in Washington, the boys look after his interests while suffering a series of creepy encounters.

The story is related, as flashback, to a young reporter (Stanley Brown) by Professor J. O. Dunkfeather (Lew Kelly), a skinny, dotty gent whose connection to the story is purposely kept obscure. Director Del Lord cuts regularly between the Stooges and Dunkfeather, whose story simultaneously intrigues the reporter and drives him buggy.

As Dunkfeather's recollection begins, Larry, Moe, and Curly are door-to-door salesmen of a ridiculous-looking electronic weight-loss device. At Graves's doorstep, the inventor and his cadaverous butler (Charles Middleton) mistake the boys for the new caretakers. Graves insults Curly mightily by suggesting that he might be "a Jap spy" and then boasts about his death ray. "It will kill *millions!*" he says happily.

He continues in that apocalyptic vein and adds a warning: "If an emergency arises, use this bomb. [A comical round thing with a long fuse] It will destroy *everything and everyone!* . . . Now remember, boys—you will defend my property until your life's blood goes down the floor in rivers!"

As night falls, the Stooges are tormented by clutching hands, a revolving bookcase, boxing gloves that dart from behind books, weird laughter, and three fiendish figures: a devil, a skeleton, and a sinister man in black. (The boys would see the same costumes two years later in *Three Pests in a Mess.*)

In an especially peculiar bit, a helium balloon adorned with a hideously grinning face attaches itself to the back of Curly's jacket and follows him through the shadowed halls, lightly bumping his head and making him jump. When Curly stops, the balloon floats between his legs and right up into his face, provoking a good scare. He runs off, the albino balloon bobbing along behind. When Curly pauses at a mirror, the balloon face floats up from behind his back and scares him all over again.

Larry opens the front door and there is the skeleton man, eerily lit from below, silently daring Larry to step outside. Elsewhere, a capuchin monkey panics Moe when it jumps onto his shoulder and curls its tail around his neck, like human fingers.

These droll elements are heightened by John Stumar's imaginatively shadowed photography, which incorporates a full palette of black and grays that highlights the house's marvelous details, such as an enormous stuffed bear, guttering candelabrum, a desiccated mummy, and a Russian clock with a human face that lugubriously tolls the hour with, "Yo. Ho. Yo. Ho."

And then there is a mysterious, unseen thrower of pies who laughs maniacally before hurling the gooey things at propitious moments—for instance, flush into the face of the man in black (Stanley Blystone) as he's preparing to dispatch Moe with a shotgun.

At the house, the Stooges are backed against the wall by the trio of fiends. Curly remembers the bomb and lifts it above his head, inadvertently lighting its fuse on a decorative wall candle.

The fiends are blown right through the wall, and all seems well—until crazed laughter and ricochet sounds announce the arrival of three pies, one for each of the boys.

"Professor," the reporter cries, "I can't stand it any longer! *Who was throwing those pies?*"

"Oh, *I* threw the pies!" The professor bursts forth with the familiar, insane laugh—and then is hit square in the face with a pie.

You've completed the ride. You've had fun. What does it mean?

Does it matter?

I CAN HARDLY WAIT (1943) ISN'T SIMPLY ONE OF THE STOOGES' WEAKEST shorts. It's also one of the most difficult to classify. The fact that the boys hold defense jobs at an airplane plant firmly positions the short as a wartime offering, but other than a modest gag predicated on rationing (the boys gorge at night behind drawn shades so the neighbors can't see) and an unfunny verbal jibe from Moe directed to "those Japs," the film does nothing to exploit the wartime mood.

When the boys aren't struggling with their food—Curly slathers Moe's hand with mustard and is later given eggshells and a teeny hambone while Moe and Larry enjoy ham and eggs—they're concerned with Curly's tooth, which is killing him. Some of the tooth gags take place in the boys' bedroom and in their triple-decker bunk bed, which suggests that *I Can Hardly Wait* is an "At Home" comedy. Soon, though, the action shifts to a dental office, where Dr. Yank (Bud Jamison) pulls Moe's tooth instead of Curly's.

If you're wondering if that gag was a lot funnier when it was done by Laurel and Hardy in *Pardon Us* (1930), the answer is yes.

Much of the tooth-related action is part of a fanciful nightmare that begins as Curly falls asleep in the uppermost bunk. Via an image of the suffering Curly that's cleverly superimposed, like a comic-strip thought balloon, above the sleeping Curly's head, we are drawn into his miserable dream.

In the bedroom as dreamt by Curly, Moe ties the tooth to a deep-sea fishing line and struggles with the gigantic rod as Curly fights him like a marlin. The tooth stays put and doesn't come out after Moe's other ideas, which involve a stepladder, a ceiling light, and a doorknob. An enormous firecracker (a brainstorm from Larry) also fails. From there, it's on to the dentist.

Moe finally rouses Curly from his restless nightmare by pistoning punches into his face—a singularly unfunny image. But the blows do loosen the bad tooth, and although the bed has collapsed, the boys are at least able to sleep.

I Can Hardly Wait is from the cold-cocoa school of comedy. A gag with a hot-water bottle, though telegraphed, is cute, and the noir-like opening, during which the boys creep into their darkened kitchen to raid the icebox, is clever. The dental routines produce a few smiles, but Jules White doesn't stage them very imaginatively, and it's obvious that Clyde Bruckman felt like coasting when he wrote the script.

Five years later, for director Ed Bernds's *Pardon My Clutch* (1948), Bruckman revisited the tooth material in almost identical fashion but with far better results. In that one, it's Shemp who suffers the torments of the dentally damned.

IDLE ROOMERS (1944) IS AN OLD DARK HOUSE COMEDY WITHOUT AN OLD DARK house. The action is set inside a swank hotel that employs the Stooges as bellboys, and it's only a matter of time until a pretty woman catches their eye. She's Mrs. Leander (Christine McIntyre, in her first appearance with the Stooges), an elegant blonde who has a big, burly husband (Vernon Dent) in the carnival business. Leander's latest attraction—which he inexplicably brings into the hotel lobby inside a steamer trunk—is Lupe the Wolf Man (Duke York), a hunchbacked brute who looks like the offspring of a Dandie Dinmont terrier and Rasputin.

The short is at its most satisfying before the boys and Lupe become acquainted. Although Moe fancies himself the leader of the bellboy corps, Larry makes a near-fatal error when he assures Mrs. Leander about her trunk: "I'll have my boy carry it up later!" Moe overhears the remark and catches Larry's head between the closing doors of an elevator, and then shoves his noggin all the way down to the floor. Del Lord, who co-wrote the short with Elwood Ullman, had a flair for absurd images, and this is a particularly good one.

With Larry put out of commission at the elevator, Moe triumphantly strides into the Leanders' room. He spies Mr. Leander in a corner with his feet up, smoking and reading the paper. Oops, the fellow isn't Mr. Leander at all. It's Curly, whose knack for making himself at home is to be envied.

Curly ends up hauling the Leander trunk on his back. The thing is so heavy that, in a beautiful cutaway, Curly's legs bow outward like overburdened tent poles, creaking and groaning like *Old Ironsides*. After a quick rest, Curly extends his arms behind him and hoists *Mrs. Leander*, not the trunk, onto his back—a bit of presumption that upsets Mr. Leander so much that he whips a few knives Curly's way.

When Curly has gone, Leander pulls his wife aside and describes his new attraction:

MR. LEANDER
There's nothing to be afraid of! He's absolutely harmless—
except when he hears music!
Then he goes insane!

An ill-mannered wolf man (Duke York) invades a hotel in *Idle Roomers* (1944). York's makeup recalls a design supervised by Clay Campbell, the head of Columbia's makeup department, for actor Matt Willis in an atmospheric 1943 thriller starring Bela Lugosi, *Return of the Vampire.*   *Photo courtesy of the Stoogeum*

Apparently, Mr. Leander has forgotten that carnivals are awash in music. Or maybe that's the whole point. Alone in the room with the trunk, Curly happily switches on the radio (he calls it "a boogie-woogie box"). The music drives the wolf man nuts and causes him to bend the bars and escape into the room without Curly knowing. In a gag that's well edited by Henry Batista, Lupe tears the radio from the wall and hurls it across the room, missing Curly's head by inches when Curly bends over, and catching Moe—who's in the room across the hall— in the back of the skull.

Lupe decides to go for a nighttime creep on the ledge to scare the hell out of two women (Joanne Frank and frequent Preston Sturges player Esther Howard) who are asleep inside. The creature's dark image, backlit through the drapes by cinematographer Glen Gano, runs against a silent soundtrack and is full of menace. But the brief sequence is the short's only atmospheric one; the rest of the story plays out in normally lit rooms and corridors.

The wolf man roams back to the Leanders' room, where, in a reprise of the mirror routine from the Marx Brothers' *Duck Soup* (which came from Max Linder's 1921 comedy *Seven Years' Bad Luck*, which borrowed it in turn from Chaplin's 1916 short *The Floorwalker*), Curly gazes into an empty frame, sees the wolf man, and imagines he's seeing himself. Yikes!

Curly and Duke York maintain pretty good synchronicity of movement as they stroke their chins, bare their teeth, and clean the "glass" with their palms.

A minute later, all three boys are being chased by the wolf man through the corridor and in and out of various rooms. Del Lord's handling of this runaround isn't bad, but Ed Bernds brought considerably more brio and precision to virtually the same gags, with Shemp, in *Shivering Sherlocks* (1948)—coincidentally, with Duke York again cast as the boys' misshapen antagonist.

The finale finds Lupe and the boys inside the same elevator, with Lupe at the controls. Stock footage of an elevator car speeding upward in its shaft culminates in a contrived, disappointingly phony shot of Stooges and wolf man flying upward into the night sky, superimposed against clouds and standing on nothing at all.

It's a weak conclusion that should have stayed in left field.

THE CONVENTIONS OF THE "OLD DARK HOUSE" GENRE HAD BEEN ESTABLISHED by novelist Mary Rinehart Roberts in her 1908 book *The Circular Staircase*. When the story was adapted to film in 1915, and again in 1926 as *The Bat*, the genre's conventions were set: a shadowy mansion, a mysterious killer, sliding panels, clutching hands, a dead body or two.

Jules White, working from a script by Jack White (story by Gilbert Pratt), uses the earliest scenes of *If a Body Meets a Body* (1945) to establish that Larry, Curly, and Moe are so poor that they live in a barely furnished shack, and banish Curly for serving horse-bone soup. But the pair changes their tune when a newspaper story reveals the hunt for Curly Q. Link, heir to the $3 million fortune of the late Bob O. Link. Horse-bone soup or not, Moe and Larry wouldn't *dream* of letting Curly venture into the world alone.

At the gloomy Link estate, the boys and other interested parties are anxious to learn how the loot will be divvied up, but the will has gone missing, and Detective Clancy (Fred Kelsey, who played the same role in a 1930 short, *The Laurel and Hardy Murder Case*) orders everyone to stay put.

During the agonizing night that follows, a parrot is toppled from his cage by a gust of wind and makes merry in the dusty laboratory of Bob O. Link, crawling up the ribs of a specimen skeleton and finally inserting itself into a loose skull. In a gag that would be repeated in two shorts with Shemp, *The Ghost Talks* and *Scotched in Scotland*, the parrot waddles around inside the skull. At first, only Curly sees this improbable vision. Jules White's timing of the skull's movements is impeccable: The thing silently waddles in the background as Curly pleads his case, and the *instant* it's out of our sight, Moe and Larry turn to look—at nothing. Curly's frustration is palpable.

Larry begins to see the light, and a few stars, when the skull teeters on the headboard of the bed and noisily conks him on the head. Larry turns to the nightstand, and there's the skull—staring at him.

A moment later, the parrot becomes tangled in a handkerchief that trails behind the skull as the bird flies around inside it. The sight is weirdly funny thanks to clever handling of the mechanical effect and to Benjamin Kline's lighting, which creates ominous layers of horizontal and diagonal shadows. Tight, shadowed close-ups on the beleaguered Curly are especially effective.

The night grows even more frightful when the corpse of Bob O. Link (Al Thompson) turns up in bed next to the boys. Moe yanks open a closet to reveal a squirming couple, bound and gagged. A quick detour brings the boys back to their bed, which is now occupied by the seated, staring corpse of the Link family lawyer (John Tyrrell). The last time we saw *him*, he was sprawled in the kitchen with a knife in his chest. (The off-camera death gurgles are audio of Columbia player Stanley Blystone.)

With Jules White and Benjamin Kline at the top of their technical games, Jack White's confidently derivative script, and a large, lively cast, *If a Body Meets a Body* has the stuff to be a classic. The only thing it lacks is a healthy Curly. The short was released on August 30, 1945, and was filmed not long after the first of Curly's strokes. He seems a little sluggish in the short immediately preceding this one, *Idiots Deluxe*, but now his debilitation is pronounced. When he protests bad treatment from Moe with "Stop it! *Stop* it!" he sounds genuinely distressed, and his entreaty to get some light in the bedroom comes out as, "Let's turn a light a candles an' look under the bed!"

Curly finally gets his hands on the will, which was stolen by the housekeeper, a man (Joe Palma) who's been masquerading in drag. As Curly prepares to read, Moe stands close to him and says, rather too seriously, "Don't shake, take it easy." The line is peculiar because it has little comic value, and because Moe seems to step out of character, as if anxious to help his younger brother through the scene.

The final revelation, that Curly has been left "sixty-seven cents, net," leads to a chorus of wails and some alarming pulling at his own hair by Larry. The moment is a very funny study in frustration, but we can only guess at Curly's frustration with the limitations imposed by his illness.

Performer Profile: Fred Kelsey
1884–1961

With Fred Kelsey, it was all about the eyebrows: fabulous, caterpillar-like tufts that worked expressively above glaring eyes and a perpetually downturned mouth. He was ideal for roles as impatient cops, jailhouse guards, bartenders, and splenetic police detectives. He may, in fact, have played police detectives more frequently than any other actor in Hollywood.

In a very long career amounting to more than 400 appearances from 1911 to 1958, Kelsey freelanced all over town, finding most of his work in features after 1917 but showing up as a welcome presence in short subjects produced by Universal, Hal Roach, and Columbia.

Stooges fans enjoy him as the befuddled police detective in *If a Body Meets a Body*—an unauthorized remake of *The Laurel-Hardy Murder Case*, in which Kelsey plays . . . the befuddled police detective.

From 1946 to 1955 he took a variety of roles in Warner Bros.' one-reel Joe McDoakes *Behind the 8-Ball* comedies, nearly always as an uncooperative authority figure or other impediment to the progress of beleaguered star George O'Hanlon.

If a Body Meets a Body (1945): A creepy old house, the reading of a will, and multiple murders. A detective (Fred Kelsey, far left) and the butler (Ted Lorch, far right) try to keep things under control.

PROFESSOR PANZER (VERNON DENT) HAS A GORILLA. CURLY HAS A BRAIN—OF sorts. Panzer wishes to bring gorilla and brain together to prove that he's a very ballsy researcher, and also to prove that the surgery can be done. If he pulls off his scheme, he'll rate a mention in Winchell and twenty to life at Folsom. Well, given his German accent, he's already escaped the hangman's noose of the Allies, so he can probably do a stretch at Folsom standing on his *kopf.*

This is *A Bird in the Head* (1946), written and directed by Ed Bernds and featuring Curly in what is perhaps the most "up" performance from his protracted period of illness. Only a slight tiredness is evident in his face, and he has no trouble with dialogue. His voice is a bit on the low side but is much more antic than in *If a Body Meets a Body.* He's engaged and very much in the moment and is up to the short's physical demands. His body had given him a reprieve.

In the first of two discrete sections, the boys are paperhangers assigned to redo an office belonging to Mr. Beedle (Robert Williams). Curly becomes enamored of the wallpaper paste, which he seasons with pepper and salt, and begins to eat. Larry lifts a heavy ladder and catches Moe's head between two of the rungs, nearly breaking Moe's neck and shattering part of the ladder. Larry and Curly carelessly paper Moe to the wall, and Curly has a devil of a time getting a rolled section of wallpaper to stay *unrolled.* (Ed Bernds wrote that Curly had a great deal of difficulty with the last, forcing Bernds to do a lot of cutaways in order to make the gag work. But the cutaways are no more frequent than you might expect, and Curly wrestles with the wallpaper very nicely.)

When Beedle returns, he can barely force his way in from the hallway outside. That's because the boys have papered over the door and doorframe. Strips of paper angle across the walls every which way; even the ladder has been affixed to the wall with paper.

Beedle is stunned. "No! No!" he says. "This is silly! This is silly! It can't be! It *can't* be!"

Moe flashes a fat grin. "Oh, yes it is! I *said* you wouldn't know the joint!"

Performer Profile: Ted Lorch
1873–1947

Tall, lugubrious, and stentorian of voice, this intimidating-seeming character actor excelled as criminals, noblemen, physicians, "foreigners," and lawyers. This made Lorch a useful fellow to have around, and he worked steadily from the early 1920s until his death in 1947. (The last of his films to be released, the Stooges' *Hot Scots*, came to screens in July 1948, more than six months after his death.)

Lorch is good fun as Jerkington the butler in *If a Body Meets a Body* ("If you need anything, just wail!"); as the crazed inventor, Mr. Graves, in *Spook Louder*, who happily reports that his death ray "will kill millions"; and as the thief who masquerades as a cadaverous mummy in *We Want Our Mummy.*

Lorch also worked extensively in features, nearly always in uncredited bit parts.

Beedle blows a gasket and causes the boys to scramble across the hall, into the office occupied by Professor Panzer. (No pricey old dark house for this crazy scientist; he probably was lucky to escape Germany with his life, never mind his *Reichsmarks*.)

Panzer is delighted when he overhears Moe call Curly "birdbrain." The scientist introduces himself and makes a peculiar fuss over Curly's widdle head.

Larry offers, "Maybe he's a headhunter."

Moe: "If he's a headhunter, he's huntin' small game!"

Sensing in each other kindred souls, Curly and Igor the gorilla become fast friends, which leads to a hilarious turnabout sequence in which the ape objects to Moe's rough treatment of his new pal. Moe has no choice but to suffer in silence when Igor encourages Curly to cuff Moe around. The smallest shrug of retaliation from Moe brings a thudding slap from Igor.

Eventually, Igor gets into a beaker of Panzer's grain alcohol and then grabs that favorite tool of every scientist, a tommy gun. Subsequent squib work, as Panzer's lower back is stitched with bullets and the Stooges take likewise across their butts, is too realistic to be funny. That anybody at all is still alive afterward seems absurd.

That was a lapse of judgment by Ed Bernds. His other lapse relates to logic: Panzer orders Igor to stop bothering the boys, and instead of seizing the moment to run away, the boys blithely follow the prof into his lab. Curly might be expected to stay (after all, he likes Igor), but why do Moe and Larry remain?

When Panzer places Curly's head behind a fluoroscope, we see silhouetted cartoon animation of a cuckoo clock and an exhausted, collapsing cuckoo. Many Web sources claim that the sequence is uncredited work by master animator Tex Avery, but Avery's involvement is unlikely. He was under contract to MGM's cartoon unit at the time and had his hands full with complex short cartoons featuring Droopy and other characters. Also, the wording of every Web claim about the sequence is virtually identical, suggesting that it originated with a single source and has been repeated but never verified.

Although scheduled as a standard four-day shoot, production of *A Bird in the Head* was suspended for a day, April 12, 1945, when word reached the set that President Roosevelt had died.

So unnecessarily concerned was Bernds with the quality of Curly's performance that, although *A Bird in the Head* was his first job as a director, he asked producer Hugh McCollum to release what Bernds thought was a better short, *Micro-Phonies*, first. McCollum complied.

CREATIVE TYPES WHO LABORED UNDER THE STRICTURES OF THE STUDIO system didn't have the luxury of hitting the wall or coming down with writer's block. They weren't allowed *not* to be able to create. An assembly line can function only if each part of it functions. And in the movie business, as elsewhere, the assembly line must function. If the line stalls, revenue stalls. So even if, say, a writer or director was unable to perform creatively—that person *had to* perform creatively.

All of this may explain the sheer awfulness of *All Gummed Up* (1947) and its miserable 1953 redo, *Bubble Trouble.* In the first instance, writer Felix Adler clearly hit the wall. He may have seen it coming. He may have known that, for the moment, his faculties had deserted him and that what he had turned in to producer-director Jules White was terrible.

Jules White was a competent, very experienced filmmaker and executive, so he surely could have had no illusions about Adler's script. Still, *it was a script*, and it had been delivered in time to shoot, which meant that the unit would have *something* for the December '47 release slot.

Moe, Shemp, and Larry are proprietors of the Cut Throat Drug Store. They've been in the same location for ten years, but now their bearded, skinflint old landlord, Mr. Flint (Emil Sitka), wants to toss them out in order to strike a better deal with a larger business.

Flint wants to remake his own life, as well as the boys'. When his frail wife, Serena (Christine McIntyre), enters the store, Flint uncharitably yells, "I'm tired of lookin' at an old hag like you!"—not pausing to consider that Serena may be equally as tired of looking at an old fart like *him.*

Flint's cruel remark is not the stuff of big yoks, and neither is his decision to throw his wife out of their home. Heartbroken, Mrs. Flint accepts the Stooges' offer of a bed in their back room.

Shemp has a brainstorm: Synthesize a youth vitamin!

Well, sure.

The boys get to work with mortar and pestle. When Moe conks Larry, Porcupine utters one of the short's few funny lines: "Put that pestle down, man!" (The word in the popular song is "pistol.")

When Mrs. Flint is made young by the Stooges' concoction, skinflint Flint demands the same rejuvenation, and he gets it—with a slight surprise.

Meanwhile, movie audiences across the nation are sitting in the dark, wondering what time the laughs are scheduled to arrive.

To be fair to Felix Adler, Jules White must be held to account here, too. Did Adler's script specify that the Flints shuffle and quaver like the caricatures of old folks found in second-rate comic strips or was that White's idea? Did Adler insist that Serena's return to youth be achieved via the cheapest, most clumsy sort of optical superimposition?

The boys' vitamin unexpectedly regresses Mr. Flint all the way back to about age twelve. Pre-pubescent Flint (child actor Norman Ollestad, with beard) pulls a gun on the Stooges, but did Adler insist that the boy wail like an infant after tripping on his own trousers? Cripes, even in this crazed narrative, boy-Flint's babyish cry doesn't make a lick of sense.

It doesn't make anybody laugh, either.

Could Adler have hoped that when the boys eat Serena's celebratory cake (which Shemp has unknowingly garnished with bubble gum instead of marshmallows), White would shoot the sequence flatly and perfunctorily, and with little mouth-balloons that look nothing like bubble-gum bubbles?

And if it was Adler alone who came up with the final shot, of teeny "bubbles" forcing their way from Shemp's ears, Adler deserved to be banned from Friars Club lunches for a month.

However, the Stooges being the Stooges, *All Gummed Up* does pinch off a few good moments. Early on, a customer (Cy Schindell) dashes into the store with a prescription hastily written by the doctor on Schindell's shirt. Moe whips up the medication and then rips Cy's shirt from his body, insisting that it's needed for the store's records.

Later, as the now-young Mrs. Flint dances with the boys, Moe and Shemp end up in each other's arms and come up with this exchange, which plays like ad lib:

MOE
Say, you're not a bad dancer!

SHEMP
Oh, I'm from Missouri, the Waltz State!

As the boys prepare the cake, Shemp has a question that also smacks of ad lib:

SHEMP
Has marshmallows got pits?

MOE
No, it's empty, like your skull!

Larry struggles to eat Serena's cake and is startled to pull a small, lighted candle from his mouth. He quickly blows it out, gives it a closer look, shrugs, and then eats it. That's pure Larry, and it's wonderful.

A gag involving a spilled box of Mexican jumping beans is poorly staged and just dies, but things become much livelier when the rejuvenated Mrs. Flint joyously tears away the long sleeves of her black dress (visibly exciting the boys: "Ooh! Ohh!") and then tugs at her hem until it's been raised to her knees. At this, the boys are in danger of publicly embarrassing themselves, getting banned in Boston, and becoming fast friends of Henry Miller. Their spastic twitches and hops, with eyes shining, are underscored by blurts of "Ooh, woo woo, nyahhh!" Welcome to the orgasm-in-your-pants school of comedy. The moment is startlingly funny and is the story's most honest and human display.

Come cake time, Christine McIntyre plays her reaction to her unladylike exhalations of bubbles beautifully, and, as always, it's fun to hear the boys go Yiddish with one of their formula's ingredients, *mishigas* ("craziness").

Because Felix Adler and Jules White had gone down in flames back in 1947, and because Jules decided in the early autumn of 1952 that the October '53 release slot would be filled with a rehash of *All Gummed Up*, scripter Jack White was essentially thrown into the swimming pool with a cinder block tied to his neck. To Jack's credit, *Bubble Trouble* improves the story's structure with a shift of the unfunny bubble-gum cake sequence from the end of the short to the middle, and with five minutes of new business (which was shot on October 13, 1952) to close out the narrative.

Emil Sitka returned for the new shoot. He again swallows the formula, becoming not a little boy but a gorilla in Mr. Flint's suit. Sitka growls, "Even my muscles are growing! I feel like I could tear the building apart!"

That's swell, but we're still wondering what's holding up the bus with all the laughs.

Flint glimpses himself in a mirror and goes berserk until Larry knocks him cold with chloroform. Shemp wants to exhibit "the talking gorilla!" Not a bad idea, but *two* talking gorillas would be better. In the ensuing struggle to jam the gooey formula down Shemp's gullet, Moe ends up swallowing the stuff.

The White brothers conclude *Bubble Trouble* with a close shot on Moe, who grunts and scratches his head, his tongue pushed against the inside of his lower lip to make a monkey face. What's worse, he moves into the camera, as if insisting that we witness his embarrassment.

And the bus with the laughs? We hear it ended up in Hoboken, where everybody had a swell time.

A COMMON CHILDHOOD WISH IS TO BE ABLE TO DO MISCHIEF WITHOUT BEING seen or heard. What fun! Zion Myers understood the fantasy's allure and exploited it nicely with his script for *Heavenly Daze* (1948), in which Shemp is granted the ability to move about surreptitiously but only so that he can reform his cousins, Moe and Larry. Oh, and Shemp is dead. That is, he's an angel.

The Stooges' occasional novelty shorts, involving such things as giant canaries, angels, and talking horses, don't always succeed as comedy, but they are nearly always intriguing. *Heavenly Daze* is certainly that, but it's also satisfying as knockabout comedy, as a verbal joust, and as an example of an amusing fantasy setting—heaven itself.

As created by art director Charles Clague and cinematographer Allen Siegler, heaven is a brightly illuminated, featureless plain that suggests both serenity and purposefulness. It's a place where time simultaneously moves forward and stands still. Shemp's Uncle Mortimer (Moe) alludes to this when he informs Shemp that he died many years before Shemp was born—and yet Mortimer knows Shemp very well.

Heaven is the traditional place of rest and reward, and yet, as on Mt. Olympus, mortal-time events on Earth can be observed and influenced. Part of the joke is that instead of the interference of Zeus and other petulant Greek gods, the heavenly observer of *Heavenly Daze* is Uncle Mortimer, a fair-minded but vaguely humorless civil servant. According to Myers and director Jules White, heaven is as much a place of business as it is a landscape of eternal bliss. Angels who have unfinished business on Earth, or who can influence the living to lead better existences, are put to work.

In this, *Heavenly Daze* doesn't draw simply on Christian belief and cultural archetypes (Uncle Mortimer, for instance, is the archetypal "Wise Old Man") but takes cues from Hollywood. *Especially*, it takes cues from Hollywood. Assigned to a specific task of reformation, angel-Shemp follows in a line of movie angels that includes Clarence (*It's a Wonderful Life*), George and Marion Kerby (*Topper*), Joe Pendleton (*Here Comes Mr. Jordan*), and Pete Sandidge (*A Guy Named Joe*). Like these phantoms, when Shemp completes his task, he will have left behind an improved earthly world, and ensured the best possible afterlife for himself.

Particular fun arises from the fact that Shemp is a reasonably new angel who doesn't quite grasp heavenly protocol. The arrival of Uncle Mortimer's lovely blonde secretary, Miss Jones (Marti Shelton), causes Shemp to *peepeepeepeepeep* in desire, and elevate his wings in a visual metaphor for erection. It's a brazen joke, and a good one. Later, Shemp dashes to catch the Heavenly Express ("Going to the Big Dipper, Little Dipper, Earth, Mars, Venus, [and, à la *The Jack Benny Program*] Cucamonga, Anaheim, and all points south"). He collides face-first with a belligerent rain cloud that wobbles into his path, and then gives him a good spraying. The obvious falseness of the grumbling, plywood cloud, with visible nozzles to allow the flow of water, only makes it funnier.

Moe and Larry have caught Uncle Mortimer's attention because they're con men who have used the money left to them by Shemp (a fulsome $140) to rent a swank apartment and a butler in order to swindle a naïve wealthy couple, the DePuysters (Vic Travers and Symona Boniface), out of $50,000. And just how do the boys propose to do that? By selling the DePuysters the rights to an absurd pen that writes beneath whipped cream.

Through a variety of mischievous means, Shemp thwarts the scheme, though not before the DePuysters and Moe and Larry are nearly suffocated in whipped cream. (At about this time, Chicago businessman Milton Reynolds appropriated an Argentinean design, the Biro ballpoint, and passed it off as his own, claiming that, among other things, the pen would write underwater. Reynolds was assisted in his promotional campaign by actress/swimming star Esther Williams.)

For longtime Stooges fans, the novelty of observing Shemp abuse Moe and Larry with impunity is a perverse joy. Shemp slaps Moe, who assumes the blow came from Larry, and he splashes the boys' drinks into their faces.

Shemp also takes charge of the bills that are his inheritance, preventing Moe from cheating Larry during the count. Exercising his skill as a heavenly pickpocket, Shemp transfers bills from one person to another, and even manages to see that the boys' conniving lawyer (Vernon Dent), walks out the door with nothing—though the lawyer won't know it until he checks his pockets.

Moe and Larry's rent-a-butler, Spiffingham, responds to a query by answering from off screen in a cultivated British accent. He strides into frame, and we see that he's African American. Actor Sam McDaniel (the brother of Oscar winner Hattie McDaniel) is a hoot as Spiffingham, mainly because angel-Shemp can't resist pulling his chain: He deposits a coat and hat in Spiffingham's arms, sneezes loudly (after receiving special dispensation from Uncle Mortimer so that the sneeze can be heard), and makes the coat and hat dance on the floor.

When Moe and Larry uneasily express the thought that Shemp may have come back to haunt them, Spiffingham reacts with the short's best line: "Says *which?*"

Performer Profile: Symona Boniface
1895–1950

The grande dame of Stooges comedies, stately Symona Boniface exuded high-society haughtiness but was never afraid to take a pie in the face.

She came to films at the tail end of the silent era and henceforth divided her time between shorts and features. Like many day players, Symona had her best roles in shorts, and it's to her credit that although she was nearly always cast as a society type, she was invariably funny (either directly or in counterpoint) and enthusiastic.

Stooges fans recall her best for two films, *Half-Wits Holiday*, in which she plays the perfectly charming Mrs. Smythe-Smythe and is rewarded with a pie that comes unglued from a the ceiling and plummets directly onto her face; and *Vagabond Loafers*, in which, as wealthy Mrs. Norfleet, she's soaked in front of guests by a gush of water from her television set, caused by Shemp and the other boys, who bumble around the house as plumbers.

Larry and Moe intend to swindle the DePuysters (Vic Travers and Symona Boniface) by encouraging them to invest in a fountain pen that writes under whipped cream; invisible angel Shemp has been sent to Earth to prevent the scam, in *Heavenly Daze* (1948).   *Photo courtesy of the Stoogeum*

The boys ask Shemp for a sign of his presence, and Shemp obliges by stick-ing their keisters with pins. The beauty of Moe and Larry is that, despite their awareness of Shemp's presence, they decide to go ahead with the swindle anyway. When the DePuysters ring the bell, Spiffingham very slowly opens the door from a protective crouch, staring at Mr. DePuyster's midsection.

MR. DePUYSTER
Why, you look as if you've seen a ghost!

SPIFFINGHAM
Mister, you don' know de half of it!

The DePuysters, particularly the missus, are elegantly turned out, and the boys' apartment is handsome, too—which makes Moe's friendly, Yiddish-tinged invitation to "Sit. *Plotz*" all the more absurd.

Shemp sees to it that the demonstration of the pen, which involves a mixer full of cream, goes awry. The pen flies free of its anchor and zings across the room like a harpoon, burying itself in Larry's forehead. (Larry's yelp of pain is real, because the pen cut through a protective plate and penetrated Larry's flesh, contrary to the assurances of Jules White.)

The conclusion of *Heavenly Daze*, although dominated by an ambitious and very well-executed fire gag, is disappointing: Everything, you see, has been Shemp's nightmare.

A 1955 remake, *Bedlam in Paradise*, picks up the greater part of the original footage but eliminates Spiffingham and adds new material by Jack White, includ-ing an opening sequence in which Moe and Larry attend to Shemp as he lies dying in bed. As you might imagine, the death throes (complete with gurgles) are not very amusing.

Philip Van Zandt makes a rakish but perfunctory appearance as the Devil aka Mr. Heller, who has already made Moe and Larry rich, and who eggs them on to swindle the DePuysters.

The real treat of *Bedlam in Paradise* is dancer/actress Sylvia Lewis, who plays the Devil's sexy aide, Helen Blazes. A Cyd Charisse type, and costumed very much as Cyd had been in *Singin' in the Rain*, the dark, impossibly leggy Lewis pops up in heaven to seduce angel-Shemp with dance. (Shemp's clubfooted attempts to follow Lewis's slinky moves are underplayed and hilarious.) As Jerry Feldman's (probably Jerry Fielding's) jazz soundtrack builds to a cre-scendo, Lewis extends her arms and strides directly into the camera, testing *our* mettle as well as Shemp's. The dancer later became a very successful television choreographer.

When Lewis bends Shemp back and kisses him, the music explodes in a disso-nant blare of brass. Jules White was often content to coast, but here he executed something fresh and startling. It's the best moment of this so-so remake.

IF YOU'RE SHOOTING A MOVIE THAT HAS A THIN PREMISE AND WEAK GAGS, YOU need to be sure that the craft elements—like mechanical effects—are working great, because if you botch them, your picture is in real trouble.

A bad film can't be saved with sound or lighting or effects work, but if those things are good, the viewer has *something* to grab onto, and the whole experience might be bearable. Jules White forgot that, or had no time to remember it, when he took Zion Myers's script and directed *The Ghost Talks* (1949).

Here is the purportedly scary stuff:
- Rain. Thunder. Lightning.
- A smallish castle with no electricity.
- A talking suit of armor.
- A skeleton unfolds itself from a dresser drawer, and walks and talks.
- The skeleton removes its own head and tosses it to the Stooges.
- Two wisecracking skeletons sit at a table and play cards.
- One of the skeletons identifies himself as Red. Shemp cracks, "Oh, Red Skeleton!"
- A bullfrog hops into Shemp's cap.
- The same frog hops down the back of Shemp's shirt.
- An owl flies into a human skull.
- The owl hoots.
- The owl sticks its wings through the sides of the skull and flies around the room, trailing a handkerchief.
- The eyes of the skull glow.
- The mounted head of a dog snarls and barks.

These are the craft elements that fall flat:
- Except for a moving visor, the suit of armor is inanimate.
- The bullfrog doesn't hop. It's simply pulled and dragged to where it needs to go.
- So that the frog can be dropped down Shemp's back, his shirt is pulled out a good six inches by wire before the frog budges from Shemp's shoulder.
- The (fake) owl doesn't fly through the window; it's simply *maneuvered* through, and then allowed to drop, like a lead weight, onto a chair.
- The skeleton that unfolds itself from the drawer shakes and wobbles on its wire rig.
- When the skeleton walks, it moves with that one-hip, other-hip gait of a poorly manipulated marionette.
- The wall-mounted dog head is so boneless and rubbery that Moe is obliged to remark, "It's a fake!" (No follow-up gag, by the way—just an acknowledgment that what we're seeing is phony.)

A few mechanical effects succeed:
- The excellent storm effects cleverly combine sound with M. A. Anderson's moody, very handsome photography.
- A glass of milk left on a tabletop is mysteriously drained dry.

- A crossbow lets fly with an arrow that pierces Larry's rear.
- Wire work performed with the skeleton that removes its own head is so slick, and the frame jumps so subtle, that for an instant the effect looks like stop-motion animation.
- The owl & skull & handkerchief soars around the room very smoothly—as it better have, because the effects people working on films with the Stooges and Columbia's other two-reel stars had been asked to execute the gag countless times before.

The driving force behind all this folderol is the suit of armor, which the Stooges encounter in their jobs as movers. (Why they're at work in the dead of night is never explained.) The armor imprisons the ghost of Tom the Tailor. A thousand years ago, Tom innocently opened his shutter as his sweetheart, Lady Godiva, rode past in the altogether. A non sequitur (but funny) pie struck Tom flush in the face, but what's more important is that the citizenry had been ordered not to peek at the Lady. Tom was branded "Peeping Tom" and sentenced to one thousand years' captivity inside the metal suit.

TOM
That shutter! That confounded shutter!

SHEMP
I shutter to think about it!

MOE (plinking Shemp's nose)
Shutter up!

Tonight, Tom's sentence is up, and the tailor awaits Godiva's return. (Godiva lived between 1040 and 1080, so her return here is about a hundred years premature.)

Voice actor Phil Arnold, though lively and expressive, doesn't even attempt a British accent. Neither does Lady Godiva (Nancy Saunders), who listlessly rides a sleepwalking horse into the castle's main room at the climax. Wearing a black Jantzen swimsuit, her back bowed as though carrying the weight of the world, she exhibits all the élan of a beach bunny with mono. And never mind the British accent: Saunders should never have been allowed to open her mouth at all, because her delivery of the line "Whoa, Charger" is as listless and flat as a car-squashed armadillo on a two-lane road in the Texas panhandle.

A moment later, with Tom seated on the horse behind her, Saunders summons the strength to murmur, "Giddap, Charger."

The horse plods out of frame.

All of this is not breathlessly exciting.

Because White and the Stooges were professionals, *The Ghost Talks* does manage a few good moments. Shemp hides his fear with an enthusiastically delivered verbal spoof of Raymond, the host of radio's *Inner Sanctum*, by calling himself "Desmond, of the Outer Sanctum" and promising "a nice, bloody murder" and other "strange happenings."

MOE *(to Shemp)*
One of us is nuts and it can't be you!

SHEMP *(triumphantly)*
Rrightt! *(Moe seizes Shemp's throat)*

SHEMP *(eyes bulging)*
Urk!

As Godiva and Tom ride off, the Stooges rush to a window to watch, and although the gag has been telegraphed—three kissers, three pies—it's still pretty funny.

To fill out his 1953 release schedule, White rehashed *The Ghost Talks* as *Creeps*. A bit more than five minutes of the short is new material written by Jack White; the rest is pickup from the original.

Much of the new material is a framing device in which the boys, lying three abreast in a crib, play squalling infants who their dads (via slick split-screen work) hope to cajole into sleep with a bedtime story. Baby Larry wants to hear about ghosts. Baby Shemp wants a story about knights.

Baby Moe: "Killings and murders I want!"

Phil Arnold returns for some fresh voice work to establish that he's Sir Tom; the Peeping Tom business is dropped. Also gone, mercifully, are the owl and Lady Godiva.

The Stooges shot a couple of quick expository inserts, as well as a fresh set piece inside a trophy-torture room, where Shemp is nearly decapitated—twice—by a guillotine.

Tom is livelier this time around and even engages the boys in swordplay.

Because the storybook tale fades out with the fight, the Baby Stooges are unsatisfied. They screech for "a story that'll put us to sleep!"

Their dads, wise in the ways of childrearing, conk the babies with hammers. *Zzzzzz!*

WORLD WAR II BROUGHT OUT THE BEST AND WORST IN SCIENCE AND MEDICINE. Prompt, smartly improvised treatment of battlefield trauma led to significant improvements of surgical technique, and many patients survived because of a newly developed antibiotic called penicillin. On the other hand, monstrously unethical surgeons and scientists ensconced in labs inside Nazi extermination camps conducted experiments so cruel that they beggar description. In those places, medicine slipped back to the Dark Ages.

All of that, plus the good-bad realities of atomic research and a collective American memory of such fictions as *Frankenstein* and *Donovan's Brain*, contributed to a postwar resurgence of general public unease about scientific work.

The times were dead perfect, then, for *Dopey Dicks* (1950), a mad-science spoof that, like so many successful spook comedies, gives the protagonists opportunities to be alternately cowardly and heroic.

Shemp is eager to be a private detective, and all three boys get their opportunity one stormy night, when they abandon their jobs as custodians for shamus Sam Shovel (get it?) to trace an abducted blonde (Christine McIntyre) to her isolated mansion. Inside, they meet a crazed professor (Philip Van Zandt) who needs human brains to perfect his dream of self-directed automatons. His prototype, a tuxedoed figure with no head, prowls around the mansion, whirring like an infernal clockwork, bumping into things and scaring the bejesus out of the Stooges.

After nearly losing their heads, the boys and Christine (the name of her character, Louise, is noted in the script but is never spoken on screen) escape the house and hitch a ride to freedom.

Elwood Ullman wrote two-reel and feature scripts for decades because he maintained his comic edge and knew how to bring fresh life to familiar plots and gags. And Ed Bernds, by 1950, had already become the Stooges' best and most inventive director.

Right from the start, the congenial-seeming professor and his peculiar butler-accomplice, Ralph (Stanley Price), give the boys a hard time.

MOE
Where's the young lady that lives in this house?

RALPH
Young lady? About five feet two, with golden hair?

STOOGES
Yes yes!

RALPH
Blue eyes?

STOOGES
Yes yes!

RALPH
Long, curling lashes?

STOOGES
Yes yes yes!

RALPH
Haven't seen her.

Even in 1950 that gag was old enough to have whiskers, but because it's directed and delivered so well here, it seems brand new, even as you wait for the payoff that you know is coming.

Later, Moe is alone with the professor. "Queer sort of duck," Moe says, gesturing toward Ralph.

Professor: "Yesss, ahahahahahahahaha!"

Moe takes this obvious madness in stride. "You're all right!" he says.

Ullman and Bernds are careful to distinguish the professor (manic and high-spirited) from Ralph (dark of mood and considerably more aware than the professor of the illegality of what he's doing). They're equally menacing, but their personalities encourage the boys to react a little differently to each.

A particularly funny bit of business involves Shemp, who *cannot* remember the phone number (MAine 2468) of the State Hospital, the place that the professor and Ralph call home. He has to sort again and again through a ridiculous pile of phone books: "Central section," he mutters to himself, "Northeastern section, Western section, if I don't hurry we'll *all* be in sections!" Every time Shemp gets through to the operator, his memory fails him: "Operator, I want MAine—MAine? . . ."

When Larry sticks his head up between the leaves of a table and goes "Psst!" he shocks the hell out of Shemp, who's positive his pal has been decapitated: "They got him and he's still talkin'!"

Later, Shemp blunders through a secret panel and finds the girl gagged and trussed to a chair—and the beauty of Shemp is that he's dumb enough to keep his cool. "What's the matter, kid," he asks carelessly, "ya got a toothache?"

Cinematographer Vincent Farrar, who was given so little to work with on the two-dollar *Hugs and Mugs*, does beautiful work on *Dopey Dicks*, devising velvet shadows that angle along the walls and crisscross the floors of Charles Clague's handsome sets. Editor Henry DeMond maintains a breathless pace.

So Ralph and the professor will be returned to the laughing academy, and the robot—well, he pilots the car that the Stooges and Christine hop into at the conclusion.

Lacking a head, he's really not a good driver at all.

IN THE DAYS WHEN MOST INTERIOR MOVIE WORK WAS SHOT ON SOUND STAGES, low-budget filmmakers surely appreciated sequences set in warehouses. A warehouse could be designed and dressed cheaply. A grid of well-placed cartons and crates provided visual interest. The camera could prowl at eye level, or it could take a higher, more omnipotent view. Thoughtful arrangement of crates and other props brought opportunities for lively movement of the actors.

A warehouse setting is especially fun when the place is full of breakable china and the bozos in charge are Moe, Larry, and Shemp.

Ed Bernds's *Three Arabian Nuts* (1951) casts the boys as warehouse laborers. Naturally, Moe has given himself command of the bills of lading, to ensure that crates are properly moved from here to there. True to form, he treats Larry and Shemp like flunkies. Partly because they resent that, and partly because they're just inept, the pair toss containers around as if they were beach balls and cause the soundtrack to vibrate with the awful noise of shattering glass and china.

Although Moe is a hopeless manager, he's a reasonably skilled schmoozer who blithely assures Mr. Bradley (Vernon Dent), the owner of a large delivery of breakable Middle Eastern artifacts, that "We're as gentle as a flock of kittens!"

At that moment, Shemp, somewhere in the bowels of the warehouse, loses his grip on a small crate and smashes everything inside.

MR. BRADLEY
Merciful heavens, what was that?

MOE
(with a vaguely panicked smile)
Oh, it could be any number of a thousand things!

Yes, or a thousand *pieces* of things.

Shemp doesn't realize that two scowling Arabs observe him from behind a riser of boxes. The Arab-Israeli War of 1948 was still fresh in people's minds, and during 1950–51, American newspapers regularly carried alarmist stories about a nationalistic, anti-monarchy movement in Egypt. For these and other reasons, both political and folklorish, Middle Easterners delineated in the shorthand of propaganda were ideal for use as villains. The schemers who watch Shemp have cleverly hidden in plain sight by undertaking their mission while attired in keffiyah headdresses and flowing thawbs. One of them, Ahmed (Philip Van Zandt), hefts a scimitar that's the size of a piece of ductwork. The other, Hassan (Dick Curtis), carries a wicked dagger.

Shemp opens a packing case and pulls out a traditional-looking Arab lamp. He thinks it's a "pretty little syrup pitcher" and polishes it with a good rub. *Poof!* Shemp has released the ebony-skinned genie of the lamp (Wesley Bly)—whom Shemp cheerfully addresses as "genius" or, alternatively, as "Amos."

The remainder of *Three Arabian Nuts* is a set-bound but very active chase comedy. The murderous Arabs want the lamp. Shemp wants to make wishes. Moe and Larry want to stay alive. Mr. Bradley wants to stop absent-mindedly resting his ass on a hot plate every time Moe invites him to sit down.

Elwood Ullman's script decrees that almost everyone will experience severe pain. Larry makes coffee and accidentally spills it down the front of Moe's pants, so Moe pours a stream of the scalding stuff onto Larry's palm. The gag is undeniably cruel but also one of the short's funniest because of Moe's dark pique and Larry's leather-lunged howls of agony.

As Moe pries nails, he raps himself in the forehead with his claw hammer. Later, at Bradley's apartment, Ahmed fries his fingers when he snatches the red-hot lamp from a fireplace.

The most inventive gag involves Larry's struggle to heft a long crate, facing forward with his arms extended behind as Moe lifts at the rear. When Moe lets go of the crate and steps away to retrieve something, Larry proceeds as before, the entire back end of the crate magically suspended in air. Larry continues with his burden, through a doorway and out of sight. Ed Bernds cuts to Shemp, holds on him for a long beat—and *then* adds the tremendous, distant crash we've been waiting for.

Tall, muscular Wesley Bly (in the only credited role of his modest career) is the soul of patience as the deep-voiced genie, granting the boys' request for lots of loot and Shemp's wish for "a new set o' threads"—a zoot suit and an outrageous "skimmer" hat that disappear as Shemp runs to show Moe. The genie even conjures up three very attentive harem girls, at no extra charge.

Mr. Bradley endures a very bad day, and the worst part is that he's given the lamp to Shemp because it was a trifle he picked up at a bazaar for fifty cents. As the harem girls stroke the boys' egos and other things, Mr. Bradley grabs a club hammer and gives his skull a good pounding, to conclude this very well-crafted celebration of fantasy and the bright side of Arab/American relations.

SPOOKS (1953) IS THE FIRST OF TWO STOOGES SHORTS FILMED AND RELEASED in 3-D, that miracle of the age that excited studios and filmgoers for about eighteen months before disappearing with such conclusiveness that nobody gave it another thought for thirty years.

But because you're dying to know and because you have a *right* to know, these are the 3-D effects that make life exciting for the boys and lovely young Mary Bopper (Norma Randall) in *Spooks*:

1. In a rare instance of a pre-title sequence, Moe, Larry, and Shemp (draped in black against a black background) approach the camera, their heads seemingly floating in a void. Larry, in the center, comes closest to the camera before dropping back to join Shemp and Moe. All three boys bring their heads lower in the frame and put on silly expressions. Cue first title card: "The Three Stooges."
2. Moe carefully aims a pen and throws it into the camera. In the next cut (flat), the pen embeds itself in Shemp's nose.
3. Moe gives the camera the old two-finger eye poke.
4. Crazed scientist Dr. Jekyll (Philip Van Zandt) shoves the needle of an enormous hypodermic in our direction.
5. Moe winds up to kick Shemp in the pants and directs the kick right at us.
6. Inside Jekyll's dark, creepy house, a bat with the face of Shemp (and his vocabulary, too: "Peepeepeepeepeep!") flies toward the camera. Shemp is beside himself: "What a hideous, monstrous face! Oh!"
7. Dr. Jekyll goes after Shemp with a heavy blade, which is thrust right at us.
8. In the most effective dimensional effect of *Spooks*, Dr. Jekyll appears behind a sliding panel and wings a cleaver at Larry and right into our faces.
9. Director Jules White dollies in on the proverbial skeleton in the closet and lets the bones fall toward Shemp and into our laps.
10. Jekyll's giant-size aide, Mr. Hyde (veteran comic Tom Kennedy), swings a sickle at the camera and finishes the motion by embedding the blade in the wall, around Moe's neck.

Performer Profile: Philip Van Zandt
1904–58

One of the most colorful of the Stooges' stock-company players, Phil Van Zandt was born in the Netherlands in 1904 and was active in Hollywood from 1939 to 1958. With his narrow eyes and pencil mustache and a silky voice that could be turned to officiousness, he specialized in stock villains: card sharps, Nazis, kidnappers, and assorted henchmen—many of them faux exotics called Kushmet, Ahmed, Rom Zingh, and Yusef.

Like many character players of the day, Van Zandt moved freely among shorts, features, and TV. He has a nice role in *Citizen Kane* (1941) as a curious reporter and a good bit in *Sweet Smell of Success* (1957) as a radio-show director.

He first worked with the Stooges in *Squareheads of the Round Table* and often supported other short-subject stars, including Hugh Herbert, Andy Clyde, and (at Warner Bros.) George O'Hanlon (in numerous "Joe McDoakes" *Behind the 8-Ball* comedies).

During the '50s Van Zandt taught acting. A very late Stooges short, *Fifi Blows Her Top*, was Van Zandt's final screen appearance. He died from an overdose of sleeping pills in February 1958, a probable suicide.

Beautiful Mary Bopper (Norma Randall) is momentarily at the mercy of fiends Tom Kennedy (left) and Philip Van Zandt in *Spooks* (1953), the first of two Stooges shorts shot and released in 3-D.
Photo courtesy of the Stoogeum

11. Hyde chases the boys with an acetylene torch and shoots a jet of flame into the camera lens.
12. Moe deals with Hyde, and the fire in Larry's pants, by squirting the camera with a stream of water.
13. Hyde grabs a pitchfork (Jekyll keeps his house supplied with *everything*) and stabs it into the camera.
14. See #4.
15. Kongo the Gorilla (Steve Calvert)—who's been penciled in by Jekyll to receive Mary Bopper's brain—pushes his hairy head at the camera.
16. The Stooges accidentally light some loose Roman candles (see parenthetical note, #13), which flame and spit into our faces.
17. The boys take the starch out of Jekyll and Hyde by pelting them with pies that also pelt the camera.
18. See #15, with the added 3-D thrill of the ape's furry hands.
19. Kongo wings pies at the boys and at Mary Bopper, sending the gooey pastries right at our much-abused friend, the camera.

So. Nineteen gags in 3-D. That's a lot of contrived business that undermines the short's pacing and makes *Spooks* one of the most "forced" of the Stooges' comedies. But the cast, Jules White, scripter Felix Adler, and the rest of the crew worked hard to overcome the requirements and limitations of the bolt-on 3-D technology.

After a frantic man (Frank Mitchell) enters the Stooges' Super Sleuth Detective Agency and identifies himself as George B. Bopper, the father of an abducted girl, Shemp gets that jive feeling: "Ohh, a *bee*-bopper! Dig that craaazy bopper name! Meemeemeemeemeemee! Cool, man! Real George! Gimme some skin! Gimme some skin!" (This outburst prompts 3-D effect #2 and Shemp's follow-up line, "Ooh, ow, gimme a blotter, willya, gimme a blotter!")

When B. Bopper shows the boys a photograph of his fetchingly décolletage daughter, Shemp enthuses, "That girl has a beautiful pair a' eyes!" After that saucy slap at the Production Code, Jules White dissolves from the smiling face in the photo to a tight shot on the face of the same girl, trussed to a chair by the fiends, her eyes darting with panic.

"Scare" music by Mischa Bakaleinikoff that plays under the main title is sterling, and careful lighting by cinematographer Lester H. White brings an air of dim, silky menace. A hearty nod, also, to the sound effects crew for smartly inserted noises of crickets, owls, and a keening wind.

On the other hand, *Spooks* resurrects the awful rubber dog-head from *The Ghost Talks* and takes the easy path with one of those insufferable "everybody's laughing at once" conclusions.

That's comedy in a desultory dimension.

AS JACK WHITE PREPARED TO WRITE *HOOFS AND GOOFS* (1957), HE LOOKED with envy—or perhaps with just a lazy eye—at one of Universal-International's most popular feature franchises. *Francis the Talking Mule* was released in 1950 and grossed three million dollars on an investment of about $150,000. It established the formula for the rest of the Francis pictures: naïve Army recruit has misadventures with his best pal, a clever, gravelly voiced mule. Seven Francis comedies were made, one a year, from 1950 through 1956. All entries but the first, which had a February 1950 release, arrived in the late spring or summer to cash in on the kiddie trade.

Donald O'Connor and Chill Wills (who went without credit as the voice of Francis) star in the first six; the last, *Francis in the Haunted House*, features Mickey Rooney, with voice actor Paul Frees stepping in for Wills.

The small trick of making the mule move his mouth was accomplished with a piece of filament attached to his gums. When the filament was tugged, Francis (who was a female named Molly) moved his mouth to clear the obstruction. The same technique was used with Tony the Wonder Horse, who plays Birdie, Moe, Larry, and Joe's deceased, and reincarnated, little sister.

Jack White's script establishes that Birdie has been dead for a year. Moe and Larry have apparently recovered, but Joe continues to mourn and to hope that Birdie will be reincarnated. Because Moe is Moe, he hides behind a chair, puts on a spooky falsetto, and identifies himself as Birdie. He promises to see Joe the next day—at a specific intersection!

The next day, Joe's belief in reincarnation is confirmed when the boys come upon a junk-cart horse that calls to them. Well, bless me, it's Birdie! The remainder of the short divides its attention between two story elements: the boys' attempts to get Birdie into their upstairs apartment and conceal her from their landlord; and Birdie's periodic complaint of sharp stomach pains. Stomach pain, hmm. Can you spell C-O-L-T?

Hoofs and Goofs was the first Joe Besser/Stooges short to see release, on January 31, 1957. Hired on the fly, Besser acquits himself as well as the script allows, appearing alternately fussy and petulant—and even using his fist to give Moe a good crack on the head. Although most comfortable in character-based comedy that was a little foreign to Moe and Larry, Joe nevertheless gives the impression that he's been with the other two for ages.

Still, to introduce Joe in a short in which the focus is a talking animal is unwisely distracting and prevents him from emerging full blown in his debut appearance as a Stooge.

The boys' shooting schedules had been reduced from four days to three by 1956, and it's to the credit of producer-director Jules White that the film—though obviously inexpensive—doesn't look threadbare. Cast and crew went outside to shoot the early scenes with Birdie, and the schedule allowed the use of four serviceable standing sets: the entryway and staircase of the boys' apartment building, an upstairs hallway, the boys' flat, and the apartment of the nearsighted landlord, Mr. Dinklespiel (Benny Rubin), which is directly beneath.

Stock-company player Harriette Tarler appears as Dinklespiel's solicitous daughter and also provides the voice of Birdie. Besser and the other Stooges do what they can with the material, and Rubin is very funny with a put-on

A career low for all concerned? Quite possibly. The Stooges take tea with their reincarnated sister (played by Tony the Wonder Horse) in the noticeably unfunny *Hoofs and Goofs* (1957). *Photo courtesy of the Stoogeum*

"Cherman" accent, but if anybody is clearly better than the material, it's Harriette Tarler. A lively and expressive on-screen actress, Tarler's post-production readings mark Birdie as believably feminine *and* forceful.

In a clever touch, Birdie isn't completely sympathetic. In fact, she acts a lot like a horse—resisting when the boys pull her away from her cart and angrily swishing her tail in their faces. Once inside the tiny apartment, she thumps so noisily on the floor that her hoof breaks through and sends a chip of plaster into Mr. Dinkelspiel's soup. "Zank you for der cracker," he murmurs to his daughter before he's splashed and finally knocked cold by progressively larger pieces. Later, when Joe passes out after carelessly dousing himself with ether (the stuff is to help Birdie through childbirth), he collapses and lets the liquid pour through the hole in the floor and right into Mr. Dinklespiel's glass of milk.

Much of the humor is perfunctory. Mr. Dinkelspiel gets flypaper stuck on his face and falls down the stairs. Birdie belches loudly. Face to face with the landlord when Birdie whinnies, Moe pretends to have bronchitis. Larry pushes open the kitchen door and knocks over Moe, who's been carrying a pan of water. A drunk (Joe Palma) observes the boys sneaking Birdie upstairs and tosses his bottle on the floor.

Birdie finally gives birth. The colt is beautiful, and Joe cries, "I'm an uncle!" but the scene is too cutesy to be a comfortable fit for the Stooges.

Although the final sequence of *Hoofs and Goofs* establishes that Joe has been dreaming and that Birdie (played by Moe in drag) is alive, the short was given a sequel five spots later on the release schedule. We've talked already about the Stooges and sentimentality, concluding that the two coexist as disastrously as army ants and a honeymoon suite. In a bad decision, then, the sentimentality meter goes into the red zone with *Horsing Around* (1957). This time, Birdie (again voiced by Harriette Tarler) is frantic because the love of her life, a circus stallion named Schnapps, has been badly injured and is about to be put down. (This is a variation on an unpleasant gag in the boys' *Three Little Twirps* [1943].)

Once at the circus, and for no sensible reason, Moe and Larry hide in a two-man horse costume, and quite inadvertently outwit the elderly, nearsighted caretaker (Emil Sitka) who's been ordered to dispose of Schnapps. (When Sitka approaches with a mammoth hypodermic, the papier-mâché horse head eyeballs the needle and gives a good, funny start.)

Joe has already spirited Schnapps to safety, and at the conclusion, the Stooges look on with egg-sucking glee as Birdie and Schnapps kiss. And kiss.

"Birdie declares, "You're the most!"

There's little to like here except the performances. Joe is noticeably more aggressive than in *Hoofs and Goofs* and less willing to put up with Moe's crap. He reacts with particular vehemence after Moe loses control of a drumstick and smacks him in the face:

JOE
Ooh, that *hurrts*!

MOE
I'm sorry, Joe. I'm sorry, Joe.

JOE
"I'm sorry, Joe, I'm sorry, Joe!" Can't you ever say anything like "I'm *glad*" once?

MOE
Yeah! So I'm glad I'm sorry once!

JOE *(mollified)*
That's better!

Felix Adler's script gives Joe another good moment when, after being ordered to "get rid of the dishes," he neatly gathers them up in the tablecloth and then flings the whole bundle out the window.

Joe would have much more to do in later shorts. In the meantime, *Hoofs and Goofs* and *Horsing Around* stand as eerie precursors of the feature films Moe and Larry would make with Joe DeRita in the 1960s. Rather than be smart and allow the Stooges to do their shtick for ninety minutes, Columbia and Fox felt obliged to burden the boys with the dead weight of cloying, killingly dull romantic subplots played out by young contract mannequins. The seeds of that are sown here, with the boys overshadowed by mother issues and young love.

Horsefeathers.

As movie audiences trended younger in the 1950s, science fiction became an especially popular and exploitable genre. Columbia's B-picture unit, in the charge of Sam Katzman, had caught onto the fad and perpetuated it with *The Man Who Turned to Stone, Creature with the Atom Brain, Earth vs. the Flying Saucers*, and a beloved misfire, *The Giant Claw*. At American International Pictures (AIP), Allied Artists, Universal-International, and Paramount, producers like Roger Corman, Bert I. Gordon, Herman Cohen, William Alland, Albert Zugsmith, and George Pal created entertaining sci-fi thrillers that were virtually guaranteed to show profits. Even giant MGM experimented with the genre, translating Shakespeare's *The Tempest* into a hyper-ambitious thriller called *Forbidden Planet.*

Columbia's two-reel unit noticed all of this and put the Stooges into their first science fiction adventure, *Space Ship Sappy* (1957). There are three sci-fi Stooge adventures (the others are *Outer Space Jitters* [1957] and *Flying Saucer Daffy* [1958]). These three aren't just the best of the Joe Besser/Stooges shorts but some of the most oddly funny of the Stooges' 1950s output. The science fiction elements give each tremendous topicality, as rocketry, space travel, missile technology, and Futurism absorbed many Americans. Further, although all of the boys' Columbia shorts, all the way back to 1934, have an ageless appeal, the sci-fi trio seems particularly modern—and *aware* of that modernity. The boys are pulling us along for the ride and also want us to notice how hip they've become. Sixtyish when they shot the sci-fi comedies (Joe Besser was a bit younger), the boys seem rejuvenated, almost lighthearted. Hairstyles, at Joe's suggestion, are more restrained than before. As the two-reel era was ending, the Stooges looked to the future.

Jack and Jules White, free for the moment of remakes and talking horses, designed *Space Ship Sappy* as a picaresque adventure. The boys are hungry vagabonds who read a want ad posted by a professor who seeks three experienced sailors. In a sylvan rural area, the boys find the address, a startlingly modern house topped with a dramatic, needle-like spire. Joe is enthused: "Dig the crazy house the professor lives in!" Moe laughs so hard he lights his nose instead of the stub of his cigar.

Inside, the boys meet Professor A. K. Rimple (Benny Rubin) and his statuesque blonde daughter (Doreen Woodbury). Almost before the boys know it, the "house" has blasted off for the planet Sunev—"Venus" spelled backwards, as the professor helpfully reveals.

Joe is convinced he's doomed: "I don't wanna die, I-I *can't* die! I haven't seen *The Eddy Duchin Story* yet!"—an absurd and amusing plug for the latest film starring Columbia's most valuable property, Kim Novak.

Benny Rubin, with skills honed on showboats and in burlesque and vaude-ville, is a stitch as the "Cherman" professor. He can't wait to finish the journey. "Ah, de anticipation!" he enthuses. "Ohh! I tink somewhat we're approaching Sunev! Vait until you see Sunev! It is de most beautiful—in my life, I haff never—dis is de most gor—I vonder vot it looks like!"

After landing, the boys are sent outside to investigate flora and fauna—"Oh, boy," gushes Joe, "dames!"—and run into sexy Sunevian cannibal chicks and a dinosaur.

Although *Space Ship Sappy* follows the strictures of contemporaneous sci-fi cinema—which mandate a reckless male scientist, a good-looking gal scientist, a giant monster, exotic but dangerous babes (as in Howco's 1953 release *Mesa of Lost Women* and many others)—it also replicates the cheapness and illogic of those films, with patently phony, and very funny, spaceship model work; alien primitives who wear mascara and high heels; a completely confabulated alien language ("Eye yi yi! Be bop!"); Larry's ability to open the door of the ship after it's already "above the world"; and more, including the fact that the professor has actually invited the Stooges on this scientific journey of a lifetime.

Although space travelers in *Rocketship X-M* and countless other sci-fi thrill-ers of the period encounter meteor swarms during their travels, Larry spies something even more unusual as he stares from a porthole: "Look! There's a big funny-lookin' bird and he's layin' eggs all over the sky! *Dozens* of 'em!"

Larry's astonished excitement is wonderfully expressed, and it's all a setup for a gag so intentionally dopey that it's hilarious: hen-sized eggs that fly through the porthole to splatter Moe in the face.

The sexy cannibal girls (Harriette Tarler, Lorraine Crawford, and Marilyn Hanold—who would be *Playboy*'s Playmate of the Month for June 1959) don't know how to kiss (they bite). The boys decide to teach them. "I know all about it!" Larry declares. "When I walk down the street, all the girls say, 'Lookit that kisser!'" But in a heartbeat, the boys are tied to posts, and the girls tickle their feet preparatory to donning hideous claws and fangs, a stewpot nearby. Only the dinosaur (well-integrated stock footage from the 1939 Hal Roach produc-tion *One Million B.C.*) diverts the women from dinner and gives the Stooges an opportunity to get away. But the boys enter the ship too quickly and knock the professor and his daughter cold. Moe isn't deterred: "Hey, fellas, I know how to run this! I used to fly a kite!"

The ship goes up and then, perilously, straight down. "Help!" Moe yells. "*Gevalt!*"

We dissolve to a Liars Club banquet, where the chairman (Emil Sitka) recognizes the boys as "the biggest liars in the world today."

Not all viewers like the ending (which has a nice payoff as Moe struggles to make an acceptance speech), but the bigger consideration of *Space Ship Sappy* is that Joe Besser comes into his own. He shows physical energy equal to Shemp's and handles his dialogue with robust enthusiasm. His gestures are broad and demonstrative, and he merges his prissy, scairdy-cat persona with the Stooges' more physical style. He's very much a Stooge.

Offhand references to IBM and Elvis Presley situate the short a consider-able cultural distance from the boys' Depression and wartime comedies. This is Modern America, and with this and the other sci-fi shorts, the Stooges position themselves for the fresh adulation and professional success that was just over the horizon.

Performer Profile: Benny Rubin
1899–1986

With vast experience in burlesque and vaudeville, dialect comic Benny Rubin was kept busy in movies and TV from 1928 to 1985. He was well liked by Red Skelton and Jack Benny and appeared with them frequently on their TV series. Rubin also showed up in many of Jerry Lewis's features of the 1960s.

Rubin's welcome appearances with the Stooges include the overenthusiastic sci-entist in *Space Ship Sappy*; the silly bearded gent in *Income Tax Sappy* who turns out to be an Internal Revue agent; and the boys' landlord in *Hoofs and Goofs*, who's sent to dreamland when Joe accidentally dribbles ether into his milk.

Rubin (and audiences) had particular fun when he trotted out his fractured "Cherman" accent and when he was given the freedom to ad lib.

A privately published autobiography, *Come Backstage with Me*, appeared in 1980.

Professor A. K. Rimple (Benny Rubin) looks on with no small horror as daughter Doreen Woodbury raises the alarm in *Space Ship Sappy* (1957), the first and best of the Stooges' science-fiction shorts.
Photo courtesy of the Stoogeum

Finally, a somber note: Over the years, stories have persisted that Columbia chief Harry Cohn was grooming lissome Doreen Woodbury for stardom. That may be, but her film career never got beyond the embryonic stage. During a February 1957 visit to New York City (more than two months before the April 18 release of *Space Ship Sappy*), Woodbury took an overdose of pills and committed suicide. She was thirty years old. Her death is a tragic coda to one of the Stooges' most exuberant two-reelers which, ironically, is the work for which Woodbury is best known today.

IN THE UNINTENTIONALLY HILARIOUS FEATURE *CAT-WOMEN OF THE MOON* (1953), a rocketship crew discovers a civilization of gorgeous, skimpily attired women. The male crewmembers fall for the beauties—one of whom has murderous powers of seduction that are literally hypnotic. The '50s produced a lot of these "lost women" sci-fi thrillers. *Queen of Outer Space* (directed by Ed Bernds), *Missile to the Moon*, and *Fire Maidens from Outer Space* are other examples, and in every one, men are manipulated like Play-Doh. The Stooges' *Outer Space Jitters* (1957) is a clever, imaginative parody of this peculiar sub-genre.

A title card informs us that we're about to visit the planet Sunev, "Somewhere in Outer Space." Opening without prelude or setup, *Outer Space Jitters* is all about the premise and how it unfolds, and in that, it's focused and pleasingly concise.

Although the Grand Zilch (Gene Roth) extends a cordial greeting to the boys and to their friend, Professor Jones (Emil Sitka), Sunev is a snake pit of conspiracy. The Zilch and the High Muckey Muck (Philip Van Zandt)—whose Sunevian veins run with electricity rather than blood—scheme to conquer Earth with an army of electronically controlled zombies. The bothersome visitors must be destroyed.

The short's primary set piece is the boys' encounter with a trio of sexy, electrically charged women (Harriette Tarler, Diana Darrin, and Arline Hunter), whose winged headpieces hold spark plugs. The girls' high-voltage kisses pack wallops: Unpopped popcorn that Larry has brought as a gift explodes right in his pocket, and a Cornish hen brought by Joe is cooked to a cinder.

At the banquet, the boys struggle mightily to manage the standard Sunevian fare of clamshells and battery acid. Out of patience at last, the High Muckey Muck reveals his intentions, so the boys grab Joe's hot-water bottle and spray Muckey Muck's back, producing a shower of sparks (a very good on-set effect) and a fatal short-circuit.

Young Dan Blocker (mistakenly billed on the title card as "Don") is Sunev's "showpiece" zombie, a gargantuan thing in coveralls, and with a face that looks like an unflattering caricature of a caveman. Cinematographer William Bradford often lit Blocker from below, so that the zombie's bushy brows, fangs, and enormous pug nose are highlighted. (Note to Dan: Better days are coming.)

Following the Stooges' energetic, panicked dashing through shadowy corridors, with the zombie close behind, Professor Jones locates a switch on the main control panel and shuts off the creature's power supply. As the boys set about destroying the mind-control machine, Larry accidentally catches Moe with a hammer. A moment later Moe is back with a wood plane, which he vigorously runs back and forth against Larry's forehead, raising an alarming amount of sawdust. The gag is one of the most violent the Stooges ever did, and one of the most grossly funny, too.

After the boys escape (Joe has put so much Sunevian gold in his pockets that his pants fall down, and he has to tie off the legs and hoist them like a sack), we discover that the adventure has been a bedtime story told to Baby Moe, Baby Larry, and Baby Joe by their dads, in a split-screen setup identical to the one used in *Creeps.*

The surreal final joke of Jack White's script is that the polite, middle-aged babysitter who arrives at the Stooges' door has a face like the zombie's—so the boys naturally abandon their kids and leap from the nearest window (their shadows quite visible on the skyscraper backdrop).

Stooges fans are not divided about the merits of *Outer Space Jitters.* They dislike it. Intensely. Much of the loathing is grounded in the obvious, and point-lessly noted, fact that Joe is neither Curly nor Shemp. Some hypercritical fans admit that the women are cute, but because of their antipathy to Joe, they will-fully ignore (or miss) the parodist elements and the quickly paced, linear plot.

When *Outer Space Jitters* was filmed in the early spring of 1957, the boys' shooting schedules for all-new shorts had been reduced from three days to two (the longtime standard, of course, had been four). Remakes carried on with one- and two-day shoots. *Outer Space Jitters* runs for more than sixteen minutes, which means that director Jules White got more than eight minutes of usable footage in the can each day—a blistering pace, particularly for aging stars who appear in virtually every scene.

As Steve Martin reminded us years later, "Comedy is not pretty." It's a lot of hard work, so although we're grateful that the boys save the world, we're even more grateful that they didn't collapse in exhausted heaps.

A point of trivia for sensualists is that starlet and August '59 *Playboy* Playmate Arline Hunter (who is paired with Joe in *Outer Space Jitters*) had been the sole player in an already notorious 1948 soft-core stag reel that was given the title *The Apple-Knockers and the Coke* when it was distributed by Grove Films in the 1970s. So startling is Hunter's resemblance to Marilyn Monroe that the grainy reel was for years attributed to MM.

JOE BESSER IS THE SOLID CENTER OF *FLYING SAUCER DAFFY* (1958), THE Stooges' final two-reel adventure into the fantastic. As written by Jack White (from a story by Warren Wilson), the short is an emotionally violent take on the Cinderella tale in which Joe is terribly abused by his loutish cousins, Moe and Larry, and by his slatternly aunt (Gail Bonney). And like Cinderella, Joe is sweet by nature, almost saintly—to a point.

The science fiction that propels the plot involves Moe and Larry's unreal-istic desire to photograph a flying saucer and walk away with *Facts and Figures* magazine's $10,000 prize. When Joe expresses his own desire to win, Larry scoffs, "He couldn't win ten thousand jelly beans!"

Joe inadvertently snaps a saucer as he's photographing a squirrel. Moe and Larry pass the image off as their own and blow the ten K on booze and broads. When the pair are accused of fraud (Joe had inadvertently snapped a paper plate driven in front of his lens by a gust of wind), Joe innocently follows their earlier orders by insisting that they took the photo. Driven from the family, Joe returns to a favorite pastime, camping.

And then a mechanical whirring causes Joe to look to the heavens . . .

The Stooges specialized in déclassé characterizations, but they never suggested "white trash"—until *Flying Saucer Daffy*. Selfish, crude, alternately mocking and angry, and immune to filth and clutter, Moe and Larry could be characters in a *MAD* magazine spoof of Tennessee Williams (whose unsparing eye and wide popularity probably inspired—and allowed—the awful nature of the boys and their mother). Mom spends her days drinking; Moe and Larry practically live at the racetrack. When Joe shows up with groceries, Moe and Larry fight over the goodies, and they try to take Joe's camera, too, a state-of-the-art Polaroid Speedliner Land Camera that's particularly appropriate in this tale of interstellar high tech.

As the fable unreels, Joe is punched, cracked, and poked. He absorbs the punishment, not because he's cowardly (he's not) but because he's the classic victim who's become complicit in his own abuse.

Still, he's curious about that abuse. After Moe painfully flicks Joe's nose— *bink!*—Joe says, "Do that again."

Bink!

"Again."

Bink!

"You," Joe says with mild disappointment, "do everything I tell you to!"

The exchange is smart as well as funny because it suggests that Joe, although on the receiving end of physical and psychic insult, is the person in charge.

Because of the inflated melodrama of much of White's script, and because Joe is emotionally and often physically separated from the others, the short plays like a Joe Besser film with a couple of other actors in unsympathetic support. Joe does his "Ooh, not so *hard*!" shtick a few times, but what he really wants to do is please Moe and Larry. To be able to do so would please *him*. But in their angry meanness, Moe and Larry prevent him.

That whirring sound we mentioned earlier is a real flying saucer, which arcs out of the sky and toward Joe in stock footage from the fine 1956 Columbia thriller *Earth vs. the Flying Saucers*. The saucer comes from the planet Zircon and is piloted by Electra (Diana Darrin) and Tyra (Bek Nelson), two ladies so beautiful, and so sweet, that Joe happily blurts, "Wow, what *mamas*!"

The girls snuggle close to help him take a photo of their ship, kiss him goodbye, and even leave him a Zirconian advertising card from a new and used

spaceship joint called
Sputnik-G.i-8, 200 Vapor
Boulevard, phone BLEEP
BLUEP BLOP.

Joe is so excited he can't
wait to get home, but when
he does, Auntie and the
cousins start in on him, and
the worm finally turns. Joe
double-punches Moe and
Larry, knocks out Auntie
with the backstroke of a
bottle, and nails his cousins
on their heads. Because the
outburst is justified, and
because we've been hoping
for it, it's even more satisfying to us than to Joe.

Now it's Joe's turn to
be feted in the pages of
Facts and Figures, and in a
later ticker-tape parade,
too. He's an international
hero, dressed to the nines
and greeting his public
from a limo, comfortably
ensconced between his new
best friends, Electra and Tyra.

Much-abused Joe finally gets evidence of extraterrestrial
visitors, courtesy of glam-aliens Bek Nelson (left) and Diana
Darrin, in *Flying Saucer Daffy* (1958).

Photo courtesy of the Stoogeum

Meanwhile, overlooking the parade route, Moe and Larry stew in a jail
cell, securely wrapped in strait-jackets and so miserable with their stupidity
that they bang their heads against the cell wall.

In Joe's overdue reward, and Moe and Larry's well-deserved punishment,
Flying Saucer Daffy defines itself as a morality tale. And with the Polaroid
camera, the comic reference to Russia's *Sputnik* (which, in real life, upset and
even terrified many Americans), the flying saucer scare/craze, and, especially,
its exploration of bad family mojo, the short is very modern.

The world was changing, rushing forward, becoming increasingly absorbed with the *new*—as Moe, Larry, and Joe discovered on December 20,
1957, the day shooting wrapped on *Flying Saucer Daffy*, and the day Jules
White had to inform the boys that, after a professional association with
Columbia Pictures dating to 1934, the Three Stooges had been fired.

They would prosper for another decade, but their greatest work was now
behind them.

Three Stooges Columbia Two-Reel Filmography

This is a filmography of all 190 Columbia shorts starring the Three Stooges.
Films are listed in order of release, not in the order in which they were shot.
When applicable, each title is followed by a working (pre-release) title, in [brackets] and plain *italics*.
Each short has been given a subjective but considered star rating on a * to **** scale.
Date of original theatrical release is followed by the uncut running time in minutes and seconds (00:00). The running times were noted during viewings and timings of each short, done expressly for this book.
A brief synopsis, in *italics*, follows each cast list.
Remakes and redos are noted in roman text following the synopsis.
KEY: P (producer). D (director). W (writer). Ph (photographer/cinematographer). w/ (with).

The Three Stooges

Moe Howard, Larry Fine, Curly Howard

1. ***Woman Haters*** ****½** May 5, 1934. 19:15. P: Jules White. D: Archie Gottler. W: Jerome S. Gottler. Ph: Joseph August. w/Marjorie White, Monte Collins, Bud Jamison, Snowflake, Walter Brennan. *"Woman hater" Larry tries to hide his engagement from his pals.*
2. ***Punch Drunks*** [*A Symphony of Punches*] ******* July 13, 1934. 17:29. P: Jules White. D: Lou Breslow. W: Moe Howard, Jerry Howard, Larry Fine (story), Jack Cluett (script). Ph: Henry Freulich. w/Arthur Houseman, Dorothy Granger, Billy Bletcher. *Curly is transformed into an unstoppable boxer whenever he hears "Pop Goes the Weasel."*
3. ***Men in Black*** ******* September 28, 1934. 18:04. P: Jules White. D: Raymond McCarey. W: Felix Adler. Ph: Benjamin Kline. w/Dell Henderson, Billy Gilbert, Ruth Hiatt, Jeanie Roberts. *Three undisciplined doctors run amuck in a hospital.*
4. ***Three Little Pigskins*** *****½** December 8, 1934. 18:24. P: Jules White. D: Raymond McCarey. W: Felix Adler, Griffin Jay. Ph: Henry Freulich. w/Walter Long, Lucille Ball, Gertie Green, Phyllis Crane. *A tough gambler mistakes three knuckleheads for college football stars and inserts them into a high-stakes game.*

5. *Horses' Collars* *** January 10, 1935. 18:02. P: Jules White (likely). D: Clyde Bruckman. W: Felix Adler. Ph: John Boyle. w/Dorothy Kent, Fred Kohler, Fred Kelsey. *The Stooges travel out west to help a young woman take back her ranch from a crooked gambler.*

6. *Restless Knights* ***½ February 20, 1935. 16:12. P: Jules White. D: Charles Lamont. W: Felix Adler. Ph: Benjamin Kline. w/Geneva Mitchell, Walter Brennan, George Baxter. *The queen's royal bodyguards get wind of a kidnap plot.*

7. *Pop Goes the Easel* *** March 29, 1935. 17:54. P: Jules White. D: Del Lord. W: Felix Adler. Ph: Henry Freulich. w/Bobby Burns, Phyllis Crane. *Three louts on the run from the cops take refuge inside an art academy.*

8. *Uncivil Warriors* **** April 26, 1935. 19:32. P: Jules White. D: Del Lord. W: Felix Adler. Ph: John Stumar. w/Ted Lorch, Bud Jamison, Phyllis Crane, James C. Morton, Heinie Conklin. *Three Union spies go behind Confederate lines to snatch valuable battle plans.*

9. *Pardon My Scotch* *** August 1, 1935. 18:44. P: Jules White. D: Del Lord. W: Andrew Bennison. Ph: George Meehan. w/James C. Morton, Nat Carr, Billy Gilbert. *Three handymen masquerade as the McSnort brothers, distillers of the world's finest Scotch.*

10. *Hoi Polloi* **** August 29, 1935. 17:50. P: Jules White (likely). D: Del Lord. W: Felix Adler. Ph: Benjamin Kline. w/Harry Holmes, Robert Graves, Bud Jamison, Phyllis Crane, Geneva Mitchell, James C. Morton. *A professor who believes that environment is the key to behavior bets a colleague that he can turn three trash collectors into gentlemen.*

11. *Three Little Beers* **** November 28, 1935. 16:11. P: Jules White. D: Del Lord. W: Clyde Bruckman. Ph: Benjamin Kline. w/Bud Jamison, Harry Semels, Eddie Laughton, Stanly Blystone. *Careless beer deliverymen get distracted and decide to play golf.*

12. *Ants in the Pantry* [*Pardon My Ants*] **** February 6, 1936. 17:42. P: Jules White. D: Preston Black (Jack White). W: Al Giebler. Ph: Benjamin Kline. w/ Clara Kimball Young, Isabelle LaMal, Bud Jamison, Harrison Greene, Vesey O'Davoren, Phyllis Crane. *Exterminators bombard a house with mice and other vermin in order to drum up business.*

13. *Movie Maniacs* [*G-A-G Men*] ***½ February 20, 1936. 17:11. P: Jules White. D: Del Lord. W: Felix Adler. Ph: Benjamin Kline. w/Bud Jamison, Mildred Harris, Kenneth Harlan, Harry Semels, Hilda Title. *Three boobs are allowed to take over a movie studio when they're mistaken for executives from the New York office.*

14. *Half Shot Shooters* ***½ April 30, 1936. 18:24. P: Jules White. D: Preston Black (Jack White). W: Clyde Bruckman. Ph: Benjamin Kline. w/Stanley Blystone, Vernon Dent. *Three inept soldiers raise the ire of their sergeant when they get their hands on an enormous cannon.*

15. *Disorder in the Court* [*Disorder in the Courtroom*] ***½ May 30, 1936. 16:32. P: Jules White. D: Preston Black (Jack White). W: Felix Adler. Ph: Benjamin Kline. w/Suzanne Kaaren, Bud Jamison, Harry Semels, Edward Le Saint, James C. Morton. *The Stooges go to court and swing into their nightclub act with friend Gale Tempest in order to clear Gale of murder.*

16. *A Pain in the Pullman* ***½ June 27, 1936. 19:46. P: Jules White. W/D: Preston Black (Jack White). Ph: Benjamin Kline. w/Bud Jamison, James C. Morton, Eddie Laughton, Phyllis Crane, Joe the Monkey. *Unemployed vaudevillians hop a night train out of town and create chaos.*

17. ***False Alarms*** **** August 16, 1936. 16:41. P: Jules White. D: Del Lord. W: John Grey. Ph: Benjamin Kline. w/Stanley Blystone, June Gittelson. *The world's dumbest firemen oversleep, meet some dames, and make life hell for their captain.*

18. ***Whoops, I'm an Indian!*** [*Frontier Daze*] **½ September 11, 1936. 17:20. P: Jules White. D: Del Lord. W: Searle Kramer, Herman Boxer (story); Clyde Bruckman (script). Ph: Benjamin Kline. w/Bud Jamison. *Three gamblers in Northwest Territory run afoul of a bad-tempered trapper.*

19. ***Slippery Silks*** *** December 27, 1936. 17:17. P: Jules White D: Preston Black (Jack White). W: Ewart Adamson. Ph: Benjamin Kline. w/Vernon Dent, Symona Boniface. *Furniture makers inherit a dress shop and become fashion designers.*

20. ***Grips, Grunts and Groans*** ***½ January 15, 1937. 18:42. P: Jules White. D: Preston Black (Jack White). W: Searle Kramer, Herman Boxer (story), Clyde Bruckman (script). Ph: Benjamin Kline. w/Harrison Greene, Casey Columbo, Blackie Whiteford, Elaine Waters. *Curly goes berserk when he smells Wild Hyacinth—a reaction that comes in handy when he has to impersonate a famed wrestler.*

21. ***Dizzy Doctors*** *** March 19, 1937. 17:39. P: Jules White. D: Del Lord. W: Al Ray. Ph: Benjamin Kline. w/Vernon Dent, Bud Jamison, Cy Schindell, June Gittelson. *Three saps invade a hospital to peddle the miracle elixir Brighto, which is good mainly for taking paint off cars.*

22. ***Three Dumb Clucks*** *** April 17, 1937. 16:50. P: Jules White. D: Del Lord. W: Clyde Bruckman. Ph: Andre Barlatier. w/Lynton Brent, Eddie Laughton, Lucille Lund. *The Stooges try to prevent Pa (played by Curly) from marrying a gold digger.*

23. ***Back to the Woods*** **½ May 14, 1937. 19:25. P: Jules White. D: Preston Black (Jack White). W: Searle Kramer (story), Andrew Bennison (script). Ph: George Meehan. w/Bud Jamison, Vernon Dent, Ted Lorch. *At Plymouth Colony, the Stooges try to make nice with the Indians.*

24. ***Goofs and Saddles*** *** July 2, 1937. 17:08. P: Jules White. D: Del Lord. W: Felix Adler. Ph: Benjamin Kline. w/Ted Lorch, Stanley Blystone, Hank Mann. *Three bumbling undercover agents are dispatched to bring in a cattle rustler.*

25. ***Cash and Carry*** [*Golddigging in the Treasury*] *** September 3, 1937. 18:19. P: Jules White. D: Del Lord. W: Clyde Bruckman, Elwood Ullman. Ph: Lucien Ballard. w/Harlene Wood, Sonny Bupp. *The Stooges upset the U.S. Treasury when they help themselves to stacks of greenbacks to pay for a crippled kid's operation.*

26. ***Playing the Ponies*** **½ October 15, 1937. 17:06. P: Jules White. D: Charles Lamont. W: Will Harr, Irving Frisch (story), Al Giebler, Elwood Ullman, Charley Melson (script). Ph: Allen Siegler. w/Nick Copeland, Lew Davis, William Irving, Billy Bletcher. *The boys are conned into trading their restaurant for a racehorse that won't run.*

27. ***The Sitter Downers*** *** November 26, 1937. 15:34. P: Jules White. D: Del Lord. W: Ewart Adamson. Ph: George Meehan. w/James C. Morton, Betty Mack, June Gittelson, Marcia Healy. *The father of the boys' sweeties says "no marriage" until the boys provide his daughters with a house.*

28. ***Termites of 1938*** ***½ January 7, 1938. 16:38. P: Charley Chase, Hugh McCollum, D: Del Lord. W: Elwood Ullman. Ph: Andre Barlatier. w/Bess Flowers, Bud Jamison, Dorothy Granger. *Three exterminators who are mistaken for professional escorts make a mess of a society party.*

29. *Wee Wee Monsieur* [*The Foreign Legioneers*] *** February 18, 1938. 17:34. P: Jules White. D: Del Lord. W: Searle Kramer. Ph: Andre Barlatier. w/Bud Jamison, Vernon Dent, William J. Irving, John Lester Johnson. *The Stooges accidentally join the French Foreign Legion and must rescue their captain from a bloodthirsty Arab chieftain.*

30. *Tassels in the Air* *** April 1, 1938. 17:02. P: Charley Chase, Hugh McCollum. D: Charley Chase. W: Al Giebler, Elwood Ullman. Ph: Allen Siegler. w/Bess Flowers, Vernon Dent, Bud Jamison. *A society dame mistakes Moe for a famous interior decorator and hires all three boys to redo her home.*

31. *Healthy, Wealthy and Dumb* [*Cuckoo Over Contests*] ***½ May 20, 1938. 16:23. P: Jules White. D: Del Lord. W: Searle Kramer. Ph: Allen Siegler. w/James C. Morton, Bud Jamison, Lucille Lund, Jean Carmen, Earlene Heath. *When Curly wins a jingle contest, the boys take a swank hotel room and arouse the interest of a trio of gold diggers.*

32. *Violent Is the Word for Curly* *** July 2, 1938. 17:49. P: Charley Chase, Hugh McCollum. D: Charley Chase. W: Al Giebler, Ellwood Ullman. Ph: Lucien Ballard. w/Gladys Gale, Marjorie Dean, Bud Jamison. *Three gas station attendants are mistaken for college professors and make some changes at a stuffy school for women.*

33. *Three Missing Links* ** July 29, 1938. 18:01. P/D: Jules White. W: Searle Kramer. Ph: Henry Freulich. w/Monte Collins, James C. Morton, Jane Hamilton, John Lester Johnson, Ray "Crash" Corrigan. *The Stooges are aspiring actors who travel to a remote isle to star in* Jilted in the Jungle.

34. *Mutts to You* [*Muts to You*] **½ October 14, 1938. 18:02. P: Charley Chase, Hugh McCollum. D: Charley Chase. W: Al Giebler, Elwood Ullman. Ph: Allen Siegler. w/Bess Flowers, Lane Chandler, Vernon Dent, Bud Jamison. *Operators of a dog-wash service take in a baby they believe has been abandoned.*

35. *Flat Foot Stooges* ** November 25, 1938. 15:24. P: Charley Chase, Hugh McCollum. W/D: Charley Chase. Ph: Lucien Ballard. w/Chester Conklin, Dick Curtis, Lola Jensen. *Small-town firemen are put to the test when a salesman who wants them to upgrade their equipment resorts to sabotage.*

36. *Three Little Sew and Sews* [*Three Goofy Gobs*] *** January 6, 1939. 15:46. P: Jules White. D: Del Lord. W: Ewart Adamson. Ph: Lucien Ballard. w/Harry Semels, Phyllis Barry, James C. Morton, Bud Jamison, Vernon Dent. *Three sailors pose as officers and get mixed up with spies.*

37. *We Want Our Mummy* ***½ February 24, 1939. 16:26. P: Jules White. D: Del Lord. W: Searle Kramer, Elwood Ullman. Ph: Allen Siegler. w/Bud Jamison, James C. Morton, Robert Williams, Dick Curtis, Ted Lorch, Eddie Laughton. *Three addled investigators travel to Egypt to locate a missing professor and the mummy of King Rutentutin.*

38. *A Ducking They Did Go* *** April 7, 1939. 16:14. P: Jules White. D: Del Lord. W: Andrew Bennison. Ph: Lucien Ballard. w/Lynton Brent, Bud Jamison, Vernon Dent, Cy Schindell. *The boys are bamboozled into selling memberships to a nonexistent duck club.*

39. *Yes, We Have No Bonanza* [*Yes, We Have No Bonanzas*] ***½ May 19, 1939. 16:02. P: Jules White. D: Del Lord. W: Elwood Ullman, Searle Kramer. Ph: Lucien Ballard. w/Dick Curtis, Lynton Brent, Vernon Dent, Suzanne Kaaren, Lola Jensen, Jean Carmen. *Gold prospectors who want to help their sweeties dig up stolen loot.*

40. *Saved by the Belle* ** June 30, 1939. 17:21. P: Charley Chase, Hugh McCollum. D: Charley Chase. W: Elwood Ullman, Searle Kramer. Ph: Allen Siegler. w/ Carmen LaRoux, Leroy Mason, Gino Corrado. *Authorities in a banana republic accuse three clothing salesmen of plotting to assassinate the president.*

41. *Calling All Curs* [*Dog Hospital*] *** August 25, 1939. 17:20. P/D: Jules White. W: Elwood Ullman, Searle Kramer. Ph: not credited. w/Lynton Brent, Cy Schindell, Beatrice Blinn, Dorothy Moore, Isabelle LaMal. *Dog doctors Larry, Curly, and Moe chase down thugs who have kidnapped a prize pooch.*

42. *Oily to Bed, Oily to Rise* **** October 6, 1939. 18:12. P/D: Jules White. W: Andrew Bennison, Mauri Grashon. Ph: Henry Freulich. w/Dick Curtis, Richard Fiske, Eva McKenzie, Eddie Laughton, James Craig, Lorna Gray. *The Stooges pursue swindlers who have the deed to oil-rich land beneath a widow's ranch.*

43. *Three Sappy People* [*Three Sloppy People*] *** December 1, 1939. 17:17. P/D: Jules White. W: Clyde Bruckman. Ph: George Meehan. w/Lorna Gray, Don Beddoe, Bud Jamison. *A man mistakes the boys for psychiatrists and asks them to cure his thrill-seeking young wife.*

44. *You Nazty Spy* [*Oh, You Nazty Spy!*] ***½ January 19, 1940. 17:57. P/D: Jules White. W: Clyde Bruckman, Felix Adler. Ph: Harry Davis. w/Dick Curtis, Don Beddoe, Richard Fiske, John Tyrrell, Lorna Gray, Florine Dickson. *Industrialists who want to go to war tap a brainless paperhanger to be dictator.*

45. *Rockin' Through the Rockies* [*Nell's Belles*] **½ March 8, 1940. 17:20. P/D: Jules White. W: Clyde Bruckman. Ph: Henry Freulich. w/Dorothy Appleby, Lorna Gray, Linda Winters. *The boys guide three beautiful showgirls through Indian country.*

46. *A Plumbing We Will Go* **** April 19, 1940. 17:32. P: Del Lord, Hugh McCollum. D: Del Lord. W: Elwood Ullman. Ph: Benjamin Kline. w/Bess Flowers, Symona Boniface, Bud Jamison, Eddie Laughton, Dudley Dickerson. *The Stooges pose as plumbers and make a mess of a house during a swanky dinner party.*

47. *Nutty but Nice* *½ June 14, 1940. 17:44. P/D: Jules White. W: Clyde Bruckman, Felix Adler. Ph: John Stumar. w/Vernon Dent, John Tyrrell. *A doctor implores the boys to cheer up a little girl who misses her father.*

48. *How High Is Up?* ***½ July 26, 1940. 16:25. P: Del Lord, Hugh McCollum. D: Del Lord. W: Elwood Ullman. Ph: Allen Siegler. w/Vernon Dent, Edmund Cobb. *Three handymen pass themselves off as high-iron workers.*

49. *From Nurse to Worse* **½ August 23, 1940. 16:43. P/D: Jules White. W: Clyde Bruckman. Ph: Benjamin Kline. w/Vernon Dent, Lynton Brent, Dorothy Appleby, Cy Schindell. *A "friend" convinces the boys that they can grab a big insurance payoff if Curly acts like a dog.*

50. *No, Census, No Feeling* *** October 4, 1940. 16:30. P: Del Lord, Hugh McCollum. D: Del Lord. W: Harry Edwards, Elwood Ullman. Ph: Lucien Ballard. w/Vernon Dent, Symona Boniface. *Census takers make a mess of a football game and a society lady's bridge party.*

51. *Cookoo Cavaliers* [*Beauty a la Mud*] *** November 15, 1940. 17:24. P/D: Jules White. W: Ewart Adamson. Ph: Henry Freulich. w/Dorothy Appleby, Lynton Brent, Jack O'Shea. *The boys travel to Mexico to operate a beauty parlor.*

52. *Boobs in Arms* [*All This and Bullets Too*] ***½ December 27, 1940. 17:55. P/D: Jules White. W: Felix Adler. Ph: John Stumar. w/Richard Fiske, Evelyn Young. *The Stooges join the army and discover that their tough sergeant is a guy they annoyed in civilian life.*

53. *So Long, Mr. Chumps* *** February 7, 1941. 17:21. P/D: Jules White. W: Clyde Bruckman, Felix Adler. Ph: Barney McGill. w/Eddie Laughton, Dorothy Appleby, Vernon Dent, Bruce Bennett. *The boys go to prison to free an innocent man.*

54. *Dutiful but Dumb* **½ March 21, 1941. 16:47. P: Del Lord, Hugh McCollum. D: Del Lord. W: Elwood Ullman. Ph: Benjamin Kline. w/Vernon Dent, Bud Jamison, James C. Morton, Fred Kelsey. *In the unstable nation of Vulgaria, the boys get in trouble when they try to photograph a new invisible-ray machine.*

55. *All the World's a Stooge* ***½ May 16, 1941. 16:04. P: Del Lord, Hugh McCollum. D: Del Lord. W: John Grey. Ph: Benjamin Kline. w/Emory Parnell, Lelah Tyler, Olaf Hytten, Bud Jamison, Symona Boniface. *When a rich man's wife decides she wants to adopt a refugee, her husband dresses the Stooges like little kids and brings them home.*

56. *I'll Never Heil Again* *** July 11, 1941. 18:04. P/D: Jules White. W: Felix Adler, Clyde Bruckman. Ph: L. W. O'Connell. w/Mary Ainslee, Vernon Dent, Bud Jamison, Don Beddoe, Duncan Renaldo. *Power brokers in Moronica send a sexy spy to get rid of dictator Hailstone.*

57. *An Ache in Every Stake* ***½ August 22, 1941. 18:06. P: Del Lord, Hugh McCollum. D: Del Lord. W: Lloyd A. French. Ph: Philip Tannura. w/Vernon Dent, Bess Flowers, Bud Jamison, Gino Corrado, Symona Boniface. *Three icemen fill in as cooks at the birthday party of a man they'd upset earlier in the day.*

58. *In the Sweet Pie and Pie* [*Well, I'll Be Hanged*] **** October 16, 1941. 17:25. P/D: Jules White. W: Ewart Adamson. Ph: George Meehan. w/Dorothy Appleby, Richard Fiske, Mary Ainslee, Ethelreda Leopold, John Tyrrell. *Three dames who need to get married in a hurry get hitched to three cons who are scheduled to hang—and then must live with them when the boys are pardoned.* Stock footage: *Hoi Polloi.*

59. *Some More of Samoa* *** December 4, 1941. 16:46. P: Del Lord, Hugh McCollum. D: Del Lord. W: Harry Edwards, Elwood Ullman. Ph: L. W. O'Connell. w/Mary Ainslee, Symona Boniface, Tiny Ward, Louise Carver, Duke York. *Three tree surgeons travel to the isle of Rhum Boogie to locate a rare persimmon tree.*

60. *Loco Boy Makes Good* [*Poor but Dishonest*] ** January 8, 1942. 17:24. P/D: Jules White. W: Felix Adler, Clyde Bruckman. Ph: John Stumar. w/Dorothy Appleby, Vernon Dent, Bud Jamison, John Tyrrell, Eddie Laughton. *The boys help a widow remodel her hotel dining room into a ritzy supper club.*

61. *Cactus Makes Perfect* ***½ February 26, 1942. 17:16. P: Del Lord, Hugh McCollum. D: Del Lord. W: Elwood Ullman, Monte Collins. Ph: Benjamin Kline. w/Monte Collins, Vernon Dent, Ernie Adams. *The Stooges take Curly's gold-finding device out west and strike it rich.*

62. *What's the Matador?* [*Run, Bull, Run*] **½ April 23, 1942. 16:18. P/D: Jules White. W: Jack White, Saul Ward. Ph: L. W. O'Connell. w/Suzanne Kaaren, Harry Burns, Dorothy Appleby, Eddie Laughton. *Comedy bullfighters in Mexico pique a jealous husband and meet a real bull.*

63. *Matri-Phony* *** July 2, 1942. 17:05. P: Del Lord, Hugh McCollum. D: Harry Edwards. W: Elwood Ullman, Monte Collins. Ph: George Meehan. w/Vernon Dent, Marjorie Deanne. *A horny, Romanesque emperor falls in love when he gets a load of Curly in drag.*

64. *Three Smart Saps* [*Father's in Jail Again*] ***½ July 30, 1942. 16:39. P/D: Jules White. W: Clyde Bruckman. Ph: Benjamin Kline. w/Bud Jamison, John Tyrrell,

Eddie Laughton, Julie Gibson, Julie Duncan, Ruth Skinner. *The Stooges' fiancées send the boys to rescue their father, a warden who's being held in his own jail.*
65. ***Even as I.O.U.*** *½ September 18, 1942. 15:36. P: Del Lord, Hugh McCollum. D: Del Lord. W: Felix Adler. Ph: L. W. O'Connell. w/Stanley Blystone, Bud Jamison, Ruth Skinner, Billy Bletcher (voice). *When they try to help an evicted woman and her daughter, the Stooges become the owners of a run-out racehorse.*
66. ***Sock-a-Bye-Baby*** [*Their First Baby*] **½ November 13, 1942. 17:48. P/D: Jules White. W: Clyde Bruckman. Ph: Benjamin Kline. w/Julie Gibson, Clarence Straight, Bud Jamison, Joyce Gardner. *A baby left on the boys' doorstep turns out to have been kidnapped.*
67. ***They Stooge to Conga*** *** January 1, 1943. 15:30. P: Del Lord, Hugh McCollum. D: Del Lord. W: Elwood Ullman, Monte Collins. Ph: George Meehan. w/ Vernon Dent, John Tyrrell, Lynton Brent, Dudley Dickerson. *Three roving handymen stumble into a house full of Axis spies.*
68. ***Dizzy Detectives*** [*Idiots Deluxe*] *** February 5, 1943. 18:33. P/D: Jules White. W: Felix Adler. Ph: Benjamin Kline. P/D: Jules White. W: Felix Adler. Ph: Benjamin Kline. w/John Tyrrell, Bud Jamison, Lynton Brent. *Three rookie cops go up against the "Ape Man" gang that's terrorizing the city.*
69. ***Spook Louder*** *** April 2, 1943. 16:00. P: Del Lord, Hugh McCollum. D: Del Lord. W: Clyde Bruckman. Ph: John Stumar. w/William Kelly, Ted Lorch, Stanley Blystone, Symona Boniface, Charles Middleton. *Door-to-door salesmen have a peculiar adventure inside the home of a crazy inventor.*
70. ***Back from the Front*** [*A Sailor's Mess*] **½ May 28, 1943. 17:51. P/D: Jules White. W: Jack White, Ewart Adamson. Ph: John Stumar. w/Vernon Dent, Bud Jamison, Stanley Blystone. *The Stooges are Merchant Mariners who wind up aboard a German raider.*
71. ***Three Little Twirps*** ** July 9, 1943. 15:26. P: Del Lord, Hugh McCollum. D: Harry Edwards. W: Monte Collins, Elwood Ullman. Ph: John Stumar. w/ Stanley Blystone, Bud Jamison, Chester Conklin, Duke York. *After they wreck a batch of circus posters, the boys are put to work beneath the big top.*
72. ***Higher Than a Kite*** *** July 30, 1943. 17:28. P: Del Lord, Hugh McCollum, D: Del Lord. W: Elwood Ullman, Monte Collins. Ph: Benjamin Kline. w/Vernon Dent, Dick Curtis. *Three RAF mechanics outwit Nazi officers in Germany.*
73. ***I Can Hardly Wait*** [*Nothing but the Tooth*] ** August 13, 1943. 18:29. P/D: Jules White. W: Clyde Bruckman. Ph: John Stumar. w/Bud Jamison, Dick Curtis, Adele Mara. *After a night gobbling rationed food, Curly gets a toothache that gives him a terrible nightmare.*
74. ***Dizzy Pilots*** [*Pest Pilots*] **½ September 24, 1943. 16:52. P/D: Jules White. W: Clyde Bruckman. Ph: Benjamin Kline. w/Richard Fiske, Harry Semels, Al Thompson. *The boys demonstrate their new airplane for representatives of the military.*
75. ***Phony Express*** **½ November 18, 1943. 17:11. P: Del Lord, Hugh McCollum. D: Del Lord. W: Elwood Ullman, Monte Collins. Ph: John Stumar. w/Bud Jamison, John Merton, Snub Pollard, Chester Conklin. *Patent-medicine salesmen who are mistaken for lawmen are enlisted to capture a notorious bandit.*
76. ***A Gem of a Jam*** **½ December 30, 1943. 16:26. P: Hugh McCollum. W/D: Del Lord. Ph: John Stumar. w/Bud Jamison, Fred Kelsey, Dudley Dickerson. *Crooks who mistake the Stooges for doctors chase them into a creepy warehouse.*
77. ***Crash Goes the Hash*** *** February 5, 1944. 17:35. P/D: Jules White. W: Felix Adler. Ph: George Meehan. w/Vernon Dent, Bud Jamison, Dick Curtis, Symona

Boniface. *Laundrymen who are mistaken for reporters try to get the goods on a con man who wants to marry a society matron.*

78. **Busy Buddies** *½ March 18, 1944. 16:45. P: Hugh McCollum. D: Del Lord. W: Del Lord, Elwood Ullman. Ph: George Meehan. w/Vernon Dent, Fred Kelsey, Eddie Laughton, John Tyrrell. *Curly enters a cow-milking contest.*

79. **The Yoke's on Me** [*Fowled by a Fowl*] * ½ May 26, 1944. 16:10. P/D: Jules White. W: Clyde Bruckman. Ph: Glen Gano. w/Bob McKenzie, Emmett Lynn. *The boys run into three escapees from a stateside internment center for Japanese.*

80. **Idle Roomers** **½ July 16, 1944. 16:50. P: Hugh McCollum. D: Del Lord. W: Del Lord, Elwood Ullman. Ph: Glen Gano. w/Christine McIntyre, Duke York, Vernon Dent, Eddie Laughton. *A wolf man invades a hotel where the Stooges work as bellmen.*

81. **Gents Without Cents** [*Tenderized Hams*] **½ September 22, 1944. 18:59. P/D: Jules White. W: Felix Adler. Ph: Benjamin Kline. w/Lindsay, Laverne, Betty, John Tyrrell, Lynton Brent. *The boys and three female dancers put on a variety show for shipbuilders.*

82. **No Dough Boys** [*The New World Odor*] *** November 24, 1944. 16:54. P/D: Jules White. W: Felix Adler. Ph: George Meehan. w/Vernon Dent, Christine McIntyre. *The Stooges are mistaken for Japanese soldiers and then run into Nazi spies.*

83. **Three Pests in a Mess** *** January 19, 1945. 15:17. P: Hugh McCollum. W/D: Del Lord. Ph: Benjamin Kline. w/Vernon Dent, Christine McIntyre, Victor Travers, Snub Pollard. *After shooting a mannequin, the Stooges think they've committed murder and try to hide the "body" in a pet cemetery.*

84. **Booby Dupes** **½ March 17, 1945. 17:02. P: Hugh McCollum. W/D: Del Lord. Ph: Glen Gano. w/Vernon Dent, Rebel Randall, John Tyrrell, Snub Pollard. *The boys buy a boat and are mistaken for Japanese sailors by an American pilot.*

85. **Idiots Deluxe** [*The Malady Lingers On*] *** July 20, 1945. 17:29. P/D: Jules White. W: Elwood Ullman. Ph: Glen Gano. w/Vernon Dent. *In a courtroom, Moe explains why he assaulted Larry and Curly during a rustic getaway.*

86. **If a Body Meets a Body** [*Nearly in the Dough*] *** August 30, 1945. 18:10. P/D: Jules White. W: Jack White. Ph: Benjamin Kline. w/Fred Kelsey, Ted Lorch, Joe Palma. *In a spooky mansion, the boys are scared silly before the reading of a will.*

87. **Micro-Phonies** ***½ November 15, 1945. 16:49. P: Hugh McCollum. W/D: Edward Bernds. Ph: Glen Gano. w/Christine McIntyre, Symona Boniface, Gino Corrado, Sam Flint, Bess Flowers, Lynton Brent. *A talented singer from high society wants to succeed on her own merits and goes along when Curly impersonates her at a party.*

88. **Beer Barrel Polecats** [*Three Duds in the Suds*] **½ January 10, 1946. 17:20. P/D: Jules White. W: Gilbert W. Pratt. Ph: George Kelley. w/Vernon Dent, Eddie Laughton. *The boys are sent to prison for bootlegging.* Stock footage from *In the Sweet Pie and Pie* and *So Long, Mr. Chumps.*

89. **A Bird in the Head** *** February 28, 1946. 17:17. P: Hugh McCollum. W/D: Edward Bernds. Ph: Burnett Guffey. w/Vernon Dent, Robert Williams, Frank Lackteen, Art Miles. *A crazed scientist with a big gorilla covets Curly's brain.*

90. **Uncivil War Birds** [*Three Southern Dumbbells*] *** March 29, 1946. 17:33. P/D: Jules White. W: Clyde Bruckman, Jules White. Ph: Philip Tannura. w/Robert Williams, Ted Lorch, Faye Williams, Eleanor Counts, Marilyn Johnson. *The boys have to stay a step ahead of soldiers from both sides when Moe and Larry join the Union Army and Curly enlists with the Confederates.*

91. *Three Troubledoers* *** April 25, 1946. 17:02. P: Hugh McCollum. D: Edward Bernds. W: Jack White. Ph: George Kelley. w/Christine McIntyre, Dick Curtis. *Out west, the boys run afoul of Badlands Blackie.*

92. *Monkey Businessmen* [*Sanitarium Stooge*] *** June 20, 1946. 18:00. P: Hugh McCollum. W/D: Edward Bernds. Ph: Philip Tannura. w/Kenneth MacDonald, Fred Kelsey, Jean Donahue (Willes), Snub Pollard. *The boys uncover fraud at a crooked rest home.*

93. *Three Loan Wolves* [*In Hock*] *½ July 4, 1946. 16:41. P/D: Jules White. W: Felix Adler. Ph: George Kelley. w/Harold Brauer, Beverly Warren, Jackie Jackson. *The Stooges are pawnbrokers who explain to their boy how they came to adopt him.*

94. *G.I. Wanna Home* **½ September 5, 1946. 15:43. P/D: Jules White. W: Felix Adler. Ph: George Kelley. w/Ethelreda Leopold, Judy Malcolm, Doris Houck, Symona Boniface. *A housing shortage forces the boys to set up housekeeping in a vacant lot and then, after they're married, in a minuscule cottage.*

95. *Rhythm and Weep* [*Acting Up*] **½ October 3, 1946. 17:38. P/D: Jules White. W: Felix Adler. Ph: Philip Tannura. w/Jack Norton, Ruth Godfrey, Nita Bieber, Gloria Patrice. *The boys team with three dancers to develop an act for a new show.*

96. *Three Little Pirates* *** December 5, 1946. 18:00. P: Hugh McCollum. D: Edward Bernds. W: Clyde Bruckman. Ph: Philip Tannura. w/Christine McIntyre, Vernon Dent, Robert Williams, Dorothy DeHaven. *The boys impersonate Arabian royalty on a strange island still ruled by pirates.*

97. *Half-Wits Holiday* [*No Gents—No Cents*] **½ January 9, 1947. 17:28. P/D: Jules White. W: Zion Myers. Ph: George Kelley. w/Vernon Dent, Barbara Slater, Ted Lorch, Symona Boniface, Emil Sitka. *A professor claims he can make gentlemen of the Stooges.* The final Stooges short to feature Curly.

The Three Stooges

Moe Howard, Larry Fine, Shemp Howard

98. *Fright Night* *** March 6, 1947. 17:14. P: Hugh McCollum. D: Edward Bernds. W: Clyde Bruckman. Ph: Philip Tannura. w/Harold Brauer, Dick Wessel, Cy Schindell, Claire Carleton. *When the Stooges let a boxer get out of condition, the guy's manager comes after them.*

99. *Out West* *** April 24, 1947. 17:36. P: Hugh McCollum. D: Edward Bernds. W: Clyde Bruckman. Ph: George Kelley. w/Christine McIntyre, Jack Norman, Jacques O'Mahoney, Stanley Blystone. *A slick owlhoot who has kidnapped a girl's father thinks the Stooges have struck gold.*

100. *Hold That Lion!* [*The Lion and the Louse*] *** July 17, 1947. 16:26. P/D: Jules White. W: Felix Adler. Ph: George Kelley. w/Kenneth MacDonald, Emil Sitka, Dudley Dickerson, Jerry (Curly) Howard. *The boys board a train to chase after a swindler.*

101. *Brideless Groom* [*Love and Learn*] **** September 11, 1947. 16:50. P: Hugh McCollum. D: Edward Bernds. W: Clyde Bruckman. Ph: Vincent Farrar. w/Dee Green, Christine McIntyre, Emil Sitka, Doris Colleen (Houck). *Shemp is besieged by old girlfriends who find out he must marry within hours or lose an inheritance.*

102. *Sing a Song of Six Pants* [*Where the Vest Begins*] **½ October 30, 1947. 16:52. P/D: Jules White. W: Felix Adler. Ph: Henry Freulich. w/Harold Brauer, Virginia

Hunter, Vernon Dent, Phil Arnold, Cy Schindell. *Owners of a tailor shop are visited by a fugitive bank robber.*

103. ***All Gummed Up*** [*Sweet Vita-Mine*] **½* December 18, 1947. 18:17. P/D: Jules White. W: Felix Adler. Ph: Allen Siegler. w/Christine McIntyre, Emil Sitka. *The boys are pharmacists who concoct goop that restores youth.*

104. ***Shivering Sherlocks*** ***½ January 8, 1948. 17:08. P: Hugh McCollum. D: Del Lord. W: Del Lord, Elwood Ullman. Ph: Allen Siegler. w/Christine McIntyre, Kenneth MacDonald, Frank Lackteen, Duke York. *When the boys visit an abandoned mansion that's been inherited by a friend, they discover the place is a hideout for criminals.*

105. ***Pardon My Clutch*** ***½ February 26, 1948. 17:40. P: Hugh McCollum. D: Edward Bernds. W: Clyde Bruckman. Ph: Allen Siegler. w/Matt McHugh, Emil Sitka, Alyn Lockwood. *A friend of Shemp's who suggests the boys take a restful trip sells them his old car.*

106. ***Squareheads of the Round Table*** [*Three Stooges in King Arthur's Court*] ***½ March 4, 1948. 18:05. P: Hugh McCollum. W/D: Edward Bernds. Ph: Allen Siegler. w/Christine McIntyre, Vernon Dent, Philip Van Zandt, Jacques O'Mahoney. *Three troubadours facilitate the romance between the king's daughter and a blacksmith.*

107. ***Fiddlers Three*** *** May 6, 1948. 17:08. P/D: Jules White. W: Felix Adler. Ph: Allen Siegler. w/Vernon Dent, Philip Van Zandt, Virginia Hunter. *The king's daughter must marry before three royal fiddlers can wed.*

108. ***The Hot Scots*** [*Scotland Yardbirds*] *** July 8, 1948. 17:13. P: Hugh McCollum. W/D: Edward Bernds. Ph: Allen Siegler. w/Christine McIntyre, Herbert Evans, Ted Lorch, Charles Knight. *Gardeners who become "yard men" for Scotland Yard meet crooks and ghosts in a Scottish castle.*

109. ***Heavenly Daze*** [*Heaven's Above*] *** September 2, 1948. 16:59. P/D: Jules White. W: Zion Myers. Ph: Allen Siegler. w/Vernon Dent, Sam McDaniel, Victor Travers, Symona Boniface. *Angel Shemp is sent from heaven to reform Moe and Larry.*

110. ***I'm a Monkey's Uncle*** *** October 7, 1948. 15:56. P/D: Jules White. W: Zion Myers. Ph: George Kelley. w/Dee Green, Virginia Hunter, Nancy Saunders, Cy Schindell, Joe Palma. *The Stone Age Stooges fight rivals for their women.*

111. ***Mummy's Dummies*** *** November 4, 1948. 15:47. P: Hugh McCollum. D: Edward Bernds. W: Elwood Ullman. Ph: Allen Siegler. w/Philip Van Zandt, Ralph Dunn, Vernon Dent, Dee Green, Suzanne Ridgeway. *Used-chariot dealers in Ancient Egypt help the king expose a crooked prime minister.*

112. ***Crime on Their Hands*** ***½ December 9, 1948. 17:34. P: Hugh McCollum. D: Edward Bernds. W: Elwood Ullman. Ph: Henry Freulich. w/Kenneth MacDonald, Christine McIntyre, Frank Lackteen. *The boys impersonate reporters and get into a jam when Shemp swallows a valuable diamond.*

113. ***The Ghost Talks*** [*That's the Spirit*] ** February 3, 1949. 16:17. P/D: Jules White. W: Felix Adler. Ph: M. A. Anderson. w/Phil Arnold (voice only), Nancy Saunders. *Inside a creepy castle, three cartage men meet a talking suit of armor.*

114. ***Who Done It?*** **** March 3, 1949. 16:31. P: Hugh McCollum. W/D: Edward Bernds. Ph: Ira H. Morgan. w/Christine McIntyre, Kenneth MacDonald, Emil Sitka, Dudley Dickerson, Duke York. *Inside a dark mansion, three inept detectives run into killers, a talking corpse, and "The Goon."*

115. ***Hokus Pokus*** [*Three Blind Mice*] ** May 5, 1949. 16:08. P/D: Jules White. W: Felix Adler. Ph: Vincent Farrar. w/Mary Ainslee, Vernon Dent, David Bond,

Ned Glass. *The Stooges inadvertently uncover an insurance scam when a hypnotist orders them to dance on a flagpole.*

116. **Fuelin' Around** **** July 7, 1949. 16:50. P: Hugh McCollum. D: Edward Bernds. W: Elwood Ullman. Ph: Vincent Farrar. w/Emil Sitka, Christine McIntyre, Vernon Dent, Philip Van Zandt, Jacques O'Mahoney. *When Larry is mistaken for an atomic scientist, he and the other boys are spirited to the State of Anemia—and then discover that the real scientist has been kidnapped, too.*

117. **Malice in the Palace** [*Here We Go Schmow*] *** September 1, 1949. 16:13. P/D: Jules White. W: Felix Adler. Ph: Vincent Farrar. w/Vernon Dent, George Lewis, Frank Lackteen, Johnny Kascier. *Café owners in the Middle East recover a valuable diamond from the Emir of Schmow.*

118. **Vagabond Loafers** *** October 6, 1949. 15:53. P: Hugh McCollum. D: Edward Bernds. W: Elwood Ullman. Ph: Vincent Farrar. w/Kenneth MacDonald, Christine McIntyre, Symona Boniface, Emil Sitka, Dudley Dickerson. *Half-baked plumbers mess up a society party but expose art thieves. Remake of A Plumbing We Will Go, with stock footage.*

119. **Dunked in the Deep** **½ November 2, 1949. 16:49. P/D: Jules White. W: Felix Adler. Ph: Vincent Farrar. w/Gene Roth. *A Communist spy tricks the boys into joining him as stowaways on a storm-tossed freighter.*

120. **Punchy Cowpunchers** ***½ January 5, 1950. 17:17. P: Hugh McCollum. W/D: Edward Bernds. Ph: Vincent Farrar. w/Kenneth MacDonald, Christine McIntyre, Jacques O'Mahoney. *Three cavalry soldiers impersonate desperadoes to shut down the Killer Dillon gang.*

121. **Hugs and Mugs** *½ February 2, 1950. 15:18. P/D: Jules White. W: Clyde Bruckman. Ph: Vincent Farrar. w/Christine McIntyre, Nanette Bordeaux, Kathleen O'Malley, Joe Palma. *Three beautiful ex-convicts involve the Stooges in a scheme to recover stolen pearls.*

122. **Dopey Dicks** **** March 2, 1950. 15:43. P: Hugh McCollum. W/D: Edward Bernds. Ph: Vincent Farrar. w/Philip Van Zandt, Christine McIntyre, Stanley Price. *A beautiful girl is held captive at the scary mansion of a scientist who needs a human brain to complete his robot.*

123. **Love at First Bite** [*New Grooms Sweep Clean*] **½ May 4, 1950. 16:01. P/D: Jules White. W: Felix Adler. Ph: Rex Wimpy. w/Christine McIntyre, Yvette Reynard, Marie Monteil. *Three dopes have trouble getting to the dock in time to meet their European sweethearts.*

124. **Self Made Maids** *** July 6, 1950. 15:47. P/D: Jules White. W: Felix Adler. Ph: Vincent Farrar. w/the Stooges, in multiple roles. *A doting father can't stand the three reprobates his daughters have chosen for mates.*

125. **Three Hams on Rye** [*How Hammy Was My Hamlet*] *** September 7, 1950, 15:43. P/D: Jules White. W: Clyde Bruckman. Ph: Allen Siegler. w/ Emil Sitka, Christine McIntyre, Nanette Bordeaux, Ned Glass. *A theatrical producer orders three stagehands to prevent a snarky drama critic from entering the theater.*

126. **Studio Stoops** **** October 5, 1950. 16:00. P: Hugh McCollum. D: Edward Bernds. W: Elwood Ullman. Ph: Vincent Farrar. w/Christine McIntyre, Kenneth MacDonald, Vernon Dent, Charles Jordon, Joe Palma. *The boys are mistaken for movie-studio publicity men and set up a fake kidnapping of a new starlet that turns out to be real.*

127. **Slaphappy Sleuths** ** ½ November 9, 1950. 16:08. P/D: Jules White. W: Felix Adler. Ph: Vincent Farrar. w/Stanley Blystone, Emil Sitka, Gene Roth, Nanette

Bordeaux. *Gas station attendants chase down a robbery gang that specializes in service stations.*

128. *A Snitch in Time* *** December 7, 1950. 16:28. P: Hugh McCollum D: Edward Bernds. W: Elwood Ullman. Ph: Vincent Farrar. w/Jean Willes, Henry Kulky, John Merton. *The Stooges are furniture makers who run into crooks when they make a delivery to a boardinghouse.*

129. *Three Arabian Nuts* [*Geni with the Light Brown Hair*] *** January 4, 1951. 15:42. P: Hugh McCollum. D: Edward Bernds. W: Elwood Ullman. Ph: none credited. w/Vernon Dent, Philip Van Zandt, Dick Curtis, Wesley Bly. *Arabs pursue the Stooges after the boys come into possession of a magic lamp.*

130. *Baby Sitters Jitters* ** February 1, 1951. 16:09. P/D: Jules White. W: Felix Adler. Ph: none credited. w/Lynn Davis, Myron Healey, David Windsor. *The Stooges are professional babysitters who get caught between warring parents.*

131. *Don't Throw That Knife* [*Noncensus Takers*] *½ May 3, 1951. 15:50. P/D: Jules White. W: Felix Adler. Ph: Fayte Browne. w/Dick Curtis, Jean Willes. *The Stooges ask census questions of a beautiful woman and arouse the jealous nature of her knife-throwing husband.*

132. *Scrambled Brains* [*Impatient Patient*] ***½ July 7, 1951. 15:42. P/D: Jules White. W: Felix Adler. Ph: Henry Freulich. w/Babe London, Vernon Dent, Emil Sitka. *Shemp's addled mental state encourages him to believe that his homely nurse is gorgeous.*

133. *Merry Mavericks* *** September 6, 1951. 15:47. P: Hugh McCollum. W/D: Edward Bernds. Ph: Allen Siegler. w/Don Harvey, Marion Martin, Dick Curtis, Emil Sitka. *Townies terrorized by a bandit mistake the Stooges for famous marshals.*

134. *The Tooth Will Out* [*A Yank at the Dentist*] *** October 4, 1951. 15:59. P: Hugh McCollum. W/D: Edward Bernds. Ph: Fayte Browne. w/Vernon Dent, Margie Liszt, Emil Sitka. *The boys muddle their way through a two-bit dental school and set up a practice out west.*

135. *Hula-La-La* *** November 1, 1951. 16:05. P/D: Hugh McCollum. W: Edward Bernds. Ph: Henry Freulich. w/Kenneth MacDonald, Jean Willes, Emil Sitka, Joy Windsor, Lei Aloha. *When a movie studio sends the boys to a South Sea isle to teach the natives how to dance, they nearly lose their noggins to a headhunting witch doctor.*

136. *Pest Man Wins* [*Mousers in the Trousers*] *** December 6, 1951. 16:01. P/D: Jules White. W: Felix Adler. Ph: Fayte Browne. w/Margie Liszt, Nanette Bordeaux, Emil Sitka, Vernon Dent, Symona Boniface. *Three exterminators wreck a high-society party.* Partial remake of *Ants in the Pantry*, with stock footage from that film and from *Half-Wits Holiday.*

137. *A Missed Fortune* ***½ January 3, 1952. 16:07. P/D: Jules White. W: Searle Kramer (source script), Jack White (new scenes). Ph: Fayte Browne. Nanette Bordeaux, Suzanne Ridgeway, Vivian Mason, Vernon Dent, Stanley Blystone. *Shemp wins big bucks on a radio contest and attracts gold diggers when he and the boys take a room at a swank hotel.* Remake of *Healthy, Wealthy and Dumb*, with stock footage.

138. *Listen, Judge* *** March 6, 1952. 17:05. P: Hugh McCollum. D: Edward Bernds. W: Elwood Ullman. Ph: Ellis Carter. w/Vernon Dent, Kitty McHugh, John Hamilton, Emil Sitka. *The boys are maladroit repairmen who turn out to be even worse as cooks when they cater a judge's birthday party.*

139. *Corny Casanovas* ***½ May 1, 1952. 16:23. P/D: Jules White. W: Felix Adler. Ph: Henry Freulich. w/Connie Cezan. *A gold digger is engaged to each of the boys simultaneously and without their knowledge.*

140. *He Cooked His Goose* [*Clam Up*] *** July 3, 1952. 15:38. P/D: Jules White. W: Felix Adler. Ph: Fayte Browne. w/Mary Ainslee, Angela Stevens, Theila (Diana) Darrin. *Womanizing pet-store owner Larry makes the mistake of interfering in Moe and Shemp's love lives.*

141. *Gents in a Jam* *** August 4, 1952 (likely). 16:14. P: Hugh McCollum. W/D: Edward Bernds. Ph: Fayte Browne. w/Kitty McHugh, Emil Sitka, Dani Sue Nolan, Mickey Simpson. *The boys innocently end up in a compromising situation with a pretty neighbor whose husband is a professional strongman.*

142. *Three Dark Horses* [*Small Delegates at Large*] ***½ October 16, 1952. 16:32. P/D: Jules White. W: Felix Adler. Ph: Henry Freulich. w/Kenneth MacDonald, Ben Welden. *Cynical politicos pay the boys to be delegates at a presidential convention.*

143. *Cuckoo on a Choo Choo* [*A Train Called Schmow*] **½ December 4, 1952. 15:28. P/D: Jules White. W: Felix Adler. Ph: Henry Freulich. w/Patricia Wright, Victoria Horne, Reggie Dvorak. *Railroad dick Moe tracks down two dopes who stay with their fiancées in a stolen Pullman car.*

144. *Up in Daisy's Penthouse* *** February 5, 1953. 16:36. P/D: Jules White. W: Clyde Bruckman (source script), Jack White (new scenes). Ph: Henry Freulich. w/ Connie Cezan, John Merton. *Shemp's dad is going to be knocked off as soon as he marries a gold digger.* Remake of *Three Dumb Clucks*, with stock footage.

145. *Booty and the Beast* [*Fun for the Money*] *** March 5, 1953. 15:52. P/D: Jules White. W: Felix Adler (source script), Jack White (new scenes). Ph: Fayte Browne. w/Kenneth MacDonald, Vernon Dent, Jerry (Curly) Howard. *The boys hop a train to chase after a crook who has tricked them into blowing a safe.* Partial remake of *Hold That Lion!*, with stock footage.

146. *Loose Loot* [*Filthy Lucre*] *** April 2, 1953. 15:52. P/D: Jules White. W: Felix Adler (source script), Jack White (new scenes). Ph: Fayte Browne. w/Kenneth MacDonald, Tom Kennedy, Emil Sitka, Suzanne Ridgeway. *The boys have violent trouble with the executor of Shemp's uncle's estate.* Stock footage from *Hold That Lion!*

147. *Tricky Dicks* [*Cop and Bull Story*] *** May 7, 1953. 15:54. P/D: Jules White. W: Felix Adler. Ph: William Whitley. w/Benny Rubin, Connie Cezan, Ferris Taylor, Phil Arnold, Murray Alper, Suzanne Ridgeway. *Three dedicated but obtuse police detectives try to capture a fugitive killer.* Stock footage from *Hold That Lion!*

148. *Spooks!* **½ June 15, 1953. 15:42. P/D: Jules White. W: Felix Adler. Ph: Lester White. w/Philip Van Zandt, Tom Kennedy, Norma Randall, Frank Mitchell, Steve Calvert. *Three pie salesmen encounter a kidnapped girl, a nutty scientist, and a gorilla.* Shot and released in 3-D.

149. *Pardon My Backfire* ***½ August 15, 1953. 15:53. P/D: Jules White. W: Felix Adler. Ph: Henry Freulich. w/Benny Rubin, Frank Sully, Phil Arnold, Barbara Bartay, Fred Kelsey, Ruth Godfrey, Theila (Diana) Darrin, Angela Stevens. *Vicious crooks who invade the boys' garage live to regret it.* Shot and released in 3-D.

150. *Rip, Sew and Stitch* [*A Pressing Affair*] ** September 3, 1953. 16:43. P/D: Jules White. W: Felix Adler (source script), Jack White (new scenes). Ph: Ray Cory. w/Harold Brauer, Vernon Dent, Phil Arnold. *Three tailors encounter a notorious bank robber.* Composed primarily of stock footage from *Sing a Song of Six Pants*.

151. **Bubble Trouble** [*Drugstore Dubs*] * October 8, 1953. 16:29. P/D: Jules White. W: Felix Adler (source script), Jack White (new scenes). Ph: Ray Cory. w/Christine McIntyre, Emil Sitka. *Three goofy pharmacists create a fountain of youth.* Heavy use of stock footage from *All Gummed Up.*

152. **Goof on the Roof** ***½ December 3, 1953. 16:22. P/D: Jules White. W: Clyde Bruckman. Ph: Sam Leavitt. w/Frank Mitchell, Maxine Gates. *The boys make a mess of their buddy's house as they struggle to install a new TV and antenna.*

153. **Income Tax Sappy** [*Tax Saps*] *** February 4, 1954. 16:28. P/D: Jules White. W: Felix Adler. Ph: Ray Cory. w/Benny Rubin, Margie Liszt, Nanette Bordeaux, Harriette Tarler, Vernon Dent, Joe Palma. *The boys cheat on their taxes and help others do the same.*

154. **Musty Musketeers** **½ May 13, 1954. 15:53. P/D: Jules White. W: Felix Adler (source script), Jack White (new scenes). Ph: Gert Anderson (Andersen). w/ Vernon Dent, Philip Van Zandt, Diana Darrin, Ruth Godfrey, Norma Randall. *Three royal fiddlers want to marry their sweethearts but must first rescue a kidnapped princess.* Heavy use of stock footage from *Fiddlers Three.*

155. **Pals and Gals** [*Cuckoo Westerners*] **½ June 3, 1954. 16:37. P/D: Jules White. W: Clyde Bruckman (source script), Jack White (new scenes). Ph: Gert Anderson (Andersen). w/Norman Willes, Christine McIntyre, Vernon Dent, Stanley Blystone. *The boys try to rescue their girls from a notorious frontier gang leader.* Extensive use of stock footage from *Out West,* plus footage from *Goofs and Saddles.*

156. **Knutzy Knights** ** September 2, 1954. 15:23. P/D: Jules White. W: Edward Bernds (source script), Jack White (new scenes), Ph: Ray Cory. w/Christine McIntyre, Vernon Dent, Jacques O'Mahoney. *A princess who is betrothed to an evil prince loves a blacksmith.* Extensive stock footage from *Squareheads of the Round Table.*

157. **Shot in the Frontier** [*Low Afternoon*] *** October 7, 1954. 15:52. P/D: Jules White. W: Felix Adler. Ph: Ray Corey. Kenneth MacDonald, Emil Sitka, Ruth Godfrey, Diana Darrin, Vivian Mason, Joe Palma. *In a shoot-out at high noon, the boys protect their brides from the murderous Noonan brothers.*

158. **Scotched in Scotland** [*Hassle in the Castle*] ** November 4, 1954. 15:32. P/D: Jules White. W: Elwood Ullman (source script), Jack White (new scenes). Ph: Ray Cory. w/Charles Knight, Christine McIntyre, Philip Van Zandt. *Three inept detectives guard valuables at a spooky Scottish castle.* Extensive stock footage from *Hot Scots.*

159. **Fling in the Ring** ** January 6, 1955. 16:15. P/D: Jules White. W: Clyde Bruckman (source script), Jack White (new scenes), Ph: Ray Cory. w/Dick Wessel, Claire Carleton, Frank Sully, Harold Brauer, Cy Schindell. *The Stooges cross a criminal when they fail to soften up a prizefighter to take a dive.* Extensive stock footage from *Fright Night.*

160. **Of Cash and Hash** [*Crook Crackers*] **½ February 3, 1955. 15:50. P/D: Jules White. W: Del Lord, Elwood Ullman (source script), Jack White (new scenes). Ph: Ray Cory. *The Stooges clear themselves of armored-car robbery by nabbing the real crooks inside a shadowy mansion.* A variation on *Shivering Sherlocks,* with extensive stock footage.

161. **Gypped in the Penthouse** [*Blundering Bachelors*] **½ March 10, 1955. 15:59. P/D: Jules White. W: Felix Adler. Ph: Ray Cory. w/Jean Willes, Emil Sitka. *At a women*

haters club, the boys reminisce about the dame who did them wrong—and realize they're talking about the same person.

162. **Bedlam in Paradise** [*Gruesome Threesome*] ****½** April 14, 1955. 15:52. P/D: Jules White. W: Zion Myers (source script), Jack White (new scenes). Ph: Ray Cory. w/Vernon Dent, Philip Van Zandt, Sylvia Lewis, Symona Boniface. *Angel Shemp has to resist temptations offered by the Devil before he can return to Earth and reform his brothers.* A redo of *Heavenly Daze,* with extensive stock footage.

163. **Stone Age Romeos** [*Caved In Cavemen*] ******* June 2, 1955. 15:42. P/D: Jules White. W: Zion Myers (source script), Felix Adler (new scenes). Ph: Ira Morgan. w/Emil Sitka, Dee Green, Nancy Saunders, Virginia Hunter, Joe Palma, Cy Schindell. *The Stooges pose as explorers and try to swindle a museum curator into purchasing their faked film footage of cavemen.* A redo of *I'm a Monkey's Uncle,* with extensive stock footage.

164. **Wham-Bam-Slam!** [*Enjoying Poor Health*] ******* September 1, 1955. 15:53. P/D: Jules White. W: Clyde Bruckman (source script), Felix Adler (new scenes). Ph: Fred Jackman. w/Matt McHugh, Alyn Lockwood. *A friend suggests that Shemp and the boys take a trip for Shemp's nerves.* Extensive stock footage from *Pardon My Clutch.*

165. **Hot Ice** ******* October 6, 1955. 16:19. P/D: Jules White. W: Elwood Ullman (source script), Jack White (new scenes). Ph: Fred Jackman. w/Kenneth MacDonald, Christine McIntyre, Barbara Bartay. *Three gardeners from Scotland Yard track down a stolen diamond.* Extensive stock footage from *Crime on Their Hands,* plus footage from *Hot Scots.*

166. **Blunder Boys** [*Cuckoo Cops*] ******* November 3, 1955. 15:55. P/D: Jules White. W: Felix Adler. Ph: Ray Cory. w/Benny Rubin, Angela Stevens, Kenneth MacDonald, Barbara Bartay. *Three deadpan police detectives track a slippery crook called The Eel.*

167. **Husbands Beware** [*Eat, Drink and Be Married*] ******* January 5, 1956. 15:51. P/D: Jules White. W: Clyde Bruckman (source script), Felix Adler (new scenes). Ph: Henry Freulich. w/Dee Green, Emil Sitka, Maxine Gates, Lou (Lu) Leonard, Doris Houck. *Because Shemp has talked Moe and Larry into miserable marriages, they scheme for Shemp to endure the same torture.* A variation of *Brideless Groom,* with extensive stock footage.

168. **Creeps** [*Three Brave Cowards*] ****** February 2, 1956. 15:36. P/D: Jules White. W: Felix Adler (source script), Jack White (new scenes). Ph: Henry Freulich. w/ Phil Arnold (voice only). *The Stooges tell their baby boys about their adventure in a haunted castle.* A redo of *The Ghost Talks,* with stock footage.

169. **Flagpole Jitters** ****** April 5, 1956. 15:54. P/D: Jules White. W: Felix Adler (source script), Jack White (new scenes). Ph: Irving Lippman. w/Vernon Dent, Mary Ainslee, David Bond, Don Harvey, Frank Sully, Barbara Bartay. *The boys get mixed up with a crooked hypnotist.* A variation of *Hokus Pokus,* with extensive stock footage.

170. **For Crimin' Out Loud** [*Nutty Newshounds*] *****½** May 3, 1956. 15:57. P/D: Jules White. W: Edward Bernds (source script), Felix Adler (new scenes). Ph: Irving Lippman. w/Kenneth MacDonald, Christine McIntyre, Emil Sitka, Duke York, Barbara Bartay. *Half-wit detectives visit a spooky mansion to protect a councilman's life.* A redo of *Who Done It?,* with extensive stock footage. This is the last Three Stooges short with all-new footage of Shemp.

The Three Stooges

Moe Howard, Larry Fine, Shemp Howard (stock footage only), Joe Palma

171. *Rumpus in the Harem* [*Diamond Daffy*] *** June 21, 1956. 15:57. P/D: Jules White. W: Felix Adler (source script), Jack White (new scenes). Ph: Ray Cory. w/Vernon Dent, George Lewis, Harriette Tarler, Suzanne Ridgeway, Diana Darrin, Ruth Godfrey White, Helen Jay. *If the Stooges are to pay off their sweethearts' debts, they must retrieve a stolen diamond from a powerful emir.* A variation of *Malice in the Palace*, with extensive stock footage. The short is the first of four in which contract player Joe Palma doubles Shemp, who passed away before production began.

172. *Hot Stuff* [*They Gassed Wrong*] *** September 6, 1956. 16:09. P/D: Jules White. W: Elwood Ullman (source script), Felix Adler (new scenes). Ph: Irving Lippman. w/Emil Sitka, Christine McIntyre, Vernon Dent, Philip Van Zandt, Connie Cezan, Evelyn Lovequist. *The Stooges are assigned to guard an atomic scientist and his daughter, but the whole lot of them is spirited away to Anemia.* A redo of *Fuelin' Around*, with extensive stock footage.

173. *Scheming Schemers* [*Pixilated Plumbers*] *** October 4, 1956. 15:50. P/D: Jules White. W: Elwood Ullman (source scripts), Jack White (new scenes). Ph: Ray Cory. w/Christine McIntyre, Kenneth MacDonald, Symona Boniface, Emil Sitka, Dudley Dickerson. *The Stooges are called to a mansion to retrieve a diamond ring from a drain and proceed to wreck a high-society party.* A variation of *Vagabond Loafers*, with extensive stock footage from that film, plus footage from *A Plumbing We Will Go* and *Half-Wits Holiday*.

174. *Commotion on the Ocean* [*Salt Water Daffy*] ** November 8, 1956. 16:32. P/D: Jules White. W: Felix Adler. Ph: Ray Cory. w/Gene Roth, Emil Sitka, Harriette Tarler. *The boys impersonate reporters and end up on the high seas as stowaways with a spy.* A variation of *Dunked in the Deep*, with extensive stock footage.

The Three Stooges

Moe Howard, Larry Fine, Joe Besser

175. *Hoofs and Goofs* [*Galloping Bride*] ** January 31, 1957. 15:30. P/D: Jules White. W: Jack White. Ph: Gert Anderson (Andersen). w/Benny Rubin, Harriette Tarler (character part, plus the voice of the horse), Tony the Wonder Horse. *Joe's intuition that the boys' late sister has been reincarnated turns out to be true—she's a horse.* This is the first Three Stooges short to feature Joe Besser.

176. *Muscle Up a Little Closer* [*Builder Uppers*] *** February 28, 1957. 16:49. P/D: Jules White. W: Felix Adler. Ph: Irving Lippman. w/Maxine Gates, Matt Murphy, Harriette Tarler, Ruth Godfrey White. *Joe's fiancée is convinced that someone at work has stolen her engagement ring.*

177. *A Merry Mix-Up* [*A Merry Marriage Mix-Up*] *** March 28, 1957. 15:51. P/D: Jules White. W: Felix Adler. Ph: Irving Lippman. w/Nanette Bordeaux, Ruth Godfrey White, Jeanne Carmen, Suzanne Ridgeway, Harriette Tarler, Diana Darrin, Frank Sully. *An unexpected reunion of three sets of identical triplets confounds various wives and girlfriends.*

178. *Space Ship Sappy* [*Rocket and Roll It*] ***½ April 18, 1957. 16:16. P/D: Jules White. W: Jack White. Ph: Henry Freulich. w/Benny Rubin, Doreen Woodbury, Harriette Tarler, Marilyn Hanold, Lorraine Crawford, Emil Sitka. *The boys sign on with an eccentric scientist and his daughter for a rocketship ride to the planet Sunev.*

179. *Guns a Poppin!* [*Nerveless Wreck*] **½ June 13, 1957. 16:30. P/D: Jules White. W: Elwood Ullman (source script), Jack White (new scenes). Ph: Henry Freulich. w/Frank Sully, Joe Palma, Vernon Dent. *Moe is on trial for assaulting Larry and Joe but explains that it was the boys' encounter with a notorious bandit that drove him over the edge.* Remake of *Idiots Deluxe*, with stock footage.

180. *Horsing Around* [*Just Horsing Around*] * September 12, 1957. 15:28. P/D: Jules White. W: Felix Adler. Ph: Ray Cory. w/Harriette Tarler (character part, plus the voice of the horse), Emil Sitka, Tony the Wonder Horse. *The boys' sister, who has been reincarnated as a horse, frets because her equine lover is about to be put down at a circus.*

181. *Rusty Romeos* [*Sappy Lovers*] *** October 17, 1957. 16:20. P/D: Jules White. W: Felix Adler (source script), Jack White (new scenes). Ph: Henry Freulich. w/Connie Cezan. *The boys are engaged to the same gold digger and don't find out until chance meetings at their sweetie's apartment.*

182. *Outer Space Jitters* [*Outer Space Daze*] *** December 5, 1957. 16:19. P/D: Jules White. W: Jack White. Ph: William Bradford. w/Emil Sitka, Gene Roth, Philip Van Zandt, Harriette Tarler, Diana Darrin, Arline Hunter, Don (Dan) Blocker. *The Stooges accompany a scientist to the planet Sunev, where they discover electrically charged schemers who want to take over Earth with atomic zombies.*

183. *Quiz Whizz* **½ February 13, 1958. 15:25. P/D: Jules White. W: Searle Kramer. Ph: Irving Lippman. w/Gene Roth, Greta Thyssen, Milton Frome, Bill (Harold) Brauer, Emil Sitka. *Joe loses a TV-show jackpot to murderous swindlers.*

184. *Fifi Blows Her Top* [*Rancid Romance*] *** April 10, 1958. 16:33. P/D: Jules White. W: Felix Adler. Ph: Henry Freulich. w/Vanda Dupre, Philip Van Zandt, Christine McIntyre, Harriette Tarler, Suzanne Ridgeway. *As the boys reminisce about their wartime sweethearts, Joe is amazed to learn that his now-married old flame has moved into the apartment across the hall.* A variation of *Love at First Bite*, with stock footage.

185. *Pies and Guys* [*Easy Come, Easy Go*] **½ June 12, 1958. 16:15. P/D: Jules White. W: Zion Myers (source script), Jack White (new scenes). Ph: Irving Lippman. w/Gene Roth, Milton Frome, Greta Thyssen, Harriette Tarler, Emil Sitka. *A professor insists to a colleague that he can turn three rabble into gentlemen.* Remake of *Half-Wits Holiday*, with extensive stock footage.

186. *Sweet and Hot* *** September 4, 1958. 16:20. P/D: Jules White. W: Jerome S. Gottler, Jack White. Ph: Irving Lippman. w/Muriel Landers. *Joe's sister has loads of talent, but her repressed memory of childhood trauma discourages her from performing in public.*

187. *Flying Saucer Daffy* [*Pardon My Flying Saucer*] **½ October 9, 1958. 16:11. P/D: Jules White. W: Warren Wilson (story), Jack White (script). Ph: Fred Jackman. w/Gail Bonney, Diana Darrin, Bek Nelson, Emil Sitka. *Joe's aunt and cousins abuse him until he wins a flying saucer photo contest.*

188. *Oil's Well That Ends Well* *** December 4, 1958. 16:09. P/D: Jules White. W: Andrew Bennison, Mauri Grashon (source script), Felix Adler (new scenes). Ph: Irving Lippman. *While prospecting for uranium, the boys discover an oil well.*

Partial reworking of *Oily to Bed, Oily to Rise*, with a few moments of stock footage.

189. **Triple Crossed** [*Chiseling Chiseler*] **½ February 2, 1959. 15:50. P/D: Jules White. W: Felix Adler (source script), Warren Wilson (new scenes). Ph: Fred Jackman. w/Diana Darrin, Angela Stevens, Mary Ainslee, Connie Cezan. *Womanizer Larry causes trouble between Moe and Joe, and their women.* Remake of *He Cooked His Goose*, with extensive stock footage.

190. **Sappy Bull Fighters** [*That's Bully*] **½ June 4, 1959. 15:17. P/D: Jules White. W: Jack White, Saul Ward (source script), Jack White (new scenes). Ph: Irving Lippman. w/Greta Thyssen, George Lewis. *The Stooges anger a jealous husband in Mexico and end up in a bullring.* Remake of *What's the Matador?*, with extensive stock footage.

Working titles courtesy www.threestooges.net

The Stooges Short That Never Was

Gus Schilling and Richard Lane

Pardon My Terror *** September 12, 1946. 16:50 P: Hugh McCollum. W/D: Edward Bernds. Ph: Glen Gano. w/Gus Schilling, Richard Lane, Christine McIntyre, Lynne Lyons, Dick Wessel, Kenneth MacDonald, Philip Van Zandt, Vernon Dent, Dudley Dickerson. *Two bumbling private detectives experience a wild night inside a dark mansion as they investigate the owner's apparent murder.*

Bibliography

Books

Bernds, Edward. *Mr. Bernds Goes to Hollywood*. Scarecrow Press. Lanham, MD: 1999.
Besser, Joe with Jeff and Greg Lenburg. *Not Just a Stooge*. Excelsior Books. Orange, CA: 1984.
Boyne, Walter J. *Classic Airplanes*. Publications International, Ltd. Lincolnwood, IL: 2001.
Bruskin, David N. *The White Brothers*. Directors Guild of America & Scarecrow Press. Metuchen, NJ: 1990.
Carone, James, with Larry Fine. *Stroke of Luck*. Siena Publishing. Hollywood: 1973.
Feinberg, Morris. *Larry: The Stooge in the Middle*. Last Gasp. San Francisco: 2000.
Flink, James J. *The Automobile Age*. MIT Press. Cambridge, MA: 1990.
Halberstam, David. *The Fifties*. Villard Books. New York: 1993.
Hardy, Phil, ed. *The Encyclopedia of Western Movies*. Woodbury Press. Minneapolis: 1984.
Hillenbrand, Laura. *Seabiscuit: An American Legend*. Random House. New York: 2001.
Hogan, David J., ed. *American West Chronicle*. Legacy Publishing. Lincolnwood, IL: 2007.
———, ed. *Civil Rights Chronicle: The African-American Struggle for Freedom*. Legacy Publishing. Lincolnwood, IL: 2003.
———. *Dark Romance: Sex and Death in the Horror Film*. Equation/Thorsons Publishing Group. Wellingborough, UK: 1988.
———, ed. *World War II Chronicle*. Legacy Publishing. Lincolnwood, IL: 2007.
Howard, Moe. *Moe Howard & the 3 Stooges*. Citadel Press. Secaucus, NJ: 1977.
Juhnke, Eric S. *Quacks and Crusaders: The Fabulous Careers of John Brinkley, Norman Baker, and Harry Hoxsey*. University Press of Kansas. Lawrence: 2002.
Ketchum, Milo Smith. *Structural Engineers' Handbook*. McGraw Hill. New York: 1918.
Kisseloff, Jeff. *The Box: An Oral History of Television, 1920-1961*. Viking. New York: 1995.
Knaebel, Nathaniel. *Step Right Up: Stories of Carnivals, Sideshows and the Circus*. Carroll & Graf. New York: 2004.
Kogos, Fred. *The Dictionary of Popular Yiddish Words, Phrases and Proverbs*. Citadel Press. New York: 2000.
Larkin, Rochelle. *Hail, Columbia*. Arlington House. New Rochelle, NY: 1975.
Lenburg, Jeff with Joan Howard Maurer and Greg Lenburg. *The Three Stooges Scrapbook*. Citadel Press. Secaucus, NJ: 1982.
Lev, Peter. *The Fifties: Transforming the Screen, 1950-1959*. University of California Press. Berkeley: 2003.

Maltin, Leonard. *The Great Movie Shorts.* Crown. New York: 1972.

Maurer, Joan Howard. *Curly.* Citadel Press. Secaucus, NJ: 1988.

Okuda, Ted with Edward Watz. *The Columbia Comedy Shorts: Two-Reel Hollywood Film Comedies, 1933-1958.* McFarland. Jefferson, NC: 1986.

Shukter, Elfreda B. and Barbara S. Scibetta. *War Brides of World War II.* Penguin. New York: 1989.

Skretvedt, Randy. *Laurel and Hardy: The Magic Behind the Movies.* Moonstone Press. Beverly Hills, CA: 1987.

Snyder, Robert W. *The Voice of the City: Vaudeville and Popular Culture in New York.* Oxford University Press. Oxford, UK: 1989.

Weinberg, Gerhard L. *A World at Arms: A Global History of World War II.* Cambridge University Press. Cambridge, UK: 1994.

Wolverton, Basil. *The Culture Corner.* Fantagraphics Books. Seattle: 2010.

Periodicals

"Beer Shortage Cuts Play in Many Popular Places." *The Billboard.* July 31, 1943. p. 104.

"Ed Bernds: A Tribute." Aubrey Menezes. *The Three Stooges Journal* #95, Fall 2000. pp. 9–11, 14.

"False Alarms, True Locations." Jim Pauley. *The Three Stooges Journal* #100, Winter 2001. pp. 4–6, 22.

"Flashback: Featuring Connie Cezon." Stephen Cox. *The Three Stooges Journal* #62, Summer 1992. pp. 8–9.

"Nanette Bordeaux, A Brief Biography." Bill Cappello. *The Three Stooges Journal* #72, Winter 1994. pp. 6–7.

"Obituaries, Connie Cezon." *The Three Stooges Journal* #110, Summer 2004. p. 3.

"Pardon This *Unfilmed* Stooge Script." Brent Seguine. *The Three Stooges Journal* #108, Winter 2003. pp. 10-11.; #109, Spring 2004. pp. 12–14.

"The Real Miss Lapdale. An Interview with Diana Darrin." Gary Lassin. *The Three Stooges Journal* #118, Summer 2006. pp. 6–8, 14.

"Stooges Locations, Then & Now: *No Census, No Feeling,* 'Count This Location.'" Jim Pauley. *The Three Stooges Journal* #110, Summer 2004. p. 8.

"Stress-Related Suicide by Dentists and Other Health Care Workers." Roger E. Alexander, D.D.S. *The Journal of the American Dental Association* Vol. 132. No. 6, 2001. pp. 786–94.

"The Three Stooges' Hidden Hollywood: *False Alarms . . .* True Finale." Brent Seguine. *The Three Stooges Journal* #125, Spring 2008. pp.12–13; #126, Summer 2008. pp. 13–14.

"The Three Stooges' Hidden Hollywood: *Hoi Polloi & Potpourri.*" Brent Seguine. *The Three Stooges Journal* #128, Winter 2008. pp. 12–13.

"The Three Stooges' Hidden Hollywood: *Pardon Us Polecats.*" Brent Seguine. *The Three Stooges Journal* #135, Fall 2010. pp. 12–14.

"Three Stooges Locations, Then and Now: *Back to the Barrel.*" Jim Pauley. *The Three Stooges Journal* #118, Summer 2006. pp. 4–5.

"Three Stooges Locations, Then and Now: *Movie Maniacs . . .* Looney Location." Jim Pauley. *The Three Stooges Journal* #127, Fall 2008. p. 5.

"Three Stooges Locations, Then & Now:. *Punch Drunks*: Larry Gets the Radio . . . But Where?" Jim Pauley. *The Three Stooges Journal* #131, Fall 2009. p. 5.

"The Three Stooges Supporting Players, Mini-Biographical Profiles: Connie Cezon." Ed Shifres. *The Three Stooges Journal* #72, Winter 1994. p. 9.

"The Three Stooges Supporting Players, Mini-Biographical Profiles: Dorothy Appleby." Journal Staff. *The Three Stooges Journal* #132, Winter 2009. pp. 9–10.

"The Three Stooges Supporting Players, Mini-Biographical Profiles: Harriette Tarler." Ed Shifres. *The Three Stooges Journal* #117, Spring 2006. p. 10.

"The Three Stooges Supporting Players, Mini-Biographical Profiles: Lei Aloha." *The Three Stooges Journal* #131, Fall 2009. p. 8.

"The Three Stooges Supporting Players, Mini-Biographical Profiles: Matt Murphy." Ed Shifres. *The Three Stooges Journal* #103, Fall 2002. p. 10.

"What's a Yucca? Why, It's a Stooges Location! *Three Little Pigskins* Stooges Locations, Then and Now." Jim Pauley. *The Three Stooges Journal* #103, Fall 2002. pp. 4–6.

Web Sites

http://chnm.gmu.edu/sidelights/who-invented-body-odor/ "Q: Who Invented Body Odor? A: Advertising Men."

http://googlebooks.com

http://www.abebooks.com

http://www.cdc.gov

http://www.columbiaranch.net

http://www.fashion-era.com/make_up.htm "Make-Up Fashion History Before 1950." Pauline Weston Thomas.

http://www.housing.com/categories/prefab-homes/history-prefabricated-home.html "History of the Prefabricated Home."

http://iconicphotos.wordpress.com/2009/05/13/an-execution-at-sing-sing/ "An Execution at Sing Sing."

http://www.imdb.com

http://www.mayflowerhistory.com

http://www.nitabieber.com

http://www.theshortsdepartment.com

http://www.threestooges.net

http://www.usmm.org (American Merchant Marine at War)

http://www.youtube.com/watch?v=QtpsmqrvV0

———. *McHale's Navy*. "Beauty and the Beast." (1963).

Films

Buster Keaton Collection (Columbia shorts). Sony Pictures. 2006.

Crime Does Not Pay: Coffin on Wheels. (1941). Private copy.

The Lost Stooges. Turner, 1998.

Pardon My Terror (1946). Private copy.

The Three Stooges Collection, Vols.1–8. Sony Pictures. 2007–10.

Correspondence and Conversation

Larry Fine, 1972–74.
Moe Howard, 1973.

Recordings

Callas: La Divina 2. Maria Callas. *Lucia di Lammermoor.* EMI Classics: 1993.

Index